To Michael,
with gratitude and …

Nigel

The Correspondence of Zwingli and Oecolampadius

Studies in Medieval and Reformation Traditions

Edited by

Christopher Ocker (*Melbourne* and *San Anselmo*)

In cooperation with

Tara Alberts (*York*) – Sara Beam (*Victoria, BC*) – Falk Eisermann (*Berlin*) – Hussein Fancy (*Yale*) – Johannes Heil (*Heidelberg*) – Martin Kaufhold (*Augsburg*) – Ute Lotz-Heumann (*Tucson, Arizona*) – Jürgen Miethke (*Heidelberg*) – Marjorie Elizabeth Plummer (*Tucson, Arizona*) – Ulinka Rublack (*Cambridge, UK*) – Karin Sennefelt (*Stockholm*)

Founding Editor

Heiko A. Oberman †

VOLUME 248

Texts & Sources

Edited by

Falk Eisermann (*Berlin*)

VOLUME 17

The titles published in this series are listed at *brill.com/smrtts*

The Correspondence of Zwingli and Oecolampadius

Translated and introduced by

Nigel Harris
Sharon van Dijk

BRILL

LEIDEN | BOSTON

Front cover: portraits of Huldrych Zwingli and Johannes Oecolampadius, by Hans Asper, 1550

The Library of Congress Cataloging-in-Publication Data is available online at https://catalog.loc.gov
LC record available at https://lccn.loc.gov/2024051082

Typeface for the Latin, Greek, and Cyrillic scripts: "Brill". See and download: brill.com/brill-typeface.

ISSN 1573-4188
ISBN 978-90-04-53790-3 (hardback)
ISBN 978-90-04-53791-0 (e-book)
DOI 10.1163/9789004537910

Copyright 2025 by Koninklijke Brill BV, Plantijnstraat 2, 2321 JC Leiden, The Netherlands.
Koninklijke Brill BV incorporates the imprints Brill, Brill Nijhoff, Brill Schöningh, Brill Fink, Brill mentis, Brill Wageningen Academic, Vandenhoeck & Ruprecht, Böhlau and V&R unipress.
All rights reserved. No part of this publication may be reproduced, translated, stored in a retrieval system, or transmitted in any form or by any means, electronic, mechanical, photocopying, recording or otherwise, without prior written permission from the publisher. Requests for re-use and/or translations must be addressed to Koninklijke Brill BV via brill.com or copyright.com.
For more information: info@brill.com.

This book is printed on acid-free paper and produced in a sustainable manner.

Printed by Printforce, the Netherlands

Contents

Acknowledgements VII
Abbreviations VIII
Major Figures in the Letters X
Preface: Imbalances and Initiatives XVIII

Introduction 1
1 Zwingli and Zürich   1
2 Oecolampadius and Basel   13
3 Zwingli and Oecolampadius   23
4 Zwingli, Oecolampadius and Strasbourg   30
5 Zwingli, Oecolampadius and the Wider World   37
6 Zwingli, Oecolampadius and Letter-Writing   41
7 Manuscripts and Editions   45
8 Translation, Then and Now   51

The Letters   55

Bibliography   429
Index of Personal Names (of Early Modern Figures)   451
Index of Place Names (Contemporary Swiss and Others)   457
Index of Personal and Place Names (Antiquity and Middle Ages)   461
Index of Bible References   463

Acknowledgements

This book owes its existence above all to the Leverhulme Trust, who funded its production by means of a Research Project Grant held at the University of Birmingham between January 2021 and December 2022. To the Leverhulme Sharon van Dijk owes two years' salary, Nigel Harris two semesters' research leave, and both of us numerous opportunities to travel, to purchase necessary research materials, and to engage in fruitful discussion with many colleagues. The Trust has our enthusiastic and lasting gratitude.

As to individuals, we must give prime billing to the distinguished classical scholar and translator Christopher Stace. When we first approached Christopher, we asked him to act as a kind of 'back stop', who might prevent us from making too many egregious errors of translation. But he became far more than that: an ever willing source of both reactive and proactive advice, an ever gentlemanly encourager, and an ever enthusiastic proponent both of fidelity to the Latin original and of good English style.

We are grateful also to many other friends and colleagues for their interest in and active support of the project. We wish to mention particularly (in strict alphabetical order): Caroline Ardrey, Peter Auger, Phyllis Benedikz, Paul Botley, Michael Dodd, Falk Eisermann, Bruce Gordon, Mark Greengrass, Elystan Griffiths, Daniel Hadas, Catherine McMillan, Lucy Nicholas, Peter Opitz, Claire Peters, Ivo Romein, Ron Speirs and Andrew Watts.

Finally, and of course, we acknowledge and are eternally grateful for the support of our partners and families: Katharine, Elizabeth and David Harris; Felix Gilding, and Jos and Martha van Dijk.

To all these people, and to any we have forgotten, we wish to say, with Oecolampadius: "we are thankful that you are so concerned for us, and that you advise us at the right time".

Nigel Harris and Sharon van Dijk
Hall Green and Groningen, May 2024

Abbreviations

AE	Jaroslav Pelikan et al., eds, *Luther's Works: American Edition*, 79 vols to date (St. Louis: Concordia or Philadelphia: Fortress Press, 1955–2022)
AGBR	Emil Dürr and Paul Roth, eds, *Aktensammlung zur Geschichte der Basler Reformation in den Jahren 1519 bis Anfang 1534*, 6 vols (Basel: Verlag der Historischen und Antiquarischen Gesellschaft, 1921–1950)
BBKL	Hans-Wilhelm Bautz et al., eds, *Biographisch-Bibliographisches Kirchenlexikon*, 42 vols to date (Hamm et al.: Bautz, 1975–2021)
BC	Reinhold Friedrich et al., eds, *Martin Bucer: Briefwechsel/ Correspondance*, 10 vols to date (Leiden: Brill, 1979–2016)
Bernstein, GH	Eckhard Bernstein, *German Humanism* (Boston, MA: Twayne, 1983)
Burnett, Debating	Amy Nelson Burnett, *Debating the Sacraments: Print and Authority in the Early Reformation* (New York: Oxford University Press, 2019)
BWK	*Blätter für württembergische Kirchengeschichte*
BZGA	*Basler Zeitschrift für Geschichte und Altertumskunde*
CC	Erika Rummel and Milton Kooistra, eds and trans., *The Correspondence of Wolfgang Capito*, 3 vols (Toronto: University of Toronto Press, 2005–2015)
CoE	Pieter G. Bietenholz and Thomas B. Deutscher, eds, *Contemporaries of Erasmus: A Biographical Register of the Renaissance and Reformation*, 3 vols (Toronto: University of Toronto Press, 1985–1987)
EC	Alexander Dalzell et al., trans., *The Correspondence of Erasmus*, 21 vols to date (Toronto: University of Toronto Press, 1974–2022)
Füglister, Handwerksregiment	Hans Füglister, *Handwerksregiment. Untersuchungen und Materialien zur sozialen und politischen Struktur der Stadt Basel in der ersten Hälfte des 16. Jahrhunderts* (Basel: Helbing & Lichtenhahn, 1981)
Füssel, DD	Stephan Füssel, ed., *Deutsche Dichter der frühen Neuzeit (1460–1600): Ihr Leben und Werk* (Berlin: Schmidt, 1993)
Gäbler, Zwingli	Ulrich Gäbler, *Huldrych Zwingli: His Life and Work* (Edinburgh: Clark, 1986)
Gordon, Swiss	Bruce Gordon, *The Swiss Reformation* (Manchester: Manchester University Press, 2002)
Gordon, Zwingli	Idem, *Zwingli: God's Armed Prophet* (New Haven, CT: Yale University Press, 2021)

KJV	*The Holy Bible: King James Version* (originally London: Barker, 1611); accessed online via https://www.biblegateway.com/
KTR	Erwin Iserloh et al., eds, *Katholische Theologen der Reformationszeit*, 6 vols (Münster: Aschendorff, 1984–2004)
Leu/Weidmann	Urs B. Leu and Sandra Weidmann, *Huldrych Zwingli's Private Library* (Leiden: Brill, 2019)
Locher, ZR	Gottfried W. Locher, *Die Zwinglische Reformation im Rahmen der europäischen Kirchengeschichte* (Göttingen: Vandenhoeck & Ruprecht, 1979)
MBW	Heinz Scheible et al., eds, *Melanchthons Briefwechsel* (38 vols to date, Stuttgart: Frommann Holzboog, 1977–2022)
OeBA	Ernst Staehelin, ed., *Briefe und Akten zum Leben Oekolampads: Zum vierhundertjährigen Jubiläum der Basler Reformation*, 2 vols (Leipzig: Heinsius, 1927–1934)
OER	Hans J. Hillerbrand, ed., *The Oxford Encyclopedia of the Reformation*, 4 vols (New York: Oxford University Press, 1996)
Potter, *Zwingli*	Idem, *Zwingli* (Cambridge: Cambridge University Press, 1976)
Schindler, BD	Alfred Schindler et al., eds, *Die Badener Disputation von 1526. Kommentierte Edition des Protokolls* (Zürich: Theologischer Verlag, 2015)
Staehelin	Ernst Staehelin, *Oekolampad-Bibliographie*, 2nd edn (Nieuwkoop: de Graaf, 1963)
Staehelin, *Lebenswerk*	Idem, *Das theologische Lebenswerk Johannes Oekolampads* (Leipzig: Heinsius, 1939)
TRE	Gerhard Müller et al., eds, *Theologische Realenzyklopädie*, 38 vols (Berlin: De Gruyter, 1977–2007)
VL 16	Wilhelm Kühlmann et al., eds, *Frühe Neuzeit in Deutschland, 1520–1620: literaturwissenschaftliches Verfasserlexikon*, 7 vols (Berlin: De Gruyter, 2011–2019)
VL DH	Franz Josef Worstbrock, ed., *Deutscher Humanismus 1480–1520. Verfasserlexikon*, 3 vols (Berlin: De Gruyter, 2009–2014)
WA	Karl Knaake et al., eds, *D. Martin Luthers Werke. Kritsche Gesamtausgabe* ("Weimarer Ausgabe"), 73 vols (Weimar: Böhlau, 1883–1929)
WA BR	Gustav Bebermeyer et al., eds, *D. Martin Luthers Werke. Kritsche Gesamtausgabe: Briefwechsel* ("Weimarer Ausgabe"), 19 vols (Weimar: Böhlau, 1931–1983)
Wackernagel, *Basel*	Rudolf Wackernagel, *Geschichte der Stadt Basel*, 3 vols (Basel: Helbing & Lichtenhahn, 1907–1924)
ZW	Emil Egli et al., eds, *Huldreich Zwinglis Sämtliche Werke*, 20 vols to date (Zürich: Theologischer Verlag, 1905–2013)

Major Figures in the Letters

Note: our translations of the letters refer back to these biographies by means of an asterisk placed before the name of the person in question (e.g. *Bucer).

Blarer, Ambrosius (1492–1562) was a member of an influential family in Konstanz, and a friend of Zwingli, Oecolampadius, Melanchthon, Bullinger and Calvin. He was active as an evangelical preacher in his home city from 1525, and, along with Johannes Zwick, became its leading reformer. He was later (from around 1534) to be a seminal reforming influence in several parts of Württemberg, and developed a reputation as a hymnologist. On him see Moeller, *Blarer*; *CoE* I, 151 f.; *OER* I, 174 f.; *TRE* VI, 711–714; *BBKL* I, 612–614; *VL 16* I, 285–291.

Brenz, Johannes (1499–1570) was a Swabian Lutheran who had been taught Greek by Oecolampadius at Heidelberg, and seems to have remained on good personal terms with him in spite of radical differences over eucharistic theology. He was based at Schwäbisch Hall from 1522 to 1548, gradually introducing Lutheran reforms, and was an influential adviser to both Duke Ulrich of Württemberg and Margrave Georg of Brandenburg-Ansbach. On him see *BWK* 100 (2000), a special number devoted to him; James Martin Estes, *Christian Magistrate and State Church: The Reforming Career of Johannes Brenz* (Toronto: University of Toronto Press, 1982); *CoE* I, 193 f.; *OER* I, 214 f.; *BBKL* I, 743 f.

Bucer, Martin (1491–1551), from Sélestat, was a Dominican who left the order under the influence of the writings first of Erasmus and then of Luther. He met Oecolampadius at Ebernburg in 1522 and settled in Strasbourg in 1523. A major force for many years in attempts to unite the Swiss and Lutheran reformers (not least over the Eucharist), he ended his career—from 1549 onwards—in England. In the letters below, we witness him being recommended by Oecolampadius to Zwingli soon after his arrival in Strasbourg, and, especially from 1527 onwards, gradually becoming a more important and influential figure within the Northern Swiss/Upper Rhenish circle of reformers, and beyond. See Greschat, *Bucer*; Krieger/Lienhard, *Bucer*; Simon, *Bucer*; *CoE* I, 209–212; *OER* I, 221–224; *TRE* VII, 258–270; *BBKL* I, 782–785; Locher, *ZR*, 456–459.

Bugenhagen, Johannes (1485–1558), originally from Wolin in Pomerania, studied at Greifswald and, having converted to Lutheranism in around 1520, moved to Wittenberg in 1521. He was to become a distinguished reformer, theologian and pastor, initially in Wittenberg and, from the late 1520s onwards, in various parts of North Germany and Scandinavia; to Zwingli and Oecolampadius, however, he was primarily a troublesome opponent in the eucharistic debate of the later 1520s. On him see Wolf-Dieter Hauschild, "Johannes Bugenhagen (1485–1558) und seine Bedeutung für die Reformation in Deutschland", *Lutherjahrbuch* 77 (2010): 129–154; *CoE* I, 217–219; *OER* I, 226 f.; *BBKL* I, 805–807.

Capito, Wolfgang Fabritius (1487–1541) was originally from Hagenau, and was educated at Pforzheim, Ingolstadt and Freiburg. Identified from an early stage as an outstanding humanist, he moved to Basel as cathedral preacher in 1515, where he became an intimate associate of Erasmus, Pellikan and, not least, Oecolampadius (see also p. 26). Following a sojourn at Mainz, he settled in Strasbourg in 1523 as provost of the Chapter of St Thomas. For the next few years he was the city's leading reformer, until misfortunes and errors of judgement (recorded in some cases in the Zwingli-Oecolampadius correspondence) led to his career waning as Bucer's waxed. On him see Kittelson, *Capito*; Milton Kooistra, "Bucer's Relationship with Wolfgang Capito", in Simon, *Bucer*, 187–204; *CoE* I, 261–264; *OER* I, 259 f.; *TRE* VII, 636–640; *BBKL* I, 921–923; *VL 16* I, 470–478.

Cratander, Andreas (c. 1490–1540). Born in Strasbourg, he was active as a printer, publisher and bookseller in Basel from 1518 to 1536. He was a committed evangelical, but retained wide humanist interests—a combination of sympathies that significantly influenced his choice of books to publish. Personally and professionally close to Oecolampadius, Cratander was also a frequent bearer of letters and messages between Basel, Zürich and Strasbourg. On him see Eugen Meier et al., *Andreas Cratander—ein Basler Drucker und Verleger der Reformationszeit* (Basel: Helbling & Lichterhahn, 1966); *CoE* I, 357 f.; *OER* I, 451.

Eck, Johannes (1486–1543) was a theologian and controversialist based at the conservative University of Ingolstadt. Already well known following his confrontations with Luther at Leipzig in 1519, Eck remained one of Luther's and the Swiss reformers' most prominent critics. Indeed, "during the years 1524–1526, Eck emerged as Zwingli's most capable enemy" (Gordon, *Zwingli*, 123). On him see Jürgen Bärsch, ed., *Johannes Eck (1486–1543): Scholastiker, Humanist, Kontroverstheologe* (Regensburg: Pustet, 2014); Erwin Iserloh, ed., *Johannes Eck (1486–1543) im Streit der Jahrhunderte* (Münster: Aschendorff, 1988); *CoE* I, 416–419; *OER* II, 17–19; *TRE* IX, 249–258; *BBKL* XLI, 282–302; *VL DH* I, 576–589; *KTR* I, 64–71; Schindler, *BD*, 653–674.

Erasmus of Rotterdam, Desiderius (c. 1466–1536) was a humanist scholar of towering significance, who had a profound influence on both Zwingli and Oecolampadius. Although Erasmus's brand of Christian humanism suffused their thought throughout their careers, the Swiss reformers' references to him in their correspondence are almost always disparaging. This reflects not only a growing intellectual gulf on such questions as ecclesiology and free will, but also the acrimonious way in which Erasmus broke off personal contact with both men in the 1520s. Recent work on Erasmus includes William Barker, *Erasmus: The Spirit of a Scholar* (London: Reaktion, 2021), and Michael Massing, *Fatal Discord: Erasmus, Luther, and the Fight for the Western Mind* (New York: Harper, 2018). See also *OER* II, 55–59; *TRE* X, 1–18; *BBKL* I, 1524–1532; *VL DH* I, 658–804; Füssel, *DD*, 235–257; Bernstein, *GH*, 105–116.

Faber (or **Fabri**), **Johann** (1478–1541). Like Zwingli and Oecolampadius's other most feared and vilified opponent, Johannes Eck, Faber was once on friendly terms with them. He remained a committed Catholic, however, and had a prominent career as a theologian and polemicist, and latterly as Bishop of Vienna. He was also a prominent adviser to Archduke Ferdinand of Austria and other Catholic princes—causing the Swiss reformers to fear, and almost certainly to exaggerate, his level of potentially baleful political influence. On him see Leo Helbling, *Dr. Johann Fabri und die schweizerische Reformation* (Einsiedeln: Benziger, 1933); idem, *Dr. Johann Fabri, Generalvikar von Konstanz und Bischof von Wien, 1478–1541. Beiträge zu seiner Lebensgeschichte* (Münster: Aschendorff, 1941); *CoE* II, 5–8; *OER* II, 87 f.; *TRE* X, 784–788; *BBKL* I, 1588 f.; *KTR* I, 90–97; Schindler, *BD*, 675–689.

Ferdinand of Habsburg (1503–1564) was Archduke of Austria from 1521, King of Bohemia, Hungary and Croatia from 1526, and Holy Roman Emperor from 1556. For many years before becoming Emperor, however, he was his brother Charles V's principal representative in the German-speaking lands. The Swiss reformers feared him in his capacity as a Catholic figurehead and would-be counter-reformer, but also as overlord of the various Habsburg possessions of *Vorderösterreich* ('Outer Austria'), parts of which were close to both Zürich and Basel. See Fichtner, *Ferdinand*; Alfred Kohler, *Ferdinand I.: Fürst, König, Kaiser* (Munich: Beck, 2003); *CoE* II, 17–20; *OER* II, 103; *TRE* XI, 83–87; *BBKL* XVIII, 404–414.

Froschauer, Christoph, the Elder (c. 1490–1564) was an invaluable associate of both Zwingli and Oecolampadius—as printer, publisher, bookseller and, not least, messenger between them and further afield. Originally from Bavaria, he acquired a printer's workshop in Zürich in 1517. He became one of Zwingli's earliest supporters and, through his extensive network of contacts—developed especially at the biannual Frankfurt Book Fair—was to be "crucial in making the work of Zwingli known in Germany" (Gordon, *Swiss*, 240). On his career see Urs B. Leu, "Reformation als Auftrag: Der Zürcher Drucker Christoph Froschauer d. Ä. (ca. 1490–1564)", *Zwingliana* 45 (2018): 1–80; *OER* II, 150; Locher, *ZR*, 582 f.

Hätzer, Ludwig (c. 1500–1529) was an early supporter of Zwingli, who grew disillusioned with the latter's relative caution and became attracted to anabaptist ideas. He was exiled from both Zürich and Augsburg in 1525, whereupon he travelled to Basel. There he took refuge with Oecolampadius, in whose house he stayed and with whom he worked closely from October 1525 until December 1526—when he was forced to flee the city in the wake of a sexual scandal involving Oecolampadius's serving maid. Thereafter Hätzer again frequented anabaptist circles and, together with Hans Denck, translated the Old Testament into German in 1528—a version which Zwingli criticised for excessive literalism. He was executed, nominally at least for adultery, in Konstanz on 4th February 1529. See Goeters, *Hätzer*; *OER* II, 213 f.; *BBKL* II, 453–456.

Haller, Berchthold (c. 1494–1536) was from Württemberg, and an early friend of Melanchthon. He studied at Cologne, and became People's Priest at St Vincent's Cathedral in Bern in 1520. From around 1523 he was a leading reformer there. He was a loyal disciple particularly of Zwingli, but also provided important support to Oecolampadius at the Disputation of Baden in 1526. Later his warm relations with both Bullinger and Farel made him an effective mediator between Zürich and Geneva. On his career see *OER* II, 208 f.; *TRE* XIV, 393–395; *BBKL* II, 485–493; Schindler, *BD*, 94–96, 694–697.

Karlstadt, Andreas Bodenstein von (1480–1541) had a much-travelled and often controversial career. He was one of the earliest evangelical reformers, and a close colleague of Luther until their split in 1524—whereafter he espoused views that were generally closer to those of Zwingli and Oecolampadius. In their correspondence he is presented consistently positively: in 1524 as a controversialist on the sacraments with whom Oecolampadius essentially agrees, and in 1530 as an exile deserving and receiving assistance as he moves regularly between Strasbourg, Zürich and Basel—in which city he was to reside, and exert considerable influence, for much of the 1530s. See Barge, *Bodenstein*; Burnett, *Karlstadt*; *CoE* II, 253–256; *OER* I, 178–180; *TRE* XVII, 649–657; *BBKL* I, 62–65 and III, 1147–1171; *VL 16* VII, 124–134.

Leo Jud (or 'Keller', c. 1482–1542) was probably Zwingli's closest associate and widely expected to be his successor in Zürich as he had been in Einsiedeln.

Jud was appointed People's Priest at St Peter's Church in Zürich in February 1523. A considerable theologian in his own right, he is also important for his German translations of works by Zwingli and many others. On him see Karl-Heinz Wyss, *Leo Jud: Seine Entwicklung zum Reformator, 1519–1523* (Bern: Lang, 1976); Wilfried Kettler, *Trewlich in Teütsch gebracht: Lateinisch-deutsches Übersetzungsschrifttum im Umkreis des Schweizer Humanismus* (Bern: Lang, 2002), 117–212; *CoE* II, 248–250; *OER* II, 356; *BBKL* XIV, 1118–1122; *VL 16* III, 488–496; Locher, *ZR*, 568–575; Gordon, *Zwingli*, 75–77.

Luther, Martin (1483–1548), the first evangelical reformer, at one stage enjoyed the unequivocal and passionate support of both Zwingli and Oecolampadius. By the time of his first mention in their correspondence, in 1525, it is nevertheless clear that the Swiss reformers regarded him with a mistrust and a certain personal hostility. This was no doubt inevitable given Luther's very different views on the Eucharist and, not least, his consistent refusal to recognize the Swiss reformers as his Christian brothers—an attitude which culminated in his notorious refusal to shake Zwingli's hand at the conclusion of the Colloquy of Marburg in 1529. Recent work on Luther includes Lyndal Roper, *Martin Luther: Renegade and Prophet* (London: Bodley Head, 2016); Alberto Melloni, ed., *Martin Luther: A Christian between Reforms and Modernity (1517–2017)*, 3 vols (Berlin: De Gruyter, 2017). See also *CoE* II, 360–363; *OER*, II, 461–467; *TRE* XXI, 514–567; *BBKL* V, 447–482; Füssel, *DD*, 324–344.

Marius, Augustinus (1485–1543), originally from Ulm, was an Austin Canon and Suffragan Bishop of Freising (1522–1526), Basel (1526–1529) and Würzburg (1529–1543). Throughout his time in Basel, during which he also served as Cathedral Preacher, he was something of a *bête noire* for Oecolampadius: an energetic and able Catholic apologist, he seems also to have possessed a rather flamboyant and irascible temperament that Oecolampadius found distasteful on a personal level. On him see Birkner, *Marius*; *CoE* II, 391 f.

Melanchthon, Philipp (1497–1560). Influenced by the humanists Johannes Reuchlin (his uncle) and Jakob Wimpfeling, he became a prodigious Greek scholar at an early age. Soon after his appointment to the chair of Greek at Wittenberg in 1518, he came under the influence of Luther, whose closest and most trusted colleague he soon became. His appearances in the Zwingli-Oecolampadius correspondence occur mainly in letters from 1529 onwards: here it becomes clear above all how adversely his once close relationship with his fellow-Swabian Oecolampadius was affected by the eucharistic disputes of the age. On this see Jeff Fisher, "The Breakdown of a Reformation

Friendship: John Oecolampadius and Philip Melanchthon", *Westminster Theological Journal* 77 (2015): 265–291. More generally see Günter Frank, ed., *Philipp Melanchthon: Der Reformator zwischen Glauben und Wissen. Ein Handbuch* (Berlin: De Gruyter, 2017); Timothy J. Wengert, *Philip Melanchthon: Speaker of the Reformation* (Farnham: Ashgate, 2010); *CoE* II, 424–429; *OER*, III, 141–145; *TRE* XXII, 371–410; *BBKL* V, 1184–1188; Füssel, *DD*, 428–463; Bernstein, *GH*, 133–138.

Myconius, Oswald (1488–1552) studied in Rottweil and Basel, and came to Zürich as a schoolmaster in 1516. Having enthusiastically supported Zwingli's appointment to the *Grossmünster*, he became one of the latter's closest colleagues (and first biographer). He was later to be Oecolampadius's—arguably less gifted and successful—successor in Basel. On his career see Ulrich Gäbler and Martin Wallraff, "Ulrich Myconius im Lichte seines Briefwechsels", in *Oswald Myconius, Briefwechsel 1515–1552: Regesten*, ed. Rainer Henrich, 2 vols (Zürich: Theologischer Verlag, 2017), I, 1–71; *CoE* II, 475; *OER* III, 118; Locher, *ZR*, 580 f.

Pellikan, Konrad (1478–1556) was active in Basel from 1519 as Guardian of the Franciscan monastery and a member of Erasmus's circle: he collaborated with the latter on various editions of patristic authors. Pellikan's views became increasingly aligned with those of Zwingli and Oecolampadius, however, and in early 1526 he succeeded Ceporinus at the *Grossmünster* School in Zürich, teaching Greek, Hebrew and Old Testament. He is nowadays best known for his remarkable seven-volume commentary on the entire Bible (Zürich: Froschauer, 1532–1539). In the correspondence, however, he is mentioned most often in the protracted lead-up to his move to Zürich. On him see Zürcher, *Pellikan*; *CoE* III, 65 f.; *OER* III, 241 f.; *BBKL* VII, 180–183; *VL DH* II, 421–434; Locher, *ZR*, 605 f.

Philipp I, Landgrave of Hesse (1504–1563) was a leading Protestant prince who became particularly concerned to reconcile Lutheran and Swiss positions on the Eucharist, and to defend reformed cities and states against imperial power. He became a regular correspondent of Zwingli from the late 1520s on, and was instrumental in organizing the Colloquy of Marburg in 1529. Philipp's somewhat idiosyncratic marital arrangements are moreover alluded to by Oecolampadius in his very last letter to Zwingli. See Cahill, *Philipp*; Gerhard Müller, "Huldrych Zwingli und Philipp von Hessen", in Schindler, *ZR*, 177–187; *CoE* II, 187–189; *TRE* XXVI, 492–497; *BBKL* VII, 476–479.

Pirckheimer, Willibald (1470–1530) was an illustrious humanist and lawyer based in Nürnberg. He was a close friend of Dürer, Erasmus and, at one time,

Oecolampadius—whom he nevertheless vehemently opposed in the eucharistic debates of 1526–1527. His fundamental theological convictions were seldom entirely clear: "Neither a good Protestant nor a good Catholic, he was too much his own man, too complicated, too scholarly, and too skeptical to accept blindly either the old faith or the new Protestant creed" (Bernstein, *GH*, 105). On his career see Willehad Paul Eckert and Christoph von Imhoff, *Willibald Pirckheimer: Dürers Freund*, 2nd edn (Cologne: Wienand, 1982); *CoE* III, 90–94; *OER* III, 276 f.; *BBKL* VII, 628–633; *VL DH* II, 465–487; Füssel, *DD*, 258–269; Bernstein, *GH*, 95–105.

Reinhart, Anna (c. 1485–1538), the daughter of a Zürich innkeeper, was first married to the minor aristocrat and mercenary Hans Meier von Knonau, who died in 1517. She nursed Zwingli through his serious dose of the plague in 1519, and was generally regarded as a model of piety. Zwingli married her in secret in 1522, before having their union blessed in church on 2nd April 1524. After his death she was accommodated and looked after in his successor Bullinger's household. On her life see Raymond Potgieter, "Anna Reinhard Zwingli—'Apostolic Dorcas', 'dearest housewife', 'angel-wife', 'ziel van mijn ziel' and 'mater dolorosa of the Reformation': From Woman to Valued Citizen", *In die Skriflig* 50/3 (2016): 1–8; Oskar Farner, "Anna Reinhart: Die Gattin Ulrich Zwinglis", *Zwingliana* 3 (1916): 197–211, 229–245; Edward J. Furcha, 'Women in Zwingli's World", *Zwingliana* 19/1 (1992): 131–142; Gordon, *Zwingli*, 68–70.

Rosenblatt, Wibrandis (1504–1564), born at Säckingen in Outer Austria to an official of Emperor Maximilian I, was married successively to the humanist Ludwig Keller (d. 1526), Oecolampadius, Capito and Bucer. Following the latter's death in Cambridge in 1551, she lived the rest of her life in Basel. She sought to play no role in public life, but was plainly regarded as a morally ideal and pragmatically able consort for busy evangelical divines. On her see Roland H. Bainton, *Women of the Reformation in Germany and Italy* (Minneapolis, MN: Augsburg, 1971), 79–95; Susanna Burghartz, "Wibrandis Rosenblatt—Die Frau der Reformatoren", *Theologische Zeitschrift* 60 (2004): 337–349; Ernst Staehelin, *Frau Wibrandis: Eine Gestalt aus den Kämpfen der Reformationszeit* (Bern: Gotthelf, 1934); *CoE* III, 172.

Strauß, Jakob (c. 1480–c. 1527), a Basler by birth, was a Dominican who became a convinced Lutheran and had a much-travelled career as an evangelical reformer. He is probably best known for his social radicalism (which brought him legal difficulties in the light of the Peasants' War), and for his protracted conflict with Oecolampadius over the Eucharist in 1526. On him see Barge, *Strauß*;

Jennifer Smyth, "Running at the Devil with God's Word. The Pamphlets of the Early-Reformation Preacher, Jacob Strauss" (PhD diss., Trinity College Dublin, 2010); *OER* IV, 118 f.; *TRE* XXXII, 246–249; *BBKL* XI, 34–37.

Ulrich VI, Duke of Württemberg (1487–1550) ruled his Duchy from 1498 to 1519, and again from 1534 to 1550. After his deposition as Duke (following military defeat by the Swabian League in 1519), Ulrich spent a good deal of time in Basel. Around 1523–1524 he may well have converted to the evangelical cause under the influence of Oecolampadius. The correspondence suggests that Zwingli was initially hostile to Ulrich, but that the latter came increasingly to be trusted as an ally, due above all to his personal and political closeness to Philipp of Hesse and his implacable opposition to the Habsburgs. On his career see Frasch, *Ulrich*; *CoE* III, 464 f.; *BBKL* XII, 900–902.

Vadian (Joachim von Watt, 1484–1551) was a humanist polymath: poet, philologist, medical doctor, geographer and historian. Following several years in Vienna, he returned to his native St. Gallen in 1517: he was its city physician, several times its mayor, and, from 1522, its most prominent proponent of evangelical reform. He was a long-term and trusted associate of both Zwingli and Oecolampadius. On him see Rudolf Gamper, *Joachim Vadian, 1483/84–1551: Humanist, Arzt, Reformator, Politiker* (Zürich: Chronos, 2017); *CoE* III, 364 f.; *OER* IV, 211 f.; *TRE* XXXIV, 489–492; *BBKL* XII, 1003–1013; Füssel, *DD*, 345–358; Locher, *ZR*, 48–51.

PREFACE

Imbalances and Initiatives

In contemporary Zürich, Huldrych Zwingli (1484–1531) remains prominent. Over the main door of the *Grossmünster*, the 'great minster' church where he preached from 1519 until his death, one reads the words: "Huldrych Zwingli's reformation began in this house of God".[1] Moreover the *Grossmünster* stands in what is now known as *Zwingliplatz*; and numerous buildings throughout the city display plaques proclaiming their roles, however minor, in the life of the great reformer. Above all, perhaps, the visitor to Zürich can hardly avoid encountering an impressive late nineteenth-century statue of Zwingli outside the so-called *Wasserkirche* ('Water Church'), adjacent to the river Limmat.[2]

The average visitor to Basel, however, is far less likely to encounter memorials to Johannes Oecolampadius (1482–1531). He is buried in the city's cathedral, but is commemorated within the building only in a three-panelled epitaph in its cloisters, on which he is given equal billing with the city's first reformed mayor Jakob Meyer zum Hirzen[3] and his own scholarly protégé Simon Grynaeus.[4] Outside, Oecolampadius is also commemorated in a relatively modest statue;[5] but this is rather difficult to find. It is hidden behind a tree in the cathedral's close and, in order to see it properly, one has to position oneself strategically between a variety of vigorous plants. Even in the Church of St Martin, the prime focus

---

1   *In diesem Gotteshaus nahm die Reformation Huldrych Zwinglis ihren Anfang.*
2   The sculptor was the Austrian Heinrich Natter (1844–1892); his work was first unveiled in 1885. Its presentation of Zwingli carrying both a Bible and a sword remains to some degree controversial.
3   Meyer was an important lay ally of Oecolampadius; a prosperous and influential figure in Basel, he was Chief Guild Master from 1522 to 1529, and Mayor of the city from 1529 to 1541. On him see Paul Meyer, "Jakob Meyer zum Hirsen [sic] (1473–1541)", *BZGA* 23 (1925): 97–142; *CoE* II, 440 f.; Füglister, *Handwerksregiment*, 321 f.; Wackernagel, *Basel*, III, 19.
4   Grynaeus (c. 1494–1541), a distinguished classicist and evangelical reformer previously based in Heidelberg, was encouraged by Oecolampadius to come to Basel in 1529 as a kind of replacement for the great humanist Erasmus, who had recently fled the city. He was to play a particularly important role in the city's spiritual life after Oecolampadius's death in 1531. On him see Walter Rominger, "'Der größte Gelehrte seit Erasmus'—und dennoch zu wenig bekannt und beachtet: Simon Grynaeus (1493–1541): 'Großer Gelehrte und kleiner Reformator'", *BWK* 116 (2016): 323–339; *CoE* II, 142–146; *OER* II, 200 f.; *BBKL* II, 377.
5   By Ludwig Keiser (1816–1890), from Zug, who sculpted the original in 1861–1862; the current copy dates from 1917.

FIGURE 1   Statue of Zwingli outside the Zürich *Wasserkirche*

of Oecolampadius's preaching and pastoral ministry from 1523 onwards, the reformer is conspicuous only by his absence. A small plaque of recent vintage commemorates Wibrandis Rosenblatt (1504–1564), who was first married to the humanist Ludwig Keller (d. 1526), then to Oecolampadius, and then in succession to the Strasbourg reformers Wolfgang Capito (d. 1541) and Martin Bucer (d. 1551);[6] but of the career of her distinguished second husband there is no mention.

On one level, of course, the glorified tourist information with which we have begun is neither here nor there; but it is also highly significant. This is because it reflects the markedly different levels of scholarly attention and understanding that have hitherto been enjoyed by the two men whose correspondence this volume translates and interprets. Zwingli is, quite simply, much better known than Oecolampadius. His complete works have been published in a reliable modern edition;[7] he is the subject of several major biographies and other book-

---

6 For brief introductions to Bucer, Capito and Rosenblatt see pp. x, xi and xvi respectively.
7 *zw*. Much is also online: see https://www.irg.uzh.ch/static/zwingli-werke/index.php and https://www.irg.uzh.ch/static/zwingli-briefe/index.php (accessed 14th December 2022).

FIGURE 2   Statue of Oecolampadius outside Basel Cathedral

length studies, in English as well as German;[8] he is the principal focus of an eminent scholarly journal;[9] and in 2019 he became the eponymous hero of an internationally distributed biopic, released to coincide with the 500th anniversary of the start of his ministry in Zürich.[10] For sure, Zwingli's profile also needs raising: he is still standardly seen as, at best, the "third man" of the Reformation, lagging some way behind Luther and Calvin;[11] and his reputation in the English-speaking world in particular has suffered from the lamentable absence of any systematic attempt to translate into English either his theological works or—still less—his voluminous and thematically rich correspondence.[12] A case in point here is the 183-letter strong correspondence between Zwingli and Oecolampadius, only one item of which has hitherto been published in a (partial) English translation.[13]

An imbalance remains, however: if, particularly outside Switzerland, Zwingli has suffered at times from a combination of facile pigeon-holing and benign scholarly neglect, Oecolampadius has been consigned to a much deeper level of obscurity. We still owe much of what we know about him to the rigorous research of a single scholar, the eminent Basel theologian Ernst Staehelin (1889–1980). Alongside several articles, Staehelin bequeathed to posterity three books that remain of fundamental importance for anyone interested in Oecolampadius: a two-volume collection of letters and other documents, presented either in full or—as is the case for his correspondence with Zwingli—in German-language summaries; a monumentally learned intellectual biography of the reformer; and a comprehensive and detailed bibliography of early modern works both by and about him.[14] That said, hardly any of Oecolampadius's predominantly Latin writings have appeared in modern editions or been trans-

---

8   See especially Gordon, *Zwingli*. Distinguished earlier studies include Potter, *Zwingli*; Stephens, *Theology*; and, translated from the German, Gäbler, *Zwingli*. The most important recent book in German is Peter Opitz, *Ulrich Zwingli. Prophet, Ketzer, Pionier des Protestantismus* (Zürich: Theologischer Verlag, 2015).
9   *Zwingliana*: see https://zwingliana.ch/index.php/zwa/index (accessed 14th December 2022).
10 *Zwingli*, directed by Stephan Haupt and with Max Simonischek in the title role.
11 Astonishingly, this cliché found its way into the title of the best-known French biography of the reformer: Jean Rilliet, *Zwingle: Le troisième homme de la Réforme* (Paris: Fayard, 1959).
12 We are aware only of the volumes translated by Jackson, Hinke, Bromiley, Potter (*Documents*) and Pipkin/Furcha (see bibliography).
13 See Potter, *Documents*, 49 f. (part of letter 552).
14 These are, respectively: *OeBA*; Staehelin, *Lebenswerk*; Staehelin. Also still worth reading is Karl Rudolf Hagenbach, *Johann Oekolampad und Oswald Myconius: Die Reformatoren Basels. Leben und ausgewählte Schriften* (Elberfeld: Friderichs, 1859).

lated, even into modern German;[15] and Staehelin remains the reformer's most recent major biographer. One wonders, indeed, whether the sheer weight and authority of his contributions might almost have deterred others from making serious studies of Oecolampadius's life and works: certainly for several decades scholarship on him seemed to be in a state of almost complete stagnation.[16]

It is only in recent years, and thanks almost entirely to American scholars,[17] that Oecolampadius has resurfaced as a relatively regular subject of academic publications. Some of these contributions, admittedly, have done little more than revisit the known contours of Oecolampadius's life and career, at times interpreting these in an uncritical manner that can border on the hagiographical.[18] Other work, however, has achieved much more than this. This is true of the late Eric W. Northway's examination of the relationship between two centrally important aspects of Oecolampadius's thought: his nuanced and influential views on the Eucharist, and his significant indebtedness to the writings of the church fathers.[19] Northway focuses especially on Oecolampadius's pioneering reception and exegesis of the eucharistic theology of Irenaeus of Lyon. Jeff

---

15   The only translations into English that we know of are: Iohannes Oecolampadius, *An Exposition of Genesis*, ed./trans. Mickey Mattox (Milwaukee, WI: Marquette University Press, 2013—includes only the first three of sixteen chapters); and Johannes Oecolampadius, *Sermons on the First Epistle of John* (*A Handbook for the Christian Life*), trans. Timothy Matthew Slemmons (s.l.: Slemmons, 2017). An edition of selected Latin and German works on the Eucharist has recently appeared, closely based on the relevant sixteenth-century prints: Johannes Oekolampad, *Ausgewählte Abendmahlsschriften*, ed. Florence Becher-Häusermann and Peter Litwan (Leipzig: Evangelische Verlagsanstalt, 2023). A modern German translation of excerpts from these (as well as eucharistic works by Luther and Zwingli) is in preparation. The Oecolampadius versions are being made by Professor Sven Grosse (Basel), whom we thank for providing us with detailed information about the project.

16   From between the 1930s and the 1990s one can point only to: Akira Demura, "Church Discipline According to Johannes Oecolampadius in the Setting of his Life and Thought" (ThD diss., Princeton, 1964); Gordon Rupp, *Patterns of Reformation* (London: Epworth, 1969), 1–46; Hughes Oliphant Old, "The Homiletics of John Oecolampadius and the Sermons of the Greek Fathers", in Boris Bobrinskoy et al., eds, *'Communio Sanctorum'. Mélanges offerts à Jean-Jacques von Allmen* (Geneva: Labor et Fides, 1982), 239–250; Ed L. Miller, "Oecolampadius: The Unsung Hero of the Basel Reformation", *Iliff Review* 39/3 (1982): 5–25.

17   The sole exception of note is Peter Opitz, "The Exegetical and Hermeneutical Work of Johannes Oecolampadius, Huldrych Zwingli and Jean Calvin", in Saebø, *Hebrew Bible*, 407–451.

18   This is true to some extent of Thomas A. Fudge, "Icarus of Basel? Oecolampadius and the Early Swiss Reformation", *Journal of Religious History* 21 (1997): 268–284; and especially of Diane Poythress, *Reformer of Basel: The Life, Thought, and Influence of Johannes Oecolampadius* (Grand Rapids, MI: Reformation Heritage Books, 2011).

19   Northway, "Reception".

Fisher, meanwhile, has helpfully illuminated Oecolampadius's approach to biblical study by highlighting its Christo-centric, or more precisely Christo-scopic nature, another perspective that owes much to patristic influence, and one which arguably enabled the Basel reformer to do an unusual degree of justice to both the "history" and the "mystery" of scripture.[20] Most importantly perhaps, Amy Nelson Burnett, in her magisterial study of the eucharistic debates of the second half of the 1520s,[21] has demonstrated the key role played within them by Oecolampadius's 1525 treatise *De genuina verborum Domini "Hoc est corpus meum" iuxta vetustissimos auctores expositione liber* (Strasbourg: Knobloch). This work not only proved a potent catalyst for printed controversies with both Catholics and Lutherans, but constituted in its own right "a sophisticated and eloquent defense of a symbolic understanding of the Lord's Supper, far more significant than anything Zwingli had written to date".[22] As we shall see, the *Genuine Exposition* in many ways crystallized important aspects of Oecolampadius's unique contribution to sixteenth-century intellectual history: his exceptional erudition and scholarly rigour, his respectful but creative reception both of the fathers and of Erasmus of Rotterdam, and the marked originality of his theological thought. The latter was every inch the equal of Zwingli's, and fully capable of exerting a direct, independent and powerful influence of its own—as it did, not least, on the intellectual development of Jean Calvin.[23]

The present volume has been informed and motivated by all these gaps, imbalances and scholarly achievements. Responding especially to the damaging paucity of source texts in English, it translates for the first time the full correspondence of Zwingli and Oecolampadius, as recorded in volumes VII–XI of Zwingli's complete works (zw): not least in the light of research into the manuscript copies held in the Staatsarchiv and Zentralbibliothek in Zürich, we are confident that this edition is both reliable and comprehensive. Our translations are accompanied by detailed explanatory and linguistic notes, which—we hope—will enable the reader to navigate the choppy and sometimes confusing waters of the letters themselves. The introduction that follows, however, seeks to provide some necessary orientation of a more general kind,

---

20 Jeff Fisher, *A Christoscopic Reading of Scripture: Johannes Oecolampadius on Hebrews* (Göttingen: Vandenhoeck & Ruprecht, 2016). Cf. p. 53: "Oecolampadius operated by the fundamental principle that Christ is the "goal" or "scope" (*scopus*) of all of Scripture, and therefore, everything written in Scripture was about him and for the benefit of his church".
21 Burnett, *Debating*.
22 Burnett, *Debating*, 105.
23 See below, p. 40.

whilst at the same time offering a new interpretation of the individual and joint achievements of Zwingli and Oecolampadius—especially between 10th December 1522 (when Oecolampadius first wrote to Zwingli) and 11th October 1531 (when the latter died in battle at Kappel).

Our introduction works outwards from Zürich and Basel. We begin by establishing the two very different local contexts within and out of which our two reformers wrote to each other. Zürich must be discussed first, because its reformation began earlier and progressed more swiftly than that of Basel, and because it developed, in the first half of the 1520s, a kind of theological and ecclesiastical template—often contested but never ignored—which Basel and other evangelically-minded Swiss and South German cities increasingly followed as the decade progressed.

Having thus considered Zwingli and Oecolampadius's relationships with their respective cities, we move on to the epistolary relationship of the two men themselves. We take account, for example, of the similarities and differences it evinces between them; of its fascinating mixture of warm personal regard and goal-oriented professional collaboration; and of a certain weakening of their working relationship as their approaches and, above all, preoccupations begin to diverge.

The introduction's fourth and fifth sections are wider in geographical and intellectual scope. We begin by pursuing a thread that pervades much of the correspondence, namely the existence of a particular closeness between Zwingli's Zürich, Oecolampadius's Basel and the Strasbourg of Bucer and Capito. We assess some theological and personal aspects of the relationships involved, and argue that the three cities' most notable joint achievement was a series of scholarly, in many respects Erasmian commentaries on books of the Old Testament which appeared from 1525 onwards. Section 5, for its part, discusses aspects of the wider influence of the Swiss Reformation, arguing in particular that, while Zwingli's contribution to developments in Southern Germany, in England and in Geneva is now reasonably well appreciated, that of Oecolampadius—on such matters as the theology of the Eucharist and of church discipline—requires greater emphasis and further study. Then in three further sections we turn to practical issues concerning the letters themselves and our translations of them. We discuss what they tell us about the everyday practicalities and constraints of sixteenth-century epistolography, such as the involvement of scribes and messengers, and the use of codes for security reasons; we give an account of the surviving original manuscripts, and examine questions posed by them and by the edition of them we have used; and we describe our methods of translation, in the light of what is known of Zwingli and Oecolampadius's own practices.

IMBALANCES AND INITIATIVES   XXV

FIGURE 3   't Licht is op den Kandelaer gestelt
            AMSTERDAM, RIJKSMUSEUM, RP-P-OB-78.422

All in all, we hope that our volume will make a material contribution to raising the profile of both Zwingli and, above all, Oecolampadius, especially but not only in the English-speaking world. Certainly the classic, in essence Calvinist view of the Reformation portrayed in the much-copied seventeenth-century engraving *'t Licht is op den Kandelaar gestelt* ('the light has been placed upon the candlestick') is still in need of revision, at least as far as our two Swiss reformers are concerned.[24]

In this work, they are both positioned towards the back of the space illuminated by the reformers' candle, some way back from the obvious 'stars', Luther and Calvin, and also behind such figures as Jerome of Prague, Girolamo Zanchi and William Perkins. Moreover, they are portrayed as facing each other, rather than the viewer, in a way that seems to suggest an inward-looking focus on the purely Swiss context; and, whilst Zwingli is at least positioned fairly centrally

---

24   Amsterdam, Rijksmuseum, RP-P-OB-78.422. The image was first published by Hugo Allart. For a treatment of the vigorous and long-lived tradition to which it belongs see Spaans, "Faces".

on the horizontal axis, Oecolampadius is literally marginalized—featuring as he does as an apparent afterthought in the extreme top right-hand corner. At least the Dutch engraving names him, unlike its likely source, Thomas Jenner's *The Candle is Lighted*, in which he is the only one of the fifteen depicted divines to remain anonymous;[25] but his relatively lowly status in the scheme of things could hardly be expressed more clearly in visual terms.

In reality, as both his original German and later Grecized names make clear, Oecolampadius possessed a powerful, distinctive and historically important light of his own;[26] but that light has hidden for too long under a bushel, for the design and manufacture of which he himself may have been partly responsible. Translating and interpreting his letters to Zwingli will represent, we hope, at least one stage in the no doubt lengthy scholarly process of enabling Oecolampadius's light to emerge into a clearer and more widely appreciated focus.

---

25 See Spaans, "Faces", 408–411, 415.
26 The German name is variously rendered Heussgen, Hussgen or Huszgen, which Oecolampadius clearly took to mean 'house-light' (*Hausschein*): Οἰκολαμπάδιος (*Oikolampádios*) is derived from οἶκος ('house') and λαμπάς ('light, lamp').

Introduction

1   Zwingli and Zürich

When he was first written to by Oecolampadius,[1] Zwingli was 38 years old, at the height of his powers, and a major and increasingly influential figure both within Zürich and beyond. The extent of his reputation is reflected immediately in the tone Oecolampadius adopts towards him—which, even allowing for the latter's innate modesty and use of humanist rhetorical conventions, clearly reflects a belief that Zwingli (although the younger man by more than a year) is in some way his superior, or at least the senior partner in their relationship. Indeed this sense, however subjective and arguably misguided, of Zwingli occupying a higher place in the theological and political pecking-order pervades almost the whole correspondence—and it is one which Zwingli does little to discourage. On the contrary, he sometimes positively encourages it, as for example when he points to the superiority of Zürich's ecclesiastical arrangements over those of Basel,[2] and, not least, when he uses the royal 'we'.[3]

Zwingli's ascent to this position of real and assumed eminence by late 1522 had not been meteoric or straightforward. Neither in his correspondence nor elsewhere does he reveal much about his early life, but it is plain that his background was both rural and, to an extent, privileged. He was born in 1484, in the village of Wildhaus, in the eastern Swiss region of Toggenburg, where his father—also called Ulrich[4]—owned land and served as *Amtmann*, that is to say as mayor or chief magistrate. Young Ulrich was plainly intellectually gifted, and underwent an extensive education—first with his uncle Bartholomäus, parish priest of Weesen, then at Latin schools in Basel and Bern, and eventually, between 1498 and 1506, at the universities of Vienna and Basel. It is not clear how far, at this early stage, Zwingli was affected by the humanist circles that were then burgeoning particularly in Vienna, with their emphasis on the scholarly study of classical antiquity and the ethical principles to be

---

1 See letter 258 (10th December 1522).
2 See for example his letter about divisions in Basel concerning the Eucharist, 367 (especially lines 13–19), or his *ex cathedra* advice (albeit in response to a specific request) on how to deal with the local Council in 569, lines 1–49.
3 This feature first appears in letter 268, lines 10–19.
4 The name 'Huldrych', or 'Huldreich', by which he later went, is a punning self-stylization: the term means 'rich in grace' (or 'rich in God's favour'). See Oecolampadius's allusion to it in 258, line 20f.

derived from this. He did, however, make the acquaintance of several progressively inclined figures who later became evangelical reformers, such as Vadian (Joachim von Watt), Leo Jud and, not least, Thomas Wyttenbach, his mentor at the University of Basel, from whom he appears to have learnt the rigorously disciplined approach to Bible study that was to remain a hallmark for the rest of his career.[5]

Between 1506 and 1518 Zwingli was active as a Catholic priest. For a decade he served in Glarus, the capital of the small independent state of the same name and the nearest major settlement to his home village; and from November 1516 he was People's Priest[6] of the Benedictine abbey of Einsiedeln (Canton Schwyz). One assumes that many of the duties Zwingli performed at this stage of his career were both routine and entirely typical of late-medieval Catholicism; but two very different sets of experiences towards the end of it shaped his future thinking with particular potency. First, he saw military action as chaplain to Swiss mercenary forces campaigning in Northern Italy, most notably at the disastrous battle of Marignano near Milan on 13th September 1515. Here he must have witnessed almost unprecedented carnage: roughly half of the participating soldiers (including 10,000 Swiss) were killed, and Zwingli was left "deeply troubled, scarred by the brutality of war and haunted by a vision that divine judgement had fallen at Marignano on the duplicity of those who had profited from the sale of Swiss mercenaries".[7] In a sense Marignano radicalized him in political terms, confirming him as an implacable enemy of the mercenary trade and of the concomitant system of pension payments made by foreign powers in return for political and military influence.[8] It also made him into a pacifist, one who vigorously underlined the phrase *Dulce bellum inexpertis* ('war is sweet to those who have not experienced it') in his copy of Erasmus of Rotterdam's *Adagia*.[9]

Erasmus was, in fact, the other seminal discovery of Zwingli's Glarus and Einsiedeln years. The latter was always a voracious reader, and spent a great deal of his time in Glarus in the systematic study of classical writers, of the

---

5   On Leo Jud and Vadian see above, pp. XIII–XIV and XVII respectively. On Wyttenbach (c. 1472–1526) see Hans Rudolf Lavater, "Thomas Wyttenbach (†1526), le maître de Zwingli", *Mennonitica Helvetica* 39 (2016): 83–91; *BBKL* XIV, 264–266.
6   We use 'people's priest' throughout as the equivalent of the German *Leutpriester*. This term refers to a person appointed to give pastoral care in a parish that was incorporated into an otherwise non-parochial ecclesiastical institution, such as a monastery or a collegiate church.
7   Gordon, *Zwingli*, 32.
8   That he persisted in these views is evident not least from letter 552, lines 18–47 (29th November 1526).
9   See Gäbler, *Zwingli*, 32.

church fathers, and also of certain scholastics such as Duns Scotus.[10] Erasmus, however, stood out. In 1514–1515 Zwingli came across the Dutch scholar's *Enchiridion militis Christi* ('Handbook of a Christian Soldier'), his collection of proverbs known as the *Adagia*, and various volumes of biblical exegesis; and these, together with Erasmus's Greek New Testament of March 1516—to the preparation of which his future correspondent Oecolampadius made a material contribution[11]—had an overwhelming impact on the still young priest. Zwingli's personal relationship with Erasmus was to prove neither unproblematic nor particularly long-lived: only six years, for example, separate their sole face-to-face meeting in April 1516 (to which Zwingli reacted with almost embarrassing euphoria)[12] from Erasmus's angry repudiation of the former's *Apologeticus Archeteles* in a letter of 8th September 1522.[13] Nevertheless Zwingli remained for the rest of his career deeply indebted to several of the Dutchman's key priorities and insights: his rigorously bibliocentric scholarship, his Christocentric theology, his ethical idealism, his outrage at ecclesiastical corruption and, not least, his clear distinction between flesh and spirit, the visible and the invisible.

Zwingli's official ministry in Zürich began on 1st January 1519, his 35th birthday. His appointment as People's Priest of the *Grossmünster* was not unanimous (the minster's canons voted for him by seventeen votes to seven), and had been preceded by some controversy: as one of his better-known letters acknowledges,[14] he had recently impregnated a sexually experienced barber's daughter in Einsiedeln. The letter, to the *Grossmünster* canon Heinrich Utinger, is a strange mixture of disarming honesty, genuine penitence, desperate self-justification and of-its-time misogyny; but it clearly did the trick, and Zwingli's appointment was confirmed—aided, no doubt, by the fact that his preaching will have been heard by numerous Zürich citizens while on pilgrimage to

---

10   For lists of the relevant authors see Gäbler, *Zwingli*, 34.
11   On this see Jeff Fisher, "The Old Testament Editor of the First Published Greek New Testament: Johannes Oecolampadius (1482–1531)", *Journal of Early Modern Christianity* 5 (2018): 35–55.
12   In the only surviving letter *from* Zwingli *to* Erasmus—ed. ZW VII, 35f. (no. 13); trans. EC III, 239f. (no. 390).
13   *Apologeticus archeteles adpellatus, quo respondetur Paraenesi, a Re. Do. Constantiensi ad senatum praepositurae Tigurinae quem Capiulum vocant missae* (Zürich: Froschauer, 1522; Leu/Weidmann 191)—ed. ZW I, 256–327 (no. 13). Erasmus's letter is in ZW VII, 582 (no. 238; 8th September 1522); trans. EC IX, 186f. (no. 1315). For a full account of Erasmus and Zwingli's relationship see Christ-von Wedel, "Erasmus", especially 77–124.
14   Ed. ZW VII, 110–113 (no. 48, 5th December 1518). There is a modern German translation in Alfred Schindler, "Zwinglis «Fehltritt» in Einsiedeln und die Überlieferung dieses Ereignisses", *Zwingliana* 36 (2019): 49–57.

Einsiedeln and that his political opinions (including a profound mistrust of France) chimed well with those of many members of the city's governing Council.[15]

That Council was a complex, bi-cameral body. It was dominated by Zürich's craft guilds, twelve of which sent delegates to the Large Council. Also represented in that chamber was the so-called *Constaffel* ('Constabulary'), a grouping of "knights, merchants, property owners, and financiers"[16] which in the early years of Zwingli's ministry at least, proved often to be a locus of conservative opposition to his reforms. This aptly named Large Council (which numbered around 200 members) was supplemented by a 24-strong Small Council, by two mayors (*Bürgermeister*) serving successively for six months each, and by largely *ad hoc* advisory commissions, which made recommendations and prepared legislation—and on whose composition and activities Zwingli seems to have had considerable influence. The Council's decision-making processes were inevitably complicated, sometimes opaque, and certainly not democratic in any modern sense; but it is important to remember that the mayors and Large Council in particular afforded Zwingli very considerable support from an early stage. It is certainly possible to exaggerate the straightforwardness of his relationship to Zürich's legislators—it was by no means problem-free, and deteriorated somewhat towards the end of his life. To Oecolampadius, however, perennially beset in Basel by a range of powerful internal opponents, Zwingli's relatively secure political position in Zürich must have seemed enviable indeed.

The latter's strong initial impact in his new city, however, was due almost entirely to the power of his own preaching. He began both programmatically and provocatively, by preaching his first sermon on the beginning of St Matthew's Gospel, rather than on the lectionary readings set for the day. Thus began a practice of preaching systematically through entire biblical books which recalled the practice of such early fathers as St John Chrysostom and had recently been revived in Basel by Wolfgang Capito,[17] but which was strikingly unmedieval in its implied priorities. As far as can be discerned from relatively scanty records, the subject matter of Zwingli's early sermons could also be incendiary: he condemned the mercenary trade and pensions, attacked ecclesiastical tithes, and cast serious doubt on the theological validity of venerating Mary and the other saints. He also showed signs of having read Luther's early

---

15 Potter (*Zwingli*, 45f.) reminds us also that Zwingli's rival candidate, the Swabian Laurentius Maer, was believed to have fathered eight children.
16 Gäbler, *Zwingli*, 8.
17 See below, p. 15.

INTRODUCTION

works, as he attacked such targets as the monastic system, the selling of indulgences and, at least implicitly, the pre-eminence of the papacy.

Topics such as these inevitably attracted both enthusiastic support and intense opposition; one has the impression the violent storm in Zürich's religious affairs that finally broke in 1522 had been long in the brewing—especially perhaps after the Council's somewhat confused mandate of November 1520, to the effect that preaching in the city's churches should be based exclusively on the Bible, but excluding "Lutheran" teachings. The storm's eventual catalyst, however, was the so-called *Wurstessen* of 9th March 1522, at which, in an action provocatively reminiscent of the Last Supper, sausages were eaten by a group of men seated at a table in the house (or shop) of the printer Christoph Froschauer.[18] The group included Zwingli, who did not eat, but who plainly masterminded this unequivocal breach of Lenten regulations, and indeed defended it in a sermon that was printed almost immediately afterwards.[19] The *Wurstessen*, which was soon much imitated elsewhere in the city, led in turn to a disciplinary visitation by representatives of the Bishop of Konstanz, which the Zürich Council declined almost ostentatiously to support: they invited Zwingli to debate before them against the bishop's men and imposed "the burden of proof on the ecclesiastical authorities, who were required to justify existing [Lenten] practice on the basis of the Scripture principle".[20] Much emboldened, Zwingli proceeded to engage in other openly rebellious acts: on 2nd July 1522 he and ten colleagues signed a petition in favour of clerical marriage; at some point during that year he got married (semi-secretly) himself;[21] in the autumn he published his first truly substantial and unequivocal statements of evangelical doctrine;[22] and on 10th October he formally broke with the Roman Catholic Church by resigning his priestly office—only to be appointed by his Council to a preaching role instead.

It is roughly at this point that Zwingli's correspondence with Oecolampadius begins, and some of their early letters find them discussing the seminal event of 29th January 1523, namely the so-called First Zürich Disputation.[23]

---

18 For a biographical note on Froschauer see above, pp. XII–XIII.
19 *Von erkiesen vnd fryheit der spysen. Von ergernus vnd verboesrung* (Zürich: Froschauer, 16th April 1522)—ed. ZW I, 88–136 (no. 8).
20 Gäbler, *Zwingli*, 55.
21 On Zwingli's wife Anna Reinhart see above, p. XVI.
22 His *Archeteles* (see p. 3, n. 13); also *Von Clarhayt und gewüsse oder unbetrogliche des worts gottes* (s.l., s.n., 6th September 1522)—ed. ZW I, 338–384 (no. 14); trans. Bromiley, 49–95.
23 See 268, lines 37–41; 269, lines 1–37; 271, lines 24–43; 280, lines 1–13. Accounts of the disputation include those in Gordon, *Zwingli*, 89–94; Gordon, *Swiss*, 57–60; Potter, *Zwingli*, 97–125; Gäbler, *Zwingli*, 63–71.

Called by the Council at Zwingli's urging, the disputation was an attempt to establish theological and political clarity and to ward off growing opposition both within and, especially, beyond Zürich. In no sense a purely academic debate, it was rather "a civil legal proceeding in the Swiss tradition of a civic or rural communal gathering, which recognized the "true divine scripture" as the formal legal rule for clarifying the situation of the church";[24] and the prime question to be tried was the purity or otherwise of Zwingli's doctrine. Whilst attended by over 600 people, the proceedings were dominated by Zwingli himself, in dialogue for some of the time with the leading Catholic apologist Johann Faber, Vicar-General of Konstanz.[25] The verdict was a foregone conclusion: Zwingli was exonerated of all error, was allowed to continue preaching with the Council's blessing, and all priests under the latter's jurisdiction were required to follow his example. In the history of the Zürich Reformation this forceful assertion both of the Council's power and of Zwingli's personal prestige was a decisive, if not yet definitive moment—and one which, for Oecolampadius and doubtless many other evangelicals, gave rise to unequivocal congratulation.[26]

Even after the First Disputation, however, the religious and political situation in Zürich, and particularly its rural hinterland, was by no means stable. Switzerland was far from immune from the intense socio-economic pressures that were to lead, in much of Germany, to the Peasants' War of 1525; and, like Luther in Saxony, Zwingli could be accused with some justification of incautiously stoking these fires. Moreover his Erasmian emphasis on the spiritual, invisible dimensions of Christianity was understood in some more radical quarters as justifying the removal, indeed violent destruction, of icons and other devotional items, themselves "seen by many as images of economic oppression".[27] The so-called Second Zürich Disputation of 26th to 28th October 1523,[28] a still larger affair than its predecessor, failed adequately to resolve these issues, and over the course of the next two years the Council, willed on by Zwingli, was more or less forced to take matters into its own hands.

With the benefit of hindsight, five measures above all can be seen as important staging posts. On 15th June 1524 the Council officially endorsed the removal

---

24 Campi, "Zurich", 74.
25 On Faber see above, p. XII. On this episode in his career see Keith D. Lewis, "Johann Faber and the First Zürich Disputation: 1523. A Pre-Tridentine Catholic Response to Ulrich Zwingli and his Sixty-Seven Articles" (PhD diss., Catholic University of America, 1985).
26 See 280, lines 1–5.
27 Gordon, *Zwingli*, 103.
28 On its proceedings see Gordon, *Zwingli*, 104 f.; Potter, *Zwingli*, 131–133; Gäbler, *Zwingli*, 76–81.

of images from Zürich's churches. In August 1524, in response to growing threats from radical anabaptists, it mandated the baptism of all new-born infants. On 5th December 1524 Zürich's monasteries were officially dissolved—though some of them had already ceased their activities voluntarily. On 12th April 1525, in a crucial if controversial move, the Latin Mass was abolished and replaced by a simple vernacular service of the Lord's Supper, underpinned by a very different sacramental theology. Finally, on 19th June 1525 a theological school, funded from tithes and other ecclesiastical payments, was set up in the choir of the *Grossmünster*.[29] All in all, these and other measures amounted to the imposition of a new ecclesiastical order: "the reforms of 1525 placed Zürich outside the Catholic Church: the sacraments had been denied and the authority of the pope spurned".[30] There was no going back.

Self-evidently, by no means everyone was happy with these developments. Indeed, the second half of the 1520s were to see Zwingli and his Zürich supporters defending their achievements on various sometimes inter-related fronts in ways that sapped their energies and frustrated many of their plans. The Second Zürich Disputation in particular had revealed the extent of radical evangelical opposition within the city, as—remarkable though this might now seem—certain former supporters of Zwingli found the pace of change too slow and the manner of its espousal too hesitant. These enthusiasts were in the main anabaptists—or, as Zwingli and Oecolampadius preferred to call them, "catabaptists".[31] In principle at least, such radical thinkers posed a serious threat to Zürich's new polity, not least because their theological differences with the Zwinglians were profound, going far beyond questions of when, how or by whom people should be baptized. Above all, anabaptist views and practices were often decidedly separatist in character, based on an understanding of the primitive church which saw it as an exclusive, fully liberated body of faithful Christians, which as such bore no allegiance and owed no obligation to the local secular powers. Such a view was fundamentally irreconcilable with Zwingli's insistence on the need for close, symbiotic collaboration between

---

29 "Encouraged by the example of Erasmus of Rotterdam, who had inspired the founding of the *Collegium trilingue* in Louvain as an independent educational institution alongside the local university, Zwingli planned a reform of education that would assure the training of future pastors"—Campi, "Zurich", 77. This institution, known as the *Prophezei* and later the *Lectorium*, was to prove influential elsewhere, not least in Basel.
30 Gordon, *Swiss*, 68.
31 See especially 391, lines 11–15 and n. 6. *Catabaptistae* means 'opponents of baptism', *anabaptistae* 're-baptizers'. The former no doubt suggested itself because of anabaptists' tendency to leave children unbaptized.

church and state. In practice, however, one suspects that the threat posed by the Zürich anabaptists was seldom as great as it seemed. Their activities were sporadic, they were deeply divided, and they were never coherently led. Moreover Zürich's authorities were often determined and grimly effective in their treatment of them. On 17th January 1525, for example, the Council reinforced its requirement for infant baptism with the threat of banishment for those who did not comply; in the aftermath numerous anabaptists were indeed expelled; and on 5th January 1527 the leading anabaptist Georg Blaurock was flogged and banished, and—notoriously—his colleague Felix Manz executed by drowning in the Limmat. Commenting to Oecolampadius on these events, Zwingli suggests that they "laid the axe at the root of the tree".[32] That overstates the case: after all, three further anabaptists were to suffer the same fate as Manz within Zwingli's lifetime. It is nevertheless plausible to claim that "by 1531 the Anabaptist movement was largely eliminated in the canton of Zürich"[33]—as long as one accepts that many of its members had, in all probability, simply moved elsewhere.

If the anabaptists attacked the Zwinglians as it were from the left wing of early sixteenth-century Protestantism, then numerous Lutheran apologists can be said to have done so from the right—at least as far as the main bone of contention, the Eucharist, was concerned. Battle lines with Lutherans such as Johannes Bugenhagen, Johannes Brenz and Jakob Strauß[34] were drawn in 1525, and they remained in place up to, and to some extent beyond, the Colloquy of Marburg in 1529. In retrospect one is tempted to wonder why the disagreements between the two camps seemed as important and incendiary as they clearly did. All sixteenth-century evangelicals, after all, were united in their clear rejection of the Mass as a propitiatory sacrifice, of transubstantiation, and of communion in one kind. Differences remained, however, particularly over the question whether Christ's body and blood were really present in the consecrated bread and wine. For Luther and his followers they were, albeit in a spiritual rather than substantial form; for Zwingli and—as we shall see—Oecolampadius, they were not. This led them, from 1524 onwards, to develop a symbolic conception of the Eucharist, according to which Christ's words at the Last Supper, "this is my body", must be understood as meaning something like "this signifies my body". Such spiritual benefits as accrued from the sacrament were therefore dependent on the faith of its recipient, rather than on any qualities of the elements themselves.

---

32   See 569, lines 59–62.
33   Campi, "Zurich", 82.
34   On these three figures see below, above, pp. X–XI, XVI–XVII.

Zwingli's fundamental insights into the Eucharist are in fact conveyed very approachably in one of his letters, that addressed to the Lutheran reformer of Reutlingen Matthäus Alber on 16th November 1524 (but also printed for public consumption).[35] His letters to Oecolampadius do not feature anything comparable, but five of them (367, 401, 416, 998, 1136) contain at least some concerted discussion of the Eucharist, and very much confirm what we know of his views from elsewhere. It is particularly striking that four of these letters allude to John 6:63 ("it is the spirit that gives life, the flesh profits nothing"), which became "the key text for Zwingli. It is a wall of bronze which nothing can shake, let alone shatter ... Of itself, without any of Zwingli's other arguments, it is enough to prove that 'is' must mean 'signifies'".[36] One of these "other arguments" is the disarmingly simple one that Christ's body cannot be in two places at once; and we see this also asserted in letters 401 and 998: now that Christ has ascended into heaven, "in that flesh he is sitting at the right hand of God", and "his body has been laid aside, as far as the function it performed in his humanity is concerned";[37] hence it is a logical absurdity to suggest that any aspect of Christ's human nature can still reside in a consecrated wafer. Finally, a passage in letter 401 demonstrates that Zwingli's insistence on a symbolic—or metaphorical—interpretation of Christ's words at the Last Supper is both reasonable and eminently biblical: scripture refers to Jesus, for example, as a stone, a vine, and a lamb, but no sane person would argue that he literally *is* any of these things.[38]

At times, in these letters at least, Zwingli's eucharistic views can come across as almost shockingly simplistic, as for example when he ends a letter with the words "farewell and be steadfast against these gods: the flesh, the blood, the bread and the wine".[39] He can also be inflexible and intransigent—as he is throughout letter 1136, from November 1530, in which he crossly repudiates Bucer's attempts at reconciliation with Luther. It is disconcertingly difficult to reconcile such attitudes with his attempts elsewhere to urge unity in eucharistic theology—on the basis that there is "nothing for which we should strive as for unanimity and concord", especially in matters that, by comparison with

---

35 *Ad Matthaeum Alberum Rutlingensium ecclesiasten, de coena dominica* (Zürich: Froschauer, 1524)—ed. ZW III, 335–354 (no. 41); trans. Pipkin/Furcha, II, 131–144. It is discussed by Burnett, *Debating*, 99f.; Stephens, *Theology*, 228–231; Locher, ZR, 294–297. For a thorough summary of Zwingli's eucharistic thought see Stephens, *Theology*, 218–259.
36 Stephens, *Theology*, 232. See 367, line 83f.; 401, lines 26–31, 39–41, 56–58, 66f.; 416, line 49; 998, lines 24–26.
37 401, line 96f.; 998, 6f.
38 See 401, lines 122–141.
39 381, line 7f. (12th September 1525).

the preaching of faith, are "wholly unnecessary ornaments", inessential for salvation.[40] Context, of course, is all; and perhaps we should not be surprised to encounter such ironies in the life of a pacifist who died in a battle for which he himself was at least partly responsible.

Mention of that battle, at Kappel in 1531, serves to remind us that, for all the inter-Protestant wrangling we have been discussing, Zwingli's most numerous, powerful and implacable opponents were Catholics. When Zürich formally espoused the Reformation, it inevitably isolated itself in an ecclesiastical, but also political sense. However promisingly evangelical ideas began to spread into areas such as St. Gallen, Appenzell and indeed Basel, power in Switzerland continued to reside primarily with the vastly more numerous adherents of the old religion. Prominent among these were the long-established Five States (*fünf Orte*) of Uri, Schwyz, Luzern, Zug and Unterwalden; and, not least, the Habsburg Archduke of Austria, Ferdinand (1503–1564), who, as the *de facto* representative of Emperor Charles V in the German-speaking lands, shared his brother's determination to re-impose Catholicism wherever possible.[41]

An important demonstration of Catholic strength, and one which is discussed at length by Zwingli and Oecolampadius, occurred at the so-called Disputation of Baden, which met—in tandem with the Swiss Confederate Diet[42]—between 19th May and 8th June 1526. As at the First Zürich Disputation, and indeed most others in the sixteenth century, the outcome of the proceedings at Baden was essentially predetermined: they took place on firmly Catholic soil, and the numerically vastly superior Catholic party was led by the experienced and formidable controversialist Johannes Eck,[43] whereas Zwingli was absent—for reasons that certainly made sense in terms of his own security, but which severely discomfited Oecolampadius.[44] Inevitably therefore, the conservative Catholic articles proposed by Eck were eventually endorsed by 84

---

40   367, lines 10f., 73–76.
41   On Ferdinand see above, p. XII.
42   This institution (called in German the *Tagsatzung*), to which representatives from all cantons were invited, was the leading organ of federal government in early modern Switzerland. It met several times a year at varying locations, but its powers, particularly in domestic Swiss affairs, were severely circumscribed by the high degree of independence enjoyed by individual cantons.
43   See above, p. XI. The fullest and most authoritative study of the disputation is now Schindler, BD. In English see also Irena Backus, *The Disputations of Baden, 1526 and Berne, 1528: Neutralizing the Early Church* (Princeton, NJ: Princeton Theological Seminary, 1993), 1–78.
44   See the letters written from Baden, e.g. 483, lines 12–14; 488, lines 1–7.

votes to 24; and into the bargain, the preaching and publishing of evangelical views were proscribed, and Zwingli branded a heretic.

Such controlling, indeed bullying behaviour on the part of the Catholic majority proved, however, to be largely counter-productive. Many cities and states simply refused to recognize the disputation's provisions and, fuelled by an energizing sense of resentment, these areas' evangelical reformers grew markedly in influence: the implementation of the Reformation in Bern (1528) and in Basel (1529), for example, can be seen as at least indirect consequences of events at Baden. Overall, far from re-uniting Switzerland under the Catholic banner, the disputation had the medium-term effect of reinforcing and sharpening its growing confessional divide. Protestant cities established the so-called Christian Civic Union (*christliches Burgrecht*), a defensive, anti-Catholic and anti-Habsburg alliance. Zürich was joined in this by Konstanz in 1527, by Bern and St. Gallen in 1528, and later by towns such as Basel, Biel, Schaffhausen, Strasbourg and Mulhouse. The Five States and Archduke Ferdinand, for their part, established a "Christian Alliance" on 22nd April 1529; and this, combined with the burning soon afterwards of the evangelical reformer Jakob Kaiser in Schwyz, made some form of civil war along confessional lines appear almost inevitable. It was in fact narrowly averted already in June 1529, when the so-called First Kappel War turned out to be no such thing, but rather a show of military force by a much stronger Protestant army, followed by a treaty in which the Five States agreed to abandon their Habsburg alliance, but not to accede to Zwingli's demands for freedom of preaching throughout the Confederation and the renunciation of mercenary activities and foreign pensions—reverses for which he blamed, probably correctly, the distinctly different, independent approach adopted by the negotiators from Bern.

By this time, though, Zwingli was "spoiling for a fight".[45] He was far from satisfied with so precarious a peace; moreover, he was "certain that Reformation was God's will for the Swiss as an elect people, and convinced that exposure to the gospel would win over the common folk. He was increasingly persuaded, however, that Catholic rulers would have to be overcome if the Word of God was to be preached to the people, and his own thinking was becoming increasingly martial"[46]—to the point, indeed, of producing his own blueprint for a military campaign.

It is hard to escape the conclusion that, towards the end of his life, Zwingli's judgement was failing him. At the very least, he overreached himself—whether

---

45 Potter, *Zwingli*, 367.
46 Gordon, *Zwingli*, 183.

out of hubris, panic, a sense of betrayal, or all of these things. He also became increasingly isolated, including from close colleagues such as Oecolampadius[47] and, indeed, from a number of former supporters in Zürich itself. His remarkable decision to address the imperial Diet of Augsburg in the summer of 1530 by means of an entirely unilateral and wholly uncompromising *Account of the Faith*[48] misfired spectacularly: the work either "fell on deaf ears", as Oecolampadius had predicted,[49] or alienated rather more sensitive ones based in places such as Bern or Strasbourg. His assiduous attempts to court Landgrave Philipp of Hesse, "whom he saw as the key to a broader alliance that would secure the Reformation among the Swiss"[50] seem in retrospect misguidedly over-ambitious.[51] And, not least, his refusal in the summer of 1531 seriously to countenance Bern's proposals to put pressure on the Catholic cantons by using economic sanctions rather than military force implies a combination of bellicosity and tunnel vision that jars alarmingly with his essentially Erasmian and Christocentric world view. Zwingli, in short, was no longer quite the man he had been.

His end was undeniably tragic. Given the seeming inevitability of bloodshed, and conscious that their opponents were divided and underprepared, the Catholic states declared war on 9th October 1531. Two days later, in a surprise attack, the Zürich troops were decimated at Kappel, and Zwingli himself was killed. The ensuing peace treaty anticipated the 1555 Peace of Augsburg in according to each canton the right to choose its own religion. Hence Zürich remained a Protestant city, and was indeed to thrive as such under Zwingli's successor Heinrich Bullinger (1504–1575); but the former's dream of uniting the whole Confederation around his own version of the gospel died with him, and has never been seriously revived.

---

47   See below, p. 28f.
48   *Ad Carolum Romanorum imperatorem Germaniae comitia Augustae celebrantem, fidei ratio* (Zürich: Froschauer, 3rd July 1530; Leu/Weidmann 200)—ed. ZW VI/2, 790–817 (no. 163). On this work see Fritz Blanke, "Zwinglis *Fidei ratio* (1530): Entstehung und Bedeutung", in *Archiv für Reformationsgeschichte* 57 (1966): 96–102; Gordon, *Zwingli*, 228–231.
49   See 1062, line 13f.
50   Gordon, *Zwingli*, 218.
51   On their relationship and protracted correspondence see René Hauswirth, *Landgraf Philipp von Hessen und Zwingli: Voraussetzungen und Geschichte der politischen Beziehungen zwischen Hessen, Strassburg, Konstanz, Ulrich von Württemberg und reformierten Eidgenossen 1526–1531* (Tübingen: Osiander, 1968). On Philipp generally see above, p. xv.

2 Oecolampadius and Basel

Unlike the quintessentially Swiss Zwingli, Oecolampadius was born in Germany—at Weinsberg, near Heilbronn in Württemberg, in 1482. His mother Anna Pfister was, however, a member of a prominent Basel patrician family; and, given that his (German) father Johannes was also a respected merchant, it is fair to say that his background was a little more privileged than Zwingli's. The broad contours of Oecolampadius's education were, however, not dissimilar: following Latin school in Heilbronn, he studied at the University of Heidelberg from 1499 to 1506, where he was taught by the noted humanist and critic of ecclesiastical abuses Jakob Wimpfeling (1450–1528).[52] Thereafter his career was characterized for some years by an apparent instability and restlessness. In February 1506 he became tutor to the sons of Elector Palatine Philipp ("the Upright") in Mainz; in November 1510 he took up a preacher's post in his native Weinsberg that had been created with the financial support of his father; from 1513 he resumed his university studies, first at Heidelberg (where he befriended Capito), and then at Tübingen (where he got to know Melanchthon); in 1516–1517 he was again in Weinsberg, where his increasing theological radicalism caused conflict with the local ecclesiastical authorities; and in late 1518, at Capito's instigation, he moved to Augsburg as the city's cathedral preacher. Moreover, these engagements were interspersed with several short- or medium-term sojourns in Basel. The most notable of these were his employment, from November 1515 to March 1516, as "Hebrew editor" for Erasmus's Greek New Testament,[53] and a period in 1518 spent as a special adviser on questions of confession and penance (*poenitentiarius*) to the relatively progressive bishop Christoph von Utenheim. When he finally settled in Basel on 17th November 1522, therefore, Oecolampadius was already 40 years old, a person of wide practical experience, and indeed a much read and respected author.[54]

By this stage he was also a convinced evangelical. He seems to have had his first significant, yet decisive encounter with Luther's writings while in Augs-

---

52   On Wimpfeling and his publications see *CoE* III, 447–450; *OER* IV, 275; *VL DH* II, 1289–1375; *BBKL* XIII, 1358–1361; Bernstein, *GH*, 29–39.
53   See above, p. 3 and n. 11.
54   For a list of Oecolampadius's publications to the end of 1522 see Staehelin, 8–37 (nos 1–73). The most notable of these include a Greek grammar (which Zwingli used), *Graecae literarum dragmata* (Basel: Cratander, 1521); a treatise on confession, *Quod non sit onerosa Christianis confessio* (Basel: Cratander, 1521); and translations of Greek fathers such as Gregory of Nazianzus, John of Damascus and, especially, John Chrysostom. On the latter see Staehelin, "Väterübersetzungen".

burg in 1518; and his study of and reflection on these intensified during a period spent as a monk at the Bridgettine convent at Altomünster between 1520 and early 1522. Moreover, he left Altomünster "because they had forbidden the preaching of the gospel";[55] and during a subsequent brief appointment as chaplain to the Protestant knight and mercenary leader Franz von Sickingen (1481–1523) at the latter's castle at Ebernburg—where he met Bucer—he was already experimenting with liturgical reform, for example requiring epistle and gospel readings to be spoken out loud and in German.[56] One way or another, those who welcomed his return to Basel in 1522 must have known that they were getting someone who was no longer a hesitant Erasmian humanist, but a potentially authoritative reformer.

Basel in 1522 was in many ways a different city from the Zürich to which Zwingli had moved at the end of 1518. It had joined the Swiss Confederation as recently as 1501 (Zürich's membership dated from 1351), and in many ways had more in common with the imperial free cities of South Germany than it did with, say, the much smaller Zürich or Bern. As such Basel was somewhat more affluent, thanks especially to its ideal location for trade, on the Rhine and within easy reach of both French and German markets. Unlike Zürich also, Basel had both a university (founded in 1460) and a bishop; especially since the arrival of Erasmus in 1514, it had been a leading centre of Christian humanism; and its diverse and thriving intellectual activities were fed and supported by—for its time—an extensive and sophisticated printing industry. All this meant that Basel in the 1520s was, potentially, an unusually fertile seedbed both for educated evangelical reformers and for theologically trained Catholics who would be able to offer them sustained and effective opposition.

With regard to its institutions of government, however, Basel was similar to Zürich—at least after 1521, when, following a protracted power struggle, "the Council rejected the bishop's formal right to approve elections to it and refused to swear the traditional oath of allegiance to the bishop, thereby ending his last claim to political authority over the city".[57] This (theoretically) newly autonomous Council was, like Zürich's, divided into a 'large" and a "small" chamber, working alongside a Mayor and a Chief Guild Master, and it functioned in a similarly pragmatic way—the main differences from Zürich being

---

55   The Frankfurt-based teacher Wilhelm Nesen (1492–1524) reports this to Zwingli in a letter of 10th July 1522—ed. ZW VII, 535f. (no. 215): *quod euangelium predicari vetuissent*, p. 536, line 11f. On Nesen, who was at various times close to Zwingli, Erasmus and Luther, see *CoE* III, 12–14.
56   See letter 215 (as n. 55), p. 536, lines 13–15.
57   Burnett, "Basel", 175.

that the Small Council was generally more powerful than the Large, and that neither body was, at least until the later 1520s, quite so dominated by the artisans' guilds. Even this latter circumstance changed during Oecolampadius's time in Basel, however: the guilds' power was materially strengthened by a law enacted in 1526 to the effect that no merchants could import into the city goods that could also be made within it; and thereafter they increasingly functioned as the city's leading motor for ecclesiastical reform. Hence guild members were particularly well placed to benefit from the adoption of the Reformation in Basel in 1529, and from the ban on Catholics holding political office that followed in its wake.

Basel had taken its first steps towards its eventual reformed polity before Oecolampadius returned to the city in 1522—initially to work as a corrector for the printer Andreas Cratander[58] and to continue his translation of the sermons of St John Chrysostom. Almost all of Luther's early works had been printed in Basel, by Adam Petri, soon after their publication in Wittenberg; and Luther's influence was intensified by the actions of various figures resident in the city at the time. One of these was Wolfgang Capito, better known for his later work in Strasbourg, but who from 1518 to 1520 had used his position as Basel's cathedral preacher to engage, as from 1519 Zwingli did in Zürich, in the expository preaching of entire biblical books—first Romans, then Matthew. Other preachers also attracted both large congregations and official suspicion for their increasingly evangelical preaching: Konrad Pellikan and Johannes Lüthard at the Franciscan church, Wolfgang Wissenburg at the hospital church, and Wilhelm Reublin at St Alban's.[59] Moreover, the latter was largely responsible for giving Basel its equivalent of Zürich's iconic *Wurstessen*: he and others broke the Lenten fast on Palm Sunday (13th April 1522) by eating a roasted suckling pig in the moated castle of Klybeck outside the city; and he followed this *Spanferkelessen* by staging a comparably flamboyant performance at the Corpus Christi procession of 19th June 1522, at which he ostentatiously carried a Bible, rather than the expected monstrance or relics. Reublin was soon expelled from Basel, but the cause he represented could not be.

Oecolampadius's own contribution to it in the years down to 1531 is not always easy to define: he at no stage enjoyed as much personal authority or institutional support as Zwingli did, and one suspects that a great deal of what

---

58   See above, p. xi.
59   On Pellikan see above, p. xv. Lüthard and Wissenburg were long-time colleagues of Oecolampadius in Basel (on them see the notes to letter 367). Reublin (1484–c. 1559), the most radical of the group, became a prominent travelling anabaptist, and did not return to Basel for many years.

he achieved happened behind the scenes. There is no doubt, however, that his arrival in Basel brought its nascent evangelical movement both a perceptible impetus and a certain intellectual cachet: he was already, after all, an internationally known scholar. As such he was very much a teacher as well as a preacher; so it is surely significant that, from the outset, he was active in Basel in both these roles. Based initially in the choir of the city's cathedral, he gave a daily lecture on Isaiah in Latin, followed by a sermon on a related topic in German. These were well attended, and led in the spring of 1523 to Oecolampadius's appointment both as an—initially temporary, later permanent—preacher at St Martin's Church, and as a professor of theology at the University.

By this time Basel was already, in effect, a bi-confessional city. Support for evangelical perspectives was on the rise, and these were articulated and spread by some five or six highly effective preachers, who enjoyed the support of many guild members. On the other hand the city remained home to several important Catholic power bases: its bishop, its cathedral, to a large extent its university, and numerous prominent members particularly of the Small Council. The response of the Council as a whole was to issue a mandate in the summer of 1523 to the effect that preachers should base their sermons entirely on the Bible, ignoring all other teachings—including those of Luther. Not least because it was based on the similar one issued in Zürich in January 1523,[60] this mandate must have seemed to many to favour the evangelical party; but in fact it was probably conceived as an attempt on the Council's part to preserve its neutrality; and in practice it succeeded only in adding to a general sense of instability and confusion.

Certainly over the next few years Oecolampadius and his fellow evangelicals made progress on several fronts. In the February and March of 1524, for example, the Council permitted and indeed promoted two high-profile disputations, the first on clerical marriage, set in train by the Liestal priest Stephan Stör, and the second on more wide-ranging topics proposed by the future reformer of Geneva Guillaume Farel.[61] The same year saw the arrival, at Basel's Augustinian church, of Thomas Gyrfalk,[62] a notably energetic and charismatic, if occasionally combustible preacher, who was to remain influential well into the 1550s. In February 1525 the process of secularizing Basel's monasteries began with the

---

60   See p. 5f.
61   On these see letter 329, lines 3–12 and n. 2f., 6.
62   A vivid picture of Gyrfalk's abilities and personality emerges from some of Oecolampadius's letters to Zwingli: see 367, n. 5; 460, lines 16–20 and n. 9; 757, lines 12–18 and n. 2; 763, lines 20–39; 856, lines 1–10 and n. 1.

dissolution of its house of Austin Canons, in exchange for the former monks being given citizenship of the city—a deal which set something of a trend, as well as a precedent.[63] Last but not least, Oecolampadius and some of his evangelical colleagues were gradually introducing some far-reaching liturgical reforms, which resulted in the publication in 1526 of vernacular orders for infant baptism, the Lord's Supper and ministry to the dying.[64]

On the whole, however, Oecolampadius's tone in his letters from around the mid-1520s tends, not without reason, to be somewhat pessimistic. For much of 1523 and into 1524 he was fearful that he would be forced to leave Basel;[65] and in late 1525 and into 1526 the conservative backlash against his eucharistic treatise *De genuina expositione* led to the confiscation of copies of the work, a ban on his writings being printed or sold in Basel and, it seems, to significant financial worries.[66] In addition to such personal vicissitudes, there were—as in Zürich, and for the same blend of economic and theological reasons—disturbing outbreaks of unrest, particularly in the rural areas surrounding Basel and particularly in 1525.[67] When one takes into account also the periodic appearances in the city of potentially disruptive anabaptists and the shilly-shallying and inconsistencies of its unwieldy Council, it is easy to see why, especially between 1523 and 1525, the religious landscape of his adopted city must often have seemed to Oecolampadius both perplexing and discouraging.

On a personal level at least, his stock began to rise in 1526. Paradoxically, this was due in part to the Disputation of Baden—at which, as we have seen, Oecolampadius was on one level roundly defeated by Eck.[68] Nevertheless his performance on this very public stage won him many admirers, and indeed signalled his "emergence ... as a spiritual and doctrinal leader of the [evangelical] movement. He had courageously and ably faced Eck in the lion's den, defending his theology to a scoffing audience, patiently enduring the insults. He was by no means Zwingli's subaltern".[69] This fact was moreover reinforced by Oecolampadius's distinguished and prominent involvement in the so-called

---

63 See Wackernagel, *Basel*, III, 364 f.
64 *Form vnd gstalt wie der kinder tauff, Des herren Nachtmal, und der Krancken heymsuchung jetz zu Basel von etlichen Predicanten gehalten werden* (Basel: Cratander, 1526; Staehelin 135). See Staehelin, *Lebenswerk*, 429–447.
65 See for example 286, line 8 and n. 3; 319, lines 5–8 and n. 2.
66 See 404, lines 1–4; 443, lines 7–10 and n. 2; 449, lines 7–21, 31–38 and n. 7 f.
67 On these see Wackernagel, *Basel*, III, 467–483.
68 See above, p. 10 f.
69 Gordon, *Zwingli*, 206.

"pamphlet war" over the Eucharist that was at its zenith in 1526 and the first half of 1527. As his letters to Zwingli make plain, he became embroiled in numerous exchanges—of often high intellectual quality—with Lutherans such as Johannes Brenz, Jakob Strauß, Willibald Pirckheimer, Theobald Billican, and indeed Luther himself, as well as with leading Catholic apologists such as Jodocus Clichtove and John Fisher.[70] The last two names in particular indicate that Oecolampadius's writings were achieving an impact beyond the German-speaking world that was denied to those of Zwingli.

Oecolampadius's ability to contribute in a unique and effective way to the eucharistic debate (and indeed many others) stemmed not least from his wholly exceptional knowledge of patristic theology. This enabled him to develop and add to the arguments that Zwingli had adumbrated in writings such as his letter to Matthäus Alber, and in so doing to demonstrate that many 'orthodox' views on the Eucharist were scholastic dogmatic accretions that owed little to the perspectives and practices of the early church. In his *De genuina expositione*, for example, he uses Augustine to argue that a sacrament is in essence a mystery, a *mysterion*—though not in the sense that it is essentially incomprehensible. Rather, its meaning remains hidden to those without faith, whilst being revealed to those *with* faith as they are "led from the visible to the invisible".[71] Oecolampadius also uses Tertullian to argue that Christ's words "this is my body" should be understood as meaning "this is the figure (*figura*) of my body"—a metaphorical interpretation that of course recalls Zwingli's,[72] but has an unimpeachable philological basis and also, arguably, the capacity to inspire a much greater range of imaginative possibilities.[73] Examples from other works include his use of Augustine to reinforce the argument that the body of Christ is now uniquely localized in heaven, and hence cannot be present in earthly celebrations of the Eucharist;[74] and numerous references to the writings of Irenaeus of Lyon—used, for example, to strengthen his attempts to discredit the gnostic implications of the Roman Mass, or to emphasize the particular suitability of bread and wine as eucharistic symbols. When one adds to such a mix

---

70   See for example letters 438, 454, 471, 530, 544, 554, 586, 600, 607, 614.
71   See A4^v–A5^r; cited by Burnett, *Debating*, 105.
72   See above, p. 8.
73   B6^{r-v}; cited by Burnett, *Debating*, 105. Brooks, *Cranmer* (p. 51, n. 5), explains the origin of this interpretation as follows: "Since Aramaic—the language used by Christ at the Last Supper—has no copula, Oecolampadius maintained that the *tropus* was by no means to be found in *est* but rather in *corpus*. Hence Christ's original meaning was not *This is my body* or *This signifies my body*, but *This is the figure of my body*. The whole ingenious explanation is based on the words of Tertullian *Against Marcion*, Lib.1".
74   See Northway, "Reception", 139–141, 285.

the numerous insights Oecolampadius gained also from his reading of Erasmus (such as the parallels between the Eucharist and the Passover and—above all—the essential primacy of spirit over flesh), it is hardly surprising that he was able to put together a eucharistic theology that, even for its time, could achieve an exceptional resonance and richness.[75]

From 1527 onwards, eucharistic matters played an increasingly important role also in the ecclesiastical life of Basel. On 21st May of that year, following years of unease and controversy fuelled by the co-existence in the same city of both Catholic and evangelical practices, the Council enjoined each side to produce, within a month, "a written justification of its understanding of the mass based solely on the Bible, and in the meantime forbidding discussion of the mass from the pulpit".[76] Oecolampadius welcomed this, not least because his opponents manifestly did not;[77] but its eventual outcome amounted to no more than an official enforcement of the city's inherently problematic bi-confessionality. On 23rd September 1527, the Council decreed that no lay person would be required to attend Mass, but that all priests should celebrate it, on pain of forfeiting their benefice. Oecolampadius and the other clergy of the by now 'traditionally' evangelical parishes of St Martin, St Leonard and the Augustinian church were exempted from this requirement; but, even so, he was left feeling "tolerated rather than favoured, and that only until such time as they find some tiny excuse to attack us".[78] This, though, was not the whole story: the Council, with its studied neutrality and insistence on protecting the rights of what was now a Catholic minority, was growing more and more out of touch with the opinions of the majority of its citizens—and especially those of its increasingly powerful guilds.

In other words, a powder keg was building; and that keg seemed still likelier to explode in the light of Bern's adoption of the Reformation following a disputation (attended by both Zwingli and Oecolampadius) in January 1528. The guilds were growing increasingly impatient;[79] there were significant outbreaks of iconoclasm;[80] and substantial numbers of anabaptists were imprisoned.[81] All things considered, it seems in retrospect inevitable that, by early

---

75   See Northway, "Reception", 272–336. He also provides (pp. 182–198) a useful catalogue of patristic references found in *De genuina expositione* and the *Dialogus* of 1530.
76   Burnett, "Basel", 188.
77   See 624, lines 22–31.
78   661, lines 4–6 (15th October 1527).
79   See 699, lines 13–15; 707, lines 19–24.
80   Particularly on Good Friday: see 714, lines 1–10 and n. 1–3.
81   See 733, lines 14–21; 747, line 25f. and n. 9.

1529, Basel's Council should finally have discovered that, in Oecolampadius's words, "if one wants always to sit on two chairs, there will be times when one can sit on neither".[82]

The Council's hand was forced just before Christmas in 1528. On 23rd December a large crowd gathered at the gardeners' guildhall to draw up a petition asking them to "put an end to discord between the preachers and to the popish Mass"[83]—in other words, to adopt fully reformed ecclesiastical arrangements. When no clear response had been given by the evening of Christmas Day, armed men took to the streets, and bloodshed must have seemed likely; but the Council was able to prevent this, with the material aid over the next few days of representatives from other cities, including Zürich and Bern.[84] On 5th January 1529 the Council temporarily mollified their evangelical critics by issuing a mandate to the effect that Basel's preachers had to preach the 'pure' gospel on pain of expulsion; that they were to meet every week to determine what might and might not be taught; that there should be a formal disputation on 30th May; and that no more than three Masses per day could be celebrated in the city. Already Oecolampadius felt able to thank "Christ the peacemaker" that "to a large extent the Antichrist has fallen";[85] but, uncharacteristically, he was being unduly optimistic. Many Catholics refused to co-operate with these terms, the Council failed to enforce them, and it took a number of further protests and disturbances, sometimes accompanied by iconoclastic violence, before the Council finally acceded to the evangelicals' demands. On 1st April 1529 it issued the first of Basel's so-called Reformed Ordinances, re-organizing its parishes, setting up a synodal system, and beginning a programme for educational reform (at both school and university level) in which Oecolampadius was to play a prominent role.[86] The latter's work was not done; but he had nonetheless been consistently instrumental in bringing about a decisive evangelical breakthrough.

In the last two years of his life Oecolampadius was much less prominent than Zwingli on the wider political stage, and certainly less inclined than him to seek a military solution to the Swiss confessional divide.[87] Nevertheless he was

---

82   707, line 37 f.
83   788, line 9.
84   See 788, lines 15–26, in which Oecolampadius reveals that he has been deputed to write to Zwingli on the guilds' behalf to request the sending of "two excellent and distinguished men who might … assist these our people both in their deliberations and in their representations to the Council" (23–25).
85   796, line 22 f.
86   See for example letters 826 and 829.
87   Indeed, his later letters to Zwingli make frequent, one assumes pointed reference to the desirability of peace: see for example 856, lines 16 f., 23 f.; 870, lines 1–5; 883, line 19.

active in advising reformers in other cities and in assisting them to implement evangelical doctrines and policies. This was most notably the case in Ulm, from which city he reported to Zwingli in detail in June 1531 (letter 1228). Otherwise, he became preoccupied to a conspicuous degree with matters of church discipline, in particular with the need he perceived to develop mechanisms for the exclusion of unrepentant sinners from participation in the Lord's Supper. He argued energetically for the introduction of such measures in Basel, but also in Switzerland's other reformed cities and cantons, most prominently at a meeting of the Christian Civic Union at Aarau in September 1530 (see letter 1106). He met with scant success, however. It is indeed a poignant irony that, towards the end of their lives and after years of close collaboration, Oecolampadius and Zwingli should have almost obsessively pursued two radically different aims— the one military and political, the other ecclesiastical and ethical—and should have failed in both.

At least Oecolampadius's preoccupation with church discipline and excommunication was a logical extension of his earlier career. A concern with ethical behaviour was, after all, a characteristic of the Swiss Reformation in general— inevitably so, given its roots in Erasmian humanism. Moreover, as Olaf Kuhr in particular has shown,[88] issues of sin, penitence and punishment constituted something of a leitmotif in the course of Oecolampadius's theological formation. As we have seen, he was already seen as a specialist in such matters in 1518 (hence his appointment as Basel's *poenitentiarius*); in 1521 he had written a learned disquisition on the subject;[89] and, in his later ministry in Basel, he continually emphasized the importance of New Testament-style public penitence, rather than the more established practice of secret confession solely to a priest.

In his later years Oecolampadius came to see excommunication in particular as essential both to the preservation of the church's moral purity and to its internal integrity as the communion of saints on earth. To this end its disciplinary task had to remain at least in part independent of all secular authorities. In his letters we see him asserting, for example, that "a magistrate who usurps the church's authority is more intolerable than the Antichrist himself", and exhorting the Swiss churches "not to neglect the keys of receiving and excluding that Christ has handed to them".[90] The problem with such perspectives was, of course, that they flew in the face of much contemporary evangelical thought—

---

88   See Kuhr, "Calvin"; also idem, *Die Macht des Bannes und der Buße: Kirchenzucht und Erneuerung der Kirche bei Johannes Oekolampad (1481–1531)* (Bern: Lang, 1998).
89   *Quod non sit onerosa*: see n. 54 above.
90   Letter 1096 (17th September 1530), lines 5 f., 24 f.

including that of Zwingli,[91] who "clearly identified the church assembly with the civil community", and hence "opposed any separate ecclesiastical jurisdiction".[92]

Hence it was no doubt inevitable that Oecolampadius's excommunication plans should have been largely ignored outside Basel. Moreover, even in his own adopted city he met with opposition[93] and eventually suffered what must have been a galling defeat. In 1530 a compromise was reached stipulating that three laymen (including two Council members) would be tasked with imposing church discipline alongside the parish priest—who, however, would have only an advisory, as distinct from a decision-making role. Yet even this was not widely implemented; and eventually, in the summer of 1531 the Basel Council in effect placed all disciplinary powers under its own authority, thereby leaving the Basel churches with no more freedom to wield "the keys of receiving and excluding" than could be claimed by their counterparts in, say, Zürich or Bern.

Oecolampadius was never a physically robust man,[94] and such defeats, alongside the catastrophe that was the Second Kappel War, no doubt took their toll on him. Hence it is perhaps not altogether surprising that, when he died on 23rd November 1531, he had survived Zwingli by a mere 43 days— just long enough for him to receive, and decline, an invitation to become the latter's successor in Zürich. Nevertheless the death of these two reforming pioneers in such quick succession underlines with alarming starkness that an era had come to an end: only twelve years after Zwingli's arrival at the *Grossmünster*, the Swiss Reformation was already entering its second generation. For his part, Basel's chief first-generation reformer was buried in the city's cathedral, and—eventually—given a memorial which, for all its disappointing lack of prominence, is undeniably apt: "Master Johannes Oecolampadius, theologian by profession, most proficient in three languages, first instigator of evangelical doctrine in this city, and true bishop/overseer of this church. As pre-eminent in doctrine as in holiness of life, he lies concealed beneath this small stone."[95]

---

91 In his letters Oecolampadius always claims that he and Zwingli are of one mind on questions of church discipline (see 1106, line 1 f.; 1123, line 24 f.; 1130, lines 1–5); but, even though Zwingli seems to have been more willing to respect the Basler's views than several other reformers were, this can only have been wishful thinking.

92 Baker, "Church Discipline", 6.

93 According to Capito, even Oecolampadius's close colleagues Johannes Lüthard and Markus Bertschi (see 367, n. 1, 6) preached against him on the subject—Capito to Bucer, 13th September 1530: *BC* IV, 275–286 (no. 340); *CC* II, 433 (no. 425).

94 See for example 456, 25–36; 670, 9–12.

95 D. IO. OECOLAMPADIUS / PROFESSIONE THEOLOGVS / TRIVM LINGVARVM / PERITISSIMUS AUTHOR / EVANGELICAE DOCTRINAE / IN HAC VRBE PRIMUS, ET TEMPLI HVIVS /

3 Zwingli and Oecolampadius

The preserved correspondence between Zwingli and Oecolampadius which we translate below is a decidedly one-sided affair: we can offer only fifteen letters by Zwingli (8% of the whole), some eight of which predate the end of 1525. This is of course frustrating, even when one takes into account the facts that Zwingli's letters tend—not least because of their more extensive theological content—to be considerably longer than those of Oecolampadius, and that one can learn at least as much about people from the letters they receive as from those they send. These proportions are not dissimilar, however, to those for Zwingli's correspondence with Bucer and Capito in Strasbourg; and indeed we calculate that, of the almost 1300 letters published in the five volumes of Zwingli's complete correspondence, only some 21% were written by the Zürich reformer. The reasons for such an imbalance can only be guessed at. For one thing, Zwingli's workload was so colossal and the demands made on him so diverse that, one suspects, it was simply impossible for him to answer every letter he received. Moreover a great deal of correspondence has for certain been lost—not surprisingly so if, as Zwingli implied to Vadian in 1524, he kept no copies of his own letters.[96] Some will also have been destroyed deliberately: for example, the fact that we have some 28 letters from Glarean[97] to Zwingli (dated between 1510 and 1523) and none at all in return must surely be attributable to the fact, by the mid-1520s, Zwingli was decidedly *persona non grata* in Glarean's humanist circles and hence someone whose communications the latter will have been loath to keep.

In the specific case of Oecolampadius, however, one suspects that he actually did write to Zwingli rather more often than *vice versa*. As we have seen, he "acknowledged Zwingli as the leader of the Swiss Reformation, frequently

---

VERUS EPVS. VT / DOCTRINA, SIC VITAE / SANCTIMONIA POLLENTISIMVS, / SVB BREVE SAXVM HOC / RECONDITVS IACET.

96 Letter 331—*zw* VIII, 166 f., here 167, lines 4–6: *non est unica epistolae alicuius in omni supellectile nostra copia* ('there is not a single copy of any letter amid all our paraphernalia'). The context suggests Zwingli—again employing the royal 'we'—is referring to his own letters, which, like all his writings, are ephemera which will pass away (*omnia nostra temporaria exeunt*). The passage is cited by Gordon, *Zwingli*, 198, though he dates it to 1528 and understands it differently ("in my house there is only one copy of my letters").

97 Or 'Heinrich Loriti' (1488–1563). Glarean was a humanist friend of Zwingli, Oecolampadius and indeed Erasmus. He was a formidable intellectual, equally proficient in geography, music, history and mathematics, and was initially enthused by Luther's teachings. By 1523, however, he had decided to remain a Catholic and was keen to distance himself from Zwingli and his supporters. On him see *CoE* II, 105–108; *OER* II, 177; *BBKL* XXIII, 530–537; *VL* 16 III, 1–16; Locher, *ZR*, 48.

consulted him on a wide range of questions, and relied on his strength and fortitude".[98] In turn the perpetually overworked Zwingli came to depend on regular, concise bulletins from Oecolampadius for his information about what was happening in Basel, Strasbourg and parts of southern Germany. Finally, especially in the later stages of their correspondence, Oecolampadius often wrote to Zwingli on other people's behalf, commending them and seeking work or favour for them.[99] Given the Basel reformer's relative lack of influence, there would have been no point in Zwingli contacting him in this way.

In the translations that follow, then, we hear Zwingli's voice much less often than that of Oecolampadius; but we can nevertheless glean a great deal about their relationship and respective personalities. As we have seen, this relationship is not generally cast, at least by Oecolampadius, as one between equals; and his many expressions of inadequacy and inferiority can grate somewhat on the modern reader.[100] That said, the presence of genuine respect between the two men is palpable: there is no reason to doubt Zwingli's sincerity when he writes to Oecolampadius "you are one who has conjoined piety with humanity and learning in such a way that it is not at all easy to know which has the upper hand in you" (268, 22–24), or commends him as "a man of incomparable learning, and truly of such discretion that, if he were to transgress, he would do so out of hesitancy rather than undue haste" (367, 149–151); Similarly, Oecolampadius for certain genuinely believed that Zwingli was "a wise man, our friend, and most zealous for the good of the state" (829, 10 f.) who would "act at all times in the strength of Christ" (419, 20). Moreover, as these last words imply, their mutual esteem was accompanied by a clear sense of the other's divine calling and mission; and this, combined with their generally close agreement on doctrinal matters, continued interest in humanist scholarship and, not least, possession of many common enemies made possible a close, sustained and fruitful collaboration.

Whether Oecolampadius can justifiably be called a "close friend" of Zwingli[101] is, perhaps, more open to question. Certainly their correspondence contains expressions of affectionate mutual concern, for example about each other's health. In 1523 Zwingli urges Oecolampadius to "keep yourself as well

---

98 Gordon, *Zwingli*, 78.
99 The list of those so commended between July 1528 and July 1530 alone is substantial: Joachim Kirser (letter 734), Janus Cornarius (767), Werner Beyel (792), Gervasius Schuler (829a), Martin Germanus (838), Thomas Gyrfalk (856), Ulrich Wieland (911), Wolfgang Ruß (1005, 1021), Ambrosius Kettenacker (1065).
100 He calls himself, for example, a "camp-menial" (258, 36), a "nonentity" (269, 15), "my poor self" (600, 3), or "insignificant" (443, 10).
101 The term "enge Freundschaft" is used for example by Ulrich Gäbler in *TRE* XXV, p. 34.

as you can. On occasion take some time away from your labours, which they say exhaust you beyond measure" (319, 24–26). Likewise, in 1526, Oecolampadius tells Zwingli that he is "rather worried on your account" because "you are rumoured to be so weak that you are even having to refrain from preaching" (438, 3–5). Moreover, most letters end with a request from one correspondent to the other to be remembered, or commended, to one or more mutual acquaintance(s). Such pleasantries were, and are, often exchanged between respected colleagues as well as between intimate friends, however; and, even allowing for the very different social *mores* of the early sixteenth century, the two men's discussion of more personal issues such as Oecolampadius's marriage to Wibrandis Rosenblatt in early 1528 is strikingly bloodless. Oecolampadius first broaches this subject, using positively tortuous circumlocutions, in letter 572, telling Zwingli that Heinrich Ryhiner[102] will be coming to Zürich to discuss with him "what state our affairs are in" and asking him to "write back or share your advice with Heinrich".[103] Zwingli's response is not preserved, but was clearly regarded by Oecolampadius as a "decidedly ambiguous oracle", on the basis of which he decided to "wait on the Lord's counsel, to see whether he favours your advice or something different"[104]—one of several occasions when an element of passive aggression can be seen as emerging from beneath Oecolampadius's habitual, rather studied demeanour of Christian meekness.[105] That is then the end of the matter, until Oecolampadius makes the startlingly terse declaration a year or so later that "it has fallen to me at last to take a wife, in answer, I believe, to my prayers. I was required to do this because my mother has died" (699, 2–4). Beyond occasional expressions of best wishes to and from Zwingli, and a woefully unsuccessful attempt at (mildly) bawdy humour,[106]

---

[102] Ryhiner (c. 1490–1553) undoubtedly was a close friend of Oecolampadius. Clerk to the Basel Council from 1524 to 1534, and city scribe from 1534 to his death, he has been described as "Basel's political spokesman in Zürich"—Walther Köhler, "Zwingli und Basel", *Zwingliana* 5/1 (1929): 2–10, here p. 9. On his career more generally see August Burckhardt, "Der Stadtschreiber Heinrich Ryhiner", BZGA 2 (1903): 34–66.

[103] 572, lines 6, 13; 6th January 1527.

[104] 576, lines 17–19; 15th January 1527.

[105] Other examples are 644, 40–43, where Oecolampadius asks Zwingli to show Martin Cellarius (to whom he believes the latter has behaved unjustly) "the Christian gentleness of your heart"; or 658, 31–50, where he rebukes Zwingli in a painfully indirect and convoluted way for publishing a comment that might be weaponized by opponents of Basel's liturgical practice of warning potential communicants about the dangers of excommunication.

[106] "Since for the time being, if I may be permitted a joke, I will neither have much leisure nor will sleep much (such, as a rule, is the privilege of the first year of marriage), I will be absent from the fray ..." (726, 8–10).

that is all we hear of the remarkable and interesting figure that was Wibrandis Rosenblatt, or of Oecolampadius's relationship with her.

It is instructive to compare exchanges such as this with the way personal matters are dealt with in Oecolampadius's correspondence with his associate of much longer standing, Wolfgang Capito, whom he had known since student days and subsequently collaborated with in Basel. Here we learn rather more, for example, about Oecolampadius's plans to marry in 1527. On 22nd January Capito advises him against marrying his elderly maidservant, who is "impure, quarrelsome, intolerable".[107] Fortunately, perhaps, Oecolampadius concurs with this judgement a week later, stating that the woman in question is recommended neither by her age nor her "wanton ways", and has in any event blotted her copybook by warning off "a certain widow of good reputation ... who loves me in Christ alone and would perhaps not disdain to serve me".[108] Elsewhere Oecolampadius asks Capito if he wants to pass a message to his (Oecolampadius's) parents via Hieronymus Bothan;[109] he confides his concern for the health of his small son Eusebius;[110] and he conveys his (eventual) wife Wibrandis's thanks for a prayer book that Capito has sent her, informing him in addition that she is pregnant.[111] With the exception of a reference to a "domestic trouble" caused by his father's determination to remarry (1139, 12–16), we have nothing like this in the letters to Zwingli; and all in all it is hard to see the latter as a trusted personal, indeed family friend in the same way that Capito was.

On balance, we think that the "close friendship" between Zwingli and Oecolampadius is best characterized as a warm, effective working relationship that ebbed and flowed according to what both parties saw as the needs of the moment. It was effective not least because "as they themselves understood well, they each possessed qualities lacking in the other."[112] Zwingli brought to the partnership the status within Switzerland, drive, charisma, confidence and optimism that Oecolampadius largely lacked, whereas the latter provided it with an international reputation for scholarship, formidable linguistic and theological skills, close attention to detail, and a certain emotional subtlety and gentleness of manner that did not come naturally to Zwingli. As with

---

107 *OeBA* II, 4–6 (no. 456), here 6; *CC* II, 267 (no. 319).
108 *OeBA* II, 6–8 (no. 457), here 7; *CC* II, 269 (no. 321).
109 *OeBA* II, 44 (no. 474); *CC* II, 275 f. (no. 328).
110 *OeBA* II, 280–284 (no. 636), here 282; *CC* II, 370 f. (no. 378). Oecolampadius fears, indeed, that God might "call the boy to himself". In fact, Eusebius survived until 1541.
111 *OeBA* II, 415–417 (no. 723), here 415; *CC* II, 370 f. (no. 402).
112 Gordon, *Zwingli*, 78.

all such collaborations, theirs was not without its tensions and insecurities. Zwingli's letters evince a conspicuous desire to parade his classical knowledge and to assert his seniority in a way that implies he was actually only too aware of the fact that Oecolampadius was his superior in learning and intellect.[113] Meanwhile the latter, for his part, reminds Zwingli of the need for temperate behaviour with a regularity and insistence that betray a certain mistrust of his colleague;[114] and his repeated avowals that he and Zwingli are in complete agreement strongly suggest a deep-seated need to convince himself, as much as his correspondent, that this is actually true.[115]

What persuades us above all that Zwingli and Oecolampadius are best seen as mutually sympathetic colleagues is, however, the manifestly goal-oriented and issue-focused approach that characterizes the majority of their partnership. The correspondence suggests that their relationship can be divided into three distinct phases of unequal length. Down to mid-September 1525, their letters are intermittent and more obviously bi-lateral (eighteen have been preserved from a little less than three years, and six of these are by Zwingli). Along with their effusive overtures of friendship and promises of prayer and mutual support, these deal mainly with what is happening at the time in Zürich and Basel. On 16th September 1525, however, Oecolampadius opines that "the priests and their associates here would readily accept what we have so far taught—but for this one dogma that they will not allow to be overthrown, that of the Eucharist as propounded either by the Pope or by Luther", a dogma that constitutes "the citadel and bulwark of their impiety" (384, 19–21). In retrospect this statement seems, in its simplistically catchall way, to encapsulate the beginning of a new phase in the two men's relationship. Certainly, for a period of almost exactly four-and-a-half years, down to letter 998 of 12th March 1530, they engage in a much closer and more active collaboration that centres on what they see as their joint, and overridingly important, calling to oppose this "one dogma". Other themes do, of course, recur during these years, such as the strangely protracted negotiations surrounding Konrad Pellikan's move from

---

113 A good example of this is letter 298, in which he alludes to the battles between Alexander the Great and Darius of Persia (lines 10–15), describes his enemies—after Strabo and Solinus—as "Herostratuses" (20), makes a clever pun on Johann Faber's name (5, 16), and adopts the third person singular to protest—too much?—that "Zwingli has never done anything of which, if called to account, he could not be absolved by even the most unfavourably disposed judge" (22 f.).

114 See for example 554, 31–35; 562, 29–33; 611, 1–8; 715, 13–15.

115 Formulations of this type include "you will see, I think, that our spirits do not disagree much—if indeed they disagree at all and are not one and the same spirit" (286, 14–16); "every judgement [of mine] is yours also" (454, 22); "we in no way disagree" (1184, 5 f.).

Basel to Zürich,[116] Basel's infuriatingly stop-start progress towards its adoption of the Reformation,[117] or the complex practical arrangements for events such the Disputation of Baden (1526) and Colloquy of Marburg (1529).[118] Nevertheless the Eucharist, and above all the various contemporary publications that debated it, are their pre-eminent concern, discussed at some point in the vast majority of the 121 letters penned between September 1525 and March 1530.

We have already listed Zwingli and Oecolampadius's most significant Catholic and Lutheran adversaries; and the course of the debates in which they participated has been thoroughly charted by Amy Nelson Burnett.[119] What needs stressing here is the extent to which their fight for eucharistic truth was a concerted two-man enterprise, co-ordinated above all through their letters. Zwingli and Oecolampadius collaborated in ways that close academic colleagues tend to also today: dividing up the tasks before them,[120] exchanging drafts of their work for comment prior to publication,[121] devising strategies to deal with various people or problems,[122] negotiating jointly with publishers.[123] Moreover, Oecolampadius seems at times to have attempted to speed up Zwingli's rate of literary production, on occasion with a level of impatience that, unusually for him, he makes little attempt to disguise.[124]

Following the failed Colloquy of Marburg and its immediate aftermath, however, much of this changed. Unless provoked by the initiatives of others, such as Bucer's decision to run his November 1530 letter to Duke Ernst of Lüneburg (zw, no. 1134) past both Zwingli and Oecolampadius before sending it—a move which provoked from Zwingli the splenetic rejoinder that is letter 1136—their long-standing mutual concern with eucharistic questions largely ceased; and this had a major impact on their epistolary relationship between the spring of

---

116 See 430, 2–4; 435, 1–12; 438, 7–9; 448, 9 f.; 454, 1–6.
117 See for example letters 438, 449, 714, 786, 788, 796 f., 809, 826.
118 With regard to Baden see 443, 1–6; 454, 23–28; 473, 28–32; 483, 486, 488; to Marburg see 875; 883, 1–34; 904, 911 f.
119 See above, pp. 17–19. Burnett, *Debating*, provides useful surveys of the "contours of the printed debate" on the Eucharist between 1525 and 1529 (25–49), and of the "impact of Oecolampadius's *Genuine Exposition*" (140–148).
120 See for example 614, 1–6; 715, 18–25; 728, 9–12.
121 For this see 412, 1–6; 642, 1–6; and especially 734, 1–8.
122 See 530, 14–18 (the desirability of talking to the Margrave of Baden); 540, 87–102 (how to deal with Luther); 728, 13–26 (how to speak to princes).
123 This happened particularly around the time that Oecolampadius's works were banned from being printed in Basel: Zwingli gave him valuable help about 'finding a publisher' in Zürich: see 449, 14–24; 496, 3 f.
124 This was most obviously the case during the relatively early project (in 1525) of composing a response to Bugenhagen's *Sendbrieff wider den newen yrrthumb*: see 394, 13; 396, 45 f.

1530 and Zwingli's death in October 1531. Oecolampadius still wrote regularly, at least up to end of March 1531, and there was a brief flurry of collaborative activity in the August of that year as they co-ordinated their responses to a request for written opinions about Henry VIII's plans to divorce Catherine of Aragon.[125] Otherwise, however, their correspondence seems largely to have lost its earlier function as a forum for collaboration in pursuit of a defined common purpose. We have no sense, it must be stressed, of the two men 'falling out', or of their ceasing to co-operate entirely. On the contrary, Zwingli assists Oecolampadius in the preparation of his commentary on Job;[126] the latter is keen to arrange a meeting with Zwingli in order to discuss, amongst other things, Bucer's negotiations with Luther over the Eucharist;[127] and they communicate in advance of the Diet of Augsburg about the preparation of documents to present there.[128] We have already seen, however, that Zwingli effectively undermined such negotiations by deciding independently to proffer his *Account of the Faith*;[129] and this is somehow typical of the two men's activities towards the very end of their lives. We find them, quite simply, pursuing separate agendas. There is, for example, no real evidence of Zwingli having much interest in Oecolampadius's campaign for independent ecclesiastical discipline, or indeed in his activities in Ulm. Similarly, Oecolampadius rarely comments on Zwingli's political and military machinations and, when he does, he generally attempts to moderate or gently challenge them, rather than giving them his unequivocal backing. In April 1530, for instance, he urges Zwingli, preoccupied as he is with Swiss affairs, not to neglect potentially new alliances with Protestant German princes and cities (834); and in July 1530 he similarly encourages him to show greater interest in the overtures for pan-evangelical peace still being made by Philipp of Hesse (1064, 1–20).

Oecolampadius's very last letter to Zwingli, dated 30th September 1531, is a poignant affair. It begins with a continuation of earlier discussions about Henry VIII's divorce and re-marriage (1285, 1–13). Thereafter, however, Oecolampadius tells Zwingli that he (Zwingli) "will be able to hear from others—or to guess without needing to be told—how things stand here [in Basel] with regard to the firmness of the alliance and the sanctity of religion" (14–16). In other words, Zwingli (always assuming that he is still interested) is no longer

---

125   See letters 1259, 1263, 1285.
126   See 1074, 20–24; 1094, 1f.
127   See 1133, 1–25; 1164.
128   See 1005, 14–20; 1028, 1–18.
129   See above, p. 12. Oecolampadius's verdict on the *Fidei ratio* is an object lesson in how to damn with faint praise: "I praise it on many counts" (1062, 25).

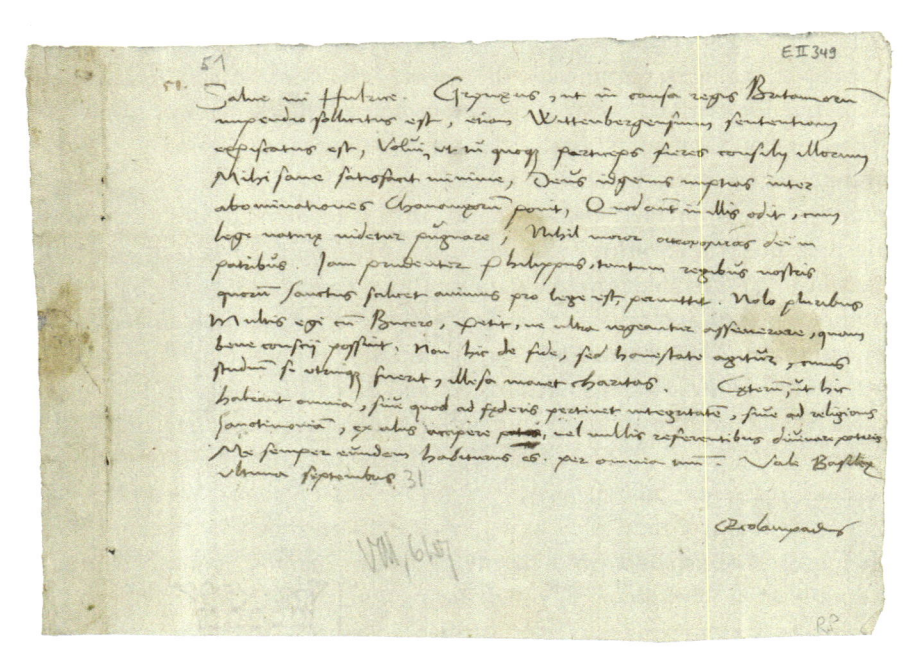

FIGURE 4   A sample of Oecolampadius's handwriting
ZÜRICH, STAATSARCHIV, E II 349, P. 51 (LETTER 1285)

dependent on Oecolampadius for his information as to "how things stand", and the latter is all too aware of the fact. In the light of this, the correspondence's very last sentence can be seen as taking on a complex significance. In a statement redolent of uncharacteristic emotional directness, even of sentimentality, Oecolampadius writes, "think of me always—as yours in all things." Was so effusive an utterance brought on by some kind of presentiment that both men would soon be dead, and that now was the time for an affectionate farewell? Or was it a backward-looking, nostalgic affirmation of the close working relationship they had once enjoyed, but no longer did to any comparable extent? One suspects it was both.

4   Zwingli, Oecolampadius and Strasbourg

Alongside Zürich and Basel, the name of one other city occurs with notable regularity in the translations that follow. Strasbourg, a large, prosperous, German-speaking town advantageously located at the confluence of the Rhein and Ill rivers, lay approximately 130 miles north-west of Zürich and 75 miles due north of Basel; and in the 1520s it underwent a tortuous process of reformation whose

INTRODUCTION 31

timeline was in many respects similar to that of Basel.[130] Moreover its principal reformers, Wolfgang Capito and Martin Bucer, both native Alsatians, were well known in Switzerland. As we have seen, Capito (born in 1478) was a long-time friend of Oecolampadius, and he also began a correspondence with Zwingli in 1520; meanwhile the somewhat younger Bucer (born in 1491) first met Capito in 1519, Oecolampadius in 1521, and Zwingli in around 1523. It was nevertheless the Zürich reformer, rather than Oecolampadius, with whom Bucer was to work particularly closely, due in part to their shared, and increasing, involvement in pan-evangelical and imperial politics and in part, it seems, to a certain temperamental affinity: both possessed a determination and robustness, allied to a tendency towards impulsiveness and impatience, which differentiated them from more naturally complaisant men of the study such as Capito and Oecolampadius.[131]

Early references to Strasbourg in the Zwingli-Oecolampadius correspondence are relatively few in number, but they already show that the three cities in question have shared interests and are in regular communication with each other. Zwingli in particular is at pains to praise "that most excellent band of teachers at Strasbourg" and to imply that he (and Oecolampadius) are in full agreement with these teachers' theology: "I have always thought it was the natural character of the doctrine we preach at Zürich, Basel and Strasbourg to make people zealous for peace and righteousness; but for that righteousness which proceeds from faith".[132] Moreover the correspondence as a whole is awash with references to letters to and from Strasbourg being sent, received, forwarded, even lost. This is hardly surprising, given that most of the letters in our corpus were written by Oecolampadius in Basel, a city which messengers would invariably go through to get from Alsace to Zürich.[133]

We hear much more about Strasbourg, however, from March 1526 onwards. As with the correspondence as a whole, so those parts of it dealing with Strasbourg entered, around then, a marked eucharistic phase, which seemed to be set in train by Oecolampadius's declaration that "Bucer has also published a work—something which in itself cheers me not a little—under his own name and that of the Strasbourg brothers, in which they have borne witness to their faith. It is a little book that gives testimony in a more than satisfactory way

---

130   See especially Miriam Usher Chrisman, *Strasbourg and the Reform. A Study in the Process of Change* (New Haven, CT: Yale University Press, 1967).
131   On the relationship between Bucer and Zwingli see Locher, ZR, 456–459; Greschat, *Bucer*, 90.
132   367, lines 132 and 68–71.
133   For examples see, among many others, 352, 1f.; 412, 12–14; 418, 34f.; 449, 10f.; 505, 38–41; 812, 28–32.

to the remarkable love they have for us" (460, 5–9). The "work" in question is Bucer's so-called *Apologia*,[134] and it is important in our context in three respects. It represents Strasbourg's first genuinely substantial contribution to the eucharistic 'pamphlet war' of the later 1520s. This was no doubt one reason for Oecolampadius's enthusiastic reception of it, along with the fact that Bucer comes down firmly on his and Zwingli's side, rather than Luther's—hardly surprisingly, given that he and Capito had also been profoundly influenced by Erasmus's clear distinction between the visible and invisible realms.[135] Second, Bucer "employed a deliberately conciliatory tone in the *Apology*, stressing the centrality of faith in Christ and presenting the question of Christ's bodily presence as of only secondary importance".[136] This was something of a leitmotif in Bucer's various comments on the Eucharist, one which Capito and Oecolampadius supported, but which Zwingli and Luther, fatefully, did not. Bucer consistently held that evangelical unity was an essential prerequisite for establishing Christ's kingdom on earth, and that it was therefore incumbent on Christians not to fall out over non-essential issues such as the nuances of eucharistic theology—especially given that one of the central purposes of the sacrament was, after all, to strengthen fraternal unity. Finally, Bucer reinforced this broad position by proposing in his *Apologia* a sophisticated new interpretation of the dominical words "this is my body." The original Aramaic version of this phrase, he argued, would not have contained a verb at all; hence to argue about what the verb supplied in the Vulgate, *est*, actually means is ultimately pointless, a "quarrel over words".[137]

Sadly, this quarrel was never truly resolved; but in the later 1520s and beyond, Bucer, now the more prominent and influential of Strasbourg's two chief reformers,[138] continued to mediate and mollify, and to suggest a sequence of potential 'magic formulae' (*significatio efficax, unio sacramentalis, vere et essen-*

---

134   *Apologia Martini Buceri qua fidei suae atque doctrinae, circa Christi Coenam* (Strasbourg: Herwagen, 1526; Leu/Weidmann 37), a response to Brenz's *Epistola Ioannes Brentii de verbis Domini, "Hoc est Corpus meum", opinionem quorundam de Eucharistia refellens* (Hagenau: Setzer, 1526). See Burnett, *Debating*, 194–197.

135   On this see especially Ernst-Wilhelm Kohls, *Die theologische Lebersaufgabe des Erasmus und die oberrheinischen Reformatoren: Zur Durchdringung von Humanismus und Reformation* (Stuttgart: Calwer Verlag, 1969).

136   Burnett, *Debating*, 194.

137   See Friedrich, "Streit", 50. He quotes from Bucer, *Apologia*, C.6ᵛ.

138   By the end of 1528 Capito's stock had fallen sharply, not least in the light of certain errors of judgement that adversely affected his reputation. One of these involved a friendship he developed with the radical anabaptist Martin Cellarius which Zwingli, Oecolampadius and Bucer all regarded as dangerously misguided (see 652, 12–15 and n. 2; 733, 8–14 and n. 5 f.; 734, 52–55; 747, 13–23 and n. 7 f.).

tialiter)[139] that might somehow succeed in combining the notion of Christ's real presence (however intangible and mysterious) with a view of the sacrament that saw it as essentially symbolic. In some ways, however, he only made matters worse: the Colloquy of Marburg, of which he was an ardent supporter, failed to produce the longed-for concord, and his own relationship with Zwingli was adversely affected.[140]

As we have seen, Oecolampadius's letters to Zwingli rarely foreground eucharistic theology. It is clear from them, however, both that he was a keen supporter of Capito and Bucer's initiatives, and that he was often used as a conduit through whom the "Strasbourg brothers" could convey their views and preferences to their geographically more remote and temperamentally less predictable colleague in Zürich. The letter which treats these matters in the greatest detail is no. 1133, from 19th November 1530. This begins with the assertion that "the representatives who were sent here from Strasbourg are very worried that you prove somewhat difficult when it comes to accepting things that might pertain to an agreement with Luther" (lines 1–3). Oecolampadius, of course, reassures Zwingli that "I do not think that, as long as proper respect is paid to the truth and to charity, there is any need to persuade you of anything" (line 4f.); but he proceeds to commend Bucer's efforts in a way that suggests that such a "need" actually does exist. With reference, one assumes, to letter 1134, a document sent by Bucer to both Oecolampadius and Zwingli on 14th November, Oecolampadius implies in effect that Bucer has succeeded in solving the hitherto intractable problem of the Eucharist: "The statement that Christ's body and blood are truly present in the Lord's Supper might perhaps be rather hard for some people to accept; but he softens this by adding that this applies to the spirit and not the body. He proceeds in the same prudent way with respect to other matters also, as when he asserts that the sacraments strengthen faith; and before long, by dint of his exposition, he closes the window on error" (lines 9–14). Zwingli's response was—to say the least—rather less sanguine,[141] but Oecolampadius's reaction to it in letter 1139 (line 4) is both skilfully phrased and exquisitely diplomatic: "your advice in it does not seem imprudent".

It is obvious, then, that—particularly by 1530—Oecolampadius was highly adept at dealing with, even manipulating Zwingli. This, combined with his academic eminence, increased standing following the Disputation of Baden,

---

139 On these attempts see Friedrich, "Streit", 51–63.
140 See the *literas iratas* (Bucer's words) he and Capito received from Zwingli on 12th February 1531—ZW XI, 339–343 (no. 1168).
141 No. 1136, in which Zwingli accuses Bucer's intervention of having "placed [us] at a great disadvantage" and "distorted and defiled" the truth (line 4f.).

geographical location in Basel and generally eirenic temperament, must have made him seem an ideal 'go-between' in negotiations involving Strasbourg and Zürich, above all on matters surrounding sacramental theology: on other topics, the Strasbourgers seem to have been more willing to deal with Zwingli directly. Certainly there is abundant evidence of Capito and Bucer using Oecolampadius in such a capacity. Particularly frequent are reminders to Zwingli, conveyed from Strasbourg via Basel, to respond to Luther's latest publications, and to do so speedily and, above all, diplomatically.[142] Typical of these is the extremely carefully worded message of 24th April 1527: "The Strasbourg brothers ... think it would be a good plan for you to answer [Luther] in German, with the gravitas with which you customarily respond to others ... But they plead with you to make your response quickly, and in your usual prudent way" (607, 26–28). Formulations such as these make one wonder who, in the end, is using or ventriloquizing whom: are the Strasbourgers employing Oecolampadius to do their dirty work for them, or is he only too glad to appeal to their authority in order to voice or reinforce his own potentially unpopular opinions? And there are occasions where one is convinced that both phenomena are at play: when, for example, Oecolampadius writes that "the Strasbourg brothers are very fearful that we are putting our adversaries under too much pressure, with the result that they will be more implacable in future" (448, 14f.), it comes as no surprise at all to see him add "I have recently written about this matter also" (line 16).

For all their respect for and conscious indebtedness to Zwingli, then, it seems that the Strasbourg evangelicals regarded Oecolampadius as on the whole a closer and more reliable ally; and this impression is confirmed when one takes account also of the three cities' other major joint enterprise during the 1520s and beyond, namely the production of scholarly commentaries on (and/or translations of) key books of the Old Testament. These activities are also alluded to at times in the Zwingli-Oecolampadius letters. In 547, 32f., for example, the latter states that he is about to "consign the last three of the minor prophets to the printing-presses", a reference to his commentary on Haggai, Zechariah and Malachi that was to appear in 1527.[143] In 883, 1–4, Oecolampadius thanks Zwingli for sending him a copy of his Latin translation of Isaiah;[144] and in 763, 12f., we find them conversing about comparable exegetical work

---

142   See 496, 4f.; 562, 29–31; 611, 1–3; 614, 3–5; 661, 9–21.
143   *In Postremos Tres Prophetas, Nempe Haggæum, Zachariam, & Malachiam, Commentarius Ioan. Oecolampadij* (Basel: Cratander, 1527; Staehelin 137; Leu/Weidmann 30). See Staehelin, *Lebenswerk*, 396–406.
144   *Complanatio Isaiae prophetae foetura prima cum apologia* (Zürich: Froschauer, 1529; Leu/Weidmann 199, 202).

being done in Strasbourg—Bucer, it seems, "has almost exhausted his strength in writing his preface to Zephaniah".[145] The fact that we are dealing with a concerted project encompassing three cities is moreover confirmed by comparable references in other letters[146] and, especially, by the presence of a common theological and methodological approach. Indeed, Bernard Roussel and Gerald Hobbs are justified in speaking of a "Rhenish" (more accurately Northern Swiss/Upper Rhenish) school of biblical interpretation—on the understanding that a "school" must involve "a body of interpreters consciously working along similar lines with analogous methods in the use of common tools, employing a mutually agreed hermeneutic in pursuit of goals at least tacitly identified".[147]

In the case of the evangelical scholars working in sixteenth-century Zürich, Basel and Strasbourg, these "methods, tools, hermeneutic and goals" were all classically Erasmian in character. Their whole interpretative edifice was founded on an expert mastery of the biblical languages (Zwingli, Oecolampadius, Capito, Bucer and their colleagues Konrad Pellikan and Sebastian Münster were—unlike Erasmus—all Hebraists); they paid meticulous attention to the historical contexts of biblical books, before seeking to apply these to the contemporary world; they showed a marked preference for a text's literal (or 'natural') meaning, whilst permitting also a *sensus moralis* and *sensus mysticus* if these could be read out of, rather than into, that literal meaning; they adopted a Christocentric and Christoscopic approach, which necessarily encompassed a willingness to apply typological approaches and an emphasis on the unity of the Bible; and, not least, they were keen to allow the words of scripture, respectfully and intelligently understood, to speak into their own, and their readers', contemporary context. There is, in short, much evidence to suggest that the scholars under discussion sought to apply to the interpretation of the Hebrew Bible many of the insights brought by Erasmus to the study of the New Testament: that, in other words, they were consciously both continuing and renewing his work as a humanist within the changed parameters of a new evangelical culture.[148]

---

145 *Tzephaniah, quem Sophoniam vulgo vocant, prophetarum epitomographus ad ebraicum veritatem versus, & commentario explanatus* (Strasbourg: Herwagen, 1528; Leu/Weidmann 39). Other examples include a slightly waspish comment on Capito's book about Hosea (747, 13–19), and Oecolampadius's periodic updates on his progress working on Daniel (763, 20–39; 774, 25–29; 786, 1–5).

146 Some examples are given by Roussel, "De Strasbourg à Bâle", 22.

147 Hobbs, "Pluriformity", 454.

148 They also, of course, made very extensive use of Erasmus's own publications. For examples see Christ-von Wedel, "Erasmus", 147–150, 155–159.

The corpus of work produced in pursuit of these ideals is impressive indeed: in Basel, Münster produced work on Proverbs (1524), the Song of Songs and Ecclesiastes (1525), Joel and Malachi (1530), and Amos (1531), whilst Oecolampadius published on Isaiah (1525), Haggai, Zechariah and Malachi (1527), Daniel (1530), Jeremiah and Lamentations (1533), Ezekiel (1534) and the remaining minor prophets (1535), with the last three named works being completed and/or edited by Capito. Meanwhile Capito himself wrote commentaries on Habakkuk (1526) and Hosea (1527), whilst Bucer translated the Psalms (1526, 1529) and commented on Zephaniah (1528). Finally, in Zürich, Zwingli worked on Genesis and Exodus (1527), Isaiah (1529), Jeremiah (1531) and the Psalms (published in 1532).[149] It is particularly striking that this list includes nearly all of the books of the non-apocryphal Old Testament from Psalms to Malachi (hence with a particular emphasis on prophecy), and that so few of these books were worked on by more than one author. In such a context one is struck also by the fact that almost all the cases of duplication involve Zwingli. It is as though, in Strasbourg and Basel's joint attempts both to unite evangelicals around a common eucharistic theology and to provide them with a humanist-inspired evangelical framework for understanding particularly the Old Testament, Zwingli and Zürich were regarded as important, valued, but not fully trusted partners—a fact underlined by the fact that, in 1534, all Strasbourg parishes were required to purchase a copy of all the Bible commentaries of Capito, Bucer and Oecolampadius, but not those of Zwingli.[150] Hobbs suggests that the latter's work on the Old Testament could not be fully integrated into that of the "Rhenish" school (and hence needed to be 're-done') in part because of his consistent, ideologically-led reluctance to use the work of Masoretic scribes and rabbinical commentators.[151] There may well be some truth in this, though in fact Zwingli's volumes on Isaiah and the Psalms postdate their Basel and Strasbourg counterparts, and seem to have arisen naturally out of the exegetical and homiletic practices of the Zürich *Prophezei*. In any case it is true that, if our Northern Swiss/Upper Rhenish school of the early sixteenth century can be "rightly understood as one of the leading centres of biblical interpretation in Europe",[152] it could not have achieved this status without Zwingli.

---

149 These details are presented in tabular form (with bibliographical information) in Roussel, "De Strasbourg à Bâle", 37–39.
150 Hobbs, "Pluriformity", 483.
151 Hobbs, "Pluriformity", 484–486.
152 Hobbs, "Pluriformity", 454.

5   Zwingli, Oecolampadius and the Wider World

The Reformation that Zwingli had begun in Zürich and that, by 1530, had also encompassed Basel and many other parts of German-speaking Switzerland proved highly influential in other parts of Europe as well.[153] This was particularly true of the South German cities—including Strasbourg, but also Konstanz, Ulm, Augsburg and Mulhouse—in which "Swiss evangelical thought spread like wildfire …, appealing to artisans and craftsmen; Zwingli's work was often read in preference to Luther's, largely on account of its emphasis on the communal nature of the church and the lucidity of the Zürich reformer's position on the sacrament".[154] All of these cities were of course different, and their reformations proceeded at different speeds and under the influence of sometimes radically different agendas; but Zwingli and his work in Zürich was in each case an essential trigger.

In England also, perspectives emanating from Zürich were crucial to the country's religious culture in the sixteenth century. Here, the key figure was in many ways Zwingli's successor Bullinger, who "at least until the 1550s, contributed more to the reformed character of the Church of England than did Jean Calvin".[155] Nevertheless much of what Bullinger developed had roots set down in Zwingli's lifetime. This is true, for example, of the latter's doctrine of a "single sphere" uniting the church and civil government, which pointed unequivocally towards the Erastian arrangements of the Elizabethan Settlement;[156] and it is true also of the Zürich Bible of 1530, a crucially important source especially for the Bible translation of Miles Coverdale—whose versions of the Psalms, which eventually found their way into the Book of Common Prayer, are based squarely on the German of Zwingli and his colleagues.[157]

In the French-speaking world also Swiss-German evangelical influence made itself felt from an early stage, not least through personal contacts of Zwingli and Oecolampadius such as Anémond de Coct, Guillaume Farel,

---

153   See the detailed surveys in Gordon, *Swiss*, 283–316; Locher, ZR, 621–680.
154   Gordon, *Swiss*, 283.
155   Carrie Euler, *Couriers of the Gospel: England and Zurich, 1531–1558* (Zürich: Theologischer Verlag, 2006), 3. This work, which focuses especially on letters and translations, is an indispensable resource for the study of relations between Swiss and English Protestants in the sixteenth century.
156   See J. Wayne Baker, "Erastianism in England: The Zürich Connection", in Schindler, ZR, 327–349, especially 328–332. Also Rudolf Pfister, "Zürich und das anglikanische Staatskirchentum", *Zwingliana*, 10/4 (1955): 249–256.
157   See Walter J. Hollenweger, "Zwinglis Einfluß in England", *Zwingliana* 19/1 (1992): 171–186, here 174–177.

Jacques Lefèvre d'Etaples and Gérard Roussel.[158] Above all, Calvin in Geneva was far more influenced by Zürich (and Basel) than he at times seemed willing to admit—to the extent indeed that one could argue that "none of [his] theological insights had not already been discussed among the Swiss Reformers in the years before Calvin started to write his *Institutio*" (in 1536).[159]

The influences summarized above have been well documented and could be added to many times over. Overall it is fair to say that the long-term achievements of Zwingli are now reasonably well appreciated, even if his importance in the history specifically of Anglicanism is still apt to be underestimated in favour of that of Calvin. As in so many other respects, however, the contribution made specifically by Oecolampadius to wider theological and ecclesiastical developments remains under-researched and insufficiently esteemed. In the context of this volume we have no scope to remedy this lack in anything approaching adequate detail. With the aid of some critical literature, however, we can offer at least a few examples of an Oecolampadianism that is clearly distinct from Zwinglianism—examples that between them constitute a few preliminary stones that might, in time, form the basis of a more extensive and coherent interpretative mosaic.

In each of the three contexts mentioned above, Oecolampadius made some real and lasting contributions. With regard to South Germany, we read in letter 1228 of him playing a key role in the implementation of the Reformation in Ulm—in company not with Zwingli but with Bucer of Strasbourg and Blarer of Konstanz (1228).[160] Moreover in the following month, July 1531, he proceeded to perform much the same service in Memmingen and Biberach. More surprisingly perhaps, given their almost complete failure in Switzerland, Oecolampadius's late-career plans for autonomous ecclesiastical discipline fell on more fruitful soil in at least some parts of Germany. At a meeting of preachers and politicians from leading South German cities held at Memmingen between 26th February and 1st March 1531, Oecolampadius's ideas on excommunication met with widespread approval, and a summary of them was incorporated into the subsequently published Memmingen Articles.[161] Thanks to the efforts of Oecolampdius's increasingly close collaborator Ambrosius Blarer, they then found their way into regulations passed by the Council of Konstanz on 5th April

---

158   See 329, 3–11 and n. 2; 347, 17 and n. 1f.; 1018, 12–20 and n. 6–8.
159   Peter Opitz, "Calvin in the Context of the Swiss Reformation", in Selderhuis, *Calvinus*, 13–28, here 26.
160   On Ambrosius Blarer see above, p. x.
161   See Wolfgang Dobras, "Zwinglische Kirchenzucht in Konstanz? Die Konstanzer Reformatoren und die Frage des Kirchenbanns", in Schindler, ZR, 131–142, here 135.

1531; and Blarer (or his successors) were subsequently able to include at least some of Oecolampadius's recommendations in comparable *Zuchtordnungen* enacted at Esslingen, Memmingen, Lindau and Isny (all in 1532), as well as—in later years—at Reutlingen, Augsburg, Kempten and Ravensburg.[162] In all of these the role of the pastor in excommunication procedures remained advisory rather than executive, but one nevertheless has a distinct impression of Oecolampadius achieving a certain victory from beyond the grave.

With regard to England, there is good reason to assume that Zwingli and Oecolampadius were regarded essentially as equals. After all, both men were asked for their opinion about Henry VIII's marital status; the works of both of them were on the Archbishop of Canterbury's list of banned literature from 1526 to 1531; and when, in March 1550, the Master of the Rolls Sir Christopher Hales commissioned Hans Asper to produce the paintings reproduced on the front cover of this volume, he took pains to ask for an image of Oecolampadius as well of one of Zwingli. As to Oecolampadius's most notable independent contribution to the development of English Protestantism, this is to be found—not surprisingly, given that it had attracted the critical attention of John Fisher as early as 1527—in his eucharistic theology. On 17th June 1533, Thomas Cranmer describes, in a letter to Archdeacon Nicholas Hawkins, the trial of the evangelical heretic John Frith, who "thought it not necessary to be believed as an article of faith, that there is the very corporal presence of Christ within the host and sacrament of the altar, and holdeth of this point most after the opinion of Oecolampadius".[163] At this point Cranmer—along with, one assumes many other Englishmen—will have been familiar with Oecolampadius's distinctive take on the Lord's Supper, but will for certain have disagreed with it. That was to change, however. In the "Lutheran phase" of his eucharistic understanding (from 1537 to around 1546), Cranmer was already mining Oecolampadius's *Dialogus* for relevant quotations from the fathers; and by the time of his contribution to the famous Debate on the Sacrament that took place in the House of Lords in late 1548, he was a convinced Oecolampadian, using Tertullian to demonstrate the essentially "figurative" nature of Christ's sacramental body.[164] Peter Brooks is no doubt correct to warn us that "if the Archbishop certainly made good use of Tertullian's *figura corporis mei*, that passage by no means assumed the same importance for him as for the Basel Reformer".[165] Nevertheless it is clear that "the Archbishop was both well acquainted with,

---

162 See Fritz Hauß, "Blarers Zuchtordnungen", in Moeller, *Blarer*, 114–127.
163 Quoted by Brooks, *Cranmer*, 3.
164 See Brooks, *Cranmer*, 34f., 50.
165 Brooks, *Cranmer*, 90.

and impressed by, the writings of that 'godly and excellent man' [Oecolampadius] .... and would have found such writings of very considerable value"[166]—not least, one is tempted to suggest, when compiling the eucharistic liturgy of the Book of Common Prayer.

Finally we turn again to Geneva, where, as we have begun to realize in the light of some relatively recent studies, Oecolampadius's independent influence was decidedly significant. We know for one thing that Calvin had access to his Old Testament commentaries, and indeed that these, along with a French translation of his work on Job, were reprinted in Geneva. Moreover, Calvin is on record as preferring Oecolampadius's work on Isaiah to that of Zwingli and Luther; and there is evidence also to suggest that he used the Basel scholar's commentary on Ezekiel and translation of Chrysostom's homilies.[167] In addition, in his own work on the Eucharist, Calvin culled the relevant publications of Oecolampadius for arguments, particularly from patristic sources, that might reinforce his own views as opposed to those of Luther;[168] and, as is perhaps rather better known, his Geneva was another city in which Oecolampadius's views on autonomous church discipline achieved a belated, posthumous influence. As Olaf Kuhr puts it, the disciplinary system proposed in Calvin's *Articles concernant l'organisation de l'église et du culte* of 1537 "shows some remarkable parallels to the Basel Discipline Ordinance and to Oecolampadian ideals".[169] Furthermore, "we are able to identify in Calvin's eucharistic liturgy of 1542 a distinct influence from Basel at one characteristic point: the solemn excommunication by which the 'unworthy' were declared to be banned from the communion table without being named."[170] None of this influence from Oecolampadius gave Calvin an easy ride as he attempted, over several years, to persuade his Council to implement his plans for an independent ecclesiastical disciplinary function; but by 1560 he had established the principle that "church and state were two separate entities. Calvin had finally secured what Oecolampadius had always envisaged but could not realize".[171]

---

166 Brooks, *Cranmer*, 91.
167 See Burnett, "Exegesis", 248 f.
168 For examples see Burnett, "Exegesis", 254 f.
169 Kuhr, "Calvin", 25 (with details).
170 Kuhr, "Calvin", 26.
171 Kuhr, "Calvin", 32.

6   Zwingli, Oecolampadius and Letter-Writing

Early sixteenth-century letter-writing differed considerably from its modern equivalent. For one thing, letters were often semi-public documents, designed to be read by more than one person. As such they have in some ways less in common with the modern letter addressed exclusively to a single recipient than they do with contemporary social media, with their potent combination of semi-public, semi-private discourses. Hence, when Zwingli was writing to Oecolampadius in Basel or Oecolampadius to Zwingli in Zürich, there was generally an understanding that the "Christian brothers" surrounding the addressee would also read the letter in question, or at least have parts of it read to them; and, as we have seen, our two reformers frequently forwarded letters to, or sent them via, Strasbourg, in order that they might be read there also.

Moreover, people other than the two named correspondents were also frequently involved not just in the reception, but also in the production and delivery of superficially 'one-to-one' letters. It is noticeable, for example, how many of Oecolampadius's letters to Zwingli are written in hands other than his own. Our analysis of the originals kept in the Staatsarchiv des Kantons Zürich has concluded that, whilst Zwingli's letters are all autographs, some 31 of Oecolampadius's were written—in part or completely—by scribes.[172] The most obvious explanation for this is, one assumes, the Basel reformer's often fragile health. This is implied above all by letter 676, written by a scribe but signed in Greek by Oecolampadius himself, in which, following reassurances about his health, the latter advises Zwingli not to be "alarmed that I am writing with the aid of a scribe" (line 40)—only to append to his concluding signature the rather poignant declaration, "I added this in my own hand" (line 45).[173] That the use of scribes was not always occasioned by physical weakness is, however, strongly suggested by the evidence of letter 505, which was written partly by a scribe and partly by Oecolampadius himself. Here Oecolampadius takes over as late as line 31, with the words "Cratander has brought a bundle of letters to the person writing this; I will now send them on to you"—whereupon, one assumes, the scribe was detailed to attend to this "sending on", leaving Oecolampadius to complete the letter himself.

Occasionally also, one is tempted to wonder whether Oecolampadius's use of a scribe might in itself have constituted a rhetorical device. It is noticeable

---

172   Our translations of Oecolampadius's letters always stipulate whether the hand of the original is—in our view—authorial or scribal.
173   Ill-health is a reason early modern authors seem generally to have felt confident in giving when explaining, or excusing, their use of a scribe. See Blair, "Erasmus", 40.

that his first two letters to Zwingli (258 and 269) are in a particularly neat and careful scribal hand; and this, combined with his flattering tone and extensive use of humanist rhetorical tropes, seems part and parcel of his all too obvious desire to create a positive first impression. Moreover, as Blair and Daybell point out,[174] many early modern letter-writers wrote in their own hands to their families, peers and friends, whilst employing scribes when writing to people they knew less well, especially if these addressees occupied a higher place in the social hierarchy. This raises the intriguing possibility that Oecolampadius's use of a scribe at the outset of the correspondence was intended to reinforce his construction of himself as Zwingli's somewhat star-struck inferior; but of course we can never really know.

We do know, however, that successful early modern communication networks such as those between Zürich, Basel and Strasbourg were dependent not just on scribes but, still more, on messengers. These are mentioned on a regular basis in the Zwingli-Oecolampadius correspondence, whether in a tone of relief that one has finally appeared (see 624, 1 f.) or, more frequently, in a tone of frustration that they are so hard to find—even when an improved level of service has recently been promised.[175] The difficulty of identifying reliable messengers must have been exacerbated by the fact that they were clearly often expected not only to deliver letters, but also to communicate in person with those letters' recipients.[176] The epistolary culture of early sixteenth-century evangelicals was, it seems, heavily if paradoxically dependent on oral as well as written methods of communication; and this was particularly the case when caution was deemed necessary. Oecolampadius in particular evinces at times an acute awareness of the dangers and limitations of letter-writing. As early as July 1526 he tells Zwingli that "we are now committing what needs to be said less openly in letters" (505, 2 f.); and in the summer of 1528 he refers somewhat disparagingly to his own letter 726, stating that "Cratander, who is delivering the letter, will be able to tell you much better [about recent developments in Basel] than it can: this letter is not so much bashful as mistrustful" (line 4 f.). At either end of the correspondence, moreover, Oecolampadius expresses regret that his communication with Zwingli cannot take place in person,[177] a form of

---

174 Blair, "Erasmus", 39; James Daybell, *The Material Letter in Early Modern England: Manuscript Letters and the Culture and Practices of Letter-Writing, 1512–1635* (Basingstoke: Palgrave Macmillan, 2012), 86–88.
175 The best example of this is Oecolampadius's complaint in 635, lines 44–47: "You can put the late arrival of these letters down to the scarcity of messengers. Heinrich [Ryhiner] promised us a courier every day; but none has appeared for almost a whole month".
176 Examples of this are 268, 37 f.; 411, 1 f.; 642, 16–18; 976, 19.
177 See 286, 1–4; 1133, 18–20; 1164, 2 f.

human interaction which, not least given his eirenic temperament, he seems consistently to have preferred: "the Strasbourg brothers", he writes for example in December 1525, "are concerned to see whether the matter can be brought forward for discussion, and I would choose this way. People oppose one another a great deal when they are apart, but less so when they are present together" (418, 10–13).

Certainly Oecolampadius was justified in seeing every letter as a potential security risk: as Mark Greengrass puts it, "even the most private letter, one that enjoined the strictest privacy upon its recipient, had the potential to be copied, extracted, collected, printed, utilized by one's friends and enemies alike, instrumentalized to tarnish a reputation, to advance an argument in a debate, or to ensure a particular outcome."[178] The dangers inherent in early modern epistolary communication were indeed made plain in the summer of 1526 by an incident alluded to in the Zwingli-Oecolampadius correspondence: the reformers' arch-enemy Johann Faber intercepted a letter from Capito to Zwingli, and printed it in a revised form which made it appear that Capito was inciting the Swiss to revolt against the outcomes of the Disputation of Baden (see 509, 1–6 and n. 3)—an "instrumentalization" of the original letter which not only "tarnished" Capito's reputation, but also landed him in considerable legal and financial difficulty.

Within the context of their own correspondence also, an awareness of the need for privacy and security led Zwingli and Oecolampadius at times to employ various forms of coded language. Hence they refer to certain individuals in indirect or opaque ways;[179] and they use Greek as a means of excluding unwanted, less educated readers—a practice which normally involves only a few words,[180] but in one case extends over slightly more than half a letter.[181]

---

178 Greengrass, "Epistolary Reformation", 431.
179 In 268, 27, for example, Johannes Romanus Wonnecker is referred to as "N. Egg"; in 960, 2, Nikolaus Guldi is "this man N."; and in 552, 77, Thomas Wellenberg is "N.N." (*nomen nescio*). Meanwhile figures such as Jakob Strauß and Johann Faber are designated routinely by punning nicknames, *Struthio* ('the ostrich') in the former case, and Τέκτων ('the workman') in the latter; and the precise identity of numerous individuals is obscured—presumably deliberately—by their being designated only by a pronoun such as *ille*.
180 Examples can be found for example in 268, 20 and 31, in which Zwingli refers to opponents as ταῶνας ('peacocks') and ὄνον ('ass'). On the use of Greek for 'coding' and other purposes in the sixteenth century see now Raf van Rooy, *New Ancient Greek in a Neo-Latin World. The Restoration of Classical Bilingualism in the Early Modern Low Countries and Beyond* (Leiden: Brill, 2023).
181 The letter in question is 673, dated 19th December 1527. At first sight its contents do not appear unusually sensitive, being concerned mainly with Capito and Bucer's desire to attend the forthcoming Disputation of Bern. This will have involved some potentially deli-

Most fascinatingly, letter 844, dated 22nd May 1529, consists almost exclusively of a list of (Latin) codewords to be used in correspondence between Zwingli, Oecolampadius, Capito and Bucer: the "good and faithful Swiss", for example, are to be referred to as "the sons of God", the "bad Swiss" as "the sons of Belial", Archduke Ferdinand as "the black one" and Philipp of Hesse as "the white one"; moreover, in moves surely guaranteed to result only in abject confusion, Speyer is to be called "Hamburg" and the Hungarians "the Danes" (lines 2–9). For all their eccentricity, indeed absurdity, the mere existence of such codewords is itself testimony to just how careful many early evangelicals felt they needed to be.

The references in our last paragraph to the smatterings of Greek that appear in the Zwingli-Oecolampadius letters serve also to remind us, of course, that we are dealing here with eminent humanists. We have already witnessed Zwingli sprinkling classical allusions liberally over some of his early letters in an apparent attempt to impress Oecolampadius;[182] and he continues to do this from time to time also in later years. In the space of three lines (6–8) near the beginning of letter 552, for example, he makes passing references to the Catilinarian conspiracy, to the Greek goddess Hestia, and to the Battle of Thermopylae. Instances of this sort of thing are not very frequent, however, and any reader coming to these letters with the expectation of witnessing a consistently sparkling display of humanist learning will be largely disappointed. In the context of Zwingli and Oecolampadius's extensive, if sometimes only reluctantly admitted indebtedness to Erasmus of Rotterdam, however, it is striking how many of their classical allusions seem to have been taken at second hand from the Dutch scholar's influential compilation of Greek and Latin proverbs, the *Adagia*. When Oecolampadius speaks, for example, of an ivy vine bereft of wine, a shrew that raises its voice, a gladiator entering the arena, or a lion whom one can know by its claw,[183] he is manifestly quoting from the proverb collection published by his distinguished former colleague.

In terms of literary form, meanwhile, only the first three letters, with their elegant circumlocutions, elaborate flattery and carefully crafted overall shape, are likely to conform to most readers' preconceptions of early modern humanist epistolography: already at the beginning of the fourth letter Oecolampadius launches into a discussion of forthcoming disputations, and that seems

---

cate negotiations with the Bern authorities, however, and Oecolampadius no doubt saw it as his duty to take more precautions than usual to prevent the letter being read by hostile eyes.
182 See p. 27 and n. 113.
183 See 359, 17; 396, 25 f.; 438, 11 f.; 812, 38 f.

to set the tone for what follows—which, with the exception of some longer letters, particularly by Zwingli, that amount to short theological treatises,[184] is a collection of predominantly brief, pragmatic pieces devoted to serving a shared cause, often composed in haste, and devoid of any literary aspirations or claims on the attention of posterity. Nevertheless it is worth remembering that humanists often saw letters as a medium situated between formal speech (*oratio*) and conversation (*sermo*); and Erasmus himself, in his influential *De conscribendis epistolis* of 1522, is at pains to stress the uniquely flexible nature of the epistolary genre. He explains that the form and content of a letter should in no way be artificially constrained, but rather should be adapted to the person to whom it is addressed and the subject with which it is concerned.[185] Hence, alongside letters designed for judicial, deliberative or demonstrative purposes, all of which have their roots in some kind of formal oratory, Erasmus places a category he calls familiar letters (*epistolae familiares*), "which include letters of announcement, narration, congratulation, lamentation, and command",[186] and which as such could, indeed should, be couched in a relatively simple style. It is eminently reasonable to think of the letters exchanged by Zwingli and Oecolampadius, and indeed by other pairs of reformers, as *epistolae familiares* in this sense—as flexibly pragmatic communications that, unavoidably constrained as they are by time, urgency and the pressure of events, nevertheless reflect the classical and humanist notion of correspondence as a conversation between absent friends.[187]

7 Manuscripts and Editions

The fact that the Zwingli-Oecolampadius correspondence remains readily available to twenty-first century readers is testimony above all to the labours of generations of Zürich-based scholars and librarians—though of course the corpus that has been handed down to us is far from complete. The surviving letters themselves contain, after all, numerous references to letters that are no longer extant.[188]

---

184 See especially 367 and 401.
185 See Jacqueline Glomski, "Epistolary Writing", in Victoria Moul, ed., *A Guide to Neo-Latin Literature* (Cambridge: Cambridge University Press, 2017), 255–271, especially 258.
186 Judith Rice Henderson, "Defining the Genre of the Letter: Juan Luis Vives' *De conscribendis epistolis*", *Renaissance and Reformation* 7 (1983): 89–105, here 98.
187 Oecolampadius indeed speaks of his own letters to Zwingli as *familiaribus scriptis* ('familiar writings') in 1041, line 5.
188 See for example 280, 5–7; 430, 11f.; 767, 1–3; 1094, 1f.; 1184, 1.

FIGURE 5   Oecolampadius's seal. The image of a light on top of a house is a visualisation of
Oecolampadius's name—see p. XXVI, n. 26.
ZÜRICH, STAATSARCHIV, E II 349, FOL. 5ᵛ (LETTER 435)

Of the 183 letters that form our corpus, the originals of some 164 are held in the Staatsarchiv des Kantons Zürich; only two of these, 812 and 1136, are by Zwingli. 160 of Oecolampadius's letters are conveniently bound together in a single volume housed in the Staatsarchiv, MS E II 349, in a collection created by the Zürich antistes Johann Jakob Breitinger (1575–1645) soon after his appointment in 1613;[189] and the originals of letters 329 and 1066 have found their way into other volumes in the same archive (MS E I 74 and E I 3 respectively). The authenticity of these Staatsarchiv manuscripts is moreover confirmed by the survival on many of them of Oecolampadius's personal seal, or at least of traces of it.

---

189   Breitinger made the first serious attempt to collect and catalogue the Zürich reformers' letters. See Randolph C. Head, "Archival Practices and the Interpretation of the Zurich Reformation, 1519–2019", in Peter Opitz and Ariane Albisser, eds, *Die Zürcher Reformation in Europa: Beiträge der Tagung des Instituts für Schweizerische Reformationsgeschichte* (Zürich: Theologischer Verlag, 2021), 389–408, here 394–396.

Two further original manuscript letters can be found in Zürich, this time in its Zentralbibliothek, where they form part of the collection known as the *Thesaurus Hottingerianus*: 401, by Zwingli, and 844, by Oecolampadius, in Msc F. 37 (fol. 193 f.) and Msc F. 47 (fol. 275) respectively.[190] Of the remaining letters by Zwingli, we know that three remain extant in their original form: 319 (Zofingen, Stadtbibliothek, StBZ Pa 14:1,17-1), 381 (Strasbourg, Archives de la Ville et de l'Eurométropole, 1 AST 162 (no. 291)), and 416 (Zofingen, Stadtbibliothek, StBZ Pa 14:1,16).[191] As far as we are aware, letter 460 is also still extant: *ZW* VIII, 545 records its location as the church library of Kamienna Góra (in Silesia, formerly 'Landeshut'; Epistolae, I, *322*). This, however, is the only letter whose existence or otherwise we have not been able to confirm. Three further Zwingli autographs have been missing since the nineteenth century—298 and 552 were last seen in Bremen, and 347 in Erlangen. They still exist, however, in copies by the Zürich pastor, teacher and church historian Johann Jakob Simler (1716–1788) which are kept at the Zentralbibliothek Zürich (MS S 8, no. 97; MS S 17a, no. 54; and MS S 11, no. 80). Simler is in our debt also for his assiduous copying, for his personal archive, of some 151 other letters whose originals *have* survived.

We are fortunate further that 496, an otherwise lost letter by Oecolampadius, is preserved in a contemporary German translation (Staatsarchiv Solothurn, AG 1,15, Eidgenössische Abschiede 1526, p. 279); and, above all, that some eight lost letters[192]—seven of which are by Zwingli—remain accessible by dint of their inclusion in a 1536 publication entitled *D.D. Ioannis Oecolampadii et Huldrichii Zvinglii Epistolarum Libri Quatuor* (Basel: Platter and Lasius). This is a fascinating collection which has yet to be adequately studied, not least because it was plainly conceived as an intervention into the theological and political debates of the mid-1530s, intent on presenting the Swiss reformers as orthodox, legitimate spokesmen for evangelicals as a whole, and as such worthy collaborators with Lutheran forces.[193] For now, however, it is important to clarify that, in spite of its title, it is in no sense an edition of the correspondence between Zwingli and Oecolampadius (only the eight letters mentioned above

---

190 The *Thesaurus Hottingerianus* is named after Johann Heinrich Hottinger (1620–1667), who made an extensive collection of letters to and from Zürich reformers, most of which had previously been in private ownership. See Fritz Büsser, "Heinrich Hottinger und der 'Thesaurus Hottingerianus'", *Zwingliana*, 22 (1995): 85–108.

191 The Zofingen letters are available online: https://swisscollections.ch/Record/991170478058705501/Holdings?openHierarchy=true#tabnav (accessed 2nd April 2023)

192 268, 359, 367, 569, 674, 960, 998 and 1217.

193 On this see particularly Andreas Mühling, "Der Briefwechselband Zwingli-Oekolampad von 1536", in Christ-von Wedel, *Basel*, 233–242.

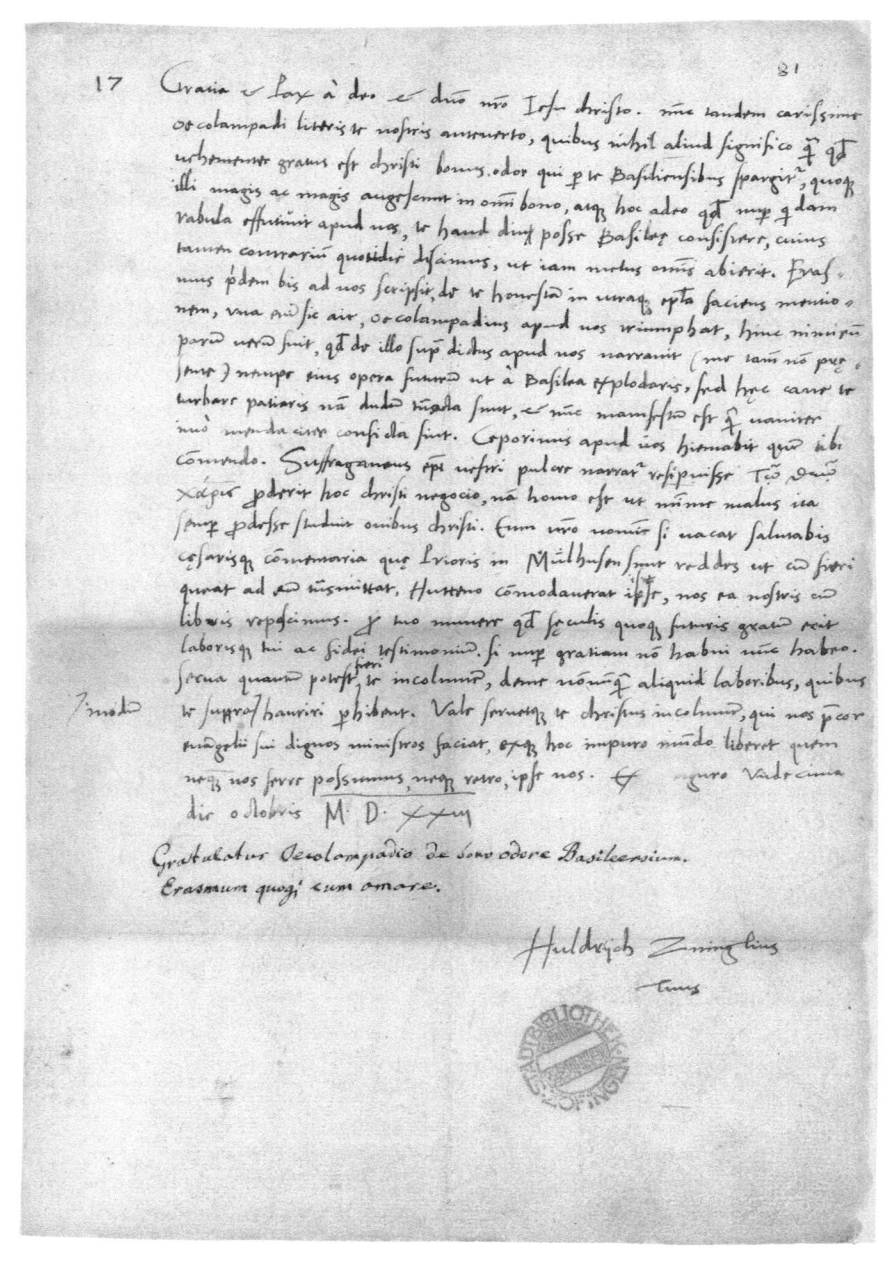

FIGURE 6   A sample of Zwingli's handwriting
ZOFINGEN, STADTBIBLIOTHEK, STBZ PA 14:1,17-1 (LETTER 319)

are included); rather, its main section is a thematically ordered anthology of their letters and other writings;[194] and this is preceded by a remarkable series of introductory pieces that include the earliest *vitae*—cast in epistolary form—of Oecolampadius (by Simon Grynaeus and then Capito) and of Zwingli (by Oswald Myconius). Altogether this volume constitutes an invaluable if rather underused resource for the study of the Zürich and Basel reformations; but, *pace* Mühling, a "Briefwechselband Zwingli-Oecolampadius" it is not.

Given this state of affairs, and the fact that the nineteenth-century edition by Melchior Schuler and Johannes Schulthess[195] has been entirely superseded, we had little choice but to use the *Corpus Reformatorum* edition of Zwingli's works (zw) as the source text for our translations. For ease of reference, we also decided to retain the numbers given to the letters in this edition, and to indicate (in italics) its page numbers. Fortunately, our study of the manuscripts—carried out, due to travel restrictions, rather later than we had hoped—confirmed the accuracy of our working hypothesis that the zw edition, whilst not ideal (particularly with regard to its now seriously outdated explicatory notes and the occasional sloppiness of its Greek), was perfectly adequate for our purpose. For the most part it offers an accurate and non-interventionist rendering of the manuscripts' wording, and departs from them—almost always with justification—mainly in the matter of punctuation. We ourselves have in some ways been influenced by these priorities, in that we have seen little compulsion to follow the editors' punctuation choices, but have made a point of ensuring that all the—infrequent—instances of our not following the actual wording of their texts have been checked against the relevant manuscripts (where possible) and properly accounted for in our notes.

The editors of zw must have appreciated the fact that the surviving manuscripts of the letters are not difficult to work with. They remain for the most part in good physical condition, and all the scribal hands involved are straightforward enough to read. There are occasional signs of haste, either in writing that is less neat than usual (as in the very short 637 and 904) or in smudges resulting from paper being folded before the ink was dry (as in 715). As one would expect also, the letters use standard sixteenth-century brevigraphs, such as *p* for *per* as part of a word (e.g. *piculum*), or a horizontal line over individual vowels to show

---

[194] These include such substantial works as Zwingli's *In catabaptistarum strophas elenchus* (fols 83ʳ–111ʳ) and Oecolampadius's *Quid de Eucharistia Veteres tum Graeci, tum Latini senserint, Dialogus* (fols 130ʳ–168ᵛ).

[195] *Huldrici Zuingli Opera*, 8 vols (Zürich: Schulthess, 1824–1842)—the letters are in vols 7 and 8.

a missing 'm' or 'n'. Similarly, *Christo* is nearly always rendered as *Chrō*, *litteras* as *lrās*, *frater/fratres* as *fr.*, and so on; but none of this causes serious problems of comprehension.

Somewhat more problematic are the sixteen cases in Breitinger's MS E II 349 where the process of cutting sheets into shape for inclusion in the bound volume has resulted in parts of the text in question disappearing from view. Worst affected is probably letter 676, from 1527, in which the meaning of three sentences has been obscured by this process, in two instances to the point of incomprehensibility.[196] In most of these cases the zw editors have sought to reconstruct lost words or phrases on the basis of the surviving manuscript evidence; again, we have checked their decisions where possible, and found them to be almost invariably plausible.

The most frustrating deficiency in the manuscripts is the absence of any unequivocal reference to the year of writing, as distinct from its day or month, in the considerable majority of the letters—strong evidence in itself to suggest that their authors tended to view them as documents intended to serve a specific short-term purpose which, as such, would no longer be relevant in any subsequent calendar year. In most of these cases the Latin editors have been able to establish the year in question with something approaching certainty, thanks to datable events, situations or publications referred to in the letter itself; and in such instances we adopt their conclusions without comment, but place the putative year of composition in brackets, so as to confirm the absence of hard manuscript evidence in support of it. Very occasionally, however, the date in question can only be a matter of interpretation; and in three such cases our weighing of the evidence differs from that of the Latin editors. Oecolampadius's letter no. 611, dated by them to 27th April 1527, has been re-dated by us—following Staehelin (*OeBA* II, 176)—to 1528, in the light of its urging Zwingli to respond urgently to Luther (lines 1–10) and its reference to negotiations between the councils of Basel and Zürich (line 20 f.). Similarly, letter 751, equivocally dated in zw to 18th August 1528, seems to us to record aspects of the lead-up to the Diet of Speyer that took place in the August of 1531,[197] and hence we have placed it there. Finally, letter 834, dated in the Latin edition to 17th April 1529, has been moved by us to the same date in 1530, on the grounds that it seems to reflect well the political and ecclesiastical climate that prevailed in the aftermath of the Colloquy of Marburg.[198] It is worth stressing,

---

196   See 676, lines 6 f., 16, 25.
197   See *OeBA* II, 643 f. (no. 910); zw XI, 578 (no. 1261b).
198   See also Staehelin's reasoning in *OeBA*, II, 435.

however, that in the vast majority of cases the chronological ordering of the letters is in little or no doubt, and that as such the correspondence possesses a certain narrative coherence.

8 Translation, Then and Now

Translation was central to early modern culture: to humanists, for example, it facilitated eloquence in Greek and Latin, as well as the acquisition of a detailed knowledge of the ancient world; and to Protestant reformers it was an essential tool for making the scriptures (and selected texts which interpreted them) available to wider sections of society. Hence it is hardly surprising that both Zwingli and Oecolampadius were active translators. As usual, Zwingli's translation work is better known, his name being indelibly associated with the monumental achievement that was the so-called Zürich Bible of 1530, a translation of the entire scriptures into German that predated that of Luther by some four years.[199] The extent of Zwingli's personal involvement in the production of this translation is a controversial question which cannot now be fully answered; but he clearly was directly responsible for independent translations (into Latin) of Isaiah and Job.[200] For his part Oecolampadius, as well as re-translating many passages in the course of his various Old Testament commentaries, was an extraordinarily prolific translator, into Latin, of some twelve church fathers.[201]

The priorities and techniques of Zwingli's and Oecolampadius's translations have not attracted much scholarly study, but the evidence we do have suggests that Oecolampadius, at least when it came to the scriptures, wanted to be as faithful to the original language as possible, while Zwingli's focus was on communicating as clearly as he could with his target audience, rather than seeking to imitate formal features of the source text. In the dedicatory epistle and preface of his *In Iesaiam* (1525), Oecolampadius explains that he is working with the Hebrew text and not using the translations of the Septuagint or St Jerome, both to aid his students of Hebrew in their understanding of the original and to enable himself to work with the actual phrases Isaiah used; he

---

199 *Die gantze Bibel der Ebraischen und Griechischen waarheyt nach auff das aller trewlichest verteütschet* (Zürich: Froschauer, 1530).
200 See above, pp. 34, 36.
201 Staehelin, "Väterübersetzungen", lists these church fathers as Peter of Alexandria, Gennadius of Constantinople, Nicephorus Chartophylax, Gregory Thaumaturgus, Gregory of Nazianzus, Thalassius, John of Damascus, John II of Jerusalem, Basil the Great, Theophylactus, Cyril of Alexandria and John Chrysostom.

even retains some Hebrew idioms in his own translations of individual verses, to the inevitable detriment of the fluency of his Latin.[202] Zwingli clearly read this preface, and indeed responded to it in the equivalent section of his own *Apologia complanationis Isaiae* (1529)—a reminder in itself that, as was the case with so many early modern figures, Zwingli and Oecolampadius communicated with each other via published works, as well as in private or semi-public correspondence. In his Isaiah preface, Zwingli states that both Jerome and Oecolampadius were able to correct many errors in the Septuagint by going back to the Hebrew sources and re-translating these,[203] thereby readily acknowledging the success of Oecolampadius's philological method. He goes on to assert, however, that his own approach to translation is a different one: he proposes to speak in a "more popular" way (*popularius loquemur*)—a procedure that involves a plainness (though, if possible, also a beauty) of utterance, and a freedom to change sentence structure and verbal tenses for the sake of clarity.[204] Moreover, in his preface to the vernacular *Prophetenbibel* of 1529,[205] Zwingli stresses that, whilst he is in no way opposed to the literal translation of a Hebrew word where an appropriate German one is available, he must at times exercise the right to translate more freely, or indeed to add words, where to do so is necessary for a satisfactory understanding of the original. That Zwingli and his Zürich colleagues were far from unaware of the tensions, indeed dangers, inherent in such a procedure is, however, demonstrated by the fact that all elucidatory German words added to the Hebrew in this way originally appear in the *Prophetenbibel* in a smaller typeface.[206]

Far from being disconcerted by such an approach, Oecolampadius seems to have approved wholeheartedly at least of Zwingli's Latin Isaiah. "Yesterday I received your letter, along with your Isaiah", he writes on 28th July 1529, "and I have spent a large part of the night on the latter. I cannot put in writing how much I liked it—and I will not attempt to do so, lest you regret the labour of reading what I wrote" (883, 1–4). Indeed, his only objection is that

---

202 Johannes Oecolampadius, *In Iesaiam Prophetam Hypomnematōn, Hoc Est, Commentariorum, Ioannis Oecolampadii Libri VI* (Basileae: Cratander, 1525; Leu/Weidmann A160), A3ᵛ–4ʳ; B4ʳ.
203 See ZW XIV, 88.
204 See Edwin Künzli, "Zwingli als Ausleger des Alten Testamentes", in ZW XIV, 871–899, here 881.
205 See the account of this in Wilfried Kettler, *Die Zürcher Bibel von 1531. Philologische Studien zu ihrer Übersetzungstechnik und den Beziehungen zu ihren Vorlagen* (Bern: Lang, 2001), 80–98.
206 See Traudel Himmighöfer, *Die Zürcher Bibel bis zum Tode Zwinglis (1531). Darstellung und Bibliographie* (Mainz: von Zabern, 1995), 311.

"you [Zwingli] exalt me with immoderate words of praise that go beyond what I deserve" (line 5f.). Furthermore, at least when translating non-biblical texts, it could hardly be said that Oecolampadius himself always favoured what modern translation theorists would call 'formal equivalence' (making the target text match the source text as closely as possible in both form and content) as against 'dynamic equivalence' (seeking the closest 'natural' equivalent to the message of the source text). Indeed, his patristic translations often privileged 'natural' communication and involved a way of treating the source that would nowadays be regarded as decidedly free. He was apt, by his own admission, to change or simply omit passages in patristic source texts with which he did not agree;[207] and, when he found that his source manuscript of Theophylactus was missing a leaf, he elected to fill the gap by composing something himself (though he did at least inform his readers that he had done so).[208] Moreover it is telling in the light of his own priorities in biblical translation that, whilst Oecolampadius's patristic translations were widely read and welcomed, they attracted criticism from humanists for their lack of attention to the formal features of their Greek sources.[209]

To claim that, in our own attempts at translation, we have been directly influenced by the procedures of Zwingli or Oecolampadius would be both precious and untrue. Nevertheless it is instructive and in a sense comforting to observe that they, like all translators—including ourselves—were manifestly aware of the tensions between formal and dynamic equivalence, lucidity and stylistic sophistication, fidelity to the source text and accessibility to their readers. In our own attempts to resolve these tensions our prime concern has been to enable our reformers' voices to speak as clearly as possible to twenty-first century readers of English. In other words, our aim has been to communicate as approachably as possible the thought processes expressed in the original letters. On the other hand, we have been very conscious that Zwingli and Oecolampadius were gifted linguists, able to make precisely nuanced grammatical, syntactical and lexical choices; and hence we have done our best also to do justice to the formal aspects of their Latin, as long as doing so does not detract from the clarity and fluency of the texts we offer. For example, we do our best to replicate such micro-level features as repetition, alliteration, and indeed puns: in letter 670, for example, we translate *intermissas missas* as "Masses he has missed", and in 687 we render *Faber ... fabricatus est* literally, as "Faber has fabricated".

---

207 Staehelin, *Lebenswerk*, 173.
208 Staehelin, *Lebenswerk*, 186.
209 Staehelin, "Väterübersetzungen", 77.

A particular difficulty when translating texts like these is how to render terms used, sometimes seemingly arbitrarily or anachronistically, to refer to particular early modern institutions, functions or publications. Here we have aimed above all for consistency. Hence, *senatus* is always "Council"; *consul* "Mayor"; *tribunus* "Chief Guild Master"; *diacosii* "Council of the Two Hundred"; *episcopus* "bishop"; *libellus* "little book" (often, though not always, synonymous with "pamphlet"); *symmistae* "members of your inner circle"; *gymnasium* "university"; and *catabaptistus* "anabaptist".

Between the text of each letter and our interpretative footnotes we have, where necessary, provided linguistic notes. These document occasions when our authors use a language other than Latin, when we have found it necessary not to follow the text of the ZW edition, and when our translation is more than usually free (in such cases we also give a very literal one). In a few instances we have found it difficult to decide between two very different but, in our view, equally plausible translations. When this occurs, we enable the reader to decide by presenting one possible version in the main body of the text, and the other in a note.

When referring to authors other than Zwingli and Oecolampadius, we have consulted modern editions that are generally regarded as reliable. Hence citations from classical texts have been taken from the OCT (Oxford Classical Texts) editions, with the exception of Cicero, *Tusculanae Disputationes* and Sidonius Apollinaris, *Epistulae*, for which we consulted the Teubner editions. Where possible, references to Erasmus are taken from the *Opera omnia Desiderii Erasmi Roterodami* (Amsterdam, 1969–) and translations of Erasmus's work from the *Collected Works of Erasmus* (Toronto, 1974–). References to the works of the main evangelical reformers are based on the standard modern editions of their complete works. Latin Bible quotations are taken from the Vulgate, a translation which our two reformers knew intimately and used extensively; for reasons of convenience we use the text of 1598 provided online by the Clementine Vulgate Project: https://vulsearch.sourceforge.net/index.html (last accessed 5th April 2023). Appropriately enough, given that many of its formulations were influenced by the Vulgate and by the Zwinglian Zürich Bible, English quotations come from the King James Version.

The Letters

∴

258   Oecolampadius to Zwingli—Basel, 10th December (1522)

Greetings, good Zwingli. It should not surprise you that, personally unknown to you as I am, I should venture to address you by letter, rather than by coming into your presence as if we were on intimate terms. Take this as a tribute to your virtues and to your reputation for benevolence—and indeed
5 to Christ himself, from whom assuredly these fragrant oils flow forth onto you. So it is that they who love him even half-heartedly—if indeed it is possible for him to be loved half-heartedly—not only love you, but are drawn together in the hope of enjoying your friendship greatly and for a long time. For what they tell us about panthers is true of you and those like you—
10 that they draw all other kinds of beast to themselves with their aroma.[1] We are, it is said, the aroma of life to some, and the aroma of death to others.[2] But to me you are the aroma not of death, but of life. | For although I have already been told so many good things about you that I cannot hear them without special delight, yet I acknowledge my own faintheartedness. And
15 so, whether I want to or not, I am drawn in my heart to introduce and commend myself to you, so that I might be renewed the more abundantly by your fragrance.

Therefore, even if I have no particular topic to write to you about, it is a great enough topic for me simply to congratulate you—which I do, most
20 warmly and from the heart. And this above all upon your name, by which you show that you are one who should be loved by all.[3] Who would not love one who does Christ's business with such diligence? Who feeds his sheep with such faith?[4] Who is so much to be feared by the wolves?[5] Who stands as a

VII, 634

VII, 635

---

3 *as if ... terms*] *iure familiarum* ('by the law of your familiars')   3f. *Take ... tribute*] *Acceptum hoc ferto*. We take this as an elliptical imperative form derived from *in acceptum ferre* ('to place something to one's credit'), though there may also be an echo of the noun *fertum* ('cake-offering to the gods')   11 *aroma ... aroma*] *in odorem ... in odorem*   19f. *most ... heart*] *multi maxime* (literally, 'a great deal, very much')

---

1 A reference to the *Physiologus* tradition (based on Pliny the Elder, *Naturalis historia* VIII, 23), in which the panther, upon awakening from three days' sleep, emits a loud, sweet-smelling roar which attracts all animals other than the dragon. The standard allegorical interpretation defines the lion as Christ and the dragon as the Devil. See most recently Nigel Harris, *The Thirteenth-Century Animal Turn* (Cham: Palgrave, 2020), 56–61.
2 Cf. II Corinthians 2:15f.
3 See p. 1, n. 4.
4 An echo of Christ's invitation to St Peter to "feed my sheep" (John 21:16f.).
5 The Bible frequently presents sheep and wolves as antithetical opposites, most influentially in Matthew 10:16 and Luke 10:3.

wall protecting the house of Israel?[6] Who interprets for us by word and deed the ancient husbandmen of religion? For I have been told these and many other things about you, and I am delighted to believe that they are true. For these reasons I congratulate you, and rejoice that an opportunity has arisen, due to our geographical proximity, for me to speak with you—not yet face-to-face, but expressing in letters (whatever their shortcomings) my heart's inclination towards you; this has not been denied me. In your humanity, you will consider this a good office, especially so in the name of him who is the source of all charity, and indeed charity itself. I pray God that he might so enrich and strengthen your spirit as to set it on fire and make it fruitful, and that I might therefore often receive joyful news of this kind about you, and indeed about the glory of the gospel and of Christ working through you—with the result that I, even though I sit only amongst the camp-menials,[7] might myself often be set on fire and, in my letters, might thank you and urge you to press on. For I permit myself not to be fearful of exhorting you by heaping such great praise upon you. And no wonder! In the amphitheatre the contestants are acclaimed not only by great people, but also by commonplace ones. Therefore, I say, carry on, and win the prize—not for yourself (you probably do not wish to hear, since you already know it, that we must seek not our own good, but that of others).[8] Rather, win it for us, win it for Christ! See to it, my Zwingli, that this letter lays the foundations for a particular friendship in Christ. I do not doubt your amicability, since you are the same towards all.

---

36 *I sit ... camp-menials*] *ad sarcinas sedentem* (literally, 'sitting amongst the burdens'). See n. 7 below   39 *by ... upon you*] *tantum applausu* (literally, 'with such great applause'). Oecolampadius is already thinking in terms of the amphitheatre

---

6   Another common biblical metaphor, used both of God (e.g. Zechariah 2:5) and of people (e.g. 1 Samuel 25:16).
7   This modesty formula seems to be modelled on Sidonius Apollinaris, 6.1.26 f. In this letter Sidonius praises the bishop Lupus, presenting himself as an unworthy sinner. Using military imagery, he counts himself among an army's camp-menials, "who because of their foolishness sit attached to the burdens of the flesh" (*qui per insipientiam suam adhuc ad carnis sarcinas sedent*).
8   1 Corinthians 10:24. There are also echoes of the previous chapter (especially 9:24–27) in the images of a race successfully run.

My host Andreas Cartander[9] also greets you.
Farewell in Christ.
Basel, 10th December.
Johannes Oecolampadius.
To Master Ulrich Zwingli, most faithful pastor of the people of Zürich, and his dearly beloved in Christ.

Original: Zürich, Staatsarchiv, E II 349, p. 1 (scribal hand). Copy: Zürich, Zentralbibliothek, Ms S 7, no. 62.

---

52 *Christ*] Greek Χριστῷ

---

9 Normally 'Cratander'. The name may be simply misspelt, or perhaps *Cartander* is intended to suggest a pun on the surname of someone who made his living from printing and publishing, hence paper (*carta*). *Cratander was in any case instrumental in facilitating the correspondence between Zwingli and Oecolampadius—see Andres Moser, "Die Anfänge der Freundschaft zwischen Zwingli und Ökolampad", *Zwingliana* 10 (1958): 614–620, especially 615. Oecolampadius lodged and worked with Cratander in the latter's house in the Petersgasse from his return to Basel on 17th November 1522 until the spring of 1524: see Staehelin, "Stellungen", 376–379.

268   Zwingli to Oecolampadius—Zürich, 14th January 1523

VIII, 3   Huldrych Zwingli to Johannes Oecolampadius, his most beloved brother in Christ. Greetings. I am tossed about in various ways, most pious and most learned Oecolampadius, yet remain steadfast, reliant as I am not on my own strength but on Christ, the rock, in whom I can do all things.[1] For it is he who comforts and revives me. Indeed, when from one quarter I am cast down by sad news of damage to the gospel, from another I am raised up and strengthened by its happy advances. If one man threatens me with a thousand deaths, another restores me with Christian writings—as you also have now begun to do[2] and, if you still love me, will continue to do often in the future. Not because I think we are worthy to have such high praise heaped on us as you burden us with; but because I see that your mind is one such as we would like to have, and we already regard it as a fertile seedbed. For when we hear that good people think rightly about Christ, we are immediately enthused by it and long to shower them with such great praise as would make us seem even foolish—unless those to whom we wrote were to respect the writer's opinion more than their own. In the same way, unless we respected your opinion more than our own, we would not be able to free you from the charge of folly; for you make us into a magnificent herald of Christ, and yourself into a camp-menial—you whom in fact I have always admired more than certain painted peacocks who are only wise in their own eyes because of the colours of their haughty speech, and turn up their noses at everyone else.[3] You are one who has conjoined piety with humanity and

VIII, 4   learning in such a way that it is not at all easy to know which has the upper hand in you.

    But from now on let us leave aside such things and discuss together matters that promote the growth of heavenly doctrine. For in these days a little

---

14 *enthused by it*] *effundimur* (literally, 'are poured forth, spread') | *shower*] *obruere* (literally, 'bury')   15f. *were to ... own*] *animum scribentis potius quam seipsos spectent* (literally, 'regarded the mind of the writer rather than themselves')   18 *charge of folly*] *ineptiis* (literally 'follies, absurdities')   19 *camp-menial*] *apud sarcinas sedentem*—see 258, line 36 and n. 7   20 *peacocks*] Greek ταῶνας

---

1   Philippians 4:13.
2   See letter 258.
3   It is unclear whether this charge is directed at any of Zwingli's opponents; but his use of a Greek word (ταῶνας) for 'peacocks', which could represent some kind of code, arguably implies that it is.

LETTER 268   61

note has been brought to us from your N. Egg[4] that is ostentatious in its use of monstrous, outlandish words—which will not be understood, as I believe, even by oracles or magicians. I beg you to laugh at that man, as he
30 deserves. Our Glarean[5] will be the most suitable person to hiss this Muse-defiling ass off the stage with his jokes and jests. When Glarean told me about it recently,[6] I made ready to say something about the matter myself; but after looking at the piece I decided it was better to stay at home—for it is by no means without danger to encounter a man who has taken leave of his senses.
35 May God be praised that the cause of the Antichrist[7] has reached such a pass as to have to depend on such champions!

The bearer of this letter will tell you, if you wish it, about the disputation which our Council has announced in a decree. A rumour is spreading that the Vicar-General of Konstanz will be there.[8] May God grant that he be not
40 prevented from attending, lest Rome or Konstanz be cheated out of the victories which they have of course grown accustomed to winning.

Farewell, and teach, admonish and exhort us often through your letters. From Zürich, 14th January 1523.

Original lost. Included in 1536 edition, fols 188ᵛ–189ʳ.

27f. *ostentatious ... words*] *verborum monstris inusitatis ambitiosa* (literally, 'ostentatious of words with strange portents')   29 *oracles*] *Sibyllas*   31 *ass*] Greek ὄνον   35 *May ... Antichrist*] Greek Τῷ θεῷ χάρις, ὅτι τῶν ἀντιχρίστων—see n. 7 below   40f. *lest ... winning*] *ne solitis triumphis fraudetur vel Roma vel Constantia: quos scilicet hactenus reportare solitae sunt* (literally, 'lest Rome or Konstanz be cheated out of the usual victories which until now they have of course been accustomed to bringing home'). Our version seeks to avoid tautology

---

4   Johannes Romanus Wonnecker (or 'Wonnegger', d. 1524), referred to by Zwingli as *Egg* or *Eck* as a play on the similarity between his name and that of Zwingli's (and Luther's) opponent Johannes *Eck. Wonnecker was a Professor of Medicine and (in 1519 and 1522/3) Rector of the University of Basel (hence the reference to "*your* N. Egg"). See *CoE* III, 463. The "little note" must be the set of theses against Lutheran doctrines which Wonnecker—in spite of having no real background in theology—had issued on 25th December 1522, with a view to provoking a disputation.

5   On Glarean see p. 23, n. 97; this letter must be one of the last occasions on which (given his increasing hostility to the evangelical cause) Zwingli or Oecolampadius can have thought of him as "*our* Glarean".

6   In letter 264, dated 30th December 1522 (zw VII, 647f.), especially p. 648, lines 4–12.

7   In the original 'Antichrists'—a striking usage, though one which occurs also in 1 John 2:18 (ἀντίχριστοι πολλοί).

8   Johann *Faber, who was indeed to be Zwingli's chief opponent at the First Zürich Disputation just over a fortnight later (29th January 1523), and remained something of a *bête noire* for him. On this episode see Keith D. Lewis, "Johann Faber and the First Zürich Disputation: 1523. A Pre-Tridentine Catholic Response to Ulrich Zwingli and his Sixty-Seven Articles" (PhD diss., Catholic University of America, 1985).

269 Oecolampadius to Zwingli—Basel, 17th January (1523)

VIII, 5 Greetings in Christ! You do a right thing and one wholly worthy of your office and your pious spirit, my Ulrich, in being ready and willing to give an account of the faith[1] and of all that you have taught hitherto—that is, of course, to follow the apostolic law and to demonstrate in all things the purity of a Christian mind. I pray to our Lord Christ that whatever seems to me to have begun in a good spirit might not be completed in the flesh;[2] for in your wisdom you know that such a thing often comes to pass. And indeed I foresee good and extraordinary things happening that will benefit the Christian flock; only may that which is sacred be done sacredly, as they say.[3] I hear that someone with a great reputation is laughing disapprovingly.[4] But good luck to him, great though he is! Who knows from whence the Lord will wish to make the rays of his light shine first and more brightly? You seem to me to be doing what is right.

If what was first rumoured came to pass, I would not entirely support it—though I am indeed aware that my judgement is that of a nonentity. For the rumour was that you are going to preside over a disputation in Zürich.[5] You know how lengthily a matter can be hotly disputed and fought over in schools; but the more we fight with words, the more we are liable to damage the truth. For even if a desire to win does not precede a disputation, then it normally follows it; and this causes strife, which in turn leads to other, far worse evils. | How, in all this, do you preserve the truth and God's wis-

VIII, 6 dom, which loves a humble and tranquil heart that trembles at the words of the Lord—a heart that would choose the greatest disgrace, nay, the deepest abyss, rather than see the merest jot or tittle lost from the truth and glory of God? So I greatly approve of your desire to defend the purity of your doctrine in person and with gentleness before your adversaries (and if only everyone

---

12 *first ... brightly*] *magis et prius* (literally, 'more greatly and before')   21 *preserve*] here we translate *salvas*, rather than the almost certainly erroneous *salva* in the manuscript and Latin edition   24f. *than ... God*] *quam ut tantillum veritati gloriaeque divinae decedat* (literally, 'than that a merest trifle should depart from divine truth and glory'). Here and in line 39 f. we have been influenced by the KJV's celebrated version of Matthew 5:18, a verse which Oecolampadius clearly has in mind here

---

1 Cf. 1 Peter 3:15.
2 Cf. Galatians 3:3.
3 Cf. Revelation 22:11.
4 Presumably *Erasmus, well enough known to both Zwingli and Oecolampadius to be referred to in these allusive and somewhat sarcastic terms.
5 The First Zürich Disputation, 29th January 1523.

LETTER 269   63

had such a spirit!), but I would deprecate what has been planned if you were
to descend into discord—which, I do not doubt, is far from so gentle a mind
as yours. Moreover, my Ulrich, you should reflect on this warning from a good
30 friend, untimely and unnecessary though it is: I seem now to see people setting up battering-rams and preparing tunnels on behalf of your adversaries,
doubtless in the hope of making you forsake your modesty and mildness and
pay less attention to what the Spirit of the Lord might dictate. If they can
succeed in this, then—in order to keep their honour intact by using human
35 regulations and customs, indeed any means whatever—they will claim most
blasphemously that divine and evangelical laws are the cause of the disturbances.
    You have the prophetic word, you have the oracles of Christ—I know that
full well. And I know that you would rather lose your life than see a jot taken
40 away from these things. You will not assign any role to yourself; rather, in all
things the leading parts will be played by the holy scriptures, and hence by
God, who speaks through them. May they alone judge between you and your
adversaries! I do not know what judges there will be in the future: I hope they
will be good and pious men who value the truth above all, though the whole
45 world may rage. But again I suspect that the wiles of the ancient enemy will
see to it that perhaps some of them will have ill-educated minds that take
greater account of what is customary, and of how long the bad customs in
question have endured, than of whatever the Lord's good and holy will might
be. I pray that they might receive the spirit of wisdom and strength. May the
50 Lord Jesus be with you, defeat and scatter his adversaries through you, and
comfort and exalt those who are his own.

Take in good part this advice of a friend in Christ, as I am fully convinced
you will.
Farewell.
55 Basel, on St Anthony's Day.
Johannes Oecolampadius, yours from the heart.
To Ulrich Zwingli, most Christian priest of Zürich, his most highly esteemed
master.

*Original: Zürich, Staatsarchiv, E II 349, p. 144f. (scribal hand). Copy: Zürich,
Zentralbibliothek, Ms S 8, no. 8.*

271 Oecolampadius to Zwingli—Basel, 21st January 1523

VIII, 11 Greetings, my Huldrych. Whenever Wonnecker, led by the Spirit, finally bursts into our inner sancta,[1] I do not much approve of disputations in general (in that they feed ostentation and contention), but least of all of the one that is to be held in our city—unless it be regarded, as it deserves to be, as what they call a carnival joke. For what good man, a man who has a Christian mind and peace in his heart (as Christ himself so strongly recommended us to have),[2] would heedlessly enter an arena[3] from which he cannot bring back anything to his advantage, but only cartloads of mockery? What else can one expect from such a meeting? Blessed is the man that walks not in the counsel of the wicked.[4] Or is it not wickedness to wish to erect again such abominable statues of idols and of doctrines? To wish to bring a ravening wolf back into our midst, in sheep's clothing and under the guise of piety?[5] To wish to defend with such obstinate madness things that are so hostile to Christian purity? Indeed, the truth is that academies are the Devil's whorehouses, as he himself has said.[6]

You are wise to think that you should stay at home.[7] All the best men will guard themselves against those dregs of humanity—although I can imagine what will happen. They will declare themselves the winners, and hence the joke will give birth to something serious: they will sell themselves as victors *VIII, 12* to the foolish masses, who are always too fond of their evil practices. | In this manner the Devil wishes to root out with evil wiles that which has not yet been properly planted. He uses against us such people as Sanballat and Tobiah—who are indeed laughable, yet wicked.[8]

14f. *Indeed ... said*] Greek Μὰ τὴν ἀλήθειαν, ἀκαδημίαι εἰσὶ τοῦ διαβόλου πορνεῖα, ὡς αὐτὸς ἔφα

---

1 See 268, n. 4. Wonnecker's anti-Lutheran theses had made his ignorance all too plain, and were treated with scorn by Zwingli, Oecolampadius and others more at home with theological discourse. In consequence the disputation he had sought to stimulate never took place.
2 Cf. Mark 9:50.
3 See the similar metaphor in 258, lines 39–44.
4 Psalm 1:1. Our translation reflects the wording of the KJV, just as Oecolampadius follows the Vulgate (*Beatus vir qui non abiit in consilio impiorum*).
5 Matthew 7:15.
6 The University of Basel will doubtless have been uppermost in Oecolampadius's mind. "He himself" is presumably *Luther, who uses the phrase διαβόλου πορνεῖα of "the Pope's universities" in his *Weihnachtspostille* (WA X/1, 447–503, here 494)—an edition of which had recently been printed in Basel by Adam Petri.
7 See 268, lines 31–34.
8 "Sanballat the Horonite, and Tobiah the servant, the Ammonite" appear in chapters 2,

I truly cannot predict what will happen here; but I have high hopes of what is happening there:[9] so much can be achieved without contention. You know, brother, that Christ comes down like rain upon wool, with neither storm nor clamour.[10] I think your Council is acting very wisely in setting it in motion of their own accord, even though no-one is urging them to do so. Only let the matter be conducted without forensic or scholastic circumlocutions or contrivances, but in the vernacular and in short and clear words—and above all, without loud insults or other sources of strife.[11] Otherwise, how would any good come out of it? How would souls that are benighted in their affections be able to see the light? By what means might truth confide in its enemies? How could a chief priest allow such uninitiated and unholy people within the holy of holies? For I hear that certain disputatious people will be present, sent there not to hunt for the truth, but to return home as victors using whatever stratagems they choose to achieve this.[12] But you, dearest brother, attend to yourself and your flock. Do not be awed by those titles borne by our learned masters, vicars and prelates. They are shadows, and not the real thing. Where there are more titles, there is less substance. You have Christ as your judge: trust him in this best of causes, and consider it sufficient to please only him. Keep an upright mind, and keep your modesty. For the rest the Lord, who knows what is expedient, will govern the whole affair. You see how intimately I treat you, carrying sand to the shore[13] and nowhere paying proper attention to my own affairs; but please show me friendliness in return. Not that, in Christ, my playing the fool can displease you.[14]

27f. *setting ... accord*] Greek οἴκοθεν κινούμενον (literally, 'set in motion from home/at their own expense')   34f. *such ... people*] τοὺς ἀμυήτους καὶ ἀνοσίους ἐκείνους   39f. *and ... thing*] Greek καὶ ἀσώματοι σκιαί (literally, 'and disembodied shadows')

---

      4 and 6 of Nehemiah. They are angered by the latter's project of rebuilding the walls of Jerusalem, and mock and plot against him.
9   A reference to the First Zürich Disputation, scheduled for 29th January.
10   A combination of Psalm 72:6 ("He shall come down like rain upon the mown grass") and Isaiah 42:2 ("He shall not cry, nor lift up, nor cause his voice to be heard in the street"). Oecolampadius's reference to wool is taken directly from the Vulgate (*Descendet sicut pluvia in vellus*, Psalm 71:6).
11   A free but not entirely misleading digest of the Zürich Council's invitation to the disputation, issued on 3rd January (see ZW 1, 466–468; no. 17/II). This at least states that the proceedings will take place in German, and that the Council are acting in the interests of "God's honour, peace and unity" (*umb gottes eer, fryden unnd einickeitt willen*, 467).
12   Oecolampadius is thinking of *Faber.
13   One is tempted to translate "carrying coals to Newcastle".
14   Presumably a reminiscence of 1Corinthians 1:18f. and, not least, *Erasmus's potent thematization of the "folly of the cross" in his *Moriae Encomium/Praise of Folly*.

I hope that Master Konrad the Commander[15] is well.
Farewell.
Basel, on St Agnes' Day in the year 1523.
Your Johannes Oecolampadius.
To Zwingli, his dearest brother.

Original: Zürich, Staatsarchiv, E II 349, p. 28 (autograph). Copy: Zürich, Zentralbibliothek, Ms S 8, no. 17.

---

15   Konrad Schmid (or 'Cunradus Faber', 1476–1531), a noted preacher and the last Commander of the Küsnacht Commandery of the Order of Knights Hospitaller on Lake Zürich. He was a friend of Oecolampadius from student days, and later a strong supporter of Zwingli, alongside whom he fell at the Battle of Kappel. On him see Alfred Egli, "Komtur Konrad Schmid, ein Wegbereiter der Reformation", *Küsnachter Jahresblätter* 1981: 30–48; Locher, ZR, 576–580.

280 Oecolampadius to Zwingli—Basel, 16th February (1523)

Greetings in Christ. The brothers have told me, dearest Zwingli, the entire story of your disputation, and again I have found it to be a matter for congratulation. It turned out as I was hoping it would—and never was any hope of mine more certain. I knew that Christ would not abandon his cause: he is near to all who call upon him in truth.[1] For the rest, I do not think that my failure to appear needs any excuse other than that your letter was not delivered in sufficient time;[2] so I am making no complaint at all about work or the rigours of winter. But even if I had been present—your adversaries, I hear, showed themselves to be so toothless that you were robbed of the chance to show your strength and power. But what is not ineffectual and feeble when it sets itself against the truth—the truth, on which, having once undertaken to defend it, you can entirely rely, since it in turn will defend you—though all the gates of hell rage against you?[3]

I desire very much to converse with you; hence I am minded to visit you as soon as I have the leisure, so that you might know my mind rather more fully than can be expressed in a letter. Meanwhile, farewell, along with your whole church and the leaders of your church, to whose love and prayers I wish to be commended.

Farewell again.
On the Day of St Juliana the Martyr. Your Johannes Oecolampadius.
To Huldrych Zwingli, most vigilant pastor of the church in Zürich, his most beloved brother in Christ.

Original: Zürich, Staatsarchiv, E II 349, p. 126 (autograph). Copy: Zürich, Zentralbibliothek, Ms S 8, no. 52.

---

22 *Christ*] Greek Χριστῷ

---

1 Psalm 145:18. Oecolampadius again quotes practically *verbatim* from the Vulgate (*Prope est Dominus omnibus invocantibus eum ... in veritate*; Psalm 144:18).
2 Zwingli must have sent or forwarded to Oecolampadius a specific invitation to the First Zürich Disputation which is now lost.
3 Cf. Matthew 16:18.

286   Oecolampadius to Zwingli—Basel, 3rd March (1523)

Greetings in Christ. Kaspar Hedio,[1] my dearest brother, indeed our brother, gave me a letter some four days ago, to which your one was also attached.[2] I have kept it with me. I was intending to visit you this week; but again my journey has been prevented. For I am again suffering enormously from the constraints of the old irksome drudgery, as if even the tinest action on my part were of such importance as to profit my brothers in Christ. So although what I want cannot happen, I must be content, as necessity itself teaches. There is still hope of my staying here for some months;[3] perhaps at some point I shall snatch enough time to be able to enjoy your company. I also know that you do not now have much free time, both because of your daily sermons and because you are responding to your antagonists.

I should like to see your disputation records, if they are ready.[4] And you will read my trifles[5] very soon. You will see, I think, that our spirits do not disagree much—| if indeed they disagree at all and are not actually one and the same spirit. And if anything has been revealed to you more fully than to me, it will please me very greatly if you teach it to me.

I hope that Master Konrad the Commander[6] is well in Christ, and that you and all of yours are also faring well, as ever.

---

5 *as if*] *nisi*, normally 'unless'

---

1 Hedio (c. 1494–1552), a humanist historian, translator and educationalist, studied and worked in Basel, and for most of his career was particularly close to Wolfgang *Capito. He followed the latter to Mainz in 1521, and thence to Strasbourg in 1523. On him see *CoE* II, 169 f.; *OER* II, 215 f.; *BBKL* II, 635 f.; *VL 16* III, 203–211.
2 Neither of these letters has survived.
3 For much of 1523 it seemed likely that, because of the powerful and multi-faceted opposition he faced, Oecolampadius would before long be forced to leave Basel. See also 319, n. 2 f.
4 These *acta* were published as Erhard Hegenwald, *Handlung der versamlung in der loeblichen statt Zürich vff den xxix tag Jenners vonn wegen des heyligen Euangelij* (Zürich: Froschauer, 1523). Whilst not written by Zwingli, they present a perspective very similar to his own.
5 It is not clear what work or works this refers to: Staehelin (nos 74–90) lists some seventeen publications by Oecolampadius for 1523 alone.
6 See 271, n. 15.

Dated at Basel, 3rd March.
Your Johannes Oecolampadius.
To Master Ulrich Zwingli, the most vigilant teacher of the Zürichers, his brother in Christ.

Original: Zürich, Staatsarchiv, E II 349, p. 143 (autograph). Copy: Zürich, Zentralbibliothek, Ms S 8, no. 65.

298 Zwingli to Oecolampadius—Zürich, 19th April 1523

VIII, 67 Greetings! I admit, most pious Johannes, that I really should write to you more often, so that I might inspire you to write more often and thereby raise our spirits, even when we are in such difficulties. But affairs do not permit us to do what we want and desire. They say that the Vicar-General of Konstanz, Johann the Workman,[1] nay rather the False Workman,[2] has been inveighing most bitterly against us, in a piece that is even now being printed in Strasbourg;[3] and that Zasius, goaded on by *Faber's spurs, is also in the process of conceiving some late-born offspring or other.[4]

But if war is to be waged I would not (by Hercules!) wish for any other opponents. One of them is such a patchwork of obvious wiles that even a half-blind person can see the joins, and the other has no more to offer than Darius's army, which, costly and beautiful though it was, distinguished itself only by falling prey to Alexander's army as soon as the latter set eyes on it[5]—an army which was certainly of no account with regard to ornaments or feminine decorations. I wish that they would come forward and take up arms openly, challenge us, and see how well Christ defends us. Nevertheless I hear that we are being overwhelmed by the Workman's[6] calumnies and slanders—definitely the last resort for people like him. But we do not fear these things, knowing full well as we do how blamelessly we have always led our lives. I do not mind those Herostratuses[7] telling cartloads of lies

---

3 *difficulties*] Greek ἀπορία   11 *the joins*] Greek τὴν ῥαφὴν (literally, 'the seam')

---

1 *Faber. This is a pun on his name: the Greek term Τέκτονα (accusative of Τέκτων) is used here to mean 'workman'; *faber* is Latin for 'workman'.
2 Greek Ψευδοτέκτονα (see n. 1).
3 *Ein warlich underrichtung wie es zu Zürch by dem Zwinglin uff den nünundzwentzigsten tag des monats Januarii nest verschinen ergangen sey* (Strasbourg: Grüninger, 1523).
4 No such work seems to have been published. Ulrich Zasius (1461–1535) was a distinguished humanist lawyer who was an early enthusiast for *Luther but later became a vituperative opponent of the evangelicals, and not least of Oecolampadius. See Steven Rowan, *Ulrich Zasius: A Jurist in the German Renaissance, 1461–1535* (Frankfurt: Klostermann, 1987); *CoE* III, 469–473; *BBKL* XIV, 357–359; *VL DH* II, 1421–1446.
5 Darius III of Persia fought two losing battles against Alexander the Great, at Issus in 333 BCE and Gaugamela in 331 BCE. Either could be meant here.
6 Faber—again referred to in a Greek pun, as ἀπὸ Τέκτονος.
7 Herostratus was an Ephesian who set fire to the Temple of Artemis at Ephesus on the night that Alexander the Great was born. The Ephesians decreed that his name should never be recorded, though in fact it is in the accounts of Strabo (14.1.22) and Solinus (*Polyhistor*, 40.3). The points of comparison between him and the likes of Faber are presumably his destructiveness and the fact that he is never to be referred to by his real name.

LETTER 298 71

about me, and even blaming on me the scandalous behaviour of others: | *VIII, 68*
Zwingli has never done anything of which, if called to account, he could not
be absolved by even the most unfavourably disposed judge. Thank God that
things have reached a point where they are pleading their case fraudulently,
25 even using botched-up slanders.

Otherwise there is no news you need to know. I commend myself to Christ
and to you. May God preserve you. Greet *Cratander, Nepos,[8] and all who
love Christ.
From Zurich, 19th April 1523.
30 Your Huldrych Zwingli.
To Johannes Oecolampadius, most pious and learned man, beloved
brother in Christ. To Basel.

Original lost; copy in Zürich, Zentralbibliothek, Ms S 8, no. 97.

---

32 *To*] German *Gen* (short form of *gegen*)

8 Jakob Näf (or 'Nepos') worked as an assistant to *Erasmus and moved with him to Basel
   in 1518. He was later active as an editor and corrector for the presses of both Froben (see
   384, n. 8) and Cratander, and taught Greek at the university and at a school he himself had
   founded. He was dead by 1527. See Blair, "Erasmus", *passim*; *CoE* III, 11f.

301   Oecolampadius to Zwingli—Basel, 27th April (1523)

VIII, 74 Greetings. May you be blessed in Christ, my Zwingli, you who visit retribution upon the arrogant and wretched daughter of Babylon, who cries out daily to her own, "tear it down, tear it down, all the way to its foundations".[1] That foolish one does not believe that the Lord has strengthened the gates of Zion,[2] and that the machines of every council of war are useless against the Lord. Blessed are you, who with pious zeal dash her little ones against the rock![3] Victory is certain, every time one takes up arms and wages war against the uncircumcised and aliens under the guidance and leadership of Christ. May God, the blessed one, himself train your hands for war and your fingers for battle![4]

Moreover we too have recently been putting our hands rather more diligently to the plough;[5] and, as soon as | the door was opened, we found many
VIII, 75 adversaries.[6] But nothing could be more foolish than they are, as I believe you have learnt from others. God is turning our work to good account, and is showing us in various ways how to attack them fearlessly and never to look back. There is good hope that the light of day will shine forth in an extraordinary way until all are destroyed who blaspheme against the Holy One of Israel.[7] Meanwhile, since we are placed in this position, far be it from us to be fearful for ourselves; and may we not only laugh at the threats, curses,

---

19 *not only laugh*] *non solum non rideamus* (literally, 'not only not laugh'); we are interpreting the second *non* as redundant

---

1   Cf. Psalm 137:7 f.
2   Cf. Psalm 147:12 f.
3   Psalm 137:9. Unlike in the previous two Psalm references, Oecolampadius is here clearly using the Vulgate: *et allidet parvulos tuos ad petram*.
4   Cf. II Samuel 22:35.
5   Oecolampadius may have in mind here the controversies surrounding Wonnecker's proposed disputation (see 271); but he is doubtless referring above all to the marked progress the cause of reform had made in Basel in April 1523. In Holy Week he had begun a series of highly influential public lectures on the Book of Isaiah; moreover, on 11th April the Council had thwarted a plot to remove reform-minded Franciscans (including Konrad *Pellikan) from their house in Basel, preferring instead to suspend four leading conservative figures (including Wonnecker) and to appoint Oecolampadius and Pellikan to professorships. For the relevant documents see *AGBR* I, 61–63 (no. 144).
6   I Corinthians 16:9.
7   Cf. Isaiah 1:4. Oecolampadius has taken the words *blasphemaverunt Sanctum Israel* from the Vulgate.

LETTER 301   73

20 reproaches, calumnies and whatever else of this kind they bring against us,
    but even receive them as blessings—strengthened by him who said we are
    blessed when they say all manner of evil against us falsely, for Christ's sake.[8]
    The sons of the Pharisees grieve to surrender any of their pride, not under-
    standing that the name of the King of Glory is to be praised; for they want the
25 name of mighty Israel to be defiled among the nations—or, certainly, they
    would not mind if it were. So it is right to be daring and to resist with tireless
    effort those enemies who are not sleeping. We see that the harvest is plen-
    teous and the labourers are few;[9] for those many lazy gluttons, who claim
    to be building but actually are destroying, and sowing weeds to ensure that
30 nothing is produced—they too are workers of iniquity.[10] Pray to the Lord
    that he might not cast us off from his children, and might even grant us a part
    of his ministry,[11] however lowly, in his household. For I am consumed with
    rage when I see the people being carried off in a different direction. You have
    long since discovered how contemptible *Faber's strength is.[12] Nor will they
35 be frightened by the derring-do of a pitiful old man as he seeks to plaster over
    the crumbling wall of his lunacies;[13] indeed, no-one need fear this. Either I
    am deceived, or fear and trepidation are reigning in all their strongholds. I
    wish you would visit us more often with your letters, seeing that we cannot
    meet face-to-face. But when there is so much business, we should be satis-
40 fied with what necessity allows. May the Lord give you increase, and may he
    bless you and your church for ever.

29f. *ensure ... produced*] the Latin again contains a double negative—*ne non operentur*
34f. *will ... frightened*] *terrebunt*—it is clear that a third person plural is intended, but not
wholly clear to whom it is referring (the people of Basel?)

---

8   Matthew 5:11. Our wording closely resembles that of the KJV, as Oecolampadius's does
    that of the Vulgate: *et dixerint omne malum adversum vos mentientes, propter me.*
9   Matthew 9:37. We stick as closely to the KJV as Oecolampadius does to the Vulgate:
    Messis quidem multa, operarii autem pauci.
10 Oecolampadius has probably taken the phrase *operarii iniquitatis* from the Vulgate's
    translation of Luke 13:27 (KJV reads "workers of iniquity").
11 This phrase is taken from Acts 1:17: Oecolampadius and the Vulgate have *sortem min-
    sterii*, KJV "part of this ministry".
12 A reference especially to Zwingli's trouncing of *Faber at the First Zürich Disputation.
13 Zasius (see 298, n. 4). See Zwingli's implicit jibe about his age in 298, line 7 f. also; at
    this point Zasius will have been 61 or 62 years old.

Nepos[14] and *Cratander greet you.
Basel. 27th April.
Your Johannes Oecolampadius.
To Huldrych Zwingli, presbyter at Zürich, most diligent of all in the ministry of the gospel, his brother.

Original: Zürich, Staatsarchiv, E II 349, p. 115 (scribal hand). Copy: Zürich, Zentralbibliothek, Ms S 8, no. 100.

---

14   Jakob Näf: see 298, n. 8.

306 Oecolampadius to Zwingli—Basel, 16th June 1523

Greetings, my brother. I too can, indeed must, plead that the great diversity of affairs hinders my writing to you—just as it delays you (as you say) from motivating me as often as you would wish to write to you on suitable occasions.[1] In truth, because these affairs are actually Christ's and not ours, we both deserve to be absolved, especially if we have no subject for discussion that would justify our taking even a short time away from the business of God. Your letters do indeed delight me enormously, as do those of all Christians; but I would not venture to demand them from anyone, unless it be also for the sake of others. I do not wish, however, to be entirely bereft of this form of comfort if it can conveniently be given; and I persuade myself that, humane as you are, you will not be deficient in performing this duty. I too would certainly not like to be accused of neglecting Christian charity in this matter, when opportunity permits.

With regard to what you write about the Vicar,[2] I do not know the book against you that he is having printed—I am not aware of anything to do with the matter. But I desire very keenly to see and read your own lucubrations;[3] for from the first beginnings of these problems I can guess what the outcome will be. No danger can threaten you from those miserable workmen and their hired works—you whose prime study it is to defend the truth. So you are acting prudently and rightly: with great courage you are standing as it were with Hezekiah in the holy city, not | fearing the most blasphemous Rabshakeh—armed as you are with faith in the Lord.[4] My detractors tear me

---

17f. *for ... be*] *nam ex problematum unguiculis, quale corpus futurum, coniecto* (literally, 'for from the tiny nails of these problems I infer that something like a body will grow') 18 *workmen*] *tectonibus*—an allusion to Zwingli's plays on Faber's name in 298

---

1 Plainly a response to the first two sentences of 298.
2 *Faber and his *Warlich underrichtung* (see 298, n. 3).
3 Zwingli's extensive commentary on his Sixty-Seven Articles, the *Ußlegen und gruond der schlußreden oder articklen* (Zürich: Froschauer, 14th July 1523)—ed. zw II, 14–457 (no. 20); trans. Pipkin/Furcha, I, 1–373.
4 A plural here (*blasphemabundos Rabsaces*), though a singular (*Rabsacen*) in the Vulgate and other Bibles (II Kings 18:17). Perhaps Oecolampadius, ever conscious of the corporate dimension of religion, envisages this figure as embodying the Assyrians as a whole. The term means 'chief priest'; and in II Kings 18:19–35 the person thus described mocks and denounces God, King Hezekiah and the people of Judah on behalf of the Assyrian king Sennacherib. Hezekiah draws his courage from the prophecy given to him by Isaiah in II Kings 19:1–7 and Isaiah 37:1–7.

to pieces also, and defame me with extraordinary lies, or else appoint some poor unfortunate to win the people's favour—they do this when they cannot attack me any more. We on the other hand should pray for them and commend them to Christ, so that in time he might lay aside his anger and have mercy upon them. For these are the prayers—and I speak as one taught by God—which he loves the most.[5]

I ask that you take care to return this packet[6] to that most excellent knight Ulrich von Hutten.[7] Let me commend *Bucer's cause to you,[8] knowing that you are most benevolent. If you can help the man, I beg you to do so. I am maimed and cannot stretch out my hand;[9] otherwise I would not shirk from doing anything on his behalf. With his character, learning, ardour, faithfulness and in many other ways, he can be of great benefit to the gospel.

27f. *taught by God*] Greek τῷ θεοδιδάκτῳ   31 *most benevolent*] Greek φιλανθρωπότατον

---

5   Cf. 1 Thessalonians 4:9.
6   Containing letters, presumably.
7   The celebrated humanist (1488–1523), who had fled to Zürich from Mulhouse in late May or early June 1523, and was helped by Zwingli not least to find accommodation—first at the spa in Pfäfers and then on the island of Ufenau in Lake Zürich, where he died on 29th August of that year. On Hutten's activities in Zürich see Ulrich Bächtold, "Ulrich von Hutten und Zwingli", *Zwingliana* 18/1–2 (1989): 12–19; Hans Gustav Keller, *Hutten und Zwingli* (Aarau: Sauerländer, 1952). More generally see Hajo Holborn, *Ulrich von Hutten and the German Reformation* (New Haven, CT: Yale University Press, 1937); *CoE* II, 267–270; *OER* II, 281f.; *TRE* XV, 747–752; *BBKL* II, 1222–1226; *VL DH* I, 1185–1237; Füssel, *DD*, 359–376; Bernstein, *GH*, 116–128.
8   Oecolampadius had got to know Bucer at Ebernburg in 1522. The latter had arrived at Strasbourg (to seek the city's protection) in late April 1523, and had commended himself to Zwingli in a letter dated exactly a week before this one (*zw* VII, 80–83; no. 304).
9   One assumes that, for all his physical frailties, Oecolampadius is here again alluding to his lack of time, and hence opportunity.

Farewell, my Zwingli, and become a great nation in Christ![10]
I wish to greet Ceporinus[11] and *Leo Jud, and your whole church, who belong to Christ.
Basel, 16th June 1523.

40 To Ulrich Zwingli, most faithful teacher of the people of Zürich, his dearest brother in Christ.

Original: Zürich, Staatsarchiv, E II 349, p. 14 (scribal hand). Copy: Zürich, Zentralbibliothek, Ms S 8, no. 117.

---

10 Cf. Genesis 12:2.
11 The short-lived Jacobus Ceporinus (or 'Wiesendanger', 1500–1525), a protégé of Zwingli, who appointed him to teach Greek and Hebrew at the *Grossmünster* school in 1522. Ceporinus will have been known to the Baslers not least from a period working as a corrector for *Cratander in 1521–1522. See Christoph Riedweg, "Ein Philologe an Zwinglis Seite. Zum 500. Geburtstag von Jacob Wiesendanger, gen. Ceporinus", *Museum Helveticum* 57 (2000): 201–219.

307 Oecolampadius to Zwingli—Basel, 8th July (1523)

Ambrosius Syragrius[1] has shown me a certain note on which he had put together parts of the work that has now been printed in your city,[2] concerning the intercession of the saints. I could not understand everything on the basis of these fragments, but they seemed to show that the saints do not intercede—as if intercession would take something away from their blessedness, and their peace would be undone by work, when it ought to be free from all activity.[3] In truth I do not see that this is adequately supported from scripture. Deal with them,[4] employing your more nuanced wisdom, either sparing them (so as not to turn them into angry wild boars), or giving them such abundant proof that, humbled, they might prostrate themselves and fall utterly silent. I ask you to consider the matter well, as sincerity requires.

You should wish Master Hutten[5] well from me, and tell him that in the meantime I have not received any letters.

Farewell.
Basel, on St Kilian's Day.
Your Johannes Oecolampadius.
To the learned and pious Ulrich Zwingli, pastor of the Zürich people, his beloved brother in Christ.

Original: Zürich, Staatsarchiv, E II 349, p. 154 (autograph). Copy: Zürich, Zentralbibliothek, Ms S 8, no. 134.

---

1 Or 'Kettenacker' (d. 1541). He spent nearly all of his career in Basel, not least as parish priest of Riehen, just outside the city, from 1518. He was in regular and supportive contact with both Oecolampadius and Zwingli. See *CoE* II, 257 f.
2 Zwingli's *Ußlegen und gruond* (see 306, n. 3).
3 This reads like a defensible if not quite accurate extrapolation from Article XIX of Zwingli's *Ußlegen und gruond* (zw II, 157–166), in which he argues on the basis of John 14:6 ("no man cometh unto the Father, but by me") that there is no biblical justification for the role of saints as intercessors. No response from Zwingli has been preserved; but his utterances on the saints were not wholly clear or consistent: see Pamela Biel "Personal Conviction and Pastoral Care: Zwingli and the Cult of Saints", *Zwingliana* 16/5 (1985): 442–469.
4 It is not clear which precise opponents Oecolampadius has in mind here.
5 See 306, n. 7.

319 Zwingli to Oecolampadius—Zürich, 11th October 1523

Grace and peace from God and our Lord Jesus Christ. Now at last, dearest Oecolampadius, I am getting ahead of you in our exchange of letters. In doing so I want only to state how very pleasing the good aroma of Christ is which you are spreading around the people of Basel,[1] and that they are growing more and more in every good work—so much so that a certain ranting advocate recently blabbed to us here that you would not be able to remain in Basel for long.[2] We, however, are learning daily that the contrary is true, so we no longer fear it. *Erasmus has already written to me twice about you, speaking highly of you both times. One of the letters says: "Oecolampadius triumphs among us".[3] So beyond doubt there was no truth in what the man I mentioned said about it here (albeit not in my presence)—namely that it is his task to ensure that you are driven out of Basel. But do not let these things disturb you, since they are now over and done with, and it is clear that the rumours were concocted vainly, indeed mendaciously.

Ceporinus will spend the winter with you,[4] and I commend him to you. Your Suffragan Bishop[5] is said to have recovered his senses splendidly, thanks

---

16f. *thanks ... God*] Greek τῷ θεῷ χάρις

---

1 Zwingli here repays Oecolampadius's compliment to him in 258 (see lines 9–12 and n. 1f.).
2 It is not known to whom precisely Zwingli is referring here; but in the second half of 1523 Oecolampadius's position in Basel was decidedly precarious. This was due mainly to his publication of four evangelically oriented theses and organization of a disputation to discuss these on 30th August—which the Council initially sought to forbid, and in which all members of the university were banned from participating. A seemingly widespread assumption that Oecolampadius could not stay in Basel (or, indeed, had already left) was articulated by the Konstanz Canon Johann von Botzheim in a letter to Erasmus dated 3rd December 1523: "I am surprised to hear that Oecolampadius is leaving Basel, for he has, I understand, a good reputation there. And whither will that worthy man betake himself in such a hurry?"—*EC* X, 127f. (no. 1401), lines 25–27.
3 No surviving letter contains these precise words. In what seems to be his last letter to Zwingli, however, dated 31st August 1523, Erasmus states that "Oecolampadius held a disputation yesterday—and it was a success"—*ZW* VIII, 114–118 (no. 315), here 117, line 25 f.; *EC* X, 80–85 (no. 1384), here line 91.
4 See 306, n. 11. Ceporinus spent the winter of 1523–1524 working in Basel with *Cratander and/or Johannes Bebel.
5 Tillman Limperger (or 'Telamonius Limpurger', 1455–after 1539), a much-travelled and well-read Austin Hermit who had been Suffragan Bishop of Basel since 1498, and who was also Cathedral Preacher there in both 1523 and 1525. An initially hesitant but later dedicated adherent of Oecolampadius's ideas, he courted controversy by attending the latter's lectures on Isaiah (see 301, n. 5); and his evangelical beliefs led to his being suspended from his ecclesiastical functions in 1525. On him see *CoE* II, 330 f.

be to God. This will further the business of Christ, for he is by no means a bad man, and has always been eager to serve Christ's flock. If you have time, please greet him on my behalf and give him the commentaries of Caesar that belong to the Prior of Mulhouse,[6] so that he might send them on to him when he can. The Prior himself had lent them to Hutter,[7] and we are now asking for them back, along with our books. If I have not already thanked you for your gift, I do so now: it will delight people also in centuries to come, and will be a fitting testimony to your work and faith.[8] Keep yourself as well as you can. On occasion take some time away from your labours, which they say exhaust you beyond measure.

Farewell, and may Christ keep you well and—I pray—make us worthy ministers of his gospel and free us from this impure world, which we cannot abide, any more than it can abide us.
From Zürich, 11th October 1523.
Your Huldrych Zwingli.
To Johannes Oecolampadius, disciple of Christ, our most beloved brother.

Original: Zofingen, Stadtbibliothek, Pa 14:1, 17-1 (21). Two copies in Zürich, Zentralbibliothek, Ms S 9, no. 42f.

---

6 Nikolaus Prug(e)ner (1488–1557), who presumably owned a copy of Caesar's *Gallic Wars*, was a friend of both Zwingli and Oecolampadius from their earlier days in Basel, and Prior of the Austin Hermits' house at Mulhouse from 1519 until late 1523—when he was dismissed for seeking to implement evangelical reforms.
7 Ulrich von Hutten (see 306, n. 7) was given refuge—and, it seems, books—by Prugner in Mulhouse between January and May/June 1523.
8 Obviously a literary gift: the likeliest candidate is Oecolampadius's Latin translation of Chrysostom's sermons on Genesis, *Divi Ioannis Chrysostomi, Archiepiscopi Constantinopolitani, in totum Genesōs librum Homiliæ sexagintasex* (Basel: Cratander, September 1523; Staehelin 75, Leu/Weidmann A105).

329   Oecolampadius and Bonifatius Wolfhart[1] to Zwingli—early March 1524

To Huldrych Zwingli, preacher at Zürich, Oecolampadius and Bonifatius wish grace and peace in Christ.

See, we are sending you a copy of the theses defended among us in Latin by that Frenchman[2] and interpreted in the vernacular by Oecolampadius before a large assembly of Christians. Nowhere have sophists been summoned to appear more often![3] | Meanwhile they are playing the roles of lofty Thrasos who shun the light in dark corners.[4] The people, however, are gradually getting wise to their idleness and tyranny with the help of the word of God. May God give the increase.[5] Now, the courier, who was present and heard everything, will soon relate to you most faithfully what was said at that disputation. Soon we will also deliver to you the recently printed record of the disputation about marriage.[6]

---

1 *preacher*] *ecclesiato*. If this is derived from *ecclesiastes* (as we take it to be), the correct dative form would be *ecclesiastae*; if from *ecclesiasticus* ('belonging to the Church'), the form would be *ecclesiastico* | *preacher*] *ecclesiasti* (see note on line 1 above)

---

1   Wolfhart (c. 1490–1543) was in Basel from 1517, as People's Priest at St Martin's Church and a lecturer at the university. An early supporter of reform, he was banned from the city in July 1524. He was later in Strasbourg and, from 1531, Augsburg. See BBKL XXIX, 1575.
2   *Gulielmus Farellus christianis lectoribus* (Basel: Cratander, 1524; Leu/Weidmann 86). "That Frenchman" is Guillaume Farel (1489–1565), an influential evangelical and later first-generation reformer of Neuchâtel and Geneva. He had arrived in Basel in the autumn of 1523, and for a while worked closely with Oecolampadius, not least on composing these thirteen theses for the disputation which took place on 3rd March 1524. As this letter suggests, however, Farel soon aroused enmity in Basel, including that of *Erasmus; and he was forced to leave in July 1525. On this episode see AGBR I, 95–107 (no. 194 f.). More generally see Borel-Girard, *Farel*; Jason Zuidema and Theodore van Raalte, *Early French Reform: The Theology and Spirituality of Guillaume Farel* (Farnham: Ashgate, 2011); CoE II, 11–13; OER II, 99 f.; TRE XI, 30–36; BBKL I, 1597 f.; Locher, ZR, 413–418.
3   This rather obscure formulation no doubt reflects the concerted efforts of the Basel Council to ensure that Farel's disputation not only took place but was well attended, especially by the "sophists" of the city's university. The Council had arranged for the disputation to take place on 23rd February; thereupon the university and its conservative supporters sought to have it banned; and on 27th February the Council issued an edict actively requiring all members of the university to be present at it, on pain of punishment.
4   Thraso is a vain and boastful soldier in Terence's *Eunuchus* (161 BCE). Whilst no clear parallel is drawn between him and contemporary figures, one wonders whether the "Thrasos" here might be Erasmus and his close circle, with whom Farel had irreparably fallen out.
5   Cf. 1 Corinthians 3:6.
6   More precisely, clerical marriage: Stephan Stör (d. 1529), the evangelically minded parish priest of Liestal, had married his long-time housekeeper and organized a disputation to

We wrote these things in the morning, whilst Oecolampadius was preaching, at the urging of a certain citizen and messenger from Zürich—at that time there was no leisure to write more.

Farewell in the Lord.
To the pious and also Christian Huldrych Zwingli, preacher at Zürich, his elder in Christ.

Original: Zürich, Staatsarchiv, E I 1.74, no. 20 (Wolfhart's hand, appended to a printed copy of Farel's theses—see n. 2 above).

---

debate the validity of enforced celibacy. This took place in Basel on 16th February 1524, with the support of Oecolampadius and Wolfhart. The proceedings appeared on 26th February: *Von der Priester Ee disputation, durch Stephanum Stör vnd andern vyl Christlichen brüdern* (Basel: Cratander, 1524).

347 Zwingli to Oecolampadius—Zürich, 9th October 1524

Grace and peace from the Lord. There is a rumour that the Duke of Württemberg[1] has joined you in espousing the gospel. At one time I had a great horror of that man; if, though, it is true that a Paul has been created out of a Saul, I cannot embrace the man in any other way than his brothers did Paul, after he had come to his senses.[2] Let me know how you feel about this matter, because, if he is a person of faith, we shall be able to discuss with him things that may be of the greatest benefit to the Christian cause. But mainly I want to know where he now is—now that you have taught him about the faith—and to know how I might safely get letters to him if he is, for example, in Montbéliard.[3] For if he is at the citadel of Hohentwiel,[4] which is my Mars, I can, if you wish, send letters to him myself, without involving you.

With regard to the provocative work by Balthasar[5] that has recently been sent to you, show me a print of it or | send me a manuscript copy—either way through our bookseller-courier.[6] Pressure of work prevents me writing more. The bookseller will tell you everything else.

---

2 *in ... gospel*] *in usum evangelii* (literally 'in the use/practice of the gospel')

---

1 *Ulrich, Duke of Württemberg. Zwingli's aversion to him may have sprung partly from the fact that he was a sworn enemy of Ulrich von Hutten, having killed the latter's kinsman Hans von Hutten in a dispute in 1515.
2 See Acts 8:1–3, 9:1–31.
3 The County of Montbéliard (part of Franche-Comté) was the only territory Ulrich possessed following his removal as Duke of Württemberg, and hence his main base.
4 A castle near Singen (and Lake Konstanz) which Ulrich von Württemberg purchased in 1521 and made into a powerful military fortress, in part with French aid.
5 The anabaptist Balthasar Hubmaier (1485–1528), who was in Basel during the winter of 1524–1525. The "provocative work" (*provocatio*) is probably the *Axiomata*, a set of 120 theses against his erstwhile patron Johannes *Eck. It is edited in Hubmaier, *Schriften*, 87–94. See also Torsten Bergsten, *Balthasar Hubmaier. Seine Stellung zu Reformation und Täufertum* (Kassel: Oncken, 1961); *CoE* II, 210 f.; *OER* II, 260–263; *TRE* XV, 611–613; *BBKL* II, 1109–1114.
6 *Froschauer.

Greet Anémond,[7] Farel[8] and Bonifatius[9] when the occasion arises.
Farewell. From Zurich, 9th October 1524.
Your Huldrych Zwingli.
To Johannes Oecolampadius, our dearest brother in the Lord.

Original: Erlangen (Universitätsbibliothek), H62/Trewbr Zwingli_Huldrich[1 (accessible online). Copy: Zürich, Zentralbibliothek, Ms S 11, *no. 80.*

---

7 Anémond de Coct (d. 1525), a French knight from the Dauphiné known to Luther from his time as a student in Wittenberg, whence he travelled to Basel in September 1523. He seems to have been based there for around a year, during which he made the acquaintance of Zwingli in Zürich—quite likely in the company of his fellow Dauphinois Guillaume Farel.
8 See 329, n. 2. In theory at least, Farel had to leave Basel in July 1524, so it comes as something of a surprise to find Zwingli sending greetings to him there some three months later. They had, however, begun a lasting friendship when Farel visited Zürich in late May 1524: see Rudolf Pfister, "Die Freundschaft zwischen Guillaume Farel und Huldrych Zwingli", *Zwingliana* 8/7 (1947): 372–389.
9 Bonifatius Wolfhart (see 329, n. 1).

352 Oecolampadius to Zwingli—Basel, 21st November (1524)

Grace and peace from God. The brothers have sent this small bundle of letters from Strasbourg.[1] To me it seems hardly possible for all churches to agree about the same ceremonies, except churches which are in the same area; for the varied opinions of weak people will not allow it. Indeed I think it is precisely through the work of the Holy Spirit (as distinct from through its absence) that people differ in such matters; for if churches had retained the same ceremonies at all times up to this day, how could we claim that Christian liberty has been preserved—a liberty which, by the way, false apostles are now rather tyrannically attacking? We, who are inactive beyond measure here, still showing no sign of abolishing abuses—we are not fit to settle this matter (though I have expressed my views in writing about certain things).

*Karlstadt, in his little books,[2] | would not have offended me if he had been merciful towards the brothers. In them, as far as I can understand, there is nothing about the Eucharist that differs from our opinion, which I expressed during our most pleasant meeting.[3] But I do not fully approve of the fact that he is rather peevish in his refusal to tolerate certain ceremonies. I have not yet read his little book on the baptism of infants, and do not think it has been printed; but, as far as I understand it from others, he certainly thinks the rite should be abolished.[4] However, I cannot yet confirm this. So far I have always followed Augustine's opinion that, when the sacrament is given to infants, it is validated by the faith of others, so that there is no imputation of original sin.[5] With regard to this matter, there is something about

---

9 *rather tyrannically*] Greek τυραννικωτέρως

---

1 By this time Zwingli and Oecolampadius were corresponding regularly with both *Bucer and *Capito.
2 These "little books" really were hot off the press: seven of them had been brought to Basel in manuscript form by Karlstadt's brother-in-law Gerhard Westerburg in early October 1524, and were printed in the matter of a few weeks. For details of this process see Hermann Barge, "Zur Chronologie und Drucksetzung der Abendmahlstraktate Karlstadts", *Zentralblatt für Bibliothekswesen* 21 (1904): 323–331.
3 No precise date is known, but it seems as though by 21st November Zwingli and Oecolampadius had finally been able to meet in person.
4 This "little book" never appeared: a treatise on infant baptism was brought to Basel by Westerburg (see n. 2), but was confiscated by the authorities before it could be printed. Nevertheless Barge, *Bodenstein*, II, 144–220, marshals evidence to suggest that Oecolampadius's brief summary of Karlstadt's views is accurate.
5 See in particular Augustine, *De baptismo contra Donatistas* (PL 43, 107–244).

which I would like you to do me the favour of teaching me at greater length, when you are at leisure to do so.⁶

I believe you have heard from his own people about how the Duke's affairs are progressing. Farel excuses himself, saying that he was urged to agree to administer the sacrament; and so his reasoning satisfied me.⁷ If his patron contacts you via an intermediary, tell him what they should do about this explanation of Farel's. | I believe the letter sent by the Luzern Diet to the Duke of Württemberg has been shown to you.⁸ What could be said that is harsher than this? Or more feeble?

May your wife⁹ remain safe in Christ, and also *Leo and *Myconius.
Farewell, excellent and brave one, in the Lord.
Basel, 21st November.
Oecolampadius.
You will see to it that Sebastian Meyer's letters are returned to him in Schaffhausen.¹⁰
To Ulrich Zwingli, most faithful minister of the word of God, his brother. Zürich.

Original: Zürich, Staatsarchiv, E II 349, p. 128 (autograph). Copy: Zürich, Zentralbibliothek, Ms S II, no. 114.

---

26 *the Duke's*] Greek τοῦ ἀρχηγοῦ (literally, 'of the (military) leader'). Oecolampadius is alluding playfully to Ulrich of Württemberg's warlike preparations at Hohentwiel (see 347, n. 1, 4)—in the awareness that Latin *dux* can mean both 'leader' and 'Duke'   40 *Zürich*] German *Zurch*

---

6   See 359, line 26f. and n. 6.
7   Following his departure from Basel in July 1524, Farel (see 329, n. 2) was at Montbéliard under the auspices of *Ulrich of Württemberg. He met with great success there as an evangelical preacher. He had scruples about celebrating the Eucharist on the grounds that he was not ordained, but reasoned that the needs of his congregation demanded this. On this phase of his career see Borel-Girard, *Farel*, 131–152.
8   On 8th November the Swiss Confederate Diet, meeting at Luzern, had written to Duke Ulrich condemning him for protecting and supporting Farel and the Lutheran preacher Johann Geyling; and on 10th November the Archbishop of Besançon had excommunicated all three of them.
9   Anna *Reinhart.
10 Sebastian Meyer (c. 1467–c. 1545), lector at the Franciscan house in Bern, who was banned from that city for espousing evangelical views in 1524. He came to Schaffhausen and assisted his fellow Franciscan Sebastian Hofmeister to propagate what were essentially Zwinglian views, before both were banned first from Schaffhausen and then from Basel in August 1525. See Bryner, "Schaffhausen", especially 222–224.

359 Oecolampadius to Zwingli—Basel, 18th January (1525)

Johannes Oecolampadius to Huldrych Zwingli, greetings.

Grace and peace from the Lord, beloved brother. Balthasar of Waldshut[1] yesterday revealed to me his opinion on the baptism of infants, and I think this should be communicated to you as a brother. He declared: "Who instituted baptism? Christ. Where? In the last chapter of Matthew. With what words? 'Go and teach all nations, baptizing them in the name of the Father, and of the Son, and of the Holy Spirit'.[2] Indeed this is right. Why therefore do we baptize infants? Baptism is a simple sign. Why do we quarrel so much about a sign? It certainly is a sign and a symbol, instituted by Christ with pregnant and most venerable words—that is to say, 'in the name of the Father, and of the Son, and of the Holy Spirit'. But anyone who diminishes this sign and abuses it does damage to a sign that has been instituted by the words of Christ. Although the sign and symbol represent an obligation by which a person binds himself to God by faith unto death, in the hope of resurrection to eternal life, the obligation should be considered more important than the sign itself. This sign, however, cannot properly be applied to infants; and hence the baptism of infants is an ivy vine without wine.[3] In baptism an obligation takes place—as today the apostolic creed[4] bears witness— as does a renunciation of Satan and all his attendant vanities, who are cast down into the water of baptism, which signifies death. In the Lord's Supper there is an obligation towards one's neighbour, by which I pledge myself to set before him the body and the blood, as Christ did for me. As our authority for this, we have the law and the prophets;[5] and I think that these will never

---

15 *more important*] *diligentius* (literally, 'more carefully')

---

1 Balthasar Hubmaier: see 347, n. 5. His core text on baptism dates from around this time: *Von dem christlichen Tauff der gläubigen* (Mikulov: Froschauer, 1526)—ed. Hubmaier, *Schriften*, 118–163. His baptismal theology is thoroughly discussed in Windhorst, *Taufverständis*.
2 Matthew 28:19. Oecolampadius's quotation from the Vulgate is again accurate: *euntes ergo docete omnes gentes: baptizantes eos in nomine Patris, et Filii, et Spiritus Sancti.*
3 An allusion to a proverb which Oecolampadius probably learnt from *Erasmus; *vino vendibili suspensa non opus est haedera* ('sellable wine does not need ivy to be hung')—see Erasmus, *Adagia*, 2.6.20 (1520). This refers to the practice of innkeepers hanging ivy on their doors to advertise that wine was available (unnecessary, presumably, if the wine were known to be good anyway).
4 Oecolampadius—or Hubmaier—seems to be confusing the Apostles' Creed (which has no mention of baptism) with the Nicene Creed (and its formulation "I acknowledge one baptism for the remission of sins").
5 Cf. Luke 16:29.

be properly taken into account in Christianity until baptism and the Lord's Supper are restored to their original purity". This is what the man said.

I think we need to respond to him in the way that you advised in your letter:[6] there is no requirement for us to examine our faith in great detail, but there is one to teach, exhort and encourage the adults carefully. The words of Christ himself indicate that he did not prescribe a specific form of words—provided that no-one rejects faith in the Holy Trinity. For even the apostles baptized simply in the name of Christ—unless perhaps they baptized in a different way that we are not told about, and Luke described things as he did in order to differentiate this baptism from the baptism of John.[7] Truly I did not say that the form of words[8] displeases me, or that I would like a different form to be introduced; I argued only that we should not attach any superstition to words. For it is enough for us to be new creations before God,[9] and indeed before the church, and to be entered in the register of the faithful by dint of a sure and sacred symbol.

Nor will Christ consider himself wronged by this, given that throughout the time of infancy and childhood boys were subject to their parents, and their blood was required of those parents.[10] So since those people were faithful and made their promises in faith, why should it be thought that God was being wronged? Moreover, when the sons have grown up | and have defied their parents, cursing them and asking "why did you circumcise me?" or similar questions, the law orders them to be killed (Leviticus 21).[11]

We are overcoming them with the stones of scripture; and, possessing as we do the symbol of the Lord's Supper, we will discern whether they wish their baptismal promise to be confirmed. Therefore I am not amazed that men of old imposed such a heavy punishment on parents whose sons would have died from their neglect. I think it is better to receive what the sign repre-

VIII, 293

40f. *were ... was required*] *in potestate parentum sunt et sanguis illorum requiritur*—both verbs are in the present, but the second in particular seems to require a past tense in English

---

6   Cf. 352, lines 23–25, in which Oecolampadius asks Zwingli for a detailed explanation of certain aspects of baptism. It seems likely that the latter responded, but that his letter has been lost.
7   Luke uses the phrase "be baptized in the name of Jesus Christ" in, for example, Acts 2:38 and 10:48.
8   That is, the form of words that conclude Matthew's Gospel—see line 6f. and n. 2.
9   Cf. II Corinthians 5:17.
10 In the context of circumcision.
11 Oecolampadius in fact means Leviticus 20:9, "For every one that curseth his father or his mother shall be surely put to death: he hath cursed his father or his mother; his blood shall be upon him".

sents than it is to discuss it. But when boys have received the Spirit of God, as I truly believe they do, the sign's meaning is not found wanting: for they are pure, and have been transformed from sons of wrath into sons of God and his kingdom. Parents, if they have been faithful, are blessed in their thousands of millions.[12] And I believe that Abraham's faith profited every single one of his innocent descendants right down to Christ. Moreover, according to the law girls benefited from the faith of their parents, even without a sign.[13]

Farewell in the Lord.

Original lost. Included in 1536 edition, fol. 65^{r-v}.

---

[12] This number is taken from Genesis 24:60 in the KJV, where it is the equivalent of *mille millia* in the Vulgate. That is also the phrase used by Oecolampadius here.

[13] Given that circumcision was seen as a covenant sign between God and the entire Jewish nation, girls—as members of that nation—were in principle included in its blessings along with circumcised boys.

367   Zwingli to Oecolampadius and the Basel Preachers—Zürich, 5th April 1525

VIII, 315   Huldrych Zwingli to Johannes Oecolampadius, Markus Bertschi,[1] Peter Frauenberger,[2] Jakob Immeli,[3] Wolfgang,[4] Thomas[5] and Johannes,[6] most pious ministers of the word at Basel, his dearest brothers in the Lord.

Grace and peace from the Lord. Even learned pagans have taught us, O dearest brothers and comrades in the army of the supreme King, that con-   5

---

1   Or 'Marcus Bersius' (c. 1483–1566), recorded as a student at Basel as early as 1512, and later People's Priest at the churches of St Theodore (1519–1523) and St Leonard (1523–1566). He seems to have been a particularly close and loyal colleague to Oecolampadius—at least until they disagreed on the matter of excommunication (see p. 22, n. 92).

2   Peter Frauenberger (or 'Petrus Gynoraeus') had a decidedly chequered career. He was appointed to the cure of St Alban's Church in Basel in 1522, only to be expelled in November 1525 for refusing to celebrate Mass. Following a period in Augsburg, he returned to Basel in 1527. Letter 728 reports, however, that he was again expelled, in the summer of 1528, this time for sexual misdemeanours—which included fathering a child by the wife of his landlord Johann Varnower. On Frauenberger see Fritz Heusler, "Petrus Gynoraeus", *Zwingliana* 1/6 (1899): 120–122; *CoE* II, 54 f.

3   Jakob Immeli (c. 1495–1543), who studied and taught at the University of Basel, and was People's Priest of St Ulrich's Church from 1523 until his suspension in February 1525 (see 376, n. 8). He was the first Basel priest to administer communion in both kinds (1523), and also to marry (1524). He remained an active supporter of Oecolampadius, accompanying him for example to the Disputation of Bern in 1528.

4   Wolfgang Wissenburg (or 'Weissenburger', 1495/6–1575), who served successively at the Franciscan Church (1518–1529), St Theodore's (1529–1541) and St Peter's (1543–1548) in Basel, as well as maintaining a distinguished academic career as a mathematician and theologian. He was the first Basel priest to celebrate Mass in German, but his eucharistic theology remained influenced by *Luther's. Hence Oecolampadius's description of him as a "brother of dubious faith" for whom Luther is a "Saxon idol" (384, lines 7–9). In the light of this one wonders whether Zwingli was writing the present letter primarily for Wissenburg's benefit.

5   Thomas Gyrfalk (d. 1559/60), an Austin Friar who was lector at their house in Fribourg before being forced to leave because of his evangelical sympathies in 1524. Thereafter he settled in Basel, serving first at the house of Austin Friars, then (from 1529) as parish priest of St Ulrich and St Elizabeth and Archdeacon of the Cathedral. After Oecolampadius's death Gyrfalk remained active in support of the former's successor *Myconius, frequently standing in for him as antistes during his last illness (1551–1552).

6   Johannes Lüthard (d. 1542), for most of his career preacher at the Franciscan monastery in Basel and a particularly close colleague of his Guardian there, Konrad *Pellikan. Even though Lüthard's evangelical views had been plain since 1519, Zwingli may have felt that he was another in need of exhortation in the matter of the Eucharist: he and Pellikan were known in 1525 still to be saying Mass (in the absence of any official instruction to the contrary). See Willy Brändly, "Johannes Lüthard, 'der Mönch von Luzern'", *Zwingliana* 8/6 (1946): 305–341, especially 315–318.

cord makes the greatest things out of little things, whereas discord stumbles and falls. So how much more should we, who | are ministers of one and the same God, learn—from his own prayer, in which he entreated the Father, "I pray that they may be one, as you and I are one"[7]—that there is nothing from which we should flee as from dissension, and nothing for which we should strive as for unanimity and concord.

Certain people tend to leave examples to the end; but here we are placing them amongst the first principles. The peace of our city, thanks be to God, has always remained so constant that up to now the storms that have assailed us have raged in vain; but do you not think that not the least reason for this tranquillity has been the concord that has existed between the ministers of the word? There is between us no animosity, no dissension, no envy, no quarrels or disputes; and from where else can this agreement of minds proceed than from a supreme and most perfect God? Are we not men? Hence we might have endured what all others endure. So it has been a gift of God that no cloud of animosity, still less of discord, has so far arisen. Therefore I ask that you will not disdain to listen to someone giving a friendly warning—someone whom you are accustomed to calling a friend. It is a bold plan of mine to admonish you—you who in many ways are our superiors in learning and piety. But justice forbids one to describe as boldness what is actually friendship—that is to say, love, indeed piety. We know your most renowned | city, we know all of you; so you cannot think that I am doing this out of any other motive than love—of piety, of your city and of yourselves. Satan tempts us too in strange ways; but he is indeed easily overcome—as long as, in our victory, we can recognize whatever he has attacked us with as a temptation. As we said, however, we have been ascribing the speed of our victory over him to nothing other than the spirit of peace and unity.

It is right for you also to be so minded. We are currently being assailed by a temptation that is by no means to be underestimated, namely our discussions about the Eucharist itself. This matter will certainly not cause us as much turmoil as some people hope it will, if only we can find a consensus, that is, an agreement in the midst of our struggle. Some otherwise weak and cowardly animals do this: they frighten the cruellest of enemies so much that they do not suffer any harm from them. Hence ducks form themselves into

---

36, 50 *consensus*] Greek συγκρητισμὸν, a term that is generally believed to have been coined by Plutarch (*De fraterno amore*, 490b) to refer to a union or alliance of two parties fighting against a common enemy. A Latin transliteration of the same word, *syncretismus*, is also translated "consensus" in line 53 f.

---

7 John 17:21.

tightly-knit wedges, so as to deprive hawks of all hope of catching them. In this way also cattle prevent bears, and harmless sheep prevent wolves from taking them as prey.

They say of Caugnista, King of Numidia,[8] that, when he was dying, he gave each of his twelve sons, one by one, twelve arrows that were tied together, and asked them to break them; one after another they all tried to do this, but in vain. Then the father untied the arrows, and ordered all his sons to break a single arrow—which they all did, as quick as a flash. Then the old man concluded: "So you too will always be invincible if you preserve peace and unity; but if each one continues to follow his own plans, you will perish before you notice the presence of any evil". If, I say, you arrive at a consensus in this way, no-one will be able to harm you. But someone will say, "How can we make such an agreement? Do we not already agree? Do we not all hold the same word in our hands?" Quite right! Be of the same mind, and the consensus is already there! But if you still disagree, you clearly do not have the same word! For even if we all have the same word in a literal sense, we do not derive from it the same meaning; therefore we do not have the same internal word, which alone is the food of the soul. For if one admits what cannot be denied, namely that there are many who rely on the same word yet disagree with each other, it follows that those who quarrel in this way over the same word are not guided by the same spirit. So when today there is no little dissension over the Eucharist, and that between brothers, it cannot be denied that some are lending their ear to a different spirit from the divine one.

VIII, 318 Now, we are tempted by the desire for glory, the fear of death, and by Satan | himself, who wishes to drag everything down into despair. For we teach in part things that bring glory to ourselves and in part things that further the cause; and some are driven by a fear of proclaiming foolish things that are abhorrent to faith and common sense. But this is not how you have taught Christ: for I have always thought it was the natural character of the doctrine we preach at Zürich, Basel and Strasbourg to make people zealous for peace and righteousness; but for that righteousness which proceeds from faith. If, therefore—above all things that pertain to God—you preach faith, that is, the righteousness that is born of faith, have you not already encom-

---

8 The king's name is a strange one, but the story of the twelve sons and the arrows was well known, going back at least as far as Aesop (c. 600 BCE). Zwingli owned a collection of fables (Strasbourg: Scherer, 1515), and wrote a note in it against the relevant story: *in hunc ferme modum XII filiis Caugnista XII sagittas simul atque scorsim confrigendas esse dicitur*—see Walther Köhler, *Huldrych Zwinglis Bibliothek* (Zürich: Beer, 1921), no. 134; Leu/Weidmann no. 2.

passed everything from beginning to end? Are not all the other things that remain wholly unnecessary ornaments? For if they were essential for salvation, Christ would have taught them in the clearest terms among the first principles.

But now I will come to the crux of the matter: some contend that the physical flesh of Christ is eaten in the Eucharist; others think that no flesh at all is present; and a third group asserts that spiritual flesh is eaten in such a way that the bread is not just bread, but at the same time also flesh—or that, when bread is eaten, flesh is eaten also. I cannot explain these things clearly, because I have not read the little books published by certain people.

See now what should dominate all our thinking: truth dictates that flesh is not eaten; for the flesh profits nothing.[9] Nor, as some mutterers say, does 'flesh' here mean 'carnal understanding'. For Christ replied in these terms to the Jews who were disputing with him about his corporeal body, and in doing so lightened their burden. Hence it is clear that he was talking about corporeal flesh when he said, "the flesh profits nothing"; they thought that was what he was talking about. Faith does not need any corporeal feeding. For if we eat Christ, that is, if we have faith in Christ, we shall never again hunger or thirst: faith requires nothing of that kind, but is content in and of itself. So it is fear that teaches us to retain these ideas about corporeal flesh. For the truth must be made known, and hypocrisy dragged into the light.

Certain people believe that the great mass of the faithful are so in thrall to this error concerning corporeal flesh that they despair of them ever being freed from it; this is where their fear and despair of gaining victory come from. So they prefer to save their own skins and their own credibility, rather than going into battle to confront a delusion. This is where such dissembling speeches as these come from: "The precious body of Christ and that noble blood of his are snatched away from us; the holiest and clearest of words are ripped from our grasp". If this were the sense of Christ's words, he would undoubtedly have spoken more clearly. As if anyone could be ignorant of the fact that there have only ever been very few priests (indeed, none at all) who believed that corporeal flesh was present in the bread! As if anyone who is already of the faith could be ignorant of what hypocrisy is! As | he that is

VIII, 319

---

73 *everything ... end*] *proram et pullim* (literally, 'prow and stern')   86 *corporeal*] *corporea*. We retain the original's use of repetition, which is itself a rhetorical device

---

9   John 6:63. Zwingli quotes here from the Vulgate: *caro non prodest quidquam*.

spiritual judges all things,[10] so truly it is well known to all the faithful that he who believes we eat corporeal flesh cannot be a person of faith. Let certain people now go and fill everyone's ears with their shouts—since those of us who are believers know from our faith that corporeal flesh cannot actually be eaten, so we do not perceive any flesh with our senses. Sensory perception was always the first to uncover the fraud, even for the unlearned.

But some people say that God can do everything, and that hence he can be at once both bread and flesh. What good, I ask, does this monstrous verbal fiction do? As if God ever meant water to be at once both water and fire! Or a leper—many of whom he healed—to be at once both leprous and clean! Or the water he had turned into wine also to remain as water![11] So these people say that spiritual eating takes place, yet they also affirm that the body is eaten; or they say that the bread really is bread and, at the same time, flesh. And they reinforce these foolish opinions, born of fear, with such insolent cries that they would have long since won the battle if they had taken such care to strengthen their case properly from the holy scriptures.

Therefore I beg of you, most virtuous brothers, let there be no dissention between you over so clear a matter! The truth will win, it will win—and when at length the truth triumphs, it will expose those who oppose it to the ridicule of all. Do not swear by the words of certain teachers; do not let anyone's authority impose itself on you.[12]

But now I will relate some of the things that have happened in our city. At Zürich we have all proclaimed the same doctrine openly. None of the faithful has taken offence, and even some of the weak ones have been strengthened by the daily teaching; so now no-one is hindering us except the impious. That most excellent band of teachers at Strasbourg feels as you do;[13] but this should be of no account, since truth is the strongest of all. So let each of you examine his faith; I already know it will teach you how worthless are those things concerning corporeal flesh that we have been garrulously grumbling about up to now. What then will be the reason for us not all being of the same

---

126 *Do not ... teachers*] *Nolite iurati esse in quorundam magistrorum verba*: likely to be an allusion to Horace, *Epistolae*, 1.1,14 (*nullius addictus iurare in uerba magistri*)

---

10   1 Corinthians 2:15. Zwingli echoes the Vulgate: *spiritalis autem iudicat omnia*.
11   Cf. John 2:1–11.
12   A less than subtle allusion to Luther and to Wolfgang Wissenburg's admiration for him (see n. 4 above).
13   Zwingli is for certain thinking of *Bucer, *Capito and perhaps Hedio (see 286, n. 1), with all of whom he was in regular contact.

mind? I hear there is a certain little murmurer[14] in your city, whom I know inside out; they say that he is sowing all sorts of discord. I beg you to avoid him, since he serves not God, but his own stomach—and, what is more, his own penis. For often in the past he has either debauched himself in adultery or in any event has given the impression of doing so. You should therefore warn such people to be sparing with their words; for we know by faith what others seek to assert with loud clamours.

| Both piety and love have compelled me, most excellent brothers, to discuss these things with you; for some talk had reached us of certain dissidents sprouting forth amongst you—if only the Lord would nip them in the bud! But what am I doing, speaking as if I thought any one of you so impudent as, in the future, to act rebelliously to the gospel's detriment?[15] For you have Oecolampadius, a man of incomparable learning, and truly of such discretion that, if he were to transgress in any way, he would do so out of hesitancy rather than undue haste. I will not in any way commend his piety, since it commends itself. For how much has he endured for the Lord's sake? How much does he endure daily, without being broken? Since you have him, you need not fear that anyone can harm you. So do not keep silent about what you think is true; but speak with moderation, lest the people be turned into swine and tear you apart.[16] That is, dispense the word prudently, so that you might hope it will bear fruit, rather than leading to the gospel's destruction. Take this our admonition in good part, dearest brothers: it is unsophisticated and jejune, but I know that it will not displease good men such as you. Be constant, and you will see the Lord's help descend upon you. The truth will win, whether those who strive against us want it or not; if only it would win easily! But may the Lord's will be done. Let us pray for each other.

VIII, 320

Farewell.
From Zürich, 5th April 1525.

Original lost. Included in 1536 edition, fols 170ʳ–171ᵛ.

---

14 This person has not been identified.
15 In fact, at least with regard to the addressees of this letter, Zwingli's fears were not borne out—in that, in spite of theological differences, they continued to work in reasonable harmony, at least until Frauenberger's disgrace in 1528 (see n. 2 and letter 728).
16 Zwingli seems here to be picking up on Oecolampadius's boar imagery in 307 (lines 8–11).

376   Oecolampadius to Zwingli—Basel, 18th August (1525)

Grace and peace from Christ. Beloved brother, in your recent letter you were excusing yourself for your extempore warning[1]—when truly no apology is needed on my account. We are united by the most sacred bond of charity, and my epistle[2] did not require any apology, as if you had charged me with things that were rather difficult to hear or to bear. Far from it—I do not in any way believe that such a thing is necessary. But as a friend I pour out the troubles of my soul into the bosom of a friend, as to a trusted confidant. For I have been allotted a people that is extremely difficult to teach, and which does not listen enough to what has been said.[3] Perhaps in these difficult times they will reject our cause, seeing that everything is very turbulent and that the kings and princes of the earth are making a stand against Christ.[4] So do not think, my brother, that I am complaining about you, or judging your letter at all severely. To be sure I take all your words in good part, even if you deal harshly with me; for I am persuaded that you are of Christ, and that he is working through you.

There is little news here. Some anabaptists have recently been thrown into prison and expelled from the city.[5] Their detractors and protectors, as well as their disciples who have not yet been rebaptized, are going about with impunity. I pray not for their punishment, but for their repentance. Daily threats are weakening the resolve of the people of Strasbourg, as I hear;[6] but the brothers | are pushing forward constantly and unitedly with the word

---

3 *most sacred*] *sanctiori* (literally 'more sacred, rather sacred')   6 *pour out*] *expuo* (literally, 'spit out')   7 *trusted confidant*] *concilii angustioris* (literally, 'rather close counsellor')

---

1   See 367, especially lines 22–25 and 144–148.
2   Presumably Zwingli wrote letter 367 in response to a (now lost) invitation from Oecolampadius.
3   A comment directed at the Baslers in general and their Council in particular.
4   Cf. Psalm 2:2.
5   The arrests must have happened between 10th and 16th August: all the anabaptist prisoners were released on 16th August, and some were expelled soon afterwards. See Hanspeter Jecker, "Die Basler Täufer. Studien zur Vor- und Frühgeschichte", *BZGA* 80 (1980): 5–131, especially 38–48; *AGBR* II, 33 (no. 46).
6   The most recent surviving letter to Oecolampadius from Strasbourg is one from *Capito, dated 28th May, in which he reports on the massacres that took place in Saverne and Scherweiler between 16th and 26th May—see *OeBA* I, 368 f. (no. 258); *CC* II, 123 (no. 245). Given that he has not written to Zwingli since April, it is certainly possible that Oecolampadius has this letter in mind, but just as likely that he has received a report of a more recent event.

of the Lord. What is to be done about Sebastian from Schaffhausen[7] will be related to you by our Wilhelm,[8] a pious man and one who sings most agreeable praises of your humanity. Immeli will not be restored to his office;[9] a wolf[10] has been chosen as his successor.

May your whole household, and your church, keep safe and well.
Farewell.
Basel, 18th August.
Your Oecolampadius.
To Huldrych Zwingli, most vigilant bishop of the Zürich church, his beloved brother.

Original: Zürich, Staatsarchiv, E II 349, p. 137 (autograph).

---

[7] Sebastian Hofmeister (1494–1533; see 352, n. 10), who had been prominent in the very early stages of the evangelical movement in Basel. He had been expelled from Schaffhausen on 3rd August, having been held responsible for the unrest which had befallen the town and its environs in the context of the Peasants' War. Wishing to return to Basel, he was required to obtain a written approval of his religious views from the University of Basel; when, inevitably, this was not forthcoming, he was expelled from the city on 14th August—see AGBR II, 31f. (no. 44). By the date of this letter Oecolampadius had hatched a plan for him to take refuge in Zürich, where Hofmeister was eventually to become a close collaborator of Zwingli. See Martin Haas, "Sebastian Hofmeister", *Schaffhauser Beiträge zur Geschichte* 58 (1981): 81–88; Bryner, "Schaffhausen", 219–224; OER II, 243; BBKL II, 983–986.

[8] Wilhelm von Zell (c. 1470–1545/6), originally from Mindelheim in the Bavarian Unterallgäu, who was with Zwingli in Zürich between June 1525 and June 1526. Thereafter he was for several years Zwingli's main representative in Southern Germany. See BBKL XVII, 1582. Instructions on the plan to help Hofmeister (see n. 7) were presumably too delicate to be consigned to paper.

[9] As People's Priest of St Ulrich's Church in Basel, Immeli (see 367, n. 3) had been under pressure from the Dean of the Cathedral since marrying his concubine in 1524; now the Council had suspended him for refusing to celebrate Mass.

[10] That is to say, a Catholic.

381   Zwingli to Oecolampadius[1]—Zürich, 13th September 1525

VIII, 357

Grace and peace from the Lord. We do not have your book on the Eucharist here,[2] nor the one which *Erasmus has recently produced, and whose contents and title we do not know.[3] This latter will doubtless eventually crawl towards us as booksellers return from the Frankfurt Fair, but I would like yours to fly across to us more quickly. I have no leisure to write more. The Lord delivers us from evil everywhere, till the day he has ordained.

Farewell and be steadfast against these gods: the flesh, the blood, the bread and the wine.
From Zürich, 13th September 1525.

Original: Strasbourg, Archives de la Ville et de l'Eurométropole, 1 AST 162 (no. 291).

---

1   Unusually, no recipient is stipulated for this letter. Oecolampadius is really the only possible addressee, however, since of Zwingli's correspondents he is the only one who had recently published on the Eucharist (see n. 2).
2   Oecolampadius's *De genuina verborum Domini "Hoc est corpus meum" iuxta vetustissimos auctores expositione liber* (Strasbourg: Knobloch, August 1525; *Abendmahlsschriften* 2–101; Staehelin 113; Leu/Weidmann A159). See Burnett, *Debating*, 103–109, 161–164; eadem, *Karlstadt*, 86 f.; Staehelin, *Lebenswerk*, 276–283; Jung, "Abendmahlsstreit", 145–148.
3   No such book by Erasmus ever appeared. Cornelis Augustijn, *Erasmus: His Life, Works, and Influence* (Toronto: University of Toronto Press, 1991), 150–152, argues that rumours circulating in Basel in 1524–1525 to the effect that Erasmus was intending to publish on the Eucharist were true, but that he changed his mind upon realizing that his views were in many respects similar to those of Oecolampadius. This interpretation is reinforced by Zwingli's profession of ignorance here, and particularly by Erasmus's characteristically equivocal reply to Basel City Council's request for his opinion of Oecolampadius's *De genuina ... expositione*: "learned, well written, and thoroughly pious, if anything could be so described which is at variance with the general opinion of the Church"—*EC* XI, 343 f. (no. 1636).

384   Oecolampadius to Zwingli—Basel, 15th September (1525)

Greetings in the Lord, beloved brother. No copy of our little book on the Eucharist has yet been made for us;[1] but it will arrive very soon, and I will make sure that some copies are brought to you via the next messenger. Your book[2] pleases me greatly. Our adversaries, because they cannot condemn it using the scriptures or rational arguments, are fools enough to reject it by sneering at it: they think everyone else is a fool, yet cannot see their own folly. That brother of ours of dubious faith,[3] to whom I sent a copy for him to read, replied that our books contained little theology but much philosophy. No doubt he is waiting to see how his Saxon idol[4] responds. Many patients, after all, are still suffering from the old illness.[5]

*Erasmus has published two books, one against a certain Carthusian called Sutor, who cannot bear there to be any other versions of the New Testament but Jerome's,[6] and another entitled *Lingua*, a book that in my view is worth reading.[7] In neither book does he oppose us. Froben[8] has also printed a Hebrew grammar by Elia Levita,[9] a book of by no means negligible learn-

---

6f. *they think ... folly*] or "they think everyone is a fool and unable to see his own folly", or "everyone thinks they are fools and unable to see their own folly" (*ut omnes stultos credant et non agnoscentes suam stulticiam*, where *omnes* could be nominative or accusative)

---

1   See 381, n. 2.
2   The *Subsidium sive coronis de Eucharistia* (Zürich: Froschauer, 17th August 1525)—ed. ZW IV, 458–504 (no. 63); trans. Pipkin/Furcha, II, 194–227. See Burnett, *Debating*, 101 f.; eadem, *Karlstadt*, 95–97; Locher, ZR, 298–300.
3   Wolfgang Wissenburg (see 367, n. 4).
4   *Luther.
5   A statement that seems to signal an increasing impatience with the continuing influence, also in Switzerland, of Luther's sacramental theology.
6   The *Apologia adversus debacchationem Petri Sutoris* (Basel: Froben, 1525), a work which unleashed a protracted controversy between Erasmus and the conservative Paris theologian Sutor (or Pierre Cousturier, c. 1475–1537; see *CoE* I, 352 f.).
7   Erasmus, *Lingua* (Basel: Froben, 1525).
8   The highly prolific Basel printer and ally of Erasmus Johann Froben (c. 1460–1527). On his career see Valentina Sebastiani, *Johann Froben, Printer of Basel. A Biographical Profile and Catalogue of His Editions* (Leiden: Brill, 2018); also *CoE* II, 60–63; *OER* II, 148 f.; *BBKL* II, 135.
9   *Sēfer haharkabah: Hebraicae Grammaticae studiosis in primis necessarium* (Basel: Froben, 1525). The author is perhaps more properly referred to as Eliyahu Baḥur (1469/70–1549).

VIII, 366 ing. I have sent | Latomus's *Elleboron*[10] via Christoph,[11] but I understand it has not yet arrived. As soon as the little book on the Eucharist arrives, I will share it with you, as long as there are messengers available.

The priests and their associates here would readily accept what we have so far taught—but for this one dogma that they will not allow to be overthrown, that of the Eucharist as propounded either by the Pope or by *Luther. For this is the citadel and bulwark of their impiety, by means of which they hope over time to regain what they have recently lost. Because this idol remains unchallenged, nobody has condemned them as truly ungodly.

Christoph has told me what the sons of Belial have tried to do against you, and I rejoice that you have been snatched out of the hands of those lying in wait for you.[12] In these early skirmishes the Lord is training us, so that, in the greater struggles that lie ahead, we might in no way doubt the eternal life that has been promised us.

Farewell.
Basel, 15th September.

Now, just as I was about to finish this letter, someone has brought letters and one or two little books, which I will send on![13] But none of them bears comparison with yours. I am also sending a work by Luther for our Wilhelm.[14]

Farewell again.
Johannes Oecolampadius.
To his dearest brother Huldrych Zwingli, bishop of the Zürichers.

Original: Zürich, Staatsarchiv, E II 349, p. 73 (autograph). Copy: Zürich, Zentralbibliothek, Ms S 15, no. 1.

---

10 This formulation is slightly confusing, in that the *Elleboron pro Jacobo Latomo* is Oecolampadius's own response to the *De confessione secreta* by the Louvain theologian Jacobus Latomus (1475–1555). The two texts were published in the same volume (Basel: Cratander, 18th August 1525; Staehelin 112, Leu/Weidmann A 161). For a brief discussion see Staehelin, *Lebenswerk*, 276. On Latomus see *CoE* II, 304–306; *TRE* XX, 495–499; *BBKL* IV, 1219–1221; *KTR* II, 7–26.
11 *Froschauer.
12 Cf. Psalm 71:4.
13 The element of excited surprise conveyed by Oecolampadius's formulation here implies that at least one of these "little books" might have been his own *De genuina … expositione*, whose imminent arrival is alluded to in lines 1–3 above.
14 Wilhelm von Zell (see 376, n. 8).

387   Oecolampadius to Zwingli—Basel, 2nd October (1525)

Grace and peace in the Lord. My brother, I am sending herewith the arrogant book by Balthasar,[1] advocate of the anabaptists—to call them by that vilest of names.[2] But what else are they? I was worried that it might perhaps have been hidden from you for a while, because, here too, certain people had the book long before I was shown it. You will reply to the man as your faith and duty instruct you; but I would have you do it as soon as possible.[3] They seem to me not to care for charity, which they regard as something to be practised elsewhere. Moreover Pomeranus, thanks to a certain remora-fish,[4] will hold back many people in the matter of the Eucharist. I beg of you, if you have no time, to respond to him through someone else—but in a little book that is no longer than his, lest the reader be put off by its prolixity.[5]

Claudius Cantiuncula,[6] in a long epistle and with consummate rhetoric, has been trying to persuade *Erasmus to write against us. I do not know what

---

1f. *arrogant book*] *arroganciam* (literally, 'arrogance')   8 *elsewhere*] *in externis* (literally 'in foreign places')

---

1   Hubmaier and his *Von dem christlichen Tauff* (see 359, n. 1).
2   This anticipates 391, line 14f., where Oecolampadius states a preference for Zwingli's designation, "catabaptists" rather than "anabaptists". On the terms see p. 7, n. 31.
3   Zwingli's response is dated as early as 5th November 1525: *Uber Doctor Balthasars Touffbüchlin waarhaffte gründte antwurt* (Zürich: Froschauer, 1525)—ed. ZW IV, 585–647 (no. 68) has a prologue dated 5th November. See Burnett, *Debating*, 151–153.
4   *Bugenhagen, called "Pomeranus" because of his origins in Pomerania. The "remora-fish" is his *Sendbrieff widder den newen yrrthumb bey dem Sacrament des leybs und blutts unsers herrn Jhesu Christi* (Wittenberg: Klug, 1525; Leu/Weidmann 42). On the controversy unleashed by this see Burnett, *Debating*, 102 f.; eadem, *Karlstadt*, 99 f. Oecolampadius is alluding to a story found in Pliny (*Naturalis historia* IX, 41) to the effect that the remora (Latin *echineis*), though a small fish, is able to prevent a ship moving by clinging tenaciously to its hull.
5   Zwingli again responded swiftly, and in person, with his *Ad Ioannis Bugenhagii Pomerani Epistolam responsio Huldrychi Zuinglij* (Zürich: Froschauer, 23rd October 1525; Leu/Weidmann 197)—ed. ZW IV, 558–576 (no. 67). See Burnett, *Debating*, 103; eadem, *Karlstadt*, 99 f. This, however, spreads over ten leaves, as against the five occupied by Bugenhagen's *Sendbrieff*.
6   The humanist Cantiuncula (or 'Chansonnette', c. 1490–1549) enjoyed a stellar academic and legal career in Basel between 1517 and 1524, when he left—for Metz, Vic-sur-Seille and later Vienna—because of the evangelicals' rising influence. His letter urging Erasmus to write against Oecolampadius's *De genuina … expositione* (see 381, n. 2) has been lost, but Erasmus's far from enthusiastic response has been preserved—see EC XI, 287–289 (no. 1616). On Cantiuncula see Guido Kisch, *Claudius Cantiuncula. Ein Basler Jurist und Humanist des 16. Jahrhunderts* (Basel: Helbing & Lichtenhahn, 1970); CoE I, 259–261; VL 16 I, 458–465.

he will do about this. Others are urging him to do it also. So there will be enough work for us to do. May the Lord help us. Let me know if there is anything you want me to do.

| Farewell.
Basel, 2nd October.
Greet the brothers.
Your Oecolampadius.
To Huldrych Zwingli, most Christian teacher of the Zürichers, his brother in the Lord.

Original: Zürich, Staatsarchiv, E II 349, p. 78 (autograph). Copy: Zürich, Zentralbibliothek, Ms S 15, no. 10.

391　Oecolampadius to Zwingli—Basel, 12th October (1525)

Greetings in Christ. My brother, with us also the state of play is unchanged, save that the hearts of the magistrates and Pharaohs are being hardened more and more, day by day.[1] They are certainly hatching something; but what will they be able to achieve against the outstretched hand of the Lord?[2] They think we are contemptible, and do not consider whose work it is that we do.

It is certain that *Erasmus is writing about the Eucharist.[3] O misery, how fruitlessly he will fight with his pen against the truth that has been revealed to him! I seem already to see what arguments he will use to tackle the question. Make sure that we have your reply to Pomeranus[4] as soon as possible! For I predict a certain victory for us. I hear the Swabian brothers[5] are stridently proclaiming that this little book has strengthened their position; for this reason their mouths need to be stopped before those of the anabaptists—whom you have more correctly been calling catabaptists (after Nazianzus).[6] For the latter, being of the baser sort, shout in corners, whereas the former shout on the housetops[7]—eminent sophists as they are, or rather not sophists but most arrogant Thrasos,[8] fonder of fighting with words than with hands, and whose own character (as they cannot deny) condemns and mocks them.

---

2 *the magistrates and Pharaohs*] Greek οἱ ἄρχοντες καὶ Φαραῶνες　　7 *about the Eucharist*] Greek περὶ εὐχαριστίας　　8f. *the truth ... him*] Greek τὴν ἀλήθειαν αὐτῷ φανερωθεῖσαν　　14 *catabaptists*] Greek καταβαπτιστάς

1　An echo of the repeated references to God hardening Pharaoh's heart in Exodus 9–11. Oecolampadius no doubt has in mind Basel Council's concerted crackdown on evangelicals in the wake of unrest in the city's hinterland in the early summer of 1525.
2　Cf. Exodus 3:20.
3　The *Expostulatio admodum pia et Christiana ad quendam amicum* (Cologne: Quentell, 1526).
4　*Bugenhagen.
5　The Lutheran reformers of Schwäbisch Hall, who, under the leadership of *Brenz, were about to present their position on the Eucharist in print: *Syngramma clarissimorum qui Halae Suevorum convenerunt virorum super verbis Coenae Dominicae ad Johannem Oecolampadium* (Augsburg: Ruff, January 1526; Leu/Weidmann A21)—ed. Brenz, *Werke*, I, 234–278. See Burnett, *Debating*, 143f.
6　Gregory of Nazianzus (c. 329–390), who dealt with baptism most influentially in his 40th *Oration* (PG XXXVI, 421). Roth, *Reformation*, I, 43, suggests that the term *catabaptistae* in fact originated with Oecolampadius, rather than Zwingli.
7　Cf. Matthew 10:2.
8　See 329, n. 4.

Farewell. 20
Basel, 12th October.
Your Oecolampadius.
To Huldrych Zwingli, most faithful pastor of the Zürichers, his brother.

Original: Zürich, Staatsarchiv, E II 349, p. 125 (autograph). Copy: Zürich, Zentralbibliothek, Ms S 15, no. 21.

394   Oecolampadius to Zwingli—Basel, 18th October (1525)

Greetings, my brother! People are saying that *Erasmus is definitely going to write.[1] He will commend Ambrose's *On the Sacraments*,[2] as the Frobens[3] are persuading him to—though he himself has never considered the book to be by Ambrose. What if perchance you were to convince him that it is not by this author, to whose works it is actually in no way similar? But what if even he has been led astray? Many will oppose us, as far as I can tell. So let us advance eagerly and with great trust in the Lord towards what lies before us.[4]

I am sending you a letter from the man from Nördlingen,[5] which seems rather | milder—though I do not know quite what it is I smell.[6] He wants Tertullian[7] to side with him. Strauß[8] wants us to propound human doctrines, as if indeed we believed in them rather than in the word of God. See to it that I get your response to Pomeranus[9] as soon as possible—for we too will be visited by both of those angry men when they emerge into the light.[10]

---

1 See 381, n. 3.
2 *De sacramentis libri sex* (PL 16, 417–462), an authority often appealed to by conservative writers on the Eucharist. In the following sentence Oecolampadius retails a common but probably erroneous belief that the attribution to St Ambrose is false.
3 Johann Froben (see 384, n. 8) and his eldest son and successor Hieronymus (1501–1563).
4 Cf. Philippians 3:13 f.
5 No such letter has survived, but it can only have come from Theobald Billican (c. 1490–1554), who—inspired in no small measure by Zwingli—had been successfully implementing evangelical reforms in the free imperial city of Nördlingen in Swabia since 1522. His views on the Eucharist had been strongly influenced by Oecolampadius's *De genuina ... expositione* (see 381, n. 2), but in general were closer to those of *Luther. On his contribution to the ongoing eucharistic debates see Simon, *Billican*, especially 99–127; also OER I, 173; BBKL I, 589–591.
6 A formulation which no doubt reflects Billican's notoriously volatile temperament.
7 Even though he did not write a treatise on the Eucharist, Tertullian was also often cited in support of various sixteenth-century positions on the subject.
8 Jakob *Strauß. Disturbed by Oecolampadius's adoption of an apparently Zwinglian position on the Eucharist, he had written to the former from Nürnberg on 7th October 1525 that he intended to oppose him in print—see OeBA I, 394 f. (no. 283). Oecolampadius did not reply.
9 *Bugenhagen. See 387, n. 4 and 391, line 10 f.
10 That is, when their works become available in Basel.

Ludwig *Hätzer greets you. He is translating our book.[11] I did not ask for this, nor did I forbid it. I will be glad of it, however, if our adversaries are troubled by seeing their empty promises exposed before the eyes of the populace. Perhaps he will see to it that it is printed in your city. I do not, however, want it to become widely known that a book is being translated in my house.

Farewell, you who are serving the Lord in good hope.
Basel, the day after St Gallus's Day.
Your Oecolampadius.
To Huldrych Zwingli, most faithful pastor of the Zürichers, his brother.

Original: Zürich, Staatsarchiv, E II 349, p. 74 (autograph). Copy: Zürich, Zentralbibliothek, Ms S 15, no. 27.

---

11   Hätzer's version of Oecolampadius's *De genuina ... expositione* (see 381, n. 2) appeared in 1526 as *Vom Sacrament der Dancksagung. Von dem waren nateurlichen* [sic] *verstand der worten Christi: Das ist mein leib, nach der gar alten Lerer erklärung* (Zürich: Froschauer; Staehelin 123). On this, and Hätzer's reasons for undertaking the project, see Goeters, *Hätzer*, 69, 74–79; Burnett, *Debating*, 148–150; Staehelin, *Lebenswerk*, 283 f.

396   Oecolampadius to Zwingli—Basel, 22nd October (1525)

Grace and peace in the Lord, my Zwingli! A certain letter is doing the rounds under *Erasmus's name—which, however, has not yet been published in print.[1] In it, he finds fault with a friend for having betrayed a secret,[2] and prays that Christ might show him little mercy if the opinion we hold on the Eucharist has ever lodged in his mind—adding that, by remembering the love of God and reflecting on the holy scriptures, he could easily have dismissed such a thought if it had even fleetingly entered his head.[3] He sets against us *Luther, who has himself shown reverence for the Catholic Church in this regard.[4] He calls Christ's taking on of flesh so as not to cause offence, and the fact that the apostles did not worship his flesh, "arguments of straw".[5] He states that the words of holy scripture support him when they say, "This is my body, etc.". Where, he asks, do these people read, "this is not my body, but a symbol of my body"? If we were to tie ourselves in knots, we would find it difficult to demonstrate with the help of other passages that the word for a thing can be seen as a symbol of that thing.[6] But we would be foolish to argue that since these words *can* be understood in this way, they *must* be understood in this way.[7] He says that we cite in vain the ancients and the orthodox, whose words we wrap up, misrepresent and twist about, but from whom we cannot cite any passage which does not clearly state that the Lord's body is present. Hence, he asks, why should he abandon the Catholic Church?[8]

These words are all found in that man's epistle, and we will be able to respond to them easily enough when the situation demands. But I wanted to make this known to you also. Not that you should expose the man to ridicule;

VIII, 395

---

1 The letter in question is Erasmus's letter to Konrad *Pellikan, from approximately 15th October 1525, EC XI, 344–350 (no. 1637). It is discussed by Christ-von Wedel, "Erasmus", 115–121.
2 In letter 1637 Erasmus chides Pellikan for claiming that he (Erasmus) agreed with the Swiss reformers on the Eucharist. In spite of Pellikan's attempts at reconciliation, the resultant breach led to the end of their friendship.
3 Along with much of this paragraph, lines 3–7 are very close to being a direct quotation from letter 1637. They correspond to lines 57–60.
4 Cf. EC 1637, lines 60–63.
5 Cf. EC 1637, lines 78–80.
6 The two sentences of lines 12–15 report *verbatim* lines 83–89 of EC 1637.
7 This sentence and the next accurately report EC 1637, lines 94–99.
8 Cf. EC 1637, lines 103–105.

for it is to be expected that, when a shrew raises its voice, what it says is passed on between its little friends.⁹

VIII, 396   For the rest, our enemies are not sleeping, | but rather are trying everything to rouse the Council of Basel against us—not that it has exactly been well disposed towards us hitherto. I was recently accused much more vehemently than ever before: Erasmus and Ber[10] were selected from amongst the theologians, and Cantiuncula[11] and Amerbach[12] from amongst the lawyers to assess my book;[13] this is what the magistracy asked them to do recently. They say that Erasmus took it badly, because he did not want to get involved in this business. The others are well enough motivated in themselves, and need no other encouragement. Glarean[14] thinks that, by slandering people, he has proved himself to be a resolute Christian.

Some of our friends have taken the view that I should leave Basel for a time; but as for me, nothing could be further from my mind. It would need them to proscribe my book or remove me from my office; otherwise I will remain steadfast, for as long as the Lord allows it. May you henceforth always be joyful in your spirit, as you are accustomed to being! For the hairs of our head are numbered,[15] and (what am I saying?) so were even the bristles of

---

9   An effectively timed reminiscence of Erasmus's *Adagia*, 1.3.65 (265): *suo ipsius indicio periit sorex* ('the shrew reveals itself and perishes'). As Erasmus explains, this is taken originally from Terence, *Eunuchus* (line 1024).
10   Ludwig Ber (or 'Baer', 1479–1554), a native of Basel who returned to work there between 1513 and 1529, following a rigorous Catholic theological training centred on the University of Paris. He was a (decidedly conservative) Professor of Theology, and several times Rector of the University of Basel. On him see *CoE* I, 84–86; *BBKL* I, 340; Schindler, *BD*, 646–648; Wackernagel, *Basel*, III, 432–434.
11   See 387, n. 6.
12   The humanist lawyer Bonifatius Amerbach (1495–1562), son of the Basel printer Johann, who, following studies at Freiburg and Avignon, returned to live in Basel from 1524 until his death. He was very active in both university and governmental circles, and remained a close friend of Erasmus, whose perspectives on the Reformation he largely shared. On him see Myron P. Gilmore, *Humanists and Jurists: Six Studies in the Renaissance* (Cambridge, MA: Harvard University Press, 1963), 146–173; *CoE* I, 42–46; *BBKL* XXII, 17–20.
13   The *De genuina ... expositione* (see 381, n. 2). The four assessors' brief was, above all, to determine whether this was a suitable work to be bought and sold in Basel. See Staehelin, *Lebenswerk*, 284.
14   See p. 23, n. 97.
15   Matthew 10:30.

LETTER 396   109

the pigs whom the demons did not dare enter until the Lord permitted it.[16]
We shall live and die by the will of the Lord who redeemed us.[17]

45   I am almost sick with desire to see your response to Pomeranus.[18] See to
it, I beg, that we get it soon. For even those whose views it does not uphold
are glorying in it.

*Hätzer greets you. He has translated our book on the Lord's Supper and
has entrusted it to Christoph the printer, with a view to his publishing it in
50   its entirety and in our shared vernacular, just as Hätzer translated it.[19] He
himself will be present and will watch over the process.

Farewell.
Basel, 22nd October.
Your Oecolampadius.
55   To Huldrych Zwingli, most faithful pastor of the Zürich church, my brother.

Original: Zürich, Staatsarchiv, E II 349, p. 11 (autograph). Copy: Zürich, Zentralbibliothek, Ms S 15, no. 36.

---

16   Matthew 8:30–32.
17   Cf. Romans 14:8.
18   *Bugenhagen. See 387, n. 4; 391, line 10 f.; 394, line 13.
19   See 394, n. 11. "Christoph" is the printer *Froschauer.

401   Zwingli to Oecolampadius—Zürich, 28th October 1525

VIII, 407   An epistle from a certain Frenchman to a certain citizen of Basel.[1]

You have not received any letters from us for a long time, because the age is so turbulent as to drag everything into suspicion and make doing wrong seem just. This has reminded us that, when the omens are bad, it is wiser to keep appropriately silent about those things you cannot fitly tell a friend, than it is to betray both yourself and that friend. Things have come to such a pass that what one discusses with a friend about truth and innocence is interpreted as criminal.

But something has happened that has caused me to resume my habit of letter-writing. A copy of a certain letter has been circulated around our city, which both *Luther's supporters and those of the Roman pontiff have attributed to *Erasmus.[2] Its diction supports this attribution, but its acerbity does not—unless either Erasmus's language is not Erasmus's, or he is nourishing one thing in his heart whilst prating about quite another with his tongue—something that we do not much like hearing of anyone. At the same time rumours are spreading that there is no doubt about the letter's authorship, or about the following facts: that it was sent by him to Konrad *Pellikan, | and that it was read in public to your Council before they considered Oecolampadius's book.[3] All this has made me so uncertain and puzzled that I am going to await your explanation of the matter before I make up my mind to believe anything. For I find it hard to be convinced that this epistle is by Erasmus, given that the arguments being marshalled here seem to be not just weak ones, but no arguments at all. For what is the point of saying, "your argument is nothing but straw",[4] without demonstrating what parts of it are strawy? Or of not being able to adduce a cast iron argument that might break one of straw? Who indeed cannot see how inept it is to

VIII, 408

---

7 *discusses*] *commentatum esse* (literally, 'has been commented on')   19 *puzzled*] Greek ἄπορον (literally, 'helpless, trapped')

---

1   The true identity of author and recipient is confirmed not just by the content (see particularly lines 134f., 233–244), but above all by the fact the letter is plainly in Zwingli's hand. One sometimes has a sense that Zwingli is enjoying the subterfuge (see for example 144–146, 174–184), but the fact that it was felt necessary confirms the precarious nature of Oecolampadius's position in Basel at this point.
2   See 396, n. 1. In spite of Zwingli's—presumably honestly held—doubts, there is no reason to suppose that Erasmus's letter was not genuine, or that Pellikan was not its intended recipient.
3   The *De genuina ... expositione* (see 381, n. 2).
4   An allusion to EC 1637, line 78f.: *Rationes stupee sunt*.

write, "he (that is, Christ) took flesh upon himself once, so as not to give offence"[5]—where this is understood as meaning that Christ only once said that the flesh profits nothing,[6] and that therefore one cannot hold on the basis of this passage that, when he says "this is my body",[7] this should be understood as not referring to bodily flesh? For one can assert that it is of no consequence whether he, who is God, said "this is my body" more than once or once only. Only once did he say, "Let it not be so with you".[8] Will it then be permissible not only to seek authority but to destroy things by exerting authority over them? Only once did he say, "you shall not steal".[9] Is it then permissible to steal someone else's dole money, or to live on a pension given by a prince? Those things which proceed from the mouth of God cannot be made null and void. For heaven and earth must pass away before one jot or tittle is removed from his words.[10] Hence one should argue in this way: Christ once expressly stated, "the flesh profits nothing"; therefore he never offered it to anyone. For God does not offer things that are of no benefit to people. And when the disciples did not wonder at this, he, with all his authority, neither rejected nor condemned them. What can you say to all this—especially given that the letter-writer has stated a short while before, "Hitherto, along with all other Christians, I have worshipped in the Eucharist the Christ who suffered for me"?[11] Now if, like this man, the apostles had worshipped Christ in the Eucharist, they would have greatly wondered at the fact;[12] but we see no trace of this. And if they neither wondered at it nor worshipped it, then it was not they who established what has been passed down to us about the Eucharist. This is no light matter: the apostles evinced no wonder at the Eucharist; hence they did not celebrate it as we do. And which of us is content with wonderment? We even worship the thing whose very name means 'thanksgiving'.

38f. *For ... is*] *quasi vero* (literally 'as if indeed')

---

5   Quoted from *EC* 1637, line 79f.—in which, however, the writer attributes the words to Pellikan's "friends" and describes their arguments as constituting "nothing but straw".
6   John 6:63.
7   See Matthew 26:26, Mark 14:22, Luke 22:19, 1 Corinthians 11:24.
8   Luke 22:26.
9   Exodus 20:15.
10 Cf. Matthew 5:18.
11 Quoted from *EC* 1637, lines 69–71.
12 One assumes that, in this elliptical statement, the transubstantiated bread is understood.

VIII, 409 | And now this: "we are told to be spiritual, as if the flesh offered in the sacrament were a hindrance to the spirit".[13] It needs no effort to see how lazy and stupid this argument is! For no-one thinks that the physical sense as a whole is excluded by the words, "the flesh profits nothing"—except a person who is either in error or has no wish to be led back on to the path of truth. What is excluded is the view which the Jews had formed about Christ's flesh; that is, they thought they were being compelled to eat his corporeal flesh. Now when it is said here that Christ, in this entire speech, is urging us to be spiritual people, the main point of the argument comes into view— which is, in essence, that we should have faith in Christ. But the Jews did not read it in this way, as meaning that "eating flesh" should be understood as "having faith in Christ"—rather, they feared the spectre of flesh under their teeth. Therefore Christ did away with this reason for error, when he said, "the flesh profits nothing". Although he gave voice to this only once, he will never in perpetuity give his corporeal flesh to be ground down by teeth.

Now when our letter-writer asks whether the flesh offered in this way is harmful to the spirit, it becomes clear that he is not Erasmus: for the latter sees plainly that it hinders spiritual understanding to think that flesh is eaten at such a feast; and the Jews, in holding such an opinion, did not understand the force of the gospel that is preached here. And no more do those people understand it who still today are in thrall to the Jews' error. The disciples, with Simon as their spokesman, do however state that they believe, that is, that they have faith in Christ: for he is "the Son of the Living God".[14] Moreover, this flesh which they claim to have eaten in carnal yet invisible form certainly hinders spiritual understanding, and for this sole reason: that neither faith nor the senses can ever accept such an opinion. Even if an insolent mouth might boast otherwise—guided no doubt by hypocrisy—that mouth itself must see that it can hardly impress a faithful person of experienced judgement. "In some ineffable way", these people say.[15] Those words

---

65 *spectre*] Latin *glaucoma*   81–83 *that ... judgement*] there is no negation in the Latin, but the sense strongly suggests that one is understood. Hence we have added "hardly" (Latin *vix*)

13   Quoted from EC 1637, line 80f.
14   John 6:69.
15   Erasmus writes: "It accords wonderfully well with the ineffable love of God for all mankind that he should have wished those whom he redeemed with the body and blood of his Son to be nourished in some ineffable way by that same flesh and blood" (1637, lines 39–42).

LETTER 401   113

are their Telamonian shield;[16] to it they all flee. They have been defeated on
the basis of scripture, faith, reason; so they immediately retreat to this sanc-
tuary of theirs, "in some ineffable way". But Christ is light,[17] and one of the
most powerful reasons for his incarnation was that he might uncover darkness and hypocrisy, and destroy them. Who, then, can have brought about
afresh such impenetrable darkness? Who can have made hypocrisy stand
more securely than ever? What hypocrisy is greater than everyone pretend-
ing to hold a certain opinion which in fact no-one holds? We all wanted to
seem to believe that Christ's flesh is eaten here; but no-one actually believed
it.

    The epistle continues thus: "it is flesh, though perceived by none of our
senses".[18] In what way, then, is it flesh? You say: in the same way as the
flesh with which Christ was clothed when he went up to heaven. But in that
flesh he is sitting at the right hand of God. We have invented | these things.   *VIII, 410*
When we speak in this way we are disregarding scripture, faith and sensory
perception—that is, when we wish to fight without regard for the truth.

    Again it continues: "it is a pledge of God's love towards us, the consola-
tion of hope".[19] I have always thought that this pledge was the seal of the
Spirit,[20] with which we believe in Christ, the Son of God, who has been sent
into our hearts. For our part we say this: Christ called it a commemoration,
not a pledge; he himself is that pledge, insofar as he suffered death, not insofar as—sitting on his Father's throne—he is figuratively devoured by teeth.
Again, when he says, "it is the consolation of hope", I would ask, whose consolation? Is it for the eyes or for the soul? Not for the eyes: for they assert
that it is eaten invisibly, that is, "in some ineffable way". What remains, then,
is that it must be a consolation for the soul; but how can flesh (call it by
whatever name you will) comfort the soul? This requires the spirit, which
can dwell in the soul. They say, "these are philosophical matters, not theological ones"—as if such things as "it is a pledge of God's love towards us,
the consolation of hope" truly came from Delphi, or had been brought from

---

101 *seal*] *arrobonem*, more correctly *arrobonam* ('pledge, earnest')

---

16   A reference to Homer's *Iliad* (books VI–VII, XIV, XVI): the Telamonian Ajax has a mas-
      sive shield made from seven cowhides covered with bronze, which enables him to
      escape injury even in three combats against Hector.
17   John 8:12.
18   *EC* 1637, line 81 f.
19   *EC* 1637, line 82 f.
20   Cf. II Corinthians 1:21 f.

between the Cherubim on the Ark of the Covenant.[21] What, though, is the point of inventing a new way of chewing flesh which would enable us to say that flesh is eaten spiritually—when the soul cannot feed on flesh any more than a sheep can? Now we are not at all ashamed to speak in this way: we do eat flesh spiritually. It is not that we are now taking 'eat' to mean 'believe'; but we are asserting that we eat this fleshly, physical, tangible flesh in a spiritual and non-sensual way—even if the Roman pontiff compelled Berengar to confess something different.[22]

After this it continues: "The word of God is on our side—we are told, 'this is my body, which is given for you', etc.".[23] If we do not allow that this is a trope, we also make Christ a stone: for he is indeed a stone,[24] and we have no means of satisfying a quarrelsome person that Christ is not a stone unless we understand this as a trope. For it is as abhorrent to the senses and to faith to eat Christ's flesh as it is for him to be a stone. If you said, "but Christ spoke thus", I would say: Christ also said, "I am the vine";[25] John called him a lamb;[26] and in turn Christ himself said that John the Evangelist was the son of his (Christ's) mother.[27] Nor is it difficult for those who accept tropes to demonstrate that the word for a thing can be read as a sign of that thing; for scripture clearly supports this. Circumcision is called a covenant,[28] though it is merely the sign of a covenant; | a lamb is called the Passover,[29] though it was merely the sign of Passover, etc.—just as your Oecolampadius and Zwingli have proven in published works.[30] But it should not be forgotten

---

120 *Roman pontiff*] the manuscript reads *Rom ponti*. The editors of ZW make this into an accusative, *Romanum pontificem*; but this seems to us to make less sense than a nominative, *Romanus pontifex* (which we therefore translate)

---

21 A sarcastic reference to two iconic sources of authoritative wisdom from the ancient world: the Oracle of Delphi, housed in the Temple of Apollo on Mount Parnassus, and the sacred chest containing the tablets on which the Ten Commandments had been written. Jehovah himself was said to dwell between the two golden Cherubim adorning the Ark's cover—see for example 1 Samuel 4:4.
22 Berengar of Tours (c. 1000–1088), a leading light at the influential school of progressive theology at Chartres Cathedral, who was a long-time critic of the doctrine of transubstantiation and was forced several times reluctantly to recant these views—most notably by Pope Gregory VII at the Lateran Councils of 1078 and 1079.
23 EC 1637, line 83f.
24 Cf. Psalm 118:22.
25 John 15:5.
26 John 1:29.
27 John 19:26f.
28 Acts 7:8.
29 Cf. Exodus 12:21.
30 In the former's *De genuina ... expositione* (see 381, n. 2) and the *latter's Subsidium* (see 384, n. 2).

that no-one argues these words are understood in this way simply because it is possible to understand them in this way;[31] rather, as far as I can tell, this is how their argument proceeds. Physical flesh does not profit anything, hence there must be a trope in the words, "this is my body"; just as in many other places the plain and obvious truth forces one to understand these words figuratively. For it is right to conclude that Christ, in Matthew, cursed a fig-tree;[32] and so in Mark it is clearly a trope when he is reported as having forgiven the tree.[33] Indeed, it is easier to regard both phrases as tropes than to deny that one of them is. How monstrous it is to misapply in this way things that have been correctly stated and put together, and then secretly to pass them on to one's little friends! Moreover when he denies that one cannot find amongst the ancients any author who states that the body of Christ is not present (in the sacrament), he is being irresponsible. For let him read in *On Consecration*, part 2, chapter 1, the sentence beginning "Why?", and he will see what Augustine says.[34] But leaving these things aside, what is the point of advancing this argument? For the fewer such references we find in the ancients, the clearer it becomes that such a foolish opinion was not commonly held at that time.

Still others say: "Let us use those words which Christ himself used". Quite right, as long as you speak to the people with whom Christ spoke, using the language that Christ used. For then it will happen that the language they both hear and speak will enter their minds in no other way but figuratively. Now in truth, if you use figurative speech with people who have no knowledge of it—see how impudent and perfidious you are, allowing people who cannot comprehend the figurative meaning to draw a perverse one from it.

As I say, all these things which this person has blabbed so idly mean that I cannot in any way believe that the letter is by Erasmus. And he would never

---

140 *truth forces*] *veritas alio in loco cogit* (literally, 'in another place the truth forces')—we read *alio in loco* as tautological   141 *fig-tree*] *virga* (literally, 'twig'). Our version follows all standard English translations, and also the Vulgate (*fici arborem*)

---

31 A response to words put by Erasmus into the mouths of his opponents in letter 1637: "What weight are we to attach to an argument like this: 'These words can be interpreted in this way, therefore they *must* be interpreted in this way'" (line 94f.).
32 Matthew 21:19.
33 Cf. Mark 11:21–23.
34 A reference to Augustine as cited in the *Decretum Gratiani*, the third part of which is entitled 'De consecratione'—see *Corpus Iuris Canonici*, ed. Emil Friedberg, 2 vols (Leipzig: Tauchnitz, 1879–1881), I, col. 1331 (D. 2 de cons. c. 47). The sentence in question is *Ut quid paras dentem et uentrem? Crede, et manducasti* ('Why do you make ready your teeth and belly? Believe, and you have eaten').

inveigh so sharply against his friend *Pellikan.[35] It seems to be by someone else, someone who hopes to hide under another person's skin. | The fact, however, that the reading of this epistle before the Council is said to have influenced it so much that Erasmus, Ber, Cantiuncula and Amerbach were immediately appointed as assessors of Oecolampadius's book,[36] leads one to suspect a trick. I exempt Erasmus here, for he has acquired a far from mediocre knowledge of Hebrew letters. But what, I ask, will the others do on this battlefield? One of them is not only a sophist, but also entirely ignorant of sacred or humanist literature. How, after all, could a she-bear[37] learn her letters? The other two are lawyers, who are perhaps not to be despised; but what do they know of the figurative expressions of sacred texts and Hebrew literature? Let everyone practice what he has learnt.[38] Fabius[39] has asserted that skills are not only to be perfected by experts, but also to be judged by them. Consider for me, I ask, the opposite case: if Cantiuncula had written something about estates, aqueducts or dealing with a contractor, and the Council had appointed Oecolampadius to assess this book; would not all of you burst out in uproarious laughter, just as you would if a pig came into the room wearing boots? Thanks be to God if you do indeed have so many men who can assess what Oecolampadius has written; but I am very much afraid that in this matter it would be more appropriate to require Oecolampadius to sit in judgement over the scholars not just of your city, but of the whole world, than that he should be subjected to anyone else's judgement. Why, I ask, are we now turning to these weapons? Or does it escape people's memory how much all of us who toil in the service of learning and piety have striven to ensure that no violence is done to anyone's writings? That what is sacrosanct should not be subjected to the judgement of a few? That matters should be regulated by the scriptures, not by a secular authority? Why then do we appeal to the consensus of the world and of councils? Ought we indeed to speak of consensus, when not only does no-one consent, but no-one even has an opinion? How much store the author of this epistle

---

35 Deliberately or not, Zwingli here significantly overstates the extent to which Erasmus would at this point have viewed Pellikan as his friend. Much of the language in letters 1637 and 1640 is vituperative indeed.
36 See 396, lines 29–35 and n. 10–13.
37 Latin *ursa*: a not particularly subtle or tasteful reference to Ludwig Ber (see 396, n. 10).
38 An allusion to Cicero, quoting a Greek proverb, in *Tusculanae Disputationes* 1.18.41: *quam quisque norit artem, in hac se exerceat*; we might translate this as 'let the cobbler stick to his last'. See also Erasmus, *Adagia* 1.6.15 (515).
39 Presumably the historian Quintus Fabius Pictor (3rd century BCE), whose works— including the statement cited here—are now lost.

actually sets by the judgement of the church and the consent of the world and of councils can be seen at the very start, when he writes the following about both Pellikan's opinion and his own: "For you thought one should profess that the Lord's body is indeed present in the sacrament, but that how it is present is an issue that is best left to God, who knows all things. My comment about your position on that was that it seemed to be rather simplistic: various complex puzzles of theology could be evaded if a Christian man were permitted to dissent from anything that had been established on the authority of councils and endorsed by every church and nation over so many centuries".[40] That is what the man wrote. Do you see, my dear X., what the author of this letter thinks in private and says in public? He would like to think that the body is present in the sacrament, but how is this matter to be "left to God"? For him, the very idea of transubstantiation has fallen by the wayside, as has the idea of eating sensorially-perceptible flesh that was forced upon Berengar.[41] So how much value do you think he places on the judgement of the church—hearing that he plainly holds a different view, but keeps it secret because | it is dangerous to state it openly in the midst of tyranny? Why therefore is that man allowed to form his own opinion— which the Roman church does not share—without regard to the judgement or testimony of the sacred letters, whereas Oecolampadius, basing his case on so many scriptures, is not allowed to state the truth? For that is why both the (in my view) false Pellikan and the false Erasmus dare to make pronouncements like this: "It seems to us very easy to declare that the Lord's body is eaten, but not in the way that the Pontiff of the church or the consensus of the world teaches". Is this view based on scripture? "But", they might say, "because of the authority of the churches we do not declare openly what we think". Learn, then, that this consensus of the world, just like your consensus, only exists because of the church and the Pontiff. If the latter were not standing in your way, you would be thinking differently; hence your opinion is not your own, but that of the church. This is what the mind of all mortals must seem to you to say: "If such a thing were permitted by the authority of the Pontiff, the church, the councils, and by my fear of them, I would never believe that flesh was eaten in the Mass." This is that "consensus of the world, the councils, etc." of yours. And I should add something else. Just as that man swears by Christ that he has never held the opinion that the body of Christ is

VIII, 413

---

202 X.] N., similarly denoting someone whose name is unknown or withheld

---

40   Erasmus, letter 1637 (lines 30–36).
41   See n. 22 above.

not present in the Mass, I in turn will swear as follows: may Christ indeed be angry with me for ever if those who pretend to think that corporeal flesh is eaten spiritually do so solely out of fear of the Jews—and not because they believe the body is actually eaten. What need is there of more? Those who are spiritual discern all things.[42]

Examine everything with care, my friend, and tell me as soon as you can which parts of this comedy are true. For here we are gripped by a desire for the truth: we will not change any aspect of our opinion if Erasmus disagrees with Oecolampadius on this question, or if the former provokes the Council into violence by directing the full flood of his eloquence against the latter; but we are not prepared to get accustomed to accepting everyone's fictions as though they were true. The group of those who protest but are reluctant to speak openly agree with the view of Oecolampadius and Zwingli. Be persuaded of this, you who worship Christ at Basel: Zwingli and Oecolampadius are able to bear the burden of this disputation on their own, as long as the matter is governed by the scriptures and the scholars of your city have some sense.

Farewell for now, and take care that the Council does not lord it over scripture, but handles it carefully.
From Christ. 28th October 1525.

Original: Zürich, Zentralbibliothek, Msc F. 37, fol. 193f. (Thesaurus Hottingerianus). Copy: Zürich, Zentralbibliothek, Ms S 15, no. 43.

---

244 *sense*] *nasus* (literally, 'nose')

---

42   Cf. 1 Corinthians 2:15.

404   Oecolampadius to Zwingli—Basel, 4th November (1525)

Grace from Christ, my brother. Nothing new has been heard since my little books were confiscated from the booksellers by the Council.¹ Silence reigns, and this is feeding a certain sense of mystery. There is a little rumour to the effect that I am to be driven out. But that is always around.² Fear is seizing the flock. I, hoping in the Lord, think it is unworthy to look back from the plough;³ hence even on All Saints' Day, as I was observing the feast with the living saints, I took it upon myself to celebrate the Lord's Supper in a rather simpler way.⁴ It may be that this has aggravated our opponents again. But when are they not irritated, save perhaps at our misfortunes? People are saying that the Council have been gifted an opportunity by *Erasmus's letter⁵ and *Karlstadt's trifling recantation;⁶ and no doubt the fauns will dance, especially when they have seen the pipe they will be dancing to. Your response to Erasmus⁷ pleased me beyond measure—I am sending back the handwritten copy you sent me. This is the way to discern those lying spirits!

I commend *Hätzer to you.⁸ He is beloved by our friends at Augsburg not least on account of his faith, even though he was forced to leave there by the power and authority of those who preached a breaded Christ more diligently than a crucified one | and could not prevail over his opinion.⁹ And so these

VIII, 417

VIII, 418

---

2 *the Council*] Greek τῇ βουλῖ (*sic*, one might expect βουλῇ)   14 *handwritten copy*] Greek αὐτόγραφον

---

1   See 381, n. 2.
2   See for example 319, n. 2 f.
3   Cf. Luke 9:62.
4   See above, p. 17 and n. 64.
5   See 396 and 401, *passim*.
6   *Erklerung, wie Carlstat sein lere von dem hochwirdigen Sacrament und andere achtet vnd geacht haben wil* (Wittenberg: Rhau-Grunenberg, 1525; Leu/Weidmann A109)—ed. WA XVIII, 455–466; trans. Burnett, *Pamphlets*, 258–269. Oecolampadius exaggerates in calling this pamphlet a "recantation" (*revocatio*), but its tone of compromise, publication in Wittenberg and appearance alongside an introduction by *Luther certainly imply a rapprochement with the Lutherans. On it see Barge, *Bodenstein*, II, 366–369; Burnett, *Karlstadt*, 75 f.
7   No. 401 above.
8   Following Hätzer's arrival in Basel, Oecolampadius made successful efforts to reconcile him with Zwingli—see Goeters, *Hätzer*, 69–73.
9   The elephant in the room here is Oecolampadius's friend (and successor as Cathedral Preacher at Augsburg) Urbanus Rhegius (or 'Rieger', 1489–1541), now that city's leading reformer and a continuing proponent of Christ's 'real presence' in the bread and wine. Hätzer's criticism of Rhegius's eucharistic theology was the trigger for the former's expulsion from Augsburg—see Goeters, *Hätzer*, 66 f. Rhegius was in fact a distinguished human-

people are now writing that he is an outlaw, because he has caused trouble for you and *Leo, and is numbered among the catabaptists[10]—although I can see clearly that he has long since come to his senses, and that he is utterly devoted to the two of you. Perhaps, when he has purged himself before you, it will also be easier for him to return to Augsburg.[11] Until now nothing about his behaviour has displeased me. He will bring with him my book about the Eucharist, which he has translated.[12] We will follow your advice in the matter of whether or not it should be published.

Sebastian Meyer is to be brought before the Council today; the reason for this is not known.[13] My soul has a foreboding of something sinister, I do not know what. For our adversaries leave no stone unturned, and do harm in any way they can.

May your soul be joyful, and may you triumph over the new baptists.[14]
Farewell.
4th November. Basel.
Your Oecolampadius.
To Huldrych Zwingli, most pious minister of Christ in word and deed, antistes of the Zürichers, his brother.

Original: Zürich, Staatsarchiv, E II 349, p. 62 (autograph). Copy: Zürich, Zentralbibliothek, Ms S 15, no. 48.

---

29 *our adversaries*] Greek ἐχθροί

---

ist and conciliatory Lutheran with Zwinglian sympathies, who remained in amicable contact with several Swiss evangelicals—though attempts by Zwingli to win him over entirely to the Zürichers' cause foundered on what the latter saw as Rhegius's "chameleon-like" nature: see Zschoch, "Zwingli und Augsburg", 168; Zschoch, *Existenz*; *CoE* III, 151–153; *OER* III, 429 f.; *TRE* XXIX, 155–157; *BBKL* VIII, 122–134; *VL 16* V, 282–289.

10 A reference above all to Hätzer's behaviour while still in Zürich in late 1524 and early 1525: at that stage he was close to such anabaptists as Konrad Grebel and Felix Manz, and supported them at the First and Second Anabaptist Disputations, resulting in his expulsion on 18th January 1525. See Goeters, *Hätzer*, 46–53.

11 Hätzer proved to Zwingli that he had "come to his senses"—at least temporarily—during a short visit to Zürich between 5th and 9th November: he supported Zwingli at the Third Anabaptist Disputation there between 6th and 8th, and had what was obviously a mutually satisfactory personal meeting with him on 9th (see Goeters, *Hätzer*, 70–73). Oecolampadius is, however, being over-optimistic about Hätzer's chances of returning to Augsburg.

12 See 394, n. 11.

13 Meyer (see 352, n. 10) had come to Basel following his expulsion from Schaffhausen. The reason for the Council's action remains unknown, but it resulted at least indirectly in Meyer being driven out of Basel along with Sebastian Hofmeister (see 376, n. 7).

14 In the forthcoming disputation (see n. 11 above).

405 Oecolampadius to Zwingli—Basel, 11th November (1525)

Grace and peace from Christ, my brother. There is nothing new this week. And nothing happened to Sebastian Meyer[1] in his trial, though Satan tempted him somewhat, with the result that he was expelled from here, just as Farel was;[2] that is how we take care of our guests, true Sodomites that we are![3]

I am sending you *Karlstadt's recantation[4]—only to recite such a palinode in the way that he does is not to recant! Indeed, even such tenuous arguments as those that Martin[5] now opportunistically regards as fit for use can uphold the truth against him.

They say that the Landgrave of Hesse[6] has written to the Margrave of Baden[7] that he should be steadfast in spirit with regard to the gospel, and that he himself will protect those who preach it. They say the same about the Count Palatine.[8] But we do not make flesh our arm.[9]

Some of our Augsburg friends have strongly recommended *Hätzer to me. So I will be at pains to see whether, in our dealings, he departs from the manners he has shown up to now. I am indeed much exercised by this on a daily basis, for it is in the nature of letters that what they have set down can easily be shown to be false when confronted by the reality of a living person. He told me about the absurdities and folly of the catabaptists.[10]

---

1 See 352, n. 10 and 404, n. 13.
2 See 329, n. 2.
3 Cf. Genesis 19:4 f., where the men of Sodom seek to do violence to the two angels visiting their city, in contrast to the hospitality just shown them by Abraham and Lot.
4 See 404, n. 6.
5 *Luther.
6 *Philipp of Hesse.
7 Philipp I, Margrave of Baden-Sponheim (1494–1533).
8 Ludwig V ("the Pacific"), Count Palatine of the Rhine (1478–1544).
9 Cf. Jeremiah 17:5. Our version reflects the diction of the KJV, just as that of Oecolampadius echoes the Vulgate: *Maledictus homo qui confidit in homine et ponit carnem brachium suum.*
10 Hätzer had been present at the recent disputation between Zwingli and anabaptist representatives in Zürich—see 404, n. 11.

VIII, 420 | Thanks be to God, who has been faithful to you and, in his mercy, will not forsake you.
Farewell.
Basel, 11th November.
Your Oecolampadius.
To Huldrych Zwingli, most faithful servant of Christ, his brother.
Zürich.

Original: Zürich, Staatsarchiv, E II 349, p. 87 (autograph). Copy: Zürich, Zentralbibliothek, Ms S 15, no. 55.

406   Oecolampadius to Zwingli—Basel, 13th November (1525)

Grace from Christ, my brother. Lest any of our affairs should escape your notice: yesterday the parish priests of St Alban's and St Leonard's Churches[1] were summoned by the Mayor[2] and Chief Guild Master[3] and were asked to sacrifice (as they call it) according to the old practice, that is, to cele-
5   brate Mass—or, alternatively, to cease their ministry of the word. St Alban's did not have anything to hand that he could use to plead his case; so he was willing to give in and to accept such an impiety, as long as the people did not intervene to prevent it.[4] How little faith that man has! St Leonard's, armed with letters from his congregation, stated that he was not neglect-
10   ing anything that pertained to his office, and that he had been subjected to this harassment once before.[5] I do not know what will happen next. I wonder why they have not summoned me also. Perhaps they reckon they will find something offensive in my little book,[6] and that this will make it easier for them to attack me. Certainly we see that Satan is leaving no stone
15   unturned.

On that same day I had again celebrated the Lord's Supper,[7] so that the people, seeing our simplicity and integrity, might not suspect that anything serious was afoot. Given that the papists are forever shouting that we are doing away with all the sacraments, necessity requires us to speak openly

VIII, 421

---

16 *celebrated*] *adornaram* (more correctly, *adornaveram*; literally 'adorned, prepared')

---

1   Respectively Peter Frauenberger (see 367, n. 2) and Markus Bertschi (367, n. 1).
2   Between 1522 and 1529 the mayoralty alternated between Adelberg Meyer zum Pfeil (1474–1548), whose support for evangelical reform tended to be moderate and equivocal, and the former mercenary Heinrich Meltinger (d. 1531), who emerged as its leading political opponent. On Meyer see *CoE* II, 440 f.; Schindler, *BD*, 712 f.; Füglister, *Handwerksregiment*, 338 f.; Wackernagel, *Basel*, III, 418 f. On Meltinger see *CoE* II, 430 f.; Füglister, *Handwerksregiment*, 302 f.; Wackernagel, *Basel*, III, 419.
3   Jakob Meyer zum Hirzen. See above, p. XVIII, n. 3.
4   In fact it was Frauenberger (of St Alban's), rather than the apparently more recalcitrant Bertschi (of St Leonard's), who was required to resign his office and leave Basel.
5   Bertschi had been tried by the Council in May 1525 in the wake of a controversial sermon and accusations that he had been inciting rebellion against the city government. See Wackernagel, *Basel*, III, 367–369.
6   The *De genuina ... expositione*—see 381, n. 2; 394, n. 11; 396, n. 13.
7   One assumes, not least from Oecolampadius's use of "again" and "simplicity", that he has been continuing to use his new vernacular Eucharistic liturgy—see 404, n. 4.

about the Eucharist—because they do not really believe their own teachers. As you advised,[8] I will write carefully to Urbanus about unction[9]—he will not take it amiss, even if perhaps he will not go along with it.

| Ludwig[10] has given an eye-witness report, quite brilliantly and with abundant spirit, on certain aspects of the disputation you instigated.[11] See to it, I beg, that these things are communicated at your leisure to those who are eager for news. For those who listened to the proceedings cannot report every single thing, as the importance of the occasion really demands.

I hope that all the brothers are well: *Leo, *Myconius and Ceporinus.[12] And you—be happy with your wife,[13] and not disturbed by the efforts of our fellow-countrymen! They will not be able to achieve anything against Christ. If he has chosen the people here for himself, he will guide them by his shepherds.

Basel, 13th November.
Oecolampadius.
To Huldrych Zwingli, his dearest brother.

Original: Zürich, Staatsarchiv, E II 349, p. 159 (autograph). Copy: Zürich, Zentralbibliothek, Ms S 15, no. 58.

---

20 *the Eucharist*] *re ipsa* (literally, 'the thing itself')

---

8 No letter from Zwingli containing such advice has survived.
9 Urbanus Rhegius (see 404, n. 9). This letter also appears to have been lost. From the context, one assumes that Oecolampadius means specifically the sacrament of Extreme Unction.
10 *Hätzer.
11 See 404, n. 11.
12 See 306, n. 11. Ceporinus was in fact to die the following month.
13 Anna *Reinhart.

411 Oecolampadius to Zwingli—Basel, 24th November (1525)

Grace and peace from Christ. *Hätzer[1] will tell you, my brother, what is happening here. There is one thing of which I would not wish you to be ignorant, namely that my fellow-citizens have not received my little book[2] very favourably—for they had been hoping that your doctrine had already been defeated, and now they see it sprouting forth again with such support as I can give it. They were, however, civil enough to act in accordance with their old way of rejecting our ideas—by releasing the book in the first instance,[3] rather than condemning it without a hearing. And so I have responded to them briefly, amicably and fearlessly—otherwise, certainly, than they deserve. I will make sure that a copy is made, so that I can share it with you also. You will see that the enemy does not pass up any opportunity for consolidating | his rule.

Our people here are doing everything in their own way, and unless the Lord blesses his little flock, there will be dire consequences one day. They will not be able to cover over their hidden wound for long. At some point they will relieve their own pain in an unexpected and inopportune way. It may be that they will fall into the trap they are preparing for others. Hätzer will tell you more.

Farewell, together with your household and the brothers.
Basel, 24th November.
Your Oecolampadius.
To Huldrych Zwingli, overseer of the Zürich church, his dearest brother.

Original: Zürich, Staatsarchiv, E II 349, p. 82 (scribal hand). Copy: Zürich, Zentralbibliothek, Ms S 15, no. 70.

---

3 *fellow-citizens*] Greek ξυμπατριῶται (literally, 'fellow-countrymen')

1 One assumes he is delivering the letter.
2 This must refer to a handwritten draft of what was to become his *Ad ecclesiastas Suevos Antisyngramma* (see 443, n. 2), a response to the *Syngramma* of *Brenz. See 391, n. 5; Staehelin, *Lebenswerk*, 287–291; Jung, 'Abendmahlsstreit', 150–153.
3 In the sense of permitting the publication of a volume currently circulating only in manuscript form. Oecolampadius is contrasting the Basel Council's behaviour favourably with their treatment of his *De genuina ... expositione* in the previous month—see 381, n. 2; 396, lines 28–35 and n. 13; 404, lines 1–3 and n. 1.

412   Oecolampadius to Zwingli—Basel, 26th November (1525)

Grace and peace from the Lord, my brother. Let us know if anything in our reply to the Swabian brothers displeases you.[1] To me, certainly, they seem to err most grossly when they ascribe divine majesty not just to the symbols but also to the words.[2] Perhaps you will not have enough leisure to read what has been written on both sides of the argument. But steal away whatever time you can when the occasion arises. It is best to know what our adversaries are objecting to, for even the least of them is not to be despised. On this issue they are certainly not holding back from bludgeoning us, because they despise us beyond measure.

Otherwise we have no news here. The magistracy will not support the Suffragan[3] in his ministry of the word. Hence the others will need to be more vigilant. The attached letter should be returned to Christoph.[4] It came from Strasbourg, but came back to me again within a week inside someone else's letters.

Farewell, together with your wife and the brothers. Admonish Ludwig *Hätzer freely, as you need to. But if he does not heed you, let me know. Farewell again.
20th November.
| Also greet dearest Wilhelm von Zell[5] heartily on my behalf—if he is still with you.
Your Oecolampadius.
To dearest Huldrych Zwingli, most vigilant bishop of the Zürich church, his brother.

Original: Zürich, Staatsarchiv, E II 349, p. 133 (autograph). Copy: Zürich, Zentralbibliothek, Ms S 15, no. 71.

---

1 On the "Swabian brothers" see 391, n. 5. On Oecolampadius's reply see 411, n. 2; 443, n. 2. For Zwingli's view of *Brenz see 416, lines 1–27.
2 A reaction to the Swabians' essentially Lutheran position that, for a rite to constitute a sacrament, it needs to involve not only a physical sign, but also divine words of institution, quoted *verbatim*.
3 Tillman Limperger (see 319, n. 5). Oecolampadius's designation of him is not entirely misleading, in that he was allowed to remain as titular Suffragan Bishop of Basel even after his suspension from active ministry on account of his evangelical sympathies.
4 *Froschauer.
5 See 376, n. 8.

416 Zwingli to Oecolampadius—Zürich, 1st December 1525

Grace and peace from the Lord. Most learned Oecolampadius, I have read *Brenz's book.[1] My judgement of it was such that, believe me, if Ludwig[2] had not reassured me from *Capito and you verbally that he has now written you an entirely friendly and Christian letter,[3] I would have been on the point of leading a major attack on that man. The reason for this is that, though he seems to be eloquent and moderately learned in languages, he ties things together very badly; he rages impudently when it is out of place to do so; he does violence to the holy scriptures; and he brazenly brings such calamity upon us that, as we said, if your words had not restrained us, we would have abandoned all hope of him. We have read half of the work of yours that we mentioned,[4] because Ludwig took it back straightaway, in order to return it to you. What you say is sound, but a man like him—unless he really is other than his words make him appear—will turn up his nose at it. May I perish if I ever encounter anything more arrogant or foolish! Is Brenz a good man? Brenz, who reveres his teacher less than a dog reveres sacred things? Who accuses us of hypocrisy, sedition and I know not what else? Who, having combined youthful boldness with all too little eloquence, foolishly sallies forth in this way to denounce people's good name? He is a Lutheran scholar: one of those who know only one thing, namely to twist scripture as much and in as many directions as possible, and to storm about uncivilly, going about their business with a populist clamour rather than with measured eloquence. If his book is published by some printer or other, please see to it that yours comes out at the same time.[5] Then I or another | of our people will make an appropriate response—one that you will not find lacking

VIII, 446

VIII, 447

---

12 *What ... sound*] *Solida sunt tua* (literally, 'yours are sound')—we are assuming that *verba* or *argumenta* is understood   21 *with ... clamour*] *tribunitiis clamoribus* (literally, 'with the loud noises of the tribune')

---

1 The *Syngramma*: see 391, n. 5.
2 *Hätzer.
3 Probably a reference to a letter addressed by Brenz to Capito and *Bucer in Strasbourg, and dated 22nd November 1525—in which his tone is firm but essentially conciliatory. Capito forwarded it to Oecolampadius, along with a letter of his own, later in November—see *OeBA* I, 421–426 (no. 307). Brenz's letter is printed in *BC* II, 59–70 (no. 112).
4 The draft of the *Antisyngramma*—see 411, n. 2.
5 This seems more or less to have happened: certainly *Froschauer's edition of the *Antisyngramma* came out in early 1526.

in modesty, but which uses levity and ridicule to teach this bold young tyro to fight more cautiously in future.[6] We want to have sport with him, rather than to triumph over him.

You be constant, as you are wont to be! For our people are constant also. They made no concession of any kind to the Berners when asked to allow Mass to be celebrated in just one small chapel.[7] We will be sending a delegation to Bern in the same way that they sent one to us;[8] I believe they will set out all the ways in which certain Helvetians have hitherto been putting pressure on our city, and will ask us in turn to begin discussing in public questions of both peace and heavenly doctrine.[9]

Christoph will endeavour to publish your book for the Germans by 4th December at the first attempt.[10] Next spring will bring with it unbridled disturbances, | but for the princes, rather than the cities to deal with—if the latter are but careful.[11] Let not your arms grow weary:[12] no-one has ever fought for a more just cause than we do! What of it that we have many adversaries? The truth will overcome, it will overcome all of them, and the thoughts of many hearts will be revealed;[13] hypocrisy will be made known; and finally the truth, wherever it has been hidden hitherto, will rise at last undefeated,

VIII, 448

---

6   As far as is known Zwingli did not write a response aimed specifically at Brenz, but his cogent vernacular treatment of the Eucharist, *Ein klare Underrichtung vom Nachtmal Christi*, appeared as early as 23rd February 1526 (Zürich: Froschauer)—ed. ZW IV, 789–862 (no. 75); trans. Bromiley, 185–238. On it see Burnett, *Debating*, 179–183; eadem, *Karlstadt*, 88–90.
7   A delegation from the Bern magistrates had arrived in Zürich two days earlier, on 29th November, to negotiate at least unofficially on behalf of the Helvetic Confederation as a whole. Bern had emerged as the likeliest broker of a deal with Zürich following the latter's highly contentious abolition of the Mass in Holy Week 1525.
8   In fact these representatives arrived in Bern only on 21st December.
9   "Certain Helvetians" could refer to the conservatively Catholic Cantons, or to those representatives of the more theologically moderate Cantons who had visited Zürich in September 1525. Attempts to reach a compromise failed, but Zwingli here at least seems sanguine about the prospect of a disputation—of the kind, presumably, which did eventually take place at Baden in May 1526.
10 Froschauer; see n. 5 above. By "the Germans" Zwingli presumably means Brenz's circle in and around Schwäbisch Hall.
11 Given that he refers to potential rural, rather than urban unrest, Zwingli is perhaps fearing—alongside, no doubt, many theological and political conflicts—a return to the violence of the Peasants' War, which had been at its height between March and June 1525.
12 Cf. Galatians 6:9.
13 Cf. Luke 2:35.

for all those who are themselves undefeated. The world agrees fully with our opinion—not this evil world, but the one which truly is written in the heavens.[14]

Farewell, and press on! There is nothing we cannot do through Christ.[15] One thing had slipped my mind: see to it especially that you deflect Brenz from waging such a diffuse campaign and make him contend instead within certain limits; for the flesh profits nothing, etc.[16] We have also recommended to Hätzer that he write to you.

From Zurich, 1st December 1525, in haste.
Your Huldrych Zwingli.
To Johannes Oecolampadius, evangelist of Basel, his dearest brother.

Original: Zofingen, Stadtbibliothek, StBZ Pa 14:1,16 (20); accessible online. Two copies: Zürich, Zentralbibliothek, Ms S 15, no. 75f.

---

14   Cf. Hebrews 12:23.
15   Philippians 4:13.
16   John 6:63: Zwingli's formulation (*caro non prodest quicquam*) quotes directly from the Vulgate.

418 Oecolampadius to Zwingli—Basel, 6th December (1525)

VIII, 451

May the grace of Christ always be with you, my brother! Your opinion of my good friend *Brenz¹ seems to me (alas!) all too true. A few years ago this man was the mildest of all the people I knew; but I don't know what Fury might now be pricking him. I fear for this Absalom, lest he tend the hairs of his rhetoric in a way that leads him into very great harm.² I pray that God might lead him into better things. I gave him sufficient warning—if only he did not spurn such admonitions! He has also been admonished by the Strasbourg brothers, especially by *Capito. I hear that a rather arrogant letter to *Bucer about my book is being spread about in Brenz's duchy.³ I have not yet seen it, however.⁴ The Strasbourg brothers are concerned to see whether the matter can be brought forward for discussion, and I would choose this approach.⁵ People oppose one another a great deal when they are apart, but less so when they are present together. Besides, since a friend has taken the trouble to have a book published and been roundly censured for it, I will (following your advice) make him see that it is juvenile to play around with such great matters.⁶

My spirit has been greatly refreshed by the constancy of your citizens, who cultivate the things of God so faithfully and behave in the wisest way

---

4f. *lest ... harm*] *ne capillos rethoricationis suæ in damnum suum maximum nutriat* (literally, 'lest he nourish the hairs of his rhetoric into the greatest harm')

---

1   See 416, lines 1–27.
2   An allusion to the baleful end met by David's arrogant son Absalom in the Wood of Ephraim (II Samuel 18:6–15): his hirsute head is caught in an oak tree as he seeks to ride past, leaving him hanging defencelessly before his eventual assassin, Joab.
3   Schwäbisch Hall was strictly speaking an imperial free city, but Oecolampadius presumably has in mind its geographical and Brenz's personal links to Württemberg and Duke *Ulrich.
4   The letter from Brenz to Bucer dated 3rd October 1525 and published as *Epistola de verbis Domini, "Hoc est Corpus meum", opinionem quorundam de Eucharistia refellens* (Hagenau: Setzer, 1526)—ed. BC II, 39–45 (no. 104). Alongside clear statements of his sacramental theology that might indeed be regarded as "arrogant", Brenz remains, on a personal level, complimentary to Oecolampadius—"whom, even if I now differ from him, I with good reason both admire and venerate greatly" (*cui ... etiamsi nunc dissentiam, sed iussta causa summe et admiror et veneror*, line 32 f.).
5   This discussion took place at the very end of 1525, at Guttenberg Castle on the Neckar, under the auspices of the Lutheran aristocrat Dietrich von Gemmingen (d. 1526). In the end neither Oecolampadius nor the Strasbourg reformers were present; but they were represented by Simon Grynaeus—see p. XVIII, n. 4. His report on the proceedings, addressed to Oecolampadius and dated 7th January 1526, is printed in *OeBA* I, 449 f. (no. 323).
6   See 416, lines 23–27.

possible. If God is for us, who can be against us?[7] If God is not for those who trust in him, whom will he be for at the last? Would that the citizens of Basel followed their example sometimes! But they are of tender years;[8] I will say no more than that.

Our Suffragan[9] has found a successor for his pulpit, the Suffragan Bishop of Freising—a wolf, if I am not mistaken.[10] He will probably accept and be installed in his office;[11] there is no danger at all in this. But they also say that Treger, | the Augustinian Provincial,[12] is going to perform the office of a preacher here. As I see it, Satan is afraid for him. We are waiting to see what new legates our Council are going to announce.[13] For our adversaries are making threats; but they will not be able to do anything aside from the Lord's will. Let us hope in him.

VIII, 452

Farewell to you and all your loved ones in Christ.
Basel, 6th December.
Johannes Oecolampadius.
It has not been possible to send this small bundle of letters from Strasbourg before.
To Huldrich Zwingli, most capable Bishop of Zürich, his dearest brother.

Original: Zürich, Staatsarchiv, E II 349, p. 13 (autograph). Copy: Zürich, Zentralbibliothek, Ms S 15, no. 79.

---

24 *wolf*] Greek λύκον (cf. John 10:12).

---

7   Romans 8:31.
8   In the sense, presumably, of being young in the faith. Oecolampadius was only too aware of how far Basel lagged behind Zürich in the implementation of the reform agenda.
9   Tillman Limperger (see 319, n. 5), suspended as Cathedral preacher due to his evangelical sympathies.
10 Augustinus *Marius. Oecolampadius's reversion to wolf imagery to describe him (see 258, n. 5; 376, line 24f.) leaves no room for doubt as to his view of Marius, who was *Faber's favoured candidate.
11 Marius visited Basel to discuss his possible appointment and 'preach with a view' in December 1525, and took up his duties on 3rd April 1526—see *AGBR* II, 290–293 (no. 350).
12 Konrad Treger (c. 1480–1543), who was born and spent much of his life in Fribourg, but was Prior of the Austin Hermits in Strasbourg between 1517 and 1525/6. By December 1525 he was already a known and detested quantity to the Strasbourg reformers, particularly after the publication in March 1524 of his polemical *Paradoxa* (Strasbourg: Grüninger), which had caused a considerable public uproar. In fact he never worked in Basel. On him see *BBKL* XII, 438–442; *KTR* V, 74–87; Schindler, *BD*, 745–749.
13 The context is the forthcoming Confederate Diet at Luzern.

419 Oecolampadius to Zwingli—Basel, 7th December (1525)

VIII, 453 Grace and peace from Christ, dearest brother. Receive herewith another bundle of letters,[1] perhaps more keenly anticipated than agreeable; but they are certainly not to be ignored, lest we remain unaware of what and how much power our adversaries have—distinguished discerners of spirits that they are! *Bugenhagen is writing against me, seeking to reprove my conscience for having (as he suggests) misquoted the opinions of the ancients.[2] They are acting boldly and, as you will read, they are not allowing the requisite article of faith to be wrested from their grasp.[3] They do not agree with you about original sin, and hence they will seek to attack you in particular.[4] I fear that more work will be created by all this; that is why, in my simple way, I warned you[5] as a friend not to do anything rash or sudden.

I do not properly understand what it is that you would not allow in the matter of inherited sin.[6] Surely you do not think that all infants are so undefiled as to be fit even to enter the kingdom through the grace of Christ? Or would you assert that certain people are made pure by the gift of God that is to come? I think you will admit that the propensity to sin does indeed weigh more heavily upon us all than it did before Adam first sinned. I will gladly differ from the Pelagians' position—as far as I can on the basis of scripture. I grieve that I did not deliberate with you more fully on this subject when we *VIII, 454* met last year,[7] for | certain thoughts had sprung to mind during the journey;

---

1 See 418, line 33. This new "bundle" also plainly came from Strasbourg (see n. 3 f. below).
2 The source of the comment attributed to Bugenhagen is impossible to identify: it does not appear, for example, in his letter to *Capito dated 5th November 1525, which is printed in *OeBA* I, 424 (no. 307, n. 2); see also *CC* II, 165 (no. 253). Moreover no published work by Bugenhagen was directed specifically against Oecolampadius.
3 "They" are presumably *Luther, who in the second of two letters to Capito dated 5th November 1525 has denied that, in Christ's institution of the Eucharist, "is" can be read as "signifies"—see *WA BR* III, 603–607 (no. 942); *CC* II, 165 f. (no. 252a).
4 See Luther's other letter of 5th November to Capito—*WA BR* III, 602 f. (no. 941); *CC* II, 164 f. (no. 252).
5 Cf. above, p. 27 and n. 114.
6 At this point in his career Zwingli's views on original sin were somewhat unorthodox and controversial. This applies particularly to his treatment of the subject in his *Vom dem touff, vom widertouff und vom kindertouff* (Zürich: Hager, 25th May 1525)—ed. *ZW* IV, 206–337 (no. 56); trans. Bromiley, 128–177 (Part I only). Here he calls original sin an unwilled *präst* ('defect'), distinguishes it from original guilt, and claims that "the children of believers cannot be damned on account of original sin, as long as they do not know the law" (p. 312). The inevitable charges of Pelagianism which followed caused Zwingli to revise these positions as early as 1526. See Stephens, *Theology*, 146–153.
7 See 352, n. 3.

but I in no way doubt that you will act at all times in the strength of Christ, that most proficient of soldiers, wherever he uses you as his instrument.

The Strasbourg priests have posted certain accusations against Capito and the City of Strasbourg on the doors of the churches, so as to embroil them in conflict.[8] But I do not know what these accusations are. What does Satan not get up to in his raging?

Farewell.
On 7th December. Basel.
Johannes Oecolampadius.
To Huldrych Zwingli, most vigilant bishop of the Zürich church, his brother.

Original: Zürich, Staatsarchiv, E II 349, p. 130 (autograph). Copy: Zürich, Zentralbibliothek, Ms S 15, no. 80.

---

23 *posted*] *inscripserunt* (literally, 'inscribed')

---

8 Very little is known about these accusations, but they plainly reflected the fears of traditionalist believers in Strasbourg in the face of the progress made by the evangelicals, the arrival of the first anabaptists in the city, and the apparently burgeoning power of the Emperor.

422   Oecolampadius to Zwingli—Basel, 19th December 1525

Grace and peace from God the Father through Christ. Things are going well, my brother. Through someone else's fault, an illness is troubling our people at the moment. Only the renewing of the Holy Spirit will cure them—as indeed all are cured on whom he has breathed.[1] The secret things, those things which it is not right for us to examine, we will leave to God. The authority of the Saxons will in no way frighten us, for they have already furnished us with a sample and taste of their spirit. As you wish,[2] I will write to our brothers with greater care than I am wont to do.

I have not yet read *Eck's letter,[3] which I am sending back, even though a copy of it was made, mainly for all the canons and the more powerful of our enemies to delight themselves in. So I raised the matter today with our most courteous Mayor[4] and offered to write a response to these lords. For we have taught nothing new, nothing seditious, nothing contrary to good morals. It is all too easy to accuse someone of heresy. I said that I would not refuse to converse or dispute with Eck, | or indeed with those whose shoes Eck is not worthy to untie:[5] but I would not wish to run foolish risks or go against the warnings of Christ. He (the Mayor) was astonished that, last year, you did not dispute with Eck, and desires to know whom you are going to put on stage this time.[6] I answered that I had high hopes of your being less fearful than I would be; for our affairs are now more secure. But I told him that he should not forget what had been done at Konstanz and attempted at Worms:[7] the

---

9 *I have ... read*] *legeram* (a pluperfect)

---

1 Cf. John 20:22.
2 Presumably in a now lost letter.
3 A letter dated 28th October 1525 and discussed at the Swiss Confederate Diet on 7th December, in which Eck accuses Zwingli and Oecolampadius of heresy with regard to the Eucharist, and challenges them to a disputation. It is printed in *OeBA* I, 408–411 (no. 293).
4 Adelberg Meyer zum Pfeil: see 406, n. 2.
5 Cf. Mark 1:7.
6 In August 1524 Eck had suggested that a disputation be organized between himself and Zwingli. By then the latter was developing the reputation as a serial non-attender of disputations, something that Mayor Adelberg Meyer (and no doubt others) seem to have held against him. In fact plans for a disputation with Eck foundered above all on disagreements about its location, Zürich or Baden: "Eck refused to enter the walls of heretical Zürich and Zwingli refused to leave. Both knew what awaited them if they ventured into hostile territory; and by 1524 there was no neutral ground" (Gordon, *Zwingli*, 124).
7 An allusion to the burning of Jan Hus at the Council of Konstanz in 1415, and to the threat to *Luther's life at the Diet of Worms in 1521.

Lord, who wishes us to be artless, commands us also to be prudent.[8] This is what I discussed with the Mayor. If I am called before the Council, I shall say the same; but they will not want to summon me.

After all, who is that wretched Eck to blaspheme against the armies of the God of Israel? Whom should we fear? Is not Immanuel our protector? What is that raving papist going to do? If, along with the Lutherans, he has rejected transubstantiation, he has already rejected his own church. If he follows that line, he can be confuted without much of a fight. But he would be yoking himself to the Lutherans! If they wanted to obey the word, they would be no less easy to confute. And if they did not want to, we would find ourselves unable to speak with such impure people. So let us be of good courage. The Lord lives, and he has spoken though the prophets and promised to give us words and wisdom.[9] So be it; let us now be blunter than fishermen![10] I wish that day might come tomorrow! But please tell me as soon as you can what your people decide in this matter. At some point we shall have to oppose the false prophets to their faces.[11]

Farewell, and trust in the constancy of my faith.
Basel, in the year of our Lord 1525. 19th December.
Your Oecolampadius.
To Huldrych Zwingli, most faithful eye and most watchful shepherd of the Zürich church, his brother.

Original: Zürich, Staatsarchiv, E II 349, p. 2 (autograph). Copy: Zürich, Zentralbibliothek, Ms S 15, no. 95.

---

32 *people*] *natos* (literally, 'sons')   41 *eye*] a literal translation (Latin *oculo*)

8 Cf. Matthew 10:16.
9 Cf. Luke 21:15.
10 A reference, one assumes, to the apostles, and not least to their untutored eloquence in the book of Acts.
11 Cf. Galatians 2:11.

430   Oecolampadius to Zwingli—Basel, 29th December (1525)

VIII, 480   Grace and peace from Christ, my brother. I did not have any contact with our friend Escher,[1] since he had left before I knew he had come. I proceeded cautiously with *Pellikan, as you will see from his letter;[2] I would prefer him to stay here, though without his cowl.[3] The Deacon's folly has made our camp stink.[4] I still believe he is innocent, although he has been thrown into prison. And our adversaries have very good eyesight, whilst ignoring the beams in their own eyes.[5]

For the rest, I approve of your plan in the matter of *Eck.[6] I have not yet consented to give an account of myself in any other location but this one: here, I am prepared. The Council has not yet deigned to summon me, and to my friends it seems ill-advised for me to ask to be heard. But if they do summon me, I will reply as you wrote.[7] If you think your letter is publishable, it will be enough that you have alerted the reader appropriately on my behalf that, when the time comes, I will not fail in my duty.

VIII, 481   I am waiting to see what the Wittenbergers are hatching: they say they are certainly going to write something | against us. And then I in turn will reprove Eck appropriately. He does not seriously want to engage with us, but to play a trick on us. We will pray to the Lord that he might bless his work.

---

1   Konrad Escher (1480–1539), a wealthy Zürich cloth merchant and Council member, who was—at least at this point—a keen supporter of Zwingli.
2   Oecolampadius has obviously had sight of Pellikan's letter to Zwingli of 28th December (no. 429; ZW VIII, 478 f.). Zwingli has invited Pellikan to succeed the recently deceased Ceporinus (see 306, n. 11) at the *Grossmünster* School in Zürich and has asked Oecolampadius to discuss the matter with him.
3   To Oecolampadius's evident frustration, Pellikan had remained a Franciscan friar.
4   Hieronymus Bothan (d. 1531), deacon at the parish of St Martin in Basel, had been implicated in a failed plot to plunder the city's cathedral and others of its churches on Christmas night in 1525. He was released, along with three others, on 30th December—see *AGBR* II, 178 f. (no. 245).
5   A play on Matthew 7:3.
6   Zwingli seems to have advised Oecolampadius to oppose Eck on behalf of both reformers (for the context see 422, especially lines 11–23 and n. 6). This is what eventually happened at the Disputation of Baden in May/June 1526.
7   In a letter that is now lost.

20 Farewell, and greet *Hätzer along with the other brothers.
    Basel, 29th December.
    Johannes Oecolampadius.
    To the most ... man Huldrych Zwingli, most faithful teacher of the Zürich church, his brother.

Original: Zürich, Staatsarchiv, E II 349, p. 60 (autograph). Copy: Zürich, Zentralbibliothek, Ms S 15, no. 109.

---

23 *To ... most ...*] the first part of a word ending in *-imo* is illegible in the original

435   Oecolampadius to Zwingli—Basel, 1st January 1526

Grace and peace from the Lord, dearest brother! The day before yesterday I wrote about what *Pellikan might be minded to do, and what my plan is with regard to *Eck;[1] but because our scrivener[2] may have been further delayed on his journey, I wanted to tell you briefly by this means also. Pellikan has been persuaded[3] and, when summoned by your letter, will very soon be hastening towards you all. Write to him, then, even if in a very few words. For if he declines the offer of this position, I do not see how he will ever be free of that superstitious sect.[4] *Hätzer is also speaking to him on your behalf today; I do not know what Pellikan's response will be. But you will get the man: he is dependable and amenable, and it is only with reluctance that I am sending him away. I prefer him, though, to act in good conscience over there than to advocate superstition here.

For the rest, if I had not had Eck's letter from you,[5] the Council would not yet have shown it to me. Since the Council has not summoned me, our friends do not think it advisable for me to write to him. For whatever I wrote would be disagreeable to certain people—although I am not unaware that, if I remain silent, they will attribute that to faintheartedness on my part (something which, praise be to God, I am not at all prey to). One thing only weighs me down, namely that some faithful Council members here are abandoning me, and that I am bearing the heavy burden of our work practically on my own. I need to keep a close watch on that most exasperating of houses.[6] But the Lord will manage the affair. Please press on, and judiciously expose the deceits of that most foolish man Eck. For the Antichrist does not have a more impudent servant.

---

4 *by this means*] *per hoc*. We take it that *modum* is understood   10 *dependable*] *non penitendum* (literally, 'not to be regretted')

---

1 See 430, lines 8–14. The letter is in fact dated 29th December.
2 *Froschauer, a regular bearer of letters between Basel and Zürich.
3 That is, to take on the role of teaching Hebrew and Greek at the *Grossmünster* school. See 430, n. 2.
4 The Franciscans, whose habit Pellikan still wore. For the context see 430, n. 2f.
5 See 422, n. 3 and 430, n. 6.
6 That is, the Basel Council.

25 | Simon,⁷ the man who is delivering this letter, has allowed his son to be baptised here, even though at first he thought highly of the catabaptists. But we will not by any means re-open old injuries that the Lord has long since forgiven—so that the Lord might forgive us our trespasses also.

Farewell, and live most happily with your wife.⁸
30 On the first day of the year 1526.
Your Johannes Oecolampadius.
Greet Wilhelm von Zell also.⁹
To his dearest Huldrych Zwingli, brilliant in every kind of virtue and most eminent in Christian learning.

Original: Zürich, Staatsarchiv, E II 349, p. 5 (autograph). Copy: Zürich, Zentralbibliothek, MS S 16, no. 2.

---

7 Simon Stumpf, who had been expelled from his post as a priest at Höngg near Zürich in 1523, in consequence of his involvement in iconoclasm: see Robert Hoppeler, "Zur Charakteristik des Leutpriesters Simon Stumpf von Höngg", *Zwingliana* 4/11 (1926): 221–229. In November 1523 he was also banned from the entire Zürich territories for anabaptist activities (which, by the time of this letter, he appears to have renounced).
8 Anna *Reinhart.
9 See 376, n. 8.

438   Oecolampadius to Zwingli—Basel, 12th January (1526)

VIII, 496   Grace and peace from Christ, my Zwingli! If you are well, that is a good thing; we are in good health, and are being treated with the usual goodwill. In truth we are rather worried on your account, as to how good your health is: for you are rumoured to be so weak that you are even having to refrain from preaching.[1] If this is true, we pray that the Lord will comfort both you and us. See to it, therefore, that you free us from this worry as soon as you can—if you are well enough. Please also write to *Pellikan, if you want him to replace Ceporinus.[2] There is no cause for delay other than the fact that he has not yet been summoned by your letter.

Today I presented my little book of requests to the Council.[3] I would have sent you a copy if one had been made. With a thankful heart I have taken on the task of descending into the arena[4]—as long as the disputation takes place here, is conducted in the vernacular, is judged according to the word of God, and takes place before learned men summoned from elsewhere. I have laid bare *Eck's tricks to some degree. Perhaps he will be brought to Luzern.[5] The Council has not yet asked me for a response; hence my appearance in the form of an epistle,[6] even though I have not been summoned.

---

8 *he*] or 'it', i.e. a letter or publication by Eck

---

1   Probably a coded reference to a false rumour emanating from Strasbourg to the effect that Zwingli had either been banished from Zürich or forced into hiding. In a letter also dated 1st January, Zwingli reassures Capito that there is no substance to this—see *ZW* VIII, 487f. (no. 434), here 487, lines 1–11; *CC* II, 178f. (no. 271).
2   See 430, n. 2.
3   This is in essence the "plan with regard to Eck" and the proposed disputation that Oecolampadius has mentioned in 435, line 2f. The contents of the "little book" are printed in *AGBR* II, 197–202 (no. 260), and summarized in *OeBA* I, 450 (no. 324).
4   Cf. Erasmus, *Adagia*, 1.11.83 (883): *in harenam descendere pro eo quod est certamen inire* ('to descend into the arena means to enter the fray'). The original context was of course gladiatorial combat.
5   Presumably for the Confederate Diet to be held there on 18th–19th January, at which the proposed disputation was to be discussed. In fact the Diet was attended by *Faber, rather than Eck. See Schindler, *BD*, 76f.
6   That is, in the form of the "little book" (see line 8 and n. 3).

Billican's little book has been sent here, with the epistle of Urbanus Rhegius alongside it.[7] But they do not discuss anything of substance in it. My little book does not yet exist; if it did, it would already have flown to Zürich.[8] He (Billican) boasts of making a single argument against both Tertullian and ourselves, namely: if we say that the body is a symbol of Christ's body, we are obliged also to say that a symbol of his blood has been handed down for our benefit—and this he disputes, in vain, but with many words. For if I say of an image of Maximilian: this is Maximilian, who begat Philipp—what does Billican intend us to understand by that? That the symbol begat Philipp?[9] But I would want other such tropes to be supplied from scripture. For example, there is this one from Exodus: "'Here are the gods who have led you out of Egypt', they taunt".[10] And they exert themselves to no avail in trying to explain that a lamb can be the Passover sacrifice.[11] Moreover they assert that my Swabian friends are printing their nonsense to the great acclaim of the Augsburgers.[12] We will have to respond to them. I do not yet know if they have removed anything from the book or added anything to it; if they have, we should take steps to prevent them. I have sent a letter to Augsburg, so as to be more certain about this.[13] Perhaps our friends will send the letter to you first. We will act with a common purpose, since God has joined us together in this cause.

VIII, 497

---

7   *De verbis coenae dominicae et opinionum uarietate, Theobaldi Billicani ad Urbanum Regium Epistola. Responsio Urbani Regij ad eundem* (Wittenberg: Klug and Augsburg: Ruff, 1526; Leu/Weidmann 33). Rhegius (404, n. 9) had taken Billican (394, n. 5) to task for his increasingly Oecolampadian leanings on the Eucharist, and this volume contains both men's contribution to the debate. On the letters see Simon, *Billican*, 103–106; Zschoch, *Existenz*, 185–191; Burnett, *Debating*, 140–143.
8   A reference to the *Antisyngramma* (see 411, n. 2; 443, n. 2).
9   The names are far from randomly chosen: the image of Emperor Maximilian I (1459–1519), father of Duke Philipp 'the Handsome' (1478–1506) appeared, for example, on innumerable coins.
10 These are the words of the Israelites in Exodus 32:4 (quoted from the Vulgate, *Hi sunt dii tui … qui te eduxerunt de terra Aegypti*). They have just made Aaron construct a pseudo-divine golden calf, during Moses's extended absence on Mount Sinai. Oecolampadius's point is, presumably, that the golden symbol is not really God, any more than the eucharistic elements are really Christ's body and blood.
11 Cf. Exodus 12:21.
12 A new edition of the *Syngramma* (see 391, n. 5) was printed by Simprecht Ruff in Augsburg in January 1526, apparently without the involvement of *Brenz.
13 No such letter has survived.

I have not received a letter from Strasbourg for many days now. Furthermore, let us know the outcome of the disputation at Chur;[14] otherwise we shall learn of it rather tardily. *Hätzer commends himself to you. And help to comfort and advise the man who brings this letter.

Farewell, and write to us soon.
Basel, 12th January.
Your Oecolampadius.

After my response to them, my Swabians met again at the seat of a certain nobleman[15] and, as a certain friend has indicated,[16] they condemned it strongly—as you, very much a true prophet, had predicted.[17] Just look at them triumphing over an opponent | they have neither seen nor defeated! But premature rejoicing is sure to end in grief—unless God wants people to be ignorant of the truth on account of their sins.

*Melanchthon is also said to have composed something on the subject of the Eucharist.[18] The coming market days will have a plentiful supply of scourges on offer[19]—if we have time to read them. The truth will overcome the many and the few with equal facility. We know in whom we believe.[20]

Farewell.
I wish good health also to our friend Wilhelm von Zell,[21] along with your household and the brothers.
To Huldrych Zwingli, most faithful superintendent of the Zürich church, his dearest brother in Christ.

Original: Zürich, Staatsarchiv, E II 349, p. 79 (scribal hand). Copy: Zürich, Zentralbibliothek, Ms S 16, no. 15.

51f. *on ... Eucharist*] in materia εὐχαριστίας   52f. *plentiful ... on offer*] uberem μαστίγων proventum

---

14　Generally referred to as the Disputation of Ilanz, 8th–9th January 1526. See Gordon, *Swiss*, 96f.
15　The meeting at Guttenberg Castle—see 418, n. 5.
16　Simon Grynaeus—see above, p. XVIII, n. 4.
17　See 416, line 12f.: Zwingli here refers specifically to *Brenz who was the Lutherans' chief spokesman at Guttenberg.
18　No such publication(s) actually appeared.
19　A reference to the forthcoming Frankfurt Book Fair.
20　Cf. II Timothy 1:12.
21　See 376, n. 8.

443 Oecolampadius to Zwingli—Basel, 25th January (1526)

Grace from Christ. If, my Zwingli, the disputation is to be held at all—as a rumour, which I do not yet believe, reports that it will be—it will perhaps be better at some point to print the letters that need to be published,[1] if we are to refute our opponents' impudence the more vigorously. Such a plan by no means displeases me: it would play to our strengths, and there is many a slip 'twixt cup and lip.

*Cratander will see to it that my writings are printed in Strasbourg, if I give him copies of them; and I am bound to him because of a debt, so that I cannot blithely do a service to a different printer against his will. I would have preferred to make an arrangement with Christoph.[2] Insignificant as I am, I will respond to Billican[3] carefully and at length. I will ignore Urbanus[4] in public and admonish him rather sharply in private. And since he mentions my friends the Swabians, they too will have a part to play. I will add to this two sermons of apologetics, in which we will wipe away much that is hateful—assuming the hearers have ears. It will not matter much if we do not share copies | with each other, since our prime concern is for both faith and love, and we will not allow this to be jeopardized—though I would always prefer you to have had the chance to apply your judgement to my writings. But needs must. I am afraid that what I feared would happen here might finally be happening, namely that I have laboured in vain and that the glory of God will not shine forth from us in any other way than that we

VIII, 508

VIII, 509

5f. *there is ... lip*] *multa inter rem et spem* (literally, 'many things between the matter and hope')   7 *my writings*] *mea* (literally, 'my' or 'my things')   18f. *to my writings*] *meis* (literally, 'to my' or 'to my things')   19 *needs must*] *necessitati parendum* (literally, 'necessity is to be obeyed')

---

1   Including, as the most obvious example, the missive from *Eck that began the whole process (see 422, n. 3). For an account of the complex exchanges of letters and pamphlets that preceded the Disputation of Baden see Schindler, *BD*, 70–79.
2   *Froschauer. The context is that Oecolampadius's works are banned from being printed and sold in Basel, so he has to look elsewhere. The group of works listed in lines 10–15 were eventually printed by Froschauer in Zürich, in one volume, later in 1526: *Apologetica Ioannis Oecolampadii: De dignitate eucharistiae Sermones duo; Ad Theobaldum Billicanum, quinam in uerbis Caenae alienum sensum inferant; Ad ecclesiastas Sueuos Antisyngramma* (Staehelin 124; Leu/Weidmann A163). See Staehelin, *Lebenswerk*, 292–300; Burnett, *Debating*, 144–148. The *Antisyngramma* is edited in *Abendmahlsschriften*, 104–216.
3   See 394, n. 5 and 438, n. 7.
4   Rhegius: see 404, n. 9 and 438, n. 7.

shall be without excuse on that day.[5] So pray to the Lord that he might look mercifully upon us. And may he also keep you, with your household and the brothers, safe for a long time for our sake.

Basel, 25th January.
Johannes Oecolampadius.
To Huldrych Zwingli, my dearest brother.

Original: Zürich, Staatsarchiv, E II 349, p. 157 (autograph). Copy: Zürich, Zentralbibliothek, Ms S 16, no. 27.

---

5 Cf. Romans 1:20.

448 Oecolampadius to Zwingli—Basel, 7th February (1526)

Grace and peace. Your letter, my dearest brother, in which you made clear the reasoning behind your trope, pleased me beyond measure.[1] I do not care by what means the truth prevails and these slanderous beasts are answered. I think I have responded to Billican and the Swabians at sufficient length.[2] Today *Cratander is going to ask the Council for permission to print these works here; if this is denied him, it will be safer to print them elsewhere.[3] For it is incumbent upon us to humble ourselves in every way before the magistrate, as far as God allows.

*Pellikan is waiting for the Chief Guild Master[4] to arrive, and then, I believe, he will hasten his journey towards you. I have a hard task, working here always under such circumstances. But in time the Lord will provide, and will not allow us to be tempted beyond our strength;[5] he will protect you also. I estimate that my book will run to fourteen sheets.

The Strasbourg brothers are very fearful that we are putting our adversaries under too much pressure, with the result that they will be more implacable in future.[6] I have recently written about this matter also.[7] There is danger from the papists who are watching us; for if we defeat our enemies, they will stir up their people against Christian teachers in other ways. So when there are bishops in fewer places, the few of them that remain will, when circumstances dictate, be in great demand. In short, the whole affair is in the hands of God, by whose grace our work will prosper.

---

12 *and ... strength*] *nec permittet tentationem ultra vires nostras increscere* (literally 'will not allow temptation to grow beyond our strength')—a slightly different rendering of 1 Corinthians 10:13 from the Vulgate and KJV   20 *when ... dictate*] *rerum necessitudine* (literally, 'due to the necessity of things')

---

1 As so often with Zwingli, this letter—which presumably touched upon his eucharistic doctrine—is lost.
2 See 443, n. 2.
3 See 443, lines 7–9 and n. 2.
4 Jakob Meyer zum Hirzen (see p. XVIII, n. 3), who had arranged for his stepson Heinrich Billing to accompany Pellikan from Basel to Zürich. In fact the journey did not take place until 22nd–25th February.
5 1 Corinthians 10:13.
6 *Capito expresses such a sentiment also in a letter to Zwingli dated 3rd February—ZW VIII, 517f. (no. 447), here 517, lines 2–4; CC II, 183 (no. 276).
7 No letter with this content has been preserved.

I do not yet know what has been decided at Baden.[8] They will impede the disputation in every way possible, even if it is held tomorrow. And they will attack us in other ways as well. But we will fear the Lord, whose work we do, and we will be kept safe and well.

Farewell.
Basel, 7th February.
Your Oecolampadius.
To Huldrych Zwingli, the most Christian bishop of the Zürichers, his beloved brother in Christ.

Original: Zürich, Staatsarchiv, E II 349, p. 120 (autograph). Copy: Zürich, Zentralbibliothek, Ms S 16, no. 41.

---

8 At the Confederate Diet that began on 3rd February.

449   Oecolampadius to Zwingli—Basel, 9th February (1526)

Grace and peace, dearest Zwingli. Seeing that our names are on almost everyone's lips, and that the *Brenzes and Rhegiuses[1] and their sort are leaping about in triumph, even some of those who seemed pious in their thinking are starting to grow weak. We need to press on with the Lord's work, to press on!

You, I do not doubt, will offer your words for sale at the marketplace.[2] For you have printers to hand. In this respect they seem to be behaving as though my words—which the Lord gave me—are not wanted. Satan is thwarting me here. All that *Cratander obtained from the Council was an order not to print anything at all that I have produced, be it large or small, good or bad.[3] So I shall be free of Cratander.[4] The Strasbourg brothers have written to suggest that I send them a copy. But it is only in my power to do this if Christoph[5] cannot take on the work. I will by no means ask him for a copy straightaway, unless he sends me some of his own accord: for I would wish him to have sufficient leisure to do this. Please take pains, out of the concern you have for Christ's church, to ensure that, if possible, an opportunity arises to print our lucubrations[6] also. Nothing now distresses me so much as to see the prince of darkness leaving no stone unturned to prevent the light advancing. It will be up to us not to yield. For I am persuaded that the Lord does not wish us to be idle in any way. | So please urge Christoph as much as you can to take on this work, which will doubtless not inconvenience him at all, and which will not be without value to the pious. And I will be very grateful to have it printed in Zürich, because then you too will be able to have a taste of what I have written; for though I assume you would wish to read all of it, pressure of work does not permit this. But if you encounter anything that is unworthy of the glory of Christ, you will have every right to refute it in full. For in these days we do not write for ourselves or for our glory; rather, we want Christ to reign. And so may your love seek to find an opportunity in your city for my little books also to be printed. I think they will not displease you.

5–7 *your words, my words*] *tua, mea* (literally 'your, my'; we take *verba* as understood)

---

1 *Brenz and Rhegius (see 404, n. 9) respectively.
2 Oecolampadius no doubt has the Frankfurt Book Fair in mind.
3 See 448, lines 5–8.
4 This statement chimes with the one in 443, line 9f., where Oecolampadius suggests that he would rather have "made an agreement with Christoph (Froschauer)".
5 *Froschauer. It seems that, by this time, an "arrangement with Christoph" *had* been made, at least in principle.
6 The *Apologetica*—see 443, n. 2.

Although our Council's decree[7] has not gone so far as to give pleasure to the flesh that flees the cross, yet I pray to Christ that it will not break my spirit, to the extent that I desist from preaching him. For the rest, because in your blessedness you wished to relieve my impecunity, I am most grateful to you all and to Christ, who put the thought into your head. I have enough money for several months. There are certain private citizens who have also assisted me. But I will be glad to shake hands on an agreement.[8] It will be more honest and more Christian to settle this domestic matter in a way that is burdensome to no-one. But for now I thank you. I pray to the Lord that he might preserve your strength. If it can be done, pray, urge, insist and ensure that my little books can be printed in your city. *Hätzer, who greets you, is writing to Christoph about what conditions he might agree to.[9] For myself, I ask for no reward.

Farewell.
9th February, Basel.
Your Oecolampadius.
Pray also for me.
To Huldrych Zwingli, most pious antistes of the Zürich church, his brother in Christ.

Original: Zürich, Staatsarchiv, E II 349, p. 33 (autograph). Copy: Zürich, Zentralbibliothek, Ms S 16, no. 43.

---

7   Presumably the ban on printing Oecolampadius's works.
8   The precise nature of Oecolampadius's plight and of Zwingli's generous offer are unknown, but one is probably justified in assuming that his salary as a professor at the University of Basel had been, or was liable to be, suspended. Certainly he made an agreement on 26th February with the trustees of St Martin's Church that his salary as People's Priest there would be increased should other sources of income fail—see *OeBA* 1, 471 (no. 338).
9   It seems that Hätzer has impressed Froschauer sufficiently for the latter to offer him work.

454 Oecolampadius to Zwingli—Basel, February (1526)

Peace and grace from Christ. *Pellikan, who has been chosen and so often summoned, is finally coming,[1] my Zwingli. I do not need to commend him to men endowed with such kindness and piety, especially since—in his integrity and virtue—he is well able to commend others in your midst. It may be that in his first months he still exudes the aroma of a monk;[2] but he will quickly adapt to your ways.

Things are going well for the Strasbourg brothers—though *Capito is physically less than strong. *Bucer is going to publish a response to *Brenz.[3] For a certain epistle by Brenz has been printed, namely the one he wrote to Bucer about the Eucharist;[4] but the editors did not print Bucer's response alongside it. See how guileless the Swabians are! Also in a letter (which I have not yet seen), *Luther has counselled the citizens of Reutlingen against supporting our cause, and has promised to do prodigious things against us.[5] But what power shall the flesh have over the truth? Billican recently sent me quite a friendly letter:[6] he seems to be coming around somewhat to our way of thinking. He prefers, | however, to think in terms of an allegory, rather than a metaphor of parts; and he says that a good deal of his letter was suppressed by Urbanus.[7] Again we see the candour with which our adversaries go about their business! And though they are like that, they still try to deny they are playing tricks on us! They are complaining about the letter to the Reutlingers that you published, even though you did not send it to their master.[8]

You know that every judgement in our *Apologetica*[9] is yours also; for we are serving a common cause. And I cannot explain why most people do not properly understand why you do not consent to the disputation being held

---

1 See 430, n. 2 f.; 435, lines 1–12; 438, lines 7–9; 448, line 9 f.
2 See 430, n. 3.
3 Bucer's "response" was the *Apologia* of 1526 (see p. 32 f. and n. 134).
4 See p. 32, n. 134.
5 In a letter of 4th January 1526, printed in WA 19, 118–125 (Leu/Weidmann A226). This was in essence a response to Zwingli's letter to Matthäus Alber (see p. 9, n. 35), which had been forwarded to Luther by its Reutlingen recipient(s).
6 Billican (see 394, n. 5) sent his letter from Nördlingen on 16th January. It is printed in *OeBA* I, 451–453 (no. 326).
7 Zschoch, *Existenz*, 190, argues that this claim was false.
8 See n. 5 above. Even though it was not addressed to "their master" Luther, he clearly had read and responded to the letter.
9 See 443, n. 2.

here[10] and do not wish to leave Zürich. In truth those who speak in this way do not care about either you or me. I am not yet convinced that the disputation needs to take place at all; but nothing is being done—apart from people setting traps. For if those people were lovers of the truth, with what profit they could attend the disputation!

Let us pray to the Lord Jesus that he might bestow also on us the spirit of wisdom, so that we might sin neither by commission nor by omission in anything that pertains to the glory of his name. For this life is short; and we should ardently desire the things we hope for, and preach that others should hope for them too.

Farewell, happy and brave one in the Lord.
Basel, in the year 1525, on a day in the month of February.[11]
Johannes Oecolampadius.
To *the most* [*pious*] Huldrych Zwingli, minister of Christ, his dearest brother.

Original: Zürich, Staatsarchiv, E II 349, p. 3 (autograph).

---

26 *care ... me*] *nec tui nec mei rationem habent* (literally, 'have care neither of your nor of my')   30–32 *might ... anything*] *ne quid vel agamus vel omittamus* (literally, 'lest we commit or omit anything')   38 *To the most*] *issimo*—the first part of the adjective was lost when the letter was folded. We surmise that its likeliest original reading is *pietissimo*

---

10   At this stage it was still widely assumed that the disputation that was eventually organized at Baden would take place in Basel instead—as Oecolampadius himself wanted (see 438, lines 9–14).

11   "In the year 1525" is clearly wrong, given the events the letter describes.

456   Oecolampadius to Zwingli—Basel, 7th March 1526

Grace and peace from Christ. Writing a foreword to Pindar was in no way unworthy of you, dearest brother.[1] For the die has fallen fortunately, if it ever has for anyone, and this is an opportune time. For there are some who are selling themselves as poets and orators using titles and boasts; those people
5 are lamenting today that all the Muses are dead and buried because of the evangelists of Christ (as they rather contemptuously call us), and they are trying, by the use of this term, to make us seem odious if we even once grumble a little that the philosophy of Christ is as far removed as possible[2] from worldly wisdom. Would that they were less concerned about their bellies,
10 that they had an equal concern for young people,[3] and were not so querulous when we are weighed down by caring for the flock that has been committed to us! As in other things, so also on this occasion, you are on hand at the right time to protect the weaker brethren. To them, we are seditious, a plague on the good arts,[4] Lernean hydras of vice,[5] masters of debauchery. But, thanks
15 be to God, we will be vindicated even if you alone are left unharmed; for our hope is in the Lord, whom we preach. We will teach peace and love even towards our enemies—standards which some of them cannot keep even towards their friends and well-wishers. We will praise the arts in such a way that they might justly be honoured. We will preach the cross, rather than
20 vice and debauchery. Meanwhile Christ will watch over us and will mock our adversaries—if indeed we have rightly perceived him and have not—as

VIII, 534

---

8 *as far ... possible*] Greek δὶς διὰ πασῶν (*disdiapason*, literally 'a double octave'). See n. 2
10 *querulous*] Greek μεμψίμοιροι   14 *Lernean hydras*] *Lernae*. See n. 5 below

1   Zwingli had in fact contributed both a foreword and an afterword to the Pindar edition of the recently deceased Ceporinus (see 306, n. 11): *Pindari Lyricorumque omnium principis, Olympia, Pythia, Nemea, Isthmia* (Basel: Cratander, 1526)—ed. zw IV, 867–879 (no. 76).
2   A metaphorical use of δὶς διὰ πασῶν is recorded by Erasmus, *Adagia*, 1.2.63 (163): "By this proverb was signified a great difference or a very long interval: hence things which seemed most incompatible with each other, and totally different in kind, were said to differ *disdiapason*". This reference, along with that to the "philosophy of Christ" (literally *Christianam philosophiam*, 'Christian philosophy') confirms one's suspicion that Oecolampadius's critique of non-evangelical humanists is aimed at least in part at Erasmus.
3   Ceporinus had himself been young; and his Pindar edition (as n. 1) was intended for learners of Greek.
4   On classical and medieval uses of the term "good arts" (*bonae artes*) see Henry Mayr-Harting, *Church and Cosmos in Early Ottonian Germany: The View from Cologne* (Oxford: Oxford University Press, 2007), 135–137.
5   A reference to the second labour of Hercules, in which he slew the Lernean hydra at the Spring of Amymone. See for example Hesiod, *Theogony*, 313–318; Alcaeus, *Fragment*, 443.

the world has—gone over to the worship of the Baals.[6] Forgive my long-windedness, my brother; I feel as though I am talking, not writing to you.

| Besides, just as your foreword gives pleasure, so do your afterword and colophon. For some time now, however, I have been complaining of being afflicted by a certain lethargy, as though I have been working excessively hard; hence I will be fulfilling my duties at some danger to myself. There is something in me—I do not know whether it is arrogance or vanity—that makes me want to be of service and contribute something to the community. Certainly I have not the strength to respond to our adversaries (far from it), and this also affects my health somewhat. I will not complain about this, however. For I know that in the past I exerted myself more and was constantly unwell; and for this reason my present weakness seems a kind of consolation, coming as it does from nowhere other than from the one whom we serve. And may he himself grant us never to grow inactive, whether we are to serve him for a long or a short time. Nevertheless, your divinely inspired exhortation[7] did caution me quite profoundly.

Please see that *Cratander[8] attends to everything most diligently. And I will be vigilant. He has not told me much, other than that you were not able to visit Christoph's[9] workshop. It is the Lord's plan that *Hätzer[10] should be afflicted in his head, and you by ulcers. Now, the trifles I produce are not worthy of the hours they steal from you. Perhaps you think I am a flatterer; but that is entirely alien to me. Truly your lucubrations have pleased me in a way that my own never really can. You alone could have tamed the Brenzes, Billicans and Rhegiuses of this world. So why do I bother? Nevertheless, having once ventured forth into the light, it will be better if I do not recoil from fighting, rather than rashly and foolishly yielding to our vainglorious enemies. But why do you sometimes honour me with your praise, so very undeserving as I am? I wish these praises would cease, for the sake of Christ's gospel! For how do unmerited hymns of praise benefit me? In truth they would have moti-

---

22f. *my long-windedness*] Greek τῇ περιττότητι   24 *your foreword*] Greek τὸ προοίμιον | *afterword*] Greek καταστροφή   42 *flatterer*] Greek κολακεύειν

6   Cf. (for example) Judges 2:11, 3:7.
7   Delivered, one assumes, in another letter that has been lost.
8   *Cratander was currently engaged in preparing the Pindar edition (see n. 1) for publication.
9   *Froschauer.
10 The context implies that Hätzer was now at Zürich, presumably in Froschauer's employ (see 449, n. 9 and line 71 below).

vated me, but thrift comes too late when you find it at the bottom of your purse.[11] May you increase boundlessly! But it will be a great thing for me to move forward slowly, as long as I do not go backwards. For truly the fathers said: "I take heed of many things, for meaning is not to be found in just one thing".[12] What is there to wonder at, therefore, if my offspring are misshapen? I rejoice nevertheless: for though I am the least when it comes to words, | yet I am certain I will say nothing that would dishonour our Christ, or that our benevolent Father himself would not willingly forgive.

VIII, 536

Please give *Pellikan, that dearest of men, a greeting on my behalf and a blessing from the Lord. There has been no time recently for me to write to him. When he has cast off his cowl, I will be able to greet in my letters not a monk, but a man.[13] He has made me into a liar: for I wrote to our Strasbourg friends, who were congratulating him, that he had removed his habit.[14] But he will not allow me to remain a liar for long. I will talk nonsense, my Zwingli, and with you of all people!

Truly those people who wrote to Utinger[15] that the worst-printed book ever was about to appear in your city had the gift of prophecy; I definitely agree with them. For I would never have thought that so corrupt a copy could emerge from my house.[16] But we hope in the Lord that even a barren woman will give birth to seven children.[17] Hence I am sending a list of some of the crasser errors to be corrected. But talk to Hätzer about these things.

---

51 *thrift ... purse*] *sera parsimonia fundi* (literally, 'thrift at the bottom (is) too late'). We use the standard English equivalent of the proverb (see n. 11)   54f. *I take ... thing*] *Pluribus intento, non est in singula sensus*—a dactylic hexameter, presumably a mnemonic

11   Oecolampadius is here alluding to a proverbial saying attributed to Seneca (*Epistula morales ad Lucilium*, I, 5), though the latter refers to the bottom (dregs) of a cup, not a purse. See note on line 51 above.
12   See the note to line 54f. One suspects the saying is of scholastic, rather than patristic origin.
13   Pellikan's continued reluctance to discard his Franciscan habit was by this stage becoming something of a running joke in Oecolampadius's letters to Zwingli: see also 430, line 3f. and n. 3; 454, line 4f.
14   *Capito expressed congratulations to Pellikan for removing his habit in a letter to Oecolampadius of 23rd January—printed in *OeBA* I, 453–459 (no. 327), here 456. There is no extant letter from Oecolampadius giving him this information.
15   Heinrich Utinger (c. 1470–1536), a canon at the Zürich *Grossmünster* and friend of Glarean (see p. 23, n. 97). He had been a prominent member of the city's pre-Zwinglian church establishment, but favoured the reformer's initial appointment at the *Grossmünster* and remained his loyal supporter. On him see BBKL XVII, 1444–1449.
16   Oecolampadius is complaining about a draft copy of his *Apologetica* (see 443, n. 2).
17   Cf. Isaiah 54:1.

I wish you good health, along with all the brothers.
Farewell.
Basel, in the year 1526. 7th March.
Your Oecolampadius.
To Huldrych Zwingli, his dearest brother in Christ.

Original: Zürich, Staatsarchiv, E II 349, p. 4 (autograph). Copy: Zürich, Zentralbibliothek, Ms S 16, no. 69.

460 Oecolampadius to Zwingli—Basel, 14th March (1526)

Grace and peace from Christ, my brother. Your arguments about the Eucharist[1] have rightly been received with both pleasure and profit by the pious here—thanks be to Christ! So I will not torture myself (as you warn) about mine having not turned out very well.[2] I am reminded, though, to do everything more carefully in future. *Bucer has also published a work— something which in itself cheers me not a little—under his own name and that of the Strasbourg brothers,[3] in which they have borne witness to their faith. It is a little book that gives testimony in a more than satisfactory way to the remarkable love they have for us. Moreover, because *Brenz's words are now being read in the vernacular,[4] custom will perhaps require us to produce an explicatory *Antisyngramma* in brief summary form[5]—thereby driving out one nail with another nail.[6] But I have compassion on the people, who, unless they are well established, are driven about hither and thither.[7] Please let me know | what I need to do.

Our position here is rather more tranquil; but tranquillity is not to be trusted, since undoubtedly it can set in motion more violent waves. Yet the Lord will not forsake his own.[8] The Augustinian and the Fransciscan[9]

1f. *Your ... Eucharist*] tua περὶ εὐχαριστίας   5 *Bucer ... work*] Bucerus quoque (literally, 'Bucer also')

---

1 *Ein klare underrichtung* (see 416, n. 6).
2 The *Apologetica*, in Froschauer's edition (see 443, n. 2 and 456, lines 66–71 and n. 16).
3 Bucer's *Apologia* (see p. 32, n. 134).
4 A German translation of Brenz's *Syngramma* (see 391, n. 5) was soon to be published, accompanied by a preface by *Luther: *Genotigter und fremdt eingetragener schrifft auch mislichens dewtens der wort des abentmals Christi. Syngramma* (Wittenberg: Klug, 1526). Luther's contribution is edited in *WA* XIX, 457–460 and translated in *AE* LIX, 150–162. On its contents see Staehelin, *Lebenswerk*, 308 f.; Burnett, *Debating*, 150 f.
5 This vernacular rejoinder was to appear in the late summer of 1526: *Billiche antwurt Joannis Ecolampadij auf D. Martin Luthers bericht des Sacraments, halbsampt einem kurtzen begriff auff etlicher Prediger in Schwaben schrifft die wort des Herren nachtmals antreffend* (Basel: Wolff, 1526; Staehelin 129; edited in *Abendmahlsschriften*, 218–234). It consisted of a response to Luther's preface, along with an abridged German version of Oecolampadius's *Antisyngramma*. See Staehelin, *Lebenswerk*, 309–312.
6 Cf. St Jerome, *Epistulae* 125, 14: *Philosophi saeculi solent amorem veterem amore novo quasi clavum clavo expellere* ('The philosophers of the world are accustomed to drive out an old love with a new one, as if they were driving out one nail with another one').
7 Cf. Matthew 9:36.
8 Cf. Psalm 37:28.
9 That is, the preachers of the Augustinian and Franciscan churches in Basel—Thomas Gyrfalk (see 367, n. 5) and Johannes Lüthard (367, n. 6) respectively. They had presumably offended against the preaching mandate introduced in 1523 and thereafter often confirmed.

have recently been admonished by the Council for preaching rather free sermons. They replied steadfastly and left their accusers in perplexity; the Augustinian even received praise. So they are still teaching in a manner contrary to our adversaries' expectations, and we have high hopes that, as Easter approaches, we will be able to proceed straightforwardly and without impediment. A rumour that the people of Schaffhausen and Appenzell were turning back from the plough[10] alarmed us not a little; but the rumour is dying down and is nothing to worry about.

Please greet *Pellikan[11] and the other brothers again and again on my behalf.
Farewell.
Basel, 14th March.
Your Oecolampadius.
To Huldrych Zwingli, bishop of the Zürich church and his brother.

Original: Kamienna Góra (Silesia, formerly 'Landeshut'), Church Library, Epistolae, I, 322 (as recorded in ZW VIII, 545—we have not been able to verify or update these details).

---

10 Cf. Luke 9:62. In Schaffhausen, various evangelical iniatives taken in 1523–1524 (such as the removal of images and the celebration of the Mass in German) had yet to attract the unequivocal support of the city authorities. In Appenzell, not all had accepted the authority's adoption of the principle of *sola scriptura* on 24th April 1524, and tensions persisted: a decision was taken on 30th April 1525 to permit individual parishes to choose their own religion, and in 1525–1526 anabaptist influence in the town was also strong—see Bryner, "St. Gallen", 259–261.
11 Plainly by this time Pellikan was safely ensconced in Zürich (see 454, lines 1–4 and n. 1 f.).

466 Oecolampadius to Zwingli—Basel, 9th April (1526)

May the grace of Christ be with you, my brother. I approve of the tactic of wearing the enemy down. Our spear has indeed been sharpened; and if there were ever anyone who could wield it expertly and bravely against the foe, then it is you, having demonstrated its great value. For this one thing is always in their mouths: we have the expression, to be "wolves in sheep's clothing".[1] Those who are coming here from Wittenberg say that the Swabians' *Syngramma* is being reprinted there, in a vernacular version together with an exposition by *Luther of the sixth chapter of John.[2] Erhard Hegenwald[3] and a certain Silesian[4] have also been here recently. You know the former, and once painted him in his true colours; he has now returned, adorned with the title of 'doctor'. The latter is truly a man of integrity and, as far as I can tell, of sound judgement; he will visit you soon, and will tell you some remarkable things about the censor.[5] They are beginning to imitate the papists very well. They are banning our books, so that only their own are read, and they are prevailing because people have not heard the views of the opposing party.

VIII, 559

5f. *wolves ... clothing*] Ἔνδυμα τῶν προβατοσχήμων λύκων (literally, 'the clothing of wolves resembling sheep'; see n. 1 below)   13 *about the censor*] περὶ τοῦ γραφοτυράννου (literally, 'the tyrant of writing')

---

1 Matthew 7:15. The precise purport of this sentence is unclear; one suspects that Oecolampadius is responding to a letter from Zwingli that has now been lost.
2 It is not clear who the "visitors from Wittenberg" were, though they seem likely to have included Erhard Hegenwald (see n. 3 below). For details of the German *Syngramma* see 460, n. 4. This includes a foreword and afterword by Luther, but nothing that could accurately be described as an "exposition" of, say, John 6:63.
3 Hegenwald is best known as the compiler of the main printed record of the First Zürich Disputation of 1523 (see 286, n. 4). Otherwise his life is not well documented: he is known to have taught at the Benedictine monastery at Pfäfers, and to have studied medicine at Wittenberg from 1524 and 1526 (see lines 9–11 above). At this time he was personally acquainted with Luther, and negotiated on his behalf with the anabaptist Konrad Grebel (see 552, n. 13). Clearly he was no longer in the orbit, or the favour, of Zwingli and Oecolampadius; but the precise reasons for this are unclear.
4 Matthias Wickler. His visit first to Oecolampadius and then to Zwingli in early 1526 proved fruitful in forging links between the Swiss reformers and those based around Caspar Schwenckfeld in Liegnitz (now Legnica). These Silesian evangelicals had already broken with Luther, not least over the Eucharist; and, in spite of differences, they shared with the Swiss a firm rejection of the notion of a 'real presence'—see Zwingli's letter to them of 17th April 1526—ZW VIII, 567–570 (no. 470). On Wickler's trip to Switzerland see Weigelt, *Tradition*, 78–80.
5 In Wittenberg, that is, where Luther's ways were becoming—in the eyes of some observers—increasingly tyrannical.

VIII, 560   But to return to what I wanted to say: | it would seem to be worth waiting, and delaying our response until we can see what Martin[6] has said. In the meantime, perhaps, a disputation will take place—something which is often mentioned here, but which seems to me extremely dangerous. Not because I mistrust the motive behind it, but because the location is suspect and not at all suitable—especially at the time in question, when a most lawless crowd of men flock together at the baths.[7] And I am not ignorant of the loyalty, nor yet of the anger that very many feel towards us—people who, if they had wanted to learn the truth, would not have rejected for so long the pious teachers who have been sent to them. But we will have to have faith in Christ that, when a date for the assembly is made known, it will be just as the glory of Christ requires. When you know something more certain about the disputation, let me know as soon as possible. My Baslers are rather slow to tell me what it would be to my advantage to know. Nor should you be silent if there is anything you want me to do. In these days of Easter the people should have been singing Psalms, but have been forbidden to do so by the magistracy.[8] This has revived the spirits of the papists, who had been utterly disconcerted by the number of people sharing worship with us. But they will rejoice only for a short time.

Farewell.
Basel, 9th April.
Greet *Pellikan along with the other brothers.
Your Oecolampadius.
To Huldrych Zwingli, most Christian teacher of the Zürichers, his brother.

Original: Zürich, Staatsarchiv, E II 349, p. 161 (autograph). Copy: Zürich, Zentralbibliothek, Ms S 16, no. 100.

---

6   Luther. Oecolampadius presumably has in mind the putative exposition of John (see n. 2).
7   Baden im Aargau was not only a Catholic stronghold, but also much visited in summer for its thermal baths.
8   This ban on congregational singing in the vernacular was evidently unpopular. At some point in the summer of 1526 Oecolampadius petitioned the Basel Council to rescind the ban (see *OeBA* I, 571 (no. 417)); and the practice had resumed by 10th August at the latest (see 518, line 7f. and n. 3).

471 Oecolampadius to Zwingli—Basel, 19th April (1526)

Grace and peace from Christ. Beloved brother, I am still no more certain about the disputation that is to take place.[1] Let me know what you have heard, and tell me what you intend—if you conveniently can. All of our friends suspect there will be tricks and hindrances to piety; and indeed one can already observe these things to some extent. Yesterday I saw in the bookshop *Eck's *Commonplaces*,[2] in which, having advanced some ridiculous views on the subject, he concludes that there is no need to dispute with *Luther and the Lutherans. Yet this distinguished master of ours had earlier decreed that heretics should be burnt.[3] This makes it clear with what level of integrity this honest man has been seeking to dispute with us[4]—with us, whom he repeatedly describes as heretics who have yet to be defeated.

I am sending a foolish little book by *Pirckheimer,[5] whom I consider to be the voice of the Nürnberg preachers—even though I would never have believed he wholeheartedly supported them. I have undertaken to respond to him as a friend.[6] You will also be able to say what you think needs to be emphasized—as long as you have the time to read such inept stuff. He is taking great care not to clash with you. Those who do not allow our little books to be sold in their cities will be judged accordingly. But what if it had pleased the Lord | to open a window on to his word via such adversaries as these?

---

1   The Baden Disputation was in fact to begin in exactly a month's time, on 19th May.
2   *Enchiridion Locorum Communium adversus Lutheranos* (Cologne: Quentell, 1525)—ed. Pierre Fraenkel, Münster: Aschendorff, 1979.
3   He does this also in the *Enchiridion*, in a section headed 'De haereticis comburendis' (ed. Fraenkel, 270–279). This question was of more than academic interest given that Eck had specifically described both Zwingli and Oecolampadius as heretics.
4   Eck had been the instigator of the push to hold a disputation in Switzerland—see 422, n. 6.
5   *Bilibaldi Birckheimheri De vera Christi carne et vero eius sanguine, ad Ioan. Oecolampadium responsio* (Nürnberg: Petreius, 1526; Leu/Weidmann 151)—ed. Helga Scheible, *Willibald Pirckheimers Briefwechsel*, vol. 6 (Munich: Beck, 2004), 80–85, 435–502. See Burnett, *Debating*, 164–166; Staehelin, *Lebenswerk*, 301.
6   This response is printed in *OeBA* I, 482–484 (no. 350).

Greet *Pellikan and your wife,[7] as well as all the other brothers.
Farewell.
Basel, 19th April.
Your Oecolampadius.
Tell Pellikan that Adam Petri[8] has not yet spoken with me.
To Huldrych Zwingli, my dearest brother.

Original: Zürich, Staatsarchiv, E II 349, p. 132 (autograph). Copy: Zürich, Zentralbibliothek, Ms S 16, no. 113.

---

7   Anna *Reinhart.
8   The prolific Basel printer Adam Petri (1454–1527), active in that capacity from around 1505, and something of a specialist in evangelical and moral theological material, not least in the vernacular. He was a close collaborator of Pellikan.

473   Oecolampadius to Zwingli—Basel, 24th April (1526)

May the grace of Christ be with you. Beloved brother, let us take courage in the Lord, who will not forsake his own in eternity. For we see the madness of the world, and the instruments of Satan raging entirely unchecked—in order, of course, that Christ might defeat him the more gloriously.

To my friends it does not seem at all a good idea for me to approach the Council before being summoned by them,[1] because some of them simply cannot abide seeing my face; hence I am bashful about showing it to them again. Then, if I do produce something, they will think it inimical to our city's innocence and modesty. They will think we are embroiled in a web of deceit; for they will interpret everything—even the most sacred of things—in the worst possible light. It bothers me above all that the Baslers have forbidden me in the strictest terms to make any representation to the Swiss[2] that might affect their reputation to even the smallest degree; hence if I so much as mention my beloved Basel masters, I will put myself in danger. They have not yet said a single word to me about the disputation; and most people do not expect it to take place.

Our enemies are boasting a great deal; they are singing victory songs in advance of the battle. What could be more arrogant than *Faber's letter?[3] Was there ever anything more full of lies? I fear that it will reach you at rather an inopportune time; so when a printed copy in the possession of a certain canon was shown to me in secret, I saw to it that it was copied by three people in less than two hours—so that, if you had not yet received a copy, you would be able to ensure that such impudent lies were made known to your Council. For it is quite plain that they wish to deceive us; and I would hardly dare | believe that anyone ever had such licence to lie. I hope that, if this impudent stuff is read before your Council, it will strengthen their resolve.

12f. *might ... degree*] nomen eorum vel minimo digito attingens (literally, 'touching their name even with the least finger')   17f. *they ... battle*] Greek ἐπινίκιον πρὸ μάχης ᾄδοντες   24 *it ... us*] ex illis fraus maxime manifestatur (literally, 'from them deceit is very much revealed')

1   Frustrated by the Basel Council's deafening silence about the proposed disputation, Oecolampadius had been considering approaching them in person on the subject since the beginning of 1526 (see 435, lines 14–18); but he clearly remained wary of doing so.
2   That is, the Confederate Diet.
3   *Epistola Doctoris Johannis Fabri ad Ulricum Zvinglium de futura disputatione Baden in Ergau die XVI. Maii habenda* (Tübingen: Morhart, 16th April 1526)—ed. FGR I, 235–246. A German version was also published, by *Froschauer in Zürich. This open letter formed part of the extensive polemical exchanges over Zwingli's non-participation in the disputation. For an account of these see Schindler, BD, 101–112.

Otherwise, I am writing a letter to *Pellikan about the *Eck affair.⁴ If you wish to, see to it that it is published in a vernacular translation. I am not reluctant to join others in facing danger; but I do not think it is advisable to do so. I am not inclined to go to Baden, unless some power or other impels me to go there. I will not refuse to go to Zürich, Bern or St. Gallen, as soon as they agree to the conditions you are proposing.⁵

Let us pray to the Lord that he might be present in his work.
Farewell.
24th April.
Your Oecolampadius.
To Huldrych Zwingli, most faithful pastor of the Zürichers, his dearest brother.

Original: Zürich, Staatsarchiv, E II 349, p. 94 (autograph). Copy: Zürich, Zentralbibliothek, Ms S 16, no. 118.

---

29 *join ... danger*] συγκινδυνεύειν (literally, 'incur danger along with others')

4 According to Staehelin (*OeBA* I, 486, n. 3), Oecolampadius was at this point considering not attending the Disputation of Baden in person (see line 30 f. above), but instead defending himself against Eck's various charges (not least in the *Enchiridion*—see 471, n. 2) in the form of an open letter to his friend Pellikan. To avoid falling foul of the Basel Council, this was to have been printed anonymously by *Froschauer in Zürich, ideally in both Latin and German (see line 27 f. above). Probably wisely, Oecolampadius eventually decided against this plan.

5 One suspects he is thinking here of the need for a reliable safe conduct, on which Zwingli and the Zürich Council were particularly insistent. See letter 488 below; also Schindler, *BD*, 103–105.

483 Oecolampadius to Zwingli—Baden, 18th May (1526)

Greetings. May you brothers also be of good courage! We will wait on the Lord's help. He will not forsake his own.

At the first session I will urge with all my might that we should reconvene at an appropriate location;[1] and I hope that the Schaffhauseners will not make themselves unpopular if other arrangements remain as they are.[2] We will not be called to appear before lunch. They are said to be getting chairs ready in the church. Berchthold has not yet arrived,[3] and nor has Hess from Appenzell.[4] But many opponents are here. Praise be to God! I have read your letter to Berchthold, and liked it.[5] If a disputation does take place, we will not fail to do anything that you have advised. But we will avoid having a disputation if we can, and for one reason only—namely that, if it turns out well, we will not be damaged by your absence and that of the other Zürichers. If only there were some way to bring you here! But I would not want to put you in danger in any way.

Farewell.
18th May.
Your Oecolampadius.
To the most wise Zwingli.

Original: Zürich, Staatsarchiv, E II 349, p. 43 (autograph). Copy: Zürich, Zentralbibliothek, Ms S 16, no. 149.

---

17 *your*] *vester*. Generally Oecolampadius addresses Zwingli in the singular at this point in a letter, but here he uses the plural form, presumably in order to address the Zürich "brothers" as a group   18 *To ... Zwingli*] Τῷ Ζουιγλίῳ τῷ σοτάτῳ (literally, 'to the most your Zwingli')—we are assuming that the last word should be σο⟨φω⟩τάτῳ ('most wise')

1 For an account of this first session see Schindler, BD, 128–131. Oecolampadius was unsuccessful in pleading for the disputation to be re-arranged, or indeed—given the paucity of evangelical attenders—replaced by a more informal discussion.
2 In fact the Schaffhausen delegates proved to be firm supporters of Oecolampadius.
3 *Haller. The Bern Council had been markedly unenthusiastic about the disputation taking place, and may well have deliberately delayed his departure.
4 Johannes Hess, a member of a prosperous Appenzell family who had studied in Freiburg; he was banished from his home town for his evangelical beliefs shortly after his return from the Disputation of Baden. See Schindler, BD, 96, 698 f.
5 This letter giving advice about how to act at the disputation has been lost.

486   Oecolampadius to Zwingli—Baden, 22nd May (1526)

VIII, 604   Greetings in Christ, my brother. The citizens of Basel, who were anxious for us, entreated us not to take part in the disputation. But the messenger did not come in time.[1] Now, yesterday morning, as you have heard, we enjoyed no small success—praise be to God! How unwilling they are to hear me speak! But my Mayor and Councillor acted quickly,[2] sternly reprimanding the other delegates if they did not give me an opportunity to speak about essential matters; because of this there is a good chance that they will treat us more equitably from now on.[3] But neither we nor our cause will be in danger, because the Lord will not in any way abandon his glory—which we wish to see preserved.

Meanwhile, may you be of good courage. We were not able to turn the discussion appropriately in the direction of shifting the disputation to a different location. Some brothers are being sent to us from Basel to reinforce us: the Suffragan and the Franciscan,[4] with their companions; we must wait for them to arrive. I would have preferred the disputation to continue, since I am not unaware of the tricks that our adversaries are setting up in the meantime. I hope the Lord will vanquish them.

---

1   The context here is the fact that evangelical representatives at Baden were massively outnumbered by Catholic ones, and that in consequence the Basel Council wanted the disputation to be adjourned until more delegates could be sent. In fact their messenger arrived in Baden after the gathering had broken up for lunch; and only at that point was the Baslers' request considered and granted. The disputation was adjourned until Thursday 24th.

2   The two Basel delegates to the Diet, Mayor Adelberg Meyer zum Pfeil (see 406, n. 2) and Chief Guild Master Urban von Brunn (d. 1526). On the latter see Füglister, *Handwerksregiment*, 357 f. Their joint report of this incident is in *AGBR* II, 331 f. (no. 398).

3   For an account of this meeting see Schindler, *BD*, 132–134. It seems that Oecolampadius did not altogether help his own cause by reading from notes for three hours in a quiet voice.

4   Tillman Limperger (see 319, n. 5) and Johannes Lüthard (see 367, n. 6) respectively. In fact Limperger was prevented by illness from making the journey, and was replaced by Jakob Immeli (see 367, n. 3).

Farewell; and pray that our work may prosper.

22nd May, Baden.

Oecolampadius.

| All the brothers greet you.

The faithful Schaffhauseners also support my view.[5]

I have received a letter meant for Chur;[6] we should expect to witness many tricks.

To his Zwingli.

Original: Zürich, Staatsarchiv, E II 349, p. 37 (autograph). Copy: Zürich, Zentralbibliothek, Ms S 16, no. 154.

---

[5] The Schaffhausen preachers present were Ludwig Oechsli (see 488, n. 4), Heinrich Lincki and Konrad Wehrli. See Schindler, *BD*, 61.

[6] It is not clear what communication is meant.

488   Oecolampadius to Zwingli—Baden, 23rd May (1526)

VIII, 610 May the grace of Christ be with you, my brother. We are not now as worried about our own reputation as we are about yours—because (as you will understand) the Berners have now also assented to the safe conduct,[1] and have been mocking you for not wanting to be present here amid so great an assembly. So it seemed to me, as to certain other good brothers, that you ought not to be absent from the disputation—if indeed this can be brought about without danger. We do not fear for our cause. Even for our adversaries, *Eck's impudence is wearisome. Berchthold is expected.[2] The Suffragan is not coming.[3] Bovillus[4] and Piscatorius[5] are here along with another man—they are all excellent men.

VIII, 611 We are fearful that your city might be beginning to prepare for a civil war.[6] What if, in this context, the safe conduct breaks up | the alliances between the Five Cantons and Bern until the disputation is over, and everybody returns to looking after their own affairs with the following clause inserted into the letter: "as long as no confederates object and all injuries are forgiven"? And you will bring with you an escort of fifty men at your side; you will even bring your own food supplies with you. For I do not see how we can stop our rivals' mouths either on the basis of what has been written, or by

---

18 *our rivals*] τῶν ἀντιπάλων

---

1 Unsurprisingly, given the experiences of Hus and *Luther (see 422, line 20f. and n. 7), the issue of a safe conduct to Baden for the reformers was a fraught and contentious one. A series of general guarantees was given; and a specific one for Zwingli, allowing also for an escort of between twenty and thirty men (*sic*—cf. line 16 above) was issued by the Diet of Luzern on 12th May 1526 and confirmed at Baden—also by the Bern delegates—on 18th May. Suspicions and legal uncertainties persisted, however. See Schindler, *BD*, 103–105.
2 *Haller.
3 See 486, n. 4.
4 Ludwig Oechsli (d. 1569), who ran the Latin School in Schaffhausen and was a loyal supporter of Zwingli and Oecolampadius. *Bovillus* is a latinized version of his surname. On him see Jakob Wipf, "Ein Schulmeisterschicksal aus der Reformationszeit (Hans Fehr, lateinischer Schulmeister in Schaffhausen 1530–1541)", *Zwingliana* 4/13 (1927): 379–400, here 379–381; Schindler *BD*, 729f.
5 Johannes Fischer (d. 1565), formerly a Dominican at Ulm and later Parish Priest of Mammern in the Thurgau, who is the likely author of a partial account of proceedings at Baden: *Quibus praeiudiciis in Baden Helvetiorum sit disputatum* (Strasbourg: Prüß, 1526). He is called *Piscatorius* for the same reason that Oechsli is *Bovillus*.
6 It is not clear how widespread such fears were: this letter does not show Oecolampadius in his calmest or most balanced state of mind. What is certain is that Zwingli's non-appearance at Baden was to some extent a political manoeuvre on his part and that of the Zürich Council—albeit one that arguably backfired (see Schindler, *BD*, 101–112).

any other means. If this cannot happen, I do not see that a similar opportunity will ever offer itself again. If you are in danger, then all of us will be in danger with you. But perhaps you know more than I could know myself. See what may promote the glory of the gospel of Christ. May our lives be dedicated to him—however little of them remains.

Farewell,
23rd May.
Oecolampadius.
To Huldrych Zwingli, his dearest brother.

Original: Zürich, Staatsarchiv, E II 349, p. 163 (autograph). Copy: Zürich, Zentralbibliothek, Ms S 16, no. 155.

495   Oecolampadius to Zwingli—Basel, 12th June 1526

Grace and peace from Christ, my brother. We have arrived home safely,[1] amidst high expectations and many congratulations on the part of all the faithful. I fear, however, that the rejoicing may last hours only, and that Satan may turn it into mourning. We have not yet been forbidden to assemble— which, when the Swiss had left, the princes are said to have instructed the delegates to do.[2] We must pray to Christ that he will not abandon his own, and will soon trample Satan underfoot.[3] I thank you for the frequent letters and greetings I received from you in Baden, through which the Lord greatly cheered and strengthened me. The Basel delegates were not able to obtain a transcript of the disputation, which most of us here find highly disagreeable.[4]

I found these letters at home. Urbanus has not yet broken off our friendship.[5]

Farewell.
12th June, Basel.
Your Oecolampadius.
To Ulrich Zwingli, his dearest brother.

Original: Zürich, Staatsarchiv, E II 349, p. 142 (autograph). Copy: Zürich, Zentralbibliothek, Ms S 16, no. 167.

---

12 *these letters*] could mean 'this letter' (*literas*)

---

1   From the Disputation of Baden.
2   This injunction was passed at the Diet of Baden on 25th June, though it was aimed specifically at prohibiting evangelical sermons and books. See Schindler, *BD*, 165–167.
3   Romans 16:20.
4   The issue of how the proceedings of the Disputation of Baden were to be recorded proved very controversial. Three decisions in particular fuelled the evangelicals' suspicion: the employment of Johannes Huber, city scribe of Catholic Luzern, to act as a kind of *primus inter pares* alongside the four scribes (two from each confessional camp) originally appointed to take minutes; the stipulation that, after the Diet, their four records should be kept by the Catholic *Landvogt* ('Governor') of Baden and compared with Huber's only after the latter had produced a revised, 'clean' copy of his notes; and the Confederate Diet's repeated rejection of requests from Basel and Bern to see the sets of minutes. See Schindler, *BD*, 142–144, 171–181.
5   Urbanus Rhegius: see 404, n. 9. In the light of recent disgreements about both *Hätzer and the Eucharist, Oecolampadius might well have had grounds to fear that their amicable contact would end. Neither man seems to have borne a grudge, however; and in any event Zwingli clearly felt it worthwhile to spend much of 1526 trying to win Rhegius's support (see Zschoch, *Existenz*, 194–202).

496   Oecolampadius to Zwingli—Basel, 13th June (1526)

To Huldrych Zwingli, bishop at Zürich, his dearest brother. Greetings in Christ, my brother!

My servant has returned without your letters. But I am grateful for your efforts in getting my little book published;[1] may God reward you for it. The brothers at Strasbourg think we should respond to *Luther. But I think it is better to wait for his prologue to the Swabians' little book which they call *Syngramma*,[2] and then do what would be appropriate to the Lord's honour. For the Devil is making work for us everywhere, and we must take good care to ensure that our enemy nowhere achieves anything against us that he could justifiably boast of. I will send | Luther's prologue on to you; you should keep it until the time is right, because he alone confirms more people in this error[3] than all the papists do.

The papists have long since sent the little book that the Strasbourgers printed,[4] so as to anger the angry Swiss still more; but it is in their nature to be angered or aroused by very little. Our man Ber has been behaving badly, and has called me before the Mayor to give testimony that he did not ask me to distance myself from one thesis and enter into negotiations about the others.[5] When I exonerated him in respect of this, he said that he would not be satisfied unless I exonerated him also before the Council. Whoever

---

1–34 The entire letter is German (the Latin original having been lost)   17 thesis] artickel

---

1 His *Ad Billibaldum Pyrkaimerum de re Eucharistiae responsio* (Staehelin 131; Leu/Weidmann A164), which was shortly to be printed by *Froschauer at Zürich, thanks no doubt to Zwingli's good offices. Parts of it are printed in *OeBA* 1, 546–551 (no. 402). It is analysed in Burnett, *Debating*, 166–169, and Staehelin, *Lebenswerk*, 301–304.

2 See 460, n. 4.

3 A reference, inevitably, to the ongoing eucharistic controversy, and specifically to Luther's doctrine of consubstantiation.

4 The anonymous *Warhaftige handlung der disputation im obern Baden des D. Hanß Fabri, Jo. Ecken unnd irs gewaltigen anhangs gegen Joan Ecolampadio und den dienern des worts* (Strasbourg: Köpfel 1526), an unofficial and tendentious account of the disputation which fuelled further controversy (see 495, n. 4). The main part of it is published in Schindler, *BD*, 524–530. Oecolampadius is surely exaggerating to say that copies had arrived in Basel "long since" (*langest hër*), given that the disputation had only ended on 8th June.

5 The *Warhaftige handlung* claims that Ludwig Ber (see 396, n. 10) visited Oecolampadius at his lodgings in Baden and offered him a cloak-and-dagger deal according to which he would drop his objections to the disputation's first thesis (on the Mass) in exchange for an agreement (*rachtung*) on the others—see Schindler, *BD*, 529 (lines 209–215). Ber unsurprisingly feared for the damage this—almost certainly untrue—story might do to his reputation.

it is that wrote that statement,[6] he was not wise to do so; for Ber and all the others were saying that if the first thesis were dealt with, the others would be dealt with soon afterwards. May God grant that everything will be written down reliably;[7] because in truth many things were discussed crudely (I will not say in a godless manner), in order to further their cause. And many brothers let things pass negligently. When I spoke, I did not have the time or leisure to think of everything; and now I have still less time and opportunity. The others have other things to do; and meanwhile the papists, protected by their lies, are happy and are boasting of victory as if they were friends of the truth! We should urge the churches to pray daily and live pure lives, in case the Father of mercy wishes for once to placate those vicious wolves who always seek to destroy his flock.

May the Lord preserve you.
13th June,[8] Basel.
Your Oecolampadius.

The Latin original is lost. Copy of contemporary German translation: Solothurn, Staatsarchiv, Abschiede 14, p. 279. See also n. 8 below.

---

6 In the *Warhaftige handlung* (see n. 4f.).
7 See 495, n. 4.
8 The Solothurn copy of this translated letter, on which the zw edition is based, is dated *Am xiij. Heumonats*, that is to say, 13th July; but the copy printed in the *Warhaftige handlung* (see n. 4) and edited by Staehelin in *OeBA* 1, 543f. (no. 400) has the much more plausible *Am xiii. Junii.*

497   Oecolampadius to Zwingli—Basel, 20th June (1526)

Grace and peace from Christ, my brother! We have not yet complied with the resolutions and decrees of our adversaries (that is to say, the enemies of truth), which are designed to drive us out of our pulpits. Rather, we continue to teach and preach, because the people have a great thirst for the Word of the Lord. The Council will doubtless demand a copy of the disputation records.[1] Yet we must pray to the Lord that Satan, who is always opposing us, will never prevail. There is a rumour about papists everywhere lying extravagantly and boasting of sweet victories over us; I hope it will benefit our cause if their lies are exposed some time, and they lose all credibility.

I am now sending a response to *Pirckheimer's follies.[2] I pray that one of your people—*Pellikan or *Myconius or some other trusty person—will see to it that it is printed correctly, and that anything which needs amending or deleting or in any other way correcting is submitted to you for your opinion. I had added some words about our disputation at Baden, but have now deleted these again. It might be worth publishing them, however, for a different reason and in some other letter. For they are priding themselves on having won the debate on the first two theses[3] solely by using Irenaeus's statement, | which I myself had cited against that impious papist notion of transubstantiation.[4] Otherwise, I did not think the Nürnbergers needed to be reminded much about why our books are banned there; I complained only about a few things just before the end, in these words: "Zwingli", I say, "also refuted it at length. The truth is discussed well there. Wagonloads of insults come out through the gates of your cities, but not even tiny threepenny basketfuls of harmless explanations enter through them. God, however, the judge and defender of truth, will take care of these things".[5] If you, my Zwingli, have anything that will help advance the truth, attend to it, in accordance with your duty.

VIII, 629

VIII, 630

23f. *tiny basketfuls*] *corbiculi* (literally, 'little baskets'), though one would normally expect the feminine, *corbiculae* | *threepenny*] *triobolares* (literally, 'worth three oboles')

1   They did this for the first time (of many) on 24th June. See 495, n. 4.
2   The *Ad Billibaldum Pyrkaimerum ... responsio* (see 496, n. 1).
3   These dealt respectively with the real presence and transubstantiation, and with the Mass as a sacrifice. For details of the relevant debates see Schindler, *BD*, 145–154.
4   The records of the Baden Disputation do indeed show Oecolampadius and Eck quoting Irenaeus of Lyon at each other (Schindler, *BD*, 309–313). See also p. 18 above.
5   A direct quotation from fol. H.3^r of the *Responsio* (as n. 2).

Farewell, together with the brothers, and commend my business to Pellikan, so that he might watch over the printer.
Basel. 20th June.
Your Oecolampadius.

It helped us that the Berners acted so adroitly in protecting their Berchthold.[6] And we are not unaware either that the St. Gallen brothers have been restored to their duties; those from Mulhouse have also not been hindered.[7] We have not yet heard how they are faring in Appenzell, Glarus and Schaffhausen.

To the dearest man Huldrych Zwingli, bishop of the Zürich church, his brother and teacher.

Original: Zürich, Staatsarchiv, E II 349, p. 52 (autograph). Copy: Zürich, Zentralbibliothek, Ms S 17, no. 2.

---

6 On 8th June, not long after his return from Baden, the Bern Council had invited Berchthold *Haller to resume his preaching activity—even though his position had seemed somewhat precarious given his refusal (since Christmas 1525) to celebrate Mass, and his repeated denials of the rite's validity.

7 The evangelicals from these two cities also seemed to experience a certain boost in consequence of the Baden Disputation: both sets of city authorities formally encouraged their preachers to resume preaching the word.

498   Oecolampadius to Zwingli—Basel, 20th June (1526)

Greetings in Christ, my brother! Your letter, along with the little book by *Luther,[1] was delivered after my assistant had gone. And because the scrivener[2] has advised me to copy it, I will keep Luther's epistle until my assistant returns and transcribes it. Then I will send it back by the next messenger. It does not seem appropriate for us to respond to him now. For it is rumoured that he has written a sixteen-page preface to the Swabians' book;[3] when we have received that, we shall be able to demonstrate to the world both our own innocence and the clear teaching of scripture. Praise be to God that our churches do not care much what that man might bleat against us.

Farewell, along with the entire Zürich church.
Basel, 23rd June.
Your Oecolampadius.
To Huldrych Zwingli, most faithful bishop of the Zürich church, his beloved brother.

Original: Zürich, Staatsarchiv, E II 349, p. 40 (autograph). Copy: Zürich, Zentralbibliothek, Ms S 17, no. 7.

---

1   Zwingli's letter has been lost, and Luther's *libellus* (or *epistola*) is also impossible to trace.
2   Presumably *Froschauer.
3   See 460, n. 4.

505   Oecolampadius to Zwingli—Basel, 12th July (1526)

VIII, 657 Grace and peace through Christ. It is not through any fear of our enemies, dearest brother, that we are now communicating what needs to be said less openly in letters; but as the Lord taught us, let us for the time being agree with our adversaries, lest those who are making trouble for us deliver us to the judge, and hence impede the progress of the gospel.[1] As we are 5
avoiding greeting disciples in the road,[2] so also we have agreed not to write unnecessary letters. And again, nothing makes us fearful, even when custom demands that we should be—for to us even death is gain.[3] Nor do you suggest otherwise, in your most agreeable letter.[4] Our ambassadors have
VIII, 658 received a response.[5] | I think that the town clerk of Luzern's[6] copy should 10
be put in order and, at the next assembly, collated by our scribe[7] with his own version—and then be circulated in that form. I have, however, heard nothing about any New Testaments being confiscated by decree; and so, as you already know, the little book against *Faber in which you seek to oppose such a practice has not been favourably received.[8] It pleases me greatly that 15

9f. *Our ambassadors ... response*] *Responsum est τοῖς ἡμῶν πρεσβευτῆ*   12 *version*] *antitypo* (transliterated from the Greek)

---

1 Cf. Matthew 5:25. Oecolampadius here uses key phrases from the Vulgate: *consentiens adversario tuo* ('agreeing/ coming to terms with your adversary') and *ne forte tradat te adversarius judici* ('lest perchance your adversary hand you over to the judge'); hence our translation reflects the phraseology of the KJV.
2 Cf. Luke 10:4.
3 Cf. Philippians 1:21.
4 This has been lost.
5 To the decision made on 25th June at the Diet of Baden (in the aftermath of the disputation held there), that evangelical preachers should either be exiled from Switzerland, or at least banned from preaching. Basel decided, in effect, to ignore this (see 495, lines 1–5); and a formal response confirming this policy was about to be delivered to the Diet.
6 Johannes Huber—see 495, n. 4. He was working on 'writing up' his notes between 9th June and the beginning of the Diet at Luzern on 1st August.
7 In fact Basel provided two of the four scribes originally appointed to take minutes at Baden (see 495, n. 4), Egmunt Rysysen and Christof Wyssgerber; so either of them could be meant here. In any event both re-appeared in Baden some time in August to compare their notes with Huber's and certify an agreed version. On Rysysen and Wyssgerber see Schindler, *BD*, 742 f. and 750 respectively.
8 Zwingli knew that the recent Diet of Baden had decreed that Luther's writings be banned and their sale forbidden; but he mistakenly believed that this proscription applied also to the former's German New Testament, and that Faber was behind this atrocity. Hence his programmatically titled piece, *Ein kurtze gschrifft warnende von dem unchristlichen*

the church is being reminded of what is right in the matter of interpreting decrees. But your little book has not been given to me in a transcription, as is usually the case; see to it that I get this as soon as possible. Wilhelm,[9] you see, brought only your letter.

Our representatives will again be steadfast in their views when they attend the next Diet: having not read the records that are in dispute, they will not remove us from our posts. Meanwhile, however, they have been frightened by a new rumour emanating from the Diet of Speyer: they fear and believe that an imperial mandate will change matters.[10] I am sending you a copy of this.[11] So Christ never does want his people to be free from care— though these threats from here and there do not greatly disturb me. But the wavering of a fainthearted flock that is in large measure inclined towards the acorns of yesteryear[12] is sowing the seeds of suspicion. | Indeed it is for him who orders us to plant and to water also to give the growth.[13] Let us pray to him.

*Cratander has brought a bundle of letters to the person who is writing this;[14] I will now send them on to you along with my own. You know well enough what they want for themselves, and do not need my advice. If we do not reply to Luther, I really do not see how we can dare to call ourselves faithful servants of Christ. *Bucer gives the wisest counsel; his letter to me is attached to yours.[15] A letter by a certain Bavarian[16] warns us that *Luther

VIII, 659

---

fürnemen Fabers, der nit allein die newlich getruckten bücher etlicher gleerten, sunder ouch daz nüw testament ze brennen sich vndernimpt (Zürich: Froschauer, 30th June 1526)—ed. ZW V, 262–271 (no. 92).

9   Presumably Wilhelm von Zell (see 376, n. 8).
10 The Imperial Diet met at Speyer from 25th June to 27th August 1526. Many evangelicals will have been worried that the imperial party (represented by the Emperor's brother Archduke *Ferdinand) would seek to enforce a rigid implementation of the fiercely anti-evangelical Edict of Worms of 1521; but in fact Ferdinand's attention was focused more on the perceived military threat from the Turks.
11 Presumably a broadsheet or pamphlet describing how "matters" might be "changed". This reads like an example of Oecolampadius expressing himself "less openly" (see line 3).
12 That is, Catholic tradition.
13 Cf. 1 Corinthians 3:6.
14 This part of the letter was written by a scribe, not by Oecolampadius himself. The letters brought by Cratander came originally from *Capito and Bucer in Strasbourg. For details see *OeBA* I, 562 (n. 1).
15 Bucer had written a letter to Oecolampadius, for forwarding to Zwingli, on 8th July 1526—ZW VIII, 646–650 (no. 502); *OeBA* I, 560 (no. 408). He then sent another one to Zwingli on 9th July—ZW VIII, 651–654 (no. 503); BC II, 137–140 (no. 133).
16 It is not clear whom Oecolampadius means here.

has said he wishes to respond to us all in a single work—if he is mad enough to do so. This too shows what he is like. His letter to the brothers at Reutlingen[17] disappeared along with the messenger from Strasbourg. I have copied the part in which he reprimands us, and will send this if you need it. But I did not copy all of it. *Pirckheimer is being very aggressive: he is threatening to vex my spirit and has roused the rabble against me. What shall I say? He is angry and wants to intimidate me. But may we attend to what the Lord wants, and may those who deserve it be struck down. *Melanchthon has said to Pirckheimer that, even though he has not written, he has been wanting to write. I believe this was said to humour the man.

Justus Jonas[18] writes to Bucer: "I will strive with all my strength to ensure that people here think thoughts of peace. It is clear that you are cheering on a runner,'[19] but we will not accept this doctrine."[20] You see that the whole world is raging. But the truth is extremely powerful. Take care that *Capito's letter is sent on to the Helvetian masters by appropriate messengers.[21]

And write to me about what I need to do. I will get ready to write a discrete *Syngramma* next week.[22] Send Bucer's letter to me.[23] And also exhort Christoph to finish off my piece against Billibald.[24]

---

17   See 454, n. 8.
18   Jonas (originally 'Jodocus Koch', 1493–1555) was an Erfurt-educated humanist who became a leading reformer in Wittenberg (from 1521), and later Halle an der Saale (1541–1547). A staunch supporter of Luther, whose funeral oration he gave, he was noted in particular as a translator and polemicist. See *CoE* II, 244–246; *OER* II, 352f.; *TRE* XVII, 234–238; *BBKL* III, 636f.
19   Latin *incitas currentem*, literally 'you are inciting a runner'. The saying is included twice in Erasmus's *Adagia*, as 1.2.46 (146; *currentem incitare*) and 3.8.32 (2732; *incitare currentem*), and had been used by Cicero (e.g. *De oratore*, 2.186 and *Philippicae*, 3.8.19) to refer to someone offering unnecessary encouragement.
20   Oecolampadius here accurately reproduces the postscript to a letter sent by Jonas from Wittenberg on 23rd June, in which he expresses a strong desire for peace among the evangelical factions, but stresses that the Lutherans cannot agree with the eucharistic teachings of Bucer, Zwingli, Oecolampadius et al. See *BC* II, 121–123 (no. 130), line 49f.
21   His letter to the twelve delegates of the Twelve Cantons at Baden, 8th July 1526—trans. *CC* II, 230–232 (no. 292).
22   He means the second part of his *Billiche antwurt* (see 460, n. 5).
23   Presumably the one of 9th July: *ZW* VIII, 651–654 (no. 503).
24   The *Ad Billibaldum Pyrkaimerum ... responsio* (see 496, n. 1), which Froschauer was in the process of printing in Zürich.

Greet *Pellikan, *Leo, *Myconius and the brothers.
Farewell.
Basel, 12th July.
Oecolampadius, who is truly yours.
60 To Huldrych Zwingli, his brother.

Original: Zürich, Staatsarchiv, E II 349, p. 135 (scribal hand to "writing this", line 31f.; autograph thereafter). Copy: Zürich, Zentralbibliothek, Ms S 17, no. 40.

---

59 *who ... yours*] Greek ὁ σώτατος (literally, 'most yours')

509   Oecolampadius to Zwingli—Basel, 18th July (1526)

VIII, 666   Greetings in Christ. Dearest brother, I am sending you the Workman's[1] toolkit, in which he is his usual most cunning self. He ridicules Berchthold[2] with an insufferable lie. He changes *Capito's word for 'to come before' the disputation (*fürkeren*, I think) to *verkeren*.[3] I do not know for a fact—though I am convinced of it—that our Capito is more honest than to distort a single jot or tittle. As you will see, he is interpreting everything in the most malign way. It is through such deceptions that a kingdom such as this becomes strong. I have responded to *Luther's epistle; now I am starting to revise the *Syngramma*.[4] May Christ help us through his Spirit. The Council has permitted our printers to publish my works, as long as they contain nothing dangerous.[5] I am waiting for my response to *Pirckheimer.[6]

1f. *Workman's toolkit*] *Fabrilia* ('workman's tools' or 'products'), here used as a play on Johann *Faber's name—see also 298, n. 1, 6

---

1   Faber. The work in question is *Newe Zeittung vnd heimliche wunderbarliche Offenbarung etlicher sachen vnd handlungen, so sich vff dem tag der zw Baden in Ergöw gehalten worden* (Würzburg: Müller, 1526).
2   *Haller. Faber had claimed that, when summoned by the Bern Council on 8th June (see 497, n. 6), Haller had stated that he approved of the Mass—when in fact he had again taken the opposite view.
3   *Verkeren* here means 'to overturn'. In late June 1526 Faber had intercepted a letter by Capito intended for Zwingli, and eventually published as *Epistola W. Fabritii Capitonis ad Hulderichum Zwinglium, quam ab Helvetiis forte interceptam* (Strasbourg: Köpfel, 1526; Leu/Weidmann A34); *CC* II, 242 (no. 299). Faber proceeded to translate this into German, gloss it (often misleadingly), and then publish it: see *BC* II, Annexe III, 248–266; trans. *CC* II, 213–230 (no. 290). His linguistic mischief primarily involved the Latin version, however: he reproduced Capito's *vehementer opus esset, ut catastrophe disputationis excudetur* ('there would be an urgent need for the conclusions of the disputation to be published') as *vehementer opus est, ut evertatur disputatio* ('there is an urgent need for the disputation to be overturned'). Having thus appeared to incite revolt, Capito was reprimanded by the Confederate Diet and prosecuted at the Imperial Diet of Speyer (see 505, n. 10). On this episode see Kittelson, *Capito*, 125–128.
4   This sentence refers to the second part of Oecolampadius's *Billiche antwurt* (see 460, n. 5).
5   The ban on Oecolampadius's works being printed and sold in Basel had clearly been lifted.
6   *Froschauer was obviously still working on te *Ad Billibaldum Pyrkaimerum ... responsio* (see 496, n. 1; 505, n. 24).

Farewell.
18th July.
Your Oecolampadius.
15   To his dearest brother Huldrych Zwingli, bishop of the Zürichers.

Original: Zürich, Staatsarchiv, E II 349, p. 106 (autograph). Copy: Zürich, Zentralbibliothek, Ms S 17, no. 49.

518   Oecolampadius to Zwingli—Basel, 12th August (1526)

VIII, 686

The grace of Christ, beloved brother. The person delivering this letter is, in my opinion, a pious man, and has been commended to me as such by *Bucer.[1] He is keen to be recruited to deliver your correspondence. For the rest, I will send your bundle of letters to *Capito via the first messenger. Capito too has opposed the Workman's wiles, and is about to send a message to the Imperial Diet.[2]

Moreover, today and on St Lawrence's Day[3] German Psalms were sung by the congregation in my church. The priests[4] had anticipated that this was going to happen, on the basis of my sermons: I had been discussing certain things from the Psalms—about joyful songs of the spirit and of the mouth—that had a bearing on the issue. So they urged the Council to prevent it if they could, and obtained from the Council an edict to ban singing from door to door. I knew nothing of this before. Truly, just as we all strive for what is forbidden, so we are emboldened when piety excuses it. The Council's prohibition was in vain. I do not know what will now happen in consequence. Some of the evils will fall on my head; and I will bear them willingly, if indeed they need to be borne. Nothing happened at my behest, but the glory of the Lord has been revealed. If the Lord prospers what has been set in train, I hope it will greatly benefit the cause of the gospel. Pray to the Lord for us.

Farewell.
12th August.
Oecolampadius.
To Huldrych Zwingli, my dearest brother.

Original: Zürich, Staatsarchiv, E II 349, p. 149 (autograph). Copy: Zürich, Zentralbibliothek, Ms S 17, no. 56.

---

5 *has opposed*] *obviam ivit* (literally, 'has gone to meet') | *Workman's wiles*] *Fabrilibus technis* (another pun on Faber's name—see 509, line 1f.)   13f. *we ... forbidden*] *In vetitum nitimur omnes*. This looks like an allusion to Ovid, *Amores* 3.4 17: *nitimur in vetitum semper cupimusque negata* ('we always strive for what is forbidden and desire what is denied')

---

1 The identity of this person is unknown.
2 See 509, n. 3. Capito had just written *Der nüwen Zeytung heymlichen wunderbarlichen Offenbarung, so D. Hans Fabri jungst ufftriben und Wolffgang Capitons Brieff gefälschet hat, Bericht und Erklerung* (Strasbourg: Köpfel, 1526). It is dedicated to the counsellors of Cardinal Elector Albrecht of Mainz, a highly influential figure at the Diet of Speyer, which had begun on 28th June and was still sitting. See *cc* II, 242–249 (nos 298 and 300).
3 10th August.
4 Presumably the Catholic ones; on the issue of vernacular Psalm singing see also 466, n. 8.

525   Oecolampadius to Zwingli—Basel, 3rd September (1526)

May the peace of Christ be with you, my brother. It is not that we are perturbed by the ferocity of those who oppose us. Have we not spoken words of peace, as the Lord taught us?[1] Are we not doing this for the Lord's glory? What parents, what friends, what teachers, what created thing will we acknowledge as our own?[2] We ought by no means to be true descendants of Phineas:[3] if the Father's glory can be vindicated by using gentleness, we will not act in such a way as to merit the name of savages. If balm can teach people zeal, we will leave it to the Spirit to achieve this. However, we will await what Martin is about to write;[4] and we will pray that he does not give free rein to his wit. Herewith I am sending the successful pieces that *Capito wrote in response to *Faber's calumnies.[5] I do not know if you have read the German ones, which are much more successful.

Xylotectus[6] departed this life on the fourth day after the Feast of the Assumption—in a Christian way, certainly, but in great torment. I often visited him when he was ill, but it was hard to understand him, babbling with confused speech as he was; but I understood clearly that, at the hour of his greatest suffering, Christ reigned in his heart.

I have received your little books, for which I am grateful. In the bundle of Petrus Gynoraeus's letters | (the Alban, as we call him here),[7] I have found nothing apart from *Eck's little book.[8] I too shall learn very soon what it

---

6f. *we will ... savages*] non patiemur, ut immites iure arguamur (literally, 'we will not suffer to be rightly termed savages')

---

1 Cf. Luke 10:5.
2 Cf. Matthew 10:37.
3 In Numbers 25:4–8 Phineas, son of Eleazar, demonstrates his zeal for the Lord in a decidedly violent fashion: by killing with the spear an Israelite man and an infidel Midianite woman, he "stops the plague" of the Israelites' idolatrous worship of the Baal of Peor.
4 Oecolampadius may well be thinking of *Luther's letter to Johannes Herwagen, which is dated 13th September 1526—ed. WA, XIX, 471–474; trans. AE LIX, 163–174.
5 See 509, n. 3; 518, n. 2.
6 Johannes Xylotectus (or 'Zimmermann', 1490–1526) was a humanist friend particularly of Zwingli. He was a member of a patrician family in Luzern, where he worked as a Latin teacher from 1510 until late 1524, when he was obliged to move because of his evangelical views. He settled in Basel, only to die there of the plague less than two years later.
7 Peter Frauenberger: see 367, n. 2. At this point he was active primarily in Augsburg, which is where this "bundle" has come from.
8 His *Ad invictissimum Poloniae regem Sigismundum, de sacrificio missae contra Lutheranos libri tres* (Augsburg: Ruff, 1526; Leu/Weidmann 66).

is like; but Gynoraeus would not give us anything that did not call Eck's very being vividly to mind.[9]

Farewell.
3rd September.
Your Oecolampadius.
The man who is delivering the letter[10] wishes to be commended to you.
To Huldrych Zwingli, most faithful minister of the gospel among the Zürichers, his most cherished brother in Christ.

Original: Zürich, Staatsarchiv, E II 349, p. 86 (autograph).

---

9 Frauenberger ('Gynoraeus') has given Zwingli a brief characterization of Eck's new work in letter 520 (ZW VIII, 688–690), dated 22nd August 1526 and sent from Augsburg.
10 We do not know who this was.

530   Oecolampadius to Zwingli—Basel, 24th September (1526)

Grace and peace through Christ, dearest Zwingli! Today I have received that infamous little book by *Strauß,[1] an intemperate and arrogant man who is just made for contentions and disturbances. For a long time his clamouring has held back the Margrave of Baden from entertaining fully correct thoughts about the Lord's Supper.[2] He rages more against you, and is actually milder towards me. Some months ago, when he was threatening to write against me, I advised him with all goodwill to turn his attentions elsewhere (if he was indeed minded to write), since he was not even-handed in this business.[3] He interpreted this as meaning that I was afraid of him. He carps at one thing I asserted in my little book, namely that nothing new occurs in the Eucharist that surpasses the understanding of the human mind: he expounds this in such a way as to imply that the bread of the Lord is not at all different from ordinary, common bread. He declines to write against me at greater length, however, and turns all his wrath on you instead. It will be worth your while responding to him in a few words—or, rather, not to him, but by offering advice as soon as you can to the Margrave of Baden. Beyond question, Strauß's works have brought about the banning from sale of our lucubrations in his principality.[4] We will need to seek access to the Margrave. We will be forgiven by all who have spoken ill of us if it is made known | that, in spite of himself, he does not deny the scriptures and is allowing himself to support us.[5] Yet for this reason all sorts of insults will rain down on him.

Otherwise nothing has changed here. The plague is not yet over. I believe others have described how much trouble the city has suffered from the light-

VIII, 722

VIII, 723

---

8 *was not even-handed*] *impares habet humeros* (literally, 'has unequal shoulders')

1   *Wider den unmilten Irrthum Maister Ulrichs Zwinglins, so er verneünet die warhafftig gegenwirtigkait dess allerhailligsten leybs und bluots Christi im Sacrament* (Augsburg: Ramminger, 1526). The work was dedicated to Margrave Philipp of Baden-Sponheim. On it see Barge, *Strauß*, 140–146; Burnett, *Debating*, 191.
2   As preacher at the Margrave's monastery in Baden-Baden since early 1526, Strauß had been preaching against the eucharistic views of the Swiss reformers. Oecolampadius also held him responsible for the ban on selling his and Zwingli's books referred to in lines 16–18.
3   Subsequent to his letter of 7th October 1525 (see 394, n. 8), Strauß had written to Oecolampadius again on 9th November—see *OeBA* I, 415–417 (no. 300). Again, there is no evidence of Oecolampadius having replied.
4   See n. 2 above.
5   In general Philipp of Baden's attitude towards reform was tolerant but equivocal: Locher describes him as having followed an "Erasmian line" (see *ZR*, 489–491, here 489).

ning strike.[6] For it struck a tower containing sulphur, saltpetre, gunpowder and other appurtenances of war. It completely destroyed the tower from top to bottom and blew apart a whole section of the city wall, killing people who were harvesting grapes nearby. I believe eighteen lives were lost, reminding us in this respect of the tower of Siloam.[7] Many people are also injured, and very many houses in the surrounding area have been severely damaged. May the Lord be praised in all his works. Greet *Pellikan on my behalf, and wish him a happy marriage.[8]

What if someone else in your city were to give the impudent Ostrich[9] a sound cudgelling on your behalf, just as he deserves? I would prefer that to your responding yourself—after all, you will be waiting for what Luther might be about to produce.

Farewell.
Basel, 24th September.
Your Oecolampadius.

If you mention the Margrave, please make sure not to incite him to act against other pious people; for he supports many exiles, whom no-one else has treated as well before. I would advise you to manage this work with all possible prudence.

Farewell again.
To Master Huldrych Zwingli, his dearest brother, who teaches Christ so impeccably to the Zürichers.

Original: Zürich, Staatsarchiv, E II 349, p. 101 (autograph).

---

6 This catastrophe had occurred on 19th September.
7 Cf. Luke 13:4.
8 Pellikan had married Anna Fries on 7th August.
9 Strauß.

534 Oecolampadius to Zwingli—Basel, 6th October (1526)

Grace and peace from God the Father through Christ, beloved brother! Johann *Faber's book of blasphemies and slanders[1] is being sold here—I do not know if it has been delivered to you. Nothing more impudent has appeared anywhere, and it conveys clearly the nature of the follies perpetrated at Baden. You do not need my advice as to what you should do. For the Spirit of the Lord will suggest it. But if that beast were not prowling around in all the princely palaces,[2] we would condemn him outright. For who would entrust his soul to a common forger, a wheedler who deals in such obvious lies—except perhaps someone who wants to be deceived? For such a person gets the lid he deserves. Moreover, since he is striving to make me seem to differ from you, and since he asserts that I conceded certain things in Baden about the invocation of the saints, I have decided to give an account of my church's thinking in a little book.[3] For I know that we have seldom disagreed on any church doctrine. Perhaps in passing I will also refute certain other arguments, if the Lord's favour does not abandon us—so that Faber's inopportune book might become an opportunity for us. I could not send you the letters from our Strasbourg friends any sooner. I fear that Bucer's letter is too obscure for you to understand.[4] And that man Jakob Sturm, the Strasbourg senator, is now one of us.[5] But Faber is | a most dangerous enemy, and you can see what lengths he will go to in order to ruin us.

9f. *For such ... deserves*] *Ei enim dignum obtingit operculum* (literally, 'For a suitable cover falls to his lot'). Oecolampadius surely has in mind Erasmus, *Adagia* 1.10.72 (972): *Dignum patella operculum* ('the lid is worthy of the pan', or perhaps 'the two of them deserve each other')

---

1 The *Christenliche beweisung doctor Johann Fabri über sechs artickel des unchristlichen Ulrich Zwinglins* (Tübingen: Morhart, 1526; Leu/Weidmann 84)—ed. *FGR* I, 265–283. See Staehelin, *Lebenswerk*, 347f.
2 Faber was exceptionally well connected in aristocratic Catholic circles, so that the Swiss reformers tended to fear the extent of his political influence—not least on Archduke *Ferdinand, whose confessor he was.
3 This was to appear as *Von Anruoffung der heylgen, Joannis Ecolampadij, uff ettlicher widersecher, und zuovorab Doctor Fabri, unnutz gegenwurfflich tandt, andtwort* (Basel: Petri, 1526; Staehelin 134; Leu/Weidmann A162). See also Staehelin, *Lebenswerk*, 348–351. In fact Oecolampadius takes issue with a wide range of points Faber raises in his *Underweisung*.
4 This letter has been lost.
5 Jakob Sturm (1489–1553) was a distinguished humanist and patrician with Erasmian-Zwinglian sympathies, who was to spend much time working for the reconciliation of the various groups of Protestants. Along with *Bucer, he was especially important in the negotiations surrounding the Colloquy of Marburg and Diet of Augsburg. See Thomas A. Brady,

The Turk is attacking with great force; yet the princes have been treating this with total unconcern, save for a few evangelical ones, who have been destroyed.[6] There are those who think that the Turk has been helped by the Pope, and indeed summoned by him to attack the Hungarians. Also there are rumours that they have a pile of money from the Roman mint which they are distributing among the soldiers in the Turkish camp; that, following the defeat of the King of France,[7] Turkish weapons have been found in the Pope's camp; and that a papal legate has been intercepted on his way to see the Turk. But these things may not be true.[8] The Italian Wars are teaching us well enough whether or not he is on Christ's side, and showing us above all how his followers rage against the gospel of Christ.

The plague has not yet ceased, and I hear it has been creeping forward also in your city. I would not want people to be so fearful that, at first, they neglect to take steps that might keep them safe, only to act later on as though there were nothing to be afraid of. For here it was mainly the anxious ones who perished, and those who set little store by their health. If you advise me against responding to Faber, let me know about it; and if you have not yet received his book, I will send it. But I think that our friends have already sent it. They say that the Ostrich has been answered,[9] and that Karlstadt has ceased preaching in Rothenburg ob der Tauber.[10]

    Protestant Politics: Jacob Sturm (1489–1553) and the German Reformation (Atlantic Highlands, NJ: Humanities Press, 1995); *CoE* III, 293 f.; *OER* IV, 121 f.; *BBKL* XI, 141–145.

6   Suleiman the Magnificent's army had defeated the Hungarians at the battle of Mohács on 29th August 1526, in which the Jagiellonian king Louis II (1506–1526) had been killed—not least because he had been unable to muster support from the Emperor or other Central European princes.

7   At the Battle of Pavia in February 1525.

8   They were no more than propagandistic fictions. In reality, "the people of [Pope] Clement's administration regarded apprehensively the Ottoman advances, and sought, albeit without much success, to stem the tide in Hungary"—Charles L. Stinger, "The Place of Clement VII and Clementine Rome in Renaissance History", in Kenneth Gouwens and Sheryl E. Reiss, eds, *The Pontificate of Clement VII. History, Politics, Culture* (Aldershot: Ashgate, 2005), 165–184, here 176.

9   Zwingli's response to *Strauß did not in fact appear until January 1527: *Antwurt über Doctor Straussen Büchlin, das Nachtmal Christi betreffende* (Zürich: Froschauer)—ed. *ZW* V, 464–547 (no. 103). See Burnett, *Debating*, 192.

10   This had happened as long ago as May 1525.

Greet *Pellikan, *Myconius, *Leo and the remaining brothers.
Farewell.
Basel, 6th October.
Your Oecolampadius.
To Huldrych Zwingli, most faithful teacher of the Zürich church.

Original: Zürich, Staatsarchiv, E II 349, p. 57 (autograph). Copy: Zürich, Zentralbibliothek, Ms S 17a, 25.

536 Oecolampadius to Zwingli—Basel, 13th October (1526)

VIII, 735 Greetings in Christ, my brother! Vitus, who delivered both your letter and *Luther's childish little book,[1] has left for Strasbourg. I have written to the brothers there that they should let us know the plan which, for certain, they are about to put into practice.[2] In attacking Luther you will have my support—for all who rely on him bark when he barks, and are silent when he is silent. Very many Augsburgers want Urbanus Rhegius to show firmness of character. He is said to have spoken soundly in his sermon on Matthew 26.[3] May the Lord continue to protect him.

I believe that Sichard has been pleasing the impious *Faber, and seeking to gain for himself a certain episcopal palace by celebrating Clement *VIII, 736* with unworthy shouts of praise.[4] | I do not condone a deed that needs to be repented of. Of the Swiss Cantons only Schaffhausen and Glarus were represented here; they have embraced the idea of the federal oath, without mentioning the gospel.[5] We have heard nothing about the other Cantons. I commend myself to you and the brothers.

5f. *silent ... silent*] *obmutescente obmutescunt et sui* (literally, 'his people are also silent when he is silent'—we read *the et sui* as redundant)

---

1   His *Sermon von dem Sacrament des leibs und bluts Christi widder die Schwarmgeister* (Wittenberg: Lufft, 1526)—ed. WA XIX, 482–523; trans. AE XXXVI, 329–361. See Burnett, *Debating*, 199 f. We do not know who "Vitus" was.
2   There is no surviving letter to either *Capito or *Bucer from around this time.
3   No published work on this topic by Rhegius (see 404, n. 9) has survived, but Matthew 26:26–29 was a key passage in contemporary debates about the Eucharist.
4   Johannes Sichard (c. 1499–1552) had taught Roman Law at the University of Basel since 1525, and was later active in Freiburg (from 1530) and Tübingen (from 1535), where he became an important adviser to Duke *Ulrich of Württemberg. On 18th August 1526 he had published a commentary on Rufinus of Aquileia's Latin translation of Book X of Pseudo-Clement's *Recognitiones*, which contained a flattering dedicatory epistle to Bishop Bernard of Trent, Chancellor to the Emperor's brother Ferdinand of Austria. On him see *CoE* III, 247; Wackernagel, *Basel*, III, 431 f.
5   At the ceremonial swearing of the federal oath of allegiance at Bern on 29th July, the Catholic Cantons had participated only on the condition that the representatives of Zürich and Basel be excluded. Immediately after the main event there was then a separate ceremony involving just Zürich, Basel and Bern; and on 30th September another one took place in Basel, this time involving Schaffhausen and Glarus. See Wackernagel, *Basel*, III, 484 f.

Farewell.
13th October.
Your Oecolampadius.
To Huldrych Zwingli, his dearest brother. Zürich.

Original: Zürich, Staatsarchiv, E II 349, p. 140 (autograph). *Copy: Zürich, Zentralbibliothek, Ms S 17a, no. 26.*

540   Oecolampadius to Zwingli—Basel, 17th October (1526)

Greetings in Christ, dearest Zwingli! Although *Faber's poisonous abuse[1] is blasphemous beyond measure and causes no little damage to Christian unity, I do not know if it would be advantageous to respond to him soon. Certainly he is unworthy of any good man's conversation; and, to avoid your taking on work that will need to be repeated, it does seem to me worthwhile delaying a response. For there is a rumour here that Christoph[2] will tell us the disputation records are to be published with a preface and afterword—the author of which, they think, is a charlatan from Konstanz, namely the Suffragan Bishop.[3] This is a summary of these pieces:

A worthy enough greeting comes first. Then, at the start of the preface, he inveighs against the new prophets, especially *Luther: he says that our faith and our religion are being defiled by their perverse doctrines and heretical statements, as well as by their contempt for the sacraments, depraved exegesis of the sacred letters, ridiculing of Councils, prohibition of the Mass and confession, abolition of ceremonies and church laws, and above all by their failure to pray to the saints; from these things stem mutinies, rebellions, scandals, errors, devastation, the spilling of blood, etc.[4] He laments that the admonitions, teachings, bulls and edicts issued by the heads of the Christian church (the Pope and the Emperor) to chastise Luther have achieved nothing—indeed, he has been made worse by being given such attention.[5] You are said to be his (Luther's) most obedient disciple, | you who have achieved amongst the Swiss what he achieved amongst the Saxons; and you have commended Luther in your writings.[6] Thereafter, having dismissed Luther, he chases after you with only loose reins, in a kind of short summary of the insults we find in Faber's book.[7] The Zürichers, hav-

---

1 A reference to the *Christenliche beweisung* (see 534, n. 1).
2 *Froschauer.
3 Melchior Fattlin (c. 1490–1548), a staunch defender of Catholic orthodoxy who had been Suffragan Bishop of Konstanz since 1518. He had debated with Zwingli as early as 1522 (see 569, n. 3), and was a leading player at the Disputation of Baden. See *CoE* II, 13 f.; Schindler, *BD*, 689–691.
4 This list summarizes the text reproduced in Schindler, *BD*, 254 f., lines 17–29.
5 Cf. Schindler, *BD*, 255, lines 29–43.
6 Cf. Schindler, *BD*, 255, lines 43–52. In fact Fattlin calls Zwingli only Luther's *gehorsamen junger und guotwilligen nachvolger* ('obedient disciple and willing follower').
7 This "short summary" is in fact quite extensive and signally damning: see Schindler, *BD*, 255–257, lines 53–93.

LETTER 540   191

ing relentlessly churned out ripostes from your printing works, have been
admonished about these things so often that they ought to have come to
their senses.[8] Also, you did not want to be bothered with doctrines or exhortations, taking refuge instead in the scriptures—which you tear to pieces as
it suits you, on the basis of your own opinions and in contempt of everyone
else's interpretations.[9] And so, as the Swiss delegates were deliberating how
to oppose this evil alliance, the triumvirate of *Eck, *Faber and Murner[10]
offered themselves—spontaneously, not by summons—to come and defeat
you; and they asked that an opportunity might be created for them to dispute
with you.[11] This request was granted and decided upon, with the consent of
the bishops of four provinces. The location was made known and the day
named.[12] The bishops were invited, along with other learned men.[13] Great
pains were taken in negotiations with the Zürchers to ensure that both you
and other learned men of your city would be present. And yet, after a safe
conduct had been issued that offered the greatest possible security, you all—
on a baseless pretext—disdained to appear.[14] Pretty well all of this is in
the preface. Then we are promised an account of the disputation, as written down by the notaries.[15] Finally we are promised a catalogue naming all
those who supported either myself or Eck,[16] and are told a yarn about Faber
lamenting that your absence had cheated him out of a famous victory, and
then presenting his book. It is also related how Murner submitted himself
to the judgement of the Swiss delegates, even at risk to his life, and how he
in turn presented a book in which, he boasted, he was going to demonstrate

---

8   Cf. Schindler, BD, 257, lines 94–103.
9   Cf. Schindler, BD, 259, lines 140–152 and 158–160.
10 The Franciscan Thomas Murner (1475–1537) had been a hated and much mocked opponent of the Swiss Reformers at least since the First Zürich Disputation of 1523, and this antipathy had increased following Murner's arrival in Luzern in 1525. He had for example set up his own press to publish polemical works against the evangelicals, and eagerly engaged in vitriolic personal attacks against the absent Zwingli at the Disputation of Baden itself. On him see CoE II, 471f.; OER III, 102f.; TRE XXIII, 436–438; BBKL VI, 366–369; VL DH II, 299–368; VL 16, IV, 511–526; KTR III, 18–32; Füssel, DD, 296–310.
11 Cf. Schindler, BD, 259, lines 153–157 and 162–167.
12 Cf. Schindler, BD, 260, lines 174–180.
13 Cf. Schindler, BD, 260, lines 188–194.
14 Fattlin includes the text of this safe conduct in his preface—Schindler, BD, 262–264, lines 243–319.
15 Cf. Schindler, BD, 265, lines 338–340.
16 Cf. Schindler, BD, 268, lines 418–445. From this point Oecolampadius's account of Fattlin's preface parts company at least with the printed version of the full text.

your infamy in forty articles.[17] Finally a conclusion is appended, in which you are upbraided for your absence, and those of us who did attend are condemned for teaching heretical doctrines and—following our defeat—for not accepting instruction; hence we deserve to be treated as heretics, as defined in the precepts of the holy fathers. They, however, seeing themselves as victors, have set down certain things that henceforth are to be kept inviolate:

1. They want the gospel to be taught according to the interpretations of the fathers and the saints, so that there might be no opposition to the hallowed ancient customs; and those who do not comply are to be punished.

2. No-one should be allowed to preach without first being examined by his bishop and found to be suitable.

| 3. No innovations should be made to the Mass, the administration of the sacraments and the other customs and constitutions, such as fasts, prayers, confessions, offerings, festivals or commemorations of the dead; rather, all such things should be observed as we have received them from the fathers. They are threatening punishments for those who do not make confession before taking communion, or who seek to take the sacrament in both kinds.

4. They state that persons will be punished who are stumbling blocks to others in the matter of eating meat or other prohibited foods.

5. A law has been enacted that printers should not publish books or pictures unless these have been examined and permitted by bishops. Moreover, in their regions no Lutheran or Zwinglian works should be bought, sold, or given as presents. In addition, as well as administrators, inspectors (that is to say, informers) are to be appointed.

6. If anyone has been expelled from one Canton because of a transgression against the aforementioned regulations, he will be expelled also from the other Cantons; and there should be no place of safety in them for people who have fled in fear of punishment.

Behold, my brother, the wisdom of the world, which the Lord will surely confound and thwart.[18] I have high hopes that the Baslers will not put

---

17 These interventions by Faber and Murner are described in the latter's *Die disputacion vor den xij orten einer loblichen eidtgenoschafft* (Luzern: Murner, 18th May 1527; Leu/Weidmann A156)—ed. *FGR* I, 404–415. The book by Faber referred to here is his *Christenliche beweisung* (see 534, n. 1), and the one by Murner his *Worhafftigs verantwurten der doctors und herren, die zuo Baden uff die disputacion gewesen sind* (Luzern: Murner, 1527; Leu/Weidmann A155)—ed. Wolfgang Pfeiffer-Belli, *Thomas Murner und der Schweizer Glaubenskampf* (Münster: Aschendorff, 1939), 7–38.

18 Cf. 1 Corinthians 1:19.

LETTER 540   193

80   their signatures to this—unless the Lord is downright angry with them.[19] So
     whether or not the records are published with the preface and afterword by
     these oh-so-saintly men, there will be a major opportunity for us to respond
     with eager gentleness. For if the records are not published, you can pretend
     you have been waiting for them in vain for such a long time that you can
85   now kill two birds with one stone; and if they are published, that will be a
     wonderfully apt opportunity to respond to them.
        Now, I would like you and your friends to advise us on how to deal with
     Luther.[20] If we are lenient towards him, his arrogance may prove useful to
     us—if there is some way of pandering to it without doing damage to the
90   truth. For if it comes to pass that this preface is published,[21] his making
     common cause with us, if expressed in a short text, could assist the cause
     of the pious a good deal—even though they are not followers of the man.[22]
     Indeed, throughout the records he is portrayed negatively, just as we are. On
     the other hand, up to now it has seemed wise for us to be confrontational
95   towards him—given that we are placed in no less peril by the followers of
     Luther than we are from any other quarter—for he has nothing else to offer
     beyond what he always asserts: "This is my body". But perhaps there might
     be a middle way: namely, if you were to rebuke *Strauß sharply, but also to
     explain gently at the end of the book[23] that | he, Strauß, actually agrees with   VIII, 748
100 Martin's writings—something it will be easy to refute once it has become
     clear what those writings are actually like. But why do I, a swine, address
     Pallas?[24]
        Carry on courageously, as you are accustomed to doing; and the Lord will
     endue his servant with great strength.

---

85 *kill ... stone*] *una opera satisfacias duobus exactoribus* (literally, 'pay off two creditors with one deed')

---

19   These hopes at least were fulfilled.
20   Presumably Zwingli had responded to Oecolampadius's comments on Luther in 536 (lines 1–6 and n. 1), but no relevant letter has survived.
21   The preface by Fattlin summarized above (see especially lines 10–42 and n. 3–14 above).
22   Oecolampadius is presumably reckoning on Luther being as aggrieved at being equated with Zwingli as vice versa.
23   This was to become the *Antwurt über doctor Strussen büchlin* (see 534, n. 9).
24   Presumably Pallas Athene, in her capacity as goddess of wisdom. Oecolampadius is also no doubt deliberately inverting Christ's warning (in Matthew 7:6) against "casting pearls before swine".

Farewell.
Basel, 17th October.
Your Oecolampadius.
To Huldrych Zwingli, his dearest brother.

Original: Zürich, Staatsarchiv, E II 349, p. 145 (autograph). Copy: Zürich, Zentralbibliothek, Ms S 17a, no. 31.

105

542   Oecolampadius to Zwingli—Basel, 19th October (1526)

Greetings in Christ. The author of this little book has asked me to attend to its printing. But since it might be difficult for the printers here to do this because of the severity of the censors, I will say only that it would be unworthy of the church and harmful to it to leave unexposed the deceptions of so many rascals, who grievously hinder us everywhere and prevent the word from bearing fruit.[1] Therefore I ask you, my brother, in the name of Christ, whose glory we seek in this, to see to it that it is published there, either by Christoph[2] or by someone else. The person who wrote it is a good man, although he does not give his name. In this regard, we should make our suffragans of Konstanz and Freising[3] a present of this book, so that they might rage against it—that is, if they do not wish to be improved by it.

Keep well along with your church, my brother.
Basel, 19th October.
Your Johannes Oecolampadius.
To Huldrych Zwingli, his dearest brother. Zürich.

Original: Zürich, Staatsarchiv, E II 349, p. 90 (autograph). Copy: Zürich, Zentralbibliothek, Ms S 17a, no. 32.

9f. *In this ... book*] *Gratificemur in hoc nostris Constantiensi et Frisingensi suffraganeis* (literally, 'Let us please our Suffragans of Konstanz and Freising in this')

---

1 The work in question is the anonymous *Was Missbreuch im wychbischofflichem ampt* (Staehelin 146), to which Oecolampadius wrote a prologue—printed in *OeBA* I, 589f. (no. 435). This polemic against the powers and ritual duties of suffragan bishops (such as the two mentioned in line 8) was eventually printed in Basel, by Thomas Wolff in 1527.
2 *Froschauer.
3 Respectively Melchior Fattlin (see 540, n. 3) and Augustinus *Marius.

543 Oecolampadius to Zwingli—Basel, 20th October (1526)

Greetings in Christ. In a few days we shall, I think, have more reliable information from the Wittenbergers. So it is worthwhile preparing a response to Martin[1] in quite a measured way and, in the mean time, praying to the Lord to help us with his Spirit, so that we might not do anything unworthy of our ministry. You will learn from *Capito's letter what, at the moment, the Strasbourg brothers judge to be useful for suppressing the Ostrich.[2] Nothing else is on my mind, other than the fact that you were to have given advice to the Margrave.[3]

But I would not want us to respond to *Faber soon[4]—for the reason which I recently gave (along with Christoph).[5] As far as I can find out from friends, our city is not going to sign the preface and appendix to the Baden Disputation records. But I hope that they will win support for their decision amongst the other Cantons, so that the plans of the wicked might be frustrated through Christ.[6] May the Lord strengthen you with his Spirit more and more every day.

Greet *Pellikan and *Leo. I have also added to yours the letters that I received from the Strasbourg brothers, so that you can study their thinking more thoroughly for yourself. Beyond this there is no need to urge you to do anything.

Farewell.
Basel, 20th October.
Your Oecolampadius.
To Huldrych Zwingli, his dearest brother. Zürich.

Original: Zürich, Staatsarchiv, E II 349, p. 100 (scribal hand).

18f. *there ... anything*] *nullo tibi opus calcare* (literally, 'you have no need of any spur')

---

1 *Luther. Oecolampadius is thinking of his *Von dem Sacrament des leibs und bluts* (see 536, n. 1).
2 See Capito's letter of 17th October 1526: ZW VIII, 749–752 (no. 541), here 749 f.; CC II, 255 f. (no. 306). "The Ostrich" is *Strauß.
3 Philipp I of Baden-Sponheim: see 530, lines 14–21.
4 See 534, lines 1–7 and n. 1 f.
5 *Froschauer. For the context see 540, lines 1–9.
6 Cf. Psalm 33:10.

544 Oecolampadius to Zwingli—Basel, 30th October (1526)

Grace and peace from Christ, beloved brother. Our people did not like the idea that the Lord might smile on other people. So you were right to predict that he is about to overthrow the plans of the wicked.[1] For all is well with us here—as long as our people do not sign.[2]

The Strasbourg brothers are continually insisting that *Luther must be answered.[3] I am sending on a letter from *Bucer admonishing you in faith;[4] you should read it. We shall be able to excuse Martin in one respect, namely that he is fearful of any violence that might be done to the divine words, lest at some point this open a window to the violation of all sacred things. In other respects I do not see how we can agree with what he has written. If I had a copy of Luther's work to hand, I would certainly try to respond to his objections. So go ahead, and then—with your honour intact and the necessary insults and reproaches duly hurled—dispatch the response as soon as you can; for it will be more useful than spending hours on that most inept and mendacious man *Faber.[5]

Today two little books by the Ostrich[6] have been sent over from Strasbourg. I do not know to what end; perhaps for us to detect their grosser errors and to taunt him with them. Why, actually, should we take so much notice of the faults of others? I am sending you the copies; if you do not need them, make sure they are returned to me, because I have not yet read them. Moreover, if the little book about the suffragans' deceptions is not to be taken up for publishing by the printers,[7] see to it that I get that back also—because the author is asking for it. It would be good, though, if these people's dishonesty and stupidity were to be exposed. The Cathedral Preacher[8] here is playing the fool irresponsibly and with immoderate flattery; it is clear even to the most obsequious what he is like.

---

26 *most obsequious*] *pituitosis* (literally, 'full of phlegm, slimy')

1 Cf. 543, lines 10–15—though there is no surviving evidence of Zwingli having made such a prediction.
2 That is, the records and decisions of the Disputation of Baden.
3 See 536, n. 1 and 543, lines 1–5.
4 This has not been preserved.
5 Specifically, his *Christliche beweisung* (see 534, n. 1).
6 *Strauß. On the basis of a dedicatory note from Oecolampadius to Zwingli, Leu/Weidmann (170, no. 175) suggest that one of these books was *Wider den unmilten Irrthum* (see 530, n. 1).
7 See 542, lines 1–8 and n. 1.
8 *Marius, who was also a suffragan bishop.

Return Konrad *Pellikan's greeting for me, in Christ.
Farewell.
Basel, 30th October.
Oecolampadius.
To Huldrych Zwingli, most faithful pastor of the Zürich church, his brother.
Zürich.

Original: Zürich, Staatsarchiv, E II 349, p. 108a (scribal hand).

547 Oecolampadius to Zwingli—Basel, 9th November (1526)

Greetings in Christ, dearest Zwingli! It is certain that the disputation records have been printed. Our notary Egmund of Rottweil, whom we used at Baden,[1] has seen them, and has acknowledged that he has signed his name on them. He was not allowed to read the rest. They say the Ostrich has recanted in Baden-Baden in the presence of the Margrave; but the Strasbourg brothers have not written anything about this.[2] Billican of Nördlingen has written to *Bucer that he cannot oppose us.[3] Our Augsburg friends write that Rhegius is of our party (that is, the party of Christ), and that the Frog and the Farmer are taking it badly.[4] As I hear it, the Landgrave is mellowing,[5] and the Frankfurters and Vangiones are agreeing with us.[6] The Dutch admire your erudition.[7]

Meanwhile we are being scattered about in all directions and derided as the worst of all mortals; but what would we not bear, so as not to be estranged from the truth? Also, *Eck is said to have slighted the city of Konstanz and that most pious man *Blarer in his notorious little book full of insults.[8]

---

1 Egmund Rysysen. See Schindler, BD, 742 f.
2 Jakob *Strauß and Margrave Philipp I of Baden-Sponheim. The report of Strauß's recantation had no obvious basis.
3 No such letter has been preserved. On Billican see 394, n. 5.
4 On Urbanus Rhegius see 404, n. 9. "The Frog and the Farmer", Johann Frosch (c. 1485–1533) and Stephan Agricola (c. 1491–1547), were Rhegius's fellow Lutheran reformers in Augsburg.
5 *Philipp of Hesse, whose "interest in Zwingli seems to have been piqued in the summer of 1526". They had in common their support for Duke *Ulrich of Württemberg, whom Philipp had come to see as "a key factor in his reaching out for Swiss support" (Gordon, *Zwingli*, 186).
6 That is, the inhabitants of Frankfurt am Main and Worms.
7 Contact between the Swiss and Dutch reformers dated from 1522–1523, when Johannes Rode and Georg Saganus had visited Zwingli, Oecolampadius and others, and familiarized them with the eucharistic thought of Cornelis Hoen. The influence was clearly two-way and ongoing: Bucer had, for example, recently informed Zwingli of the enthusiasm with which his ideas had been adopted in Holland and Friesland, thanks to the advocacy of Rode and others—see ZW VIII, 651–654 (no. 503, 9th July 1526), here 652, lines 9–11.
8 His *Antwurt uf das ketzerbuochlein Ambrosi Blarers*—ed. Karl Meisen and Friedrich Zoepfl, *Johannes Eck, Vier deutsche Schriften* (Münster: Aschendorff, 1929), pp. 41–52. This represents Eck's intervention in an epistolary quarrel between Blarer and the Dominican Prior of Rottweil, Georg Neudorffer.

VIII, 765 | The Turk has retreated, having abandoned Pannonia and left the immigrants unharmed.[9] A certain Zápolya,[10] the leading count of the Pannonian kingdom and a man of ill repute who brought the Turk there, is now summoning a meeting of the princes; he desires the royal crown for himself.[11] People say, on the same authority, that the Turk has abandoned Syria and Egypt to the Sufis; but few believe this.[12] They also state, groundlessly, that the Turk has been committing such great cruelty that certain powerful men are discussing in open letters how the common people might now be despoiled still more. *Ferdinand is not a Lutheran,[13] but he is melting down the gold and silver vessels of all the churches and monasteries in the South Tyrol—no doubt he is intending to fight against the Turk.[14]

Nothing could trouble me more deeply than the fact that the magistracy allows such contradictory things to be taught here.[15] They make many concessions to our adversaries which we would be ashamed to grant them. But

---

16f. *immigrants*] Metanastis, from the Greek μετανάστης   22f. *powerful men*] Greek τῶν κρατούντων   25f. *South Tyrol*] ad Athesin (literally, 'near the (river) Athesis'). The modern name of this river continues to feature in the Italian term for the South Tyrol, *Alto Adige* ('Upper Adige')

---

9   "Pannonia", the former Roman province, is Oecolampadius's word for Hungary. Following their victory at the battle of Mohács and burning down of Buda, the Ottoman army under Suleiman the Magnificent had begun to retreat on 17th September. They left much destruction in their wake, but avoided Transylvania with its significant population of "immigrant" Saxons—by prior arrangement, many suspected, with the local prince John Zápolya (c. 1490–1540). On the latter see Firchner *Ferdinand*, 50 f.; *CoE* III, 241–243; *BBKL* XIV, 343 f.
10 Here called "Hallweyda"; but it is impossible to imagine anyone other than Zápolya (as n. 9) being meant.
11 Zápolya (as n. 9) was indeed crowned King of Hungary at Székesfelérvár the day after this letter was written.
12 "Recognizing their important functions, the Ottomans encouraged the spread of Anatolian sufism in the Balkans by giving land grants to [sufi] brotherhoods"—Metin Kunt and Christine Woodhead (eds), *Süleyman the Magnificent and His Age* (London: Longman, 1995), 18. There was, however, never any likelihood of such grants being made in respect of the recently conquered lands of Syria (1516) or Egypt (1517).
13 Ferdinand, Archduke of Austria, was, in fact, an unimpeachably devout Catholic; Oecolampadius's statement of the obvious is presumably intended to counter the view that Ferdinand's court was populated by an excessive number of influential German Lutherans.
14 Ferdinand was himself a candidate for the throne of Hungary, and was to defeat the Ottoman-supported Zápolya at the battle of Tokaj in August 1527. On his involvement in Hungary see Firchner, *Ferdinand*, 45–52 and 58–65.
15 A reference to the Council's ongoing policy of permitting both Catholics and evangelicals to preach without hindrance.

30 perhaps it is pleasing to the Lord that we should be exercised in this way. They are not learned enough for us to dispute with them; yet they are forever singing the same old song. Next week I will consign the last three of the minor prophets to the printing-presses.[16]

Farewell.
35 Basel, 9th November.
Your Oecolampadius.
To Huldrych Zwingli, most faithful teacher of the Zürich church, his brother in Christ.

Original: Zürich, Staatsarchiv, E II 349, p. 80 (scribal hand). Copy: Zürich, Zentralbibliothek, Ms S 17a, no. 47.

---

16 Oecolampadius's commentary on Haggai, Zechariah and Malachi. See p. 34 and n. 143.

552 Zwingli to Oecolampadius (and Others)—Zürich, 29th November 1526

VIII, 778   Grace and peace from the Lord. Dearly beloved brothers, I am indeed ignorant of what Jodocus's father communicated to his son by letter; but I do know that whatever he did eventually write is not much for you to worry about.[1] The man is always driven by affection for his brother, whom (given that we are the last to discern the vices of those close to us) he believes to be   5
a good or at least a just man—even though he is in fact the most depraved of the Catilinarian band.[2] But this is the state of Hestia's affairs.[3]

Meanwhile they have held a Diet at Baden,[4] where they agreed to exhort the Council and people of Zürich again to allow just one little Mass. When this was announced in Bern by a man who had acted as a delegate,[5] a cer-   10
tain honest and faithful friend of our city[6] countered him in this way: "Why
VIII, 779   do you all take on this | work to no purpose? Do you not see that every day there is less and less for you to do in Zürich? And not without cause. Not

---

7 *But ... affairs*] Sic autem ἀφ ἑστίας res habet—see also n. 3 below   8 *at Baden*] Greek ἐν Θερμοπύλαις—see also n. 4

---

1   The former Provost of St Peter's monastery in Embrach, Heinrich Brennwald (c. 1478–1551), a supporter of Zwingli, had written about developments in Zürich to his (illegitimate) son Jodocus, an associate of the Strasbourg reformers, who had passed on its contents to *Capito—a circumstance which motivated the latter to write to Zwingli urging the use of carefully coded language. See zw VIII, 771–773 (no. 550), here 771f.; CC II, 259 (no. 309). Hence Zwingli's reassurance that no damage has been done. On Brennwald see Robert Hoppeler, "Zur Biographie des Embracher Propstes Heinrich Brennwald", *Zwingliana* 3/2 (1920): 509–514; 4/1 (1921), 51f.
2   Heinrich Brennwald's brother Felix, a prominent Zürich politician and 'pensioner' (see n. 7) who opposed Zwingli. He and his associates are compared to Lucius Sergius Catilina (108–162 BCE) and his fellow participants in the Catilinarian conspiracies that sought to overthrow the Roman Republic.
3   Hestia was the Greek goddess of hearth and home; so a freer translation might read "this is the state of affairs here in Zürich".
4   Zwingli refers to Baden as Θερμοπύλαι, 'Thermopylae'. This is a play on the toponym ('baths', in Latin *Thermae Helvetiorum*), but for certain also an allusion to the battle of Thermopylae in 480 BCE—at which the Greek army fought bravely but eventually suffered a heavy defeat at the hands of the numerically vastly superior Persians. It is not difficult to imagine parallels suggesting themselves between this event and the evangelicals' still recent experiences at the Disputation at Baden.
5   The knight Kaspar von Mülinen (1481–1538), an active Catholic member of the Bern Council.
6   The Zürichers had numerous friends in Bern, so a specific identification here is impossible.

only they themselves but everyone everywhere is saying that they are doing away with the Mass." Then the man who had been a delegate replied: "We would not have made this decree lightly if there were not Zürichers who had worn us down with their (albeit silent) requests." Our friend told us of these words. So what could we say? To those who were paying attention to all this it seemed entirely right to suppurate a little this ulcer of the pensioners (or rather traitors or transgressors),[7] especially since everyone could see that all the deliberations of the Diet were corrupted by the paying of wages. And not only this, but also that the wage-earners were hired by these same means to resist the gospel, thereby assisting their leaders to work against the good of their nation. Something else was also apparent, namely that the Catilinarian band[8] always came together and congratulated each other if anything adverse had befallen the church, and that all those who were suspected of taking foreign money took a very pertinacious stand against the gospel. What more is there to say? It was apparent that they were doing all the things that corrupt men usually do—men who cannot be unknown to you from your reading of your Sallusts and Ciceros[9] and who are only too familiar to us, experiencing as we do their ardent treachery.

So since this was the way things stood, and since these men were showing at every opportunity by their words and deeds that they were more to be feared than the enemy themselves, I have, I confess, inveighed most resolutely against the scandal that is treachery, and have shaken it to its foundations using all my battering-rams[10]—with the result that those involved have clearly seen its wall collapse, whilst some (out of fear) have feigned anger or indignation, whereas others have—because of the situation—hardly dissembled at all. In the course of my orations I let slip—not for the imprudent, but for those willing to learn—the following analogy: goldfinches live on

---

14f. *that ... Mass*] a play on words in the original, *missam esse missam faciendam*   18 *So ... say*] *Quid ergo nobis oscitandum erat?* (literally, 'what was there for us to yawn/open our mouths wide')   21 *by ... wages*] Greek μισθοδοσία   22 *wage-earners*] Greek μισθοφόρους

---

7   Zwingli and his supporters had long inveighed against the practice of foreign powers giving money ('pensions') to Swiss politicians in exchange for their support, not least on matters of faith and ecclesiology. The Zürich Council had formally forbidden this practice by a law enacted on 15th November 1522, and increased the levels of punishment for it in one passed on 13th December 1526.
8   See n. 2 above.
9   These two authors wrote the most important records of the Second Catilinarian Conspiracy of 63 BCE (in which Cicero was also actively involved, as the Consul who suppressed the revolt).
10 In this paragraph and the next Zwingli refers to what he has said in sermons—and perhaps in representations to the Zürich Council—rather than in published works.

hemp seed, but only if the seed has been ground. And so, if these traitors and mercenaries cannot be convicted on the basis of evidence (an anchor to which they always have recourse), who would be so foolish or so careless of their own safety as to allow judges to deliberate over such a crime? So here we examine a traitor by subjecting him to rope torture—using hemp ropes that are twisted and ground like seeds; but we believe that no-one should be tried by torture unless some evidence exists against him.

I said that I too knew something about this matter, and I did not do so without foundation. Certain letters were found that everyone thought I knew nothing of, but about which, in fact, all excellent men carefully consulted me in secret; and I had also learnt much about it elsewhere, by many different ways and means. An autocracy has been set up | to combat this present evil, not based on the Roman model of one person alone having full charge of everything, but rather involving eleven eminent persons, to whom is entrusted the duty of investigating crimes and dispensing justice.[11] Enquiries are being made and many things, both trifling and incriminating, are being discovered—with the upshot, however, that those who previously spoke of what they were privy to are now thinking about denying it. This is the way with the common people and with that faint-hearted kind of man who grows pale before the sword of justice.

Grebel, a distinguished and highly influential man hereabouts[12] and the father of Konrad Grebel,[13] who was | the ringleader of the anabaptists, has been beheaded for accepting more than 1,500 florins from the Emperor, the French and the Roman pontiff, ostensibly for his son. In addition | (some-

---

42 *mercenaries*] *mistophoros*, derived from the Greek   52 *autocracy*] *dictatura*

11 This commission (*dictatura*!) had begun the work of enquiring into 'pensioners' on 11th October 1526. On the immediate context see Gordon, *Zwingli*, 206 f.

12 Jakob Grebel (c. 1460–1526), an influential Zürich iron merchant who had been an early supporter of and spokesman for Zwingli, but who seems to have fallen victim to the reformer's desire to make an example of a prominent 'pensioner'. His execution had taken place on 30th October. On his career see Wirz, "Familienschicksale", 473–499, 537–544.

13 Jakob Grebel's son (c. 1498–1526), a Greek scholar and friend of both *Vadian and Zwingli, whose increasingly radical views had led him to break with the latter around 1523, and who had incurred renewed hostility by performing adult re-baptisms at Zollikon in January 1525. He predeceased his father, dying of the plague in Maienfeld (Graubünden) in the summer of 1526. On him see Hans-Jürgen Goertz, *Konrad Grebel: Ein Radikaler in der Zürcher Reformation* (Zürich: Theologischer Verlag, 2004); OER II, 191–193; BBKL II, 295 f.

thing I could not believe at first) his son Konrad's wife,[14] following her husband's death some months previously, had been petitioning her father-in-law for her inheritance (here widows are entitled to a third of the estate); but he had turned her away, saying that his son had not owned any property. Later, though, 400 gulden were found which Grebel had put into his own purse in his son's name. Following Grebel's execution some people are fleeing, the gates having been locked in vain; Jodocus's uncle left in an empty shit cart.[15] So it is that those who betray their country for the sake of their stomachs and their shit must also seek their salvation in shit. They are now working towards returning, feigning innocence and saying that Grebel was a better man than to become involved in the business of such men, even if he was imprudent in so far as he allowed them to know his business.[16] Another man, called N.N., was also tortured:[17] a maimed man whose left arm—which was shorter than his right—was dislodged very early in the process, he is dissolute and overly bold, and it is the Lord who has brought about this delay to his mounting number of shameful crimes. The autocracy and its enquiries continue to thrive. In all this we have not only urged all to be constant in destroying evil, but also have made certain examples, so as to make men of this sort known to those who have been unaware of them. But so much for that.

The printer will finish the response to the Ostrich[18] before Christmas Day. We have not yet begun our Latin complaint against *Luther,[19] but we will present it, if the Lord wills, at the Frankfurt Spring Fair. Plutarch's "Lives" I regard as profitable to read; but the Aldine edition, whilst excellent, is very

---

77 *N.N.*] an abbreviation for *nomen nescio* ('I do not know the name')   83f. *But ... that*] Greek Καὶ ταῦτα μέν ταῦτα

14 Barbara Ziegler, of whom Konrad's parents had never approved, and with whom he himself seems to have had a difficult relationship—see Wirz, "Familienschicksale", 479f.
15 Felix Brennwald (as n. 2), who was also strongly suspected of being a 'pensioner'.
16 Brennwald succeeded in obtaining a pardon and returning to Zürich in October 1527.
17 A letter from Capito dated 10th December (zw VIII, 798–800, no. 557, here 798f.; CC II, 261, no. 312), makes it plain that this is a reference to the torture, in Winterthur, of the Zürich 'pensioner' and mercenary Thomas Wellenberg. He may well have fled Zürich after Jakob Grebel's death.
18 *Strauß. Zwingli's "response" is *Antwurt über Doctor Strussen Büchlin* (see 534, n. 9), a rejoinder to Strauß's *Wider den unmilten Irrthum* (see 530, n. 1).
19 *Amica exegesis, id est, Expositio eucharistiae negocii, ad Martinum Lutherum* (Zürich: Froschauer, 1527; Leu/Weidmann 198)—ed. zw V, 562–758 (no. 104), trans. Pipkin, II, 238–369. See Burnett, *Debating*, 201–203.

expensive,[20] so it would be best if *Cratander divided it into two volumes, offering the first at the abovementioned Fair, and the second at the Autumn Fair.[21] If | people in Strasbourg, Basel and Nürnberg agreed with this view of ours, he would set about this work sooner, knowing that he could sell a hundred or two hundred copies. When I think of all the authors, it certainly seems to me that he is the one we should place in the hands of our Greek students, not so much for his style as for his most excellent arguments.

Farewell, beloved brothers, and pray to the Lord for us.
On the penultimate day of November 1526, by lamplight.
To Oecolampadius and the brothers at Strasbourg, especially *Capito.

Original lost (formerly in Bremen). Copy: Zürich, Zentralbibliothek, Ms S 17a, no. 54.

---

20 Zwingli is presumably referring to the complete Venice edition: *Plutarchi Opuscula LXXXXII* (Venice: Aldus Manutius, 1509).
21 The biannual Frankfurt Book Fairs are meant. Cratander's Plutarch did not in fact appear until considerably later: *Plutarchi Chaeronei philosophi clarissimi opuscula, quae quidam extant omnia* (Basel: Cratander, 1530).

554 Oecolampadius to Zwingli—Basel, 1st December 1526

Grace and peace from Christ. What an exceedingly gratifying thing you have done for me, beloved brother, in allaying some of my anxieties by your letter![1] Rumour had it that altogether graver things had happened,[2] and your welfare is of very great concern to us. *Capito has been asking again and again for more reliable news of you, but I had nothing certain to tell him. Now we shall both rest easier in our minds—praise be to God, who is seeing to it that this evil will very soon be removed from us, both here and there.[3] At no other time, I believe, has Mammon so shamefully opposed the business of the gospel. You are perhaps not unaware of how many bondsmen he has. At every hour they long for the death of him whom they crucify and blaspheme. But we hope that our God will give better things to our pious and holy people—he who is our protector in heaven. They fear that they will be crushed by the good fortune of the Emperor and *Ferdinand, who are reported to be making new threats against the people of God and the cities that have embraced the gospel.[4] But invincible Zion is accustomed to hearing blasphemies and defeating armed men by prayer.

Nothing has reached Strasbourg from Wittenberg except for that most inhuman letter in which he most ungratefully flays *Bucer, that most honest and best deserving of men.[5] This friend of ours had written a preface to the fourth volume of lucubrations that *Luther had given us in Latin, a preface glowing with Christian gentleness and piety, and full of learning.[6] And in it, he also gave advice about the Eucharist, along with an honest account of your and my views about it. But that wretched man is waxing so indignant that he will brook no end to his fury. He sent his letter to Setzer,[7] the Hagenau printer, for him to print it if Herwagen[8] does not want to. Bucer thinks that Herwagen will print it, but alongside Bucer's antidote—that is, the apolo-

---

1 No. 552 above.
2 In the light of Oecomlampadius's comments here, and their tone, it seems likely that rumours of Zwingli's death had been circulating.
3 Oecolampadius is presumably thinking of Zwingli's campaign against pensions (see 552).
4 In the wake of the battle of Pavia and Treaty of Madrid, there were widespread fears that a resurgent Charles v and Ferdinand of Austria would focus their attention more squarely on suppressing the Reformation.
5 Luther's letter to Herwagen of 13th September: see 525, n. 4.
6 *Praefatio M. Buceri* (see n. 9 below).
7 Johann Setzer (or 'Secer', d. 1532), who printed many works by Luther and his followers, as well as by humanists, between 1523 and his death.
8 Johann Herwagen (1497–c. 1558), who printed many works by Lutherans in Strasbourg between 1522 and 1528, and thereafter moved to Basel. See *CoE* II, 186 f.

gia in which he will also respond to the calumnies of Pomeranus.[9] May God grant it success! Who does not fear the judgement of God? If the blast of his voice breaks down the cedars of Lebanon,[10] who thereafter can trust in his own strength?

It will be for you, my brother, to assess the letter thoroughly, and not to ignore the furious words it so contemptibly hurls at us as if we were enemies of Christ and his kingdom, but rather to refute these with Christian gentleness. Above all, refute them according to the perenniel guiding principle: use words that are clear and appropriate.

Let us have as soon as you can what you have written against the Ostrich.[11] I am sending you my sermon "On the Invocation of Saints", in which I respond to *Faber.[12] I hope it will be clear from this that we do not | disagree at all on the matter; and if you wish perchance to respond to his lies at some point, you can do so without delay.

There is still a persistent rumour that the proceedings of the Baden Disputation which were so scandalously printed at Tübingen are being given only to our enemies, under the strictest oath of silence. They say that there are also some copies at Schaffhausen.[13] How the trust we have in our lands will be exposed to ridicule! Write to Bovillus[14] about it.

I have not yet met with *Cratander, but fear that it will not be convenient for him to give us Plutarch.[15] At the moment he has in press Hesychius, an ancient scholar of Leviticus[16] who is helpful on the subject of the Eucharist,

---

44 the trust ... lands] Greek ἡ τῆς ἡμετέρας χώρας πίστις (χώρας, 'land, country', is a singular, but a plural form seems necessary in a Swiss context)

9 This did indeed happen, in the following composite volume: *Praefatio M. Buceri in quartum tomum postillae Lutheranae continens summam doctrinae Christi, eiusdem Epistola explicans locum 1. Corinth 10, Epistola M. Lutheri ad Iohannem Hervagium superiora criminans, Responsio ad hanc M. Buceri, item ad Pomeranum satisfactio de versione Psalterii* (Strasbourg: Herwagen, 1527; Leu/Weidmann 38). "Pomeranus" is *Bugenhagen.
10 Psalm 29:5.
11 *Strauß. See 552, n. 18.
12 See 534, n. 3.
13 The text in question was in fact Faber's *Christliche beweisung* (see 534, n. 1).
14 Ludwig Oechsli (see 488, n. 4).
15 See 552, n. 20 f.
16 *Isychii Presbyteri Hierosolymorum* [Hesychius of Jerusalem] *In Leviticum libri septem* (Basel: Cratander, 1527).

and my Zechariah[17] and Theophylactus;[18] perhaps he will do what we want him to do after Easter.

They say that Balthasar of Waldshut[19] has re-baptized a certain nobleman in Styria, and is still consolidating his doctrine. I have heard about the | miserable anabaptists who are attacking you, but this has caused me no pain: they are only showing their folly and their malignity, and in this they are destroying themselves, not you. We are having to keep busy in various ways. I recently came across a certain dialogue, in which this same Balthasar spits at me and the Basel brothers.[20] It was intercepted in its flight. It contains nothing that is pressing, except for asking us to find in the scriptures where Christ or the apostles baptized children; but it makes one ill with its insults, idiocies and taunts.

Greet *Pellikan, *Leo, *Myconius and your wife.[21]
Basel, 1st December 1526.
Your Oecolampadius.
To Huldrych Zwingli, his dearest brother, teacher of the church at Zürich.

Original: Zürich, Staatsarchiv, E II 349, p. 6 (autograph). Copy: Zürich, Zentralbibliothek, Ms S 17a, no. 57.

---

17 See 547, n. 16.
18 *Theophylacti Arciepiscopi Bulgariæ, in quatuor Euangelia enarrationes, diligenter recognitæ Ioanne Oecolampadio Interprete* (Basel: Cratander, 1527; Staehelin 138). On this see Staehelin, *Lebenswerk*, 185 f.; idem, "Väterübersetzungen", 64–66.
19 Hubmaier (see 347, n. 5). The "certain nobleman" is Leonhart von Liechtenstein (1482–1534), a member of the Styrian/Moravian aristocratic family which owned the town of Nikolsburg (now Mikulov in the Czech Republic). Following Hubmaier's arrival there in 1526, this swiftly became an important stronghold of the anabaptist movement, thanks not least to Leonhart's support.
20 *Ein gesprech der Predicanten zu Basel vnd Balthasaren Huebmörs von Fridberg von dem Khindertauf.* This has survived only in the edition by Simprecht Sorg (Nikolsburg, 1526; Leu/Weidmann A93), so Oecolampadius had presumably seen a version of the work in manuscript or in an edition that was banned before it could be printed (cf. the phrase "intercepted in its flight"). The controversy over baptism between Oecolampadius and Hubmaier is discussed by Windhorst, *Taufverständnis*, 113–121.
21 Anna *Reinhart.

562   Oecolampadius to Zwingli—Basel, 23rd December (1526)

Greetings in Christ, my Huldrych! I have opened your letter to the Strasbourg brothers,[1] and am pleased to see that another way has at last been found to communicate the disputation's proceedings to the world. That good man Murner is worthy of commendation; but we will wait and see how faithfully he performs his task.[2] I fear that our fellow-countrymen will get little glory from it, and I certainly grieve, not so much for ourselves as for them—however they feel about me. But we shall be able without much effort to deflect whatever they devise or decide against us, so that the cause of the gospel will not only not be hindered, but will even be furthered. If only we could get a copy straightaway!

Now, how can I adequately praise the example set by St. Gallen in abolishing images and Masses?[3] We are trying to do this here. But God's anger is greater than anything we can achieve with our words. We must endure the Lord's judgement until he shows us greater favour. Our adversaries are still teaching and preaching their lies with impunity, and there are people who like | such things. But by now there are also a good many who love Christ in the right way.

We recently asked the Suffragan Bishop of Freising[4] in the friendliest of letters to teach from the scriptures (or listen to us teach from them) what he had told the people about the opinion of the church—things that we were perhaps in danger of preaching erroneously. Otherwise there is no way in which those who contradict us can be restored to order. Most of us are now preaching more freely, so they might be forced to convict those who have been accused. But I am telling a story to deaf people. Let us know if you can

---

24 *I ... people*] *surdis fabulam* (literally, 'a story to the deaf'; we assume a verb such as *narro* is understood)

---

1 No. 560 (ZW VIII, 807–809; 18th December 1526). In it, Zwingli passes on a rumour that a version of the events at Baden is to be printed at Luzern, albeit "with the most impudent prejudice" (*cum impudentissimo praeiudicio*, 807, line 2f.) in favour of the Catholic party. The letter is also printed in BC II, 185–187 (no. 143) and summarized in CC II, 261f. (no. 313).

2 A reference to Murner's *Die disputacion vor den xij orten*: see 540, n. 17. Oecolampadius's praise of him is all too obviously ironic. On Murner see 540, n. 10.

3 Reform in St. Gallen had been proceeding apace since the election of *Vadian as mayor in December 1525, but here Oecolampadius is probably referring to a raft of decisions made by the Council in December 1526: they removed all images from St Laurence's Church, introduced a new ecclesiastical calendar, and established a marriage court. See Bryner, "St. Gallen", 246f.

4 *Marius. The "we" refers to Basel's evangelical preachers, who wrote jointly to Marius on 4th December. The letter is printed in *OeBA* I, 596f. (no. 444).

think of any way in which Christ can, at last, be taught here in concord. All five of us[5] are in entire agreement that we will each do his utmost to leave nothing undone that might redound to the glory of Christ. But this is always hindered by false prophets fomenting against us.

The Strasbourg brothers often write me to advise you, in a friendly way, not to treat Luther as he deserves, but rather as our cause (which is the cause of the gospel) demands. It requires gentle ministers. In your case, it does not seem to me necessary for me to do this: you yourself will moderate your pen. What can Luther say that is graver than that we have never truly known Christ or taught him? So we cannot be silent; but it is still less fitting to trade insults with him. May the Spirit of Christ anoint you and teach you. Please send us what you have said in reply to the Ostrich.[6]

| Farewell.
Basel, 23rd December.
Your Oecolampadius.
To Huldrych Zwingli, pastor of the Zürichers, his beloved brother.

Original: Zürich, Staatsarchiv, E II 349, p. 70 (autograph). Copy: Zürich, Zentralbibliothek, Ms S 17a, no. 67.

VIII, 816

---

5 In the published German version of the Basel preachers' letter to Marius, *Widerlegung der falschen gründt, so Augustinus Marius, Thumbpredicant zu Basel, zu verwenen das die Meß ein Opffer sey, eynen Ersamen Radt doselbig überantwort hat* (Basel: Wolff, 1528; Staehelin 150), there are in fact seven signatories: Oecolampadius, Markus Bertschi, Wolfgang Wissenburg, Johannes Lüthard, Thomas Gyrfalk, Peter Frauenberger and Jakob Immeli (see 367, n. 1–6).

6 *Strauß. See 552, n. 18.

564 Capito and Oecolampadius to Zwingli—Strasbourg and Basel, 26th December 1526

*This is not a jointly authored letter. Rather, it consists principally of a letter by *Capito which Oecolampadius is to pass on to Zwingli, followed by a short note in Oecolampadius's hand. Capito's contribution is summarized in CC, II, 263f. (as no. 314). Its themes include the forthcoming publication of the records of the Baden Disputation, a discussion between *Bucer, Capito and the anabaptist Hans Denck (which had resulted in the latter's expulsion from Strasbourg), and the need for caution in troubled times. This latter is the reason, one assumes, why Capito's letter has not been sent to Zwingli directly. We translate below the note in Oecolampadius's hand.*

VIII, 821 | Hieronymus of Chur[1] delivered your letter, and that of Capito. We are well here, as we usually are. We are waiting to see what the meeting in Luzern will bring.[2] I have some not insignificant business to deal with.[3] In your presence I would gladly hear your advice; but in your absence I will content myself with prayers. May the Lord's will be done. Fare well, along with *Pellikan.

To his Huldrych Zwingli, pastor of the Zürich church, his superior, who merits respect. Zürich.[4]

Original: Zürich, Staatsarchiv, E II 349, p. 178.

---

1 Hieronymus Artolph (d. 1541) was a close associate of Bonifatius Amerbach (see 396, n. 12) who had studied in Basel, and had a lengthy teaching career at its university, whose Rector he became in 1538. See *CoE* I, 73f. The letter from Zwingli he delivered has been lost; that by Capito is presumably the one to which Oecolampadius is adding his note.
2 The Confederate Diet was to meet on 29th December.
3 This is probably a veiled reference to Oecolampadius's marriage plans—see letter 572 below.
4 This somewhat more distant form of address no doubt reflects the fact that this letter is primarily a missive from Capito—who, for example, uses the term "his superior", *maiori suo*, also in other letters from around this time (e.g. 578, 632, 705).

LETTER 569   213

569   Zwingli to Oecolampadius—Zürich, 3rd January 1527

Huldrych Zwingli to Johannes Oecolampadius.   IX, 7
   Grace and peace from the Lord. You urged me recently to advise you as
to how an end might be put to the anti-Christian gatherings that take place
among you;[1] but it has escaped my mind to do what, in that letter, you asked
5 me to do. For it often happens that, buried as we are under so much work,
the most important things get forgotten; but we will now send the advice we
had it in mind to give you—not, by Hercules, that we are anticipating anything on the basis of foresight, but rather of experience. So we do not know
whether it was a deliberate decision on your part to advise the Suffuran (for
10 which, understand 'Suffragan') in a friendly fashion by letter;[2] but you should
act the same way towards the other false prophets, warning them also that,
unless they come to their senses, you will refute their doctrine openly and in
detail. That way they will burn all the more with anger—unless Satan is not
at work so venomously in your citizens as he has been in ours. You must try
15 to place some people in their congregations who are not at all seditious (for
some are wont to report more than they have heard), and get them to pass
on verbatim the lies and vain babblings that are uttered; then you or someone else of our persuasion should publicly and repeatedly tear these words
to pieces without mentioning the name of the person who spread the lies,
20 but threatening to reveal it if he is unwilling to desist. You will proceed in this
way until such time as the originator of them is publicly disgraced; for by this
means the Council will be compelled to summon you all to a disputation.
In our city there were good citizens who protested against false prophets to
their faces—and the latter were rebuked by the Council and then instructed
25 to keep peace and order; some were thrown into prison.
   We have already been given an opportunity to inveigh against him, but it
did not achieve anything.[3] Then at last our *Leo went to a sermon preached

---

9 *Suffuran*] *suffuraneum*. Zwingli appears to be attempting a rather recondite pun on *suffuror*
('to steal secretly, filch')

---

1   See 562, line 19f.
2   *Marius; for the present context, see 562, lines 18–24 and n. 4.
3   Following this abrupt reversion to the subject matter of lines 8–10, Zwingli seems—
    perhaps deliberately—to be confusing his Suffragans. He is not believed to have come
    across Marius before late 1525, and here recounts events that took place some years earlier,
    under the aegis of Suffragan Bishop Melchior Fattlin (see 540, n. 3). In particular Zwingli
    famously disputed with Fattlin before the Zürich Council in April 1522 in the immediate
    aftermath of the infamous *Wurstessen* (see p. 5 above). He described this in the *Epistola
    Huldrici Zuinglii ad Erasmum Fabricium de actis legationis ad Tigurinos missae diebus 7*.

by the Augustinian;[4] and while this man was wittering like an old woman in his usual fashion, he interrupted the sermon in the friendliest manner and addressed him thus: "Listen for a little while, O Reverend Father Prior", and then: "And you, most excellent citizens, let nothing disturb you; | I will do everything in a Christian spirit, etc.". It would be tedious to relate everything. In short, a tragedy nearly ensued, for there were some who insisted that Leo be beaten for his audacity (you are not unaware of what kind of man frequents these people's meetings); but equally there were some present who rescued him from danger—and at length it descended into a comedy. For when the Council was forced by this method to pass judgement on the altercation, not only was justice done, but also the malice of the worst of men was uncovered.[5]

There might also be another approach, but I do not know how appropriate it would be for you all; so disregard it, if all of you who stand by the gospel intend to address the Council and explain (if you are allowed to) what a divisive thing it is that in one and the same city the people are rent asunder by conflicting sermons—especially when those on whom an excellent and righteous part of the populace depend never appear at services, but rather seek to avoid and flee from those whom they should be serving. Therefore you would be neither adequate Christians, nor indeed human beings, if you abandoned those who despair of victory—that is, the common people, simple and eager for the truth, who are committed to your faith.

There is no news of the collated documents[6] being issued by the magistracy; but those in Zürich, Strasbourg and St. Gallen, etc., have recently done this. Haner wrote to me from Nürnberg the other day, asking me first of all to greet you, and then telling me that *Luther has absented himself from the lecture hall in order to have enough time to write against you.[7] Some are

---

45 *never*] *nunquam non* (literally, 'never not'; we read the double negative as if it were a single one)   51 *etc.*] in the edition, this word occurs, bizarrely, at the end of the sentence. We have moved it to a place where it makes sense

---

8.9. *aprilis 1522* (Zürich: Froschauer, 1522)—ed. ZW I, 142–154 (no. 9); trans. Jackson, 113–129.
4   Leo Jud interrupted the Augustinian Lector in this fashion at some point early in 1523.
5   On 4th July 1523 the Council decided that Jud had committed no punishable offence, but that the Lector/Prior had contravened the edict published following the First Zürich Disputation that required all preaching to be in line with the Bible.
6   That is, the records of the Disputation of Baden.
7   ZW VIII, 810–813 (no. 561), here 810, lines 12–14. Johann Haner (c. 1480–c. 1549) had a somewhat volatile career, as a supporter variously of *Erasmus, Zwingli and *Philipp of Hesse. He had returned to his home city of Nürnberg in the Autumn of 1526 after having spent

55 warning that he is going to attack us; but, alas for you, it is hard for Saul to kick against the pricks.[8] Let us not be at all troubled while they are preparing their words against us. My apologia against *Strauß is now groaning under the press.[9]

60 Farewell, you and all the brothers, and start the year (15)27 happily. The catabaptists who were recently rightly consigned to the ravens[10] are disturbing the peace of the pious among us; but I believe the axe has been laid at the root of the tree.[11] May the Lord be with his church. Amen.

Zürich, the third day of January 1527.

Original lost. Included in 1536 edition, fols 193ᵛ–194ʳ.

---

60 *to the ravens*] Greek εἰς κόρακας

---

less than a year as Cathedral Preacher in Würzburg. On him see *CoE* II, 161–163; *BBKL* II, 513. The work being prepared by Luther is *Das diese wort Christi "Das ist mein leib. Etce" noch fest stehen widder die Schwermgeister* (Wittenberg: Lotter, 1527; Leu/Weidmann A140)—ed. *WA* XXIII, 63–283; trans. *AE* XXXVII, 3–150. See Burnett, *Debating*, 223–226.

8 Acts 26:14. Zwingli quotes from the Vulgate (*durum est tibi contra stimulum calcitrare*), as do we from the KJV.

9 The *Antwurt über Doctor Straussen Büchlin* (see 534, n. 9).

10 That is, to their deaths. Zwingli must be thinking particularly of Felix Manz, who was drowned in Zürich on 5th January; his associate Georg Blaurock survived, having merely suffered banishment from the city.

11 Cf. Matthew 3:10.

572   Oecolampadius to Zwingli—Basel, 6th January (1527)

IX, 13   May the grace and peace of Christ be with you, most beloved Zwingli! Our Heinrich, the clerk to our Council,[1] a truly worthy man who is easily the most dependable of all the brothers at work here and the most adept at proclaiming the gospel, would derive great pleasure from talking to you. You will be able to tell us through him what you would wish us to do for the glory of the gospel. And you will hear from him what state our affairs are in.[2] I wrote certain things to *Pellikan the day before yesterday, in order to get his advice.[3] Heinrich here is also aware of the issue, for I hide nothing from him. Now the opportunity has arisen, you will be able to speak with him—though previously I asked Pellikan to disclose the matter to you. It is certainly not my intention to do anything in this regard that could justly damage the gospel; it will be for the Lord to give us grace. Hence, if there is time, you or Pellikan should either write back or share your advice with Heinrich. For the rest, Heinrich will relate how Masses are becoming valueless, etc.

Given at Basel, 6th January.
Your Oecolampadius.
To his Huldrych Zwingli.

Original: Zürich, Staatsarchiv, E II 349, p. 95 (autograph). Copy: Zürich, Zentralbibliothek, Ms S 18, no. 9.

---

11 *justly*] *iure* (literally, 'with regard to the law')

---

1   Heinrich Ryhiner. See above, p. 25, n. 102.
2   The letter's delicate, circumlocutory tone reflects the personal nature of the matter in hand, namely Oecolampadius's plan to marry.
3   This letter is lost.

576 Oecolampadius to Zwingli—Basel, 15th January 1527

Greetings in Christ, beloved brother! We would indeed take your advice if the criterion of righteousness were used—even the pagans who do not know God embrace this principle.[1] Our adversaries have hardened their hearts, united as they are at least in this one thing that they strenuously protest about to their friends. But the Lord will find them out, and he uses them to try us. They call us disorderly and seditious—we who have to bear all manner of insolence. But we are catching a whiff of what they themselves are concocting. It is good that the Lord does not stretch out the rod of the wicked over the fate of the just, since otherwise they would long since have swallowed us up alive.[2] Eventually we shall have to resolve to think of our opponents as antichrists—since the darkness is more contemptible when the truth about it has been acknowledged, and we will then walk in greater fear of the Lord. We have not failed to do anything that you advised, but so far very great plagues have remained with us, and we are enduring them patiently.

Now, with regard to the business of mine that I wrote to *Pellikan about, Heinrich has delivered a decidedly ambiguous oracle from the two of you.[3] So I will wait on the Lord's counsel, to see whether he favours your advice or something different. I myself will strive to ensure that I do no injury to the word of the Lord—Christ help me, I would rather endure every vexation and every trouble that may be heaped upon me than turn back from the plough.[4] Your defence against *Strauß delights me beyond measure.[5] Any honest reader will think it pardonable to single out this ridiculous writer for well-merited sneers, given that in the past he has not blushed to play the fool with the truth. I have forwarded a copy I was given to the Strasbourg brothers.

---

1 There is no surviving evidence of Zwingli offering specific advice to Oecolampadius on the question of whether non-Christians could be saved, but it was something on which he held quite radical and—to modern readers—progressive views. See W.P. Stephens, "Zwingli and the Salvation of the Gentiles", in idem (ed.), *The Bible, the Reformation and the Church. Essays in Honour of James Atkinson* (Sheffield: Sheffield Academic Press, 1995), 224–244.
2 Psalm 124:3. Oecolampadius's formulation *alioqui nos vivos deglutissent* is very close to the Vulgate's.
3 See 572 (especially n. 2).
4 Cf. Luke 9:62.
5 See 534, n. 9.

IX, 22 | The catabaptists who came here as exiles from Strasbourg are making trouble for us again.[6] They love subterfuge, and disguise their dubious doctrine by claiming they are being persecuted. I am sending the Erasmian letters that you asked for.[7] I fear that Baden will pay little attention to things that might promote peace.[8] Our brothers greet all of you and commend our church to your prayers.

Farewell.
15th January, Basel, in the year 1527.
Your Oecolampadius.
To Huldrych Zwingli, his beloved brother.

Original: Zürich, Staatsarchiv, E II 349, p. 8f. (autograph). Copy: Zürich, Zentralbibliothek, Ms S 18, no. 15.

---

6 These are likely to have included Hans Denck and Michael Sattler, who had been expelled from Strasbourg in December 1526.
7 While Zwingli's request has not been preserved, it almost certainly pertained to the recently published *D. Erasmi Rotherodami Epistolae tres, nuper in apertum prolatae. Ad christianissimum regem Franciscum. Ad parlamentum. Ad theologicam facultatem* (s.l.: s.n., 1526; Leu/Weidmann A63).
8 The Confederate Diet had convened at Baden on the previous day (14th January), to discuss not least the controversies surrounding the records of the previous year's disputation there.

586 Oecolampadius to Zwingli—Basel, 2nd February (1527)

Grace and peace from Christ our Lord. Amen. Three days ago, my brother, after I had read Murner's calendar[1]—half-laughing at the man's imbecilic impudence and half-grieving over such boldness in stirring up all manner of evils—I did not think it was possible for those opponents of ours to come up with anything more vainglorious or more malign. But when I read that most poisonous little book by *Pirckheimer,[2] I realized that Murner is a mere novice in the art of abusing people, and that the other man really is far and away its most proficient master—so much so that I hardly have a greater aversion to anything than to the prospect of responding to him. It is a proper full-length book, and he is a man of leisure—he will not | be laying aside his studies because of any reproaches or kindnesses. Time is short,[3] there is much to do and there are a great many arguments to deal with; but if I leave even one unanswered, Pirckheimer will rejoice at it. I hope, however, that God, the defender of my innocence, will be with me, so that this man's vituperation will not injure either me or the church of Christ. May you, together with your church, assist me with your prayers, so that I might proceed as you wish me to—namely by responding cheerfully, with no spirit of bitterness and in few words (and those witty ones) within a few days. For although that man would make me into the chief and most mendacious of all hypocrites, I find that I am nothing unless I do something with all my heart. But may Christ be praised, who wished first to experience such abuse himself, so that we also might learn to endure it—certain as we are that eventually, on that great day that will make known the secrets of every heart, such abuse will be transformed into glory.[4]

---

19 *chief*] Greek κορυφαῖον

---

1 *Der Lutherischen evangelischen Kirchen Dieb und Ketzer Kalender* (Luzern: Murner, 1527)—ed. Ernst Götzinger, *Zwei Kalender aus dem Jahre 1527* (Schaffhausen: Schoch, 1865), 30–47. On Murner see 540, n. 10.
2 *Bilibaldi Pirckheymheri De vera Christi carne et vero eius sanguine, aduersus conuicia Ioannis, qui sibi Oecolampadij nomen indidit, responsio secunda* (Nürnberg: Petreius, 1527). See Burnett, *Debating*, 169–171.
3 Oecolampadius is thinking particularly of the forthcoming Frankfurt Book Fair. In the event his rejoinder to Pirckheimer, the *Responsio posterior* (see 594, n. 2), was ready in time for Frankfurt.
4 Cf. Romans 2:16.

I can promise very little with regard to the Swabian cities, since they have some very timid prophets.⁵ What some of them acknowledge amongst their friends about the true nature of the Eucharist they oppose most disputatiously from the pulpit. They listen to *Luther as their teacher, and you should respond to him as soon as possible—so that at the next book fair,⁶ where there will be a large crop of invectives against us, we will not lack for something with which to keep our adversaries in check. This will be much more worthwhile than publishing the commentary on Genesis, if indeed this could not be printed at the same time as the apologia—though I trust that nothing can be more praiseworthy than your commentary.⁷ For I have tasted a few passages from it, and they have whetted my appetite wonderfully.

Our Duke of Württemberg, who is staying with the Landgrave of Hesse, asks me in the letter I was given to greet you in particular.⁸ I have heard from a servant that, every day, they are mindful of our affairs; but the Landgrave has so far stuck to his guns on the issue of the Eucharist; otherwise, he is said to be the most zealous prince when it comes to furthering the gospel.⁹ A few months ago he sent your arguments and mine to | Luther, urging him to write against us and saying that if Luther omitted to do so, then he (the Landgrave) would no longer read his writings. So, on the advice of the Strasbourg brothers, I have arranged to write him a few things on the matter, in the hope that the Lord might perhaps see fit to open his heart.¹⁰ For he is no tyrant, and he is said not to wish me ill. Now, though, that most vainglo-

---

38 *our affairs*] *nostri*. We have supplied *negocii*, as a noun for the adjective *nostri* to qualify
41 *your ... mine*] *tua et mea*, 'yours and mine'. Again we need to supply a noun, in this case *argumenta*

---

5   For certain Oecolampadius means *Brenz. He seems to have been justified in thinking that the latter's thinking was not as fixed or uncompromising as his *Syngramma* had suggested. Jung, "Abendmahlsstreit", 153–155, argues that some of Brenz's slightly later publications (from 1528 and 1529) articulate a position on the Eucharist that owes much to Zwingli and Oecolampadius, as well as to Luther.

6   That is to say, the Frankfurt Spring Fair.

7   In fact *Froschauer did succeed in publishing Zwingli's Genesis commentary (*Farrago Annotationum in Genesim*) in advance of the Fair, as well as two polemics against Luther: the *Amica exegesis* (see 552, n. 19) and the *Früntlich verglimpfung und ableynung über die predig des treffenlichen Martini Luthers wider die Schwermer* (Zürich: Froschauer, 1527)—ed. ZW V, 771–794 (no. 106).

8   This letter has not survived.

9   On *Philipp of Hesse's dealings with *Ulrich of Württemberg see 547, n. 5. Around this time the latter, in exile, was a close ally and frequent guest of Philipp's—see Frasch, *Ulrich*, 226–228.

10   There is no evidence that Oecolampadius ever did write to Philipp in this way.

LETTER 586   221

rious senator[11] is sowing confusion and pulling him away from the process we have begun; but he will not disrupt it entirely. Here, we are managing our affairs in the usual way.

50 Farewell in Christ, and give *Pellikan a greeting from me—I will reply to his letter as soon as I have time.[12]
I also wish your wife well.[13]
Farewell again.
Basel, 2nd February.
55 Your Oecolampadius.
To Huldrych Zwingli of Zürich, pious and sincere preacher of Christ, his dearest brother.

Original: Zürich, Staatsarchiv, E II 349, p. 36 (autograph). Copy: Zürich, Zentralbibliothek, Ms S 18, no. 40.

---

47 *pulling him away*] retrahit (literally, 'pulling away'; we supply an object, such as *eum* or *illum*)

---

11 *Pirckheimer, who held the title of "imperial counsellor" (*Kaiserlicher Rat*), and was perceived to be influential in Protestant political circles.
12 No such letter has survived.
13 Anna *Reinhart.

588   Oecolampadius to Zwingli—Basel, 4th February (1527)

Grace and peace from Christ, excellent Zwingli! It is not necessary to write a long letter at present, and nor is there much time to do so. In place of a letter, let M. Bertschi,[1] who is one of those whom you believe can assist our church, keep you informed. You know that he is both a faithful and a sound man, who truly conducts himself as a faithful servant in the house of the Lord.

The Strasbourgers have not yet done away with the Mass altogether;[2] so Satan is everywhere obstructing the endeavours of pious people. As to *Luther, we hope that either you will win him over to our cause or will be able in large measure to draw him away from his errors. If only the Lord would permit both these things! Please devote yourself to this task.[3] It is said here that my friends the Swabians are coming together again, no doubt to play the fool still more.[4] Certain people have abandoned them. If Luther ever gives glory to Christ, some people somewhere will grow dumber than a fish. In my marital matter, I shall do nothing precipitately; otherwise, I am being kept busy in various ways.

Farewell.
4th February, Basel.
Your Oecolampadius.
To Huldrych Zwingli, bishop of the Zurichers, his brother.

Original: Zürich, Staatsarchiv, E II 349, p. 63 (autograph). Copy: Zürich, Zentralbibliothek, Ms S 18, no. 30.

---

1   Markus Bertschi (see 367, n. 1).
2   Until 20th February 1529, Mass could still be celebrated in four of the city's churches.
3   That of writing the two works against Luther that were to be published in February/March (see 586, n. 7).
4   Plans for a second conference at Guttenberg (see 418, n. 5) do not seem to have come to fruition.

594   Oecolampadius to Zwingli—Basel, 28th February (1527)

Grace and peace from Christ, my brother! I have almost devoured the melancholy meal, so to speak, which Nürnberg sent us.[1] It contains as much charity as the Devil himself. I have responded.[2] I am copying this response. It will be on sale at the Fair.[3] Afterwards, the demented beast will try to rip the whole thing to pieces and eat it alive. You also, if you can, press on with the pieces you are writing against *Luther, so that they can be printed.[4] For those men do not sleep, but rather rouse up the whole world against us. We must walk carefully in the midst of a perverse generation;[5] and we must trust in the Lord.

Farewell in the Lord.
Greet *Pellikan. Pray to the Lord for me, all of you.
The last day of February, Basel.
Your Johannes Oecolampadius.
To Huldrych Zwingli, his dearest brother.

Original: Zürich, Staatsarchiv, E II 349, p. 54 (scribal hand). Copy: Zürich, Zentralbibliothek, Ms S 18, no. 57.

---

1   *Pirckheimer's *Responsio secunda* (see 586, n. 2).
2   This was to appear as *Ad Bilibaldum Pykraimerum de Eucharistia, Responsio posterior* (Basel: Cratander, 1527; Staehelin 140; Leu/Weidmann A167). See Burnett, *Debating*, 171 f.
3   The Frankfurt Spring Fair.
4   See 586, n. 7.
5   Cf. Acts 2:40.

600   Oecolampadius to Zwingli—Basel, March (1527)

IX, 73   Greetings in Christ. My brother, I am sending herewith what I have written on Zechariah,[1] and also my response to that most impertinent slanderer *Pirckheimer[2]—such things as could be produced by my poor self in the midst of all this confusion. For you know that I am still engaged in other business. It is enough that they are not impious, even though they will not satisfy the fastidious stomachs of our age. The first part of your *Exegesis*[3] pleased me very much—so much so that I straightaway sent the pages in question on to the Strasbourg brothers.[4]

Billican writes to me about Luther in the following terms:[5] "*Luther is already preparing a greater task for you.[6] For he has utterly contradicted himself in this debate by assuming that the words of the Lord "this is"[7] mean that, in the sacrament, the body and blood of Christ give life for the development of the inner man, by the power of the Holy Spirit who works through faith, and through the death and resurrection of Jesus Christ. You will do the duty of a good Christian man and pastor. But even Luther acknowledges the absurdity of the notion of flesh and blood forming part of the Lord's Supper; and no doubt he also accepts the impossibility of flesh and blood possessing a twofold nature. For how can mortal and corruptible flesh nourish someone out of death into resurrection? How can blood do this, when children are born not from blood, but from the word? Now you see. The dispute will be about faith, and about the mystery of the divine working within us in such a way that we are born and grow in Christ".

This is what he writes. If I understand him correctly, he will be somewhat milder in future, and the path to public peace will open up—something I pray in every way that God might grant us. We have enough enemies, after all.

---

1 His commentary on the last three minor prophets is meant—see 547, n. 16.
2 See 594, n. 2.
3 See 552, n. 19.
4 This fact is confirmed in a letter sent to *Capito on 18th March—*OeBA* 11, 44 (no. 474); CC 11, 275f. (no. 328).
5 The letter, sent from Nördlingen, is printed in *OeBA*, 11, 14 (no. 460). On Billican see 394, n. 5.
6 An allusion to *Das diese wort Christi* (see 569, n. 7), which was to be published in March.
7 Oecolampadius is referring in abbreviated form to Christ's words of institution, *hoc est corpus meum* (Matthew 26:26, Mark 14:22, Luke 22:19).

| Clichtoveus of Paris has written a most asinine volume against me.[8] I will not reply to it until I have also received abuse from other people at the Book Fair; and then, having asked your advice and with the Lord's help, I will do what seems good to you. For he has already been answered in large part; and he has written many quite unworthy things, things that do not merit a response from us.

As yet we have heard no news from the assemblies at Bern.[9]

Our newly elected bishop Philipp von Gundelsheim seems to be threatening our people and the people of Solothurn; he is surrounding himself with more knights than bishops of Basel have been accustomed to doing.[10] But if he chooses to insult those who wish us ill, he will perhaps incite them to look upon us with rather greater favour.

Farewell.
Basel, 26th March.
Greet *Pellikan and the brothers.
Your Oecolampadius.
To Huldrych Zwingli, his dearest brother. Zürich.

Original: Zürich, Staatsarchiv, E II 349, p. 162 (autograph). Copy: Zürich, Zentralbibliothek, Ms S 18, no. 69.

---

40 *26th March*] the original reads *die Marcii 26* (literally, 'the day of March 26th'). It is possible also that the year 1526 is meant, but this would be a curious way of expressing it; and a contemporary note on the manuscript states that the events described occurred in 1527 (*omnino ad a. 1527 pertinet*)

---

8   *De Sacramento Eucharistiae, contra Oecolampadium, opusculum* (Cologne: Quentell, 1527). Jodocus Clichtoveus, or 'Josse Clichthove' (1472–1543), was a Flemish humanist theologian based in Paris and later Chartres, who by the 1520s had become the evangelicals' most prominent French opponent. On him see *CoE* I, 317–320; *OER* I, 368f.; *BBKL* XXII, 208–213; *KTR* II, 82–91.

9   On 18th and 19th March representatives of Bern, Basel, Schaffhausen, Appenzell and St. Gallen had met in Bern to discuss policy towards the seven Catholic Cantons.

10   Philipp von Gundelsheim (1487–1553) had been elected Bishop of Basel on 28th February—see *AGBR*, II, 443f. (no. 602). Despite some initially robust actions (see 661, n. 1), he in fact proved powerless to resist the spread of reform, and was forced to move his residence outside the city in 1528. His origins as a Franconian aristocrat seem also not to have enhanced his personal popularity in Basel. The reference to Solothurn is an oblique one to ongoing negotiations about the status of former episcopal vassals now under the protection of the Basel Council—see Wackernagel, *Basel*, III, 402f.

607   Oecolampadius to Zwingli—Basel, 24th April (1527)

IX, 100   Grace and peace from Christ, dearest brother! This man Fabian, who is learned and pious, was sent to us by the most Christian Duke of Legnica;[1] please greet the brothers there with kindness, as you are wont to do, and treat Fabian as someone who comes recommended. The Duke wishes to find some learned and distinguished men of his own to direct the affairs of the university he has decided to found there. He deigned to write to me personally, so as to be more confident that the process will be successful.[2] In fact I could not point to anyone here who either would or could take on so great a duty.[3] Perhaps in Zürich, with its greater number of people, there is someone who will be glad to take on the task.[4] Please think if there is someone you can identify; for it would be a sin against charity not to do the bidding of such faithful brothers if it were possible to do so. In the past year Matthias Wickler, himself a Silesian, has visited both of us;[5] he commended us to the brothers in such a way that they anticipate hearing only the best things about us. You will learn this from a letter by Krautwald:[6] we and they have Martin as a common enemy.

I have finally received, from the Frankfurt Fair, *Luther's most poisonous book against me and you, which is written in the vernacular and bears the title *That these words (this is my body, etc.) still hold true against the cranks*.[7]

IX, 101   It concedes nothing in fury to either *Pirckheimer or *Faber. | So what, in the end, will happen to the church of Christ? How much scope is Satan to be given? How great is God's anger towards the sons of men? In the meantime, undeserving as we are of even a mild rebuke, we are being pursued

---

1   Fabian Geppart (c. 1499–1545), city scribe of Legnica (Liegnitz), and a leading light at the short-lived Protestant University which existed there from 1526 to 1529. It was founded by the "most Christian duke" Friedrich II (1480–1547), who was attracted to the Swiss evangelicals' doctrine of the Eucharist and by their anti-Habsburg stance. On relations between Legnica, Zürich and Basel see Weigelt, *Tradition*, 82f.
2   No such letter from the Duke has survived.
3   See, however, lines 45–61 below.
4   Eventually Zürich sent the Oecolampadius pupil and noted Hebrew and Greek scholar Theodor Bibliander (1506–1564) to teach at Legnica. He remained there until 1529. On him see *CoE* I, 145f.; *BBKL* I, 577f.; *VL 16* I, 238–243.
5   See 466, n. 4.
6   Valentin Krautwald (1465–1545), Lector in Theology and Canon of the Cathedral Church at Legnica since 1523. His spiritualist views, along with those of Caspar Schwenckfeld, were to prove divisive, and contributed both to the early demise of the Protestant University (see n. 1) and to his own exile in 1529. On him see *OER* I, 451f.; *VL 16*, III, 598–604. The letter referred to here has not survived. On the Silesian context generally see Weigelt, *Tradition*.
7   *Das diese wort Christi* (see 569, n. 7).

by a demon; we are desperate and full of discord; and if we were to excuse ourselves with even a single word, we would be the most arrogant of all men.

The Strasbourg brothers (who were themselves trodden on by the heel of Luther's book) think it would be a good plan for you to answer him in German, with the gravitas with which you customarily respond to others, and for you to show by what passions he has been driven to his ruin. [8] They will also work on something themselves.[9] But they plead with you to make your response quickly, and in your usual prudent way. I do not know whether *Froschauer has sent a copy across to you. If you do not have one, I will gladly send you mine; but at present I need it for myself. For, given that he is bearing down on me more than on others, I will not be able to remain completely silent. So I will offer a brief apologia,[10] which I will give you to read (if only time allows) before it is printed—to ensure that nothing injudicious comes out of it.

I am sending herewith the catabaptists' articles,[11] and some things written against you. Our magistracy is rather feeble in repelling these. The reason for this is easy to guess. They are tolerant even towards the papists—indeed, they defend them whilst hurling every kind of insult at us.

Farewell, happy in the Lord.
Basel, 24th April.
Oecolampadius.

| Before I sealed this letter, our Petrus Gynoraeus,[12] whose erudition and integrity I recently commended to Fabian, came with what I believe to be a

---

26f. *who ... book*] or, "were also touched on near the end of Luther's book" (*quos et ipsos sub calcem libri perstrinxit Lutherus*)

8   Zwingli's response was to appear on 20th June: *Das dise wort Jesu Christi: Das ist min lychnam, der für üch hinggeben wirt, ewigklich den alten eynigen sinn haben werdend* (Zürich: Froschauer, 20th June 1527)—ed. ZW V, 805–977 (no. 107). See Burnett, *Debating*, 227–229.
9   This plan seems to have come to nought.
10 This was to be *Das der miszverstand D. Martin Luthers, uff die ewigbstendige wort ('Das ist mein leib') nit beston mag. Die ander billiche antwort Joannis Ecolampadij* (Basel: Cratander, 8th June 1527; Staehelin 143, Leu/Weidmann A168; edited in *Abendmahlsschriften*, 236–333). See also Staehelin, *Lebenswerk*, 313–318; Burnett, *Debating*, 227.
11 The so-called Schleitheim Articles, presented by Michael Sattler in February 1527. On them see James M. Stayer, 'Swiss-South German Anabaptism', in idem and John D. Roth (eds), *A Companion to Anabaptism and Spiritualism, 1521–1700* (Leiden: Brill, 2007), 83–117, here 90–102.
12 Or 'Peter Frauenberger'; see 367, n. 2.

good omen: he pleaded with me to invite him to perform this duty. So I spoke to Petrus at length, and in the end I concluded that he had not made a case for himself. If only he were equal to the task and one could trust he has been called to it by the Lord! That, anyway, is what we discussed, and we made the following decision: first of all, Fabian should enquire diligently of you and *Leo in Zürich as to whether anyone more suitable can be persuaded to undertake this duty; Petrus himself should remain with us, awaiting a separate opportunity. If there is no-one over there who is minded to travel to other lands, and if you and Leo—who know the man inside out—also give your view as to whether or not Petrus is an appropriate person to go to Silesia, he will go or stay according to what you decide. And so, my Huldrych, this is what we have to bear in mind with regard to the Silesian brothers and to our Petrus: they should not have cause to complain of a rather inept person being thrust upon them, and he should not be exiled from here in perpetuity. I know, my brother, that we must take care to retain learned and honest men in our region, lest perchance we too might need to recruit them from somewhere else, at great danger to ourselves. But charity dictates that we be somewhat imprudent in this regard and, casting our care on the Lord,[13] seek not our own advantage, but that of Jesus Christ.[14] Certainly our adversaries are nourished by the single hope that we, being so few, cannot hold out for long, and for that reason they lie in wait to kill us—as if, indeed, Christ were not able to raise up people who are much more suitable than we are. But we strive to follow a different plan, and we trust in the Lord with great hope that he will protect his church against them—even though the hypocrisy of the age frightens me a great deal. The church deserves something very different from the most appalling state of spiritual poverty it finds itself in. In accordance with your faith and love, please support Fabian, who has been commended to you, and help him in this matter.

Farewell again.
To Huldrych Zwingli, his dearest brother.

Original: Zürich, Staatsarchiv, E II 349, p. 39 (scribal hand). Copy: Zürich, Zentralbibliothek, Ms S 18, no. 90.

We date letter 611 to 1527. See below, p. 286 f.

---

13   Cf. 1 Peter 5:7.
14   Cf. 1 Corinthians 10:24.

614 Oecolampadius to Zwingli—Basel, 1st May (1527)

Greetings in Christ. There is nothing that I would now like more, my Huldrych, than to know what course of action you have chosen to adopt concerning *Luther. To the Strasbourg brothers it seemed best for you to reply quickly in German:[1] they wanted me to oppose the Frenchman and the Englishman, that is, Clichtoveus and Rochester.[2] But neither our people nor I myself approve of their idea: whilst we, amidst the greatest possible provocations, are constantly calling on our adversaries to meet with us, they have already brought out their books and are declaring themselves the victors— they say that we have actually been defeated! There is no point in dealing with such obstinate people, since they attack me more than anyone, and I can see that the heart of man is extremely sick. Pray therefore to the Lord, along with your church, that we might write things that are worthy of Christ. He[3] plays the fool uncommonly well when he declares that the body and blood are present wherever the divine is present. They believe it is not at all unworthy of Christ for the body of Christ now to be discussed by unworthy people. And there is also conflict about whether the spiritual flesh is profitable to eat. Let me know what you have given the Silesians, whom I commended to you: are they going to take our Gynoraeus from us, or have they found men over there who meet their expectations?[4]

Farewell.
Basel, 1st May.
Oecolampadius.
To Huldrych Zwingli, his brother.

Original: Zürich, Staatsarchiv, E II 349, p. 71 (autograph). Copy: Zürich, Zentralbibliothek, Ms S 18, no. 104.

---

1 See the discussion in 607, lines 26–29.
2 On Clichtoveus, and Oecolampadius's dealings with him, see 600, n. 8. "Rochester" (*Roffensi*) is a reference to John Fisher, Bishop of Rochester (1469–1535), who had recently published *De veritate corporis et sanguinis Christi in eucharistia, adversus Iohannem Oecolampadium* (Cologne: Quentell, 1527). See Staehelin, *Lebenswerk*, 330. Oecolampadius did not in fact respond directly to Fisher's work. On Fisher see *CoE* II, 36–39; *OER* II, 109 f.; *TRE* XI, 204–206; *BBKL* XVII, 383–385; *KTR* II, 49–65.
3 Luther.
4 See 607, lines 1–16 and 45–61.

624   Oecolampadius to Zwingli—Basel, 22nd May (1527)

IX, 152   May the grace of Christ be with you, my brother! Just now a messenger at last appeared, so that I can now send my letter and *Bucer's to you.[1] This has happened at a time when it is particularly expedient for us to share our counsels about our common enemy. The insolence of our adversaries, who have even started praising *Luther and flaunting his book from the pulpit, has forced me to rush into print before I have properly finished my book.[2] I could not entirely restrain myself from adding some bitterness to the mix: it is very difficult to refute and condemn so many insults, so many lies, so many traps. So I am sending a few folios, from which you can get a flavour of the work as a whole. Let us give thanks to the Lord that truth is so powerfully on our side. I do not think I have left anything out that I needed to respond to.

There is one passage on which he attacks you specifically, whereas elsewhere he seems virtually to disregard you, seizing rather on me.[3] This is
IX, 153 where we read in John 3, | "What is born of the flesh is flesh, what is born of the spirit is spirit".[4] I have indeed interpreted that reference as meaning that this "flesh" can be understood as the flesh of Christ. For, both in this chapter and in chapter 6,[5] Christ wanted to draw us away from his flesh and towards his Spirit; so why would he not speak of his flesh at times as the flesh that is shared by humankind? You will have to write at length about that verse; but be mindful also of what Bucer advises. I hold on tenaciously to one rule: that, when we speak of sacraments, we are speaking of signs.

Yesterday we of the evangelical party and also the papist preachers were summoned to the Council chamber and told to describe, in written form and within a month, the basis on which we either assert or deny that the Mass is a

---

24 *in ... form*] *in libellis* (literally, 'in little books')

1 The relevant volume of Bucer's correspondence contains no letter addressed by Bucer to Zwingli between late March and 8th July 1527; so—unless the letter in question is lost—this must be a reference to Bucer's letter to Oecolampadius of 11th May (no. 158; BC III, 62–65). This too focuses mainly on recent controversies with Luther concerning the Eucharist.
2 *Das der miszverstand* (see 607, n. 10).
3 A reference to Luther's *Das diese wort Christi* (see 569, n. 7). Using a viticultural image, Luther condemns Zwingli for trying with excessive force to "press" (*keltern*) the meaning "this is the sign of my body" from Christ's words "this is my body" (WA XXIII, 274 f.).
4 John 3:6. Oecolampadius quotes almost exactly from the Vulgate: *Quod natum est ex carne, caro est: et quod natum est ex spiritu, spiritus est.*
5 Cf. John 6:63.

sacrifice and a good and useful work to be offered on behalf of the living and the dead.[6] We may use only the canonical scriptures, in accordance with the decree that was published some time ago.[7] This matter greatly terrifies our sacrificing opponents, but pleases us exceedingly: for we hope that the Lord will look favourably upon us at the last; we must pray to him that all might redound to his glory. Meanwhile nothing else has happened that I need to tell you about. We hope to read your words as soon as possible.

Basel, 22nd May.
Johannes Oecolampadius.
To Huldrych Zwingli, his brother.

Original: Zürich, Staatsarchiv, E II 349, p. 153 (autograph). Copy: Zürich, Zentralbibliothek, Ms S 18, no. 123.

---

32 *your words*] *tua* (literally, 'yours')

6 This event had taken place two days earlier, on 20th May. On it, and on the ensuing debate, see Wackernagel, *Basel*, III, 387–392; Roth, *Reformation*, I, 38–41.
7 Presumably the written form of the Council's summons, published on 16th May—see *AGBR*, II, 487–489 (no. 657).

625   Oecolampadius to Zwingli—Basel, 31st May (1527)

Greetings in Christ, dearest brother. I am again sending you some quires;[1] there are seven or eight still to come, and the printers will produce these by Pentecost.[2] I cannot wonder enough at God's opinion of *Luther. *Bucer has not yet published anything on behalf of the Strasbourgers; but he will give us something.[3] Those brothers here who enjoy your confidence greet you, and are keen to spur on your response.[4] There is nothing to redeem our situation here today, other than that they no longer disagree on the subject about which, in the past, they used to quarrel beyond measure.[5] Thanks be to Christ. For if we were in disagreement today, the matter would be much harder to manage, since even the papists are taking delight in that single mad book.[6] As I wrote recently, the Council have enjoined us to give an account of why the papist Mass is an abomination—this is what has been agreed.[7] So I am now sweating over this, seeking to expose its abominations clearly from the scriptures. I still do not know what our adversaries are up to. They are being evasive, or are pretending to be, and these days they are inventing stratagems of every kind in their daily meetings. They seem to be rather downcast in spirit. The bishop and canons have replied to the magistracy that matters such as these are their concern. One can only conclude that they propose to govern their people in silence; | but if they do this, they will be attending to their affairs in an ill-advised way. The Strasbourg brothers wish to learn from me how far your people are in agreement with the other Helvetians.[8] So far I have not learnt anything certain here that I could give them by way of an answer.

---

1   See 624, lines 4–10 and n. 2.
2   *Das der miszverstand* (see 607, n. 10), was in fact published on 8th June, the day before Pentecost.
3   See 607, lines 26–29 and n. 8.
4   That is to say, *Das dise wort Jesu* (see 607, n. 7).
5   The Eucharist. The issues addressed by Zwingli in letter 367 (5th April 1525) had clearly been resolved.
6   Luther's *Das diese wort Christi* (see 569, n. 7), which provided grist to the mill of all the Swiss evangelicals' opponents.
7   See 624, lines 23–31 and n. 6.
8   The tense antagonism between Zürich and in particular the Catholic Cantons had recently been exacerbated by claims made by Luzern—and hotly denied—to the effect that Zürich wished to incorporate Konstanz into the Helvetic Confederation and to conquer the Thurgau by force.

Farewell.
25 Basel, the last day of May.
Johannes Oecolampadius.
To Huldrych Zwingli, his dearest brother.

Original: Zürich, Staatsarchiv, E II 349, p. 59 (autograph). Copy: Zürich, Zentralbibliothek, Ms S 18, no. 130.

627 Oecolampadius to Zwingli—Basel, 15th June (1527)

IX, 158 Grace and peace from Christ. Beloved brother, the more loyal to us the couriers are, the more it will be possible to discuss this briefly in a letter: and who is either as able or as suitable as our Heinrich to relate to you faithfully what is happening here?[1] Now I am sending another part of my book against *Luther, or as much of it as has yet been printed—in anticipation of yours.[2] The records of the Disputation of Baden are to be offered for sale at the Zurzach Fair;[3] I beg you to consider what remedy needs to be used against them. It will not be possible to remain entirely silent, since the published version is corrupt and does not seem to have been well enough thought through to expose the tricks that were played. Powerful people pay for liars; and perhaps some prominent men will use this opportunity for their own ends, so as to make more work for us. You will probably get the dispu-

IX, 159 tation records first. | So let us know what you and your people would want us to do. Otherwise I am minded to attack Rochester and Clichtoveus, and just to include an account of the disputation in that same work;[4] for they are all attacking us from the same battle line, namely the papist one. Some people are talking nonsense here, claiming that *Faber has been drowned along with Salamanca.[5] If the rumour proves true, the noble lords will finally be able to recognize the judgement of God—unless their eyes are utterly beguiled.[6]

10f. *pay for liars*] *sunt mendaciorum patroni* (literally, 'are patrons of liars')

---

1 Heinrich Ryhiner (see p. 25, n. 102), who plainly delivered this letter.
2 Oecolampadius's *Das der miszverstand* (see 607, n. 10; here sent, presumably, as the last of three instalments) and Zwingli's *Das dise wort Jesu* (see 607, n. 7).
3 Copies of Huber's disputation records had in fact been available at Zurzach since 9th June (see Schindler, *BD*, 179).
4 In fact neither Zwingli nor Oecolampadius—despite much soul-searching—ever published a refutation of the disputation records. On the references to "Rochester and Clichtoveus" see respectively 614, n. 2 and 600, n. 8.
5 Gabriel von Salamanca-Ortenbourg (1489–1539) was an aristocrat of Spanish origin who had served as treasurer to Ferdinand of Austria from 1521 to 1526, and thereafter—in spite of proven financial improprieties—continued to advise both him and Charles v. Salamanca and Faber had recently been sent by *Ferdinand as emissaries to England and the Netherlands; reports of their demise *en route* were wholly inaccurate. On Salamanca see *CoE* III, 189.
6 Presumably Oecolampadius is thinking especially of the arch-Catholic *Ferdinand.

Farewell.
Basel, 15th June.
Your Oecolampadius.
To Huldrych Zwingli, his brother.

Original: Zürich, Staatsarchiv, E II 349, p. 96 (autograph). Copy: Zürich, Zentralbibliothek, Ms S 19, no. 5.

635   Oecolampadius to Zwingli—Basel, 14th July (1527)

IX, 173   Grace and peace from Christ, dearest brother! It will be safer to overlook the machinations that took place at the Disputation of Baden and—the flesh being what it is—more dangerous to expose them; and I do not even see what such a thing could achieve or contribute to the advancement of truth.[1] Amongst the pious the truth was made known long ago; but the impious will not accept any explanation we give, however holy. Hence we would incur danger in vain—and danger would also threaten us if we spoke either about the corrupt copies or about the fact that they cannot be trusted. If they were not accompanied by the preface and appendix,[2] I myself could certainly neither sanction the records nor reject them. Some things have been formulated so carelessly that, when I read them, I did not recognize myself as having spoken in that way; and some things refute our enemies so clearly and incontrovertibly that even those who are not spiritual would regard them as damaging to *Eck. Now they are bracing themselves for the most violent reproaches. And so, now that Eck's desire even to read the work has died away, why do we waste valuable time in vain? There are some who desire what you also want, namely that I myself might point out in a letter where the records are deficient in terms of clarity; others, however (*Capito is one of them) would prefer you to undertake the task.[3] I certainly am not
IX, 174   minded to respond to such vile | men, and hence would not willingly impose so odious and superfluous a task on anyone else. If, however, you consider it wholly advisable to do so, I will abandon my wish and, in obedience to you, will entrust to my pen the words that the Lord gives me—even though such behaviour on my part might frighten our Council not a little.

As to how that business of the Mass is going,[4] you should learn more details from those delivering this letter than it would be appropriate to write down.[5] What the Council has decreed in the matter of the anabaptists, you will learn from the attached mandate.[6]

---

1   Over the previous month Oecolampadius had obviously read the disputation records and Zwingli had not (see Schindler, BD, 179). This experience had plainly led the former to conclude that they were not as biased and inaccurate as he had anticipated (cf. 627, lines 4–9).
2   That is, the accompanying texts attributed to Melchior Fattlin and summarized above in 540, lines 10–55.
3   Capito expresses such a sentiment in his letter to Zwingli (no doubt seen also by Oecolampadius) dated 7th July. See ZW IX, 167 f. (no. 632), here 167, lines 1–3; CC II, 293 f. (no. 333).
4   See 624, lines 21–31 and 625, lines 11–14.
5   Letter 636, line 1, implies that the letter was delivered by *Cratander.
6   This must refer to the mandate of 6th July outlawing anabaptists and their supporters.

The Duke of Württemberg greets both you and me in a letter which his secretary Kornmesser has given me.[7] At the time of writing he had clearly not yet seen our apologias,[8] for he had sent a book of Martin's to *Capito, which the latter has kept, on the grounds that it was of no use to us and a little cumbersome for the courier to carry. It is enough for us to have been able to recognize the Duke's benevolent soul.

The Strasbourg brothers would like us to prepare our responses[9] in Latin in time for the next fair, because they have learnt that Justus Jonas is going to elucidate the Lutheran calumnies in Latin.[10] In fact, although I have already translated some pages, I doubt that it is worthwhile publishing them. For what if Martin, having read our works, were to be enlightened by the readings the Lord has given us, and hence were to prevent our version from being printed or to offer a more mild-mannered one instead? Then we would again be accused of having shown too little charity. How I wish that what has been written on both sides had been absorbed into a sponge of reliable truth! I would like to hear your views on this also some time. You can put the late arrival of these letters down to the scarcity of messengers. Heinrich[11] promised us a courier every day; but none has appeared for almost a whole month.

| Farewell, and keep safe and sound.
Basel, 14th July.
Your Oecolampadius.
Greet *Pellikan, whom I congratulate warmly and from my heart on the birth of Samuel.[12]
To Huldrych Zwingli, most sincere teacher of the Zürichers, his brother.

Original: Zürich, Staatsarchiv, E II 349, p. 299 (autograph). Copy: Zürich, Zentralbibliothek, MS S 19, no. 18.

---

7   The letter is lost. Johannes Kornmesser, originally from Uhingen near Stuttgart, was a loyal and long-serving assistant to Duke *Ulrich.
8   Most notably, one assumes, Zwingli's *Früntlich verglimpfung* (see 586, n. 7) and Oecolampadius's *Das der miszverstand* (see 607, n. 10).
9   See n. 8. This is another suggestion made by Capito in letter 632 (ZW IX, 167, lines 4–7).
10 On Jonas see 505, n. 18. The translation project attributed to him here never came to fruition.
11 Heinrich Ryhiner: see p. 25, n. 102.
12 Samuel Pellikan was born on 1st June 1527, and was himself to become a distinguished scholar and teacher (see Zürcher, *Pellikan*, 27–29).

636 Oecolampadius to Zwingli—Basel, 19th July (1527)

May the grace of Christ be with you. I wrote to you via Chartander,[1] my brother, about how perplexed and ambivalent I am concerning our plan for dealing with the Disputation of Baden.[2] But I am still awaiting your advice, and would like to have it soon. You know very well what our Council is like: if they are not consulted, they take it amiss, and if they are consulted, they will not connive at any scheme. I have told the Franciscan of a way in which one might show mercy towards the Helvetians and the bishops and make the Ecks, Fabers and suchlike monsters shoulder the blame.[3] So write back soon. It is undeniable that the copies were printed in a very careless and rather confusing way, but one could not immediately detect any dangerous falsifications or distortions. I will write if you request it; but how can you request it if you have not yet read the records?[4] It is true that we could make better use of our time; but there is something decidedly useful in being aware of our adversaries' deceits.

As to the little books by Balthasar[5] that need to be sent, nobody has talked to me about them. I did send one a while ago;[6] and now I have received two copies. I am sending one on and keeping the other. Since it is directed against a dialogue | that was once held under my roof,[7] it is right that I should pen a response to it—and I have decided to do this, so that the wiles of the deceivers might be exposed.[8] In this book he falsely accuses me of saying

---

7f. *and ... shoulder the blame*] *fabaque ... cudatur* (literally 'and a bean is pounded'). This expression goes back at least as far as Terence (*Eunuchus*, line 381): *istaec in me cudetur faba*— 'this bean will be pounded on me', i.e. 'I must smart/take the blame for this'. The expression can also be found in Erasmus's *Adagia* 1.1.84 (84)

---

1 *Cratander is of course meant, but (rather more strongly than in 258, n. 9) one suspects this may be a deliberate pun on the printer's name (Latin *charta* = 'paper').
2 See letter 635 (especially lines 1–24), which presumably had been delivered by Cratander.
3 Johannes Lüthard (see 367, n. 6), preacher at the Franciscan church in Basel. Oecolampadius refers to him as "the Franciscan" also in 460, line 17 and 486, line 14.
4 See also 627, lines 6–14 and 635, lines 1–24.
5 Hubmaier: see 347, n. 5.
6 Hubmaier's *Ein gesprech der Predicanten*: see 554, n. 20.
7 In the summer of 1525 Oecolampadius had hosted talks between himself, his colleagues Jakob Immeli, Wolfgang Wissenburg and Thomas Gyrfalk (see 367 n. 3–5), and representatives of the anabaptists. Hubmaier's *Ein gesprech der Predicanten* is a somewhat slanted report of this occasion.
8 This was to appear as the *Antwort auff Balthasar Hübmeiers büchlein wider der Predicanten gespräch zuo Basel, von dem kindertauff*. It was printed as part of a composite volume that also contained Oecolampadius's *Underrichtung von dem Widertauff, von der Oberkeit,*

that I deny the existence of original sin in children, and claims that, in doing so, I am speaking not with my own voice, but rather with yours, the voice of my master in Zürich. In fact he charges you with four errors: first, that you defend the (in his words) impious baptism of infants against the accepted truth, by means of your pen, your doctrine and the hangman.[9] And because you are defending what is not true, God may be punishing you in such a way that you fall into a further error: you openly proclaim that original sin is not sin. When this was pointed out to you by the learned scholar Urbanus Rhegius,[10] using abundant evidence from the scriptures (Romans 7),[11] and also by others, you immediately fell into a third error, writing that Paul had not spoken properly or appositely (German *artlich*) about sin, but that you *do* speak properly about it, thereby implying that Paul had not spoken with the Holy Spirit's voice, but had misunderstood the nature of sin! Then, finally, you rush from that error into the fourth one, and state with an impure mouth that almighty God, the supreme creator, formed the woman Eve from the rib of the sleeping Adam under an inauspicious sign. These are four great and intolerable errors, which you have freely spread about by mentioning them in your published letter to Urbanus Rhegius on original sin.[12] This is as it usually happens—that God allows those who defend one untruth to fall into others also. Finally he prays that God might vouchsafe you to acknowledge these blasphemies and might graciously lift you up, you who have fallen so low. That is what the dialogue contains about you. Otherwise, the entire dialogue is directed against us, and reproaches us with the same degree of frankness that it does you. Somewhere else again he says of me that I commend infant baptism on the basis of Exodus[13]—just as you claim in your

---

       und von dem Eyd, auff Carlins N. widertauffers artickel (Basel: Cratander, 5th September 1527; Staehelin 145; Leu/Weidmann A169). See Staehelin, *Lebenswerk*, 384–390; an excerpt appears in *OeBA* II, 85f. (no. 504).

9   A reference to the judicial drowning of the anabaptist Felix Manz in Zürich on 5th January 1527.

10   See 404, n. 9. Hubmaier is alluding to Rhegius's *Responsio* to Theodor Billican (see 438, n. 7). On relations between Zwingli and Rhegius between 1525 and 1527 see Zschoch, "Zwingli und Augsburg", 167–171.

11   In particular Romans 7:7 f.

12   *De peccato originali declaratio ad Urbanum Rhegium* (Zürich: Froschauer, 25th August 1526); ed. ZW V, 369–396 (no. 97); trans. Hinke, 2–32.

13   An allusion to the argument that infant baptism is the Christian equivalent of circumcision, made on the basis of passages like Exodus 4:24–26 (Zipporah's circumcision of Moses).

work that "is" means "signifies" on the basis of Genesis.[14] Otherwise he does not mention you. So for this reason I will keep the little book here, unless you ask for it again.

Rumour here has it that Franz Kolb is intending to leave Bern and go somewhere else (where, I do not know), because as yet no stipend has been agreed for him.[15] | Write a letter, to try to keep him there. I shall write too.

Farewell. 19th July.
Your Oecolampadius.
To Huldrych Zwingli, his dearest brother.

Original: Zürich, Staatsarchiv, E II 349, p. 32 (autograph). Copy: Zürich, Zentralbibliothek, MS S 19, no. 19f. From "This is" (line 38), the beginning of its last recto page, the remainder of the letter is treated as a separate piece; hence the double numbering.[16]

---

14 A reference to Joseph's interpretation of Pharaoh's dream in Genesis 41. He consistently uses the verb 'to be' when explaining the dream's meaning (e.g. v. 26, "The seven good kine are seven years; and the seven good ears are seven years"). As such the passage was used in support of certain understandings of the Eucharist.

15 Kolb (c. 1465–1535) studied in Basel, became a Carthusian, and was later an evangelical reformer in Nürnberg, Wertheim and, from April 1527, Bern. In fact he did not "leave the Berners", but rather remained in their city until his death. The question of his stipend was resolved as early as 14th August 1527; but it is not known whether, or to what effect, Zwingli or Oecolampadius intervened on his behalf. On him see *BBKL* IV, 322 f.

16 We are grateful for this information to Dr André Junghänel, Zürich.

637   Oecolampadius to Zwingli—Basel, 19th July (1527)

Greetings in Christ. Re-reading my letter to you, my brother, I noticed that you are still waiting for certain things in addition to what I have sent, namely Balthasar's paradoxes.¹ I read these on some sheet of paper sent here by *Faber. Now I have no faith in that man, and I do not think that the impu-
5 dence it contains comes from Balthasar. But the sheet says that he, Balthasar, has taught that the Virgin Mary also had other sons, and that Christ was conceived in original sin and is not the true Son of God. Certainly I would not be able to believe that Balthasar had asserted such things, even if someone other than Faber was spreading such blasphemies; for this would be | to
10 refute the whole of Christianity in one go. I do not have the sheet containing these blasphemies to hand.

IX, 179

IX, 180

Once again, farewell.
19th July.
Oecolampadius.
15 To his Huldrych Zwingli.

Original: Zürich, Staatsarchiv, E II 349, p. 103 (autograph). Copy: Zürich, Zentralbibliothek, MS S 19, no. 21.

---

1 *my letter to you*] *literas tuas* (literally, 'your letters'). It is plain Oecolampadius has been rereading 636, lines 15–20, composed on the same day and presumably not yet sent   3 *paradoxes*] Greek παραδοξότατα

---

1 These "paradoxes" are the so-called Nikolsburg Articles, compiled by Balthasar Hubmaier (see 347, n. 5) to discredit the radical anabaptist Hans Hut (c. 1490–1527) in advance of a disputation with him at Mikulov (Nikolsburg) in the summer of 1527. Hence Oecolampadius was correct to surmise that these articles did not reflect Hubmaier's own views. On this episode see J. Denny Weaver, "Hubmaier versus Hut on the Work of Christ. The Fifth Nicolsburg Article", *Archiv für Reformationsgeschichte* 82 (1991): 171–192. On Hut see also OER II, 280 f.; TRE XV, 741–747; BBKL II, 1213–1217.

642 Oecolampadius to Zwingli—Basel, 18th August (1527)

The grace and peace of Christ. Brother, I am sending you herewith what I wrote to the Landgrave of Hesse about the first chapter of Ezekiel.[1] Would you mind reading your copy and letting me know if it leaves anything to be desired—and I do not doubt that there are many such things—so that in future I might write in a better informed and more reliable way? For there is danger in those Sphinxes.[2]

Today I gave the printer what I wrote against the catabaptists[3]—in which, as charity requires, I make mention of your work.

There is a rumour that Balthasar has been burnt; but his book is still alive, and it is not right for us to be silent about it, until such time as it is turned to ashes by the fire of the word.[4]

| *Pirckheimer is writing against me for the third time,[5] or so the person delivering this letter tells me. What is the man going to say now? How many charges will he trump up this time? Whatever he writes will hardly be worth responding to. But it distresses me that so noble a city is now oppressed by so great a tyranny.[6] O profane Osiander![7] The courier—whom I ask you to

---

3 *letting me know*] *indicanto*, a third person plural imperative; we read *indicato*, the equivalent singular   16 *profane*] Greek ἀνόσιον

---

1 Oecolampadius seems to have lectured on Ezekiel roughly between March 1527 and the summer of 1528 (see Staehelin, *Lebenswerk*, 408). These lectures were worked up into a full commentary by *Capito only after Oecolampadius's death; but a commentary on the first chapter, with a preface and dedication to *Philipp of Hesse, was published on 12th August 1527: *Das erst Capitel des propheten Jeheskiels uszgelegt durch Joannem Ecolampadium. Von dem ampt der Oberen vnd der vnderthonen* (Basel: Cratander; Staehelin 144; Leu/Weidmann A166).
2 Presumably a reference to the monstrous "four living creatures" described at length in Ezekiel 1.
3 See 636, n. 8.
4 Balthasar Hubmaier (see 347, n. 5) was eventually burnt at the stake, in Vienna on 10th March 1528; but the rumour mentioned here was plainly false. "That book of his" is *Ein gesprech der Predicanten* (see 554, n. 20). On Oecolampadius's eventual response see 636, n. 8.
5 This was published as *Bilibaldi Pirkheymeri de conuitiis Monachi illius, qui graecolatine Caecolampadius germanice vero Ausschin nuncupatur, ad Eleutherum suum epistola suum epistola* (Nürnberg: Petreius, 1527; Leu/Weidmann A181). See Burnett, *Debating*, 173. Oecolampadius did not in fact reply to it.
6 Nürnberg, where Pirckheimer was active and where the sale of books by the Swiss reformers had been banned.
7 Andreas Osiander (1496–1552), a distinguished Hebrew and Greek scholar who had become the chief Lutheran reformer in Nürnberg, and whom Zwingli blamed for the ban on

commend to the brothers—will tell you the rest, if perhaps he can stay and talk to you for a while.

The Strasbourg brothers have sent a suitable preacher to Worms, a certain Fontanus.[8]

At Ulm there is a ban on papist preachers who refused to abandon their doctrinal system.[9] We cannot by any means get such a ban out of our Council, but you know what is preventing it; perhaps one day the Lord will be mindful of us.

I hear that both *Bucer and *Capito are unwell physically; but they have not been afflicted by the plague. Great lights like them, who guide us as they do, would not be snuffed out before their time unless the Lord were angry. May the Lord keep you safe for us for a long time!

Farewell.
Basel, 18th August.
Your Oecolampadius.
To Huldrych Zwingli, his dearest brother.

Original: Zürich, Staatsarchiv, E II 349, p. 110 (autograph). Copy: Zürich, Zentralbibliothek, Ms S 19, no. 34.

---

19 *to Worms*] *Wormaciensibus* (literally, 'to the people of Worms')

　　his and Oecolampadius's publications. On him see Gottfried Seebaß, *Das reformatorische Werk des Andreas Osiander* (Nürnberg: Verein für Bayerische Kirchengeschichte, 1967); *CoE* III, 35 f.; *OER* III, 103–105; *TRE* XXV, 507–515; *BBKL* VI, 1298 f.

8　Leonhard Brunner (c. 1500–1558), a biblical scholar who was a Deacon at Old St Peter's Church in Strasbourg, and was now given the difficult task of calming church affairs in Worms after controversies occasioned by local anabaptists.

9　Ulm did not become officially Protestant until 1530, but since 1526 its Council had been taking steps to restrict the activities particularly of the city's Franciscans—one of whom, a certain Ulrich, had been expelled in early August. See Specker/Weig, *Ulm*, 250.

644 Oecolampadius to Zwingli—Basel, 20th August (1527)

The grace and peace of Christ. I have found it hard to believe (and am still not inclined to do so) that you are rather annoyed with our Cellarius[1] about all that pertains to baptism. He himself and the Strasbourg brothers themselves fear this is the case, and are praying about it; and they have written me a letter on the subject,[2] urging me—on account of our friendship and brotherly love—to take steps to stop you bringing up again anything that might once have given offence through the somewhat imprudent boldness of its language. For those who know him better on the basis of long acquaintance can indeed bear witness to who he is and what he is like now. Hitherto he has remained entirely unknown to me, save for the little that rumour had asserted about his reputation—and this, as is usually the case, was very different from the reality of things. Perhaps the same is true of you; but I do not know what conversation once took place between the two of you.[3] Whatever it was, however, both his letter and the one from our brothers remind us well enough to regard him with honour and friendliness. For the rest, I do not yet have a view as to whether his little book[4] merits a somewhat indignant reaction. After all, it is causing very great trouble for the catabaptists, and will be an intolerable nail in the coffin of all our adversaries, to whatever ends they eventually attack us. It is very hostile towards the papists. It tramples *Luther underfoot on many counts. It makes *Erasmus himself nervous: he is now arming his new *Hyperaspistes* of his own free will.[5] It strengthens

---

7f. *through ... language*] *sermonis licentia prudentius* (literally, 'impudently, by the boldness of language')   10 *unknown*] Greek ἄγνωστος   15 *to ... friendliness*] *ut honeste de eo sentiamus et amice* (literally, 'that we might feel in an honest and friendly way about him')   21 *of his own free will*] *pro suo* αὐτεξουσίου—a punning reference to the fact that Erasmus's most public debate with *Luther concerned the reality and power of human free will (see n. 5 below)

---

1   Or 'Martin Borrhaus' (1499–1564). He had studied at Tübingen and Ingolstadt, and had been associated with prominent anabaptists both in Wittenberg and in Switzerland. From 1527 to 1536 he lived in Strasbourg, where he developed a close relationship with *Capito, but continued to be mistrusted by *Bucer (and Zwingli) for his anabaptist and chiliastic leanings. He later taught at the University of Basel. See *CoE* I, 287; *OER* I, 202 f.; *BBKL* I, 707 f.
2   This letter has not been preserved.
3   Zwingli had met Cellarius in Zürich in 1524.
4   *De operibus Dei* (Strasbourg: Herwagen, 1527; Leu/Weidmann A20). Its contents—highly controversial at the time—are discussed in Williams, "Cellarius", 479–486.
5   This work was to be the second part of the *Hyperaspistes Diatribae Adversus Seruum Arbitrium Martini Lutheri* (Basel: Froben, 1527; Leu/Weidmann A62), the first volume of which had appeared in 1526.

our cause here in every way. And so, my brother, whatever some people are saying about it, the little book should by no means be discounted. And apart from anything else, it is surely of great importance that he wants our advice; and I do not doubt that he will hear us with gratitude whenever, | through weakness, he is unable to achieve what in all piety he has tried to do. If, at the wholesome behest of charity, he defends our freedom to baptize infants and condemns catabaptism, I do not see what danger there is. We also have sinned in this respect: for we have never dared to teach infant baptism as a doctrine, but—prompted by charity—we have simply affirmed that pious people will by no means overlook this duty. And the works against Balthasar[6] that are now in press will say the same things: I do not wish the baptism of infants to be regarded in the same light as matters irrelevant to religion, but nor do I wish to limit anyone's freedom. Moreover, since in all ways we are of one heart and hold all things in common in Christ,[7] we must strive to demonstrate this fact, lest our adversaries suspect any discord or, rather, rivalry. In other respects the whole world is raging against us—not so that we should turn a blind eye to any falsehoods or strange doctrines, but so that we should not be more severe on our friends than on our enemies, whose countless sins we both desire and are compelled to forgive. I pray, however, that in dealing with this honest man who is also (as I see it) zealous for your reputation, you in turn might allow him to taste the Christian gentleness of your heart, even if only in a few letters.[8] If he needs to be admonished, admonish him; and if he takes this admonition well, you can banish your concerns about him. For he does not want you to be his enemy. By the way, I am also sending on a letter of his;[9] perhaps until now his admiration and respect for your reputation have held him back from taking the initiative to greet you in a letter.

---

33 *in the same light*] ἀδιάφορον (literally, 'not different')

---

6 Hubmaier (see 347, n. 5). The works in question are the two treatises on baptism that *Cratander was to publish together on 5th September (see 636, n. 8).
7 Cf. Acts 4:32.
8 No letter from Zwingli to Cellarius survives, but the latter wrote to Zwingli (distancing himself from anabaptist perspectives) on 31st August—see ZW IX, 206–208 (no. 649).
9 Presumably the one sent to Oecolampadius from Strasbourg earlier in August, which is printed in *OeBA* II, 91 f. (no. 508).

There is a rumour that Luther is again thundering against us, and I do not know what new hells he is threatening.[10] Glory be to Christ, for by this means he will not let the truth be hidden any longer from these ferocious men.

I commend Cellarius to you as a friend, my brother.
Farewell.
Basel, 20th August.
Your Oecolampadius.
To Huldrych Zwingli, his dearest brother.

Original: Zürich, Staatsarchiv, E II 349, p. 58 (scribal hand). Copy: Zürich, Zentralbibliothek, Ms S 19, no. 35.

---

[10] Luther's response to both Zwingli's *Früntlich verglimpfung* (see 586, n. 7) and Oecolampadius's *Das der miszverstand* (see 607, n. 10) was in fact to be delayed until the following year: *Vom abendmal Christi Bekendnis* (Wittenberg: Lotter, 1528; Leu/Weidmann A141)—ed. WA XXVI, 261–509; trans. AE XXXVII, 161–372. See Burnett, *Debating*, 229–231.

648 Oecolampadius to Zwingli—Basel, 31st August (1527)

Grace and peace from Christ. My Zwingli, I recently sent you, via a certain Bavarian, our Ezekiel and a letter from Cellarius.[1] Now I am learning from frequent letters that the Strasbourg brothers are preoccupied by the same concern about him.[2] I am wondering where this suspicion might have sprung from; but whatever it is, let me know. I think, however, that there is no danger, and that the brothers' concerns have been fuelled by someone's idle fancy. If the prayers of Oecolampadius, prayed in the name of Christ, have any force at all, please see to it that their concerns are alleviated, lest even the suspicion of discord between us encourage our Philistines. I hope to see soon what you have written in Latin against the catabaptists.[3] Our works are still in press.[4] As far as I can deduce from your words in the vernacular,[5] we will not disagree at all.

The bearer of this letter is a Dutchman,[6] a lover of Christ: he is commended as such by the brothers, and his every utterance confirms the fact. It would benefit the work of the gospel if we showed greater kindness to those who sincerely seek our company—so that the mouths of the detractors who heap the worst insults upon us, and of those who vainly desire by such means to thwart the gospel, might to some extent be stopped by true friends.

The day before yesterday the pieces we have written about the need to abolish the Mass were read here before the Council.[7] Would that those with ears to hear had listened![8] I fear they will again delay their verdict for some time;[9] I understand nothing has been decided as yet.

---

13 *lover of Christ*] φιλόχριστος

---

1 For Oecolampadius's commentary on Ezekiel see 642, n. 1; for Cellarius's letter see 644, lines 45–48 and n. 8f. We have no way of knowing who the "certain Bavarian" was.
2 That is to say, by the same concerns about the apparent anabaptist tendencies of Cellarius (see 644, n. 1) that Oecolampadius attributes to Zwingli in 644, lines 1–9. For an account of the controversies surrounding him in Strasbourg, see Williams, "Cellarius", 492–497; Kittelson, *Capito*, 178–181, 184–186.
3 *In catabaptistarum strophas elenchus* (Zürich: Froschauer, 31st July 1527)—ed. ZW VI/1, 21–196 (no. 108).
4 See 636, n. 8.
5 In the original, *vernaculis tuis*. The reference is presumably to Zwingli's *Früntlich verglimpfung* (see 586, n. 7).
6 Again there is no record as to who this might be.
7 For the context see 624, lines 23–31 and n. 7.
8 Cf. Matthew 13:9.
9 In fact the Council was to act with reasonable speed: its official response was published on 21st September.

Farewell, and love me in Christ, as you are wont to do.
The last day of August.
Your Oecolampadius.
To Huldrych Zwingli, his dearest brother. Zürich.

Original: Zürich, Staatsarchiv, E II 349, p. 75 (autograph). Copy: Zürich, Zentralbibliothek, Ms S 19, no. 42.

652 Oecolampadius to Zwingli—Zürich, 4th September (1527)

Grace and peace from Christ, my brother. I will read your *Refutation*[1] with great eagerness, and will compare it with my own writings. Truly I do not wish to disagree with you on any matter of any importance, and I hope that you in turn will not disagree with us—although we permit people either to
5 baptize or not to baptize healthy little children, using charity as our prime criterion when considering whether baptism should be brought forward or deferred. But when I have read your book on the subject, I hope that you will have sufficient leisure, when you have read my little apologia, to make a note of what displeases you about this matter.[2] For I have written nothing which I
10 would not wish to be corrected, should the truth require it. When I have seen *Pirckheimer's book,[3] I will respond to it (if it seems to be in readers' interest for me to do so), and will do so briefly, as you advise.[4] Now with regard to Cellarius, I do not anticipate anything bad happening, though our *Capito is extremely credulous; and, when it came to Hätzer's wiles, we should have
15 been more cautious about not welcoming just anyone.[5]

Farewell, together with *Leo, *Pellikan, Megander[6] and the other brothers.
Basel, 4th September.
Your Oecolampadius.
To Huldrych Zwingli, his dearest brother.

Original: Zürich, Staatsarchiv, E II 344, p. 509 (autograph). Copy: Zürich, Zentralbibliothek, Ms S 19, no. 47.

---

1 The *Elenchus*: see 648, n. 3.
2 Oecolampadius may well have been right to fear that Zwingli would not approve specifically of his liberal views as to the most desirable timing of baptism; these were after all in line with the opinions of Cellarius (see 644, n. 1 and 4; also Williams, "Cellarius", 483–485).
3 See 642, n. 5.
4 No such advice from Zwingli has survived.
5 *Hätzer had had to leave Basel in December 1526, when he became embroiled in a sexual scandal with Oecolampadius's serving maid.
6 Kaspar Megander (or 'Grossmann', 1495–1545), a theologian who was born and died in Zürich and remained loyal to Zwingli throughout his career, but is best known for his reforming activities in Bern between 1528 and 1537. See *OER* III, 41; *BBKL* XIV, 1245–1249.

658   Oecolampadius to Zwingli—Basel, 30th September (1527)

Greetings in Christ, my brother. O, what bold champions the bready idol has at Nürnberg! They have been assembling all kinds of insults against us, and they firmly believe that they have been right to do so. A response from me to *Pirckheimer would be in vain.[1] His verbal diarrhoea is incurable, just as—I fear—Osiander's diseased tongue will admit of no remedy.[2] I have read what he has written,[3] and everywhere I have detected the presence of a sophist. Yet you will have to do battle with him—as indeed you are about to do, even without my encouragement.[4] He is threatening to write more, and denies us salvation, as if we had been blotted out of the book of life;[5] I have seen nothing more arrogant, I have observed nothing more vainly adorned with grandiose rhetoric. But you, boil down and encapsulate your answer in a very few words: perhaps at some point he will be grateful for this service. May the Lord direct his own work.

If you think it is prudent to discuss see the record of the Disputation of Baden as you promised to, let me know if there is anything in my words that displeases you, so that I can explain myself.[6] For the public location was forcing me to speak differently from the way | I had intended. The audience had been exasperated by blasphemous and slanderous speeches, and were very reluctant to listen to arguments about the Eucharist. This was why they were

---

4 *verbal diarrhoea*] γλωσσαλγεία (literally, 'use of the tongue until it aches')   11 *grandiose*] *maiori* (literally, 'greater')   11f. *boil down ... words*] *ut bullam, parcissimis verbis comprime* (literally, 'like a capsule [or 'papal bull'!] compress in very few words')

---

1   See 642, lines 12–15 and n. 5.
2   On Osiander see 642, n. 7.
3   This is a letter written by Osiander in response to, and published alongside, one by Zwingli: *Epistolae duae, una Hulderichi Zvinglii ad Andream Osiandrum, qua cum eo expostulat, quod novum illud de Eucharistia dogma hactenus reiecerit, ac temere impugnarit. Altere Andreae Osiandri ad eundem Hulderichum Zuinglium, Apologetica* (Nürnberg: Petreius, 1527; Leu/Weidmann A170). Both letters appear in ZW, Zwingli's as no. 617 (ZW IX, 127–130) and Osiander's as no. 659 (ZW IX, 232–276); also in Osiander, *Gesamtausgabe*, II, 537–578 (no. 90).
4   In fact no subsequent letter or longer reply from Zwingli to Osiander has survived.
5   Cf. Exodus 32:32. The full title of Osiander's letter makes it plain that he is intending to make further contributions to the eucharistic debate: *Apologeticc, qua docet, quid quam ob causam reiecerit, quid que post hac ab eo in illa causa expectandum sit. Quos si diligenter perlegeris, Christiane lector, tanto familiarius, ea que deinceps Osiander in Eucharistiae caussa scripturus est, intellexeris*.
6   We know that Oecolampadius had for some time wanted Zwingli to compose an account of the perceived failings of the Disputation of Baden's records (see 635, lines 16–19 and 636, lines 1–14); but it is not clear that Zwingli ever undertook to do so.

keen to debate this matter first at the meeting: they were hoping to overwhelm us in the initial combat. Hence I thought I should delay igniting this discussion still further, by dealing with their calumnies about the safe conduct; we listened to these in order that I might then demonstrate that we were true churchmen. For nothing worse could have happened to me than to be excluded from the true church of Christ. And seeing that transubstantiation, that grossest of errors, was supported by our adversaries, I in turn took it upon myself to expose it—in order that, when their worthlessness was revealed, some of their authority might collapse in one respect, and thereafter their deceptions might be ignored in other respects also. But we were not pleading our case before Rhadamanthus and Aeacus.[7]

In your *Refutation of the Catabaptists' Tricks*[8] you reproach in passing those who are in the habit of banning others from the Lord's Supper. Certain people are using this against us, because we celebrate the Eucharist according to our Basel liturgy—which, however, does not diverge from the word of God.[9] They are saying this because we issue a warning just before the Lord's Supper that identifies those whom we wish to participate in it. Now, I understand very clearly what you have written, and indeed I know that you are very clear about it. For, as our friend, you could advise us in a letter if | you identified anything in the rite we use that you found intolerable; and it would please us a great deal if you did this. You know the state of our churches, how much tyranny we suffer, and how much we desire to be free from tyranny. Just as the apostle wants individuals to examine themselves,[10] so we offer this advice to many—thereby taking the trouble to give our adversaries, who have been so quick to speak ill of us on other occasions, no further opportunities to do so (lest, with our consent, all the ungodly share their filth with us). That said, I do not think you are attacking us in your writings. So you can advise us on this matter at your leisure and in private; in this way you will challenge us to take account both of the need for peace and of your doctrine—in so far as the truth permits it. I have neither read nor received the letter from Berchthold you wrote about recently.[11]

---

7 Along with Minos, two of the three Greek Judges of the Dead, and presumably as such embodiments of wisdom and justice—in a way that those in charge of the Disputation of Baden palpably were not.

8 See 648, n. 3. The reference in question is in zw VI/I, 111–113.

9 Oecolampadius is referring to the sacramental liturgy published in 1526—see p. 17, n. 64. The passage mentioning those who are to be banned from the Eucharist is discussed in Staehelin, *Lebenswerk*, 433.

10 Cf. 1 Corinthians 11:28.

11 *Haller. Neither of these letters has survived.

Farewell.
Basel, the last day of September.
Your Oecolampadius.

At *Capito's urging I have opened a letter from *Bucer, in which the preachers from Ulm, who are most honest men, make a case.[12] As far as I am concerned, I gave a satisfactory answer about intercession last year, in the published sermon that I preached here on All Saints' Day against *Faber—who, foolishly as always, thought that it should be included in his blasphemous book.[13] For how can I deny to people the affection of charity, on the basis of which the saints and angels—empowered as they are by charity—look upon us with favour? And why should I refute someone who terms this a form of "intercession", unless I were to deny that they are alive in | spirit? Otherwise I have not condoned this type of invocation, on the grounds that it is unknown to scripture—though who would not want the whole body of Christ to pray with him? I will look more carefully at what I said in the course of disputations. It is no wonder that the forerunner of the Antichrist is striving to destroy that city:[14] for he is causing similar trouble in Augsburg, summoning that city's preachers to the most disreputable of towns[15] in order to dispute with him, whilst he himself is entirely free and completely safe to engage with them in their city.[16] Behold, Eck is using this pretext to induce people to recognize him as the disputer *par excellence*!

Farewell.
To Huldrych Zwingli, his dearest brother.

Original: Zürich, Staatsarchiv, E II 349, p. 114 (autograph). Copy: Zürich, Zentralbibliothek, Ms S 19, no. 67.

---

12   See letter 657 (zw IX, 225–227). Oecolampadius is here in a sense already raising the subject of *Eck, who had recently written to the Ulm evangelicals accusing them of heresy.
13   For the context see 534, lines 1–13 and n. 1–3. Eck was again raising the issue of the invocation of the saints in his polemic against the Ulm preachers.
14   Eck and Ulm are meant.
15   This is a plural form in the original, but one assumes that Ingolstadt is meant.
16   Eck had been at loggerheads with Augsburg since the city's Council had banned his writings on the Mass in 1526. Negotiations had begun, particularly between Eck and Urbanus Rhegius (see 404, n. 9) about the possibility of a formal disputation, but this did not come to pass.

661 Oecolampadius to Zwingli—Basel, 15th October 1527

Greetings in Christ, my brother. Up to now the ungodly have been sticking to their dogmas when it comes to observing the rite of the papal Mass; as a result our rural priests have been obliged either to revert to their former impiety or to carry on without their stipends.[1] We appear to be tolerated rather than favoured, and that only until such time as they find some tiny excuse to attack us. But we hope the Lord will overthrow plans that go against the glory of his name. Matters in the Council are troublesome enough, as the person delivering this letter will be able to tell you.

For the rest, *Capito writes from Strasbourg that he wants me to tell you how the tyranny of the new bishop (*Luther, he supposes) is gaining in strength every day, and how he has recently joined forces with certain representatives of the secular arm to devise a plan for | the Holy Mother Church of Wittenberg:[2] they have agreed that the articles written by heretics and the prejudices espoused by the common people must be examined, so as to ensure that no Zwinglian, or follower of Oecolampadius, or person of whatever description who has moved there from Strasbourg, is permitted to receive pastoral care.[3] We are called cranks, and also fanatics who cannot be defeated unless the Most Holy Provincial Synod imposes limits on us. They

---

12f. *the ... Wittenberg*] *sanctae matris ecclesiae Wittembergensis*: there are three genitives here, so various constructions are possible. We are assuming that Oecolampadius wants to imply the Lutherans are behaving like authoritarian Catholics   17 *cranks*] *schwermeri*, from German *Schwärmer*

---

1 As Oecolampadius had feared (see 600, lines 34–38 and n. 10), Basel's new bishop Philipp von Gundelsheim had taken a hard line against reform, and had influenced the Council to issue an edict on 23rd September stating that, whilst no-one was obliged to hear Mass, priests had to celebrate it, on pain of losing their stipends—see *AGBR*, II, 715f. (no. 728). Oecolampadius and others who had already ceased to hold Masses remained exempt from the new edict; but plainly it affected many other priests, not least those in Basel's rural hinterland.

2 A reference to the ongoing visitation of Saxon parishes, which proceeded in 1526 and 1527 with a view to increasing levels of moral, legal and administrative order in the growing Lutheran churches. The moves were much mistrusted, not least because of the material involvement of Elector Johann of Saxony and other princes.

3 In fact neither Zwingli, Oecolampadius nor Strasbourg was discussed in the written report and recommendations that followed the Saxon visitations: *Unterricht der Visitatorn an die Pfarhern ym Kurfurstenthum zu Sachssen* (Wittenberg: Schirlentz, 1528)—ed. *WA* XXVI, 195–240; trans. *AE* XL, 263–320. The text is principally by *Melanchthon, but has a prologue by Luther. As lines 9–17 suggest, a number of scare stories were circulating.

are threatening excommunication. The Saxons said this. But Capito is now thinking about what we need to write against them. And indeed every effort must be made.

I wrote to you recently via Christoph, but have not yet received a reply to this letter.[4] Almost everyone is denouncing Osiander's impudence. The kingdom of God does not exist in flowery words.[5] *Strauß has published some foolish things against me.[6] I do not wish to respond now, unless the brothers urge me to. I am translating what Cyril wrote against Julian the Apostate.[7] I have translated almost three books, without doubt the most learned ones. See to it that your church prays for ours, so that it might be strengthened and might prosper at last; for it is rather weak. And may you also fare well, victorious over the enemies of Christ, and your own.

Dated 15th October 1527.
Your Oecolampadius.
Thomas, my Augustinian,[8] greets you especially.
To Huldrych Zwingli, his beloved brother. Zürich.

Original: Zürich, Staatsarchiv, E II 349, p. 9 (scribal hand). Copy: Zürich, Zentralbibliothek, Ms S 19, no. 76.

---

4 The references to Osiander in line 22f. imply that Oecolampadius is here referring to letter 658; but it is not clear that this was delivered by *Froschauer.
5 For the context see 658, lines 4–11. Oecolampadius is echoing 1 Corinthians 4:20.
6 *Das der leyb Christi und seyn heiliges Blut im Sakrament gegenwertig sey, richtige erklerung auff das new büchlein D. Johannes Haußscheyn, diesem zuwider* (Augsburg: Steiner, 1527)— the long-threatened response to Oecolampadius's *De genuina … expositione* (see 381, n. 2). It is discussed in Barge, *Strauß*, 155–162. The latter did not in fact reply to it.
7 Oecolampadius's full three-volume Latin translation of Cyril of Alexandria's works was published in 1528: *Divi Cyrilli Archiepiscopi Alexandrini Opera, in tres partita Tomos: in quibus habes non pauca antehac Latinis non exhibita* (Basel: Cratander; Staehelin 156). On it see Staehelin, *Lebenswerk*, 454–461.
8 Thomas Gyrfalk (see 367, n. 5), preacher at the Augustinian church in Basel.

665   Oecolampadius to Zwingli—Basel, 6th November (1527)

Greetings in Christ, beloved brother. All of us good people are reflecting upon the response we presented to the Council, and which is now being printed under many of our names.[1] This was done above all because certain people have written to other cities claiming that our Council has been considering the submissions of both parties, and has decided on the basis of them that priests who do not celebrate Mass are to be banned. For the rest, we are not very anxious about the title it is to be given—you can decide on it there.[2] None of the brothers would refuse to put his name to it. I fear, however, that this letter is reaching you too late; if it were not, I would advise that we would like the following title: "Response of the Basel preachers who were asked by an honourable Council why they have preached that the popish Mass is an abomination before God, and not a sacrifice for the living and the dead". They certainly think that the signatories' names should be placed at the end. There are seven of us: Johannes Oecolampadius, People's Priest at St Martin's; Markus Bertschi, People's Priest at St Leonard's; Wolfgang Wissenburg, People's Priest at the hospital; Johannes Lüthard, Preacher at the Franciscan church; Thomas Gyrfalk, Preacher at the Augustinian church;[3] Hieronymus Bothan, Deacon at St Martin's;[4] and Balthasar Vögelin, Deacon at St Leonard's.[5] But | if the book has already been printed, it will not disturb us at all if no mention is made of our names; for it is sufficient to us if the truth confounds that greatest of abominations. At the time no messenger was available, so we were not able to advise on the title. But all is well, whatever the title is.

10–13 *Response ... dead*] German *Antwort der predikanten zu Basel, so von einem ersamen radt also ersucht, warumb sie gepredigt haben, das die bepstisch meß ein greuwel für gott und kein opfer für die lebendigen und die todten*   14–19 *Johannes ... Leonard's*] these details are given in German

---

1   For the context see 624, lines 23–31; 625, lines 11–20; 648, lines 19–22. The publication in question is *Ein Christliche vnd ernstlich antwurt der Prediger des Euangelij zu Basel, warumb sy die Mess einen grüwel gescholten habind. Uff erforschung vnd gheyß des Ersamen Radts daselbst gebennhe* (Zürich: Froschauer, 1527; Leu/Weidmann A165).
2   Zwingli and his colleagues were materially involved in arranging for the *Christliche vnd ernstlich antwurt* (as n. 1) to be published in Zürich: the "you" in line 7 is a plural, as is the one in 668, line 9.
3   For these close colleagues of Oecolampadius see 367, n. 1, 4–6.
4   See 430, n. 4.
5   Very little is known of this figure, but he appears to have come from Walenstadt (in Canton St. Gallen), and to have matriculated at Freiburg in 1504 and Basel in 1509.

Now I must tell you that your letter[6] was a source of great comfort to the brothers; throughout it, they can see your concern for us and your obviously genuine feelings towards us. Your plans were the same as ours, and indeed covered everything, without omitting any detail; as such they reveal a degree of concern and carefulness that—given our insignificance—went far beyond what was needed. Yet we will not cease to invoke and implore you in a rigorous yet friendly way. The Lord, though, is not yet looking kindly upon us: we are singing our song to the deaf, for Basel is incurable and knows of no remedy.[7] For the rest, your Andreas[8] will tell you on his return what has been happening here recently. *Capito writes that he has learnt from a reliable source that numerous truly troublesome men are dissuading *Luther from writing.[9] For my part, I would wish his bad conscience would deter him from doing so.

All the brothers greet you; I now find that they leave nothing to be desired with regard to steadfastness or prudent zeal. In the name of us all, greet *Pellikan and *Leo, along with our other colleagues.

Farewell.
Basel, 6th November.
Johannes Oecolampadius.
To Huldrych Zwingli, his dearest brother.

Original: Zürich, Staatsarchiv, E II 349, p. 119 (autograph). Copy: Zürich, Zentralbibliothek, Ms S 19, no. 89.

---

6 This seems to have been lost.
7 One assumes Oecolampadius is frustrated mainly about the Council's decision, on 21st October, to allow its citizens freedom of choice as to whether or not to attend Mass. On the immediate consequences of this decision see Roth, *Reformation*, I, 44–46. In retrospect, of course, it seems clear that such "balance-of-power politics" (*Gleichgewichtspolitik*—Roth, *Reformation*, I, 41) could in time only work to the evangelicals' advantage.
8 *Cratander or—perhaps more likely—Zwingli's associate Andreas Krämer.
9 The context cannot be deduced from any of Capito's surviving letters.

667 Oecolampadius to Zwingli—Basel, 10th November (1527)

Greetings in Christ. I have received your letter, my brother. We will deal faithfully with what needs to be sent to Strasbourg. Osiander, being mindful of such little reputation as he possesses, promised much but delivered little.[1] I have not yet been able to see what came before it, though he is not reporting anything he has not seen. But, however many artifices he employs, he will not inflict any evil on our good cause. *Bucer has sent us a letter from the Voyevoda here, and some good people want it to be printed in the vernacular.[2] Nevertheless I cannot find a suitable printer for the purpose here. I would not like to give false accusers an opportunity to suggest that we are its authors, for in that way no damage would be incurred by the Turk, that most troublesome tyrant—although | it would not be unprofitable for the injustice of princes to be exposed, if perhaps they were to vanquish their confusion and come to their senses. What, after all, can one hope for in their case? When will they be victorious, if they continue to exert their tyranny? Or perhaps this is a whip that God has wielded to punish our sins? Consider, you and your people, what is to be done.

Farewell, together with all your household.
Basel, 10th November.
Oecolampadius.
To Huldrych Zwingli, teacher of the Zürichers, his dearest brother.

Original: Zürich, Staatsarchiv, E II 349, p. 56 (autograph). Copy: Zürich, Zentralbibliothek, Ms S 19, no. 84.

---

3 *promised ... little*] nihil praeter expectationem egit (literally, 'had done nothing beyond expectation', an ironic understatement on Oecolampadius's part). See n. 1 below   14 *victorious, if*] the manuscript and edition have a sentence-ending question mark rather than a comma here; this seems to us to obscure the passage's meaning

1 Osiander has not carried out the threat that he would again write against Oecolampadius—see 658, line 8 f. and n. 5.
2 The context is unclear, not least because the manuscript of the letter contains no reference to a specific year. Around this time, however, John Zápolya (see 547, n. 9–11) was assiduously soliciting support from evangelical and other anti-Habsburg forces in the Empire, chiefly via embassies carried out by the Polish diplomat Hieronymus Laski (1496–1542). Hence the (lost) letter alluded to here is likely to have emanated at least indirectly from Zápolya, to whom Bucer elsewhere refers as "the Voyevoda"—see BC IV, 177–180 (no. 321), here 179, line 9.

668   Oecolampadius to Zwingli—Basel, 24th November (1527)

Grace and peace from Christ, dearest Huldrych! We desire to hear from you what you think we need to do in the matter of Bern, news of which delighted us in no small measure.[1] We will attend the disputation, if the Lord allows it—for we are promised a happier outcome than we had at Baden. Perhaps Christ will reveal his glory in this way. For the truth cannot be taught entirely without fruit. Would that, embracing each other, we might see in the New Year there to the glory of Christ! If you are present, you will be able to achieve a great deal through your authority and erudition—whether our adversaries are present or absent. For the rest, you did very well in ensuring that our response was published in Zürich.[2] There is nothing for Christoph to be afraid of, because nothing has been added to what we submitted. There are some who want our opponents' responses to be appended to ours.[3] Perhaps a copy of them can indeed be included; but I have instructed Immeli[4] to speak with you in person and ask how you would advise us on the matter.

Farewell.
Basel, 24th November.
Your Oecolampadius.
To Huldrych Zwingli, his dearest brother.

Original: Zürich, Staatsarchiv, E II 349, p. 117 (autograph) Copy: Zürich, Zentralbibliothek, Ms S 19, no. 102.

---

1 The first reference in this correspondence to the Disputation of Bern, which had been announced on 15th November and was scheduled for 6th January 1528.
2 See 665, n. 2.
3 In fact the evangelical and Catholic responses to the Council were to be published together, though not by *Froschauer: *Ob die Mess ein opffer sey: beyder partheyen Predicanten zu Basel antwurt, Vff erforschung eins Ersamen Radts eyngelegt* (Basel: Wolff, 1527; Staehelin 149). They are discussed by Birkner, *Marius*, 52–63.
4 See 367, n. 3.

670   Oecolampadius to Zwingli—Basel, 30th November (1527)

Grace and peace from Christ, my Zwingli! We could not have helped that   IX, 315
man Matthäus, even though he was our brother;[1] but otherwise your prayers
have been highly effective. May the Lord provide for him elsewhere. The
man Lucas is in some danger because of the Masses he has missed, indeed
stopped celebrating entirely.[2] In ways such as this our affairs always hang by
a slender thread. We are always put under pressure by those more powerful
than ourselves; but he that is stronger still does not allow us to be oppressed,
and shows his strength in our weakness. Let us trust in him. For the rest,
I shall not be absent from the Bern meeting[3] unless the Lord prevents me
from going; for I am not altogether well physically. If my health should deteriorate, I could hardly attend. Yesterday I let blood, and am now somewhat
better. Hence I do not anticipate being hindered at all. I will write earnestly
to the Strasbourg brothers, and I hope this will not be in vain.[4]

Farewell.
Basel, the last day of November.
Your Oecolampadius.
To Huldrych Zwingli, most faithful bishop of the Zürichers, his brother.

Original: Zürich, Staatsarchiv, E II 349, p. 89 (autograph). Copy: Zürich, Zentralbibliothek, Ms S 19, no. 105.

4 *Masses ... missed*] the pun is somewhat more effective in the original, *intermissas missas*

1 This person cannot be reliably identified.
2 The context is not entirely clear, but presumably relates to the Basel Council's decision to require most churches to celebrate Mass again as of 23rd September (see 661, n. 1). A "Lucas" who might well have been affected by this was the Zürich-born Lukas Rollenbutz, who is documented between 1505 and 1530. As Prior of the Austin Canons' monastery in Basel from 1505, he had been responsible for handing its house and possessions over to the City Council in February 1525 (see Wackernagel, *Basel*, III, 364f.), and was now firmly of the evangelical persuasion. On him see *CoE* III, 169.
3 See 668, n. 1.
4 In context this letter, now lost, is likely to have included an exhortation to the somewhat reluctant Strasbourg Council to allow their representatives to attend the forthcoming Disputation of Bern. See also no. 673 below.

673 Oecolampadius to Zwingli—Basel, 19th December (1527)

Greetings in Christ. I hope the brothers from Strasbourg, that is to say *Capito and *Bucer, will go to the disputation that is to take place in Bern.[1] May Christ our Saviour deign to bless them in this, to his glory. But they would like the Berners to send letters to their own Councillors, inviting the two of them to come: the brothers think this would be beneficial in many respects, aware as they are that it will take only a slight pretext for their Council to enter into friendship with the Berners—for they are not boastfully opinionated, but rather full of every good intention. But you, beloved Huldrych, assess the matter more prudently according to your wisdom, and do not neglect what needs to be done. I will also write to *Berchthold today;[2] and you do this too. Many messengers will soon be readily available to you—sooner than they will be to me. You understand the matter, I believe. Do what seems good to you. Or how would it be if your citizens were to invite them as observers, so that they might be better able to bear witness to events before princes or other cities? | For the Berners might perhaps be worried that, if they invite only Strasbourg, they will seem to be holding other cities in contempt; and Strasbourg will feel that it is offensive and rude for them to attend an assembly in another city without having received an invitation. For the rest, some printer or other will go ahead and publish blasphemous Murner's little book.[3] Farewell.

1–12 *Greetings ... to me*] Χαίρειν .... ἐμοί. This is the only substantial passage in Greek in the entire correspondence. From 'You understand' (line 12) the letter is predominantly in Latin   15 *Berners*] Greek Ἀρκτοπολίταις   16f. *other cities (...) and Strasbourg*] Greek ἄλλαι πόλεις, Ἀργεντίνῃ δὲ   19f. *some ... Farewell*] Greek τὸ τοῦ βλασφήμου Τειχαλείπτου βιβλίον ἕτερός τις τυπόγραφος φθάσας δημοσιώσει. Ἔρρωσο.

1 See 668, lines 1–4 and n. 1; 670, n. 4. The contents of this letter, as well as the caution betrayed by its being in Greek, strongly confirms the level of mistrust that still obtained between Strasbourg and Bern, which Zwingli and Oecolampadius—for perhaps slightly differing reasons—were keen to overcome.
2 *Haller.
3 The reference is presumably to the *Appellation vnd beruoff Johannis Ecken, Johannis Fabri vnd Thome Murner für die xij. ort einer loblichen Eydtgnoschaft wider die vermeinte disputation zu Bern gehalten* (Luzern: Murner, 7th December 1527), a polemical work in which the reformers' three main Catholic opponents question the legitimacy of the Bern Council's plan to hold a religious disputation.

LETTER 673

Basel, 13th December.
Oecolampadius.
To Huldrych Zwingli, his dearest brother, at Zürich.

Original: Zürich, Staatsarchiv, E II 349, p. 85 (autograph). Copy: Zürich, Zentralbibliothek, Ms S 19, no. 111.

674 Zwingli to Oecolampadius—Zürich, 15th December 1527

Huldrych Zwingli to Johannes Oecolampadius.

Grace and peace from the Lord. Today I have received a letter from Berchthold,[1] who governs his bears[2] with bridles of the word, expressing his grief about your illness. If he has learnt about it from a source other than our letter,[3] I should be very sorry about it; but I hope he has not come to know of anything worse than what we passed on to him from your recent letter.[4] So tell the messenger how you are.

We are still thinking in the same way as before. Ber[5] and *Vadian[6] have been invited by the Bern Council to preside over the disputation; but the aforementioned beast[7] will not be there. If he should appear, Vadian will tame him with more than human enchantments and enticements; and if he remains defiant, the likes of Kolb[8] will beat him into submission. But no doubt you have already understood all this perfectly well.

2f. *from Berchthold*] *a Berchtholdis*, a plural form: presumably Zwingli is attributing the sentiment expressed jointly to Berchthold *Haller and the other Berners. The conceit is carried through into line 3f., where the verbs are also plural (*reguntur, queruntur, percepissent, intellexisse* (*istos*))   12 *the likes of Kolb*] *Kolbii*: Zwingli again derives a plural form from a proper name (see n. 8 below)

---

1   *Haller. His ten theses, co-written with Franz Kolb (see 636, n. 15), formed the basis for debate at the forthcoming Disputation of Bern.
2   A far from original pun based on the similarity between the city's name (Bern) and the German word for 'bears' (*Bären*).
3   No such letter from Zwingli to Haller and/or the Berners has survived.
4   See 670, lines 8–12.
5   Ludwig Ber (see 396, n. 10). He had served as one of four 'presidents' at the Disputation of Baden in 1526, and was being asked to perform a similar function at Bern. After some hesitation, he declined the offer.
6   Vadian did indeed preside over the Disputation of Bern, along with Nikolaus Briefer (see 676, n. 4), Konrad Schmid (see 271, n. 15) and the Praemonstratensian Abbot of Gottstatt Konrad Schilling (d. 1549).
7   A play on Ber's ursine name, which Zwingli carries into the following sentence.
8   Kolb's surname too is the basis for a play on words: *Kolben* is German for a club or cudgel; and it too is used here in the plural, presumably again to suggest the image of Ber being rushed upon by several Berners.

Johannes Huber of Luzern | and the clerks from Fribourg, Solothurn and Bern will be secretaries to the meeting⁹ (see to it that all this work is remunerated). The thing will take place in the Church of the Franciscans. You should be there, if you are again able to speak. Nothing certain is being reported from Strasbourg. From Chur they will send Comander¹⁰ and the Abbot of St Lucius, a peaceable but wanton woman.¹¹ I foresee that, if God wills, the iron nerves of some people will be softened there.

Farewell.
15th December, at approximately the tenth hour before the moon rises.
1527.

Original lost. Included in 1536 edition, fol. 199ᵛ.

15f. *see ... remunerated*] or, 'see too it that all this work is fairly distributed' (*vide, ut omnia sint compensata*)

---

9   The procedure of several clerks 'taking minutes', and of their efforts then being collated by the Luzern city scribe Johannes Huber (see 495, n. 4), had already been adopted at the Disputation of Baden in 1526. In fact Huber did not attend the Bern Disputation: records of it were made by Peter Cyro and Georg Schöni from Bern, Georg Hertig from Solothurn and Eberhard Rümling from Thun.

10 Johannes Comander (c. 1485–1557), who had attended school with *Vadian and university with Zwingli. He was a highly successful reformer in Chur (and more widely in Graubünden), and had written a set of eighteen theses for the Disputations of Ilanz in 1526 which formed the basis of those prepared by Haller and Kolb for Bern. On him see TRE XIX, 378–384; BBKL I, 1105f.

11 Theodul Schlegel (c. 1485–1529), a close ally of *Faber, was Abbot of the Praemonstratensian house of St Lucius in Chur from 1515 until his death—by beheading—on 23rd January 1529. Chur had gradually espoused reform over the course of the 1520s, but Schlegel had continued stoutly to defend Catholic orthodoxy. In the event he did not attend the Disputation of Bern. The reference to him as a "peaceable but wanton woman" is a pun on his somewhat unusual forename: *tul* or *dul* is a Swiss form of MHG *tole* or NHG *Dohle*, 'jackdaw'; but the term was also used to mean a shy or foolish girl (see SI II, 12, 1697f.). On him see Vasella, *Schlegel;* BBKL IX, 250–253.

676 Oecolampadius to Zwingli—Basel, 18th December (1527)

Grace and peace from the Lord. Those Bears have already reported to us what they are writing to you; for Ber heard on Monday that he had been selected to preside over the show.[1] I do not know whether his rustic modesty has led him to delay his response right up until today. It is not certain how he will reply.[2] A date has been fixed for the papists at last to tell the Council whether they want to stay here or go.[3] They are holding the wolf by his ears.[4] *They are afraid that the Council may order (him) ... who previously was begging.* | For such delicate people should be treated gently, lest they come to harm—especially since they have treated the state and the Christian cause so well. We pray to Christ that they might reflect and come to understand what is intrinsically worthier and more useful to the cause of the gospel.

Moreover the Suffragan,[5] upon learning that his offspring is being printed, is rushing about impatiently: he has complained to the Magistrate and has demanded that the printer be stopped. This has not been finally agreed with him, but, having been summoned to plead his case before the whole Council, *he has obtained ...* We will deal with him adequately when the time comes.

Hear this from the Strasbourg brothers (who greatly desire to see you): we are expecting to see them—because the day before yesterday I received another letter[6] from them saying that they will be here before the day fixed

---

6f. *They are ... begging*] here as elsewhere, the letter is damaged and words are missing, rendering a satisfactory reconstruction impossible. We simply translate what can be read   16 *he has obtained*] again the letter has lost at least one crucial word, the object of *obtinuit*

1 See 674, lines 8–12. The "show" is the forthcoming Disputation of Bern. In the light of Oecolampadius's formulation and the absence of any surviving letter, it seems safe to assume that the Berners conveyed this news to the Basel reformers by word of mouth.
2 See 674, n. 5.
3 To Bern, for the forthcoming disputation.
4 From the ancient Latin proverb *lupum auribus tenere*, found e.g. in Terence, *Phormio*, line 506, and meaning 'to be in a difficult and dangerous situation with no obvious way out'. The Basel Catholics were in the end represented at Bern, not least by the Dean of St Peter's Church Nikolaus Briefer (1484–1548), who was one of the disputation's co-presidents.
5 *Marius. He had been asked by the Basel Council to write a response to the *Widerlegung der falschen grunt* of Oecolampadius and his evangelical colleagues (see 562, n. 5), but objected strongly to Oecolampadius's plan to publish the two pieces alongside each other. Hence Marius's work also appeared separately: *Eyngelegte Schrifft auff Anmutung eynes christenlichen Rats der loblichen Statt Basel, das Opfer der Meß belangent* (Basel: Faber, 1528)—ed. AGBR II, 639–678 (no. 688); see Birkner, *Marius*, 50–52.
6 This has not been preserved.

20 for the disputation, so that we might enjoy a fruitful discussion. There are certain things that it would be profitable to do together with them. I have written back to them[7] saying that they should indeed hasten to come here; but it would not be a sound idea for you or me to go to Bern before the appointed day[8]—partly so as not to give our adversaries fuel for suspicion,
25 and partly *because it is also less safe ... to leave home without an escort*. They have asked me to pass all this on to you. When they have set forth their case to me here, we shall perhaps fly to you together, and be your companions on the journey. Write back to me what you want to be said to them. I will see to it that firmer arrangements are also communicated by the first messenger.
30 There was no need to fear for my health. What I wrote to you about was a chill, rather than a disease. Praise be to God, I am healthier, wealthier, braver and stronger than my enemies would wish me to be. I have not interrupted any of my usual work. If the Lord wishes to use me as his instrument, I am sure that I will have enough strength. Otherwise I would not wish to be
35 granted a greater span of life: there are so many things that make this life | IX, 334
bitter.

I have also invited my friend *Brenz;[9] if I persuaded him to come, I am sure the Lord would change his mind. May the Lord keep us and direct all things to the glory of his name.

40 Do not be alarmed that I am writing with the aid of a scribe. We are used to being somewhat delicate, and now I am starting to have some care for my health.

Farewell.
Basel, 18th December.
45 Johannes Oecolampadius—I added this in my own hand.
To Huldrych Zwingli, his brother. Zürich.

Original: Zürich, Staatsarchiv, E II 349, p. 10 (scribal hand, except for line 45).
Copy: Zürich, Zentralbibliothek, Ms S 19, no. 115.

---

20 *so ... discussion*] Latin *ut ubere colloquio satiemur*, literally 'so that we might be richly satiated by discussion'   25 *because ... escort*] here there is another gap in the letter; on this occasion what remains makes more sense, though we leave the words *m (?) ... conductu* untranslated   45 *I ... hand*] Greek τῇ ἐμοῦ χειρὶ ὑπέγραψα

---

7 Again, no such letter has survived.
8 *Haller had suggested to Zwingli in letter 672 (zw IX, 318–320, here 318, lines 8–13) that he arrive in Bern some six to eight days before the disputation started. He plainly ignored or declined this offer.
9 He did not in fact travel to Bern.

687 Oecolampadius to Zwingli—Basel, 11th February (1528)

May the grace and peace of Christ be with you, my brother. We rejoice that the Lord has brought you back safely to your people.[1] We have returned safely to ours too. And indeed the Strasbourgers have come home also, having confounded the expectations of our adversaries—thanks be to Christ, who does not leave his own without help, wherever they are. But our fellow citizens have not been inspired in the slightest by the example of the Berners,[2] so that it is now clear how little we care about the things of God—to say nothing of other things. Indeed, the public cannot be expected to carry on acting prudently when the sacredness of religion is belittled. But we do not wish to tell the Lord when to bring an end to these evils. There are still some who are urging us to write an apologia to King *Ferdinand, who has cut us to the quick with such a dreadful decree.[3] I do not know if | you have read it. If a copy of it has not yet reached you, let me know, and you shall have one. These people think it will be easy for the Zürichers to find a way to deliver our response safely to the prince, namely by approaching that neighbour of ours Salamanca in his name[4]—though I myself do not know what to expect from this man. I will write a short apologia and give it to you. Once you have considered it, you will be able to produce a better one.[5] We may waste a few hours on this. Truly *Faber[6] has fabricated the edict against us alone: he is far more tolerant of the Lutherans.

---

19 *Faber has fabricated*] Latin *Faber ... fabricatus est*

---

1   From the Disputation of Bern.
2   The context is Bern's implementation of its Reformation Mandate on 7th February. The "fellow citizens" (*nostrates*) with whom Oecolampadius feels frustrated are above all his conservative opponents on the Basel Council.
3   A reference to Archduke Ferdinand's decree promulgated at Buda on 22nd August 1527, condemning evangelical doctrines and attempting to ban the works of Luther, Zwingli and Oecolampadius throughout the Empire. It is printed in *FGR* I, 484–493.
4   For Salamanca see 627, n. 5. In 1524 he had become Count of Ortenbourg (near Sélestat in Upper Alsace), and hence a kind of neighbour to the Baslers.
5   No Swiss evangelical rebuttal of Ferdinand was in fact published.
6   It is hard to see how Oecolampadius could have possessed hard evidence of his *bête noire* Faber's complicity in the composition of Ferdinand's decree, but he was in the latter's service at this point, and Oecolampadius had long feared his political influence—see also 534, lines 2–10 and n. 2.

| I have recently received a letter from the Duke of Württemberg, who greets us both. In it, he pleads with me to go and see the Landgrave,[7] stating that the latter approves of me and wishes to converse with me. But dangers stand in our way, so that I dare not commit myself to such a long journey—even though it might well enhance the reputation of us all if I were to visit so great a defender of the gospel.

The refutation of my Suffragan is in press.[8] Meanwhile they are preparing to print another book against me by the Dominican preacher[9]—as yet they have not made a copy of it for me. How easy it would have been for our magistracy | to remove it from the obstacles that stand in our midst![10] But these things have to happen, so that we might learn from them.

On my return from Bern I found my mother mortally ill. She was indeed somewhat comforted by my arrival; and a few days later she fell asleep in the Lord, leaving behind the troubles and hardships of this world. She has left me to arrange many things, and in consequence I have heavier domestic burdens to bear than hitherto.

Farewell, and greet *Pellikan, Megander[11] and Sebastian.[12]
Basel, 11th February.
Johannes Oecolampadius.
To his dearest brother Huldrych Zwingli, pastor of the Zürich church.

Original: Zürich, Staatsarchiv, E II 349, p. 141 (scribal hand). Copy: Zürich, Zentralbibliothek, Ms S 20, no. 43.

---

[7] The letter is not extant, but its mention here is an early indication of the increasingly important roles to be played by Duke *Ulrich of Württemberg and, particularly, Landgrave *Philipp of Hesse in the run up to the Colloquy of Marburg.

[8] For the context see 562, n. 5 and 676, n. 5.

[9] This was an 'unofficial' statement on the Eucharist made to the Basel Council by Ambrosius Pelargus, the Catholic preacher of the city's Dominican church. It was printed in revised form as the *Apologia Sacrificii Eucharistiae, per Ambrosium Pelargum Franckofordianum: rationem exigente inclyto senatu Basiliensi* (Basel: Faber Emmeus, 1528; Leu/Weidmann A173). A German version, dated 8th August 1527, is in *AGBR* II, 685–701 (no. 705). Pelargus (or 'Storch', 1493–1561) was an active opponent of the evangelicals in Basel between 1525 and January 1529, when he was forced to flee the city. Thereafter he was based in Freiburg and, from 1533, Trier. See *CoE* III, 63 f.; *OER* III, 241; *KTR* IV, 75–96.

[10] Presumably by banning Pelargus's work—which did happen, briefly, later in the year.

[11] See 652, n. 6.

[12] Sebastian Hofmeister: see 376, n. 7.

692   Oecolampadius to Zwingli—Basel, 2nd March 1528

IX, 371

May the grace and peace of Christ be with you! My brother, on the advice of friends I have postponed my journey to the prince of the Hessians, until such time as I am written to about it again.[1] But there are some people who have been secretly induced to press for me to be sent for. *Bucer or *Capito will go with me. I have not yet written down those very few things through which I wanted to demonstrate our innocence to King *Ferdinand;[2] but if they are written in time, I will send them by the next messenger. Not that there is any very urgent necessity, since the Diet of Regensburg will either be cancelled or will accomplish little—given that most princes will not attend.[3]

But here you have the sermon I gave at Bern.[4] *Pellikan prised it out of them by means of two letters. I could not recount all of it from memory. If you are going to oversee its printing, feel free to add to or subtract from it, or to reject it entirely, as you think fit.

About Althamer[5] I have been told nothing, other than what he did.

IX, 372

| We are now strenuously urging from the pulpit that people should be mindful of civil peace, given that a diversity of preachers has been allowed;[6] but their uncircumcised ears have become deaf.[7]

---

1   See 687, lines 21–26 and n. 7.
2   See 687, lines 10–19.
3   An imperial Diet had been scheduled to start in Regensburg on the same day as this letter was written, 2nd March; but Oecolampadius was right in surmising that it would not take place.
4   Oecolampadius's sermon on the love of God (*Von der lieben Gottes zuo siner gemeynd*) was printed as one of a collection of sermons preached at the Disputation of Bern: *Die predigen, so von frömbden predicanten, die allenthalb här zuo Bernn uff dem gespräch oder disputation gewesen, beschehen sind* (Zürich: Froschauer, 1528; Staehelin 154).
5   Andreas Althamer (c. 1500–1539) had aroused the ire of Zwingli and Oecolampadius by stoutly (and characteristically) defending specifically Lutheran positions at the Disputation of Bern. A humanistically inclined Tübingen graduate, his career had taken him from Schwäbisch Gmünd (where he had tried in vain to introduce the Reformation in 1524–1525) to Wittenberg and, by 1528, Nürnberg, where he was Deacon at St Sebald's Church. On him see *OER* I, 21; *BBKL* I, 129 f.; *VL 16* VII, 25–39.
6   Oecolampadius was worried both by the Basel Council's continuing policy of tolerating both Catholic and evangelical preachers, and by the growing antagonism among many guild members towards this policy (cf. 687, line 8 f.; 699, lines 13–15 and n. 5). See also Wackernagel, *Basel*, III, 493–496.
7   A reference to the Council, using rhetoric based on Jeremiah 6:10.

Farewell.
Basel, 2nd March 1528.
20 Your Oecolampadius.
To Huldrych Zwingli, Zürich preacher, his dearest brother.

Original: Zürich, Staatsarchiv, E 11 349, p. 12 (autograph). Copy: Zürich, Zentralbibliothek, Ms S 20, no. 59.

699   Oecolampadius to Zwingli—Basel, 15th March (1528)

Grace and peace from Christ. Most excellent Huldrych! This good man is in a hurry,[1] it seems; but meanwhile I would not wish you to be ignorant that it has fallen to me at last to take a wife,[2] in answer, I believe, to my prayers. | I was required to do this because my mother has died.[3] Our false brothers have been rather offended by it, and are using it to show how sincerely they love the gospel; pray to the Lord that the marriage might be blessed, and that it might redound to his glory.

She is a widow of good reputation, and young; her family contains some of our prominent opponents, and also some friends of the gospel; but she has brought a poor dowry (not, indeed, that I would want a more ample one). Some cartloads of lies will be spread about, I know,[4] but we are not worried about them: these things vanish in and of themselves.

Otherwise nothing has changed. Many guilds are urging the Council to impose concord amongst the preachers; and the latter in turn is going to communicate its mandate to us.[5] But such a peace will not last.

Farewell, and greet our friends.
Basel, 15th March.
Your Oecolampadius.
To Huldrych Zwingli, at Zürich, his dearest brother.

Original: Zürich, Staatsarchiv, E II 349, p. 148 (autograph). Copy: Zürich, Zentralbibliothek, Ms S 20, no. 75.

---

3 *in ... prayers*] or, 'in accordance, I believe, with my wishes' (*pro votis, opinor, meis*)
13 *guilds*] German *Zunffte*

---

1   This letter (like many others) was clearly written in the presence of a waiting messenger.
2   Wibrandis *Rosenblatt.
3   See 687, lines 32–36.
4   *Luther, for example, wrote to Nikolaus von Amsdorf on 18th April that Wibrandis was a rich widow; and *Erasmus waxed waspish in a letter to Adrianus a Rivulo dated 21st March: "Oecolampadius has recently taken a wife, a quite attractive young woman. He wishes to mortify the flesh, I imagine. Some call the Lutheran business a tragedy; to me it seems more of a comedy, because all the commotions end in marriage"—EC, XIV, 135 (no. 1979).
5   The continued pressure being placed on the Council by the guilds to change their policy of tolerating Catholic preaching confirms that guilds were "very much the motor of religious change" in Basel (Gordon, *Swiss*, 110).

704   Oecolampadius to Zwingli—Basel, 25th March (1528)

Grace and peace from Christ. It was very gratifying, dearest brother, that you wished us well on the occasion of our marriage.[1] For our supreme God will grant what people ask piously of him. My soul foresees good things. In this matter we took heed of God's command, rather than the haughty disapproval of men. Few here rejoiced in it, yet it was important to take a wife precisely so as not to give constant offence. What you have stated about the Swabian League,[2] *Capito has also reported; indeed he has written to his Council that the Swabian League have deployed 300 cavalrymen, and that these men have been seizing catabaptists and sacramentarians everywhere,[3] and are now punishing them by putting them to death without regard for justice—because the adherents of these two groups are growing in number.[4] Our Nürnbergers | have issued an extremely harsh edict preventing the records of the Disputation of Bern from being read there—doubtless on account of the Eucharist.[5]

I ask that you commend to the Berners this good man, who is capable of preaching the gospel. For he is not, as far as I can tell, one of the common horde of itinerants.[6] He would prefer to work, but we are advising against it. For that great harvest needs more labourers than the Lord is sending out.[7]

Christoph[8] has not left any copies of the Bern Disputation records here. We would like some, however, especially to send to friends who live far away.

4f. *haughty disapproval*] *supercilia* (literally, 'superciliousnesses' or 'arrogances')

1   See 699, lines 2–12 and n. 2–4.
2   That is, the association of princes, bishops and imperial free cities set up to defend their interests in 1488—but which by 1528 had become increasingly fragmented due to the confessional divide.
3   That is to say, all those who propound adult baptism and/or deny the real presence of Christ in the Eucharist.
4   In a letter to Zwingli written four days later, Capito states that these rumours were in fact untrue—*ZW* IX, 406f. (no. 705), here 407, lines 15–18.
5   The principal architect of this ban seems to have been Althamer (see 692, n. 5).
6   Presumably the (unidentifiable) bearer of this letter is meant. Following the imposition of its Reformation Mandate, Bern was searching widely for pastors and preachers, and no doubt many clerics with no fixed employment were approaching Oecolampadius and Zwingli for references.
7   Cf. Matthew 9:37f.
8   *Froschauer.

My Suffuran has written the most impudent little book against me.[9] My friends count it unworthy of a serious response; rather, they want me to welcome it with joy on account of its poetic talent and wit. But if the little book were by one of you, I would send that person some critical comments on it. What can you say about the body politic, when it lets such things as this go unpunished?

Farewell.
Basel, 25th March.
Your Oecolampadius.
To Huldrych Zwingli, at Zürich, his dearest brother.

Original: Zürich, Staatsarchiv, E II 349, p. 69 (autograph). Copy: Zürich, Zentralbibliothek, Ms S 20, no. 84.

---

22 *Suffuran*] *Suffuraneus*. See 569, line 9 f. and the accompanying note

9 *Wyderauffhebbung der warhafftigenn grunden, so Augustinus Marius Thuompredicant zuo Basel zuo beweisen, das die Meß eyn opfer sey, eynem Ersamen Radt doselbst vberantwort hat. Wider die falsche widerlegung Joannis Oecolampadij* (Basel: Faber Emmeus, March 1528; Leu/Weidmann A147). See Birkhan, *Marius*, 70–73.

707   Oecolampadius to Zwingli—Basel, 1st April (1528)

Grace and peace from Christ. Herewith, dearest brother, I am sending for your consideration some little books which would not have been printed here if God were not angry with us.[1] Up to now, I have been able to console myself to some extent with the knowledge that we have all individually denounced them from our pulpits, partly in the presence of Christ and partly in that of the Antichrist. For I was hoping that darkness was about to yield at last to the light of truth, and that the vanity of our adversaries would be revealed in all its reckless folly. I am not saying this out of arrogance. In this age there is hardly any other city in which the word of God has been proclaimed with greater patience and vigilance, or for a longer time. Once Tyre and Sidon, penitent in sackcloth and ashes, would have felt disgust at their abominations;[2] but not only do we persist in them, we seem even to get worse. So now I am greatly afraid, aware as I am of the great danger lying in wait for cities that love and cherish false prophets but have little care for the truth. They must have been blinded. The blind cannot avoid falling into ditches along with their blind guides,[3] who are unable to lead them out again because God—who alone can set people free—is angry with them. If they wanted an example to follow, only Jerusalem could teach them how to think things through more sensibly for themselves. So I am worried and anxious for the people with whom the Lord has desired me to dwell. Certainly a good part of our citizens, if not the majority of them, lament with all their heart that we have to labour under so many disagreements, and almost to compete for souls who have already been redeemed by the blood of Christ. | For this reason certain guilds also have been petitioning the Council. We ourselves are not leaving anything undone. But God has been slow to look upon us with favour—no doubt because we are praying all too halfheartedly that he might at some point remember us and not abandon us entirely. You can see from these little books what great freedom our adversaries enjoy; and they use it

---

12f. *but ... worse*] *at nos non solum non haeremus, sed et retrocedere videmur.* This could also be translated 'but we are not merely standing still, but rather going backwards'

1 Oecolampadius means *Eck's tripartite volume *Ein Sentbrieue an ein frum Eidgnoszschafft, betreffendt die ketzerische disputation Frantz Kolben des außgeloffen münchs, vnnd B. Hallers des verlognen predicanten zuo Bern. Ein annderer brieue an Ulrich Zwingli. Der drit brieue, an Cunrat Rotenacker zu Ulm* (Basel: s.n., 1528), as well as the recent Catholic apologias by Pelargus (see 687, n. 9) and *Marius (704, n. 9).
2 Cf. Matthew 11:21.
3 Cf. Matthew 15:14.

by sparing no-one. *Eck's letters have been printed here, making Basel into Ingolstadt.⁴ There is speculation as to who persuaded the printer to do this.⁵ The Council could easily have found out. The Suffuran is blaspheming still more, as he defends the trivial trifles (and indeed blasphemies) that we have refuted; he is slandering us so openly and so shamelessly that it is not worth our while opposing him.⁶ The whole city knows this, and those who could have prevented it turned a blind eye to it. Meanwhile the gospel is getting a bad reputation and we, along with Basel itself, are getting an even worse one; and I fear that if one wants always to sit on two chairs, there will be times when one can sit on neither. What must Christians think when they read that such things are taught and published here? How long will our adversaries remain silent when they hear us condemn their works in public? For my part I know nothing of civic affairs, and can glean nothing about them from the prophets; but I predict things that I am terrified to speak of. Alas, a house divided against itself ...⁷

From the same workshop also Pelargus, a truly ignorant monk, is shoving out his nonsense:⁸ he quotes from Greek and Hebrew, though he scarcely knows the rudiments of either | language. Atrocianus, the schoolmaster at St Leonard's, desires to promote our piety through such pretty poems!⁹ Is Basel not a free city, when even impious blasphemies go unpunished here? But you are not unaware of what my little books once suffered.¹⁰ For the present we have done nothing about these matters, other than to plead our

---

31 *Suffuran*] see the note to 569, line 9f.

---

4   See n. 1. Eck was of course based at Ingolstadt.
5   The printer was very likely Johann Faber Emmeus (d. 1542), originally from Jülich, who became a citizen of Basel in 1526 and printed several works there, primarily by Catholic authors such as Marius and Pelargus. He fled the city for Freiburg upon its formal adoption of the Reformation in 1529. On him see *CoE* II, 5.
6   The reference is to Marius's *Wyderauffhebbung der warhafftigenn grunden* (see 704, n. 9), and no doubt also to his violently expressive manner of preaching (see Birkner, *Marius*, 79–82).
7   Matthew 12:25.
8   See 687, n. 9. The "workshop" in question is that of Faber Emmeus (see n. 5).
9   Johannes Atrocianus (c. 1490–1540) was a Catholic humanist who studied in Basel from 1513, and was active there also during the 1520s, from which decade most of his published neo-Latin poems date. These have been edited by Christian Guerra et al., *Johannes Atrocianus: Text, Übersetzung, Kommentar* (Hildesheim: Olms, 2018). Like many of his co-religionists, Atrocianus left Basel for Colmar in 1529. On him see *VL* 16 I, 162–167.
10 The implication is that the Council should ban works like those discussed in this letter, as it once did the writings of Oecolampadius himself.

innocence in public before the people and to tell the Council that we are ready to respond if we think anyone anywhere has taught things contrary to their mandate, and ready also to point out that our adversaries are teaching many things contrary to their mandate. Or do you not think that God
55 is behaving like a wrathful man towards a city that hears such things and does not correct them? I am writing this to you, brother, in all good faith, so that you can ensure prayers are said for us in your city also, prayers that God might give us the grace we need to teach Christ in unity and purity, and might raise up for this city some friends who could warn it of the dangers it
60 faces because it has lent us only deaf ears. Perhaps the Zürichers and Berners could achieve more than others in this regard, given that they are connected to our people by a closer bond, and especially because they understand that the slanders of this faction will belittle them, along with all most excellent and holy men.
65 I hope that my marriage will be a good omen, since it greatly displeases the world,[11] and also the hypocrites here who prattle about the gospel with their mouths, but are themselves very much of the world. | I see how great *IX, 416* and secure a thing it is to live one's life with a good conscience. I have replied to Pelargus in Latin.[12] Wolfgang will translate it at the hospital.[13] I will not
70 reply to the Suffuran unless you tell me to.[14] He does not deserve a response because of his manifest calumnies—even if the popish party is now boasting about them.

51–54 *we are ... mandate*] our translation accurately reflects the repetitious nature of the original at this point

---

11   See 699, lines 2–12 and n. 2–4; 704, lines 1–6.
12   This was published as *Repulsio apologiae sacrificii eucharistiae, quam Pelargus factionis S. Dominici, senatui Basilien obtulit* (Basel: Wolff, 1528; Staehelin 151). See Staehelin, *Lebenswerk*, 374–376.
13   Wolfgang Wissenburg (see 367, n. 4), preacher at the hospital in Basel. His German version appeared as *Ableynung der schützred der opffermesz, die Pelargus Predigersorden eim ersamen radt zuo Basel soll han* (Basel: Bebel, 1528).
14   Cf. 704, lines 22–27.

Farewell, and pray to God for us.
Now Basel is sending you gifts of quality.[15] Please burn them or keep them amongst your treasures.
Basel. 1st April, 1st April.
Heinrich David has ordered his tenant to leave his house before Easter, in favour of Emmeus the printer;[16] but I do not know if he will move out, since I expect nothing of this kind can be arranged within the space of a year.
Your Johannes Oecolampadius.
To Huldrych Zwingli, most faithful teacher of the Zürich church, his brother.

Original: Zürich, Staatsarchiv, E II 349, p. 123 (scribal hand). Copy: Zürich, Zentralbibliothek, Ms S 20, no. 91.

---

76 the date is indeed given twice, as *prima Aprilis, 1. Aprilis*

15 An ironic reference to the "little books which would not have been printed here if God were not angry with us" that accompanied this letter.
16 Heinrich David was a prominent Basel citizen, master of the Bären guild and a heavy investor in various printing firms. On him see *CoE* I, 378. On Faber Emmeus see n. 5 above.

710   Oecolampadius to Zwingli—Basel, 5th April (1528)

May the grace and peace of Christ be with you. We are not sending any delightful news from here, my Huldrych, but rather from more fortunate Strasbourg. Please find herewith what *Capito has given us, but which we were unable to send on before.[1] We have seen a copy of the Bern Disputation records,[2] and we commend their remarkable diligence. I hope that when it becomes known how judiciously all the work has been done, those who forbade people to read such sacred things will be filled with regret. With regard to the sermons preached at Bern, however, nothing has yet appeared. Perhaps they will be presented in a separate little book.[3]

Farewell.
Basel, 5th April.
Greet *Pellikan.
Your Oecolampadius.
To Huldrych Zwingli, most faithful pastor of the Zürichers, his brother.

Original: Zürich, Staatsarchiv, E II 349, p. 108b (autograph). Copy: Zürich, Zentralbibliothek, Ms S 20, no. 94.

---

1 It is not clear what this refers to. Nevertheless Capito's letter to Zwingli of 29th March (zw IX, 406–408; no. 705) mentions the former's intention to send the latter a copy of his recently published commentary on Hosea (p. 406, line 4); so it is possible that this was forwarded via Basel.
2 These records, compiled under the direction of Peter Cyro (see 674, n. 9), had been published on 23rd March: *Handlung oder Acta gehaltner Disputation zuo Bernn in Üchtland* (Zürich: Froschauer). The publication's origins are traced in Hans Rudolf Lavater, "'Veritas evangelica per typographiam': Zur Genese der in Zürich gedruckten Berner Disputationsakten 1528", *Zwingliana* 45 (2018): 233–279.
3 This did in fact happen: see 692, n. 4.

714   Oecolampadius to Zwingli—Basel, 16th April (1528)

May the grace and peace of Christ be with you, dearest brother. The changeable nature of events can disrupt even the best of plans. Indeed, God himself does this: nothing can happen without his agreement. Our city is in a highly turbulent state; would that these things are not harbingers of still greater discord to come! On Good Friday[1] a group of zealots, five of them in all, removed all the images from the altar of St Martin's Church, leaving not a single one in place. They did this without the Council's permission and without my knowledge.[2] Thirty-four people then followed the brave example set by these few: after Vespers on Easter Monday[3] they swept the Augustinian church clean of all its images. On the following day the Council met and threw into prison those who had removed the images from my church. This action struck no terror into the others; on the contrary, it led them to plead with the Council on behalf of those who had been imprisoned. No fewer than 200 people joined them in this, and when the Council ordered them to go home, they would not listen until such time as they had received an answer to their protestations. Eventually they repaired to the house of the Carpenters' Guild; and the Council did indeed decree that the prisoners should be released and that all images should be removed from five churches.[4] But this has not yet appeased the conspirators, since no decision has been made about the uniformity of preaching.[5] Hence they are putting pressure on the Council, which today failed to implement what it had previously agreed. And that remains the state of affairs here up to today, 16th April. So what | do you

---

5 *removed*] *in unum locum semoverunt* (literally, 'removed to one place')   19f. *about ... preaching*] *de concordia concionatorum* (literally, 'about the concord of the preachers')
21 *what ... agreed*] *condictum senatum* (literally, 'the agreement of the Council'—we read *senatum* as the genitive *senatus*)

---

1 9th April 1528.
2 As People's Priest of St Martin's Oecolampadius had a right to be consulted in advance of such a move. An account of the iconoclasts' trial is given in *AGBR* III, 65f. (no. 86).
3 12th April.
4 St Martin's, St Leonard's, the Augustinian church, the Franciscan church and the church at the hospital—all churches whose preachers were prominently committed to the evangelical cause. The Council's mandate to this effect had been issued on the previous day, 15th April—see *AGBR* III, 67–69 (no. 87). In practice this placed the destruction of images under state control.
5 See for example 692, lines 15–17 and n. 6.

think your representatives and those of the Berners should advise our people to do?[6] If only they were here now to make peace in the midst of our discord!

When I reported your plan to our friends,[7] we were not in any way thinking that such things as this were going to happen. But I will not conceal from you what at that point seemed right to them. First, as to the city of Konstanz: it seemed to them wiser for your people | first to visit the people of Solothurn, Schaffhausen and Appenzell, with a view to establishing more clearly whether Konstanz really is under threat of war, and, if so, whether they would wish to support it;[8] then they (your representatives) would be in a position to persuade our people in earnest and with greater authority.

As far as our own affairs are concerned: it was made known to us some time ago that people from your city would be coming here with some Berners in order to persuade the Council to abolish the lack of uniformity in preaching.[9] But very many have interpreted this as meaning that they will be seeking to convert our enemies to our faith by forceful means; and in consequence we are being dragged into suspicion, as if that were what we are actually intending. What indeed would be the harm, if we were in fact the originators of so holy a deed? And so care is to be taken to ensure that the matter is dealt with openly before the Council of the Two Hundred; but one fears it will not be easy to get them to meet unless a reason for doing so is first given to the Small Council[10]—and they, when they know your people are here, will try initially to persuade the Two Hundred to adopt their own way of thinking. This process will not leave us with much hope. Why do we even have to tell those who are generally called the Two Hundred that the legates have been ordered by their home cities not to say anything until they actually appear before the Large Council (that is, the Council, of the Two

IX, 432

23f. *your ... to do*] or, 'we should advise our people to do about your representatives and those of the Berners' (*de legatione vestratium et Bernensium ad nostrates consulendum*). The context makes this latter version seem less likely

---

6   For the context see 707, lines 44–64.
7   The plans currently under negotiation to expand Konstanz's recently signed formal alliances with Zürich and Bern to include other Swiss cities.
8   Having failed in its attempt to join the Helvetic Confederation in 1527, Konstanz remained in need of Swiss help: it was surrounded by hostile territories, and Archduke *Ferdinand was making threats against it.
9   See 707, lines 56–64.
10 For a brief description of the two conciliar bodies and of the relationship between them see Hans R. Guggisberg, *Basel in the Sixteenth Century* (Eugene, OR: Wipf & Stock, 1982), 6f.

Hundred), or until some other event has taken place while they are in the city—such as our people stating that they have joined forces with our enemies? But they are less keen on this second possibility. If the occasion arose, the legates would be able to set the matter before the Large Council with great force and passion, giving an account of the dangers and the great evils to be anticipated from the other party, and stating that, if the papists were to seize power, they would certainly impose a far heavier servitude than there had ever been before.

In reply, the Large Council would begin by thanking the Berners for sending representatives and scholars to visit them | to promote concord in their city; but they would state plainly that, however much good uniformity of preaching might do in Bern, they themselves admire the letters by *Eck that were printed in Basel[11]—even though there are present in their city preachers who most strongly contradict and most impudently reject those letters in print.[12] But, they would say, your people have such piety and zeal for God and his word that if their, the Council's, interlocutors could even today adduce something sound and substantial that might be more pleasing to God, they would cease teaching what has been taught hitherto, and would be only too pleased to do so. For they would not wish to fight against God, which is the breeding-ground of all evil. And hence they would ask that, if their interlocutors can teach them things that are more to be depended upon than their own ideas, they might send such teachers and preachers as could teach these things thoroughly and publicly in Basel, and could explain the reasons behind their teachings.

Certainly, if the Basel Council were to ask such things of your people, then the Zürichers and their teachers and preachers would be compelled (whether they wanted to or not) to express their views, and they would be rejected if they turned out not to be teaching the truth. Our people think this would be useful if our adversaries here summoned leaders from other Cantons who might recommend our expulsion from here. But they will not actually dare to propose any such thing. For all of their teachers fear the light;

---

71 *could teach*] *edoceantur* (literally, 'could be taught')

11   See 707, lines 1–3, 29f., and n. 1, 4.
12   Oecolampadius is of course referring ironically to himself.

and, in defiance of ancient custom, they have not yet sworn their seventh year oath.[13] Our friends did not offer many more reflections on this topic.

For the rest, we have learned from others that a rumour is circulating which will itself offer up opportunities for our work. No doubt you have heard that the Austrians are preparing for war—though against whom it is not clear.[14] Some suspect against the Swiss. If that is true, Basel would be attacked first. But there are suspicions that *Faber has been blurting out secret information to certain noblemen to the effect that they should pay no attention to any of the leaders against whom they are to go into battle,[15] and also that all our neighbours are being advised to arm themselves and to install guns that cannot be transported easily from place to place. The Strasbourgers are asking for 200 hundredweights of gunpowder; they had promised the Austrians 100 hundredweights.[16] It is even said that a large sum of money was sent to Strasbourg for them to recruit soldiers. Likewise a great nobleman is said to be in Ensheim.[17] All these things mean that some people are regarding the Austrians with great mistrust, as though they were about to undertake something against the Swiss. Would that these suspicions might go away; certainly our people are not taking them seriously. Nevertheless, if there is fear of such a thing, a great opportunity will offer itself for your people to come here as soon as possible and calm down our turbulent city. Reflect with friends, therefore, on what might need to be done. Perhaps the Lord will soon look with favour upon us; if not, he will lose all of us in this generation, so that he might show compassion elsewhere.

*Capito and *Bucer have written about *Luther's little book,[18] to the effect that they have never seen anything more deceitful or slanderous. It rages against both of us, but much more so against you; and therefore Capito is

IX, 434

---

13 A reference to the fact that seven years had passed since the significant changes made to Basel's constitution in 1521, according to which the city's Council no longer owed obedience to its bishop. Traditionalists no doubt hankered after the former state of affairs.

14 By "the Austrians" Oecolampadius essentially means the Habsburg Archduke *Ferdinand, who was increasingly worried about the threat of invasion by the Ottoman Turks.

15 On Faber's perceived political influence see 534, lines 2–10 and n. 2; 687, n. 6.

16 On 12th March this amount had been negotiated by Salamanca (see 627, n. 5), for use in the service of Emperor Charles v in Italy.

17 Almost certainly Salamanca. Given the closeness of his links with Alsace (see 687, n. 4), one wonders whether Eguisheim is meant.

18 Both letters have been lost; the 'little book' is *Vom abendmal Christi Bekendnis* (see 644, n. 10).

asking me to remain silent and you to respond, given that you have been attacked more and that you can at the same time demonstrate my innocence.[19] I myself have not yet seen the book; it is said to consist of 30 quires.[20]

Bucer expresses himself in these words: "Luther agrees with us on the matter, as far indeed as it pertains to the presence of the body of Christ. | For he asserts that Christ's body is in the bread in a definitive, rather than circumscriptive sense. Also, the assertion that the bread is the body of Christ does not mean that the two are identical; nor is the union of the bread and the body of Christ the same as that of the humanity and divinity of Christ, or of fire and the nature of an angel—when an angel was said to go before the Hebrew people in a pillar of fire.[21] Nor was the dove an angel, or the Holy Spirit a species of dove—when he was seen above Christ.[22] He calls this a unity of operation. But he says that between the bread and the body of Christ there exists a sacramental union, according to which the one element is made known by the other. Moreover he adds that the body of Christ is present in non-believers when they speak the words of Christ as we have instructed them to speak them, etc.".

Bucer hopes that, in our response, we will vigorously and unequivocally repel the slanders, and also show that Luther agrees with us on the matter, as far as the presence of Christ's body is concerned. He advises us to read the four-leaf quires 't' and 'u' carefully.[23]

I am also sending you another letter from Capito,[24] from which you can learn what little faith Luther has in himself, and how he even alienates many of his closest friends.

112f. *in ... sense*] *definitive, non circumscriptive*

---

19 In fact Zwingli and Oecolampadius issued a joint response: *Uber D. Martin Luters Buch, Bekentnuß genant, zwo antwurten Joannis Ecolampadii und Huldrychen Zwinglis* (Zurich: Froschauer, 1528; Staehelin 155). For Zwingli's contribution see ZW VI/2, 22–248 (no. 125); for Oecolampadius's see *Abendmahlsschriften*, 336–395, also Staehelin, *Lebenswerk*, 319–323; Burnett, *Debating*, 231f.

20 This is accurate: the 1528 edition of Luther's *Bekendnis* is indeed composed of thirty four-leaf quires.

21 Cf. Exodus 13:21.

22 Cf. Matthew 3:16.

23 These sections of Luther's work contain some of the points mentioned in the quotation from Bucer (lines 110–123), but are doubtless singled out above all because they include a systematic rebuttal of the eucharistic views of *Karlstadt, Zwingli and Oecolampadius (lumped together as "cranks", *Schwermer*). They correspond to pp. 433–444 of the WA edition.

24 See n. 18 above.

LETTER 714 283

Farewell.
These things were written on 16th April, and given to a messenger on the 17th.
Your Oecolampadius.

135 You know, my brother, what danger resides in letters: so make sure this is torn up or burnt. For matters are uncertain, and one can have LITTLE HOPE[25] in men. Our opponents are exasperated beyond measure. Moreover today they also pleaded with the Council, I do not know what about. Hence I fear that this discord among our preachers will last a long time, and that unless your
140 people are able to master the situation, it would be better for us to forget the matter completely or to delay it for some time. So weigh up this business rather better than I have written about it, and destroy the letter.

Farewell again.
To Huldrych Zwingli, most faithful pastor of the Zürich church, his brother
145 in Christ.

Original: Zürich, Staatsarchiv, E II 349, p. 150 f. (autograph). Copy: Zürich, Zentralbibliothek, Ms S 21, no. 7.

---

25   The words PARVM SPEI are capitalized also in the manuscript.

715   Oecolampadius to Zwingli—Basel, 20th April 1528

May the grace of Christ be with you, my Huldrych! In my most recent letter I told you about the position in our city and about what you could do.[1] But you can learn that also from the Council's mandate.[2] For me, this does not diminish discord, but seems rather to promote it. Now the house is openly divided against itself. And if such a house were to endure, Christ would be a liar.[3] If only your representatives had been able to prevent it being issued! Impious decrees are harder to rescind than holy ones—such is human nature. But because this is the Lord's work, he will be able to complete it, in order that he might reign the more gloriously[4]—as he is wont to do, especially when he is most fiercely attacked. And so the matter is to be discussed before the Two Hundred, as their dignity requires; meanwhile we also will be mindful of our duty, although I cannot wholly guarantee this in respect of all our people.

Now, it will be essential that you respond to *Luther[5] in a mild and gentle spirit—not that this master of calumnies and prince of sophists deserves it, but because it is necessary if the truth is to be defended. Moreover, since he often admonishes me also, and since you are perhaps less conversant with my affairs (in the same way that I do not have all your writings at my fingertips), I do not think it would be ill-advised for me to clear up those things he taxes me personally with, and for you to repel what he is hurling both at you in particular and at us in general. I shall touch upon general questions in passing, and you will discuss them at greater length, always keeping our audience in mind—so that the world might know that we, as ministers of Christ and of the truth, are not concerned with our own affairs, but rather reflect on those things that spring from love. But if you prefer a different approach, let me know. Indeed I cannot read such calumnies without becoming nauseous; how then will I stitch together even a modest apologia without feeling

---

2 *and ... do*] *et quae facies*: could also mean 'and what its condition is' (depending on whether *facies* is read as a verb or a noun)   20 *and ... general*] *et quae communiter tractat* (literally, 'and is saying about us in general')

---

1   See 714, especially lines 34–73.
2   The mandate of 15th April, according to which images were to be removed from five churches. See 714, n. 4.
3   Cf. Matthew 12:25.
4   Cf. Philippians 1:6.
5   For the context of this paragraph see 714, lines 104–109. Oecolampadius here articulates the reasoning behind his and Zwingli's eventual decision to respond to Luther's *Bekendnis* separately, but in the same volume.

disgust? Nevertheless, if you wish it, and trusting in the mercy of Christ, I will gird up my loins for the task; for there is no need to waste very much paper.

Farewell.
Basel, 20th April 1528.
Your Oecolampadius.
Our catabishop[6] is in town; he is always around at the right time for his flock.
To Huldrych Zwingli, most faithful teacher of the Zürich church, his brother.

Original: Zürich, Staatsarchiv, E II 349, p. 17 (autograph). Copy: Zürich, Zentralbibliothek, Ms S 21, no. 10.

---

6 *Marius. In earlier letters he has been mockingly referred to as *Suffuraneus*, "the Suffuran" (see 569, line 9f. and note); here he is called *catascopus*, an amalgam of Greek κατά ('against') and Latin *episcopus* ('bishop'). It is tempting to translate 'anti-bishop'; but we have gone with 'catabishop' because of its—certainly intended—echoes of 'catabaptists', our correspondents' preferred term for another set of enemies, the anabaptists.

611   Oecolampadius to Zwingli—Basel, 28th April (1528)[1]

Grace and peace be with you, my Huldrych! The brothers are urging you to respond to *Luther—not only our own and the Strasbourgers, but others too.[2] But may the glory of Christ and of the truth be your chief motivation. For I regard it as one of the lowest things that he is once again raging against you—something you should disregard entirely. Let him prevail by using insults and sneers, but you will prevail by using the scriptures, and with dignity and gentleness—so that the spirit of both these qualities might be made known to all who have been taught by the Lord.[3] I cannot yet see the end of the tragedy—whether we shall fall in any way. Hence there is need of great caution. I myself have decided not to respond at all as yet. But if I am urged by others to do so, I shall do nothing to mollify this loathing if I preach a long sermon. Yours will be the prize, and yours also the victory that Christ is winning. Meanwhile we shall pray that the Lord might help his own cause.

It is reported that *Melanchthon has replied to the Landgrave on the subject of the Eucharist; and what he says is recorded on a single sheet of paper enclosed in this letter.[4] From this you also can judge how trustworthy he is. *Capito has recently sent me a letter, which is to be forwarded to you.[5] I was also going to write about some other things, but my somewhat confused state of mind has not allowed this. For our Council has not responded to yours with any great civility: it has declared how wise it is.[6] | So the legates will report on this more fully than it is proper for me to do in a letter. As I see

---

1   We here follow Staehelin's suggestion (*OeBA* II, 176; cf. *ZW* IX, 116f.) that this letter can be more plausibly dated to 1528 than to 1527, not least because of the references to Melanchthon's correspondence with "the Landgrave" (line 15f.) and to the Basel Council's response to Zürich's legates (lines 20–22). See below, n. 2, 4, 6.
2   Specifically, to Luther's *Bekendnis* (see 644, n. 10). The need for Zwingli—and indeed Oecolampadius—to refute this work. but to do so with moderation, is for example a theme of *Capito's letters from around this time: to Oecolampadius on 9th April (*OeBA* II, 171f. (no. 566); *CC* II, no. 353); to Zwingli on 15th April (*ZW* IX, 424f. (no. 712); *CC* II, 355); and to Zwingli again on 22nd April (*ZW* IX, 442f. (no. 717); *CC* II, no. 356).
3   Cf. John 6:45.
4   Likely to be a somewhat garbled reference to Melanchthon's letter to Elector Johann of Saxony particularly about the eucharistic doctrines of *Karlstadt—see *MBW* T3, 255–257 (no. 645, January 1528).
5   *CC* II, no. 353 (see n. 2 above).
6   A reference to the—initially unsuccessful—attempts by representatives from Zürich and other evangelical cities to assist the progress of the Reformation in Basel—see 714, lines 34–73; 715, lines 1–6; Wackernagel, *Basel*, III, 498f.

it, Christ alone will rule his people here through his Spirit; he will deem certain people to be unworthy to exercise their ministry. Hence we shall teach with sincerity, and shall solicit the prayers of Christians that we might be delivered from the mouths of our adversaries. Later perhaps—when we have been sufficiently tested—more favourable things will follow. You should not doubt our steadfastness, unless we are abandoned by the Lord. But pray to the Lord, and farewell.

Basel, 28th April.
Your Oecolampadius.
To Huldrych Zwingli, teacher of the Zürichers, his brother.

Original: Zürich, Staatsarchiv, E II 349, p. 68 (scribal hand). Copy: Zürich, Zentralbibliothek, Ms S 18, no. 95.

---

24 *to exercise their ministry*] *ut illorum ministerio fungatur* (literally, 'that he might exercise their ministry' (*sic*); we read *fungatur* as the third person plural form *fungantur*)
32 *teacher*] Greek μυσταγωγῷ ('teacher, priest'). This is a dative; hence we have added an iota subscript which is omitted in the zw edition

726   Oecolampadius to Zwingli—Basel, 20th May 1528

The grace of Christ, my brother. If there is anything pleasant here (which I do not know about), anything different (as is often the case), or indeed anything bitter (as we not infrequently suspect), *Cratander, who is delivering this letter, will be able to tell you much better than it can: the letter is not so much bashful as mistrustful. Not to put too fine a point on it, we are still in the same mire. In addition, I would like to know from you whether you are going to reply to *Luther.[1] I have in fact promised the brothers on your behalf that you will. Since for the time being, if I may be permitted a joke, I will neither have much leisure nor will sleep much (such, as a rule, is the privilege of the first year of marriage),[2] I will be absent from the fray; but you must join battle, in the knowledge of Christ's grace towards you. Just now a certain exile showed me this decree—on the basis of which he himself was exiled, because he was unwilling to comply with it.[3] He is, however, now about to return to the lands adjoining Wittenberg. I shall write a few verses or lines to both *Melanchthon and Martin, for him to deliver:[4] from these they will be able to see whether we are fanatics and possessed by demons. It is still unclear what *Philipp of Hesse and the Saxons | are trying to achieve;[5] so various things are being reported. My mind is not foreseeing anything auspicious. Yet Christ is the King of the world and the Lord of all flesh. I rejoice that the Berners have become rather more peaceable.[6]

---

16 *and ... demons*] Greek καί δαιμονόληπτοι

---

1   See 715, lines 13–28 and n. 5.
2   See 699, line 2 f.
3   Neither the exile nor the edict can be identified.
4   A letter from Oecolampadius to Melanchthon dated 21st May 1528 is printed in *OeBA* II, 189 f. (as no. 579); but no letter to Luther from around this time has survived.
5   A reference to the leading Protestant princes *Philipp of Hesse and Elector Johann of Saxony.
6   Around 14th May there had been violence in the Bernese Oberland following attempts to celebrate Mass at Interlaken. Oecolampadius's optimism is somewhat premature: unrest continued over a period of several months, due not least to the provision of Catholic troops by the Canton of Unterwalden. See Feller, *Bern*, II, 177–182.

Farewell in Christ.
Basel, in the year 1528, 20th May.
Your Oecolampadius.
To Huldrych Zwingli, his dearest brother.

Original: Zürich, Staatsarchiv, E II 349, p. 16 (autograph). Copy: Zürich, Zentralbibliothek, Ms S 21, no. 37.

728 Oecolampadius to Zwingli—Basel, June (1528)

May the grace and peace of Christ be with you, my brother! I had put to one side the barks of that furious man *Luther without reading them properly; but now I am taking them up again, because I see this is an approach you favour,[1] and one which shows that I myself do not lack commitment to our cause—even though Cyril and Ezekiel, to say nothing of others, are almost overwhelming me.[2] But it will be good to be busy, and to remember that the enemy does not need to be pursued any harder if he is anyway hastening to his ruin: economy of words is welcome at other times, but particularly so now. I will leave it to you to refute the arguments directed at both of us and specifically directed at you; I myself, so that I might free myself as soon as I can from this work, will repel the darts that he has hurled at me—with God's help.

Now, I am very happy with your advice that we should address the princes.[3] But it would be more effective for you to do this rather than me, since you will write with your habitual brevity and avoid even the smallest digression. Perhaps when I take my pen in hand with the aim of adjusting my words to fit your style, it will be | persuaded to write in that way. Princes are sensitive and used to adulation; they will not find us very agreeable. We do not know how to flatter them, and nor should we. But if we do not flatter and worship them like gods, then (following the reasoning of evil counsellors) they will think that we despise them, and will probably be all the more irritated. They will want their apostle to emerge unscathed;[4] but we shall not be able to spare him entirely. So we need to proceed very cautiously. Above all else it will be useful if your Council and Bern's deign to commend us, and indeed our views on the Eucharist, to them in a friendly letter. Get to work on this: I will leave these things to your wisdom. In any event I will soon be able to undertake the work myself, and, in the hours that remain, will steal

---

11f. *with God's help*] τοῦ θεοῦ ῥοπῇ. We take the last word as a dative with a missing iota subscript   21 *probably*] ὡς κινδυνεύει (literally, 'as is likely')   24f. *and ... Eucharist*] Latin *imo rem ipsam* (literally 'indeed the matter itself')

---

1 If Zwingli communicated this view in a letter, it has been lost. The Luther text in question is his *Bekendnis* (see 644, n. 10).
2 For Oecolampadius's translation of works by Cyril of Alexandria see 661, n. 7. For the problematic textual history of his Ezekiel commentary see 642, n. 1.
3 Zwingli's part of his and Oecolampadius's joint refutation of Luther's *Bekendnis* (see 714, n. 19) contains a dedicatory preface to Elector Johann of Saxony and Landgrave *Philipp of Hesse.
4 Both the Elector and the Landgrave were committed Lutherans.

LETTER 728 291

what little time I can to devote to this business. See to it that you too start on the work straightaway: for you are not giving yourself much time to do it.

30 The day before yesterday I entrusted some letters from our Silesian friends to a certain exile who was intending to see you, for him to pass on to you;[5] I do not know if he has done this.

Petrus Gynoraeus, a man most ill-deserving of the gospel,[6] has been publicly flogged and driven out of here in great ignominy—it is astonishing how
35 great is the jubilation and triumph of our adversaries. He was always asking for our commendation—a man with such a guilty conscience, who threw in his lot with adulterers and was twice an adulterer himself. That is the way men beguile us every day and see to it that, in the end, we will not dare to commend anyone.

40 Farewell.
Basel, a day in June.[7]
Your Oecolampadius.
To Huldrych Zwingli, his dearest brother.

Original: Zürich, Staatsarchiv, E II 349, p. 138 (scribal hand). Copy: Zürich, Zentralbibliothek, Ms S 21, no. 45.

---

30 *some letters*] or 'a letter' (*literas*)

---

5 The "certain exile" cannot be identified, but the letters entrusted to him can: they are those sent to Oecolampadius by Valentin Krautwald on 28th April and by Caspar Schwenckfeld on 3rd May, both from Liegnitz (Legnica)—see *OeBA* II, 177–181 (no. 573 f.). On these Silesian reformers' vain attempts to forge a close alliance with their Swiss counterparts see Weigelt, *Tradition*, 77–85.

6 Or 'Peter Frauenberger', previously a close collaborator of Oecolampadius in Basel. On him and his recent sexual misdemeanour see 367, n. 2.

7 The date is incomplete: *Basileae Iunii die*. We are assuming the letter predates no. 730 (21st June) because the expulsion of Frauenberger took place on 9th or 10th June, and is spoken of in a way that implies it was a recent event (lines 34–36).

730   Oecolampadius to Zwingli—Basel, 21st June (1528)

May the grace and peace of Christ be with you, my Huldrych. The Strasbourg brothers are again warning us that we should not delay in responding to *Luther:[1] the members of his faction, as well as the Swiss, are giving us a great deal of trouble, and are boldly following the example of the papists. I have already told them that you are about to give your response; but maybe they are fearful that we are being held back by other business and are neglecting more urgent things. From what you write, *Bucer should be urged to publish the dialogue he says he has written about this matter alongside our works.[2] Tonight I have taken up my pen to address you on the subject of Luther's tyranny,[3] and I seem able to complain about things more directly than when I am addressing princes.[4] But please continue to speak to the princes using vigorous speech and moderate force—as you would resolve to do if you were addressing unbiased judges.[5]

For the rest, you will learn from those closest to you how things are here. My wife greets you and your wife.[6]

Basel, 21st June.
Oecolampadius.
To Huldrych Zwingli, his dearest brother.

Original: Zürich, Staatsarchiv, E II 349, p. 44 (autograph). Copy: Zürich, Zentralbibliothek, Ms S 21, no. 50.

---

1 For the context, see most recently 728, n. 1 and 3.
2 Bucer's work was in fact published separately from those of Zwingli and Oecolampadius (see 714, n. 19) as the *Vergleichung D. Luthers, vnd seins gegentheyls, vom Abentmal Christi: Dialogus, das ist, eyn freundtlich gespräch* (Strasbourg: Köpfel, 1528; Leu/Weidmann A25)—ed. Bucer, *Schriften*, 11, 305–383. See Burnett, *Debating*, 237–240.
3 Oecolampadius's contribution to *Uber D. Martin Luters Buch* begins with a prologue addressed to Zwingli. See 714, n. 19; 115^r–117^v.
4 One assumes that Oecolampadius has in mind here his experience of writing a dedicatory preface for his Cyril translation (see 661, n. 7) to Margrave Philipp of Baden-Sponheim.
5 Cf. 728, lines 13–23.
6 Respectively Wibrandis *Rosenblatt and Anna *Reinhart.

733   Oecolampadius to Zwingli—Basel, 3rd July (1528)

The grace and peace of Christ, my Huldrych! Please do not be concerned that you have not received my apologia[1] via this messenger. For many things have hindered it, and the matter itself is more complex than I thought. Moreover it worries me that, the more that man[2] rages, the more I pretend not to mind, and keep quiet. Konrad, my assistant,[3] has begun to transcribe it; it will be finished within four days, I think. I will make sure that this same assistant brings it to you soon. I believe *Bucer's dialogue will precede our work.[4] For I have urged him not to keep it secret. There is something I find wanting in our *Capito. The catabaptists here are boasting a great deal that he favours them, since he treats them with a certain kindness; although | I do not think that he agrees with them as yet, all the same I would also like you to warn him.[5] But I do not want you to mention me, since I have warned him already, and the rumour still persists. Perhaps we have Cellarius to thank for this.[6] Recently more than 100 catabaptists were assembled in a nearby field: some of these were taken away by force to a prison here, like captives who in former times were driven away with sticks from one place or another. They know what malady we are suffering from here, and no doubt are plotting something—but perhaps they do not yet know what. For they say that even the pestilential Kautz[7] was present there. We will keep as close a watch as the Lord enables us to. But what if such prophets are no more than hypocrites deserve?

---

1   See 728, n. 1 and 3 (etc.).
2   Luther, to whose *Bekendnis* on the Lord's Supper Oecolampadius is responding (see 714, n. 18 f.).
3   Konrad Hubert (1507–1577), who had come to study theology at Basel in 1526 and before long had begun assisting Oecolampadius in numerous, mainly clerical functions. He moved to Strasbourg in 1531 as an assistant to Bucer, and devoted much of the second half of his life to editing the works of Bucer and Capito. On him see BBKL II, 1106–1108.
4   See 730, n. 2.
5   Bucer in particular had been worried about Capito's position on baptism for some time: he had indeed written to Zwingli on the subject on 15th April and again on 24th June—respectively ZW IX, 426–429 (no. 713) and BC III, 122–125 (no. 186); and ZW IX, 492 f. (no. 732) and BC III, 167 f. (no. 198). On this controversy between Bucer and Capito see Kittelson, *Capito*, 177–181.
6   See 644, n. 1; 652, lines 12–15 and n. 2.
7   Jakob Kautz (c. 1500–1532), an anabaptist initially active in Worms, and now an itinerant preacher. His radical seven theses, published on the door of the Dominican church at Worms on 7th June 1527, had proved influential in a number of cities, including Strasbourg and Basel. On him see BBKL III, 1264 f.

Farewell.
3rd July. Basel.
Your Oecolampadius.
To Huldrych Zwingli, his beloved brother.

Original: Zürich, Staatsarchiv, E II 349, p. 76 (autograph). Copy: Zürich, Zentralbibliothek, Ms S 21, no. 55.

734 Oecolampadius to Zwingli—Basel, 9th July (1528)

May the grace of Christ be with you. Dearest Zwingli, my friend Konrad[1] is bringing you my response to *Luther,[2] which is shorter than the matter requires, but longer than I had intended. How I wish that you could steal enough time to read it! If there is anything in it that differs significantly from your interpretation, feel free to correct, shorten or embellish it, and to do this as if it were your own work. And indeed it is yours too, not only because it is Christ's work, but also because we are being tested by it equally and are making one and the same case. For when I make a statement as to our unanimity, our adversaries will think Babylon has been captured[3] if they see that we disagree in the very least. I do not think that the passage on Corinthians 10 (about communion and fellowship of the body) is inconsistent with your opinion.[4] It will be for you to ensure that it is printed faithfully by the press. If you do not have time for this, ask *Pellikan or *Leo to take up the burden. That assistant of mine[5] was very eager to see you: please encourage him to continue in my employment. For he is very useful to me, biddable and of such intelligence and gentleness that we shall one day be able to place him in a position of honour—although I do not doubt that his feelings towards me would make him reluctant to be torn away from my company. He will be able to give you a full account of my affairs, and of the City and University of Basel's disinclination to receive Christ. | Tyranny has spread deep roots. Those who perform even the smallest office on our behalf are hated—as indeed are all those people who listen to us. Those who habitually speak ill of us are admired, and advance to greater prosperity—even if they do not merit this by dint of their piety or learning. But the Lord is for us, and has preserved us thus far in the face of such things. The new Council[6] will not hold us in any greater favour than the old one, other than that our Jakob Meyer zum Hirzen[7] is now serving again as Chief Guild Master.

---

1 Konrad Hubert (see 733, n. 3).
2 His contribution to *Uber D. Martin Luters Buch* (see 714, n. 19).
3 An allusion, no doubt, to Luther's seminal 1520 treatise on the sacraments, *Concerning the Babylonian Captivity of the Church—De captivitate Bablylonica ecclesiae* (Wittenberg: Lotter)—ed. WA VII, 497–573; trans. AE XXXVI, 3–126.
4 Oecolampadius must be referring to fols 175ʳ–178ʳ of the 1528 edition (see n. 2), where he takes Luther to task in some detail for his perceived misunderstanding of the terms εὐχαριστία ('thanksgiving') and κοινωνία ('communion, participation') in 1 Corinthians 10:16.
5 Hubert.
6 A new Council was sworn in on 24th June each year.
7 See p. XVIII, n. 3. Oecolampadius here calls him *Iacobus a Stella Nigra* ('of the Black Star'),

What I am about to ask of you is no small thing: the chancellor of the younger Margrave of Baden[8] once commended to me his son, Joachim by name, and he has now been living with me for a year. He is a young man of excellent character, and biddable in every way. Having seen that humanist (especially Greek) studies are at a standstill here, and that the gospel is in a parlous state, he sought permission from his father to betake himself to a place where both letters and piety are faring better. The fond father did not deny him this, and wrote to me asking me to secure accommodation and companionship for his son, either with you or with some other pious and learned man—so that he might both have someone to watch over him and want for nothing materially. There will be no delay in paying. | My assistant will talk to you about this. If, therefore, you are able to look after him in your house, you will do something that is most pleasing to me, but also to his father, a distinguished man who serves the gospel excellently in the Margrave's household. Indeed, he alone opposed the Margrave in defending the gospel. No-one has greater integrity than he has. But if it is not convenient for you, I ask you to persuade Collin[9] to take him in. He is not in any way extravagant. You will be able to inquire of my assistant as to his character. I know that, if it is possible for him to live with you, it will be a great joy for you, and moreover will not be a cause of regret to your wife.[10] No doubt you will see to it that he can live either with you, or with Collin or *Leo. I would prefer to keep him here with me, but I would be sinning against so excellent a nature. He seems to be rather artless; but even such a defect would be remedied in your company.

31f. *humanist ... studies*] *bona studia* (literally, 'good studies')   37f. *so that ... materially*] *quo pariter et inspectorem vitae habeat et non egeat* (literally, 'by which he simultaneously has an inspector of (his) life and does not lack')

---

after an inn he owned. Meyer generally used the more familiar *zum Hirzen* ('at the Stag') after inheriting an establishment of that name by marriage in 1521.

8   Jakob Kirser, Chancellor of the Margravate of Baden and Bailiff of Pforzheim. He was a committed proponent of evangelical views in sometimes unfavourable circumstances (see for example line 41f.). The "younger Margrave" is Margrave Philipp (1478–1533), who had succeeded his less evangelically inclined father Christoph (1453–1527) in April 1527. Christoph had appointed Kirser Chancellor as early as 1513.

9   Rudolf Collin (1499–1578), a soldier, ropemaker, classicist and autobiographer, who had taken up citizenship in Zürich in 1526. He served as Professor of Greek at the *Grossmünster* school and became a trusted ally of Zwingli, particularly in political matters. He later acted as guardian to the reformer's children after the latter's death.

10 Anna *Reinhart.

The Strasbourgers have not yet been able to abolish the Mass completely. You recently heard the warning I would like to give *Capito,[11] but I would not wish to be revealed as the instigator of this. The catabaptists are certainly taking advantage of his favour and goodwill, and are boasting of it.

Greet your wife and the brothers.
Farewell.
Basel, 9th July.
Your Oecolampadius.
To Huldrych Zwingli, most faithful teacher of the Zürichers, his brother.

Original: Zürich, Staatsarchiv, E II 349, p. 84 (autograph). Copy: Zürich, Zentralbibliothek, Ms S 21, no. 62.

---

11   See 733, lines 8–14 and n. 5 f.

737 Oecolampadius to Zwingli—Basel, 22nd July (1528)

Grace and peace from Christ. My brother, I am praying to the Lord that our work against *Luther is prospering in your hands.[1] I sent the Silesians' little book[2] via *Pellikan. I wonder why it has not been delivered. I have kept another copy of it, which I am sending now. You will see from it that he has not even quoted their words accurately.[3] I have not wanted to mention these words, since I have undertaken to respond only to the parts aimed at me.[4] Besides, if there is anything you want to change in my words, you can add to or subtract from them as you think fit.[5] I would like you to consider what I wrote about the argument that there is a difference between the substantial body and the true body,[6] so that you can attack the passage in question. Indeed, it seems to me that just as there is no man who is not rational, there is no body that has no substance.

I think you have already received the work that *Bucer wrote.[7] Nevertheless I am also sending you my copy, in case it may not have reached you yet. He has acted faithfully in every way.

I commend this young man to you,[8] in case at any time you need him for your work. For at some point he will be of benefit to many—if he imbibes that Christian fervour of yours.

---

9 *argument*] Greek περιγραφῆς (literally, 'outline') 12 *that ... substance*] *nisi quantum* (literally, 'unless of a certain size')

---

1 Zwingli and Oecolampadius's joint response to Luther (see 714, n. 19).
2 Caspar Schwenckfeld, *Ein anwysunge das die opinion der leyplichen gegenwertigheyt vnsers Herrens Jesu Christi im Brote oder vnder der gestalt deß Brot gericht ist Widder den ynhalt der gantzen schrifft* (Zürich: Froschauer, 1528, with a prologue by Zwingli; Leu/Weidmann A196). Zwingli's prologue, dated 28th April 1528, is in zw VI/2, 258 f. (no. 126). On the Swiss reformers' Silesian connection see 466, n. 4; 607, lines 1–16 and n. 1–5.
3 The "he" is Luther, who had already replied to the Silesians in his *Bekendnis* (see 644, n. 10).
4 See 728, lines 9–12.
5 See Oecolampadius's invitation in 734, lines 3–8.
6 The issue of the nature of Christ's body pervades and underlies much of Oecolampadius's contribution to *Uber D. Martin Luters Buch* (see 714, n. 19) rather than being limited to one section; the most sophisticated discussion of it comes, however, at the beginning of the piece's second part, from 131ᵛ to 136ʳ.
7 See 730, n. 2.
8 A reference to an unknown messenger.

Farewell.
20 Basel, 22nd July.
Oecolampadius.
To Huldrych Zwingli, his dearest brother.

Original: Zürich, Staatsarchiv, E II 349, p. 46 (autograph). Copy: Zürich, Zentralbibliothek, Ms S 21, no. 68.

747   Oecolampadius to Zwingli—Basel, 6th August (1528)

May the grace of Christ be with you. Although, dearest brother, we in no way doubt your vigilance and speed in publishing our apologias,[1] there are some people here who are rather impatient about the delay. To comply with their wishes, please see to it that Christoph[2] sends some copies here as soon as possible. Matthias Limperger is here, the nephew of our Suffragan Bishop[3] and an upright man. He tells us how badly we are received in Hesse and Saxony. I am not surprised. Such prophets lend a willing ear to foolish rumours of this nature! According to some people we deny the Holy Trinity, and according to others we teach that Christ was simply a man; this, no doubt, is their utterly unjust interpretation of "alteration". There are high hopes that, if our little books are openly sold, our adversaries will soon wax quieter than fish. And so you acted wisely in dedicating the little books to the princes.[4] | There is also the matter of how to deliver them reliably. I hear in a letter from *Bucer that *Capito is finally becoming aware of the deceptive spirit of the catabaptists, with the result that he is trusting them less every day;[5] but in any event he does not set as much store by Cellarius[6] as he once did. He has no disagreement with Bucer, and we need fear no disorder on his account—even though he would like to see infant baptism abolished, and has crammed some other ideas from Cellarius into his Hosea.[7] Nevertheless he is defending the purity of the faith properly against them: he thinks that the leaders and heads of their faction should be expelled, and he strongly asserts that, with regard to external signs, there should be sufficient freedom for infant baptism to be permitted. We demand nothing more from him. But perhaps he himself will write to you more fully on the matter.[8]

---

8 *Trinity*] Greek Τριάδα   9 *simply*] Greek ψιλόν   10 *alteration*] Greek Ἀλλοίωσιν   23 *infant baptism*] Greek παιδοβάπτισμα

---

1   See 714, n. 19; 730, lines 1–7; 737, line 1f.
2   *Froschauer.
3   Tillman Limperger: see 319, n. 5. Nothing is known with any certainty about his nephew Matthias.
4   See 728, n. 3.
5   The letter by Bucer is no longer extant; on the context see 733, lines 8–14.
6   See also 644, n. 1; 652, lines 12–15 and n. 2.
7   *In Hoseam Prophetam v.f. Capitonis Commentarius* (Strasbourg: Herwagen, 1528; Leu/Weidmann 46).
8   Capito had in fact clarified his position to some extent in a letter to Zwingli dated 31st July—*zw* IX, 516–518 (no. 743); *cc* II, 348 (no. 366).

25   Some catabaptists, men and women, are being held in prison here. It may be that some of them are in danger of losing their lives.[9] I have here some personal effects and some money belonging to Paul Rasdorfer;[10] I will send them on via the next carrier.

I bid you and the brothers farewell.
30   My wife and assistant wish me to send a greeting.[11] Greet your wife[12] also.
Basel, 6th August.
Johannes Oecolampadius.
To Huldrych Zwingli, his dearest brother.

Original: Zürich, Staatsarchiv, E II 349, p. 30 (autograph). Copy: Zürich, Zentralbibliothek, Ms S 21, no. 97.

---

9   In fact, some at least were released in short order: Hans Zanger, Hans Walch, Claus Schwitzer and Jacob Müller on 6th August, and Konrad Winkler, Veit Öttli and Nysius Schmidt on 8th August—see *AGBR* III, 142–147 (nos 183–187).
10 According to 743 (see n. 8; p. 518, line 7 f.), Rasdorfer's effects had been forwarded from Strasbourg on or before 31st July. Originally from Kempten im Allgäu, Rasdorfer was to serve as parish priest at Betschwanden near Glarus until 1531, and thereafter both in Kempten and in other Swiss parishes.
11 Wibrandis *Rosenblatt and Konrad Hubert (733, n. 3) respectively.
12 Anna *Reinhart.

750   Oecolampadius to Zwingli—Basel, 16th August (1528)

IX, 530 Grace and peace from Christ. We found a letter for Paul[1] amongst his effects, which a young man is bringing together with the money—around eight florins in batzen.[2] You should keep these with you to pay the carrier from them, and then give the rest to Paul.

Otherwise we have no news here. Our adversaries are abusing their power a good deal, but they cannot triumph over the word of God; so their power is now diminishing. Nevertheless we always need your prayers and those of others.

It is good that *Pellikan is looking after our apologia.[3] Send it here when this can conveniently be arranged.

Greet Pellikan, your wife[4] and the other members of your inner circle.
Farewell.
Basel, 16th August.
Your Oecolampadius.
To Huldrych Zwingli, his dearest brother.

Original: Zürich, Staatsarchiv, E II 349, p. 45 (autograph). Copy: Zürich, Zentralbibliothek, Ms S 21, no. 103.

We date letter 751 to 1531. See below, p. 422

---

7 *your*] *vestris* (a plural form)

1 Paul Rasdorfer: see 747, line 26f. and n. 10.
2 A *Batz* was a small-denomination coin, roughly equivalent to the German *Groschen* or penny (see *SI* II, 4, 1464–1468).
3 Zwingli and Oecolampadius's joint response to Luther: see 714, n. 19. On the involvement of Pellikan in its production process see 734, lines 12f.
4 Anna *Reinhart.

757 Oecolampadius to Zwingli—Basel, 5th September (1528)

May the grace and peace of Christ be with you. This brother, my Huldrych, seems to me to be a man of faith;[1] he prefers to work with his hands, rather than follow the popish abomination any more. He was exiled by the princes. He asks for nothing more than to learn a particular skill. He could not find a position here. I would not wish to impose any kind of burden on you, since I know you are encumbered with more important business. But perhaps you have made the acquaintance of some pious citizen who might be able to help him; please commend the man to him. Perhaps the Lord will soon call him back to his ministry.

We are keeping going the whole time here, clashing with our adversaries and provoking them—but in vain. The truth has few patrons; hence I fear that our Day of Judgement may be drawing near. The man who struck our brother Thomas[2] only paid a single fine, for failing to keep the peace—even though he could have been convicted of many offences, which it would be embarrassing to relate. Afterwards he was punished on the authority of the magistrates. His other insults—though they were more serious—have so far gone unpunished. Thomas, who was entirely innocent, was also found to be so.

Let me know if you have not yet received *Bugenhagen's work:[3] I will send it by the next messenger. For our printers and booksellers are solicitous about acquiring such little books. Which of course shows remarkable loyalty towards us!

Farewell.
Basel, 5th September.
Oecolampadius.
To Huldrych Zwingli, his beloved brother, who teaches the gospel of Christ fruitfully in Zürich.

Original: Zürich, Staatsarchiv, E II 349, p. 122 (scribal hand).

---

1 This messenger cannot be identified, though in the context (see line 3) it is likely that he was one of the priests recently expelled from Baden—see 763, lines 45–54 and n. 13.
2 Thomas Gyrfalk (see 367, n. 5) had recently been assaulted by a Catholic priest outside a church in Basel. We learn more about this incident in 763, lines 20–39.
3 *Publica de Sacramento corporis et sanguinis Christi, ex Christi institutione confessio* (Wittenberg: Luft, 1528; Leu/Weidmann A31). See Burnett, *Debating*, 240–242.

763   Oecolampadius to Zwingli—Basel, 28th September (1528)

May the grace and peace of Christ be with you. For a long time now I have not seen any messenger heading for Zürich, and so I was forced to wait for our Christoph,[1] so as to write to you through him. In the first place I thank Christ Jesus, who assisted you in writing the defence against *Luther[2] to such an effect that—whether because he despises us or because he has little faith in himself—he has freely chosen to be silent; and now he will have to remain so, unless he wishes to spread the greatest possible confusion, even amongst his own supporters. But now his monkey, *Bugenhagen, is putting in an appearance: he too is bringing his latest confession with him,[3] and is making more of an effort to take his revenge on *Bucer and you (if he can) than he is to assail the two of you with powerful arguments. As for me, he seems somehow to be avoiding and shunning me. Bucer, in writing his preface to Zephaniah,[4] has almost exhausted his strength; but he is asking either you or me to answer the man in full. And indeed he would prefer me to reply to him, since no personal issues exist between Bugenhagen and me. But the plan does not yet strike me as a good one.[5] For no-one is better suited to contend with him than one of those whom he himself is attacking—even if the matter at hand is the church and its truth. It is not out of any uneasiness that I have declined to do this.

| Meanwhile there is nothing new here. I have begun to lecture on Daniel; as a prelude to this, after I had put up some theses for debate according to the scholastic custom,[6] it so happened that a certain sacrificer removed the sheet from the doors of the chuch and tore it up—in full view of Thomas the

---

13 *almost ... strength*] *cornu eius fere attrivit* (literally, 'almost worn away his horn'—presumably with constant butting). The alternative form of Bucer's surname, *Butzer*, can be used in German to describe horned cattle

---

1 *Froschauer.
2 See 714, n. 19.
3 See 757, n. 3. Bugenhagen's use of the word *Confessio* in his title mirrors that of Luther's *Bekendnis* (see 644, 10).
4 See p. 35, n. 145. Bucer had already announced its appearance to Zwingli two days previously—see zw IX, 558f. (no. 762), 558, lines 9–12; BC III, 204f. (no. 206), lines 7–10.
5 In fact Oecolampadius never did respond to Bugenhagen's *Confessio*.
6 Oecolampadius seems to have done this as early as 4th September (see Staehelin, *Lebenswerk*, 409, with a summary of the theses' contents). The text of his lectures on Daniel only appeared, in two separate editions, in March 1530: *In Danielem prophetam Ioannis Oecolampadij libri duo, omnigena et abstrusiore cum Hebraeorum tum Graecorum scriptorum doctrina referti* (Basel: Wolff and Bebel; Staehelin 162 f.; Leu/Weidmann 31). See Staehelin, *Lebenswerk*, 552–566.

Augustinian.[7] When Thomas remonstrated with this man, asking him why he did not prefer to destroy the holy scriptures and to vanquish us in that way, the man swiftly drew a weapon, with a view to injuring his reprover. But our Thomas was alert: he forestalled the man and threw him to the ground. If he had not controlled himself, he could have killed the murderer; but he spared him. Some men ran up and enjoined them to keep the peace; and then Thomas, unconcerned, left the man and his dagger where they were. The latter, however, having showed contempt for the public peace, seized Thomas's sword and wounded him slightly in the head. The wound is indeed a slight one, but the man's temerity and his reckless deed are not beyond reproach. For this reason fickle rumour is making a mockery of Thomas's evangelical forebearance, and is relating baseless things rather than true ones. But I would not want you to be unaware that our brother was innocent of any wrongdoing that might injure his reputation—unless, that is, someone wants to account it a crime to defend yourself against a murderer who is attacking you.[8]

For the rest, if you would like to respond to Bugenhagen, who has dedicated his little book to *Brenz, I beg you to read what Brenz has brutishly written against you just before the end of his commentary on Ecclesiastes.[9] Perhaps you can expose the insolence he shows in that work, and also in the one he has written about the sixth chapter of John.[10]

Remind my Joachim of his duty.[11] Some time ago the Strasbourg brothers advised us that the Margrave of Lower Baden[12] | had forced ten pious and learned parish priests to leave his territory, for no other reason than that they had ceased celebrating the popish Mass.[13] They are now staying with the

IX, 562

---

[7] Thomas Gyrfalk, preacher of the Augustinian church in Basel. On him see 367, n. 5.
[8] On the aftermath of this incident see also 757, lines 12–18.
[9] *Der Prediger Solomo, mit hoch gegründter auß heyliger Göttlicher geschrifft außlegung durch D. Johann Brentzen Prediger zu Schwebischen Hall* (Nürnberg: Peypus, 1528)—facsimile edition by Martin Brecht (Stuttgart: Frommann-Holzboog, 1970). From our perusal of the work it is not clear what passage or section Oecolampadius has in mind.
[10] *In D. Johannis Evangelion, Johannis Brentij Exegesis, per autorem diligenter reuisa, ac multis in locis locupletata* (Hagenau: Setzer, 1528). Brenz's section on John 6 contains an extensive discussion (118^v–130^r) of verse 63, in which he articulates a classically Lutheran understanding of the Eucharist.
[11] Joachim Kirser: see 734, lines 28–51.
[12] Here used, presumably, to draw attention to the area around Sponheim, rather than the 'Upper' Baden region around Baden-Baden, Mahlberg and Lahr.
[13] In the summer of 1528, Margrave Philipp von Baden-Sponheim, often seen by the Swiss evangelicals as an ally, had imposed the restoration of certain Catholic ceremonies—under the influence of Balthasar Merklin, Provost of Waldkirch and Vice-Chancellor

Strasbourg brothers. Worthy labourers in the Lord's harvest.[14] If any villages over there, or indeed anywhere in Switzerland, are in need of good pastors, they could call on these most superior and agreeable men—certainly Mantel, once of Stuttgart,[15] who was imprisoned for several years for the sake of the gospel, and Ambach, who also was detained in prison in Mainz for the sake of the truth.[16] It was entirely appropriate to welcome such men. Perhaps the Strasbourgers have also written letters to you on this subject;[17] they certainly wanted me to tell you about it.

Farewell.
Basel, 28th September.
Oecolampadius.
To Huldrych Zwingli, his dearest brother.

Original: Zürich, Staatsarchiv, E II 349, p. 136 (autograph). Copy: Zürich, Zentralbibliothek, Ms S 21, no. 126.

---

of Archduke *Ferdinand, to whom he was personally close. In all twenty evangelical preachers are said to have left Baden.

14 Cf. Matthew 9:37 f.

15 Johann Mantel (c. 1468–1530), a close associate of Johann von Staupitz and formerly preacher at St Leonard's Church in Stuttgart, who had been imprisoned by the Austrian government between 1523 and 1525, and then served at Iffenzheim in Baden. In exile he became the parish priest at Elgg in Canton Zürich.

16 Melchior Ambach (c. 1490–1559), who studied at Mainz from 1516, and between 1522 and 1524 introduced a number of evangelical reforms in his parish at nearby Bingen. Following a brief period of imprisonment he went to Baden, and in 1528 to Neckarsteinach, near Heidelberg. In 1541 he is recorded as having moved to Frankfurt.

17 No such letters have been preserved.

767   Oecolampadius to Zwingli—Basel, 17th October (1528)

May the grace and peace of Christ be with you, my brother! We are thankful that you are so concerned for us, and indeed for the church of Christ which is here—and that you are advising us at the right time. We pray that you will continue to do so; and, in exchange, you will certainly soon receive ample reward from Christ our Lord himself. I in turn have anxiously been asking our friends whether our Council has determined anything of the kind that the man from Zug heard from Luzern and that you have heard from him.[1] But everyone denies it, and so far no-one has admitted any involvement in the case. In fact the Council clearly had decided upon something different, and had communicated this to its representatives in writing: at the moment it would not wish to provide assistance in a matter of faith, to the people of Schwyz against those of Toggenburg, or indeed to anyone else against anyone else. But the Council has ordered that, if the affair can be settled peacefully, great pains should be taken to do so. This is what the Council has decided, whatever those men eventually suggested to the Seven Cantons. Certainly councillors have stated that they did not support anything of this kind. But since the men in question are extremely hostile to us and are not on the side of the word of God, I am almost led to suspect that the Luzerner was not entirely wrong. If they had been sufficiently convinced by reliable | testimonies how perversely they had carried out their responsibilities, they would no doubt have been induced to repent of their actions a little. But they have not yet been persuaded by their friends that they have neglected their duty in this regard. Perhaps it would be helpful if something more certain were to become known. We hope that more trustworthy people will be sent to future assemblies, and that the Council's innocence will become plain.

22f. *they have ... regard*] *Nondum amicis persuasum est, eos sic sui officio oblitos* (literally, 'it has not yet been persuaded by/to their friends that they have been neglectful of their duty in this regard'); an alternative translation might read, 'their friends have not yet been persuaded that they ...'

---

1   The letter by Zwingli alluded to in lines 1–3 is lost, but there is plenty of evidence here to suggest that Oecolampadius is referring to ongoing tensions between the Catholic Canton of Schwyz and the neighbouring, increasingly evangelical area of Toggenburg (Canton St. Gallen). At the Confederate Diet in Baden on 28th September, representatives from Basel, Schaffhausen and Appenzell were appointed to mediate—see *AGBR* III, 167–169 (no. 232). The two conservatively-minded Basel representatives, Heinrich Meltinger (see 406, n. 2) and Andres Bischof (see Füglister, *Handwerksregiment*, 317 f.) seem, however, to have overstepped their authority, and to have risked an escalation of the problem, by urging the Schwyzers to take military action against the Toggenburgers—a policy which would certainly not have found favour with the militarily cautious majority in the Basel Council.

It is possible that a mistake was made in the matter, in that the Council had agreed that the treaty should be renewed on the basis of a seven-year oath—something which the Seven Cantons have neglected to do hitherto; if they sought to do this now, such a request could not be denied, but neither could it be made in the first place. So perhaps some words were spoken about that time-honoured loyalty of the Swiss.[2] But your letter describes something quite different—something that we are not at all afraid of here. So be of good courage. What if something of this sort has been made up in Luzern? But however things stand, you are owed a debt of gratitude for your faith and concern.

Johannes Cornarius, a medical doctor, learned in Greek and Latin, who has also taught classical letters and the medical arts at Wittenberg, hearing that your people lack a physician, asks to be commended to you through me;[3] perhaps over there he could be supported by means of a public salary? I could not refuse to write a letter of recommendation for someone who has been commended to me by dear friends: from this letter you will be able to see what kind of man he is. I myself have never met him. If he cannot be given what he desires, please be so good as to write back to him in a friendly manner.

| I have warned *Capito about what is holding his people back from seeking an alliance with your city.[4]

---

42 have ... him] *modium salis cum eo non edi* (literally, 'I have not eaten a peck of salt with him'). This echoes the proverb *Nemini fidas, nisi cum quo prius modicum salis absumpseres* ('you should trust nobody except him with whom you have already taken a peck of salt')—Erasmus, *Adagia*, 2.1.14 (1014)

2 This somewhat confusing passage relates to the terms of Basel's joining the Helvetic Confederation in 1501. It was initially intended that the relevant treaty should be renewed by both parties every five, or later seven years; but in fact the practice had been in desuetude since 1506.

3 Janus Cornarius (*sic*, c. 1500–1558), originally from Zwickau, was in Basel from September 1528 to September 1529, active mainly as an editor in the city's printing houses. He returned to Zwickau as a physician in 1530, practised there and later in Nordhausen, Frankfurt and Marburg, and remained prolific also as an author and editor. On him see Marie-Laure Monfort, *Janus Cornarius et la redécouverte d'Hippocrate à la Renaissance: textes de Janus Cornarius édités et traduits* (Turnhout: Brepols, 2017); *CoE* I, 339 f.

4 Oecolampadius did this in a letter dated 15th October: see *OeBA* II, 237 f. (no. 607); *CC* II, 359 f. (no. 368). The alliance under discussion did not in fact come into being until 5th January 1530.

Greet your wife,[5] *Pellikan, and all of our friends.
Basel, 17th October.
Your Oecolampadius.
To Huldrych Zwingli, his dearest brother.

Original: Zürich, Staatsarchiv, E II 349, p. 50 (autograph). Copy: Zürich, Zentralbibliothek, Ms S 21, no. 135.

---

5 Anna *Reinhart.

768   Oecolampadius to Zwingli—Basel, 21st October (1528)

Grace and peace from Christ, my Huldrych! Some citizens returning here from Zug have openly reported to several friends of the word things which were not very different from what you recently told me about our city's representatives.[1] And so if our Council want to take a phlegmatic view and to keep themselves out of the affair, they will not be able to put the blame for it retrospectively either on God or on us. For he has given them plenty of opportunities to set the record straight, and we also have not stopped giving them friendly warnings. Meanwhile our adversaries are certainly not sleeping, and every day are hatching new plans; but they do not consider how many great plans God has thwarted, right down to this day. If this were not his work, and if he were not protecting it, it would be a great wonder that they have not swallowed us alive.[2] We hope that he, by his Spirit, will shortly reveal that he is alive and that he holds the sceptre in his hands—and that he will not allow your most faithful warning to count for nothing. If you have come to know anything more about this business, you can write to me via this man.[3] For we have decided also to exhort the people in public if necessary. We will remain grateful and obliged to you not only for these things, but also for many other kindnesses.

Farewell.
Basel, 21st October.
Your Oecolampadius.
To Huldrych Zwingli, teacher of Christ at Zürich, his dearest brother.

Original: Zürich, Staatsarchiv, E II 349, p. 47 (scribal hand). Copy: Zürich, Zentralbibliothek, Ms S 21, no. 138.

---

12 we read *absorpsissent* ('they have swallowed') for the edition's *absorpsisset* ('he has swallowed')

---

1   See 767, lines 5–25 and n. 1.
2   Cf. Psalm 124:3.
3   The unidentified messenger.

774 Oecolampadius to Zwingli—Basel, 8th November (1528)

Grace and peace from Christ. As you advised me, my Huldrych, I have faithfully hinted to *Capito about the need to approach our city.[1] He has written to me in these words:[2] "I do not know how to respond to you. We are not idle, but there must be a right time for everything. Various people are complaining about various things. The popular mood of the commonwealth is a many-headed monster. And very many people are fearful of the highly unpredictable actions of our friends. There are some who have high hopes of Konstanz as a future ally, because of our common profession of Christ. But wise people are suspicious of anything new.[3] Listen now to something else. Certain people from Metz have come here; they say that in their city excellent reports are circulating about the compact between cities that is to be ratified; and that the proposed compact will be ratified on 12th November, since—they say—the articles have already been drawn up and fully approved. It is true that, in our city, there is complete silence about the matter; but we should not doubt that the compact between the prime movers of this our German commonwealth will be like this. You can discuss and pronounce upon the other matters as the occasion arises".[4] Capito wanted me to pour out these things to you. | He does not trust every messenger. But here we will be mindful of what you have sent us via Christoph.[5] If only our people would deign to listen to us!

We hope the turmoil in Bern will soon cease, to the great glory of Christ, even though we fear that those who have betrayed the church there are leading the best people into the kind of danger from which they will barely be able to escape.[6]

---

1 Zwingli has plainly enlisted Oecolampadius's help in his attempt to negotiate a formal alliance between Zürich, Basel and Strasbourg. The letter in which this hint is dropped is no longer extant, though lines 3–17 above are also translated in CC II, 362f. (no. 370a); and Capito refers to it in a letter to Zwingli dated 1st November—ZW IX, 593f. (no. 773), here 593, line 2; CC II, 363 (no. 71).
2 The original letter has been lost.
3 Cf. Oecolampadius's cautious assessment of the suitability of Konstanz as an ally of Zürich in 714, lines 27–33 and n. 8. His reservations might well have been of a theological rather than political nature, in that the city's sacramental theology tended towards the conservatively Lutheran.
4 Such an alliance was indeed established between Nürnberg, Augsburg and Ulm; but Strasbourg refused to join.
5 *Froschauer. We do not know what this message consisted of.
6 A reference to the disturbances in the Bernese Oberland: see 726, n. 6.

I am now busy with my Daniel.[7] I will handle the calculation of the 70 weeks after the manner of Eusebius.[8] If you have a more reliable way of doing it, I beg you to let me know; for none of the other authors, be they Hebrew or Christian, are able to square the circle; and what *Bucer does with regard to Matthew,[9] or Capito with regard to Hosea,[10] is unsatisfactory also. For people expect to read reliable material about this passage.

Moreover, it will not have escaped your notice that Benedikt[11] is opposing our Erasmus[12] at Schaffhausen in the matter of Christ's descent into hell. I myself interpret it this way: that indeed Christ's divine soul, released from his body, journeyed to the fathers, who had been waiting peacefully for him in a certain place along with Abraham, and that this revelation has brought them into a state of greater joy—in that he, the firstborn son, has opened for them the gates of paradise. Indeed I know that spirits are not restricted to particular places; but they must exist somewhere or other. And hence in my view the fathers were not wrong to teach that Christ descended to these people as a liberator. If you do not disagree with this view, that is a good thing—thanks be to God, who causes us to be of one mind in everything.

---

7   See 763, lines 20–22 and n. 6.
8   Cf. Daniel 9:24, "Seventy weeks are determined upon thy people and upon thy holy city, to finish the transgression, and to make an end of sins, and to make reconciliation for iniquity, and to bring in everlasting righteousness, and to seal up the vision and prophecy, and to anoint the most Holy". Oecolampadius interpreted these weeks as representing the time between Cyrus the Great's instruction to rebuild the temple in Jerusalem, and the coming of Christ (see his commentary—763, n. 6, 109^r–124^r). Eusebius of Caesarea's detailed discussion of this passage is in his *Demonstratio evangelica*, VII, 2, and is conveniently summarized in J. Paul Tanner, "Is Daniel's Seventy-Week Prophecy Messianic? Part I", *Bibliotheca Sacra* 166 (2009): 181–200, here 194–196.
9   *Enarrationum in Evangelion Matthaei, quibus verbotim simul et quae Marcus atque Lucas cum hoc habent communia explicantur* (Strasbourg: Herwagen 1527; Leu/Weidmann A23), here 302f.
10   See 747, n. 7. For the discussion of this passage see 262f.
11   Benedikt Burgauer (1494–1576), a native of St. Gallen, who had been a close associate of *Vadian in the early years of the Reformation there, but later espoused Lutheran views, notably on the Eucharist. He attended the First Zürich, Baden and Bern Disputations and settled in Schaffhausen in 1528. In the light of his protracted quarrel with Erasmus Ritter, he was forced to leave there in 1536, and later enjoyed a lengthy ministry at Isny in the Allgäu. See *CoE* I, 222; Bryner, "St. Gallen", 242, 247; Bryner, "Schaffhausen", 225f., 230.
12   Erasmus Ritter (d. 1546), who was initially an opponent of reform at Schaffhausen, but later worked closely with Sebastian Hofmeister (see 376, n. 7). He is best known for his lengthy feud with Benedikt Burgauer between 1528 and 1536, when both were dismissed. Ritter, who had generally represented Zwinglian perspectives in their debates, later settled in Bern. See *BBKL* VIII, 410–412; Bryner, "Schaffhausen", 225f., 230.

But if you do, tell me in a few words what you think, so that if the question begins to be bandied about rather pryingly by the common people, your view will not differ from mine. I will happily submit to those who come up with better arguments.

Farewell.
Basel, 8th November.
Oecolampadius.
To Huldrych Zwingli, his dearest brother.

Original: Zürich, Staatsarchiv, E II 349, p. 34 (autograph). Copy: Zürich, Zentralbibliothek, Ms S 21, no. 156.

786 Oecolampadius to Zwingli—Basel, 15th December (1528)

Grace and peace from Christ, dear brother. You have not made any reply about the weeks in Daniel,[1] and there is no need to break sweat on these matters, occupied with other things as you are. For by the grace of Christ I have finished all of Daniel; and, if the printer does not disappoint, I will make sure that it is published.[2] As to other aspects of our affairs, read the following and reflect on what needs to be done in order to prosper Christ's work:

A few days ago a certain councillor stood up in the Council and pointed out how many disagreements there are between the preachers here, and how bad the Council's reputation is; he alluded to those blasphemies and insults with which we besmirch each other on both sides, only then to throw the blame back onto the Council. Having said which, he added that they would never be able to attend to other matters unless they first of all dealt with the cause of the discord between preachers, and put an end to this. Thereupon he walked out. He is a good and loyal man who wishes us well. For this reason people are anticipating a change in affairs. If the Council do not treat this man fairly when he gives an account for his actions before them, other councillors might follow his example. And if that happens the people, a large proportion of whom are inflamed and beginning to seethe, will be unable to hide their indignation. And so, if you learn of any disturbances arising out of all this, I beg of you in friendship to take action as soon as possible along with your best men, so that we are not lacking in peacemakers. For unless I am wrong, in the coming holidays if not before, the people will request insistently that Christ be preached in a uniform way.[3] Meanwhile please hint to them ambiguously—as it were—what can be done, what you predict will eventually happen, and what their duty is. You understand the situation, I think. | Through the grace of Christ the constancy of your city lends an element of vitality to our pusillanimous people—may he bless you all still more.

---

11 *on both sides*] for *mutum* ('silent') we read *mutuo* ('mutually')   22 *so ... peacemakers*] *ne desint paci componendae* (literally, 'lest for the making of peace are lacking'; this elliptical clause might also be rendered 'so that we do not lack what we need to make peace')

1　See 774, lines 25–29.
2　See 763, line 20–22 and n. 6.
3　Such a request was indeed submitted by representatives of the guilds on 23rd December—see *AGBR* III, 197–202 (no. 291); *OeBA* II, 272 (no. 625); letter 788 below.

30 When I have read *Eck's trifles,[4] I will let you know what I think.
Our Pelargus is also going to publish something against me here.[5] The end of those men is at hand, I think.[6]
They say *Luther is writing something against us on the external word in Isaiah.[7] Again there, he will have to work hard.

35 Farewell, my brother, and pray for me and for our church at Basel.
Basel, in the year 1529,[8] on the 15th day of December.
Oecolampadius.
To Huldrych Zwingli, preacher at Zürich, most excellent man, his faithful brother.

Original: Zürich, Staatsarchiv, E II 349, p. 22 (autograph). Copy: Zürich, Zentralbibliothek, Ms S 21, no. 204.

---

4 *Verlegung der disputation zu Bern mit grund götlicher geschrifft* (Augsburg: Weißenhorn, 1528).
5 This was to be the *Hyperaspismus Sive Propugnatio Apologiae, quo Eucharistiae sacrificium ab Oecolampadiana calumnia strenue asseritur* (Basel: Faber Emmeus, 1529; Leu/Weidmann A174). On Pelargus see 687, n. 9.
6 Presumably the Dominicans, at least those based in Basel.
7 No such work materialized. On Luther's concept of the 'external word', see 976, n. 3.
8 It is plain from the context (and the contents of 788) that 1528 is meant.

788 Oecolampadius to Zwingli—Basel, 23rd December 1528

IX, 624 Grace and peace from Christ, dearest Huldrych. Of course I know that you are occupied with various affairs; but what I am now asking of you must cause you to put off all other activities. For it is our business to promote the spread of evangelical truth, and we are now rolling this stone with great endeavour.[1] So please rush to the aid of your friends and, as soon as possible, recommend such a course of action with the utmost diligence to your most faithful mayors and councillors. The distinguished people of Basel, or at least the righteous amongst them, are today begging their Council most urgently to put an end to discord between the preachers and to the popish Mass—unless it can be proved from the scriptures to be justified and holy.[2] Moreover it suits those who are of this mind not to desist from asking until such time as the Council accedes to their most honest requests and, in addition, promises to preserve a Christian moderation in all things. We do not know how the Council will respond.[3] The people have been maintaining a sense of decorum, lest what has been embarked upon be undone. So they enjoined me to write to you about these things and to beg you, by the Christ we share and by the most sacred bonds of charity, immediately to raise the matter with your mayors and councillors, so that the people might with increased faith unite with your people and those of our dearest allies in jointly asking that, to the glory of the gospel, there might be a more abundant growth of peace and concord here; and also to request the aid of those among your people who are more fully versed in the matter of truth and pure religion, in sending two excellent and distinguished men who might on their behalf assist these our people both in their deliberations and in their representa-

IX, 625 tions to the Council.[4] There you have it. | In doing this both you and your city will put the people of Basel very much in your debt. The Berners have also been written to in the same manner.[5] Please excuse the fact that the matter

---

1 The process of—finally—implementing irreversible evangelical reform in Basel.
2 See 786, line 23 f. and n. 3.
3 Whilst the events of 23rd December 1528 were of decisive importance, the Reformation Ordinance ending the state of *de facto* bi-confessionality in Basel was not issued until 1st April 1529—see *Basler Kirchenordnungen*, 13–42; AGBR III, 383–41C (no. 473).
4 Two representatives from Zürich, Rudolf Stoll and Jakob Werdmüller, left for Basel as early as 25th December. See their report home dated 28th December—AGBR III, 207 f. (no. 300).
5 This request met with similar success: Lienhart Hübschi, Diebolt von Erlach, Nikolaus Manuel and Lienhart Willading travelled from Bern on 26th December. Their frequent reports back to Bern constitute a valuable source of information about the course of events: see AGBR III, 209 f., 212–214, 224 f., 228–230, 232 f., 238 f. (nos 301, 306 f., 322, 329, 331, 336).

LETTER 788   317

has not been carried forward by other letters or other messengers: I know
you have sufficient faith in a hand-written document from me. This matter
brooks no delay. For the people are now assembled, and are staying put.[6] See
to it that your people fly here as quickly as possible, and pray to God along
with your church that all may turn out well and to the glory of Christ.

Basel, 23rd December in the year 1528.
Oecolampadius.
To Huldrych Zwingli, most faithful teacher of the church at Zürich, his
beloved brother in Christ. Zürich.

Original: Zürich, Staatsarchiv, E II 349, p. 15 (scribal hand). Copy: Zürich, Zentralbibliothek, Ms S 21, no. 208.

---

6 An estimated crowd of 500 people had congregated outside the Gardeners' guildhall in Basel.

792 Oecolampadius to Zwingli—Basel, 3rd January (1529)

Grace and peace from Christ, my Huldrych. Werner Beyel[1] is easily the best of the notaries who work here, with regard to talent, skill and experience. Having become aware that the principal scribe of your city[2] is about to die and lay down his burden, he has asked me, along with other friends,[3] to commend him especially to you—by introducing him, rather than by making the most ardent promises as to his wholly unswerving faith and works, so that I might not live to repent of commending him, nor you of taking him under your patronage. For some time now he has been assigned to what they call the spiritual consistory,[4] but he was always striving to free himself of that post; and he now hopes that, on this occasion, he will be able to escape. And so I do not commend him to you in any commonplace way. If the post is still available, please make sure your people verify the man's faith for themselves. It ought not to harm his cause that, for some time now, he has been active in secular public life. In this important work his experience would count for a great deal, and he merits our support—not least so that we might be able, if not immediately then at least in time, to bid farewell to those Pharisees. But if he can boast of having your confidence, that might perhaps enable me to win over some of his friends also. I hope that you will appoint this trustworthy man, who will prove to be deserving of your assistance.

For the rest, I can make no promises about our affairs here; the rumours are still just as ambiguous. But the constancy of the people, who are not desisting from making their requests,[5] gives me much hope.

---

1 Werner Beyel (or 'Bygel', c. 1488–1545) was an episcopal notary with evangelical sympathies, who had worked in Basel from 1508, before being appointed city scribe of Zürich in late January or early February 1529—not least on the basis of this recommendation from Oecolampadius. Thereafter Zwingli made extensive use of Beyel's services also in his dealings outside Zürich.
2 Wolfgang Mangolt, who had been in post since May 1526.
3 Markus Bertschi (see 367, n. 1) was for example to write to Zwingli in a similar vein three days later (ZW X, 5; no. 793); and indeed Beyel himself had done so on 2nd January (ZW X, 1–3; no. 791).
4 An ecclesiastical court presided over by the Bishop of Basel.
5 Many Basel guilds especially were continuing to put pressure on the Council to accede to their formal demands of 23rd December 1528, to the effect that the Mass should be abolished and only evangelical preaching permitted. See 788, especially lines 7–10..

Farewell.
Basel, 3rd January.
Oecolampadius.
To Huldrych Zwingli, most faithful teacher of the Zürichers, his dearest brother.

Original: Zürich, Staatsarchiv, E II 349, p. 55 (autograph). Copy: Zürich, Zentralbibliothek, Ms S 22, no. 3.

796 Oecolampadius to Zwingli—Basel, 11th January 1529

Grace from Christ, my Huldrych! When your shields were delivered,[1] your representatives were already arming themselves for their journey, since their business was already complete;[2] they will have informed you amply about this. We wanted the kingdom of Christ to be untainted; but there were no Josiahs present.[3] For you know that this city is governed not by democracy but by an aristocracy. But does each and every one of these noblemen work sincerely for the gospel? Nothing is to be held against the people. For now they have been satisfied by a decree from the Council, which they hope will soon be followed by another one which, at this time, they did not wish to obtain by force.[4] The unanimous agreement of the councillors and legates has prevented the people's zeal from becoming more fervent; and the view they hold of the gospel clearly moderated their behaviour, so that outsiders did not think badly of that zeal. It is as if our magistracy thought it a bad thing to use the gospel as a basis for action, when in fact the work of the gospel loves the power of the word more than the power of the sword. Besides, there was a danger that the deceit of certain people would split them into two factions, with some of them persisting with their plans, while others actually supported the Council. Nothing good could come from that. So, at the urging of the brothers, I myself, seeing that our cause was making little progress, reminded the people of their duty in an honest sermon preached by the grace of Christ. I did this to prevent anything being done that was unworthy of the gospel. So we give thanks to Christ the peacemaker. For to a large extent the Antichrist has fallen: seeing that nobody will now dare to raise objections from the pulpit, there is hope that other things will go well also. But they will still bring their malice to bear every day; for Satan will not cease from hindering us.

---

1 We assume, along with the annotators of the ZW edition (X, 10, n. 1) that this rather strange military image refers to letters that are now lost.
2 A reference to the delegates from the Council of Zürich who had been sent to Basel in the aftermath of the events of 23rd December 1528: see 788, especially n. 4.
3 Josiah was the righteous King of Israel who "did that which was right in the sight of the Lord, and walked in all the way of David his father, and turned not aside to the right hand or to the left" (II Kings 22:2). His relevance here lies in his role as an uncompromising religious reformer, significant not least for forbidding the worship of all gods but Yahweh.
4 On the Council's mandate of 5th January see above, p. 20.

Today the bishop arrives[5]—we do not know why, but he will not achieve anything.

| Today in the Large Council Ber[6] has resigned his provostship of St Peter's and his canonry—though in such a way that his successor must pay him 300 crowns in expenses.

Christoph[7] will supply you with the *Hyperaspismus* of Pelargus,[8] in which he opposes my most innocent refutation. While the legates were here, the people asked the Council to suppress that little book, on the grounds that it was infamous; and they were granted their request. Recently, however, after your people had left, the Council returned their copies of it to the printer[9] and allowed him to sell them—with some suggesting it is a good book. If you have time, you will see from the title what it is like. I myself explained to the Council how disreputable it is, but I see that I have accomplished little.[10] From this, then, I have learnt how vigilant we must be. Pharaoh will not let the people of Israel go easily.[11] But the Lord will be with his people.

Farewell. 11th January in the year 1529.
Oecolampadius.
To Huldrych Zwingli, preacher at Zürich, his dearest brother.

Original: Zürich, Staatsarchiv, E II 349, p. 21 (scribal hand). Copy: Zürich, Zentralbibliothek, Ms S 22, no. 16f.

---

5   Philipp von Gundelsheim: see 600, n. 10. He had been living at Porrentruy in the Jura, some 50 km from Basel.
6   Ludwig Ber: see 396, n. 10. Alongside his work at the university he was Provost of St Peter's Church in Basel and a Canon of the Cathedral; his abrupt departure and that of other leading Catholics must have confirmed the evangelicals in their hope that victory was near.
7   *Froschauer.
8   See 786, n. 5. On Pelargus see 687, n. 9. He too was very shortly to leave Basel, on 9th February.
9   Johann Faber Emmeus: see 707, n. 5.
10   Oecolampadius had argued that Pelargus's work should continue to be banned after the departure of the delegates from other cities.
11   An allusion to the narrative that dominates the book of Exodus.

797 Oecolampadius to Zwingli—Basel, 17th January 1529

Grace and peace from Christ, my Huldrych! Our man Hieronymus Rhaetus[1] will tell you faithfully what state our affairs are in. The arrangements that were recently mandated are under threat; for our adversaries also have again been given the opportunity to preach.[2] How I fear that our city will finally be destroyed, unless a different version of the faith is introduced! I am indeed reluctant to urge the people to set themselves free, since I am afraid the upheaval would be prejudicial to the gospel. But, in their shameless impudence, they scorn our reproofs. They consider it a holy thing to mock the people, I believe—their papal laws teach them this. But you should take counsel with our closest friends,[3] and write to me as soon as possible. Indeed, if your legates and the Berners' had not induced our people with their friendly persuasion to accept these conditions, they would be thinking very differently about the matter today.

The man Hieronymus does not need to be commended to you, for you have already known him for some time | as one of our men and as meriting your favour. But, in his modesty, he is asking me to do so.

Also Werner, who seeks to fill the office of scribe in your city,[4] is again asking me for recommendations. I recently wrote to you about his circumstances,[5] and I do believe that he would perform this duty meritoriously.

Farewell, and pray to God for our church, lest we do anything unworthy of Christians.
Basel, the 17th day of January in the year 1529.
Oecolampadius.
To Huldrych Zwingli, most upright teacher of the Zürichers, his brother.

Original: Zürich, Staatsarchiv, E II 349, p. 18 (autograph). Copy: Zürich, Zentralbibliothek, Ms S 22, no. 24.

---

1 Or 'Hieronymus of Chur'. This man is likely to have been Hieronymus Artolph, who was recorded in Basel as early as 1509, and much later (in 1538) became Rector of its university.
2 Compare 796, lines 6–8. The stipulations of the Council's mandate (see p. 20) had not changed, but were clearly not being consistently enforced.
3 Presumably the Berners: see 788, lines 15–27 and n. 4f.
4 Werner Beyel: see 792, n. 1.
5 See 792, lines 1–19.

809   Oecolampadius to Zwingli—Basel, 31st January (1529)

Grace and peace from Christ, dearest of brothers! We still have high hopes that the evangelical cause will have a happy result here this year.[1] Meanwhile something is worrying us: Satan will be in torment, having to acknowledge the glory of Christ against his will. So we are urging on people caution and
5 concord. For the tricks of the evil one are not unknown to us. It seems a good idea for the date of the disputation not to be postponed[2] to a time when there would be no danger of the old faith prevailing; that way there would be less suspicion. Moreover the notary we recommended to you will tell you better in person things which might in different circumstances be written
10 down.[3]

A certain friend, a man known in many countries,[4] would like to know as soon as possible what case the people of Chur are making and what they have sought to achieve by trickery in Graubünden[5]—so that at the forthcoming meeting of the princes in Speyer he might be able to damage the
15 authority of certain people.[6] So tell me if you know anything for certain.

x, 45

---

5 *For ... us*] or, 'For no tricks of the evil one lie in wait for us' (*Non enim latent nos maligni versutiae*)

---

1 This optimism proved justified: on 1st April 1529, the Basel Council issued the so-called "Reformation Mandate", whose liturgical and structural measures marked the beginning of a new reformed polity in the city.

2 The Council's mandate of 5th January had stipulated that a formal disputation should take place in Basel on 30th May; but such plans were overtaken by events, and it never happened.

3 Werner Beyel: see 792, n. 1.

4 Not least because of the cloak-and-dagger rhetoric, there is no real way of knowing who is meant here. Staehelin's suggestion (*OeBA* II, 278) of the Basel town clerk Kaspar Schaller is possible, but no more than that.

5 A reference to reports that Abbot Theodul Schlegel (see 674, n. 11) had been plotting to reimpose Catholicism on Chur and its environs, in league with Gian Giacomo de' Medici (1498–1555), Marquess of Musso and Lecco, who owned a castle on the border between Graubünden and Milan. In consequence of this Schlegel had been executed on 23rd January. For more details see Zwingli's response, letter 812 (especially lines 33–57).

6 The Diet of Speyer, which convened on 15th March 1529; it is best known for re-imposing the 1521 Edict of Worms, thereby seeking to proscribe all future evangelical reform. Again Oecolampadius's formulation is so guarded as to preclude any certainty about who the "certain people" might be.

x, 46 | Farewell.
Basel, on the last day of January.
Your Oecolampadius.
To Huldrych Zwingli, most sincere teacher of Christ at Zurich, his most beloved brother.

Original: Zürich, Staatsarchiv, E II 349, p. 139 (autograph). Copy: Zürich, Zentralbibliothek, Ms S 22, no. 39.

812   Zwingli to Oecolampadius—Zürich, 4th February (1529)

Grace and peace from the Lord. The terms you have agreed amongst you in Basel[1] displeased me only insofar as so much time has been spent on your most excellent and faithful vigils over the Lord's flock, but so little on denying opportunities to those werewolves. Gods above, what rock heaps of illusions they will roll out before your eyes! They say the city will be diminished by the absence of the canons, wars will be hatched on every side, and the unity of the Swiss will be weakened. But you, complete strangers as you are to all duplicity, will make great efforts to play down these things, lest the people remain fecklessly fickle in doing their duty. The enemy will already be at the gate; already some very slothful knight of the Sundgau will be sending a wounded citizen of Basel back home to his children.[2] I know the minds of certain Baslers very well. These, as I say, are things that have been disturbing me for your sake. On the other hand it is a comfort that, unless the Lord guards the city, we will all keep watch in vain.[3] But it is grievous that the Christian peace is being granted to you only with such difficulty—to you collectively, and especially to you individually, you who were born for better things.

Those of us who are ministers of the word at Zürich have approached the Council, asking it to agree with our plans to publicize the disputation as widely as possible.[4] The Berners, now that our people have communicated our opinion to them also, are receiving our advice a little more reluctantly. And we have no desire to be taught the truth by *Eck and *Faber as if we were unsure of it—rather, for the good of the churches, we wish thoroughly to discuss controversial subjects and to defend the truth, so that even the faithless might understand it better. So now our legates are delivering further messages, lest we end up writing only to you. But we shall know some time what that Bear[5] is muttering to himself.

Our friend Melchior, who has often carried letters between us,[6] has received all of these from Strasbourg for passing on to you. On occasion indeed he has brought letters intended for other people; hence we have opened

---

1 See p. 20.
2 A reference to the perceived threat to Basel from Archduke *Ferdinand of Austria and his forces: the extensive neighbouring territory of the Sundgau, in southern Alsace, was governed by a staunchly Catholic Habsburg administration centred on Ensisheim.
3 Psalm 127:1.
4 See 809, n. 2.
5 The city of Bern.
6 Possibly Melchior Ambach (see 763, n. 16).

your letter from Strasbourg. He reminded us that *Capito had allowed him to make a copy of it for us if it did not reach you straightaway.

In Chur, the Abbot of St Lucius, a man only moderately learned in Latin,[7] was beheaded on 23rd January of this year, having been found guilty of treason. The Raetians[8] now know nearly everything about the dealings between the Pope's men and *Ferdinand's;[9] we ourselves have learnt a good deal about them through our friends; but the Raetian Council has promised to tell our Council everything. When they do, I will pass it on to you. For if you know one thing, you can work out the rest—as with a lion's claw.[10] Wanting to put the Abbot in prison, they soon examined some chests of letters; and when they went to him and questioned him about the matters to which the treacherous letters bore witness, he most resolutely denied knowing anything about them. He did this trusting that, as he thought, he would be so shielded by the protection of his fellow conspirators that the letters too would remain safe. Eventually, when he understood plainly that all the proofs of his betrayal were already in the hands of the Council, he confessed to all his treasons. In his dying words he warned faithfully against the love of money, but made not a single mention of the gospel. In short, some big names are at the head of this conspiracy.[11] The reason why the Abbot perished is that he was in the service of a bishop who was at pains to sell off his church.[12] *When ... Markus Sittich of Ems and Count*

---

36 *Ferdinand's (men)*] *Perdinandicorum*. The initial 'P' is possibly an error, but more likely part of a pun involving *perdere*, 'to lose': see also line 62 f., where Ferdinand is said to have been "given his name for his perdition'" (*a perdendo*)   48 *against ... money*] *ut Philipporum amicitias fugiant* (literally, 'that they might flee the friendships of Philips'—a reference to the *Philippes d'or*, gold coins famously minted by Philip of Macedon   51 f. *When ... [children]*] the letter is damaged at this point, and approximately five words (indicated by the dots) are omitted. The words in square brackets are conjectures suggested by the context (see n. 13)   51 *Sittich*] Latin *Psittacus* (= German *Sittich*), 'parakeet'

---

7   Theodul Schlegel: see 674, n. 11 and 809, n. 5.
8   Zwingli's standard term for the inhabitants of Chur and Graubünden, on which the early-medieval province of Raetia Curiensis had been centred.
9   The Medici Pope Clement VII (1478–1534), and Archduke Ferdinand.
10 Cf. Erasmus, *Adagia*, 1.9.34 (834)—*Leonem ex unguibus aestimare*. "To know a lion by his claws is to form an idea of an entire object from one single inference, to infer much from little evidence and great results from small indication".
11 As Vasella shows (*Schlegel*, 280–288), Zwingli's report of Schegel's crime, trial and dying words is heavily slanted and largely inaccurate. See Vasella's own account (*Schlegel*, 258–272), which explains the political and ecclesiastical motivations underlying the Council of Chur's treatment of him.
12 The Prince Bishop of Chur in 1529 was nominally Paul Ziegler (c. 1471–1541—see Locher, *ZR*, 450). In fact he had left the city in 1524, but was now involved in a plot

LETTER 812   327

Musso[13] | *pretended [to attend] the wedding of their [children]*, a cohort of a   x, 54
thousand armed men entered Chur on the occasion and pretext of accompanying the bride and groom hither and thither; but in fact they had arranged
55   to invade the city and capture the episcopal palace and whatever else they
could. Those holy and learned men Comander[14] and Baling[15] had already
gone.
   I have already suggested to *Bucer in a letter[16] that their legates ought
not to intervene in the matter of Unterwalden.[17] For that is what the mat-
60   ter requires. But now it will be possible for them to work together anywhere
with Zürich and Bern as the opportunity arises—which for sure is a source of
pleasure to you also. We found that the head of this conspiracy is he who was
given his name for his perdition[18]—an unhappy omen for his supporters,
but a very happy one for us. If God wills, you will soon see some marvellous
65   works performed to his glory.
   Beyel has been made ours by the Secret Council, on your sole recommendation.[19] For your confidence in him had such an influence on me that I set
myself openly against the proudest of families. In the event we only won
by a few votes. But he will restore everything through his faith and indus-

---

           to install as bishop Giovanni Angelo de' Medici (1499–1565), the future Pope Pius IV
           and younger brother of the *condottiere* Gian Giacomo de' Medici (or 'Musso', see 809,
           n. 5). The Medicis' ambitions were political and financial, and for certain many bribes
           were paid to church officials. What, if anything, Theodul Schlegel knew of this plot is
           unclear (see Vasella, *Schlegel*, 235 f., 319).
13   Gian Giacomo de' Medici (see 809, n. 5) and his fellow mercenary leader Markus (or
           'Marx') Sittich von Ems (1466–1533). Their families had just been united through the
           marriage of Musso's daughter Clara de' Medici and Sittich's son Wolf Dietrich von
           Hohenems. The occasion used as an "occasion and pretext" was not the wedding itself,
           but the couple's passage through Chur as they travelled from Northern Italy to Hohen-
           ems immediately afterwards. Moreover they were almost certainly not accompanied
           by 1,000 potentially bellicose armed men—this claim smacks more of evangelical inse-
           curities than of historical accuracy (see Vasella, *Schlegel*, 236–246, 311–316).
14   See 674, n. 10.
15   Nikolaus Baling (or 'Pfister', or 'Artopoeus', c. 1500–1553), an evangelical Greek and
           Hebrew scholar who taught at Chur, Thun, Brugg and (from 1547) Bern.
16   This has not been preserved.
17   The context is the Confederate Diet that had met at Baden on 1st February. On the
           "matter of Unterwalden" see 726, n. 6.
18   Ferdinand. See the note on line 36 above.
19   See 792, lines 1–19. The election of Werner Beyel as city scribe was something of a trial of
           strength between Zwingli and his supporters in the so-called Secret Council, and some
           of Zürich's more conservative families and groups. See Wirz, "Familienschicksale", 551 f.

try (perhaps he himself does not know this). In any case you can give him good advice on all matters, for it would ruin me if he did not live up to your recommendation.

Farewell, dearest brother, and may God grant us his blessing—that is, may he keep your church in faith and constancy. Amen.
Tell the Strasbourg brothers what you judge it right to tell them.
Zürich, 4th February.
The man's ability has pleased me well on other occasions—Beyel's, I mean.
Your Huldrych Zwingli.
To Johannes Oecolampadius, his dearest brother in the Lord.

Original: Zürich, Staatsarchiv, E II 337, p. 32f.

826 Oecolampadius to Zwingli—Basel, 28th March (1529)

Grace and peace from Christ. Dearest Huldrych, if affairs at Basel had not been reported to you very fully and reliably by your delegates,[1] we would have told you about them: I was setting aside some free time and considering how, if I were to write, I would describe to you what has been done. Meanwhile nothing new has happened here. Paul Phrygio[2] has been called to the preacher's post | at St Peter's; we are awaiting his arrival. Tomorrow, I believe, our ecclesiastical arrangements will be determined by decree of the Council;[3] they will be much like yours. But you will learn of the things that are to be put in place when they have been approved. Next, we shall also reform the university. Now of course the legates of the princes of Saxony and Hesse have returned from Speyer.[4] They are hurrying by this route to see the Emperor, because *Ferdinand and the bishops have rescinded the Diet's edict permitting everyone freely to practice his religion as long as the Diet judges it to be pleasing to God and defensible in the eyes of the Emperor; moreover they are trying to restore papist rule everywhere.[5] In the meantime, however, another courier has come, announcing that our people[6] have refused not only to go to war against the Turk, but also to contribute towards the cost of equipping the army, until such time as we are safe from the priests—whose thinking is already well enough known. We should in no way doubt that the Lord will be with his people.

16f. *to go to war*] *militiam* (could also mean 'to send soldiers')

1   Likely to be Jakob Werdmüller (see 788, n. 4) and Rudolf Thymysen, who are known to have reported back from Basel in mid-February. On the key events of late 1528 and early 1529 see Roth, *Reformation*, II, 9–16.
2   Or 'Seidensticker' (1483–1543), who was in fact to play the role of a professor of theology as well as a parish priest. Originally from Konstanz, he had a much-travelled career, working at various points in Eichstätt, Sélestat, Mulhouse, Strasbourg and Tübingen. He was in Basel from 1529 to 1535. On him see *CoE* III, 79 f.; *BBKL* VII, 559–561.
3   The relevant deliberations took place, and their outcome was made known, on 1st April.
4   The Diet of Speyer had begun on 15th March.
5   This is quite an accurate summary: in the absence of Emperor Charles v, his representative Archduke Ferdinand took a hard line on religious toleration, in essence revoking the arrangements made at the previous Diet of Speyer ("the Diet's edict", line 12) in 1526. Charles himself had remained in Northern Italy; hence the route through Basel alluded to here.
6   This term (*nostros*), which usually refers to the people of Basel, here must mean the Swiss evangelical delegates at the Diet of Speyer.

I wish you and your household well.
Farewell.
Basel, 28th March.
Oecolampadius.
To Huldrych Zwingli, most faithful pastor of the Zürich church, his dearest brother.

Original: Zürich, Staatsarchiv, E II 349, p. 134 (autograph). Copy: Zürich, Zentralbibliothek, Ms S 22, no. 122.

829 Oecolampadius to Zwingli—Basel, 1st April 1529

Grace and peace from Christ. Since I am employing a faithful assistant,[1] dearest brother, I will outline in just a few words the matter that he will report on more fully. The ecclesiastical and political mandates are being approved by the Large Council today; in these, the Small Council also undertakes to establish a university.[2] Therefore I want Konrad to see what arrangements you have there, and what you think will benefit our university—so that we might put an end to the idle talk that accuses us of being enemies of the good arts. For we too know that the liberal arts are gifts from God, which good people can use well. So it will please us greatly (via our assistant) to learn these things, and perhaps others too—from you, who are a wise man, our friend, and most zealous for the good of the state. Far be it from me to blush with shame, my brother: it will be a cause of great glory to us on the Day of Judgement that, in our ardent charity, we have not shunned anxiety or perils for the sake of the brothers.

My wife greets you and your wife.[3]
Farewell.
Basel, 1st April in the year 1529.
Oecolampadius.
To Huldrych Zwingli, his dearest brother.

Original: Zürich, Staatsarchiv, E II 349, p. 20 (autograph). Copy: Zürich, Zentralbibliothek, Ms S 22, no. 129.

---

1 Konrad Hubert: see 733, n. 3.
2 The University of Basel had been founded in 1460, but its activities were suspended due to a lack of students in 1528. Strictly speaking, then, Oecolampadius is referring to a reform and reorganization. A submission on this subject made by him to the Council is printed in *OeBA* II, 313–317 (as no. 654). For a discussion of his overall contribution to educational reform see Staehelin, *Lebenswerk*, 541–551.
3 Wibrandis *Rosenblatt and Anna *Reinhart.

829a   Oecolampadius to Zwingli—Basel, 2nd April 1529

Grace and peace from Christ, dearest Huldrych. You already know, without my letter, what this man[1] is like and how worthy I believe him to be of a prominent position. We were indeed intending to keep him here with us; but it was right to consider and pursue not what is in our own interests, but rather what redounds to Christ's glory and profits his church; and we know that Primaguardia, or Bremgarten as they call it, needs a man of excellent faith, learning, integrity, constancy and—above all—prudence. So we are obliged to send him there; he also has letters of recommendation for the Bremgartners, and will be able to achieve much there that is of benefit to Christ. I know that you will assist the man most diligently. But if he arrives there too late and the town has already been provided with another good man, I ask that we be told about this in good time, in case a position is left unfilled here and he can work with us.

For the rest, news of my Konrad's dealings with you[2] is spreading more and more every day.

Farewell.
Basel, 2nd April.
Oecolampadius.
To Huldrych Zwingli, most faithful pastor of the Zürich church.

Original: Zürich, Staatsarchiv, E II 349, p. 29 (autograph). Copy: Zürich, Zentralbibliothek, Ms S 22, no. 42.

We date letter 834 to 1530. See below, pp. 359–361

---

14 *news*] Greek φήμη ('rumour, report')

---

1   Gervasius Schuler (1495–1563), originally from Strasbourg, who was in Bremgarten in Canton Aargau between 1529 and 1531, its brief period of Protestant ascendancy before the reimposition of Catholicism following the Second Kappel War. He later worked in Basel, Memmingen, Zürich and Lenzburg (Canton Aargau).
2   Konrad Hubert: see 733, n. 3 and 829, lines 5–11.

838   Oecolampadius to Zwingli—Basel, 3rd May 1529

May the grace of Christ be with you. The man delivering this letter was one of the Syngrammatarians,[1] but has now—through the grace of Christ—recovered his senses to the extent that he is a burden to his erstwhile brothers, and is putting so much pressure on them that I believe he will soon bring very many of them back to the faith. You will therefore deem him worthy of your conversation, my Huldrych, from which he will learn how united we are in proclaiming Christ; and he will then be able to confute our enemies, who repeatedly claim that we are at odds with one another, and glory not a little on that account. For the rest, *Pellikan will report on how things are going here.[2]

Farewell.
Basel, 3rd May in the year 1529.
Oecolampadius.
To Huldrych Zwingli, most faithful pastor of the Zürichers, his dearest brother.

Original: Zürich, Staatsarchiv, E II 349, p. 19 (scribal hand). Copy: Zürich, Zentralbibliothek, Ms S 23, no. 7.

---

1 Martin Germanus (c. 1496–c. 1559) was "one of the Syngrammatarians" in the sense that he had endorsed, and perhaps co-written, the *Syngramma* of 1525 (see 391, n. 5). He studied in Cologne, Vienna and Heidelberg, and had been a Lutheran pastor in Fürfeld in the Rheinland Palatinate since 1520. He increasingly espoused Zwinglian views, however, had broken with *Brenz, and had arrived in Strasbourg in 1529. He later worked closely with *Bucer.

2 Pellikan was by now firmly established in Zürich, but is recorded as having travelled to Basel on 4th May to collect his books from his former home, the city's recently secularized Franciscan monastery.

844 Oecolampadius to Zwingli, Basel, 22nd May (1529)

Greetings, my Huldrych. From this letter you will be able to understand more openly what our friends write more obscurely.[1] This is what they asked me to tell you: they call a discussion a "treaty"; the good and faithful Swiss "the sons of God"; the bad Swiss "the sons of Belial"; an assembly a "senate" or "council"; Speyer "Hamburg"; the Turk "the enemy"; Ferdinand "the black one"; the Hungarians "the Danes"; likewise, bishops are "elders"; evangelical princes "juniors"; the Raetians "the nearer ones"; the Hessians and Saxons "the ones further away"; war "movement"; peace "rest"; the prince of Hesse "the white one"; the cities of the Empire "churches". Now you know these codes, you will be able to use them when writing to our friends.

Otherwise, know that they[2] have read and approved the terms of the treaty entered into by the citizens of our two cities.[3] I do not know of any hindrances apart from those which my friend Konrad[4] told you about.

Farewell.
Basel, 22nd May.
Your Oecolampadius.

Original: Zürich, Zentralbibliothek, Msc F. 47, fol. 275 (Thesaurus Hottingerianus; autograph). Copy: Zürich, Zentralbibliothek, Ms S 25, no. 31.

---

1 This fascinating letter is designed to facilitate communication between Zwingli and the Strasbourg reformers *Capito and *Bucer—in particular, it deciphers codewords used by Capito in recent letters to Zwingli (nos 840 and 842; zw x, 119–121, 124–126). Zwingli himself later adopted a similar code in his letters to *Philipp of Hesse.
2 The Strasbourg reformers.
3 The cities of Zürich and Bern had signed a Christian Civic Union (*Christliches Burgrecht*) for the propagation of the evangelical faith in June 1528, and they were joined in 1529 by Basel, Biel, Mulhouse, Schaffhausen and Strasbourg.
4 Konrad Hubert: see 733, n. 3.

856   Oecolampadius to Zwingli—Basel, 12th June (1529)

Greetings in Christ, my Huldrych. Our man Thomas[1] asks me to recommend   x, 160
him to you, though I do not think he needs me to: none of my brothers and
intimates is closer to me than he is. Given your integrity, you will not reject
the man or his conversation and, if there is a need anywhere, will employ
his services. He holds you in such regard and is endowed with a faith so
remarkable as easily to compensate for anything he leaves to be desired in
the matter of learning. He will regard it as a favour to be admonished by
you, and you will find him ready to obey commands. He is possessed of great
openness. If you want us to do anything further here[2] and do not have leisure
to tell us, you can let us know via Thomas. For at this crucial time it is possible that many things will happen that need to be rectified. At one point
there is hesitation, at another an untimely lack of funds, and at another
faintheartedness. Although indeed I am not a military man, I nevertheless
have concerns and anxiety that everything will turn out well, and I want us
not in any way to underestimate our most devious, conniving and traitorous
enemies. It may be that some final sense of desperation will impel them to
attempt something while we are hoping they will make peace; so I hope you
will not cease urging your people to work together as closely as possible, so
as to make good speed in a timely and prudent way, until such time as certain victory is ours. For as long as the poison is not entirely removed from this
domestic snake of ours, we shall not only not be safe, but we shall be exposed
to the very greatest dangers. If you do this, I will think highly of your zeal—
seeing that this knot can only be cut here by the Tenedian axe.[3] May God
establish peace, to the glory of his name.

---

9 *openness*] Greek παρρησίασ (*sic*). One would expect παρρησίας   17 *they ... peace*] *manus porrecturum* (literally, 'hands to be reached out')

---

1 Thomas Gyrfalk: see 367, n. 5. He was plainly keen to serve as a military chaplain in the First Kappel War that was about to begin (by 12th June Zwingli and the Zürichers had already been in camp for three days).
2 Some 500 troops left Basel for Kappel on the same day that this letter was written, 12th June.
3 A reference to Tenes, King of Tenedos, described by Cicero and others as possessing a sharp double axe by means of which he meted out immediate and severe justice—see also Erasmus, *Adagia*, 1.9.29 (829). Oecolampadius's reference to a "knot" implies that he may be thinking also of another myth surrounding Tenes, in which he uses his axe to cut the cord mooring the boat of his father Cycnus.

x, 161 | Farewell.
Basel, 12th June.
Oecolampadius.
Grynaeus,[4] my house guest, sends many greetings, and will write to you soon.
To Huldrych Zwingli, his dearest brother.

Original: Zürich, Staatsarchiv, E II 349, p. 72 (autograph). Copy: Zürich, Zentralbibliothek, Ms S 23, no. 67.

---

4 Simon Grynaeus: see p. XVIII, n. 4. Oecolampadius had recently brought him to Basel.

870 Oecolampadius to Zwingli—Basel, 3rd July (1529)

Greetings in Christ. Blessed be the Prince of Peace, who is allowing you to breathe again for a while and has vindicated his doctrine and indeed his glory, lest he be thought bloodthirsty.[1] May he see to it that the alliances which have been re-established grow in strength with great holiness, and are never violated. Certainly, if war is to be waged at all, it will be better for us to rage against external forces[2]—whom I very much fear Satan will incite to taunt us until such time as they destroy our patience. What Sturm has told you and me from the Strasbourgers finds us in the same mind.[3] Truly, if our adversary agrees a date with the prince,[4] I think this will augur well.

| Last month *Melanchthon wrote me a most eloquent and friendly letter;[5] but he remains of the same mind as *Luther. He is encumbered by frivolous arguments, in my view. This shows how well equipped they are.

Grynaeus is lecturing with great skill on Aristotle's *Rhetoric*, that is, of course, on those parts of it which bear on Theodectes;[6] we are expecting Münster[7] to teach Hebrew. If the Lord grants us peace, we shall not neglect any of the good academic disciplines; but if it is denied us, there will be no room at all for the Muses.

The person delivering this letter has been commended to us by the Strasbourgers as a pious and rather erudite man, tested by the cross, and suited to

---

1 A peace treaty (the "Erster Kappeler Landfriede") between the Catholic and evangelical Cantons had been signed on 26th June, before any actual fighting had taken place.
2 That is to say, Emperor Charles, Archduke *Ferdinand and such broader Catholic coalitions as they might form.
3 Jakob Sturm: see 534, n. 5. He had been representing the Strasbourg Council in the peace negotiations at Kappel and, on his way there, had called on Oecolampadius in Basel between 14th and 16th June. The context suggests they discussed plans for the forthcoming Colloquy of Marburg.
4 A reference to negotiations about the colloquy taking place between Luther and *Philipp of Hesse.
5 The letter on the Eucharist printed in *OeBA* II, 308–310 (no. 652).
6 A tragic poet, writer on rhetoric and composer of riddles (c. 380–c. 340 BCE).
7 Sebastian Münster (1489–1552), originally a Franciscan and a pupil of *Pellikan, who had been called to Heidelberg as Professor of Hebrew in 1524 and from 1528–1529 performed the same role in Basel. He published several Hebrew grammars and an edition of the Hebrew Bible, but is now best known as a cartographer (especially his *Cosmographia* of 1544). On him see *BBKL* VI, 316–326.

guiding Christ's flock somewhere.[8] But we do not have any vacant positions here. We hear that faithful ministers of the word are wanted in the Thurgau district. So please make sure to help him.

Farewell.
Basel, 3rd July.
Oecolampadius.
To Huldrych Zwingli, the foremost teacher of the Swiss both in piety and in learning, his brother.

Original: Zürich, Staatsarchiv, E II 349, p. 41 (scribal hand). Copy: Zürich, Zentralbibliothek, Ms S 23, no. 120.

---

8 Likely to be Balthasar Hirt from Pforzheim, who was one of the preachers expelled from Baden in 1528 (see 763, lines 45–54 and n. 13). He had delivered a letter from *Bucer to Zwingli on 30th June 1529, in which the former commends him—ZW x, 182–184 (no. 867), here 183, line 10 f.; BC III, 292 f. (no. 230), lines 17–19. Subsequently, one Hans Grob informed Zwingli on 25th July that Hirt had obtained a post at Lichtensteig in the Toggenburg region—ZW x, 216 f. (no. 879), here 216, lines 3–5.

875   Oecolampadius to Zwingli—Basel, 12th July (1529)

Greetings in Christ, dearest brother. *Luther and *Melanchthon have promised the Prince of Hesse to travel to Marburg for the colloquy on the subject of the Eucharist.[1] We too are now being invited to this. And I do not see how we could refuse so illustrious a man what he is asking. Indeed, how could I renege on things that I once promised to do, unless I wanted to be held in the lowest esteem, and that not unjustly? So I have undertaken to attend on the appointed day.[2] And indeed, how I would like you to be my companion— something that would also please the Prince! You will learn from his letter what the safe conduct will be like. | I could not respond to this with any certainty; but I said that I had committed the whole matter to you for your judgement. So, I ask you, write a reply on this matter that will be appropriate for both of us; for in this regard I will willingly follow your plan.[3] But however you respond, please let me know about it by the next reliable courier; and tell me what you want me to do in this matter, so that we can prepare for the journey in time.

Farewell.
Basel, 12th July.

I have written to the Prince about the safe conduct in the following terms: Furthermore, I have not yet fully made up my mind about the safe conduct, since I do not know what Master Huldrych Zwingli will find convenient, and I would like to be his travelling companion. For this reason I will write to him also and urge him to give Your Grace an answer on our joint behalf about the safe conduct. If however it is not convenient for him to travel with me, it is my firm intention to travel to Strasbourg on 21st September and then, with the advice and help of good friends, to take the road to St. Goar. It may well be that this route will suit Zwingli also. I hope to seek and find a safe conduct

---

Lines 19–28 are translated from Oecolampadius's copy of his German letter to *Philipp of Hesse, which he includes here

---

1 This eventually took place between 1st and 4th October 1529.
2 Oecolampadius's letter of acceptance is printed in *OeBA* II, 339–341 (no. 676).
3 Oecolampadius's complete deferral to Zwingli in this matter (as well as his various reassurances in the next letter) are no doubt motivated in part by painful memories of the controversies surrounding safe conducts on the occasion of the Disputation of Baden in 1526. See for example 488, lines 1–7 and n. 1. This time Zwingli made no difficulties, and indeed wrote a positive response to Philip as early as 14th July (*ZW* X, 207–209; no. 876).

from Your Grace, Count Palatine Ludwig[4] and the Governor of St. Goar. May Your Grace be kind enough to ask them for their protection.

Your Oecolampadius.
To Huldrych Zwingli, most Christian teacher of the Zürichers, his beloved brother.

Original: Zürich, Staatsarchiv, E II 349, p. 111 (autograph). Copy: Zürich, Zentralbibliothek, Ms S 23, no. 126.

---

4 Pfalzgraf Ludwig von Pfalz-Zwiebrücken (1502–1532), a Lutheran, whose protection enabled the Swiss evangelicals largely to avoid the Catholic bishoprics of Speyer, Mainz and Worms.

883 Oecolampadius to Zwingli—Basel, 29th July (1529)

Grace and peace from Christ, my brother. Yesterday I received your letter, along with your Isaiah,[1] and I have spent a large part of the night on the latter. I cannot put in writing how much I liked it—and I will not attempt to do so, lest you regret the labour of reading what I wrote. One thing pains me, namely that you exalt me with immoderate words of praise that go beyond what I deserve. But how can I be irritated by someone I know to be such a friend? If only there were the same honesty in *Melanchthon, to whom I can scarce restrain myself from replying; but, in the hope that the colloquy will happen, I am controlling myself.[2] The matter is being inflamed still more by the printer Setzer[3] boasting that he has published the letter with Philipp's knowledge and that the latter is now preparing to plead his case in a book of appropriate length. If (as has not yet been confirmed to me) this is indeed the case, what was the purpose of the letter other than to make an enemy of me? But I am not afraid of this; for we know the sum total of what he can achieve, and I am already accustomed to | being insulted by these little friends. It is best for me to bite my tongue until we return from the colloquy.[4] If this ends well, we will not regret remaining silent; if less well from our point of view, it will still be fitting for us to respond—provided that Christ allows it. Meanwhile let us think thoughts of peace.

Of course you know of the route I described to the Landgrave.[5] I do not suspect that Prince of any trickery. As I understood it from Sturm,[6] very few people will be present at the colloquy, so as to remove any opportunity for vexatious showing off or quarrelling. The Prince has also invited Sturm and, with him, *Bucer, as well as another member of their inner circle.[7] Moreover in a letter he has suggested—but not recommended—to me that I might travel up the Rhine; but, because of the bishoprics of Speyer and Mainz, this would be less safe.[8] Furthermore, when we reach Strasbourg we shall not

---

1 The letter seems to have been lost; for details of Zwingli's "Isaiah" see p. 34, n. 144.
2 This text being objected to is the letter that Oecolampadius describes as "most eloquent and friendly" in 870, line 11f. (see also n. 5); his anger has been aroused by Melanchthon publishing the letter without telling him.
3 See 554, n. 7. The letter appeared as *Epistola ad Iohannem Oecolampadium, de Coena Domini* (Hagenau: Setzer, 1529).
4 Oecolampadius did in fact reply to Melanchthon at some point in July or August 1528: see *OeBA* 11, 343–350 (no. 680).
5 See 875, lines 23–27.
6 See 534, n. 5 and 870, n. 3.
7 Kaspar Hedio: see 286, n. 1.
8 See 875, n. 4.

be of a mind to travel anywhere else unless we can also return safely. Then at the end, unless our adversaries are immodest, they will admit to sensible people that they have been defeated; and we, when we return home safely, will make this known to the churches of the faithful. And so there are good grounds for trust. Nevertheless, along with you, I would have wished for a fairer and closer location.[9] So if he responds to your city,[10] we will take care to adjust our plans in line with what benefits the church and the glory of God.

x, 228   You recently asked what my printer pays me per copy in respect of my religious | writings.[11] For a single quire we have agreed on what they call a *teston*,[12] and for three quires a florin. Sichard has looked after his own interests better.[13]

My people are telling me that Froben[14] is reprinting a hodgepodge of letters by *Erasmus, to which many have been added in which you, *Pellikan and *Capito are repeatedly censured by name.[15] I will inquire diligently as to whether there is any substance to this, and will tell you.

I thank you for Isaiah. One day something made of lead will be sent to you, in exchange for this gold.[16]

Farewell.
Basel, 29th July.
Oecolampadius.
To Huldrych Zwingli, most Christian teacher of the Zürichers, his dearest brother.

Original: Zürich, Staatsarchiv, E II 349, p. 83 (scribal hand). Copy: Zürich, Zentralbibliothek, Ms S 23, no. 146.

---

9   Zwingli had suggested Strasbourg to *Philipp of Hesse as a more appropriate location for the colloquy—ZW X, 207–211 (no. 876), here 208, lines 10–13.
10 Philipp of Hesse in fact replied to the Zürich Council on 24th July, and to Zwingli himself on 27th July, on both occasions rejecting the suggestion of Strasbourg—see ZW X, 218–222 (no. 880), here 219, lines 12–15.
11 This question is not preserved in any extant letter.
12 A low-value coin with a head depicted on it (hence French *teston*); Du Cange (VIII, 88) suggests that it equated to twelve pennies in the reign of Henry VIII.
13 See 536, n. 4. There too Johannes Sichard is portrayed as keen to further his own self-interest.
14 See 384, n. 8.
15 This revised and expanded edition of Erasmus's letters appeared in August 1529: *Opus epistolarum Des. Erasmi Roterodami, per autorem diligenter recognitum et adiectis innumeris novis, fere ad trientem auctum* (Basel: Froben).
16 Presumably a reference to the forthcoming (re-)appearance of Erasmus's letters.

895   Oecolampadius to Zwingli—Basel, 10th August (1529)

Greetings in Christ, my brother. I have written to the Strasbourgers about your exhortation,[1] asking that they might urge the Prince of the Hessians to name a location for the colloquy that is fairer to us; but I understand that, due to Sturm's absence,[2] they have not done much about it, and that the latter has been fearing that, when he returns, they will also achieve little. Moreover goodwill towards us has so diminished that even he, Sturm, has not rushed to bring anything before the Council. Certainly they do not want to be the instigators of any danger. Meanwhile, from the letters I have received, I know nothing about what they have discussed or done. When the Chief Guild Master of our city returns,[3] he will explain anything they might have agreed with him; and it is for you to determine what might tend towards the glory of God—to whom we commit his work. For he is a powerful protector.

Farewell.
Basel, 10th August.
Oecolampadius.
To Huldrych Zwingli, antistes of the Zürichers, his dearest brother.

Original: Zürich, Staatsarchiv, E II 349, p. 116 (autograph). Copy: Zürich, Zentralbibliothek, Ms S 23, no. 149.

---

1 Presumably a reference to Zwingli and Oecolampadius's joint desire for the forthcoming colloquy to be held in Strasbourg; but the letter to Strasbourg is lost.
2 Jakob Sturm: see 534, n. 5 and 870, n. 3.
3 Jakob Meyer zum Hirzen, who had been in Strasbourg. On him see p. XVIII, n. 3.

904   Oecolampadius to Zwingli—Basel, 18th August (1529)

Grace and peace from Christ. The Strasbourgers are eagerly expecting you.[1] And I would like to know what would be the most suitable time for me to join you, by whatever means I eventually make my journey.

Farewell.
Basel, 18th August.   5
Your Oecolampadius.
To Huldrych Zwingli, most faithful teacher of the Zürich church, his dearest brother.

Original: Zürich, Staatsarchiv, E II 349, p. 160 (autograph). Copy: Zürich, Zentralbibliothek, Ms S 23, no. 183.

---

1 Plans for the Colloquy of Marburg were finalized fairly swiftly in August 1529, and it is plain that Zwingli and Oecolampadius are indeed intending to travel there via Strasbourg (cf. 875, lines 23–27).

911 Oecolampadius to Zwingli—Basel, 31st August (1529)

Greetings in Christ. My brother, I have advised this man Ulrich,[1] who greatly desires to speak with you, to hasten his journey, lest his wish be perhaps frustrated if he remains here longer.[2] He is from Ulm, a preacher, and would like to know about the ceremonies of our churches; and I think this is the sole reason for his journey. Unless I am mistaken, he has a letter of recommendation for your Council; indeed, he brought one with him for ours also. Perhaps his people, having become utterly disgusted with popish superstition, will soon adopt practices similar to those of our churches. But you can hear all these things from him. It is not | very long since he arrived from Wittenberg; but he does not seem to have adopted Saxon habits. Commend him (either yourself or through *Leo) to *Blarer or Zwick[3]—for he has been instructed to visit them also.

For the rest, when the person who will be travelling with me to Strasbourg comes here, he will find a boat ready for him which will hasten forward that very day, unless my friend deceives me. If it were me, and I did not wish to follow my travelling companion, I would set sail from here rather late; but in doing so I would be following the counsel of others[4]—and the brothers[5] are urging us in daily letters not to arrive late. So I shall await that most longed-for companion on the appointed day.

Basel, the last day of August.
Your Oecolampadius.
To Huldrych Zwingli, most Christian teacher of the Zürich church, his brother in Christ. Zürich.

Original: Zürich, Staatsarchiv, E II 349, p. 42 (scribal hand).

---

1 Ulrich Wieland, who had studied under *Melanchthon in Wittenberg and returned to his home town of Ulm in 1529. He was sent on the visits to Basel, Zürich and Konstanz alluded to in this letter by the Ulm Council at the urging of the city's leading evangelical Konrad Sam. Wieland subsequently acted for many years as preacher of the hospital church in Ulm.
2 Zwingli was of course about to depart for Marburg.
3 The two most prominent reformers in Konstanz. On Blarer's cousin Johannes Zwick (c. 1494–1542) see Bernd Moeller, *Johannes Zwick und die Reformation in Konstanz* (Gütersloh: Mohn, 1961); *CoE* III, 480 f.; *BBKL* XIV, 670 f.
4 Oecolampadius is discussing, in a very indirect way, the preparations for the journey to Marburg that he and Zwingli were to undertake on 4th September. The imprecision and opacity with which these arrangements are confirmed reflect the Swiss reformers' continuing concern for confidentiality and their own personal security.
5 That is, their associates in Strasbourg.

912   Oecolampadius to Zwingli—Basel, 1st September (1529)

Greetings in Christ. You see, my brother, how much our affairs are of concern to that most dutiful hero of the faith.[1] So we should guard against any delay on our part. I will await you. You will go to the house of our Chief Guild Master,[2] and then you will steal into my house by night. We will take care to ensure that nobody knows you are there. Yesterday evening the Chief Guild Master himself showed me your letter, from which I learnt that it would not please you at all if many people knew of our journey from me.[3] Certainly I cannot wholly deny that the rumour about us attending the colloquy began here, but you can guess who the person behind it is. First of all the Landgrave's courier[4] blabbed out some secret information to the companions he was travelling up from Strasbourg with. Then certain Zürichers passed this on in public—on the bridge or at social gatherings. Hence I could no longer deny that the Prince is planning something of this kind. But I have not told anyone the time or day on which we will set sail from here, or the day on which you are expected. On the advice of the Chief Guild Master, I have disclosed the matter to the magistracy, as was right and proper. The magistrates wish the enterprise well in every way. They have also decreed that I should be given sufficient means for the journey, | and should be joined on it by an excellent and faithful Councillor. This will be Rudolf Frey[5]—even though he does not yet know he has been chosen. When you come, we will arrange everything to ensure that we arrive safely in Strasbourg, either by boat or on horseback. To this day no-one even in my household knows when you are coming. Other things could not be concealed. More in person.

Farewell.
1st September. Basel.
Oecolampadius.
To Huldrych Zwingli, most faithful teacher of the Zürich church, his beloved brother.

Original: Zürich, Staatsarchiv, E II 349, p. 147 (autograph).

---

1 *Philipp of Hesse.
2 Jakob Meyer zum Hirzen: see p. XVIII, n. 3.
3 Zwingli's letter, now lost, was presumably a reply to the upbeat letter sent to him by Jakob Meyer zum Hirzen from Baden in late August (zw x, 285; no. 910).
4 The name of this person is unknown.
5 (Hans) Rudolf Frey (d. 1551) was a clothier who became a citizen of Basel in 1501, and was an active member of the Council and a leading light of the guild *Zum Schlüssel*. On him see Füglister, *Handwerksregiment*, 308f.

934 Oecolampadius to Zwingli—Basel, 24th November (1529)

Grace and peace from Christ, my brother. Whatever the nature of that new conflict of yours with regard to the business at Marburg, I could not properly understand from your recent letter[1] whether you are going to produce something for the general public, or console with the brothers in private. The second option seems on the whole to be worthwhile. But although we parted on the terms that one party would not attack the other without advance written warning, I think this arrangement does scant justice to our gentleness—we have been superior to them in the matter of charity. And I think that you are not minded to reply, unless perhaps the Lutherans have attacked us first—though in the meantime I have not heard or learnt anything about them, except what you have told me about Osiander.[2] This (I am speaking of the latter subject) greatly pleases me. But if you still have your summary, or a copy of its consolations and instructions,[3] I ask you to make a copy for us also, so that we might in all respects be able to respond using the same words—even though, for my part, I am not greatly distressed about the matter. I do hear, however, that some of the catabaptists, papists and false brethren have been criticizing most of what has been agreed with a rather severe arrogance—| but I do not care about them. On the other hand, that single article about the ascension is vexing me day and night;[4] and if only I had the leisure to do so, I would make a list of things that argue against them and bear witness to the simplicity of the catholic faith. Does the latter not indicate that Christ has been exalted into the heavens until the day of revelation, and indeed into the heavens of the firmament? Is it not harmful to deny much of our faith, and does this not bring various errors with it? But our affairs are not giving

---

8 to ... matter] *ut hoc saxum volutem* (literally, 'that I might roll this stone'). The term is generally used of vain attempts to achieve something—see Erasmus, *Adagia*, 2.4.40 (1340); but cf. 788, line 4 f.

---

1   The letter in question has been lost, meaning that the precise context of this letter is hard to establish.
2   Osiander had had an edition of the Twelve Articles drawn up at the Colloquy of Marburg printed in Nürnberg, claiming that he and *Luther were the authors: *Was zu Marpurgk in Hessen vom Abendtmal und andern strittigen artickeln gehandelt vnd vergleicht sey worden. Andreas Osiander. Martinus Luther* (Nürnberg: Petreius, 1529; Leu/Weidmann A171). Zwingli had already complained about this in a letter to *Philipp of Hesse dated 2nd November—ZW x, 329–334 (no. 931), here 331, lines 21–23.
3   Zwingli had read and commented on the Twelve Articles from the pulpit on 24th October.
4   In fact the Twelve Articles are entirely orthodox on this topic; but it seems to have been one on which Luther and Oecolampadius had differed sharply at Marburg.

me enough time to attend to this matter. Nevertheless it will remain in my mind. And you too, my brother, should not ignore the issue, and at the same time should pray to the Lord that he might extirpate this and other errors.

Here there is nothing new. We are astonished that the Berners are being so negligent with regard to the Strasbourgers.[5] As I see it, if God in his mercy did not protect our people better than they do themselves with their own vigilance and zeal, they would have been done for long ago. Consider, moreover, that if this thing does not happen, a means of helping other brothers also is being denied us.[6]

Fare you well.
Basel, 24th November.
Greet the brothers; and our people always wish you well, especially Markus.[7]
Oecolampadius.
To Huldrych Zwingli, most faithful pastor of the Zürichers, his dearest brother.

Original: Zürich, Staatsarchiv, E II 349, p. 127 (scribal hand). Copy: Zürich, Zentralbibliothek, Ms S 24, no. 34.

---

5 Negotiations for a formal alliance between these two cities were proceeding slowly—especially, it seems, on Bern's side.
6 Presumably Oecolampadius is here returning to his earlier train of thought about the Berners.
7 Markus Bertschi: see 367, n. 1.

958   Oecolampadius to Zwingli—Basel, 15th January (1530)

Greetings in Christ. I have nothing new to communicate, save that the day before yesterday I received a letter from *Karlstadt,[1] who sends you warmest greetings, regrets that he was not allowed to be present at the Colloquy of Marburg, and tells us how many artifices and injustices lying *Luther is perpetrating on him—indeed, he wanted to urge Karlstadt by force to write against the two of us. For, amongst other things, he writes this: "If I told you what tricks and deceits, and also how many troubles and afflictions I have | been assailed by, it is certain that the Lutherans would both deserve and incur great dishonour. They were urging me with many threats to write against you and my master and brother Zwingli.[2] When I refused to do this, and afterwards said that it was an impossible burden for me to take on, and moreover that, if I were to do it, no-one should advise me on what to say, since Luther was behaving like a military commander and a prince, they compelled me to give an account of my fundamental beliefs. I did this, having obtained the Elector's[3] consent. They promised bread and gave me snakes.[4] Thereafter I wrote to the Elector[5] that there was nothing in all the books that Luther had written to express his views against Oecolampadius and Zwingli that might induce me to support Luther's opinion, save only one short little verse[6]—and that for this reason I could no longer refrain from speaking the truth in his territory, and craved his indulgence that he might either permit me to speak openly or, if this were displeasing to him, to leave his lands. I awaited a response to this letter for six months; when this was denied me, I left, and I hardly know how I was brought to East Frisia".[7] Thus writes Karlstadt. You see what kind of beast we have been dealing with.

---

16 *snakes*] *basiliscos* (literally, 'basilisks', the serpent-like monsters capable of killing with a glance)

---

1 The letter has been lost.
2 On the subject of the Eucharist, in order to strengthen Luther's case against the Swiss reformers. The request was made as early as the summer of 1528—see Barge, *Bodenstein*, II, 386 and n. 150.
3 The committed Lutheran Johann of Saxony.
4 Cf. Matthew 7:9 f.
5 Barge (*Bodenstein*, II, 389) dates Karlstadt's letter to the Elector to 12th August 1528.
6 Much of this quotation from Karlstadt is either unreliable or obscurely expressed, but here he is presumably alluding to a Bible verse (such as Luke 22:19) that describes the institution of the Eucharist.
7 On Karlstadt's spell of exile in East Frisia, which began in the summer of 1529, see Barge, *Bodenstein*, II, 399–411.

Now to our dealings here with the catabaptists:[8] when they stealthily suggest to the people that tithes and offerings should not be paid, and we refuse to teach this and call them false prophets, they lead many people astray from hearing the word of God—so much so that I fear that, by chasing after the freedom of the flesh, they will fall into error. Recently one of them, who had perjured himself three times, was beheaded.[9] Others have also been taken prisoner; they are guilty of a similar sin. And behold, when they die bravely and behave as though they were innocent, a fresh danger arises. For those who are not built upon a firm foundation begin to sway to and fro, paying more attention to constancy than to the reason for constancy, or to the cross rather than the reason for the cross—as if indeed faith could only be established through suffering. This, anyway, is a judgement on hypocrites—of whom the world is full.

X, 401 | *Erasmus also has written a certain caustic epistle,[10] which the Prior of St Leonard's[11] has said he will send to you, and in which *Pellikan, *Bucer and indeed all of us are mentioned. No doubt he wants someone to oppose him, so that, by his barking, he might curry still more favour with princes. He is not worth provoking; but he is nonetheless hostile to our cause and, what is more, to Christ's; and he deserves to be reined in. The advice he gives is not very sensible.

---

8 Following the imposition of the Reformation Mandate in the previous year, the Basel Council's attempts to discipline anabaptists had been considerably stepped up. Moreover a much publicized debate with the anabaptists had taken place very recently, on 29th December 1529.
9 Hans Lüdin, a mason by trade, had become the first anabaptist martyr in Basel, on 12th January 1530. See AGBR IV, 29 f. (no. 313).
10 This rather substantial piece, occupying some 23 leaves, had been published on 1st January, as Contra quosdam, qui de falso iactant evangelicos, Epistola (Cologne: Gymnich, 1530).
11 Lukas Rollenbutz: see 670, n. 2.

Farewell.

Basel, 15th January.

I had almost forgotten that I have had a word in the ear of that excellent man Funk about the Duke of Württemberg.[12] I think you have been admonished by his minister.[13] Funk will tell you what I have said, namely that up to now nothing could have been done in the matter, but that now it might be appropriate to do something, given that his prince has been working on our city's behalf.[14] If any prince deserves our thanks, he also deserves our help. You can achieve more in this affair than I can. Farewell again.

To Huldrych Zwingli, most faithful teacher of the Zürichers, his dearest brother.

Original: Zürich, Staatsarchiv, E II 349, p. 113 (scribal hand). Copy: Zürich, Zentralbibliothek, Ms S 25, no. 15.

---

[12] Ulrich Funk (c. 1480–1531) was a Zürich Councillor, who was returning home from Strasbourg via Basel, and presumably brought this letter with him. Funk was a close associate of Zwingli, accompanying or representing him at the Disputations of Baden and Bern, and at the Colloquy of Marburg. On him see Emil Egli, "Meister Ulrich Funk: Zwinglis Begleiter auf Synoden und Disputationen", *Zwingliana* 2/1 (1905): 13–17.

[13] The context of this statement is unclear, though the "minister" in question is likely to have been Johannes Kornmesser (see 635, n. 7).

[14] Duke *Ulrich was in the process of negotiating defensive alliances with Zürich, Basel and Konstanz.

960   Oecolampadius to Zwingli—Basel, 17th January 1530

Johannes Oecolampadius to his Huldrych Zwingli. Greetings.

Greetings in Christ, my Huldrych. This man N.[1] is going to bring you another letter: he has, I hope, entirely repented of his catabaptist ways and, even though he has been given letters of commendation by others, I wanted to add one of my own. He seems to be worthy and stands out from the crowd, someone whom we might help by jointly protecting him—so that he might be permitted to return to his homeland, where he would be able to live in peace and benefit many by working with his hands. He has already atoned sufficiently for what he did wrong.

Farewell.
17th January 1530.

Original lost. Included in 1536 edition, fol. 81ᵛ.

---

5 *one of my own*] *meam* συστατικήν (literally, 'my own commendatory ⟨letter⟩')

---

[1] This person can be identified as Nikolaus Guldi, a former anabaptist from St. Gallen who, some five days earlier, had also been commended to Zwingli by *Bucer—ZW X, 392–394 (no. 955), here 392f.; BC IV, 1f. (no. 269). He had a chequered career, having at one point for example been imprisoned in St. Gallen; his conversion was plainly genuine, however, and he later returned to his home city, becoming a trusted associate of *Vadian.

976   Oecolampadius to Zwingli—Basel, 12th February (1530)

Greetings in Christ. I am now entirely immersed in Daniel,[1] my brother; how well I expound him in my lectures is for others to judge. For this reason I am writing less at present, and there are not many matters that are forcing me to do so.

They say that *Luther has written a little book about the Colloquy of Marburg.[2] The need for us to write and complain was all the more urgent because his people are spreading rumours to the effect that we have been defeated by them and have recanted our views on original sin, on the Trinity, on the external word[3] and on other matters. Likewise, they not only do not acknowledge us as brothers, but they banish us from communion and from the church. But, God be praised, their cause is now growing weaker and weaker every day. Lambert in Hesse[4] and many others are openly thinking as we do, | and so is the Landgrave himself, along with his Chancellor.[5] *Bucer has communicated these and other things to me, and asked me to make them known to you.[6]

Otherwise there is nothing new for me to write about. You know yourself that there is turmoil in Solothurn.[7] Around fifty farmers have been

---

1 See 763, n. 6.
2 This rumour proved to be false.
3 A favourite term of Luther's (*verbum externum*), which emphasizes that God's word of promise to mankind must come from 'outside' human consciousness—that is, from the Bible, preaching and the sacraments, rather than via the kind of 'inner' illumination often appealed to by radical evangelicals.
4 François Lambert (c. 1487–1530), a French Franciscan who first met Zwingli in Zürich in 1522. Already strongly influenced by Luther, he moved to Wittenberg in 1523, became a citizen of Strasbourg in 1524, and in 1526 was called by Landgrave *Philipp of Hesse to implement the Reformation in his territories and (from 1527) to teach theology at the newly founded University of Marburg. Oecolampadius is justified in claiming his support for a symbolic interpretation of the Eucharist. On him see *CoE* II, 284; *OER* II, 387; *TRE* XX, 415–418; *BBKL* IV, 1015–1020.
5 Johannes Feige (1482–1543), a humanist, lawyer and politician from Lichtenau, who had a strong personal influence on *Philipp of Hesse, was "the most powerful person in the Hessian government next to the Landgrave"—Cahill, *Philipp*, 71. See also *CoE* II, 15.
6 No letter answering to this description has survived.
7 *Haller had been given permission to preach in Solothurn for a month, beginning on 24th January. His presence had, however, caused considerable uproar—as Haller himself reports to Zwingli in a letter written in Solothurn on 14th February—*ZW* X, 450–454 (no. 977).

arrested here, for disobeying the magistracy; they have now been released.[8]
The courier will tell you about this.

Farewell.
Basel, 12th February.
Your Johannes Oecolampadius.
To Huldrych Zwingli, his beloved brother.

Original: Zürich, Staatsarchiv, E II 349, p. 109 (autograph). Copy: Zürich, Zentralbibliothek, Ms S 25, no. 45.

---

8 These were anabaptist sympathizers, primarily from the nearby villages of Rothenfluh and Anwil. Contrary to the impression given by Oecolampadius, they were in fact imprisoned in Basel for something approaching a month, before their release on 11th February—see *AGBR* IV, 321 (no. 348).

998 Zwingli to Oecolampadius, Zürich, 12th March 1530

Huldrych Zwingli to Johannes Oecolampadius. Greetings.
Grace and peace from the Lord. Our *Leo has explained to me your opinion on Paul's words;[1] and it is really no different from the one that we hold. We understand "discerning the Lord's body" as worthily perceiving the humanity, death and resurrection of Christ; that is, perceiving what needs to be perceived about Christ. Yet the body of Christ has been laid aside, as far as the function it performed in his humanity is concerned; and this is stated no differently in the holy scriptures. For in the letter to the Hebrews it says: "he, in the days of his flesh",[2] that is, he who, when his life ended and he died, entirely laid aside his flesh, with his human function. It is the same in this passage: he rightly discerns the body of Christ who knows the body he assumed and the divinity in which he abounds to be the one saviour and Christ—and that nothing has ever been given to the world that is greater or more precious than this redeemer. Moreover this seems to me something that Paul always has in mind, and for this reason he distances himself from idol-worship: he denies that the church merits esteem when those who wish to be seen as belonging to it actually assent to idol-worship.[3] For those who do not adequately esteem Christ's human function find it all too easy to condemn his church. Why, after all, do we discuss these things in books and letters, with the result that we are constantly emphasizing what we want to discourage? Paul was gripped by anxiety about Christ being held in contempt (as you are now about Christ's | body!); for this reason he seeks to magnify and honour him at all times.

For us, the communion of Christ's blood is the church: trusting in Christ's blood, drinking his blood—but in the spirit, not in the rite (unless in a sacramental sense). Now I do not think it is strange for us to call it the church of Christ's blood: it is after all a church which drinks Christ's blood in the spirit, which believes itself to have been redeemed by Christ's blood, which has faith in Christ's blood. For even if this statement seems rather strange, Paul

---

9 *he ... flesh*] Greek ὃς ἐν ταῖς ἡμέραις τῆς σαρκὸς αὐτοῦ   22 *as you ... body*] *en tibi nunc corpus* (literally, 'behold, to you now the body')   25 *rite*] the manuscript and edition have *rictu*, 'smile'; we take it that *ritu* is meant

---

1 1 Corinthians 11:29.
2 Hebrews 5:7.
3 The Pauline passage Zwingli is here somewhat obliquely discussing is presumably his discourse on food sacrificed to idols, 1 Corinthians 8:1–13.

himself says, "because there is one bread, we, who are many, are one body":[4] by way of prosapodosis, he gives the reason why the church has been called the fellowship of the body of Christ, etc.

As to *Karlstadt: I think that you have now received letters both from us and from him. It seems to me better for him to remain in Strasbourg.[5]

If N. and N. pass on to you our advice on the French question, read it carefully:[6] for there are many reasons to be very wary of the corruption and bribery of the King.[7]

Farewell, and work well.
Zürich, 12th March 1530.

Original lost. Included in 1536 edition, fol. 46ʳ.

---

30 *because ... body*] Unus enim panis et unum corpus tota multitudo sumus (literally, 'though we, so great a multitude, are one bread and one body'; we use the familiar—and theologically sounder—liturgical formulation)   31 *prosapodosis*] Greek προσαποδόσει, a rhetorical figure in which repeated or parallel structures are used for the purpose of definition or explanation

---

4 1 Corinthians 10:17.
5 The letters mentioned here have not been preserved; but Karlstadt, who had lived mainly in northern Germany since fleeing Saxony in 1529 (see 958, lines 1–22), had recently arrived in Strasbourg, where he was enjoying the support of *Capito and others. See Capito's letter to Zwingli of 15th May 1530—zw x, 580–582 (no. 1025); cc II, 421 (no. 410). On Karlstadt's sojourn in Strasbourg see Barge, *Bodenstein*, II, 416–422.
6 Following approaches from representatives of the French government around the turn of 1529 and 1530, Zwingli did for a while consider the possibility of entering into an implausible alliance with France—see Walther Köhler, "Zu Zwinglis französischen Bündnisplänen", *Zwingliana* 4/10 (1925): 302–311; Locher, ZR, 519–521. The messengers alluded to here are likely to be two of the three whom Zwingli used in the context of these negotiations: Werner Beyel (see 792, n. 1), and the prominent Strasbourg evangelicals Jakob Sturm (see 534, n. 5) and Mathis Pfarrer (1485/6–1568).
7 François I (1494–1547).

1005   Oecolampadius to Zwingli—Basel, 30th March (1530)

Greetings in Christ. I seem to have sent you a big present, my Zwingli—if, that is, you judge at your leisure that this Daniel[1] is worth your reading, and if you tell your friend freely of anything that displeases you. For up to now I have found it very difficult to make progress on it, and for that reason I
5 would willingly listen to any better ideas that other people might bring to bear. I desire the same in respect of *Leo, though he perhaps does not have much more leisure than you do.

For the rest, Wolfgang, the future parish priest of Lengnau,[2] who is bringing this letter, is a worthy man, and deserves to be treated with love by you
10 all. For he is learned, | and has suffered a good deal for the sake of Christ— even though he only recently committed himself entirely to Christ. So given that his own virtues commend him, there is no need for me to commend him to you at greater length.

Now, in the matter of the Emperor, some people think it would be a good
15 idea for us to tell each other who will be charged with the duty of responding and pleading the case on behalf of our cities, what articles we are keenest to defend, and what false accusations we wish to refute.[3] But I think this is unnecessary, given that the delegates will select for consideration only one out of all our statements. But if even you think the plan exists, I will gladly
20 send you what little I put together, and you can send me your thoughts too.

---

19 *statements*] *apologiis* (literally, 'justifications, statements in our defence')

---

1 See 763, n. 6. The copy sent by Oecolampadius to Zwingli survives, with a handwritten dedication. See Leu/Weidmann no. 31.
2 Wolfgang Ruß, who seems to have been a rather more complex character than Oecolampadius here implies: originally from Ulm, he was a leading light in the so-called *Pfaffenstürmen* riots at Erfurt in 1521, thereafter travelled widely and restlessly, gained a reputation as a drunken prattler, and was divorced by his wife in November 1530 (see letter 1040 below). See Walther Köhler, "Zu Wolfgang Russ", *Zwingliana* 6/1 (1934): 57 f. In fact Ruß's appointment was not confirmed at the Spring Synod of the Zürich church later in 1530: on this see letter 1021 below.
3 The context is Emperor Charles V's announcement, on 21st January 1530, that the Imperial Diet would meet at Augsburg on 8th April (though in fact it did not do so until 20th June). The members of the Christian Civic Union (see 844, n. 3) had convened at Basel between 9th and 12th March and decided that a single digest should be prepared to represent the views of its various member cities at the Diet. For all Oecolampadius's support of it, however, this decision seems not to have been implemented.

I have little hope of the French.[4] For they seem to be able to make alliances on any basis apart from that of the gospel. If only they were sensible!

Farewell.
The penultimate day of March.
Oecolampadius.
To Huldrych Zwingli, most faithful teacher of the Zurich church, his most beloved brother.

Original: Zürich, Staatsarchiv, E II 349, p. 131 (autograph). Copy: Zürich, Zentralbibliothek, Ms S 25, no. 92.

---

4 See 998, n. 6.

834 Oecolampadius to Zwingli—Basel, 17th April (1530)[1]

Greetings, my Huldrych. Truly there is an old adage to the effect that one should not lightly forsake one's old friends;[2] but I do not know how profitable it is for you on that account to have cut yourself off from new ones—in whom greater faith has been observed, and from whom greater benefit can be anticipated.[3] You are not unfamiliar with what they are planning today, or what they have always attempted to do. Apart from the name, little remains of the alliance.[4] If only they would not sally forth straightaway against the most obvious enemies! It would perhaps be better for them to proceed like that.[5] On the other hand one can anticipate, on the basis of our trust in them, what to expect from those who desire the greater glory of the same Christ as ourselves. Will not those who are joined together in Christ have a closer bond than those whom fleshly desires have united? I am not by any means rejecting our old allies, as long as they are useful to us and we can hold them to their duty. But if they disdain their old allies and do not go along with them, what is the point of our not also entering into fellowship with many others? Why neglect an opportunity which might perhaps be paid for later without the need for money, entreaties or favours? There is hardly any need to remind you of how much we might be able to obtain from these people at the right time, whether in peace or in war—just as you know for certain how much our long-established alliance could do in frustrating the plans of the wicked, breaking their impudent spirits, and scaring off those who rage. And so if it is possible to deliberate further on the matter, my brother, I ask you to consider with your main advisers whether it would be expedient to reject these people entirely. Our people certainly think it would not

X, 101

---

1 We follow Staehelin (*OeBA* II, 435; cf. zw X, 101–103) in assigning this letter to the April of 1530, rather than 1529. Its contents seem consistently to reflect the political and ecclesiastical situation that prevailed after the Colloquy of Marburg and in the lead-up to the Second Kappel War.
2 A reference to Erasmus, *Adagia*, 3.3.80 (2280), *Nouos parans amicos ne obliuiscere ueterum* ('when finding new friends, do not forget the old ones').
3 The context is an attempt by *Bucer, *Philipp of Hesse and various evangelicals (including, it seems, Oecolampadius) to form an alliance between Strasbourg, Bern, Basel, Zürich and some of the Protestant German states which were later to form part of the Schmalkaldic League (established in January 1531). Zwingli—and the Berners—were resisting this.
4 That is to say, the Helvetic Confederation.
5 A cryptic reference, one assumes, to Swiss religious division at a time of perceived threats from both the Ottoman and the Holy Roman Empires.

x, 102   be. They will be buoyed up | by a new and realistic hope, until such time as an alliance (of whatever name) is solemnly ratified—if perchance our old allies come to their senses in the meantime and place less trust in our common enemies. A rumour is now beginning to be spread among our new allies to the effect that the business is fully completed and that no sticking points remain. But if our adversaries think they have suffered rejection, they will be emboldened to persecute them—since the sons of this age neglect no opportunity, and indeed are more shrewd in dealing with their own generation.[6] But I would not want the excellent church of Christ either to be imperilled or to be exposed to mockery, and this could not happen without our being to blame—unless truth is not powerful enough to reconcile the pious, or falsehood effective enough to unite the impious. Who, henceforth, will beg us to be faithful? Who will seek our friendship? Christ will not abandon his own, even without us. But meanwhile, where is our duty? And where is consolation? I am not writing to you because they are already in a state of such double-headed danger that one must anticipate a tragedy; but because that Chief Guild Master[7] of ours discussed the matter with me and advised me to write to you, I did not by any means wish to disobey his command. Work out for yourself, then, what redounds more to the glory of Christ, or to the honour and benefit of our homeland. It certainly seems to me that we can forge a bond with our new and very faithful friends without jettisoning our old ones—if indeed the latter also wish to stand firm in the faith. What the former ask is that we should vex our old allies—whereas, if they were wise, they would welcome them with open arms. But you know that I am not very good at giving advice—though I am writing with sincerity. Be sure to manage this business in such a way that our new friends are not scorned, but that nothing is neglected which might win back the goodwill of our old allies.

x, 103 | Farewell in Christ.
Basel, 17th April.
Oecolampadius.

---

40 *that one ... tragedy*] *ut opus sit τραγῳδίζειν* (literally, 'that there is need to seek a tragedy')
47 *that ... allies*] *quod veteres iure possit male habere* (literally, 'that one would be able to vex old allies justly')

---

6   Luke 16:8. Oecolampadius quotes the Vulgate accurately (*quia filii hujus saeculi prudentiores ... in generatione sua sunt*).
7   Jakob Meyer zum Hirzen: see p. XVIII, n. 3.

Advise Christoph the printer[8] that, if he does not want to print the Bible in the translation by Sante Pagnini, he should return the two quires to me, so that I can have a book assembled that otherwise (having been taken apart) will be lost.[9]

60 To Huldrych Zwingli, most faithful pastor of the Zürich church, his brother.

Original: Zürich, Staatsarchiv, E II 349, p. 93 (autograph). Copy: Zürich, Zentralbibliothek, Ms S 22, no. 146.

---

8 *Froschauer.
9 Presumably Oecolampadius possessed a copy of this translation of the Bible into Latin (Lyon: Du Ry, 1528) and was seeking in vain to persuade Froschauer to reprint it. Pagnini (or 'Santes Pagnino', 1470–1541) was a Dominican from Lucca, formidably learned especially in Hebrew. On him see OER III, 194f.; BBKL VI, 1433f.

1013   Oecolampadius to Zwingli—Basel, 26th April (1530)

Greetings in Christ. If *Karlstadt replies properly to Philipp's absurdities, this will relieve us of some work; if not, the epistle I gave that man at Marburg stands ready,[1] and this, with a few small additions, will demolish that miserable wretch's efforts—unless you think it ill-advised. However, Karlstadt will respond, and we shall be privy to his reply. That little manuscript which changed hands at Marburg must not be allowed to go to waste.[2] You know how they tried to deceive the Prince with their testimony.

I hardly know what those excellent councillors will try to do at Augsburg.[3] It is the Lord's work: may he, in good time, take vengeance on the enemies of his glory.

You will hear the rest from other people's letters.[4]

Farewell, my Huldrych.
Basel, 26th April.
Oecolampadius.
To Huldrych Zwingli, his dearest brother.

Original: Zürich, Staatsarchiv, E II 349, p. 67 (autograph). Copy: Zürich, Zentralbibliothek, Ms S 25, no. 109.

---

1 *Melanchthon had insulted Karlstadt in the dedicatory epistle to his *Sententiae veterum aliquot scriptorium, de Coena Domini bona fide recitatae* (Wittenberg: Klug, 1530). Karlstadt did not respond, so Oecolampadius did indeed publish a revised version of the letter he had given to Melanchthon, as part of his *Quid de Eucharistia veteres tum Græci, tum Latini senserint, Dialogus, in quo Epistolae Philippi Melanchthonis et Joannis Oecolampadij insertae* (Basel: Herwagen, 2nd July 1530; Leu/Weidmann 142). See Staehelin, *Lebenswerk*, 608–611.
2 Melanchthon's *Sententiae* (see n. 1), in which he seeks to marshal patristic support for the Lutheran view of the Eucharist, originated in a handwritten document given by him and *Luther to *Philipp of Hesse at the Colloquy of Marburg.
3 At the Imperial Diet: see 1005, n. 3.
4 Oecolampadius is likely to be thinking of *Capito's letter to Zwingli dated 22nd April and dealing mainly with imperial politics and the latest machinations of *Faber—*zw* x, 546–551 (no. 1012); *cc* II, 419 f. (no. 407).

1018 Oecolampadius to Zwingli—Basel, 4th May 1530

Greetings in Christ. My brother, you could still have satisfied me by sparing your eyes and writing me fewer and briefer letters, even though I read those very long ones of yours with great joy.[1] Given your trouble,[2] it would be unworthy of me, if pleasant, to chase after you and distract you from better things.

I for my part am also thinking of writing a little apologia, though not so much on my own behalf as on that of our people.

Other news that is circulating confirms that the Emperor is no longer as daunting for us as he was. For rumour has it that the Florentines have both burnt his ships and intercepted his weapons, causing no little damage to his army.[3]

France is belatedly coming to Christ. For those who came here at Easter[4] report that the bishops and theologians | are taking violent measures against those who confess Christ. In response to this the King[5] is not only remaining silent, but is threatening to burn, along with others, the most learned men Gérard Roussel[6] and Jacques Lefèvre d'Etaples,[7] unless they dissuade his sister from a course that these men have urged her to take;[8] and I see that the

---

6 *little apologia*] Greek ἀπολογίδιον

---

1   It seems likely that Oecolampadius had recently received a long letter from Zwingli; but this has been lost. No doubt it contained material about the evangelicals' preparations for the Diet of Augsburg (see 1005, n. 3). The various parties were engaged in writing separate policy statements: Zwingli was determined to write only on his own behalf, whereas Oecolampadius wished to write on behalf of the people of Basel (see 6 f. above).
2   Presumably, in context, this relates to a problem Zwingli was having with his eyes.
3   In the context of the Italian Wars, the imperial army had suffered defeats in Florence on 21st and 25th March; but the precise details given here are almost certainly untrue.
4   These people have not been identified.
5   François I.
6   Gérard Roussel (or 'Gerardus Rufo', c. 1480–1555), was a humanist and pupil of Lefèvre d'Etaples. Like his teacher, he remained a Catholic, but was attracted particularly to the teachings of Zwingli and Oecolampadius, and—as her confessor—exerted considerable influence on Marguerite de Navarre (see n. 8). Under her auspices he became Bishop of Oloron in 1526. On him see *CoE* III, 174 f.; *OER* II, 452 f.
7   The eminent Aristotelian humanist and Bible translator, also known as Jacobus Faber Stapulensis (c. 1460–1536). As a reformer who chose to remain a Catholic, he encountered considerable hostility; but he also enjoyed the protection of François I and his court, meaning that his being burnt for heresy was never a serious possibility. On him see Christoph Schönau, *Jacques Lefèvre d'Etaples und die Reformation* (Gütersloh: Gütersloher Verlagshaus, 2017); *CoE* II, 315–318; *OER* II, 415 f.; *TRE* X, 781–783.
8   Marguerite de Navarre (1492–1547), who was in many ways sympathetic to church reform,

best of our friends over there are very fearful. But if he is already resisting the Lord, there is a danger, whether he gets his sons back or not,[9] that the gospel will be aped by hypocrites.

The Abbot of St. Gallen[10] has been well described to me as a one-eyed old man.

I hope that, in the end, I will show myself to be appropriately straightforward and honest in the eyes of the reader of *Melanchthon.[11]

*Bucer has been pleading the case of all of us against *Erasmus very faithfully,[12] even though he could have done much more.

| Farewell.
Basel, 4th May 1530.
Johannes Oecolampadius.
To Huldrych Zwingli, his dearest brother.

Original: Zürich, Staatsarchiv, E II 349, p. 23 (autograph). Copy: Zürich, Zentralbibliothek, Ms S 25, no. 124.

21f. *as ... man*] Greek καί ὁ μονόφθαλμος πρέσβυς

---

though significant more for seeking to moderate between Protestants and Catholics than for actively pursuing evangelical agendas. On her see Gary Ferguson, ed., *A Companion to Marguerite de Navarre* (Leiden: Brill, 2013).

9   "His [François I's] sons" were the Dauphin François, Duke of Brittany (1518–1536) and Henri, Duke of Orléans and later King Henri II (1519–1559). Under the peace terms of the Treaty of Madrid (17th January 1526), they were held in captivity in Spain under the auspices of Emperor Charles V between February 1526 and July 1530.

10   Kilian Germann (1485–1530) had been Prince Bishop of St. Gallen since early 1529. The role of such a figure in an increasingly Protestant area had for some time been a thorn in the flesh particularly of Zwingli, and had become more acute since Germann—in exile since the First Kappel War—had been actively mobilizing Catholic support against the evangelicals. Calling him a *monophthalmos* is an accusation of primitiveness or narrow-mindedness.

11   A reference to the *Dialogus* (see 1013, n. 1).

12   This was to be published as *Epistola apologetica ad sincerioris Christianismi sectatores* (Strasbourg: Schaeder and Apronianus, 1530).

1021 Oecolampadius to Zwingli—Basel, 11th May (1530)

Greetings in Christ. Our brother Wolfgang—whom I recently commended to your charity[1]—has told me how your synod has written to his people that he is not at all suitable to lead them.[2] I truly wonder at this: for I know him to be both learned and pious enough, even though he was rather tardy in abandoning the papists. But it often happens that Satan does his work above all in the lives of the most innocent people. For I do not think that he can be rejected on the grounds either of dishonesty of life or of impurity of doctrine. And, as far as I understand it, he has not been investigated by your people; but he has caused offence to the brothers because of certain ceremonies that were not conducted in every respect in accordance with your rite. This greatly surprises me, since the man has not done anything out of obstinacy and has not yet been either admonished or interrogated. Think on this, my brother: if your people proceed with such severity, are we not presenting the Lutherans and papists on a daily basis—if the practice spreads—with something they in turn can throw back at us? But, unless I am mistaken, the ambition of certain people who, as we know, can scarcely be compared to Wolfgang when it comes to either life or doctrine, is exaggerating and exacerbating the case, which is not in itself a bad one, of a man who has nothing at all to reproach himself for—in order that they might now replace the man they themselves chose. How much we must pray to God that this plague never infects our churches! For it will be the end of us if ministers are appointed to churches in these ways. The proof of this is the brother of your city scribe[3] wanting this man to spend time abroad. In ecclesiastical affairs no-one ought to take any risk without investigating things carefully.

| Certainly, if any position had become vacant in our city, we would not have allowed him to leave us. He chose to leave the Margrave's jurisdiction,[4] in which he held an honest position, rather than continuing to conduct illicit

---

22–24 *The proof ... carefully*] Greek Τεκμήριον ἐστι τόν τοῦ ὑμετέρου ἀρχιγραμματέως ἀδελφὸν τούτου παροικίαν φιλοτιμεῖσθαι. Ἔδει ἐν ἐκκλησιαστικοῖς πράγμασιν οὐδένα κινδυνεύειν ἀζητήτως.

---

1 Wolfgang Ruß: see 1005, n. 2.
2 The Synod of the Zürich church met twice a year, in the spring and autumn: it appears that the Spring Synod of 1530 did not confirm Ruß's appointment as Parish Priest of Lengnau, only to reverse its decision in the light of this protest by Oecolampadius.
3 This must be Kaspar Beyel, brother of Werner (see 792, n. 1); but the precise context is unclear.
4 Ruß must have been active somewhere in Baden, where Margrave Philipp's attitude to the Reformation was apt to be changeable. See 763, n. 13.

ceremonies; for the Margrave is not angry with him, even though he is well instructed in piety. Therefore I could not fail to point these things out to you, knowing that you will not take ill whatever I advise you in a friendly manner; and I beg you still, on his behalf, not to remove him. For I hear that his people are pleased with him, and that even some of his adversaries have come to their senses in response to his exhortations. Moreover we need not expect him to be obstinate with regard to these external matters. I beg you to lend him a more receptive ear; for in stormy synods not everything can be assessed all that accurately.

I am sending what *Bucer has sent from Strasbourg.[5]
Farewell.
Basel, 11th May.
Your Oecolamapadius.
To Huldrych Zwingli, most faithful and beloved pastor of the Zürichers.

Original: Zürich, Staatsarchiv, E II 349, p. 158 (autograph). Copy: Zürich, Zentralbibliothek, Ms S 25, no. 125.

---

5 Probably a letter dated 4th May, which contains material of interest to both Zwingli and Oecolampadius—ZW X, 567 (no. 1019); BC IV, 96f. (no. 297).

1028 Oecolampadius to Zwingli—Basel, 22nd May (1530)

Greetings in Christ, my brother. Konrad Joham[1] and Sturm's brother[2] are here, delegates from Strasbourg. I am on familiar terms with one of them, namely Konrad; and when we were talking together about various things, he urged me to write to you, because he thinks it would be worthy of the glory of the Swiss, and also profitable to many other small evangelical towns who think like us, if the three cities of Zürich, Bern and Basel were to send some excellent man who speaks French to Augsburg.[3] This person would explain to the Emperor—if not humbly, then certainly in a friendly way—that there is no danger in our gospel, which dissuades people from fighting wars and receiving pensions, teaches them to keep their word and has the greatest respect for peace; that things would be even less tolerable if the gospel were not taught; and that we are being blamed for many things that we simply do differently, and which are anyway far from terrible. It would be good also if this man mentioned other things that honour our cause (which is most honourable in itself). Konrad thinks that written submissions would be less profitable and less acceptable than an oral one. Think about this, and if it seems to you a good plan, say so to those who need to know.

For my part, since I am ignorant of what | the Swiss consider to be worthy of them, I do not know whether this would be appropriate. But I can see how much the princes will boast of being involved in the things of God! I am not unaware of how liberal they are when it comes to fine words.

As I say, *Karlstadt is coming with his family (wife and children); he will visit you (leaving his family here), and you can talk to him further.[4] He asks us to stay our pens.

---

1 Joham (d. 1551) was a wealthy merchant-banker and trader and an influential member of Strasbourg's Council. See *CoE* II, 238.
2 Peter Sturm (d. 1563), brother of Jakob (see 534, n. 5). Like Jakob he had enjoyed a humanist education, not least under Wimpfeling (see p. 13, n. 52), and had joined the Strasbourg Council in 1524. He later often engaged in diplomatic missions for the city.
3 That is, to the forthcoming imperial Diet. Charles v did not speak German.
4 On Karlstadt's visit to Zürich in the summer of 1530 see Barge, *Bodenstein*, II, 422 f.

Farewell.
Basel, 22nd May.
Your Oecolampadius.
To Huldrych Zwingli, most faithful pastor of the Zürichers, his dearest brother.

Original: Zürich, Staatsarchiv, E II 349, p. 35 (autograph). Copy: Zürich, Zentralbibliothek, Ms S 25, no. 133.

1038 Oecolampadius to Zwingli—Basel, 3rd June (1530)

Greetings in Christ, my brother. Behold, Andreas[1] has visited you too: by comparison with others, he is highly skilled, and a very different man from the one described either by *Melanchthon or by *Luther. For a very few days we here were given a taste of his manners, and if only the requests we made of our Council had been successful, there would already be a prospect of him working in the surrounding countryside;[2] but you know that they are—not to put too fine a point on it—hesitant when it comes to advancing the interests of learned men. I fear we are unworthy of such a visitor. I ask that he might be warmly commended to you. For he merits a high reputation on many counts, not just because he is a good and learned man, but also because he was one of the first to make an impression on the adversaries of Christ, and by now has spent many years in exile. We suffer this persecution with him. This will grieve our adversaries, who used to preach in their churches that the three of us had formed three heresies out of three little words.[3] May those great Elijahs[4] and chief prophets now see whether there is any spirit of dissension between us! Moreover I do not doubt that the Strasbourg brothers also will commend *Karlstadt enthusiastically.[5]

Yesterday I finished my response to Philipp's epistles.[6] Karlstadt | has read it, and you can hear his assessment of it. The dialogue has grown longer than I had imagined. It was not appropriate to oppose the simple, loudly roared opinions that I had read with simple ones of my own. The deceits of dishonest Melanchthon had to be exposed graciously. If our printers had the gifts of Christ and Mercury, I could speedily bring its publication to fruition. At present I do not know what will happen. I wish you all the best, my brother.

---

1 *Karlstadt.
2 Oecolampadius and his allies had been keen to appoint Karlstadt as a pastor in a rural parish.
3 The "three little words" are "this [is] my body". Oecolampadius no doubt has in mind particularly Luther, whose criticism of those evangelicals who disagreed with him on the Eucharist was generally vituperative.
4 Zwingli had famously referred to Luther as Elijah (in an essentially positive sense) in letter 113 (*ZW* VII, 250–253; here 250, lines 11–15).
5 They had in fact already done this in various letters: e.g. *Bucer in *ZW* X, 574–578 (no. 1023), *BC* IV, 97–101 (no. 298); *Capito in *ZW* X, 580–582 (no. 1025).
6 See 1013, n. 1.

Farewell in Christ.
Basel, 3rd June.
Johannes Oecolampadius.
To Huldrych Zwingli, most faithful pastor of the Zürich church, his beloved brother.

Original: Zürich, Staatsarchiv, E II 349, p. 129 (scribal hand). Copy: Zürich, Zentralbibliothek, Ms S 25, no. 149.

1040 Oecolampadius to Zwingli—Basel, 17th June 1530

With regard to little Wolfgang, I am satisfied.[1] A single word of your explanation occasions more faith in me than cartloads of his complaints; nevertheless, by the mercy of Christ, we cannot deny our assistance to someone who begs us for it with entreaties. But it was not without cause that I commended him to you. Five years ago he produced an honest example of his learning, in published sermons.[2] Since then he has always been commended by his neighbours for living a more blameless life than others. I am a man, and I can err. He too is a man, and he is changeable. And so I would not wish to offend against your brotherly love on his account. Meanwhile, I gather from *Bucer and from eminent men in his city that he (Bucer) is to be sent to Augsburg,[3] as long as he is granted a safe conduct.

*Luther is said to be about to present some articles from his confession to the Emperor, in which he expresses agreement with us except in the matter of the Eucharist.[4]

| Today Herwagen[5] has received, for printing, our dialogue of patristic *sententiae* on the subject of the Eucharist.[6]

I am thankful that you are supporting *Karlstadt so humanely. I have just the same opinion of him as you. So make an effort to see if he can be provided for. Greet him from me, and tell him his wife and children are well.

x, 614

x, 615

---

1 See 1021. It seems that the appointment of Wolfgang Ruß had been ratified in the light of Oecolampadius's protest; but the story did not end well (see also 1005, n. 2).
2 Two sermons by Ruß were published in 1523: *Eyn Sermon in welcher der mensch gereytzt vnd ermant wirt zu lieb der Evangelischen lere* (Zwickau: Gastel and Nürnberg: Höltzel); *Ein gütte nutzliche predig von dem rechtten guetten glauben* (Augsburg: Nadler and Munich: Schobser). In 1524 there followed *Ein Sermon von underscheyd der werck der menschen* (Strasbourg: Schürer).
3 That is, to the Diet.
4 Oecolampadius is probably thinking of the Schwabach Articles of 1529, an early Lutheran confession of faith published as *Die bekentnus Martini Luthers auff den ytzigen angestelten Reichstag zu Augspurgk eynzulegen: In siebenzehen Artickel verfasset* (Erfurt: Sachse, 1530; Leu/Weidmann A142); and/or *Auff das schreyen etlicher Papisten, uber die sibenzehen Artickel. Antwort Martini Lutthers* (Wittenberg: Maler, 1530), a work published without Luther's knowledge or approval. Both are edited in WA xxx, 172–182, 186–197.
5 See 554, n. 8.
6 See 1013, n. 1.

Farewell.

Basel, 17th June 1530.

Johannes Oecolampadius.

To Huldrych Zwingli, most vigilant pastor of the Zürich church, his brother.

Original: Zürich, Staatsarchiv, E II 349, p. 66 (autograph). Copy: Zürich, Zentralbibliothek, Ms S 26, no. 4.

1041 Oecolampadius to Zwingli—Basel, 17th June (1530)

Greetings, my brother. I have sent you a letter today via Connard from Wittingen,[1] and one has come from that little man Wolfgang,[2] in which he makes a concerted attempt to excuse himself and seems to fear nothing so much as me disagreeing with you or you with me. Nevertheless I could not discern from your letter[3] that you are irritated by these familiar writings of mine, and there is no reason to suppose that you are. I was, however, pleased to read that he is complaining more bitterly about something which is in no danger of happening than he is about his own case. But since we should everywhere seek after the stuff of peace rather than of discord, I will tell you about those of his entreaties that tend towards excusing him. He says that at the time he complained to me nothing at all was regarded as suspicious about the letters which were later objected to.[4] Then he apologizes, no doubt genuinely. For these reasons it will not be a bad thing if his case is heard in full, and he is either entirely confuted by or reconciled to you. But whichever it is, my brother, you need not have any suspicion that I bear you any rancour; nor do I suppose that you do, however much I might seek the welfare of others. But that is enough (indeed, more than enough) about these matters.

I enclose a letter from *Karlstadt. His wife is missing him.
I wish you and yours well.
Basel, 17th June.
Your Oecolampadius.
To Huldrych Zwingli, most excellent pastor of the Zürich church, his brother.

Original: Zürich, Staatsarchiv, E II 349, p. 81 (autograph). Copy: Zürich, Zentralbibliothek, Ms S 26, no. 5.

---

1 The letter is 1040, but the messenger cannot be identified. He presumably came from Wittingen near Gifhorn in Lower Saxony, or perhaps Wettingen near Baden in Canton Aargau.
2 Wolfgang Ruß: see most recently 1040, n. 1.
3 This letter has been lost.
4 It is not clear what the letters referred to contained, or indeed precisely wherein (at this point) Ruß's fault was deemed to lie; but the context is for certain the Zürich Spring Synod's refusal to ratify his appointment as parish priest of Lengnau (see 1021 and n. 2).

1049   Oecolampadius to Zwingli—Basel, 23rd June (1530)

x, 642   Greetings in Christ, my brother. At last our people here have followed your people's example and have ordered all those who either oppose the word of God, or have hitherto refused to share the Lord's Supper with us, to retire from the Large and the Small Council; and in future all public offices are to be purged in this way, from the greatest to the least, in the city as in the countryside;[1] and then a form of church discipline is to be introduced which will take the place of excommunication, namely the exclusion from communion of all who defile our church through their incorrigible lifestyle or
x, 643   doctrine.[2] May Christ bless | what has begun so propitiously! For now the house of the Lord of Lords has been cleansed of all those iniquitous people we shall, through Christ, stand firm indeed against the world's threats. For if God is for us, who is against us?[3]

*Bucer is said to have gone to Augsburg.[4] Let us pray that he might gore our adversaries with his horns to great effect.

I wish *Karlstadt well. Though his family are well, they are missing him.

Last year's Chief Guild Master, Jakob Meyer, has been elected Mayor,[5] and Balthasar Hiltprant Chief Guild Master—you know what he is like in a war![6] Moreover, after all this, the Canons of our Cathedral Church are unwilling to behave amicably in their case against their fellow-citizens of Basel: they have replied to the Strasbourgers to this effect.[7] This will not grieve many people much.

13f. *might ... horns*] *cornupetat*. See the note to 763, line 13.

---

1   These important decisions had been ratified on 21st June—see *AGBR* IV, 479f. (no. 540). Zürich had taken similar steps as early as 9th December 1528.
2   These matters proved more difficult to regulate than exclusions from official positions: an agreement on excommunication was eventually made on 14th December 1530 (*AGBR* V, 60–62 (no. 76)), but even thereafter was not consistently implemented.
3   Romans 8:31.
4   That is, to the Diet.
5   Jakob Meyer zum Hirzen: see p. XVIII, n. 3.
6   Hiltprant (d. 1538) was known as a soldier, and had been one of the 500 troops sent from Basel to assist Zürich in advance of the abortive First Kappel War (see above, p. 11). On him see Füglister, *Handwerksregiment*, 297f.
7   The disagreement was over whether the City of Basel was still required, after the implementation of the Reformation, to pay dues to the Cathedral Chapter. The canons' letter to Strasbourg is dated 15th June 1530—see *AGBR* IV, 472 (no. 530).

Farewell.
Basel, 23rd June.
Oecolampadius.
25 To Huldrych Zwingli, his beloved brother.

Original: Zürich, Staatsarchiv, E II 349, p. 155 (autograph). Copy: Zürich, Zentralbibliothek, Ms S 26, no. 21.

1050 Oecolampadius to Zwingli—Basel, 25th June (1530)

Greetings in Christ. It has been reported here that the Emperor's ambassador has, at the outset, asked the princes of the Empire to provide due and appropriate help against the Turk, and that he now wishes them to return home to attend to this as soon as possible. The princes, however, are not willing to do so before matters of faith have also been dealt with;[1] for they do not want always to be at odds with each other over such issues. Moreover the ambassador has suggested that, even if a blind eye is turned to all other matters, his imperial majesty will use all his might to take action against errors concerning the sacrament, the Mass and confession. In sum, no grace is to be hoped for from the Emperor, but very much from God.

*Bucer left for Augsburg on Sunday, *Capito on Monday.[2] May God prosper their journeys!

*Luther is said to have written a book in which he flatters the Emperor, is hostile to our cause, and sets out an approach by which princes might take control of ecclesiastical matters.[3]

Otherwise people are playing the fool. On the feast of Corpus Christi, the Emperor, bareheaded in all the heat—having shaved his hair in a clerical fashion—and carrying a lighted candle, processed behind the Archbishop of Mainz,[4] | who was bearing a breaded God; and many princes returned home after they had accompanied them as far as the temple.

---

1 The Diet of Augsburg had begun on 20th June.
2 That is, 19th and 20th June respectively.
3 His *Vermanung an die geistlichen versamlet auff dem Reichstag zu Augsburg* (Wittenberg: Lufft, 1530)—ed. WA XXX/2, 268–356; trans. AE XXXIV, 3–61.
4 Archbishop-Elector Albrecht III of Brandenburg (1490–1545), best known as the addressee of Luther's *95 Theses*. He was in fact an in many ways enlightened humanist, though he opposed the evangelicals with greater vigour after the Peasants' War of 1525. The procession described here took place on 16th June.

Here, many enemies of the word have been driven out of their high positions.[5]

My dialogue is in press.[6]

*Karlstadt has returned safely.[7]

25 Farewell, along with our friends.

25th June.

Your Oecolampadius.

The man delivering the letter is my wife's brother, the mint master.[8] He is dear to me; may he be dear to you also.

30 To Huldrych Zwingli, his dearest brother.

Original: Zürich, Staatsarchiv, E II 349, p. 91 (autograph). Copy: Zürich, Zentralbibliothek, Ms S 26, no. 23.

---

5 See 1049, lines 1–6.
6 See 1013, n. 1.
7 This stay in Basel seems to have been a short one: by 14th July he was clearly back in Zürich—see 1062, line 20 f.
8 Adalberg Rosenblatt, about whom little is known beyond that he was Master of the Mint at Colmar.

1062   Oecolampadius to Zwingli—Basel, 14th July 1530

Greetings in Christ. It was not appropriate, my brother, for our studies to be interrupted by matters that have nothing to do with us; but we are not freed from obligation on that account. We should allow this to happen partly out of our good nature, and partly because of the integrity of those who are asking. It will be better to err on the side that brings us greater goodwill, and certainly we should not be difficult. That man Heinrich, a citizen of Basel,[1] has asked for letters of recommendation to you—even though I barely know him. I did not want to be difficult, and I ask that you also show him some kindness by helping him; I would not, however, want your people to put themselves at any risk: in their wisdom, they know the dispositions, skills and faith of men better than we do. If they have need of his labour, they must arrange this on fixed terms that involve very little risk.

I have received the things you sent to Emperor Charles,[2] and I like them—even though, I am afraid, they will fall on deaf ears. For I hear that over thirty of our master-theologians | have gathered at Augsburg and are going to stitch together some things pertaining to the faith.[3] I am expecting a letter from the brothers at any time, and they will provide a more reliable report.

The Prince of the Catti[4] and our Sturm[5] are said to be behaving excellently.

For *Karlstadt's benefit I have added to your little book some quires that concern him.[6] Greet him from me.

9f. *to ... risk*] Greek κινδυνεύειν

---

1 Possibly Heinrich Budoti, former Steward of the Antonine monastery at Issenheim in Alsace, who is known to have bought property in Basel in 1526.
2 The *Fidei ratio*. See above, p. 12.
3 Oecolampadius has in mind the preparation of the so-called Confutation of Augsburg, which was presented to the Emperor on 3rd August as a Catholic rejoinder to the Protestant Confession of Augsburg.
4 *Philipp of Hesse. The Landgraves of Hesse styled themselves, amongst other things, *Principes Cattorum*, in honour of the ancient Germanic tribe known as the Catti, who had settled in the Upper Weser area.
5 Jakob Sturm (see 534, n. 5). The context of his "excellent behaviour" is presumably the Diet of Augsburg.
6 One assumes that, in effect, Oecolampadius is sending two at least partial copies of his *Dialogus* (see 1013, n. 1 and 1050, line 23).

Farewell.

Basel, 14th July.

I have received your *Account of the Faith, to the Emperor*,[7] and have read it avidly; I praise it on many counts.

To Huldrych Zwingli, most faithful pastor of the Zürich church, his dearest brother.

Original: Zürich, Staatsarchiv, E II 349, p. 49 (autograph). Copy: Zürich, Zentralbibliothek, MS S 26, no. 42.

---

7 See n. 2 above: Oecolampadius here translates an abbreviated title of the full work: *Fidei ad imperatorem ratio(nem)*.

1064   Oecolampadius to Zwingli—Basel, 15th July (1530)

XI, 28   Greetings in Christ, dearest brother. You have perhaps heard about the business being conducted at Augsburg[1] from sources that are more authoritative and closer to home. But, in addition, read what *Capito has written to the brothers: in my opinion he is quite reliable.[2] Now look, just as we predicted, the Saxons are retreating! In accordance with their plan, no doubt, their pen has been raging against us through no deserts of our own—in order that, by thus turning their anger away towards others, they might earn greater favour for themselves. But the Lord is making a mockery of that plan in a beautiful way and—as you will read—is wreaking a terrible vengeance on them.[3] Besides, our white one (you know that the Landgrave is meant)[4] is being more than heroic—indeed, truly Christian—in his constancy, so that he truly deserves to be regarded with greater deference by our people; and it is regrettable that the Berners are so reluctant to receive him into the
XI, 29   Christian Civic Union.[5] For this reason a certain mutual | friend of ours[6] has been speaking with me about many aspects of these affairs. He enjoys a very great reputation amongst us, and has asked me to write to you, urging you to ensure that your city's leaders persuade the Berners with the greatest and sternest resolve not to break with your city or (I hope) with ours in the matter of welcoming the Landgrave's overtures. This is something which we trust you would do anyway; and it would do greater honour both to them and to us, as well as being (I would add) more pleasing to Christ by reason of its piety and charity. And, if one cares to consider temporal things, such a joining of forces would be very useful to us and very frightening for our enemies. So see, my brother, if you can consider in your wisdom what wedge you might use

---

13 Berners] Ἀρχ[τ]οπολίτας   13f. into ... Union] in civem recipere (literally, 'receive as a citizen')

---

1   The Imperial Diet of Augsburg, which was still in session.
2   This letter seems to have been lost.
3   Whilst the precise tactics used are impossible to trace, the context suggests that the Lutherans have been seeking without success to drive a wedge between the Swiss evangelicals and those representatives—German no doubt—who are sympathetic to *Philipp of Hesse.
4   See 844, line 8 f.
5   For the context see 834, pp. 359–361 above (especially n. 3).
6   Likely, though not certain, to have been someone from Strasbourg, most obviously Jakob Sturm (see 534, n. 5).

LETTER 1064 381

25 to break this difficult knot. Certainly there is a danger that they, by ceasing to do anything, will slow down the Strasbourgers also.[7] You see how things are.

There is another thing on which it also seems worth the effort to work in earnest alongside the Berners, namely the issue of the Solothurners. It
30 was right for them to make common cause with us in Christ, so fruitful were the seeds that had been planted in their region.[8] But now there is a persistent rumour that the whole area is being contaminated by the ordures of the catabaptists, whom the papists are tolerating uncomplainingly, in order to destroy the gospel; and because of this the authority of the ministers of
35 God's true word is in decline and of no account. Now, no-one will be able to argue them out of their error better or more justly than the Berners themselves. But perhaps—and this seems to me very probable—they are barely listening even to them. Nevertheless an attempt needs to be made to cleanse the region by some means, so that it might one day be fit to receive Christ.
40 Please consider what is to be done in this matter also. To what extent their preacher Philipp[9] can influence affairs I do not know.

May God be with you in everything.
Farewell.
Basel, 15th July.
45 Your Oecolampadius.
To Huldrych Zwingli, most Christian moderator of the Zürich church, his beloved brother.

Original: Zürich, Staatsarchiv, E II 349, p. 48 (scribal hand). Copy: Zürich, Zentralbibliothek, MS S 26, no. 43.

---

7 Eventually, agreements with the Hessians were signed by Zürich on 30th July, by Basel on 16th November, and by Strasbourg on 18th November.
8 The City of Solothurn had mandated preaching solely according to the Bible as early as 22nd September 1529; but the situation there remained fluid and fraught, until "the Second Kappel War tipped the balance in favour of the old faith" (Henny, "Failed Reformations", 272).
9 Philipp Grotz, a former military chaplain from Zug, had been expelled from Solothurn in 1523, but was recalled as People's Priest under Bernese influence in August 1529, only to be expelled again after the Second Kappel War.

1065 Oecolampadius and the Basel Preachers to Zwingli—Basel, 18th July (1530)

XI, 30 Greetings in Christ. Our man Ambrosius[1] has been known to you for many years, and I do not doubt that he has also been commended to you: in the case of his wife[2] he has asked for letters of recommendation from us to you— even though, given the trust you have in sincere ministers of the word, we do not really think that such letters are necessary. But because he is very dear to us and has worked faithfully alongside us in the ministry of the word from the beginning, and even in the midst of danger, we pray that the great number of your duties (with which we know you have been burdened beyond measure) will not prevent you from lending him your support when you are at liberty to do so. On your advice, he was one of the first priests to get married, and not only did he join himself in true conjugal affection to a nun—namely Agathe, the daughter of a citizen of Zürich but physically not very robust—but also (as we know by the report of all in the vicinity) the two of them have had an honest and holy marriage. Nevertheless, now
X, 31 that many who have left the convent after her | are being given—in order that they might live more comfortably—an endowment and a considerable share of the convent's possessions, he is asking that his wife should not be deprived of her share, and hence should not be denied what is being granted to many others. This certainly does not seem unfair to us. And so, my brother, since his cause is familiar to you also, and since he can call you readily to mind, we are asking you on his behalf to deign, as far as is possible, to plead his case before good men; you will be doing all of us a great favour in this regard.

Farewell.
Basel, 18th July.
Oecolampadius and the other Basel preachers who are most devoted to you.
To Huldrych Zwingli, most watchful moderator of the Zürich church, our beloved brother.

Original: Zürich, Staatsarchiv, E II 349, p. 92 (autograph). Copy: Zürich, Zentralbibliothek, MS S 26, no. 47.

---

1 Ambrosius Kettenacker: see 307, n. 1.
2 Agathe Nießlin, formerly a nun in the Convent of Poor Clares at Gnadental in Canton Aargau, over which Zürich retained some influence. The request outlined in lines 14–19 was declined.

1066 Oecolampadius to Zwingli—Basel, 20th July (1530)

Greetings in Christ. I have just received this letter from Hedio,[1] which contains various things that you should consider carefully, if you do not know them already: such as, for example, the affairs of Markus von Ems;[2] the *Account of the Faith* you have sent to the Emperor;[3] the truce with the Turk;[4] *Melanchthon; the Berners, whom he is urging to enter into an alliance with the Prince of the Catti;[5] our beloved friends from Luzern, Zug and Konstanz.[6] With our faith in the Lord, who will not lay aside his glory.

| *Karlstadt's knapsack is here; it will be sent on to him in the next shipment.

Farewell.
Basel, 20th July.
Your Oecolampadius.
To Huldrych Zwingli, his beloved brother in Christ.

Original: Zürich, Staatsarchiv, E I 3, p. 2ʳ (autograph). Copy: Zürich, Zentralbibliothek, Ms S 26, no. 49.

---

1 Kaspar Hedio: see 286, n. 1. The letter has been lost; but Hedio is known to have been dealing with the Strasbourg reformers' correspondence in the absence of *Bucer and *Capito at the Diet of Augsburg.
2 Or 'Markus Sittich': see 812, n. 13.
3 See 1062, n. 2, 7.
4 No treaty had been signed; but there was speculation that, in the light of many princes' reluctance to vouchsafe military aid against the Ottoman Empire (see 1050, lines 1–5), Emperor Charles would have to sue for peace.
5 *Philipp of Hesse: see 1062, n. 4; also 834, pp. 359–361 above (especially n. 3).
6 Oecolampadius's ironic tone suggests that Hedio has been expressing disapproval of submissions made to the Diet of Augsburg by the Catholic Cantons of Luzern and Zug, and by the Bishop of Konstanz and his followers.

1074   Oecolampadius to Zwingli—Basel, 15th August (1530)

XI, 58   Greetings, my Huldrych! Bucer has sent this speech of Pimpinella's from Augsburg,[1] for sending on to you. All it says is that the Germans are driving back the Turk. It digresses at times, laments that the tunic of the Lord has been rent asunder,[2] and calls our doctrine a diabolical thing by which even excellent and prudent princes have been led astray. I have marked that passage on B.4.[3] Elsewhere he flatters and blasphemes, claiming that the Germans will vindicate Christ himself, the redeemer of the human race and of the whole world—as long as they are obedient. But, my brother, we know there are ways in which they are more hostile than the Turks. Nothing these people are attempting to do shows a peaceable disposition towards us; but they send lavish legations to sue the Turks for peace on possibly dishonourable terms. The new things that *Bucer also writes[4] about have already become stale news there.

Rudolf,[5] however, will be able to tell you what is happening here: there are some who, like many others, need to be spurred on to attend with greater ardour to the affairs of Christ's church. You can talk the more freely with him at home because of the remarkable friendship which united you and him on your journey last year.

Please greet *Karlstadt for me.

---

17 *at home*] Greek οἴκοθεν

---

1   Vincenzo Pimpinella (1485–1534), a noted poet, orator and lecturer on the New Testament, was Archbishop of Rossano from 1525 until his death, and papal nuncio to the court of Archduke *Ferdinand from 1529 to 1532. The speech he delivered during the Mass which opened the Diet of Augsburg on 20th June was published as *Oratio Augustae habitae XII. Kal. Julii* MDXXX (Augsburg; Weyssenhorn, 1530; Leu/Weidmann A178). The same printer issued a German translation in the same year. On this period of Pimpinella's career see Gerhard Müller, "Vincenzo Pimpinella am Hofe Ferdinands I., 1529–1532", *Quellen und Forschungen aus italienischen Archiven und Bibliotheken* 40 (1960): 65–88; also *CoE* III, 85; *BBKL* XVII, 1071f.
2   Cf. John 19:23f.
3   Oecolampadius's reference is accurate: on fol. B.4^{r–v} of the Weyssenhorn edition we do indeed read that those who have divided Christendom *Tunicam illam inconsutilem multas iam in partes diuisam destruunt* and *Vera et honestissima Christi dogmata quadam diabolica persuasione eliminant*. Moreover Pimpinella regrets that they have seduced not only ignorant people, but also *optimos et prudentes Principes*.
4   This letter has been lost.
5   Rudolf Frey, who had travelled with Zwingli and Oecolampadius to the Colloquy of Marburg in 1529: see 912, lines 16–20 and n. 5.

20 Finally, if your translation of Job is ready and you can spare it, I ask you to share it with me;[6] for, having been won over by requests from friends, I have decided to adorn it with my comments to the best of my ability.[7] And you would make something that would not have been at all unpleasant into something that is truly pleasing.

25 Farewell.
Basel, 15th August.
Your Oecolampadius.
To Huldrych Zwingli, his beloved brother.

Original: Zürich, Staatsarchiv, E II 349, p. 88 (autograph). Copy: Zürich, Zentralbibliothek, Ms S 26, no. 73.

---

6 No Latin translation of Job by Zwingli has been published; but a manuscript of one exists in the Staatsarchiv Zürich, dated 4th February 1530: see Emil Egli, "Die Neuausgabe der Zwinglischen Werke", *Zwingliana* 2/9 (1909): 269–278, here 276f. Zwingli must have sent this, or a copy of it, to Oecolampadius before 13th September (see 1094, n. 1).

7 Oecolampadius's commentary on Job was published posthumously: *Ioannis Oecolampadii Doctoris Undecunque Doctissimi In Librum Iob Exegemata* (Basel: Petri, 1532; Staehelin 168). See Staehelin, *Lebenswerk*, 566–571.

1094 Oecolampadius to Zwingli—Basel, 13th September (1530)

XI, 126 Greetings in Christ. I have found at home your translation of Job, along with a letter.[1] I will take care, my brother, that this lucubration of yours comes to no harm. Otherwise no news has been reported here, except that what *Bucer wrote to you, he has now also written to me and—because that letter was written later—has added one further thing:[2] that those groups of seven people who had originally been selected to seek paths leading to peace have been appointed to do so again, given that the groups of three have achieved
XI, 127 nothing.[3] But | the evangelicals, though more had been expected of them, have not reached any agreement with the papists. In this way the enemies of the truth are continually confounded.

Farewell, and greet your whole household along with our dearest brothers—to whom I am eternally grateful for the kindness they have recently shown us.
Basel, 13th September.
My Hieronymus[4] has left my little cap there. Could it please be sent back via him?
Oecolampadius.
To Huldrych Zwingli, his beloved brother.

Original: Zürich, Staatsarchiv, E II 349, p. 53 (autograph). Copy: Zürich, Zentralbibliothek, Ms S 27, no. 3.

---

1 See 1074, line 20 f. and n. 6 (the letter referred to has been lost).
2 Bucer's letter to Oecolampadius has been lost; but his letter to Zwingli must have been one from earlier in September: ZW XI, 107–110 (no. 1087a); BC IV, 267–272 (no. 338).
3 The ultimately impossible task of achieving interconfessional harmony at the Diet of Augsburg took on various forms, including that of forming committees of seven (later three) representatives from each side, Catholic and Protestant.
4 Likely to be Hieronymus Bothan: see 430, n. 4.

1096   Oecolampadius to Zwingli, Basel, 17th September (1530)

Greetings in Christ. I rejoice that you are satisfied with our account of how excommunication, or indeed church discipline in general, is to be instituted,[1] or rather restored—given that, as our affairs stand, I cannot see how the lack of such measures could be other than highly dangerous. For a magistrate who usurps the church's authority is more intolerable than the Antichrist himself. The magistrate wields a sword, and rightly so; but Christ gave us a medicine and remedy by which we might cure fallen brothers. If the church's authority remains intact, such a brother will still be able to profit from the remedy of her admonition, even if she hands him over to Satan for the destruction of his flesh;[2] if, however, all accused persons are brought before the magistrate, either the magistrate will blunt his sword, or he will render it completely useless by sparing a few people or many, or—by raging—he will make the gospel seem odious. In such contexts we would not be correcting our brothers by setting them before a magistrate; we would be betraying them. Christ did not say | "if he does not listen, tell it to the magistrate", but "tell it to the church".[3] This does not mean that I will exclude our leading citizens from the church along with the anabaptists. But their function is different from an ecclesiastical one, and they can put up with, and do, many things that the purity of the gospel does not allow: it tolerates the Jews and their privileges; it turns a blind eye to brothels; it allows many things to go unpunished in order that still greater evils might be avoided—evils that would not be at all pleasing to the church. Hence, my brother, many things at the moment are causing me to consider it very much our pastoral duty to exhort our churches not to neglect the keys of receiving and excluding that Christ has handed to them.[4] But I am sending you a copy of the speech that

---

1 It is not clear what spoken or written statement of Zwingli's is being alluded to here. The nearest the latter is known to have come to endorsing Oecolampadius's views on excommunication is a sentence in a letter to *Vadian dated 22nd September 1530—ZW XI, 146 f. (no. 1101), here 146, line 6 f.: *Oecolampadius rationem quandam ostendit, quae fratribus non magnumopere placebat, at mihi magis et magis arridet* ('Oecolampadius expounded a view that did not much please the brothers, but which appeals to me more and more'). When speaking enthusiastically of Zwingli's support for his position, however, one suspects Oecolampadius is often guilty of wishful thinking. See also p. 21 f. above.
2 1 Corinthians 5:5; Oecolampadius's wording of this quotation is very close to that of the Vulgate, *tradere Satanae in interitum carnis*.
3 Matthew 18:17. Oecolampadius again seems to be quoting from the Vulgate: *Quod si non audierit eos: dic ecclesiae.*
4 Cf. Matthew 16:19.

I gave in the brothers' name before the Council after the end of the recent synod,[5] so that you might have our opinion in full.

The other thing you wish for, namely that this plan should be adopted by common consent in all the churches of our Union[6]—so that it might have still greater authority—is something that I too would wish to see accomplished; and I know of nothing more wholesome or necessary that might come to pass in our churches. Yet many things alarm me. For very many churches will consent only tardily and with great reluctance, and will argue that it is a new papal tyranny—when in fact it is not like that at all. Very many will fear for their own affairs. Some, perhaps, will reject it totally.[7] I know how certain citizens of Bern and Strasbourg will make un-Christian remarks, as if the destruction of the fatherland were imminent—when in fact there is not the least danger of this, if the matter be properly understood. But they will not need to pay much attention to these issues: if they want to be admired as Christian cities, they will by no means be able to oppose the teachings of Christ, and will either accept this arrangement along with the others, or will follow suit very soon. So this is the way things must be arranged.

As soon as it can be done at a convenient time, an assembly of the Christian Civic Union should be called in which this and other issues should be discussed and settled.[8] At this, each city should be represented either by one of its principal preachers or by a statement on the matter at hand drawn up by its preachers. Questions of marriage and a variety of other ceremonies could, however, also be brought up—questions which it would be good for us to attend to and resolve in a uniform way. Meanwhile the brothers in the various cities should be urged to address the issue of excommunica-

---

42 *So ... arranged*] *Tela itaque sic texenda erit* (literally, 'And so in this way the web needs to be woven')   49 *attend to and resolve*] *dirimi et servari* (literally, 'to be annulled and preserved')

5 At the Basel church's first synod, on 2nd May, Oecolampadius had been tasked with presenting a new order for church discipline to the entire Council—see *AGBR*, IV, 417–420 (no. 473 a–b). A Latin version of his eventual speech on the subject appeared posthumously in 1536, as part of the collection of letters by him and Zwingli—see pp. 46, 48 above, fols 42^r–46^r. It is printed in *OeBA* II, 448–461 (no. 750). On the early debates concerning church discipline in Basel see Roth, *Reformation*, II, 26–33.
6 See 844, n. 3.
7 Oecolampadius's pessimism was to prove justified: he was able to implement his plans for church discipline only in Basel, and even there only in watered-down form. See above, p. 21 f.
8 The Union did in fact meet in Aarau on 27th September (see 1106, lines 1–31); representatives were present from Zürich, Basel, Bern, Schaffhausen, St. Gallen, Mulhouse, Biel and Konstanz—but not Strasbourg.

tion clearly from the pulpit[9]—as being a matter that is useful and in some respects necessary for the churches.

Since, however, the Baslers decreed some time ago that excommunication should be restored, but are still hesitating to implement this (I do not know whether they are looking to | others to act or are insufficiently faithful to the cause),[10] it is certainly incumbent upon those of us who are here to urge them to proceed. If, however, there is hope of the other cities being ready to implement this ordinance, it would be easy for you to prevail on your Council to write to our Council,[11] saying that they have understood our people have decided to put in place church discipline or excommunication in accordance with the word of the Lord; that this is a praiseworthy thing of which they do not disapprove; that they nevertheless desire that the resolutions should contain nothing contrary to the wishes of their churches; and that they therefore recommend leaving the matter undecided for a while until the next meeting of the Civic Union, at which it may be possible to act together in unison both on this issue and on others concerning the church; but that, in the mean time, they do not wish on this account anything to be left unpunished that could result in the church being dishonoured. If the Zürich Council wrote to this effect, our delayers would certainly not hurry up, even if we urged them strenuously to do so; although when we in Basel understand how your churches are affected by all this, even we ourselves will be able for a time to refrain from the goading that is required of us. So please tell me how matters stand.

Upon my return[12] I faithfully mentioned to the Mayor and Chief Guild Master[13] the possibility of establishing schools and educating boys using funds from the churches,[14] and also about our presentation of the little book

---

9   This happened, at least in Basel, on 18th or 25th September (see 1106, lines 27–29).
10 A mandate to introduce excommunication in Basel was passed by the Council on 8th June, but not published or implemented in its original form. See *OeBA* II, 461–464 (no. 751); *AGBR* IV, 456–460 (no. 520).
11 The Zürich Council did indeed write to their Basel counterparts on 24th September, but in different, much more negative terms than those envisaged here—refusing, for example, to grant Zwingli permission to support Oecolampadius at the forthcoming meeting at Aarau (see n. 8). The letter is in *OeBA*, II, 491f. (no. 780); *AGBR* IV, 596f. (no. 637).
12 From Zürich (see n. 1).
13 Respectively Jakob Meyer zum Hirzen (see p. XVIII, n. 3) and Balthasar Hiltprant (see 1049, n. 6).
14 Following Basel's formal adoption of the Reformation, Oecolampadius was plainly keen to apply the Zürich model of using money from the dissolution of the monasteries and other ecclesiastical institutions to finance an ambitious educational programme.

XI, 132 of requests to the legates of the Five Inner States.[15] | They themselves have brought the book before the Council, so we did not raise the matter in vain; but they have not yet discussed how these things might most conveniently be brought about. It may be possible to deliberate about them in greater detail with the Christian Civic Union[16]—for the subject is too difficult and too necessary for it to be debated only by uneducated people. They want the little book of requests for the Five Inner States to be shorter, so as not to displease its critics.

I should be sending on the letters that *Bucer wrote in Strasbourg, but they have not been copied and are not very important for you to know about.[17] I will however send them when they have been copied.

Greet your wife[18] and children, also *Pellikan and *Leo; read and consider my speech with them, and admonish me freely.
Farewell.
17th September. Basel.
Your Oecolampadius.
To Ulrich Zwingli, his most beloved brother.

Original: Zürich, Staatsarchiv, E II 349, p. 38 (autograph). Copy: Zürich, Zentralbibliothek, Ms S 27, no. 5.

83f. *so ... critics*] Greek εἶναί τι δεῖ τῷ μώμῳ οὐκ ἀρέσκον (literally 'it needs to be something displeasing to criticism')

15 The "Five Inner States" are the Catholic Cantons of Uri, Schwyz, Unterwalden, Luzern and Zug. The "little book" was composed by the evangelical preachers of Zürich, Bern, Basel and Strasbourg, and sent on 5th September. In essence it is a plea that the word of God might be preached freely throughout Switzerland. See *OeBA* II, 483f. (no. 772).
16 This did not happen at Aarau (see n. 8), but did at the meeting in Basel on 13th February 1531.
17 It is not clear what documents Oecolampadius is referring to here.
18 Anna *Reinhart.

1102 Oecolampadius to Zwingli—Basel, 25th September (1530)

Greetings in Christ. I have no news to relate, my brother; but I expect that you have heard some from the Augsburgers.[1] I do indeed suspect that *Luther and *Melanchthon will not accept our view, however much they have encouraged *Bucer to hope for this.[2] At any rate most of the Syn-grammatarians among the Cherusci[3] are still crying out boldly against us, prophesying that we will be confounded in the end. But it is they who will be confounded—with all who have not made God their protector. We have never liked a lie.

Here you have some very manly letters from Martin to Philipp (would that they used such magnanimity in their honest judgement of others!).[4] If they already show such mixed loyalty towards that teacher, how much more will there be for us to fear? For although until now—with Christ as our judge—we have wished for many things in the midst of our people, if we continue to urge these things eagerly, nothing will be able to trouble us.

The subject of excommunication is again being discussed in our Council.[5] Although in other respects they deal somewhat negligently with offenders, they will abandon the church if it irritates them—and this in spite of Christ's holy counsel, "If even salt is deprived of taste, wherewith can it be salted"?[6] Christ wants every sacrifice to be seasoned with salt, and Paul wants an unleavened Passover.[7] O, how wretched will the church's condition be if it is forbidden to produce yeast,[8] or if shameless people bring filth into the camp of Israel! So consider, my brother, what I recently wrote and sent via Thomas Platter.[9]

---

20 *unleavened*] Greek ἄζυμον

---

1 That is, *Bucer and others still attending the Diet at Augsburg. Bucer had indeed written to Zwingli as recently as 18th September—*ZW* XI, 138–143 (no. 1099); *BC* IV, 286–291 (no. 341).
2 The principal bone of contention remained, of course, the Eucharist.
3 On the term "Syngrammatarians" see 838, n. 1. Presumably *Cherusci* here refers to the Swabians, though the term could be used loosely of a number of ancient Germanic tribes.
4 Any number of letters from *Luther to *Melanchthon could be meant here: WA BR V contains some six for the month or so leading up to the date of this letter alone (pp. 559–561, 576–579, 584f., 617f., 621–624, 626–628). Still more mysterious is how any of these (or copies of them) might have come into Oecolampadius's possession.
5 See 1096, lines 1–73. The letter from the Zürich Council discussed in that letter had clearly not yet arrived in Basel.
6 Matthew 5:13.
7 Cf. 1 Corinthians 5:7 f.
8 Cf. Exodus 13:7.
9 Letter 1096 above. The humanist ropemaker and schoolmaster Thomas Platter (or 'Blat-

Farewell, and greet *Pellikan, *Leo, Werner,[10] Collin[11] and Ammann,[12] and especially Ulrich Funk[13] and your whole household.
Farewell again.
Basel, 25th September.

Original: Zürich, Staatsarchiv, E II 349, p. 112 (autograph). Copy: Zürich, Zentralbibliothek, Ms S 27, no. 15.

---

ter', c. 1499–1582) had been known to Oecolampadius since the time of the Disputation of Baden and had spent time in Basel in 1529, before settling there as bursar of the Cathedral School in the late summer of 1530. He is best known today for his autobiography, edited by Paul Wirth as *Geißhirt, Seiler, Professor, Buchdrucker, Rektor: Ein Lebensbild aus dem Jahrhundert der Reformation* (St. Gallen: Ottmar, 1999). See also Werner Meyer and Kaspar von Greyerz, eds, *Platteriana: Beiträge zum 500. Geburtstag des Thomas Platter (1499?–1582)* (Basel: Schwabe, 2002); BBKL VII, 730–732; VL 16 v, 97–107.

10 Werner Beyel: see 792, n. 1.
11 Rudolf Collin: see 734, n. 9.
12 Johann Jakob Ammann (1500–1573), the son of a prosperous cloth merchant in Zürich, who had been a pupil of Glarean and Beatus Rhenanus, and had returned to Zürich in 1526 as a Canon of the Grossmünster and Professor of Latin at its school. See Locher, ZR, 581 f.
13 See 958, n. 12. Funk will have spent time with Oecolampadius at the Colloquy of Marburg, which no doubt explains the warmth of the greeting here.

1106 Oecolampadius to Zwingli—Aarau, 27th September (1530)[1]

Greetings in Christ. I have obeyed you, and my Council has obeyed your Council.[2] I came to Aarau, was listened to most patiently, and set out the issue as you wished me to. I warned them that there was a great difference between a secular magistrate and the authority of the church—however necessary the former's office might be in his own eyes. And I do not doubt that, if they show you the little book recording my actions,[3] you will diligently act on what pertains to church practice, and will not need to be exhorted about it. I asked for three things: first, that in this matter they assent to the teaching of the Baslers, that is of Christ. Then, if this does not seem quite sound, that preachers should be sent from all the cities of the Christian Civic Union, along with other delegates, to consider everything in accordance with the word of God, so as to decide on something better. They could come together at Basel, because of the Strasbourg brothers. Finally, if we cannot achieve anything like this, that they should not ridicule the Baslers for pursuing for themselves what is in line with the word of God. | I did not ask for anything unworthy. If only one were answered with equal fairness!

I want soon to be more certain about what one might hope for. I fear the Berners will hate us still more, since they publicly asserted at a recent synod[4] that they had transferred their authority into the hands of the magistrate—a statement that seems to me more servile than is fitting for shepherds of the Christian flock. I do not know if Megander[5] failed to understand us properly, since he spoke to his people as if the affairs of the church could not be better appointed than they are now. So both he and Berchthold[6] should be advised to consider the matter more carefully. It seems to me that their legate Negelinus[7] shares our opinion, unless he is deceiving us.

---

1 *my Council*] *Basilensi*, '(by) the Basel (Council)'

---

1   This letter was written from a meeting of the Christian Civic Union at Aarau.
2   In the sense that Oecolampadius had represented his plans for church discipline at the Aarau meeting (see 1096, n. 8; *AGBR* IV, 598–602 (no. 641)), and that the Council of Basel had reacted to its Zürich counterpart (see 1096, n. 11) by again delaying the implementation of these plans.
3   This has survived, and is printed in *OeBA* II, 494–498 (no. 782).
4   This had met on 6th September.
5   See 652, n. 6.
6   *Haller.
7   Hans Franz Nägeli (1496/7–1579), a prominent member of the Bern Council, also a noted soldier and later (1540–1566) Mayor.

Certainly we would have settled the matter at Basel already if | your Council's letter had not arrived: on Sunday we had all preached very forcefully and with one voice that the Council should not constantly put off implementing what it had once decreed.[8] But if we are to gain allies in the matter, it will be useful for our progress to be halted for a while—even if the interests of our own church will be seriously ill-served by such a remedy.

We have not yet heard anything about what *Bucer discussed with *Melanchthon in Augsburg.[9]

Please write to me via our Mayor's son[10] what you would like me to do.

Greet your wife[11] together with your children, also *Leo and *Pellikan.
Farewell.
Aarau, 27th September.
Your Oecolampadius.
Master Bannerman,[12] a good man in my opinion, will tell you what has happened; I cannot know how well my proposal was received, since my Councillor[13] left the assembly with me.
To Huldrych Zwingli, his most beloved brother.

Original: Zürich, Staatsarchiv, E II 349, p. 124 (autograph). Copy: Zürich, Zentralbibliothek, Ms S 27, no. 18.

---

8   See 1096, n. 10 f.
9   After considerable pressing Bucer had been granted a personal meeting with Melanchthon at Augsburg in late August 1530, with a view to making another attempt to iron out the two parties' disagreements on the Eucharist. The day before this letter was written, indeed (26th September), Bucer had also seen Luther at Coburg.
10 Johann Rudolf Meyer (c. 1498–1564), son of Jakob Meyer zum Hirzen (see p. XVIII, n. 3).
11 Anna *Reinhart.
12 Hans Schwyzer (or 'Schweizer', c. 1464–1531), the Zürich army's standard-bearer, in which capacity he served from 1516 to his death in the Second Kappel War. He worked extensively for the guilds and Council in and around Zürich, and from 1527 particularly often for Zwingli.
13 Rudolf Frey: see 912, n. 5.

1123 Oecolampadius to Zwingli—Basel, 28th October (1530)

Greetings in Christ. It is now a long time since I received any letters from Zürich, my brother: Thomas Platter[1] had led me to hope that I would be given a copy to read of the letter you were about to send to the Strasbourg brothers;[2] but the courier left us in extreme haste. My curiosity is not making me particularly anxious about the other matters, however. Meanwhile I am being kept busy by what I consider to be the church's affairs. I wish we were able to meet, as we were asked to at Aarau.[3] For various reasons I was confident that this would be of benefit to the church. The brothers from other churches are also requesting this urgently, *Bucer especially—but he thinks Sturm[4] should be present, | since the man's views on ecclesiastical matters (as on everything else) are not to be sneezed at. Berchthold[5] would prefer us to assemble for a disputation at Solothurn; but I could not agree to this, since a meeting will be taking place in Basel at the same time, and they will have business there.[6] It is also still unclear how well we would be received or how easy it would be for us to be let in. Indeed I do not know whether the delegates to the forthcoming Basel assembly will include any preachers, given that the cities will be sending their best spokesmen.[7] And I fear that, at the moment, what we want may be less appropriate for those cities which are faced with so many difficulties and dangers—even though I do not see that anything should dissuade us from doing it. And so, since there is no certain prospect of this happening, the second most desirable case is that the delegates who are sent here should be given instructions to raise this matter of ours, and to urge either that our people should press on with it or that

---

1f. *from Zürich*] *isthinc* (literally, 'from there')

---

1 See 1102, n. 9.
2 This does not seem to have survived.
3 A reference to the meeting of the Christian Civic Union on 27th September 1531 (see no. 1106, lines 1–31), at which the leading evangelical theologians were recommended to meet with a view to seeking agreement on the matter of excommunication. This did not happen, and before long Oecolampadius had decided to content himself with trying to make the desired reforms in Basel alone (see Staehelin, *Lebenswerk*, 514–527; also lines 14–20 of this letter).
4 Jakob Sturm: see 534, n. 5.
5 *Haller.
6 The next meeting of the Christian Civic Union was scheduled to take place in Basel on 11th November (though it was subsequently postponed to 16th November). This assembly was, however, always intended to be primarily political in nature, with its main agenda item being relations with the German Protestant princes: see 834 (pp. 359–361), n. 3.
7 See n. 6. In the event no theologians from outside Basel did attend.

we should meet at some point to discuss it. Both the Mayor's son[8] and Platter himself have indicated that this is no different from your opinion. Other matters of state should be passed on to other people as far as is possible. We are hoping to deal chiefly with issues that pertain to Christ or the church.

I believe Berchthold has commended to you the cause of the people of Solothurn—that they should not be put in danger by Treger's men[9] and the catabaptists creeping up on them; and I myself am thinking of the dangers that exist when people have not cleaned out their ears so as to hear properly. This week certain seditious farmers and | townsmen were not far away from starting a war prematurely; but the Council's discretion calmed the growing disorder in time.[10]

Farewell.
Basel, 28th October.
Your Johannes Oecolampadius.
To Huldrych Zwingli, most faithful pastor of the Zürichers, his brother.

Original: Zürich, Staatsarchiv, E II 349, p. 152 (autograph). Copy: Zürich, Zentralbibliothek, Ms S 27, no. 68.

---

8   Johann Rudolf Meyer: see 1106, n. 10.
9   Konrad Treger (see 418, n. 12), who had continued to be an influential spokesman for conservative Catholicism.
10   On 21st October some citizens of Basel had joined a potentially violent uprising by the farmers of the Laufental against their overlord, the Bishop of Basel. Since the latter group were officially also citizens of Basel, it seems as though the Council was able fairly swiftly to assert its moral authority over them.

1130 Oecolampadius to Zwingli—Basel, 7th November (1530)

Greetings in Christ. I recently wrote to you, my brother, and now I ask you again, to see to it that delegates are sent to the next meeting who support our position on excommunication and who—rather than dissuading or discouraging them—would urge our magistracy to press on with the business that has been embarked upon.[1] For our church certainly has need of such a remedy, since the magistracy connives at many things and is extremely capricious when it comes to correcting them—with the result that I remain silent also about many other matters. We take in good part the fact that our plan did not please your brothers in the synod:[2] charity is too sacrosanct in our eyes for us to let them antagonize us in the slightest. We trust that they are similarly disposed towards us. Perhaps at some point the Lord will give people to understand that our unity is very great in other respects also.

Farewell.
Basel, 7th November.
Your Oecolampadius.
To Huldrych Zwingli, his beloved brother.

Original: Zürich, Staatsarchiv, E II 349, p. 77 (autograph). Copy: Zürich, Zentralbibliothek, Ms S 27, no. 88.

11f. *Perhaps ... also*] the sentence contains two occurrences of *aliquando* ('at some point', 'one day'); we translate only one, to avoid tautology

---

1 See 1123, n. 6f.
2 The Autumn Synod of the Zürich church which had met on 25th and 26th October had rejected Oecolampadius's proposals for excommunication.

1133   Oecolampadius to Zwingli—Basel, 19th November (1530)

Greetings in Christ. The representatives who were sent here from Strasbourg[1] are very worried that you will prove somewhat difficult when it comes to accepting things that might pertain to an agreement with *Luther.[2] For my part I do not think that, as long as proper respect is paid to the truth and to charity, there is any need to persuade you of anything. In my opinion *Bucer is the more astute of the two.[3] Initially, he proposes things that might be regarded as going against us. But before long he opens up our doctrine with such clarity as to leave nothing to be desired, and in so doing he shuts Satan's mouth. The statement that Christ's body and blood are truly present in the Lord's Supper might perhaps be rather hard for some people to accept; but he softens this by adding that this applies to the spirit and not the body.[4] He proceeds in the same prudent way with respect to other matters also, as when he asserts that the sacraments strengthen faith; and before long, by dint of his exposition, he closes the window on error. Therefore I trust that what he has brought before the public will not displease you. | You are familiar with Luther's obstinate nature: to overcome it, we had to modify our mode of speech with a view to benefitting so many thousands,[5] and to do this without prejudice to the truth. But I would prefer to hear your view, and—if possible—in person rather than by letter: this is something that those delegates desire most particularly.[6] Perhaps you could also fruitfully report on other matters relating to the good of the church. Therefore come soon, if you

---

1 Niklaus Kniebis and Konrad Joham, who represented Strasbourg at the Basel meeting of the Christian Civic Union that had begun on 16th November (see 1123, n. 6). Kniebis (d. 1552) and Joham (see 1028, n. 1) were often employed in negotiating with the Swiss, representing as they did Strasbourg's heavily pro-Zwinglian 'Zealots' party, rather than the more moderate, sometimes pro-Lutheran 'Politiques' centred around Jakob Sturm—see Thomas A. Brady, *Ruling Class, Regime and Reformation at Strasbourg* (Leiden: Brill, 1978), 236–245.
2 On 14th November Oecolampadius and Zwingli had been sent copies, for comment, of a document in which Bucer seeks to find a solution to the eucharistic debate that will reconcile both the Swiss evangelicals and the Lutherans. This is found in *ZW* XI, 236–247 (no. 1134) and *BC* V, 131–145 (no. 368).
3 It is not wholly clear to whom Bucer is being implicitly compared to: Luther, or maybe Capito?
4 This is not a *verbatim* quotation from no. 1134 (see n. 2), but it does fairly convey much of its gist.
5 A reference to the so-called sacramentarians' insistence on denying that Christ is present in the Eucharist, at least in bodily form.
6 Zwingli in fact composed a written response as early as 20th November (no. 1136 below), expressing unequivocal opposition to Bucer's document.

can; but if it is not appropriate to do so, respond in a way that acknowledges us to be true and equal, as befits those who love God. It is not for the ignorant to sit in judgement on idle gossip if those of us who can pronounce with more reliable judgement delay in doing so.

Moreover I have met your delegates and the Berners';[7] but there is scant hope. It would have been better if I had never gone to Aarau, and the business in Basel had been completed beforehand.[8] Now it depends, and will continue to depend, on the moral shortcomings of those who fear the advance of the kingdom of Christ here. Nevertheless we do not yet wholly despair. Sometimes the audacity of those who ask for things wins through.

The Strasbourg delegates are also warning against a copy of the agreement[9] being transcribed or shared with anyone, until such time as we can be more certain that Luther fully consents to it; | for if that man has persuaded his brothers by some word or other not to accept the fraternal agreement, or to agree to it only in part, then nothing honourable would come of publishing it in haste.

Farewell.
Basel, 19th November.
Greet your wife, along with your children and the brothers.

Original: Zürich, Staatsarchiv, E II 349, p. 31 (autograph). Copy: Zürich, Zentralbibliothek, Ms S 27, no. 94.

---

23 *as ... God*] *iuxta amantes* (literally, 'like lovers')   35 *fraternal agreement*] *fraternitatem* (literally, 'brotherhood')

7   At the ongoing meeting in Basel (see 1123, n. 6). Zürich was represented by Werner Beyel (see 792, n. 1) and the long-serving and influential mayor Diethelm Röist (1482–1544; see Wirz, "Familienschicksale", 271). Bern, however, sent only its treasurer Bernhard Tillmann (d. 1541/2).
8   Oecolampadius is still preoccupied with the issue of excommunication. He plainly feels that it has been a tactical error to raise the matter with other cities at Aarau (see 1123, n. 4), and that this has only impeded the introduction of a code of church discipline in Basel itself.
9   See n. 2.

1136 Heinrich Engelhard, *Leo Jud and Zwingli to Diethelm Röist and Werner Beyel—Zürich, 20th November 1530[1]

XI, 250 First of all, grace and peace from God. To you, dear lords, pious, honourable, wise, gracious and benevolent, we offer all respect.

When we read the attempt at mediation made by our dear brother Martin *Bucer,[2] in which we were placed at a great disadvantage and in which the truth was distorted and defiled, nothing saddened us more than these words: the true body of Christ and his true blood are truly present in the Lord's Supper, etc.[3] Not that the words "true" and "truly" displease us, as long as they are taken in their proper sense; but the ordinary person will understand the German as meaning that the true, essential body of Christ is truly and actually eaten in the Lord's Supper—as the Lutherans have always said. And the simple man will understand by this that Christ is in his nature and essence eaten with the mouth,[4] as *Luther has also taught—though he has sometimes moved away from this and said that it is the sacrament that is eaten physically. Since we have never made any statements about the holy sacrament that were not commonly made also by the ancients, | and since the

XI, 251 Lutherans—in the person of Luther—are so effectively defended in Bucer's letter even though they have said such outrageous and unchristian things in the course of the debate, we can easily see that this epistle[5] can, in the future, give rise only to quarrelling—for by now we are well aware of the Lutherans' tricks. And since the words "true" and "truly" in ordinary German are, as things now stand and as we have described them, understood by ordinary people to mean "in his essence, in his nature, personally present"; since Bucer could not accept the clear, simple words that we had put forward, namely, "we confess that Christ's body is present in the Eucharist, not

---

11 *in ... essence*] German *natürlich wesenlich*

---

1 Whilst not explicitly a communication between our two correspondents, this vernacular German letter is included because it is written and signed (also on behalf of Engelhard and Jud) in Zwingli's hand, and because line 73 below indicates that he meant it to be read by Oecolampadius. Heinrich Engelhard (d. 1551) was a close and long-standing colleague of Zwingli and Leo Jud, active as people's priest of Zürich's *Fraumünster* and a canon of its *Grossmünster*. On Röist see 1133, n. 7; on Beyel see 792, n. 1.
2 See 1133, n. 2.
3 This is an accurate quotation from Bucer's document: *wir ... bekennen, das der ware lyb und das war blůt Christi im abendmal warlich zůgegen seye* (no. 1134—p. 237, line 6f.).
4 The phrase translated "is eaten with the mouth" (*geessen werde mit dem mund*) is underlined for emphasis in the original manuscript.
5 Bucer's letter of mid-November (see 1133, n. 2).

LETTER 1136 401

25 physically or according to nature, but sacramentally, in the pure and spotless heart of a God-fearing Christian"; and since even Bucer approached us again with those Lutheran stratagems and errors: we are letting you know that we will stick absolutely to the previously agreed position,[6] which is contained in its entirety in the following words: Christ's body is present in the Lord's
30 Supper, not physically or according to nature, but sacramentally, in the pure and spotless heart of a God-fearing Christian. For you will see that backing down in a way that is detrimental to the truth will do no good, and that this murky mixture will serve the darkness rather than the light. *Capito holds to our opinion, and Bucer himself used to be more properly right-thinking than
35 he is now. Now, from the length of time this business has been dragged out we can tell that very many things have been discussed and attempted with Luther; but since in all this time he has not assented to anything that might promote the truth, but rather is ever more stubborn, it is not right for us to let the truth be damaged in any way for the sake of these quarrelsome people.
40 Nevertheless, because of the agreements and negotiations that are now before us, we concede that Bucer should send his piece—whatever is in it—to the Prince of Lüneburg,[7] so that other matters might be brought to a more peaceable pass; but if anyone claims that the truth has been obscured, or accuses us | of having abandoned it, we wish to reserve the right to explain   XI, 252
45 ourselves and to stand by the truth, even if the whole world condemns us for failing to pursue peace. For we can see the state of dark anxiety that comes from meddling. God, who has guided us for ever and ever, will lead us on.

You know, dear lords, that all of this is just a way of protecting Luther, not the truth, since—as we always see it—the majority of all Christians agrees
50 with us; and this will reveal itself more and more, day by day.

That matters in Augsburg now stand as they do is the work of those who are of our mind and not Luther's.[8] But although the unity we now see before us might be hindered by all this, you may well know that, now we have unity and division can again flee from our hearts, it would be a cold and fragile

---

25 *according to nature*] German *natürlich*   37–39 Our switch from the singular ("he", meaning Luther) to the plural ("quarrelsome people") is dictated by the German: *so er aber nit wyter nachgibt ... umb der kybigen luten willen*

---

6   That is to say, to the position on the Eucharist arrived at in discussions between Capito, Zwingli and Oecolampadius on 2nd and 3rd September 1530.
7   See 1133, n. 2. The eventual addressee of Bucer's letter was to be the Lutheran Duke Ernst of Lüneburg (1497–1546), known as 'the Confessor' for his religious zeal. He was well known to Luther, having resided in Wittenberg between 1512 and 1520, and having implemented the Reformation in his territories in 1527.
8   A Zwinglian/Oecolampadian view of the Eucharist was currently prevailing in Augsburg.

thing if it could be driven away by these disputes; so there is no major cause for concern, we think, that we will not be able, in the midst of these tensions, to maintain friendship with them on the basis of our common faith and unity—as the papists and Lutherans do when they move against the Turk.[9] For an agreement would be made to protect people, lands, common justice and the articles[10] of faith, etc. In this we are agreed. But if they did not wish to do this, we would see this as evidence of meddling and mistrust. So there will be no need to set their interests before those of the truth. When agreements were reached over controversies of doctrine, these were recorded in a short, pure summary.[11] Although Bucer's epistle is a private letter, not a negotiated agreement, it is nevertheless a verbal seed and a plant for fighting, and we can tolerate it being printed, albeit without prejudice to us.

Moreover, console our dear lords and citizens of Strasbourg[12] with things other than this pitifully won agreement, which cannot last. God is old, but not ill, and still has strength and help sufficient for us, etc.

| God be with you.

Given on the 20th day of November 1530, after the second hour after midday.

Let Oecolampadius read this also.[13]

In steadfast obedience to your honourable wisdom, Heinrich Engelhard, Leo Jud and Huldrych Zwingli.

The messenger was given two gulden and his lodgings were paid for.

All read on the advice and with the permission of the representatives.

To the lord Röist and the City Clerk of Zürich,[14] at present messengers at Basel, or, if they have left, Johannes Oecolampadius.

Original: Zürich, Staatsarchiv, E I 3.1, p. 68 (autograph).

---

65 *verbal ... fighting*] Zwingli coins the terms *wortensaat* and *kampfsvflanzen*, implying presumably that Bucer's letter is a potential catalyst for debate

---

9   The implication of this well-nigh impenetrable sentence is that, in the light of such agreements as had been made at the Colloquy of Marburg, Zwingli felt—however naïvely—that political and military collaboration between the Swiss and Lutheran parties remained possible in spite of their doctrinal differences.

10 Latin *summa*. In this context the term seems likely to refer to the Articles of Marburg which had been (largely) agreed in 1529—see 934, n. 2f.

11 *ein kurtze lutre summ*. A further reference, one assumes, to the Articles of Marburg.

12 Röist and Beyel were in Basel for a meeting of the Christian Civic Union, at which representatives from Strasbourg were also present—see 1123, n. 6 and 1133, n. 7.

13 See 1133, n. 2; also n. 1 above.

14 Beyel: see n. 1 above.

1139 Oecolampadius to Zwingli—Basel, 26th November 1530

Greetings in Christ, beloved brother. Fuchsstein[1] sends the attached letter. You will see what it is about—and I hope it is something very favourable! Your letter about the agreement with *Luther has also been delivered to me;[2] your advice in it does not seem imprudent. I did not, however, write anything about this matter to Strasbourg because, when the messenger came, their legates[3] had already left. Then no-one came for a while, and you had not instructed anyone to do so. So *Bucer's plan can go ahead, though with the danger that, unless all appearances deceive, Luther will think less of it than we do. We can tolerate this exposition of Bucer's[4] |—though it is opaque, it is clearer than the one which the Lutherans are about to approve, unless they depart from their normal way of thinking.

What news shall I write about? A domestic trouble, almost a tragic one: that father of mine, as you know, is set on marrying someone who would be a stepmother to me, and I will not be able to oppose this with force.[5] One has to take into account the good man's circumstances; but I also have to put up with the evils of public life.

---

1 *Fuchsstein*] Greek ὁ Ἀλωπηκολάθιος; ἀλώπηξ means 'fox' and λᾶας 'stone'   3 *with Luther*] Lutheri, a genitive   15f. *but ... life*] et haec sunt cum publicis malis (literally, 'and these things exist with public evils')

---

1 A more than usually convoluted pun (see note on line 1 above), on the name of Johann von Fuchsstein (d. 1535/6), an associate and one-time Chancellor of Duke *Ulrich von Württemberg. He played a leading role in negotiations between the latter and the Swiss evangelicals. The letter referred to here has not survived.
2 Letter 1136 (see 1133, n. 6).
3 See 1133, n. 1.
4 See 1133, n. 2.
5 Oecolampadius's parents had been living with him in Basel since 1527; his mother had died in early 1528, whereupon Oecolampadius himself had married (see 699 above) and had since fathered three children. Hence his concerns about the remarriage of his now blind father Johannes Husschin to Margarethe Lopinen will have included financial and inheritance-related ones. These were dealt with in two contracts printed in *OeBA* 11, 529–533 (nos 803, 805), dated 25th and 27th November 1530; but in fact Oecolampadius's father was to outlive him.

Farewell.
26th November 1530.
Johannes Oecolampadius.
To Huldrych Zwingli, his beloved brother in Christ.

Original: Zürich, Staatsarchiv, E II 349, p. 104 (autograph). Copy: Zürich, Zentralbibliothek, Ms S 27, no. 99.

1142 Oecolampadius to Zwingli—Basel, 3rd December (1530)

Greetings in Christ. My brother, I have written diligently to *Bucer about your thoughts concerning the agreement with *Luther.[1] I am returning your letter to you,[2] though it is worth keeping; for no-one can bind those slippery eels together carefully enough.

It would be good to put a bridle on the man who is making trouble for the church at Schaffhausen,[3] lest in his wilfulness he causes more trouble for others too. But if he engages us in battle, we shall not refuse him. Every law that applies to you is a law also for us, as far as our magistracy allows it—including the right to call people to our aid as and when we need to.

Our synod of fifty bishops and deacons has again unanimously asked the Council, through its deputies,[4] to give thought to revitalizing the churches through the remedy of excommunication. We are yet to receive an answer, even though the Council—as they did before—are saying that they will reply soon.[5]

Farewell.
Basel, 3rd December.
Johann Oecolampadius.
To Huldrych Zwingli, his beloved brother.

Original: Zürich, Staatsarchiv, E II 349, p. 156 (autograph). Copy: Zürich, Zentralbibliothek, Ms S 27, no. 105.

---

9 *call ... need to*] *evocandi etiam quo libet* (literally, 'of summoning also where we wish'). The precise context is unclear

---

1 This letter has been lost.
2 Letter 1136 (see 1133, n. 2). The address of this letter stipulates that, if it reaches Basel after the departure from the city of Beyel and Röist, it is to be delivered instead to Oecolampadius (ZW XI, 253, line 12 f.). Presumably this was done.
3 Benedikt Burgauer: see 774, n. 11. Following his move from St. Gallen to Schaffhausen in 1528 he was continuing to expound Lutheran doctrines, not least on the Eucharist.
4 Latin *deputatos*; the reference is to a three-man commission recently established by the Council to supervise school, university and also church affairs.
5 Soon after this the Council finally mandated Oecolampadius's plans for excommunication: in respect of the city's churches on 14th December, and of the churches of its surrounding countryside on 15th December. See *OeBA* 11, 536–541 (809 f.); *Basler Kirchenordnungen*, 46 f.; *AGBR* V, 60–68 (nos 76–80).

1164   Oecolampadius to Zwingli—Basel, 1st February (1531)

XI, 326 Greetings. Scarcely have I read *Bucer's letter,[1] and they are again asking for it to be sent on to you. So I am sending it. But I hope that we shall be able to discuss these things in person;[2] for, as I hear, the delegates of the Christian cities are bringing some of their preachers.

XI, 327 | Farewell, and if you can come yourself, do not send anyone else![3]   5
Basel, 1st February.
Oecolampadius.
To Huldrych Zwingli, his beloved brother.

Original: Zürich, Staatsarchiv, E II 349, p. 61 (autograph). Copy: Zürich, Zentralbibliothek, Ms S 28, no. 28.

---

1 Likely to be his letter to the Basel Mayor Jakob Meyer zum Hirzen (see p. XVIII, n. 3), dated 23rd January 1531 and dealing with two major current controversies: disputes over the Eucharist, and plans for an alliance with German Protestant princes. See BC v, 210–223 (no. 381); also (extracts) OeBA II, 554–556 (no. 820).
2 At the forthcoming meeting of the Christian Civic Union, due to begin on 12th February in Basel.
3 Zwingli was in fact represented by *Leo Jud.

1173 Oecolampadius to Zwingli—Basel, 25th February 1531

Greetings, my brother. *Leo has told you enough about what the brothers recently discussed, requested, permitted and approved here.[1] I think these things will not have displeased you, in that—for example—they are conducive to peace and public concord without being detrimental to Christ's glory. But if they do not seem that way to you, let me know when you can. Truly they seemed to me to be of great benefit to our churches. Does it not matter that there should be people who teach Christ after us, or where and how they are educated? Moreover, the fact that local synods will be attended by representatives of their closest neighbours will be of greater benefit to bishops, in their isolation, than is pleasing to certain people who will get wind of it.[2] So | I am convinced that you will neglect no opportunity to promote these things, in keeping with your care for all the churches. Now, please receive favourably what that man Heinrich (our Council's scribe) suggests to you;[3] for you know that we have to handle somewhat delicate matters, that we must be united in our duty, and that we must seek to bring about changes for the better.

Farewell.
Basel, in the year 1531, on the 25th day of the month of February.
Your Oecolampadius.
To Huldrych Zwingli, his beloved brother.
The Solothurners are insistent that our Markus[4] should preach there for a time; we are hardly keen to send him. If only you could send them a man through whom they might come to Christ!

Original: Zürich, Staatsarchiv, E II 349, p. 26 (autograph). Copy: Zürich, Zentralbibliothek, Ms S 28, no. 44.

---

1 It is difficult to place this sentence in context, but one suspects Oecolampadius has in mind—at least in part—the still vexed question of church discipline. See most recently 1142, n. 4f.
2 The Basel meeting had arranged for annual synod meetings of individual cities' churches to be attended by representatives from two or more neighbouring cities. Perhaps inevitably, this caused suspicion among clergymen who feared a growth in uniformity and a loss of local independence.
3 Heinrich Ryhiner: see above, p. 25, n. 102. It is not clear what "delicate matters" he was to discuss with Zwingli—perhaps the current moves to standardize, or at least align, church practices.
4 Markus Bertschi: see 367, n. 1. There is no evidence that he ever worked in Solothurn.

1184 Oecolampadius to Zwingli—Basel, 22nd March (1531)

Greetings in Christ. We have received your letter, my brother;[1] but the Mayor threw the scribe into prison because the letter had been opened, and the Small Council[2] wrote to him about it. Otherwise, the response of your fellow Zürichers pleased our Council,[3] and yours also pleased me. There is no time now to reply to the letter, nor is it necessary to do so, since we in no way disagree—we who do not depend on anyone from outside.[4]

Now I did not want you to be unaware of what happened to Andreas Osiander's letter,[5] which you sent some months ago, but which I sent on to Strasbourg with a letter of mine to *Bucer and *Capito. I gave it to a man from Rottweil who said that he was now living at Strasbourg,[6] and that he knew our two friends. I was speaking to Bucer about this matter when he was here,[7] and revealed the whole purpose of the letters. But he said that none had been delivered. So I do not know what duplicity or accident might have prevented this.

| I am now sending the son of the Provost of Embrach, whom Capito had recommended to me, back to his father, to be told what his father wants him to do.[8] The son would have liked to stay here, but was ordered on my advice

---

3 *Small Council*] *probuleutae*, from Greek προβουλεύται. In Athens, this term referred to the members of a smaller council that considered matters to be put to the larger general assembly

---

1 This letter has been lost.
2 Adelberg Meyer zum Pfeil: see 406, n. 2. The identity of the incarcerated scribe and of his supporters is unknown.
3 A letter written from the Zürich Council to their Basel counterparts on 17th March. Both Councils had responded negatively to invitations by the cities of the so-called Tetrapolitan Confession (Strasbourg, Konstanz, Memmingen and Lindau) to join the Schmalkaldic League.
4 A rather waspish reference to the Strasbourg reformers, whom Zwingli and Oecolampadius were at this point apt to view as dangerously close to the German Lutherans.
5 These details cannot be linked to any particular surviving letter. On Osiander see 642, n. 7.
6 This person has not been identified.
7 Most likely for the meeting of the Christian Civic Union in February
8 The (former) Provost of Embrach near Zürich is Heinrich Brennwald (see 552, n. 1), his son Hans Jakob Brennwald. A letter from Zwingli to Capito has been preserved in which the former recommends Hans Jakob—ZW X, 556f. (no. 1014a); CC II, 420 (no. 408), As a result of this the latter was apprenticed to the Strasbourg city clerk Peter Butz (hence the phrase "given over to letters", line 19). No subsequent commendation from Capito to Oecolampadius has survived.

LETTER 1184   409

to go to his father. I do not know whether the father wishes him again to be given over to letters; but if he is so minded, it might be more convenient and cheaper for the son to be educated there,⁹ rather than here.

Greet *Leo, and tell him that his *Annotations*¹⁰ have been delivered to me by Ambrosius.¹¹
Also greet your wife,¹² and the other brothers and teachers of the faith.
Basel, 22nd March.
Oecolampadius.
You will excuse the young man to his father.¹³
The Berners have again responded rather harshly.¹⁴
A messenger will be sent to Strasbourg today.
May the Lord direct all things favourably.
To Huldrych Zwingli, most faithful pastor of the Zürichers, his dearest brother.

Original: Zürich, Staatsarchiv, E II 349, p. 121 (autograph). Copy: Zürich, Zentralbibliothek, Ms S 28, no. 77.

---

9   Presumably in Strasbourg.
10 Leo Jud, *Annotatiuncula ad Philippenses ex ore Huldrichi Zwingli excepta* (Zürich: Froschauer, 1531).
11 Ambrosius Kettenacker: see 307, n. 1.
12 Anna *Reinhart.
13 Presumably Hans Jakob and Heinrich Brennwald (see n. 8).
14 This could refer to a number of communications from around this time; the precise one referred to cannot be identified.

1189   Oecolampadius to Zwingli—Basel, 28th March 1531

XI, 389 Greetings in Christ. My brother, I hardly need remind you again how great a man Jakob Ziegler[1] is, and how valuable he is to our churches. And so the Strasbourgers have sent here fifteen crowns' travel money for sending on to him. *Bucer is urging us—that is, the Baslers and the Zürichers—to supplement this with a substantial sum, so that he might be able to free himself from there and journey to us the more conveniently.[2] I have not yet properly found out how sound a plan this seems to your people. For what your

XI, 390 councillor Bernhard Meyer reported[3] | was in some ways ambiguous. So tell us something more certain about the matter, and if you Zürichers do decide to send some money, send it here, either to me or to the Mayor,[4] and the Baslers will also add their contribution. If it is too burdensome for your people to send some money, tell me that also—so that our people, along with the Strasbourgers, might either hold back our money or bring the good man on our own initiative. For we have agreed with his brother a limit of a few months, within which we are to bring him here to us. And the deadline is now approaching.

Farewell, my brother.
Basel, 28th March in the year 1531.
Oecolampadius.
To Huldrych Zwingli, most faithful pastor of the Zürich church, his most beloved brother.

Original: Zürich, Staatsarchiv, E II 349, p. 27 (autograph). Copy: Zürich, Zentralbibliothek, Ms S 28, no. 86.

---

1 The noted humanist, theologian, astronomer and geographer (c. 1490–1549), who was currently in Ferrara but wished to relocate to a Protestant area of Germany or Switzerland. His amanuensis Martin Richter had recently visited Strasbourg, Basel and Zürich, in part to discuss the matter. Ziegler did in fact reside in Strasbourg from 1531 to 1534, but increasing disillusionment with evangelicalism led him thereafter to move to Baden-Baden, Vienna and Passau. On him see *CoE* III, 474–476; *BBKL* XXVIII, 1549–1596.
2 Bucer had in fact made this case to Zwingli directly and in more detail, in a letter datable to 14th January 1531 and delivered by Martin Richter: see *ZW* XI, 298–309 (no. 1157), here 304–307; *BC* V, 190–202 (no. 377), here 198–201.
3 Presumably at the meeting of the Christian Civic Union in Zürich on 5th March. Bernhard Meyer zum Pfeil was the younger brother of the Mayor Adelberg (see 406, n. 2), and often engaged in diplomatic activities on Basel's behalf. On him see Füglister, *Handwerksregiment*, 312 f.
4 Adelberg Meyer zum Pfeil.

1217 Zwingli to Oecolampadius, Konrad Sam[1] and Others—Zürich, 4th June 1531

Huldrych Zwingli to Johannes Oecolampadius, Konrad Sam and the other brothers assembled at Ulm.

Grace and peace from the Lord. Hear how things stand with us: the legates from King François are in our midst,[2] trying to make peace among the Swiss. The Five Inner States do not want the word to be preached, as the King's legates[3] demanded of them. | For as soon as they arrived here, they asked our Council to find ways and means of bringing about peace. The Council replied as follows: if there were any hope of the Five Inner States allowing the preaching of the word of God and the preservation of that law of peace which guards against them persecuting our faith either in their lands or in ours, then we would be willing to discuss peace and reconciliation. To the things the legates put to them[4] as it were in secret, they replied (as I said) that they would not tolerate the preaching of the word of God as we would understand it (etc.), but that otherwise they would do anything that was required by the terms of the agreements and by the laws of peace.

Our soldiers have returned from the siege of Musso, apart from two thousand men.[5] Today, on 4th June, it is being reported that Musso's troops have sallied forth and toppled two war-machines that had been placed atop their high mountain,[6] causing no little (that is to say: severe) carnage on their side and on ours: for, away from the places where the machines fell, there were only a few men left in the fortress and still fewer in our camp. Having attacked the Duke's army in this way, they routed them in some rural

---

19 *high*] Greek ἠλίβατον

---

1 Konrad Sam (1483–1533) was the leading reformer at Ulm and a regular recipient of letters from Zwingli since 1526. He had been instrumental in bringing Oecolampadius, along with *Bucer and *Blarer, to the city, to assist in the implementation of the Reformation. On Sam see Specker/Weig, *Ulm*, 233–268; BBKL VIII, 1280 f.
2 François I of France.
3 Lambert Maigret and Louis Dangerant (or 'Boisrigault'), who had arrived in Zürich on 19th May.
4 The representatives of the Five Inner States.
5 A reference to the so-called Second Musso War of 1531–1532, involving the Marquess of Musso (see 809, n. 5), the Duke of Milan and representatives of the Protestant Swiss Cantons, which took place primarily in the Valtelline, then under the rule of the Bishop of Chur. A prime tactic of the Swiss troops was to besiege Musso's own castle. They were in action between 8th and 24th May, leaving behind only 2,000 men fighting in the pay of the Duke of Milan, Francesco Maria Sforza (1492–1535).
6 This had happened on 30th May.

place or other. Apart from this calamity, our army is safe. It appears | that the little monarch of Milan,[7] or at least his men, are acting dishonestly. The people of Chur are sending numerous and strong reinforcements forthwith. So keep watch; for we also are on guard. By the grace of God, our Council is undaunted and steadfast.

Greet all the brothers.
Zürich, 4th June 1531.

Original lost. In 1536 edition, fol. 199ʳ.

---

7 Duke Francesco Maria (see n. 5).

1228   Oecolampadius to Zwingli—Ulm,[1] 22nd June (1531)

Greetings, my brother. We rejoice that everything is going well over there. Here, truly everything is being done as our gracious God wishes—in the right way, indeed, but extremely slowly. We spent many days just preaching, both in the city and in the countryside, waiting for the elder Besserer:[2] he is last year's Mayor, a man | of authority on account of his years, and revered for his judgement and experience of affairs; without him the Council does nothing. But when we spoke about the most important things of all, which we have condensed into eighteen articles, all the priests and monks were summoned separately and asked to give their opinion on these, and to indicate to the Council whether they should be regarded as more conducive to Christianity or to heresy. The articles were adequately explained by *Bucer; but nearly all of them protested their inexperience in such matters—as if, up to now, they had not in fact been shunning our people, dishonouring them and tearing them apart with their reproofs as if they were heretics. Two of them above all wanted to appear to resist: the pastor of the church at Geislingen,[3] and the prior of the Dominican Order.[4] They raised no objection beyond the usual one, namely that the church and the Emperor's edict[5] did not allow the faith to be discussed in the presence of lay persons—this even though no-one had asked for a disputation to take place. Moreover they asserted that they in turn would put something in writing, but would submit this to the judgement of the universities in the first instance. The Mayor[6] rejected all their evasions in his opening speech, but these impudent and wretched men continued in vain to reach for the same weapons. Having listened to them for long enough, and with greater patience than they deserved, the Council (for this is what I am calling those who presided over this matter) | dismissed them and proceeded to have friendly discussions with us

---

22 *evasions*] *effugia* (literally, 'means of escape')

---

1   See 1217, n. 1.
2   Bernhard Besserer von Rohr (1471–1542), who was indeed over a substantial period the leading light in Ulm's politics.
3   Georg Osswald, parish priest of Geislingen since 1508, who was a long-standing opponent of the Reformation.
4   Leonhard Köllin: see BBKL IV, 261f.
5   An allusion to the so-called Code of Justinian (483–565), according to which spiritual matters were placed under the authority of the See of Rome.
6   Besserer (as n. 2).

about what needed to be done in the days that followed, and to report on these things to the Large Council. The latter then ratified everything without difficulty. And so the Mass has been banished from the city and sent into permanent exile.[7] Over the course of the last three days the images and altars have been removed from the city's principal parish church,[8] and from there the workmen involved are moving on to other churches. There is a consensus in favour of this ecclesiastical and civil settlement. The ceremonies will be very similar to the rites of our churches. The monks will be sent back to their orders, and schools for the study of languages will be established. Martin Frecht has been summoned from Heidelberg to lecture on the holy scriptures, of which he is a professor there.[9] He is from Ulm, piously erudite, highly eloquent, and by no means ignorant of the languages. In the countryside it is, for now, impossible to teach anything properly. For the people are very crude and superstitious, and have been robbed of their senses by wholly unlearned sacrificers. All of them have been examined, and very few have been found suitable for the ministry of the word—so that faithful labourers are to be called to the harvest from elsewhere.[10] And we ask you also, if you know of any excellent men who are free, to tell this to our Konrad,[11] who is in charge of recruiting such people. Certainly the Council leaves nothing to be desired, and for this reason there are high hopes that they will enter into an alliance with our Christian Civic Union—and without any need to repent first.[12] Bucer is now working on an apologia and the church ordinances; | when these have been approved,[13] we hope that we will be sent home. The Augsburgers, given that they are better off themselves, are

XI, 491

---

7   This decision was taken on 16th June.
8   A slightly strange designation for Ulm Minster.
9   Frecht (c. 1494–1556) was a long-time friend of both Oecolampadius and Bucer. He became the leading reformer in Ulm following the death of Sam (see 1217, n. 1), and was influential in seeking reconciliation between the Lutheran and Zwinglian factions. See Specker/Weig, *Ulm*, 269–321; OER II, 136 f.; TRE XI, 482–484; BBKL II, 115 f.
10   Cf. Matthew 9:38. Ulm, using the good offices of Strasbourg, began to seek appropriate evangelical pastors from the relevant Swiss cities as early as 12th August.
11   Most obviously Konrad Sam (see 1217, n. 1); though ZW (XI, 490, n. 10) suggests *Pellikan.
12   The thought is presumably that, having officially mandated the Reformation, Ulm will face no confessional hindrances in any attempt to forge a political alliance with the Swiss cities.
13   This was done formally on 6th August. The ordinances are edited in Emil Sehling et al., eds, *Die evangelischen Kirchenordnungen des XVI. Jahrhunderts*, 24 vols (Tübingen: Mohr Siebeck et al., 1902–2020), XVII, 124–162.

responding coolly. The Memmingers, who are also sending for us every day,[14] are fervently embracing the gospel.

*Blarer, Bucer, Sam and Frecht greet you and the members of your inner circle.

I believe the Strasbourgers have written about what was done at the meeting in Frankfurt.[15] The Saxons and the Austrians still detest us, but the Swabian towns do not.

Farewell.
Ulm, the 22nd day of June.
Johannes Oecolampadius.
To Huldrych Zwingli, most faithful teacher of the church at Zürich, his dearest brother. To Zürich.

Original: Zürich, Staatsarchiv, E II 349, p. 164 (autograph). Copy: Zürich, Zentralbibliothek, Ms S 28, no. 158.

---

62 *To*] German *gen*

---

14 Oecolampadius and Bucer did in fact go to Memmingen, for the same purpose for which they had visited Ulm, on 1st July.

15 The members of the Schmalkaldic League had met at Frankfurt between 3rd and 11th June—and had decided against pursuing an alliance with the Swiss.

1248 Oecolampadius to Zwingli—Basel, 20th July (1531)

Greetings, dearest brother. I have returned home in good order,[1] and have found everything in good order, with the sole exception of the unrest involving the Solothurners[2]—but I trust this will be settled peaceably.

I have recommended *Karlstadt[3] in more places than one. Everywhere the innocent and excellent man labours under such hostility that, in my patronage of him, I cannot commend him enough. Even the Schaffhauseners want some distinguished man or other, and their preachers, Erasmus[4] and Benedikt,[5] have chosen to appoint him—though only if they cannot find anyone else. So they will need to be admonished. Perhaps | he can find a position at Memmingen, if you write to Simprecht[6] and tell me when you know more. I would willingly write on his behalf to the Memmingen magistracy. The man has truly behaved most honourably towards me.

A little book by Michael Servetus is doing the rounds, *Concerning the Errors of the Trinity*.[7] This is full of blasphemy and impiety in my opinion—which, indeed, is, the view of the church—even if the book is being praised

---

1f. the repetition of 'in good order' is suggested by the original (*Salvus domum redii et salva reperi omnia*)

---

1   That is, from a tour that had taken in Ulm, Memmingen, Biberach and Konstanz.
2   A reference to the so-called *Galgenkrieg* ('Gallows War') of 1531–1532: Basel and Solothurn had been engaged in territorial conflicts for several decades, and the situation had been exacerbated by religious changes and uncertainties. The situation was eventually resolved without bloodshed, following the mediation of other Cantons.
3   He did eventually find a post, in Altstätten, in September 1531.
4   Erasmus Ritter: see 774, n. 12.
5   Benedikt Burgauer: see 774, n. 11. He and Ritter had been given the task of finding a theologian and teacher to minister in Schaffhausen, but were reluctant to appoint Karlstadt because of his perceived unreliability.
6   Simprecht Schenk (c. 1485–1559), a former Carthusian and convinced Zwinglian, who had been a leading preacher at Memmingen since 1525 and had attended the Disputation of Bern in 1528. He was later active at Kempten im Allgäu.
7   *De trinitatis erroribus libri septem* (Hagenau: Setzer, 1531). Oecolampadius's report on this volume to the Basel Council is printed in *OeBA* II, 631–634 (no. 896). Servetus (1511–1553) was an Aragonese nobleman who is most famous for being burnt at the stake by Calvin in Geneva—though his radical views had already attracted opposition from both Protestant and Catholic theologians. On Oecolampadius's initially friendly relationship with Servetus see Jeff Fisher, "Housing a Heretic: Johannes Oecolampadius (1482–1531) and the 'Pre-History' of the Servetus Affair", *Reformation and Renaissance Review* 20 (2018): 35–50. On Servetus see also *CoE* III, 242f.; *OER* IV, 48f.; *TRE* XXXI, 173–176; *BBKL* X, 740–749.

by certain Strasbourgers.[8] Perhaps it has reached you over there. If you do not have it, let me know, and I will take pains to share it with you.

At Ulm we have left *Blarer, a man of the greatest integrity, to watch over the Lord's work, so that the work that has begun might grow. *Bucer's apologia and church ordinances for Ulm will be printed,[9] with Blarer guarding against any mistakes. From these one can see that they have accepted the evangelical doctrines in the true spirit.

There are those who want the meeting at Konstanz to be brought forward,[10] since our neighbouring evangelical cities and the princes from further away are not daunted by our affairs. Only our internal wars displease them, and when we have resolved these, we shall be better able to win over our friends. But unless certain people are humiliated, there will be little appetite for peace.

Farewell.
Basel, 20th July.
Your Oecolampadius.
To Huldrych Zwingli, his beloved brother in Christ.

Original: Zürich, Staatsarchiv, E II 349, p. 107 (autograph).

---

8   Presumably a reference to Bucer, who seems not to have been as negatively disposed towards Servetus's work as Oecolampadius was.
9   See 1228, n. 13.
10 This was to involve the members of the Christian Civic Union, plus sympathetic German cities. It did not take place.

1253   Oecolampadius to Zwingli—Basel, 31st July (1531)

XI, 550   Greetings. I have read everything you wrote to the Mayor,[1] my brother. He in no way doubts Funk's honesty.[2] He is taking good care to prevent even the shortest delay with regard to the other matter he knows about.

We congratulate the people of Rapperswil, who have been freed from the assaults of their enemies;[3] and we pray for steadfastness, along with vigilance. For the souls of the Pharaohs, unless they have been drowned,[4] are continually contriving new ways of persecuting the pious.

Here we have reformed our theological teaching after the example of your church.[5] For the Professor of Hebrew will lecture on the Old Testament, and
XI, 551   the Professor of Greek on the New; | I myself will add to this a theological exegesis in very grammatically correct Latin; and Paul[6] will conclude with an epilogue in the vernacular. At the moment we are enjoying the dogs' days vacation.

After three days during which I shall be away from home, I shall return to Job,[7] as long as unforeseen business does not prevent it. For I would like your copies to be returned to you all at last.

Farewell.
Basel, the last day of July.
Johannes Oecolampadius.
Greet *Leo and *Pellikan and the other brothers.
To Huldrych Zwingli, his dearest brother.

Original: Zürich, Staatsarchiv, E II 349, p. 98 (autograph).

---

10 *the New*] we read the manuscript's *nova* as *novo*

---

1   Adelberg Meyer zum Pfeil: see 406, n. 2.
2   Ulrich Funk: see 958, n. 12. The context is that Funk has been sent to negotiate with Solothurn (see 1248, n. 2).
3   The Reformation had recently been established in Rapperswil (Canton St. Gallen).
4   Cf. Exodus 14:21–28.
5   These arrangements, based squarely on those of the Zürich *Prophezei*, came into force on 5th August.
6   Paul Phrygio: see 826, n. 2.
7   See 1074, lines 20–24 and n. 6f.

1259   Oecolampadius to Zwingli—Basel, 13th August (1531)

Greetings in Christ, my brother. Almost at the same time as I returned from Swabia,[1] our Grynaeus[2] also came home from England. There he found great favour in the eyes of the notables of the realm, who are most learned men, and removed from many hearts some of the hostility under which the gospel labours there. Hence it came about that he was both consulted about the matter of the King's marriage[3] and instructed to fish for our churches' views on it. I regard this as by no means inauspicious, and do not suspect that it springs from malevolent motives. For no-one has yet complained about our people's view of the matter—not even strangers. So we should by no means neglect this opportunity: if, perhaps, he was formerly deceived by the Pope[4] | and treated most shamefully by Luther,[5] he may start to look towards us—who neither neglect the truth in favour of flattery nor, in our zeal, are strangers to compassion. We may indeed end up winning no little favour, either by offering the King some suitable words of encouragement, or by giving him the answer he wants. But it would be good to reply unanimously. In short, the case is this: the King married his wife many years ago, though previously she had been married to his dead brother;[6] the Roman pontiff gave his assent to this, and pronounced the marriage lawful. They have been living together for some years, and have produced children, among them a daughter who is still alive;[7] the others have died. Now the King is afflicted by a crisis of conscience, and wants a divorce. As you will see, there are some

---

6 *fish for*] *expiscetur*—Oecolampadius likes describing Grynaeus's actions in terms that evoke fishing, presumably on the basis of his forename being Simon. See also 1285, line 2
21 *crisis*] *erynnide* (literally, 'fury'). The term is also used in respect of Brenz in 418, line 3

---

1 There is no record of Oecolampadius having been in Swabia since his letter of 20th July (1248, n. 1).
2 See p. XVIII, n. 4.
3 Henry VIII and his desire to obtain a divorce from Catherine of Aragon. On Grynaeus's involvement in this episode see Wolfgang Simon, "Der Basler Gräzist Simon Grynaeus und die Eheangelegenheit König Heinrichs VIII. im Spiegel der Bucerbriefe", in Christ-von Wedel, *Basel*, 203–213.
4 Presumably be a reference to Julius II (1503–1513), who had granted Henry and Catherine permission to marry in 1503, though they did not in fact do so until 1509.
5 Most obviously in the *Contra Henricum Regem Angliae* (Wittenberg: Rhau-Grunenberg, 1522; Leu/Weidmann A130)—ed. *WA* X/2, 180–222; trans. *AE* LXI, 3–61. This is a rejoinder to the "King's Book", *Assertio septem sacramentorum adversus Martinum Lutherum* (London: Pynson, 1522)—ed. Pierre Fraenkel (Münster: Aschendorff, 1992).
6 Henry VII's eldest son Arthur, Prince of Wales (1486–1502).
7 The future Mary I.

illustrious universities⁸ which support him in this opinion, stating that his marriage is in every way nefarious, and openly asserting that the Pope has erred. But the King is said to be languishing with love for a certain woman who is not lowly born, and whom he would marry if he divorced his first wife.⁹ You, my brother, with your most perspicacious intellect, will be able to see plainly what is right, what is wrong, and what advice and consolation is required to deal with the royal mind gently but without flattery. I see two stumbling blocks. The first is that, if he keeps his wife, so many universities will pour scorn on the opinions that he is now busily reinforcing with the aid of so many arguments and reasons. The second stumbling block (just as big), is this: if he divorces her, how is it that he has been treating her as his lawful wife for so many years? No prudent or pious person approves of what the Pope has done. For we are not Mesopotamians or Persians, and so for our part we do not see the example set by the King as an offence against public | honour—whatever Christians pretend about it. But now that (having been deceived) they have been living together in good faith for many years and have overcome any scandal by their long period of cohabitation, it does not seem to be a good precedent to separate those who have been joined together for such a long time; for legitimate companionship creates a union between a man and a woman. And so I am reluctant to agree with the universities. Now, I am bearing in mind the underlying argument of those who say that the law found in Leviticus about not taking one's brother's widow¹⁰ is not just ceremonial or judicial, and hence is binding and—of necessity—to be observed to the letter. But I have not yet been persuaded by this, because Moses brought the law to the Hebrews, whereas now, if we believe, charity and the law of nature are sufficient for us; and because we read that many saints have done similar things without incurring disgrace. Two sisters fell to Jacob's lot.¹¹ He did not abandon his first wife, not (I would think) because this would set an example of inconstancy, but because he would not fight against a divine and natural law. For Jacob was more chaste in God's eyes

---

34 *Mesopotamians*] *Osdroeni*, that is, the inhabitants of Osroene (*sic*), an ancient kingdom centred on Edessa in Upper Mesopotamia   51f. *more chaste ... men*] *multis monogamis castis coram deo castior*

---

8   These now included Oxford, Cambridge, the Sorbonne, Orléans, Toulouse, Bologna and Padua.
9   Anne Boleyn, who was a daughter of the Earl of Wiltshire and maid of honour to Queen Catherine.
10 Leviticus 18:16.
11 Jacob married both of Laban's daughters, first Leah and then (while Leah was still alive) Rachel: see Genesis 29:15–30.

than many chastely monogamous men. We know that the kingdom of God is among us.[12] See therefore, my brother, how one might respond in the most circumspect of ways. I know that you are overwhelmed by work, but I pray that it will not vex you to weigh the evidence in this matter and to send us your opinion.[13] For there are many reasons to avoid offending so great a King; but let him see above all how sincere our conduct is—even though, as I suspect, we will not answer as he wants us to, but as we ought to.

Farewell.
Basel, 13th August.
Johannes Oecolampadius.
To Huldrych Zwingli, his brother.

Original: Zürich, Staatsarchiv, E II 349, p. 102 (autograph).

---

12   Luke 17:21.
13   Zwingli did "send his opinion", namely that the marriage "ought to be dissolved; but ... the queen should be put away honourably, and still used as a queen; and the marriage should only be dissolved for the future, without illegitimating the issue begotten in it" (taken from George Burnet's summary of a now lost letter to Simon Grynaeus, dated 17th August 1531—see *zw* XI, 579).

751 Oecolampadius to Zwingli—Basel, 18th August (1531)[1]

Greetings in Christ. I suspect, my brother, that at the forthcoming meetings your people will respond brusquely, and will no longer listen.[2] This part of the plan I myself neither approve nor disapprove of. I would prefer, however, for this initiative not to come from you or another preacher, lest—if things turn out badly—our sacred ministry be blamed for it. For I fear there are some people who wish to pass off any sort of zeal as virtue, as if they had been taught to do this by us; they do this to provoke hostility in us—in us, for whom they are never fervent enough. And it is true that they are less fervent than we would like them to be. But that zeal of theirs is hardly the fervour of the Holy Spirit, but rather comes from a world like this one. Until now our people have been listening well enough, and are to be commended for their patience. There is a danger that they will get a bad name if they refuse to listen to others who are also longing for peace. Let us not rush. The fatal hour—and a dreadful one for the enemies of God—is upon us.[3] You understand what I would like. We should attend to the gospel.

Farewell,
Basel, 18th August.
Your Oecolampadius.
To Huldrych Zwingli, his dearest brother.

Original: Zürich, Staatsarchiv, E II 349, p. 99 (autograph).

---

1 We agree with Staehelin (*OeBA* II, 642f.) and zw XI, 578—against zw IX, 531f.—that this letter is much more likely to have been written in 1531, rather than 1528. Its content and tone reflect the conflicts and tensions in Switzerland (and between our two correspondents) in the months leading up to the Second Kappel War. We have not used its suggested alternative number "1261b", however (zw XI, 578), since this strikes us as potentially confusing.

2 A reference to the Confederate Diet at Bremgarten, which began on 22nd August. Attempts to broker peace between Zürich and Bern on the one side, and the Five Inner States on the other, had been thwarted not least by Zwingli's intransigence; and on 18th August, the date of this letter, the Basel Council wrote to its Zürich counterpart urging it strongly to reconsider its rejection of the latest set of peace terms.

3 Given that Zwingli was to die in battle within two months of the sending of this letter, Oecolampadius's fears were tragically justified.

1263 Oecolampadius to Zwingli—Basel, 20th August (1531)

Greetings. We have read, dearest brother, what seems to you to be right in the matter of the King of England;[1] and we gladly support it, understanding clearly how you have weighed everything with unsullied judgement. Nor do we doubt that the future fruit of this labour will not be a matter for regret. And so we thank you. We will keep a transcribed copy, which we can even send back to you if you wish. My opinion does not differ from yours in any way, except with regard to wording; but you can read it yourself, for it is not very long, just like a letter.

Up to now *Bucer and *Capito have taken a different view;[2] but I hope that, having read your words, they will not dissent from us |—even though their opinions have been infected, especially the one that is not a little troublesome for the illustrious church.[3] They would let the King commit bigamy. But it would not be right in this regard for us to listen more to Mohammed than to Christ.

Now as to an agreement with the Five Inner States:[4] although certain people have high hopes, I (would that I were wrong!) am pessimistic about it unless the other side either humbles itself or is humbled.

I wrote a letter about three days ago to be delivered by your scribe;[5] but I could not find him when urged to by those who had written the response from our Council to yours. Nevertheless I am now sending this note, which is untimely and unnecessary; but do heed the worries of a friend, even if they are useless.

---

1 See 1259, especially n. 13.
2 The Strasbourg reformers were opposed to Henry's marriage being dissolved, encouraging him instead to engage in bigamy.
3 Oecolampadius is presumably thinking of the ubiquitous and impenetrable problem of the Eucharist, on which Strasbourg's opinion was particularly "infected" by Luther's, but which remained problematic for the Catholic party also.
4 See 751 (p. 422), n. 2. Oecolampadius's pessimism was justified: on the day this letter was sent, the Inner States had entered into negotiations with Austria, and on the following day (22nd August) their representatives did not even appear at the Diet of Bremgarten.
5 Letter 751.

Farewell, together with your wife and the brothers.
20th August.
Oecolampadius.
To Huldrych Zwingli, most faithful pastor of the church at Zürich, his beloved brother.

Original: Zürich, Staatsarchiv, E II 349, p. 97 (autograph).

1264 Oecolampadius to Zwingli—Basel, 24th August (1531)

Greetings. The Ulmers have written to me also, my Huldrych, in the same vein—as I believe—that they wrote to you.[1] Theirs is doubtless an honest request, since they are conscientious and pious men; and they are altogether worthy of our granting their wish, which is to help them appear better prepared at the forthcoming meeting. Perhaps they might make use of our published works at appropriate points. Show them that you are open to everyone's need—that is to say, that you are the same person that we described you as being when we were discussing things with them there. If there is anything of this kind, let me know.[2] Hide nothing from me.

Farewell.
Basel, 24th August.
Your Oecolampadius.
To Huldrych Zwingli, his beloved brother.

Original: Zürich, Staatsarchiv, E II 349, p. 105 (autograph).

---

1 In letter 1261a (zw XI, 576f.), sent via Strasbourg to both Zwingli and Oecolampadius, the Mayor and Council of Ulm specifically request the aid and advice of the two theologians at and in advance of the forthcoming Diet of Speyer.

2 It is unclear what Oecolampadius means here; but much of the letter, which seems to have been written in haste, is either laconic or elliptical.

1285 Oecolampadius to Zwingli—Basel, 30th September (1531)

XI, 629

Greetings, my Huldrych. Grynaeus, disturbed as he is by the efforts being made in the case of the King of the Britons, has also been fishing for the Wittenbergers' opinions.[1] I wished you also to be party to their deliberations.[2] I am not in the least bit satisfied. God numbers this kind of marriage among the abominations of the Canaanites.[3] And the thing he hates about it seems to conflict with the laws of nature. I am not in any way deterred by God's domestic arrangements in the case of the fathers.[4] Wisely Philipp is now per-

XI, 629

mitting such things to those kings | of ours whose pious spirit is so obviously in favour of the law.[5] I do not wish for many more such men. I have discussed many matters with *Bucer. He is asking us not to urge them to assert more than in good conscience they can. He is not concerned with faith here, but rather with honesty—a virtue which, if practised by both parties, in no way undermines love.

For the rest, you will be able to hear from others—or to guess without needing to be told—how things stand here with regard to the firmness of the alliance and the sanctity of religion.

---

2 *has ... for*] expiscetur (see note on 1259, line 6)   7 *domestic arrangements*] Greek οἰκονομίας

---

1   In the matter of Henry VIII's desire to divorce Catherine of Aragon (see 1259 and 1263). On Grynaeus see p. XVIII, n. 4.
2   Philipp *Melanchthon had responded to Grynaeus's request on 23rd August (*MBW* V, 175–183 (no. 1180)) and Luther on 3rd September (*WA BR* VI, 178–188 (no. 1861)). Grynaeus forwarded copies of their letters to Oecolampadius, Bucer and Zwingli; but the latter had plainly not received his, or had not responded to it.
3   In this context, Oecolampadius can only be referring to bigamy, which Bucer and Capito (see 1263, lines 9–12), as well as the Wittenbergers, recommended to Henry VIII. Essentially he is conflating, or confusing, two passages from Deuteronomy—17:17 ("neither shall he [Israel's King] multiply wives to himself, that his heart turn not away: neither shall he greatly multiply to himself silver and gold"); and the list of "abhorrent practices" associated with the Canaanites in 18:9–14. This list, however, is concerned with various forms of sorcery and divination, rather than with sexual morality.
4   A reference to the polygamy practised by such figures as Esau, Jacob, David and Solomon.
5   This is surely meant sarcastically: statements by Melanchthon (not least in his letter of 23rd August—see n. 2) had given fresh hope to the long unhappily married *Philipp of Hesse that he too might in time be given theological sanction to marry Margarethe von der Saale (1522–1566) before the death of his wife Christine of Saxony (1505–1549)—that is, in effect, to commit bigamy. In the event he did not marry Margarethe until March 1540. On the theological and spiritual issues involved see Wolfgang Breul, "'Mit gutem Gewissen'. Zum religiösen Hintergrund der Doppelehe Landgraf Philipps", *Zeitschrift für Kirchengeschichte* 119 (2008): 149–177.

Think of me in the same way always—as yours in all things.
Farewell.
Basel, the last day of September.
Oecolampadius.
To Huldrych Zwingli, most faithful teacher of the Zürichers, his brother.

Original: Zürich, Staatsarchiv, E II 349, p. 51 (autograph).

Bibliography

1   Sixteenth-Century Publications

Anon., *Warhaftige handlung der disputation im obern Baden des D. Hanß Fabri, Jo. Ecken unnd irs gewaltigen anhangs gegen Joan Ecolampadio und den dienern des worts* (Strasbourg: Köpfel, 1526)

Anon., *Was Missbreuch im wychbischofflichem ampt* (Basel: Wolff, 1527)

Eliyahu Baḥur, *Sēfer haharkabah: Hebraicae Grammaticae studiosis in primis necessarium* (Basel: Froben, 1525)

Theodor Billican and Urbanus Rhegius, *De verbis coenae dominicae et opinionum uarietate, Theobaldi Billicani ad Urbanum Regium Epistola. Responsio Urbani Regij ad eundem* (Wittenberg: Klug and Augsburg: Ruff, 1526)

Johannes Brenz, *Syngramma clarissimorum qui Halae Suevorum convenerunt virorum super verbis Coenae Dominicae ad Johannem Oecolampadium* (Augsburg: Ruff, 1526)

Johannes Brenz, *Epistola de verbis Domini, "Hoc est Corpus meum", opinionem quorundam de Eucharistia refellens* (Hagenau: Setzer, 1526)

Johannes Brenz, *Genotigter und fremdt eingetragener schrifft auch mislichens dewtens der wort des abentmals Christi. Syngramma* (Wittenberg: Klug, 1526)

Johannes Brenz, *In D. Johannis Evangelion, Johannis Brentij Exegesis, per autorem diligenter reuisa, ac multis in locis locupletata* (Hagenau: Setzer, 1528)

Johannes Brenz, *Der Prediger Solomo, mit hoch gegründter auß heyliger Göttlicher geschrifft außlegung durch D. Johann Brentzen Prediger zu Schwebischen Hall* (Nürnberg: Peypus, 1528)

Martin Bucer, *Apologia qua fidei suae atque doctrinae, circa Christi Coenam* (Strasbourg: Herwagen, 1526)

Martin Bucer, *Praefatio M. Buceri in quartum tomum postillae Lutheranae continens summam doctrinae Christi, eiusdem Epistola explicans locum 1. Corinth. 10, Epistola M. Lutheri ad Iohannem Hervagium superiora criminans, Responsio ad hanc M. Buceri, item ad Pomeranum satisfactio de versione Psalterii* (Strasbourg: Herwagen, 1527)

Martin Bucer, *Enarrationum in Evangelion Matthaei, quibus verbotim simul, et quae Marcus atque Lucas cum hoc habent communia explicantur* (Strasbourg: Herwagen, 1527)

Martin Bucer, *Vergleichung D. Luthers, vnd seins gegentheyls, vom Abentmal Christi: Dialogus, das ist, eyn freundtlich gespräch* (Strasbourg: Köpfel, 1528)

Martin Bucer, *Tzephaniah, quem Sophoniam vulgo vocant, prophetarum epitomographus ad ebraicum veritatem versus, & commentario explanatus* (Strasbourg: Herwagen, 1528)

Martin Bucer, *Epistola apologetica ad sincerioris Christianismi sectatores per Frisiam orientalem, & alias inferioris Germaniae regiones, in qua evangelii Christi vere studiosi, non qui se falsò evangelicos iactant, iis defenduntur criminibus, quae in illos Erasmi Roterodami epistola ad Vulturium Neocomum, intendit* (Strasbourg: Schaefer and Apronianus, 1530)

Johannes Bugenhagen, *Eyn Sendbrieff widder den newen yrrthumb bey dem Sacrament des leybs und blutts unsers herrn Jhesu Christi* (Wittenberg: Klug, 1525)

Johannes Bugenhagen, *Publica de Sacramento corporis et sanguinis Christi, ex Christi institutione confessio* (Wittenberg: Lufft, 1528)

Wolfgang Capito, *Epistola W. Fabritii Capitonis ad Hulderichum Zwinglium, quam ab Helvetiis forte interceptam* (Strasbourg: Köpfel, 1526)

Wolfgang Capito, *Der nüwen Zeytung heymlichen wunderbarlichen Offenbarung, so D. Hans Fabri jungst ufftriben und Wolffgang Capitons Brieff gefälschet hat, Bericht und Erklerung* (Strasbourg: Köpfel, 1526)

Wolfgang Capito, *In Hoseam Prophetam V.F. Capitonis Commentarius* (Strasbourg: Herwagen, 1528)

Martin Cellarius, *De operibus Dei* (Strasbourg: Herwagen, 1527)

Jacobus Ceporinus, *Pindari Lyricorumque omnium principis, Olympia, Pythia, Nemea, Isthmia* (Basel: Cratander, 1526)

Jodocus Clichtoveus, *De Sacramento Eucharistiae, contra Oecolampadium, opusculum* (Cologne: Quentell, 1527)

Peter Cyro et al., *Handlung oder Acta gehaltner Disputation zuo Bernn in Üchtland* (Zürich: Froschauer, 1528)

Johannes Eck, *Enchiridion Locorum Communium adversus Lutheranos* (Cologne: Quentell, 1525)

Johannes Eck, *Ad invictissimum Poloniae regem Sigismundum, de sacrificio missae contra Lutheranos libri tres* (Augsburg: Ruff, 1526)

Johannes Eck, *Antwurt uf das ketzerbuochlein Ambrosi Blarers* (Cologne: Quentell, 1526)

Johannes Eck, *Verlegung der disputation zu Bern mit grund götlicher geschrifft* (Augsburg: Weißenhorn, 1528)

Johannes Eck, *Ein Sentbrieue an ein frum Eidgnoszschafft, betreffendt die ketzerische disputation Frantz Kolben des außgeloffen münchs, vnnd B. Hallers des verlognen predicanten zuo Bern. Ein anndrer brieue an Ulrich Zwingli. Der drit brieue, an Cunrat Rotenacker zu Ulm* (Basel: s.n., 1528)

Erasmus of Rotterdam, *Moriae Encomium Erasmi Roterodami Declamatio* (Strasbourg: Schürer, 1512)

Erasmus of Rotterdam, *Adagiorum chiliades tres ac centuriae fere totidem* (Basel: Froben, 1513)

Erasmus of Rotterdam, ed., *Novum instrumentum omne* (Basel: Froben, 1516)

Erasmus of Rotterdam, *Enchiridion militis Christiani, saluberrimis præceptis refertum* (Basel: Froben, 1518)

Erasmus of Rotterdam, *Apologia adversus debacchationem Petri Sutoris* (Basel: Froben, 1525)

Erasmus of Rotterdam, *Lingua* (Basel: Froben, 1525)

Erasmus of Rotterdam, *Epistolae tres, nuper in apertum prolatae. Ad christianissimum regem Franciscum. Ad parlamentum. Ad theologicam facultatem* (s.l.: s.n., 1526)

Erasmus of Rotterdam, *Expostulatio admodum pia et Christiana ad quendam amicum* (Cologne: Quentell, 1526)

Erasmus of Rotterdam, *Hyperaspistes Diatribae Adversus Seruum Arbitrium Martini Lutheri*, 2 vols (Basel: Froben, 1526–1527)

Erasmus of Rotterdam, *Opus epistolarum Des. Erasmi Roterodami, per autorem diligenter recognitum et adiectis innumeris novis, fere ad trientem auctum* (Basel: Froben, 1529)

Erasmus of Rotterdam, *Contra quosdam, qui de falso iactant evangelicos, Epistola* (Cologne: Gymnich, 1530)

Johann Faber, *Ein warlich underrichtung wie es zu Zürch by dem Zwinglin uff den nünundzwentzigsten tag des monats Januarii nest verschinen ergangen sey* (Strasbourg: Grüninger, 1523)

Johann Faber, *Christenliche beweisung über sechs artickel des unchristlichen Ulrich Zwinglins* (Tübingen: Morhart, 1526)

Johann Faber, *Epistola ad Ulricum Zvinglium de futura disputatione Baden in Ergau die XVI. Maii habenda* (Tübingen: Morhart, 1526)

Johann Faber, *Newe Zeittung vnd heimliche wunderbarliche Offenbarung etlicher sachen vnd handlungen, so sich vf dem tag der zw Baden in Ergöw gehalten worden* (Würzburg: Müller, 1526)

Guillaume Farel, *Gulielmus Farellus christianis lectoribus* (Basel: Cratander, 1524)

Johannes Fischer (attrib.), *Epistola Quibus praeiudiciis in Baden Helvetiorum sit disputatum* (Strasbourg: Prüß, 1526)

John Fisher, *De veritate corporis et sanguinis Christi in eucharistia, adversus Iohannem Oecolampadium* (Cologne: Quentell, 1527)

Erhard Hegenwald (attrib.), *Handlung der versamlung in der loeblichen statt Zürich vff den xxix tag Jenners vonn wegen des heyligen Euangelij* (Zürich: Froschauer, 1523)

Henry VIII of England, *Assertio septem sacramentorum adversus Martinum Lutherum* (London: Pynson, 1522)

Hesychius of Jerusalem, *In Leviticum libri septem* (Basel: Cratander, 1527)

Balthasar Hubmaier, *Axiomata quae Baldazar Pacimontanus, Musca, magistraliter examinanda proposuit* (Zürich: Froschauer, 1524)

Balthasar Hubmaier, *Von dem christlichen Tauff der gläubigen* (Mikulov: Froschauer, 1526)

Balthasar Hubmaier, *Ein gesprech der Predicanten zu Basel und Balthasaren Huebmörs von Fridberg von dem Khindertauf* (Mikulov: Sorg, 1526)

Leo Jud, *Annotatiuncula ad Philippenses ex ore Huldrichi Zwingli excepta* (Zürich: Froschauer, 1531)

Andreas (Bodenstein von) Karlstadt, *Erklerung, wie Carlstat sein lere von dem hochwirdigen Sacrament und andere achtet vnd geacht haben wil* (Wittenberg: Rhau-Grunenberg, 1525)

Martin Luther, *De captivitate Bablylonica ecclesiae* (Wittenberg: Lotter, 1520)

Martin Luther, *Contra Henricum Regem Angliae* (Wittenberg: Rhau-Grunenberg, 1522)

Martin Luther, *Sermon von dem Sacrament des leibs und bluts Christi widder die Schwarmgeister* (Wittenberg: Lufft, 1526)

Martin Luther, *Das diese wort Christi "Das ist mein leib. Etce" noch fest stehen widder die Schwermgeister* (Wittenberg: Lotter, 1527)

Martin Luther, *Vom abendmal Christi Bekendnis* (Wittenberg: Lotter, 1528)

Martin Luther, *Die bekentnus Martini Luthers auff den ytzigen angestelten Reichstag zu Augspurgk eynzulegen: In siebenzehen Artickel verfasset* (Erfurt: Sachse, 1530)

Martin Luther (attrib.), *Auff das schreyen etlicher Papisten, uber die sibenzehen Artickel. Antwort Martini Lutthers* (Wittenberg: Maler, 1530)

Martin Luther, *Vermanung an die geistlichen versamlet auff dem Reichstag zu Augsburg* (Wittenberg: Lufft, 1530)

Augustinus Marius, *Eyngelegte Schrifft auff Anmutung eynes christenlichen Rats der loblichen Statt Basel, das Opfer der Meß belangent* (Basel: Faber Emmeus, 1528)

Augustinus Marius, *Wyderauffhebbung der warhafftigenn grunden, so Augustinus Marius Thuompredicant zuo Basel zuo beweisen, das die Meß eyn opfer sey, eynem Ersamen Radt doselbst vberantwort hat. Wider die falsche widerlegung Joannis Oecolampadij* (Basel: Faber Emmeus, 1528)

Philipp Melanchthon, *Unterricht der Visitatorn an die Pfarhern yn Kurfurstenthum zu Sachssen* (Wittenberg: Schirlentz, 1528)

Philipp Melanchthon, *Epistola ad Iohannem Oecolampadium, de Coena Domini* (Hagenau: Setzer, 1529)

Philipp Melanchthon, *Sentenciae veterum aliquot scriptorum, de Coena Domini bona fide recitatae* (Wittenberg: Klug, 1530)

Thomas Murner, *Die disputacion vor den xij orten einer loblichen eidtgenoschafft* (Luzern: Murner, 1526)

Thomas Murner, *Der Lutherischen evangelischen Kirchen Dieb und Ketzer Kalender* (Luzern: Murner, 1527)

Thomas Murner, *Ein worhafftigs verantwurten der doctors und herren, die zuo Baden uff die disputacion gewesen sind* (Luzern: Murner, 1527)

Thomas Murner et al., *Appellation vnd beruoff Johannis Ecken, Johannis Fabri vnd Thome Murner für die xij. Ort einer loblichen Eydtgnoschaft wider die vermeinte disputation zu Bern gehalten* (Luzern: Murner, 1527)

Johannes Oecolampadius, *Graecae literarum dragmata* (Basel: Cratander, 1521)

Johannes Oecolampadius, *Quod non sit onerosa Christianis confessio* (Basel: Cratander, 1521)

Johannes Oecolampadius, *Divi Ioannis Chrysostomi, Archiepiscopi Constantinopolitani, in totum Genesōs librum Homiliæ Sexagintasex a Ioanne Oecolampadio hoc anno versae* (Basel: Cratander, 1523)

Johannes Oecolampadius, *De genuina verborum Domini "Hoc est corpus meum" iuxta vetustissimos auctores expositione liber* (Strasbourg: Knobloch, 1525)

Johannes Oecolampadius, *Jacobi Latomi professoris de Confessione secreta. Joannis Oecolampadii Elleboron, pro eodem Jacobo Latomo* (Basel: Cratander, 1525)

Johannes Oecolampadius, *Vom Sacrament der Dancksagung. Von dem waren nateurlichen verstand der worten Christi: Das ist mein leib, nach der gar alten Lerer erklärung* (Zürich: Froschauer, 1525)

Johannes Oecolampadius, *In Iesaiam Prophetam Hypomnematōn, Hoc Est, Commentariorum, Libri VI* (Basel: Cratander, 1525)

Johannes Oecolampadius, *Apologetica Ioannis Oecolampadii: De dignitate eucharistiae Sermones duo; Ad Theobaldum Billicanum, quinam in uerbis Caenae alienum sensum inferant; Ad ecclesiastas Suevos Antisyngramma* (Zürich: Froschauer, 1526)

Johannes Oecolampadius, *Ad Billibaldum Pyrkaimerum de re Eucharistiae responsio* (Zürich: Frochauer, 1526)

Johannes Oecolampadius, *Billiche antwurt auf D. Martin Luthers bericht des Sacraments, halbsampt einem kurtzen begriff auff etlicher Prediger in Schwaben schrifft die wort des Herren nachtmals antreffend* (Basel: Wolff, 1526)

Johannes Oecolampadius, *Form und gstalt wie der kinder tauff, Des herren Nachtmal, und der Krancken heymsuchung jetz zu Basel von etlichen Predicanten gehalten werden* (Basel: Cratander, 1526)

Johannes Oecolampadius, *Von Anruoffung der heylgen, Joannis Ecolampadij, uff ettlicher widersecher, und zuovorab Doctor Fabri, unnutz gegenwurfflich tandt, andtwort* (Basel: Petri, 1526)

Johannes Oecolampadius, *Ad Bilibaldum Pykraimerum de Eucharistia, Responsio posterior* (Basel: Cratander, 1527)

Johannes Oecolampadius, *Das der miszverstand D. Martin Luthers, uff die ewigbstendige wort ('Das ist mein leib') nit beston mag* (Basel: Cratander, 1527)

Johannes Oecolampadius, *Das erst Capitel des propheten Jeheskiels uszgelegt durch Joannem Ecolampadium. Von dem ampt der Oberen vnd der vnderthonen* (Basel: Cratander, 1527)

Johannes Oecolampadius, *In Postremos Tres Prophetas, Nempe Haggæum, Zachariam, & Malachiam, Commentarius* (Basel: Cratander, 1527)

Johannes Oecolampadius, *Theophylacti Arciepiscopi Bulgariæ, in quatuor Euangelia enarrationes, diligenter recognitæ Ioanne Oecolampadio Interprete* (Basel: Cratander, 1527)

Johannes Oecolampadius, *Underrichtung von dem Widertauff, von der Oberkeit, und von dem Eyd, auff Carlins N. widertauffers artickel. Antwort auff Balthasar Hübmeiers büchlein wider der Predicanten gespräch zuo Basel, von dem kindertauff* (Basel: Cratander, 1527)

Johannes Oecolampadius, *Divi Cyrilli Archiepiscopi Alexandrini Opera, in tres partita Tomos: in quibus habes non pauca antehac Latinis non exhibita* (Basel: Cratander, 1528)

Johannes Oecolampadius, *Repulsio apologiae sacrificii eucharistiae, quam Pelargus factionis S. Dominici, senatui Basilien obtulit* (Basel: Wolff, 1528)

Johannes Oecolampadius, *Ableynung der schützred der opffermesz, die Pelargus Predigersorden eim ersamen radt zuo Basel soll han* (Basel: Bebel, 1528)

Johannes Oecolampadius, *In Danielem prophetam Ioannis Oecolampadij libri duo, omnigena et abstrusiore cum Hebraeorum tum Graecorum scriptorum doctrina referti* (Basel: Wolff and Bebel, 1530)

Johannes Oecolampadius, *Quid de Eucharistia veteres tum Græci, tum Latini senserint, Dialogus, in quo Epistolae Philippi Melanchthonis et Joannis Oecolampadij insertae* (Basel: Froben, 1530)

Johannes Oecolampadius, *Ioannis Oecolampadii Doctoris Undecunque Doctissimi In Librum Iob Exegemata* (Basel: Petri, 1532)

Johannes Oecolampadius and Huldrych Zwingli, *Uber D. Martin Luters Buch, Bekentnuß genant, zwo antwurten Joannis Ecolampadii und Huldrychen Zwinglis* (Zurich: Froschauer, 1528)

Johannes Oecolampadius and Huldrych Zwingli, *DD. Ioannis Oecolampadii et Huldrichi Zuinglii Epistolarum Libri Quatuor. Ad Haec Scriptorum Io. Oecolampadii & Huldrichi Zuinglii Purgatio. Utriusque vita & obitus, Simone Grynaeo, Wolfgango Capitone, & Osvaldo Myconio autoribus. Epigrammata Hebraica, Græca, Latina* (Basel: Platter, 1536)

Johannes Oecolampadius et al., *Ein Christliche vnd ernstlich antwurt der Prediger des Euangelij zu Basel, warumb sy die Mess einen grüwel gescholten habind. Uff erforschung vnd gheyß des Ersamen Radts daselbst gebennhe* (Zürich: Froschauer, 1527)

Johannes Oecolampadius et al., *Widerlegung der falschen gründt, so Augustinus Marius, Thumbpredicant zu Basel, zu verwenen das die Meß ein Opffer sey, eynen Ersamen Radt doselbig überantwort hat* (Basel: Wolff, 1528)

Johannes Oecolampadius et al., *Die predigen, so von frömbden predicanten, die allenthalb här zuo Bernn uff dem gespräch oder disputation gewesen, beschehen sind* (Zürich: Froschauer, 1528)

Andreas Osiander, *Epistolae duae, una Hulderichi Zvinglii ad Andream Osiandrum, qua cum eo expostulat, quod novum illud de Eucharistia dogma hactenus reiecerit, ac temere impugnarit. Altere Andreae Osiandri ad eundem Hulderichum Zuinglium, Apologetica* (Nürnberg: Petreius, 1527)

Andreas Osiander (attrib.), *Was zu Marpurgk in Hessen vom Abendtmal und andern strittigen artickeln gehandelt vnd vergleicht sey worden. Andreas Osiander. Martinus Luther* (Nürnberg: Petreius, 1529)

Ambrosius Pelargus, *Apologia Sacrificii Eucharistiae: rationem exigente inclyto senatu Basiliensi* (Basel: Faber Emmeus, 1528)

Ambrosius Pelargus, *Hyperaspismus Sive Propugnatio Apologiae, quo Eucharistiae sacrificium ab Oecolampadiana calumnia strenue asseritur* (Basel: Faber Emmeus, 1529)

Vincenzo Pimpinella, *Oratio Augustae habitae XII. Kal. Julii MDXXX* (Augsburg: Weyssenhorn, 1530)

Sante Pagnini, ed. and trans., *Biblia habes in hoc libro prudens lector Sanctes Pagninus post incunabula Luther, Tyndale, Calvine* (Lyon: Du Ry, 1528)

Willibald Pirckheimer, *De vera Christi carne et vero eius sanguine, ad Ioan. Oecolampadium responsio* (Nürnberg: Petreius, 1526)

Willibald Pirckheimer, *De vera Christi carne et vero eius sanguine, aduersus conuicia Ioannis, qui sibi Oecolampadij nomen indidit, responsio secunda* (Nürnberg: Petreius, 1527)

Willibald Pirckheimer, *De convitiis Monachi illius, qui graecolatine Caecolampadius germanice vero Ausschin nuncupatur, ad Eleutherum suum epistola suum epistola* (Nürnberg: Petreius, 1527)

Plutarch, *Plutarchi Opuscula LXXXXII* (Venice: Aldus Manutius, 1509)

Plutarch, *Plutarchi Chaeronei philosophi clarissimi opuscula, quae quidam extant omnia* (Basel: Cratander, 1530)

Wolfgang Ruß, *Eyn Sermon in welcher der mensch gereytzt vnd ermant wirt zu lieb der Evangelischen lere* (Zwickau: Gastel and Nürnberg: Höltzel, 1523)

Wolfgang Ruß, *Ein gütte nutzliche predig von dem rechtten guetten glauben* (Augsburg: Nadler and Munich: Schobser, 1523)

Wolfgang Ruß, *Ein Sermon von underscheyd der werck der menschen* (Strasbourg: Schürer, 1524)

Caspar Schwenckfeld, *Ein anwysunge das die opinion der leyplichen gegenwertigheyt vnsers Herrens Jesu Christi im Brote oder vnder der gestalt deß Brot gericht ist Widder den ynhalt der gantzen schrifft* (Zürich: Froschauer, 1528)

Michael Servetus, *De trinitatis erroribus libri septem* (Hagenau: Setzer, 1531)

Johannes Sichard, *Divi Clementis Recognitionum Libri X. ad Jacobum Fratrem Domini, Rufino Torano Aquileiense Interprete* (Basel: Bebel, 1526)

Stephan Stör et al., *Von der Priester Ee disputation, durch Stephanum Stör vnd andern vyl Christlichen brüdern* (Basel: Cratander, 1524)

Jakob Strauß, *Wider den unmilten Irrthum Maister Ulrichs Zwinglins, so er verneünet die warhafftig gegenwürtigkeit dess allerhailligsten leybs und bluots Christi im Sacrament* (Augsburg: Ramminger, 1526)

Jakob Strauß, *Das der leyb Christi und seyn heiliges Blut im Sakrament gegenwertig sey, richtige erklerung auff das new büchlein D. Johannes Haußscheyn, diesem zuwider* (Augsburg: Steiner, 1527)

Konrad Treger, *Ad reverendum in Christo P. et illustrem principem Fabianum de monte Falcone Lansanensem episcopum paradoxa* (Strasbourg: Grüninger, 1524)

Huldrych Zwingli, *Von erkiesen vnd fryheit der spysen. Von ergernus und verboesrung* (Zürich: Froschauer, 1522)

Huldrych Zwingli, *Epistola ad Erasmum Fabricium de actis legationis ad Tigurinos missae diebus 7. 8. 9. aprilis 1522* (Zürich: Froschauer, 1522)

Huldrych Zwingli, *Apologeticus archeteles adpellatus, quo respondetur Paraenesi, a Re. Do. Constantiensi ad senatum praepositurae Tigurinae quem Capiulum vocant missae* (Zürich: Froschauer, 1522)

Huldrych Zwingli, *Von Clarhayt und gewüsse oder unbetrogliche des worts gottes* (s.l., s.n., 1522)

Huldrych Zwingli, *Ußlegen und gruond der schlußreden oder articklen* (Zürich: Froschauer, 1523)

Huldrych Zwingli, *Ad Matthaeum Alberum Rutlingensium ecclesiasten, de coena dominica* (Zürich: Froschauer, 1525)

Huldrych Zwingli, *Subsidium sive coronis de Eucharistia* (Zürich: Froschauer, 1525)

Huldrych Zwingli, *Vom dem touff, vom widertouff und vom kindertouff* (Zürich: Hager, 1525)

Huldrych Zwingli, *Uber Doctor Balthasars Touffbüchlin waarhaffte gründte antwurt* (Zürich: Froschauer, 1525)

Huldrych Zwingli, *Ad Ioannis Bugenhagii Pomerani Epistolam responsio* (Zürich: Froschauer, 1525)

Huldrych Zwingli, *Ein klare Underrichtung vom Nachtmal Christi* (Zürich: Froschauer, 1526)

Huldrych Zwingli, *Ein kurtze gschrifft warnende von dem unchristlichen fürnemen Fabers, der nit allein die newlich getruckten bücher etlicher gleerten, sunder ouch daz nüw testament ze brennen sich vndernimpt* (Zürich: Froschauer, 1526)

Huldrych Zwingli, *De peccato originali declaratio ad Urbanum Rhegium* (Zürich: Froschauer, 1526)

Huldrych Zwingli, *Amica exegesis, id est, Expositio eucharistiae negocii, ad Martinum Lutherum* (Zürich: Froschauer, 1527)

Huldrych Zwingli, *Antwurt über Doctor Straussen Büchlin, das Nachtmal Christi betreffende* (Zürich: Froschauer, 1527)

Huldrych Zwingli, *Das dise wort Jesu Christi: Das ist min lychnam, der für üch hinggeben wirt, ewigklich den alten eynigen sinn haben werdend* (Zürich: Froschauer, 1527)

Huldrych Zwingli, *Farrago Annotationum in Genesim* (Zürich: Froschauer, 1527)

Huldrych Zwingli, *Früntlich verglimpfung und ableynung über die predig des treffenlichen Martini Luthers wider die Schwermer* (Zürich: Froschauer, 1527)
Huldrych Zwingli, *In catabaptistarum strophas elenchus* (Zürich: Froschauer, 1527)
Huldrych Zwingli, *Complanatio Isaiae prophetae foetura prima cum apologia* (Zürich: Froschauer, 1529)
Huldrych Zwingli, *Ad Carolum Romanorum imperatorem Germaniae comitia Augustae celebrantem, fidei ratio* (Zürich: Froschauer, 1530)
Huldrych Zwingli et al., trans., *Die gantze Bibel der Ebraischen und Griechischen waarheyt nach auff das aller trewlichest verteütschet* (Zürich: Froschauer, 1530)
See also under Oecolampadius and Osiander.

2   Secondary Literature Referred to in Abbreviated Form

Abendmahlsschriften
Florence Becher-Häusermann and Peter Litwan, eds, *Johannes Oekolampad, Ausgewählte Abendmahlsschriften* (Leipzig: Evangelische Verlagsanstalt, 2023)

Baker, "Church Discipline"
J. Wayne Baker, "Church Discipline or Civil Punishment: On the Origins of the Reformed Schism, 1528–1531", *Andrews University Seminary Studies* 23 (1985), 3–18

Barge, *Bodenstein*
Hermann Barge, *Andreas Bodenstein von Karlstadt*, 2 vols (Leipzig: Brandstetter, 1905)

Barge, *Strauß*
Hermann Barge, *Jakob Strauß: Ein Kämpfer für das Evangelium in Tirol, Thüringen und Süddeutschland* (Leipzig: Heinsius, 1937)

Basler Kirchenordnungen
Emidio Campi and Philipp Wälchli, eds, *Basler Kirchenordnungen 1528–1675* (Zürich: Theologischer Verlag, 2012)

Birkner, *Marius*
Joachim Birkner, *Augustinus Marius, Weihbischof von Freising, Basel und Würzburg (1485–1543): Ein Lebensbild* (Münster: Aschendorff, 1930)

Blair, "Erasmus"
Ann Blair, "Erasmus and his Amanuenses", *Erasmus Studies* 39 (2019): 22–49

Borel-Girard, *Farel*
Gustave Borel-Girard et al., *Guillaume Farel: 1489–1565. Biographie nouvelle écrite d'après les documents originaux* (Neuchâtel: Delachaux & Niestlé, 1930)

Brenz, *Werke*
Martin Brecht et al., eds, *Johannes Brenz, Werke: Studienausgabe*, 5 vols (Tübingen: Mohr, 1970–1986)

Bromiley
G.W. Bromiley, trans., *Zwingli and Bullinger* (London: SCM Press, 1953)

Brooks, *Cranmer*
Peter Brooks, *Thomas Cranmer's Doctrine of the Eucharist. An Essay in Historical Development* (London: Macmillan, 1965)

Bryner, "St. Gallen"
Erich Bryner, "The Reformation in St. Gallen and Appenzell", in Burnett/Campi, *Companion*, 238–263

Bryner, "Schaffhausen"
Erich Bryner, "The Reformation in Schaffhausen", in Burnett/Campi, *Companion*, 216–237

Bucer, *Schriften*
Robert Stupperich et al., eds, *Martin Bucer: Deutsche Schriften*, 18 vols (Gütersloh: Mohn, 1960–2015)

Burnett, "Basel"
Amy Nelson Burnett, "The Reformation in Basel", in Burnett/Campi, *Companion*, 170–215

Burnett, "Exegesis"
Amy Nelson Burnett, "Exegesis and Eucharist: Unexplored Connections between Calvin and Oecolampadius", in Selderhuis, *Calvinus*, 245–260

Burnett, *Karlstadt*
Amy Nelson Burnett, *Karlstadt and the Origins of the Eucharistic Controversy: A Study in the Circulation of Ideas* (New York: Oxford University Press, 2011)

Burnett, *Pamphlets*
Amy Nelson Burnett, trans., *The Eucharistic Pamphlets of Andreas Bodenstein von Karlstadt* (Kirksville, MO: Truman State University Press, 2011)

Burnett/Campi, *Companion*
Amy Nelson Burnett and Emidio Campi, eds, *A Companion to the Swiss Reformation* (Leiden: Brill, 2016)

Cahill, *Philipp*
Richard Andrew Cahill, *Philipp of Hesse and the Reformation* (Mainz: von Zabern, 2001)

Campi, "Zurich"
Emidio Campi, "The Reformation in Zurich", in Burnett/Campi, *Companion*, 57–125

Christ-von Wedel, *Basel*
Christine Christ-von Wedel, ed., *Basel als Zentrum des geistigen Austauschs in der frühen Reformationszeit* (Tübingen: Mohr Siebeck, 2014)

Christ-von Wedel, "Erasmus"
Christine Christ-von Wedel, "Erasmus und die Zürcher Reformatoren", in eadem and Urs B. Leu, eds, *Erasmus in Zürich. Eine verschwiegene Autorität* (Zürich: Neue Zürcher Zeitung, 2007), 77–165

Feller, *Bern*
Richard Feller, *Geschichte Berns*, 2nd edn, 4 vols (Bern: Lang, 1974)

FGR
Adolf Laube, ed., *Flugschriften gegen die Reformation (1525–1530)*, 2 vols (Berlin: Akademie, 2000)

Fichtner, *Ferdinand*
Paula Sutter Fichtner, *Ferdinand I of Austria: The Politics of Dynasticism in the Age of the Reformation* (New York: Columbia University Press, 1982)

Frasch, *Ulrich*
Ein Mann namens Ulrich: Württembergs verehrter und gehaßter Herzog in seiner Zeit (Leinfelden-Echterdingen: DRW, 1991)

Friedrich, "Streit"
Reinhold Friedrich, "Ein Streit um Worte? Bucers Position in der Abendmahlsfrage im Jahr 1530", in Simon, *Bucer*, 49–65

Goeters, *Hätzer*
J.F. Gerhard Goeters, *Ludwig Hätzer (ca. 1500 bis 1529): Spiritualist und Antitrinitarier: eine Randfigur der frühen Täuferbewegung* (Gütersloh: Bertelsmann, 1957)

Greengrass, "Epistolary Reformation"
Mark Greengrass, "An 'Epistolary Reformation': the Role and Significance of Letters in the First Century of the Protestant Reformation", in Ulinka Rublack, ed., *The Oxford Handbook of the Protestant Reformation* (Oxford: Oxford University Press, 2006), 431–456

Greschat, *Bucer*
Martin Greschat, *Martin Bucer: Ein Reformator und seine Zeit* (Munich: Beck, 1990)

Henny, "Failed Reformations"
Sundar Henny, "Failed Reformations", in Burnett/Campi, *Companion*, 264–290

Hinke
William John Hinke, trans., *Ulrich Zwingli: "On Providence" and Other Essays* (Durham, NC: Labyrinth, 1922)

Hobbs, "Pluriformity"
R. Gerald Hobbs, "Pluriformity of Early Reformation Scriptural Interpretation", in Saebø, *Hebrew Bible*, 452–511

Hubmaier, *Schriften*
Gunnar Westin and Torsten Bergsten, eds, *Balthasar Hubmaier: Schriften* (Gütersloh: Mohn, 1962)

Jackson
Samuel Macaulay Jackson, ed./trans., *Huldrych Zwingli: Early Writings* (New York: Putnam, 1912)

Jung, "Abendmahlsstreit"
Martin H. Jung, "Abendmahlsstreit: Brenz und Oekolampad", *BWK* 100 (2000): 143–161

Kittelson, *Capito*
James M. Kittelson, *Wolfgang Capito: from Humanist to Reformer* (Leiden: Brill, 1975)

Kuhr, "Calvin"
Olaf Kuhr, "Calvin and Basel: The Significance of Oecolampadius and the Basel Discipline Ordinance for the Institution of Ecclesiastical Reform in Geneva", *Scottish Bulletin of Evangelical Theology* 16 (1998): 19–33

Krieger/Lienhard, *Bucer*
Christian Krieger and Marc Lienhard, eds, *Martin Bucer and Sixteenth Century Europe. Actes du Colloque de Strasbourg (28–31 Août 1991)*, 2 vols (Leiden: Brill, 1993)

Moeller, *Blarer*
Bernd Moeller, ed., *Der Konstanzer Reformator Ambrosius Blarer (1492–1562)* (Konstanz: Thorbecke, 1964)

Northway, "Reception"
Eric W. Northway, "The Reception of the Fathers and Eucharistic Theology in Johannes Oecolampadius (1482–1531), with Special Reference to the *Adversus Haereses* of Irenaeus of Lyons" (Ph.D diss., University of Durham, 2008)

Osiander, *Gesamtausgabe*
Gerhard Müller and Gottfried Seebaß, eds, *Andreas Osiander d. Ä.: Gesamtausgabe*, 10 vols (Gütersloh: Mohn, 1975–1997)

Pipkin/Furcha
H. Wayne Pipkin and Edward J. Furcha, trans., *Huldrych Zwingli: Selected Writings*, 2 vols (Allison Park, PA: Pickwick, 1984)

Potter, *Documents*
G.R. Potter, ed./trans., *Huldrych Zwingli* (Documents of Modern History, London: Arnold, 1978)

Roth, *Reformation*
Paul Roth, *Die Reformation in Basel*, 2 vols (Basel: Helbing & Lichtenhahn, 1936–1943)

Roussel, "De Strasbourg à Bâle"
Bernard Roussel, "De Strasbourg à Bâle et Zurich: une école rhénane d'exégèse (ca. 1525–ca. 1540)", *Revue d'Histoire et de Philosophie Religieuses* 68/1 (1988): 19–39

Saebø, *Hebrew Bible*
Magne Saebø, ed., *Hebrew Bible/Old Testament. The History of its Interpretation. Vol. II: From the Renaissance to the Enlightenment* (Göttingen: Vandenhoeck & Ruprecht), 2008

Schindler, ZR
Alfred Schindler et al., eds, *Die Zürcher Reformation—Ausstrahlungen und Rückwirkungen* (Bern: Lang, 2001)

Selderhuis, *Calvinus*
Herman J. Selderhuis, ed., *Calvinus Pastor Ecclesiae. Papers of the Eleventh International Congress on Calvin Research* (Göttingen: Vandenhoeck & Ruprecht, 2016)

SI
Friedrich Staub et al., eds, *Schweizerisches Idiotikon: Wörterbuch der schweizerdeutschen Sprache*, 16 vols to date (Frauenfeld: Huber, 1881–2012)

Simon, *Billican*
Horst Simon, *Humanismus und Konfession: Theobald Billican, Leben und Werk* (Berlin: De Gruyter, 1980)

Simon, *Bucer*
Wolfgang Simon, ed., *Martin Bucer zwischen den Reichstagen von Augsburg (1530) und Regensburg (1532). Beiträge zu einer Geographie, Theologie und Prosopographie der Reformation* (Tübingen: Mohr Siebeck, 2011)

Spaans, "Faces"
Joke Spaans, "Faces of the Reformation", *Church History and Religious Culture* 97 (2017): 408–451

Specker/Weig, *Ulm*
Hans Eugen Specker and Gebhard Weig, eds, *Die Einführung der Reformation in Ulm: Geschichte eines Bürgerentscheids* (Stuttgart: Kohlhammer, 1981)

Staehelin, "Väterübersetzungen"
Ernst Staehelin, "Die Väterübersetzungen Oekolampads", *Schweizerische Theologische Zeitschrift* 23 (1916): 57–91

Stephens, *Theology*
W.P. Stephens, *The Theology of Huldrych Zwingli* (Oxford: Oxford University Press, 1986)

Vasella, *Schlegel*
Oskar Vasella, *Abt Theodul Schlegel von Chur und seine Zeit, 1515–1529: Kritische Studien über Religion und Politik in der Zeit der Reformation* (Fribourg: Universitätsverlag, 1954)

Weigelt, *Tradition*
Horst Weigelt, *Spiritualistische Tradition im Protestantismus. Die Geschichte des Schwenckfeldertums in Schlesien* (Berlin: De Gruyter, 1973)

Williams, "Cellarius"
R.L. Williams, "Martin Cellarius and the Reformation in Strasburg", *Journal of Ecclesiastical History* 32 (1981): 477–497

Windhorst, *Taufverständis*
Christof Windhorst, *Täuferisches Taufverständnis: Balthasar Hubmaiers Lehre zwischen traditioneller und reformatorischer Theologie* (Leiden: Brill, 1976)

Wirz, "Familienschicksale"
Hans Georg Wirz, "Zürcher Familienschicksale im Zeitalter Zwinglis", *Zwingliana* 6 (1935–1938): 194–222, 242–271, 470–499, 537–574

Zschoch, *Existenz*
Hellmut Zschoch, *Reformatorische Existenz und konfessionelle Identität: Urbanus Rhegius als evangelischer Theologe in den Jahren 1520 bis 1530* (Tübingen: Mohr, 1995)

Zschoch, "Zwingli und Augsburg"
Hellmut Zschoch, "Zwingli und Augsburg", in Schindler, ZR, 163–176

Zürcher, *Pellikan*
Christoph Zürcher, *Konrad Pellikans Wirken in Zürich 1526–1556* (Zürich: Theologischer Verlag, 1975)

3 Other Secondary Literature

Sabine Arend, "Martin Bucer und die Ordnung der Reformation in Ulm 1531", in Simon, *Bucer*, 63–82

Matthieu Arnold, "Straßburg und Basel im Briefwechsel Martin Bucers (1524–1531)", in Christ-von Wedel, *Basel*, 179–191

Cornelis Augustijn, "Erasmus und die Reformation in der Schweiz", *BZGA* 86 (1986): 27–42

Cornelis Augustijn, *Erasmus: His Life, Works, and Influence* (Toronto: University of Toronto Press, 1991)

Irena Backus, *The Disputations of Baden, 1526 and Berne, 1528: Neutralizing the Early Church* (Princeton, NJ: Princeton Theological Seminary, 1993)

Ulrich Bächtold, "Ulrich von Hutten und Zwingli", *Zwingliana* 18,1–2 (1989): 12–19

Jürgen Bärsch, ed., *Johannes Eck (1486–1543): Scholastiker, Humanist, Kontroverstheologe* (Regensburg: Pustet, 2014)

Roland H. Bainton, *Women of the Reformation in Germany and Italy* (Minneapolis, MN: Augsburg, 1971)

J. Wayne Baker, "Erastianism in England: The Zürich Connection", in Schindler, *ZR*, 327–349

Hermann Barge, "Zur Chronologie und Drucksetzung der Abendmahlstraktate Karlstadts", *Zentralblatt für Bibliothekswesen* 21 (1904): 323–331

William Barker, *Erasmus: The Spirit of a Scholar* (London: Reaktion, 2021)

Torsten Bergsten, *Balthasar Hubmaier. Seine Stellung zu Reformation und Täufertum* (Kassel: Oncken, 1961)

Pamela Biel, "Personal Conviction and Pastoral Care: Zwingli and the Cult of Saints", *Zwingliana* 16/5 (1985): 442–469

Fritz Blanke, "Zwinglis *Fidei ratio* (1530): Entstehung und Bedeutung", in *Archiv für Reformationsgeschichte* 57 (1966): 96–102

Thomas A. Brady, *Ruling Class, Regime and Reformation at Strasbourg* (Leiden: Brill, 1978)

Thomas A. Brady, *Turning Swiss: Cities and Empire, 1450–1550* (Cambridge: Cambridge University Press, 1985)

Thomas A. Brady, *Protestant Politics: Jacob Sturm (1489–1553) and the German Reformation* (Atlantic Highlands, NJ: Humanities Press, 1995)

Willy Brändly, "Johannes Lüthard, 'der Mönch von Luzern'", *Zwingliana* 8/6 (1946): 305–341

James Brashler, "From Erasmus to Calvin: Exploring the Roots of Reformed Hermeneutics", *Interpretation* 63/2 (2009): 154–166

Wolfgang Breul, "'Mit gutem Gewissen'. Zum religiösen Hintergrund der Doppelehe Landgraf Philipps", *Zeitschrift für Kirchengeschichte* 119 (2008): 149–177

Stephen E. Buckwalter, "Die Entwicklung einer eigenen Position: Bucer und die innerprotestantische Abendmahlskontroverse bis zum Tod Zwinglis und Oekolampads", in Simon, *Bucer*, 98–108

Fritz Büsser, "Bucer und Zwingli", in Krieger/Lienhard, *Bucer*, 393–402

Fritz Büsser, "Heinrich Hottinger und der 'Thesaurus Hottingerianus'", *Zwingliana* 22 (1995): 85–108

August Burckhardt, "Der Stadtschreiber Heinrich Ryhiner", *BZGA* 2 (1903): 34–66

Susanna Burghartz, "Wibrandis Rosenblatt—Die Frau der Reformatoren", *Theologische Zeitschrift* 60 (2004): 337–349

Amy Nelson Burnett, "'It Varies from Canton to Canton': Zurich, Basel, and the Swiss Reformation", *Calvin Theological Journal* 44 (2009): 251–262

Amy Nelson Burnett, "Oekolampads Anteil am frühen Abendmahlsstreit", in Christ-von Wedel, *Basel*, 215–232

Amy Nelson Burnett, "Revisiting Humanism and the Urban Reformation", *Lutheran Quarterly* 35 (2021): 373–400

Miriam Usher Chrisman, *Strasbourg and the Reform. A Study in the Process of Change* (New Haven, CT: Yale University Press, 1967)

James Daybell, *The Material Letter in Early Modern England: Manuscript Letters and the Culture and Practices of Letter-Writing, 1512–1635* (Basingstoke: Palgrave Macmillan, 2012)

Akira Demura, "Church Discipline According to Johannes Oecolampadius in the Setting of his Life and Thought" (ThD diss., Princeton, 1964)

Wolfgang Dobras, "Zwinglische Kirchenzucht in Konstanz? Die Konstanzer Reformatoren und die Frage des Kirchenbanns", in Schindler, *ZR*, 131–142

Willehad Paul Eckert and Christoph von Imhoff, *Willibald Pirckheimer: Dürers Freund*, 2nd edn (Cologne: Wienand, 1982)

Alfred Egli, "Komtur Konrad Schmid, ein Wegbereiter der Reformation", *Küsnachter Jahresblätter* 1981: 30–48

Emil Egli, "Meister Ulrich Funk: Zwinglis Begleiter auf Synoden und Disputationen", *Zwingliana* 2/1 (1905): 13–17

Emil Egli, "Die Neuausgabe der Zwinglischen Werke", *Zwingliana* 2/9 (1909): 269–278

James Martin Estes, *Christian Magistrate and State Church: The Reforming Career of Johannes Brenz* (Toronto: University of Toronto Press, 1982)

Carrie Euler, *Couriers of the Gospel: England and Zurich, 1531–1558* (Zürich: Theologischer Verlag, 2006)

Oskar Farner, "Anna Reinhart: Die Gattin Ulrich Zwinglis", *Zwingliana* 3 (1916): 197–211, 229–245

Gary Ferguson, ed., *A Companion to Marguerite de Navarre* (Leiden: Brill, 2013)

Jeff Fisher, "The Doctrine of Justification in the Teaching of John Oecolampadius (1482–1531)", in Michael Parsons, ed., *Since we are Justified by Faith: Justification in the Theologies of the Protestant Reformation* (Carlisle: Paternoster, 2012), 44–57

Jeff Fisher, "The Breakdown of a Reformation Friendship: John Oecolampadius and Philip Melanchthon", *Westminster Theological Journal* 77 (2015): 265–291

Jeff Fisher, *A Christoscopic Reading of Scripture: Johannes Oecolampadius on Hebrews* (Göttingen: Vandenhoeck & Ruprecht, 2016)

Jeff Fisher, "Housing a Heretic: Johannes Oecolampadius (1482–1531) and the 'Pre-History' of the Servetus Affair", *Reformation and Renaissance Review* 20 (2018): 35–50

Jeff Fisher, "The Old Testament Editor of the First Published Greek New Testament: Johannes Oecolampadius (1482–1531)", *Journal of Early Modern Christianity* 5 (2018): 35–55

Günter Frank, ed., *Philipp Melanchthon: Der Reformator zwischen Glauben und Wissen. Ein Handbuch* (Berlin: De Gruyter, 2017)

Thomas A. Fudge, "Icarus of Basel? Oecolampadius and the Early Swiss Reformation", *Journal of Religious History* 21 (1997): 268–284

Edward J. Furcha, "Women in Zwingli's World", *Zwingliana* 19/1 (1992): 131–142

Ulrich Gäbler and Martin Wallraff, "Ulrich Myconius im Lichte seines Briefwechsels", in Oswald Myconius, *Briefwechsel 1515–1552: Regesten*, ed. Rainer Henrich, 2 vols (Zürich: Theologischer Verlag, 2017), I, 1–71

Rudolf Gamper, *Joachim Vadian, 1483/84–1551: Humanist, Arzt, Reformator, Politiker* (Zürich: Chronos, 2017)

Myron P. Gilmore, *Humanists and Jurists: Six Studies in the Renaissance* (Cambridge, MA: Harvard University Press, 1963)

Jacqueline Glomski, "Epistolary Writing", in Victoria Moul, ed., *A Guide to Neo-Latin Literature* (Cambridge: Cambridge University Press, 2017), 255–271

Hans-Jürgen Goertz, *Konrad Grebel: Ein Radikaler in der Zürcher Reformation* (Zürich: Theologischer Verlag, 2004)

Ernst Götzinger, ed., *Zwei Kalender aus dem Jahre 1527* (Schaffhausen: Schoch, 1865)

Christian Guerra et al., eds, *Johannes Atrocianus: Text, Übersetzung, Kommentar* (Hildesheim: Olms, 2018)

Hans R. Guggisberg, *Basel in the Sixteenth Century* (Eugene, OR: Wipf & Stock, 1982)

Volker Gummelt, "Die Auseinandersetzung über das Abendmahl zwischen Johannes Bugenhagen und Huldrych Zwingli im Jahre 1525", in Schindler, *ZR*, 189–201

Martin Haas, "Sebastian Hofmeister", *Schaffhauser Beiträge zur Geschichte* 58 (1981): 81–88

Karl Rudolf Hagenbach, *Johann Oekolampad und Oswald Myconius: Die Reformatoren Basels. Leben und ausgewählte Schriften* (Elberfeld: Friderichs, 1859)

Karl Hammer, "Der Reformator Oekolampad", *Zwingliana* 19/1 (1992): 157–170

Karl Hammer, "Bucer und die Basler Theologen", in Krieger/Lienhard, *Bucer*, 403–408

Nigel Harris, *The Thirteenth-Century Animal Turn* (Cham: Palgrave, 2020)

Wolf-Dieter Hauschild, "Johannes Bugenhagen (1485–1558) und seine Bedeutung für die Reformation in Deutschland", *Lutherjahrbuch* 77 (2010): 129–154

Fritz Hauß, "Blarers Zuchtordnungen", in Moeller, *Blarer*, 114–127

René Hauswirth, *Landgraf Philipp von Hessen und Zwingli: Voraussetzungen und Geschichte der politischen Beziehungen zwischen Hessen, Strassburg, Konstanz, Ulrich von Württemberg und reformierten Eidgenossen 1526–1531* (Tübingen: Osiander, 1968)

Randolph C. Head, "Archival Practices and the Interpretation of the Zurich Reformation, 1519–2019", in Peter Opitz and Ariane Albisser, eds, *Die Zürcher Reformation in Europa: Beiträge der Tagung des Instituts für Schweizerische Reformationsgeschichte* (Zürich: Theologischer Verlag, 2021), 389–408

Leo Helbling, *Dr. Johann Fabri und die schweizerische Reformation* (Einsiedeln: Benziger, 1933)
Leo Helbling, *Dr. Johann Fabri, Generalvikar von Konstanz und Bischof von Wien, 1478–1541. Beiträge zu seiner Lebensgeschichte* (Münster: Aschendorff, 1941)
Judith Rice Henderson, "Defining the Genre of the Letter: Juan Luis Vives' *De conscribendis epistolis*", *Renaissance and Reformation* 7 (1983): 89–105
Fritz Heusler, "Petrus Gynoraeus", *Zwingliana* 1/6 (1899): 120–122
Traudel Himmighöfer, *Die Zürcher Bibel bis zum Tode Zwinglis (1531). Darstellung und Bibliographie* (Mainz: von Zabern, 1995)
Hajo Holborn, *Ulrich von Hutten and the German Reformation* (New Haven, CT: Yale University Press, 1937)
Walter J. Hollenweger, "Zwinglis Einfluß in England", *Zwingliana* 19/1 (1992): 171–186
Robert Hoppeler, "Zur Biographie des Embracher Propstes Heinrich Brennwald", *Zwingliana* 3/2 (1920): 509–514; 4/1 (1921): 51 f.
Robert Hoppeler, "Zur Charakteristik des Leutpriesters Simon Stumpf von Höngg", *Zwingliana* 4/11 (1926): 221–229
Erwin Iserloh, ed., *Johannes Eck (1486–1543) im Streit der Jahrhunderte* (Münster: Aschendorff, 1988)
Hanspeter Jecker, "Die Basler Täufer. Studien zur Vor- und Frühgeschichte", BZGA 80 (1980): 5–131
Hans Gustav Keller, *Hutten und Zwingli* (Aarau: Sauerländer, 1952)
Wilfried Kettler, *Die Zürcher Bibel von 1531. Philologische Studien zu ihrer Übersetzungstechnik und den Beziehungen zu ihren Vorlagen* (Bern: Lang, 2001)
Wilfried Kettler, *Trewlich in Teütsch gebracht: Lateinisch-deutsches Übersetzungsschrifttum im Umkreis des Schweizer Humanismus* (Bern: Lang, 2002)
Guido Kisch, *Claudius Cantiuncula. Ein Basler Jurist und Humanist des 16. Jahrhunderts* (Basel: Helbing & Lichtenhahn, 1970)
Walther Köhler, *Huldrych Zwinglis Bibliothek* (Zürich: Beer, 1921)
Walther Köhler, "Zu Zwinglis französischen Bündnisplänen", *Zwingliana* 4/10 (1925): 302–311
Walther Köhler, "Zwingli und Basel", *Zwingliana* 5/1 (1929): 2–10
Walther Köhler, "Zu Wolfgang Russ", *Zwingliana* 6/1 (1934): 57 f.
Alfred Kohler, *Ferdinand I.: Fürst, König, Kaiser* (Munich: Beck, 2003)
Ernst-Wilhelm Kohls, *Die theologische Lebensaufgabe des Erasmus und die oberrheinischen Reformatoren: Zur Durchdringung von Humanismus und Reformation* (Stuttgart: Calwer Verlag, 1969)
Milton Kooistra, "Bucer's Relationship with Wolfgang Capito", in Simon, *Bucer*, 187–204
Friedhelm Krüger, "Bucer und Erasmus", in Krieger/Lienhard, *Bucer*, 582–594
Edwin Künzli, "Zwingli als Ausleger des Alten Testamentes", ZW XIV, 871–899

Olaf Kuhr, *Die Macht des Bannes und der Buße: Kirchenzucht und Erneuerung der Kirche bei Johannes Oekolampad (1481–1531)* (Bern: Lang, 1998)

Metin Kunt and Christine Woodhead, eds, *Süleyman the Magnificent and His Age* (London: Longman, 1995)

Hans Rudolf Lavater, "Thomas Wyttenbach (†1526), le maître de Zwingli", *Mennonitica Helvetica* 39 (2016): 83–91

Hans Rudolf Lavater, "'Veritas evangelica per typographiam': Zur Genese der in Zürich gedruckten Berner Disputationsakten 1528", *Zwingliana* 45 (2018): 233–279

Urs B. Leu, "Reformation als Auftrag: Der Zürcher Drucker Christoph Froschauer der Ältere (ca. 1490–1564)", *Zwingliana* 45 (2018): 1–80

Keith D. Lewis, "Johann Faber and the First Zürich Disputation: 1523. A Pre-Tridentine Catholic Response to Ulrich Zwingli and his Sixty-Seven Articles" (PhD diss., Catholic University of America, 1985)

Michael Massing, *Fatal Discord: Erasmus, Luther, and the Fight for the Western Mind* (New York: Harper, 2018)

Mickey Mattox, ed./trans., *Iohannes Oecolampadius: An Exposition of Genesis* (Milwaukee, WI: Marquette University Press, 2013)

Henry Mayr-Harting, *Church and Cosmos in Early Ottonian Germany: The View from Cologne* (Oxford: Oxford University Press, 2007)

Eugen Meier et al., *Andreas Cratander—ein Basler Drucker und Verleger der Reformationszeit* (Basel: Helbing & Lichtenhahn, 1966)

Karl Meisen and Friedrich Zoepfl, eds, *Johannes Eck, Vier deutsche Schriften* (Münster: Aschendorff, 1929)

Alberto Melloni, ed., *Martin Luther: A Christian between Reforms and Modernity (1517–2017)*, 3 vols (Berlin: De Gruyter, 2017)

Paul Meyer, "Jakob Meyer zum Hirsen (1473–1541)", BZGA 23 (1925): 97–142

Werner Meyer and Kaspar von Greyerz, eds, *Platteriana: Beiträge zum 500. Geburtstag des Thomas Platter (1499?–1582)* (Basel: Schwabe, 2002)

Ed L. Miller, "Oecolampadius: The Unsung Hero of the Basel Reformation", *Iliff Review* 39/3 (1982): 5–25

Bernd Moeller, *Johannes Zwick und die Reformation in Konstanz* (Gütersloh: Mohn, 1961)

Marie-Laure Monfort, *Janus Cornarius et la redécouverte d'Hippocrate à la Renaissance: textes de Janus Cornarius édités et traduits* (Turnhout: Brepols, 2017)

Andres Moser, "Die Anfänge der Freundschaft zwischen Zwingli und Ökolampad", *Zwingliana* 10 (1958): 614–620

Andreas Mühling, "Der Briefwechselband Zwingli-Oekolampad von 1536", in Christ-von Wedel, *Basel*, 233–242

Gerhard Müller, "Vincenzo Pimpinella am Hofe Ferdinands I., 1529–1532", *Quellen und Forschungen aus italienischen Archiven und Bibliotheken* 40 (1960): 65–88

Gerhard Müller, "Huldrych Zwingli und Philipp von Hessen", in Schindler, *ZR*, 177–187

Christine Mundhenk, "Die Beziehung Bucers zu Luther und Melanchthon", in Simon, *Bucer*, 205–216

Leonhard von Muralt, "Renaissance und Reformation in der Schweiz", *Zwingliana* 11/1 (1959): 1–23

Hughes Oliphant Old, "The Homiletics of John Oecolampadius and the Sermons of the Greek Fathers", in Boris Bobrinskoy et al., eds, *'Communio Sanctorum'. Mélanges offerts à Jean-Jacques von Allmen* (Geneva: Labor et Fides, 1982), 239–250

Peter Opitz, "The Exegetical and Hermeneutical Work of Johannes Oecolampadius, Huldrych Zwingli and Jean Calvin", in Saebø, *Hebrew Bible*, 407–451

Peter Opitz, *Ulrich Zwingli. Prophet, Ketzer, Pionier des Protestantismus* (Zürich: Theologischer Verlag, 2015)

Peter Opitz, "Calvin in the Context of the Swiss Reformation", in Selderhuis, *Calvinus*, 13–28

Wolfgang Pfeiffer-Belli, ed., *Thomas Murner und der Schweizer Glaubenskampf* (Münster: Aschendorff, 1939)

Rudolf Pfister, "Die Freundschaft zwischen Guillaume Farel und Huldrych Zwingli", *Zwingliana* 8/7 (1947): 372–389

Rudolf Pfister, "Zürich und das anglikanische Staatskirchentum", *Zwingliana*, 10/4 (1955): 249–256

Raymond Potgieter, "Anna Reinhard Zwingli—'Apostolic Dorcas', 'dearest housewife', 'angel-wife', 'ziel van mijn ziel' and 'mater dolorosa of the Reformation': From Woman to Valued Citizen", *In die Skriflig* 50/3 (2016): 1–8

Diane Poythress, *Reformer of Basel: The Life, Thought, and Influence of Johannes Oecolampadius* (Grand Rapids, MI: Reformation Heritage Books, 2011)

Christoph Riedweg, "Ein Philologe an Zwinglis Seite. Zum 500. Geburtstag von Jacob Wiesendanger, gen. Ceporinus", *Museum Helveticum* 57 (2000): 201–219

Jean Rilliet, *Zwingle: Le troisième homme de la Réforme* (Paris: Fayard, 1959)

Walter Rominger, "'Der größte Gelehrte seit Erasmus'—und dennoch zu wenig bekannt und beachtet: Simon Grynaeus (1493–1541): 'Großer Gelehrte und kleiner Reformator'", *BWK* 116 (2016): 323–339

Lyndal Roper, *Martin Luther: Renegade and Prophet* (London: Bodley Head, 2016)

Bernard Roussel and Gerald Hobbs, "Strasbourg et l' «école rhénane» d'exégèse (1525–1540)", *Bulletin de la Société de l'Histoire du Protestantisme Français* 135 (1989): 35–53

Steven Rowan, *Ulrich Zasius: A Jurist in the German Renaissance, 1461–1535* (Frankfurt: Klostermann, 1987)

Gordon Rupp, *Patterns of Reformation* (London: Epworth, 1969)

Alfred Schindler, "Zwinglis «Fehltritt» in Einsiedeln und die Überlieferung dieses Ereignisses", *Zwingliana* 36 (2019): 49–57

Christoph Schönau, *Jacques Lefèvre d'Etaples und die Reformation* (Gütersloh: Gütersloher Verlagshaus, 2017)

Valentina Sebastiani, *Johann Froben, Printer of Basel. A Biographical Profile and Catalogue of His Editions* (Leiden: Brill, 2018)

Gottfried Seebaß, *Das reformatorische Werk des Andreas Osiander* (Nürnberg: Verein für Bayerische Kirchengeschichte, 1967)

Emil Sehling et al., eds, *Die evangelischen Kirchenordnungen des XVI. Jahrhunderts*, 24 vols (Tübingen: Mohr Siebeck et al., 1902–2020)

Wolfgang Simon, "Der Basler Gräzist Simon Grynaeus und die Eheangelegenheit König Heinrichs VIII. im Spiegel der Bucerbriefe", in Christ-von Wedel, *Basel*, 203–213

Timothy Matthew Slemmons, trans., *Johannes Oecolampadius: Sermons on the First Epistle of John* (*A Handbook for the Christian Life*), (s.l.: Slemmons, 2017)

Jennifer Smyth, "Running at the Devil with God's Word. The Pamphlets of the Early-Reformation Preacher, Jacob Strauss" (PhD diss., Trinity College Dublin, 2010)

Ernst Staehelin, *Frau Wibrandis: Eine Gestalt aus den Kämpfen der Reformationszeit* (Bern: Gotthelf, 1934)

James M. Stayer, "Swiss-South German Anabaptism", in idem and John D. Roth, eds, *A Companion to Anabaptism and Spiritualism, 1521–1700* (Leiden: Brill, 2007), 83–117

W.P. Stephens, "Zwingli and the Salvation of the Gentiles", in idem, ed., *The Bible, the Reformation and the Church. Essays in Honour of James Atkinson* (Sheffield: Sheffield Academic Press, 1995), 224–244

Charles L. Stinger, "The Place of Clement VII and Clementine Rome in Renaissance History", in Kenneth Gouwens and Sheryl E. Reiss, eds, *The Pontificate of Clement VII. History, Politics, Culture* (Aldershot: Ashgate, 2005), 165–184

J. Paul Tanner, "Is Daniel's Seventy-Week Prophecy Messianic? Part 1", *Bibliotheca Sacra* 166 (2009): 181–200

Lee Palmer Wandel, *The Eucharist in the Reformation: Incarnation and Liturgy* (New York: Cambridge University Press, 2006)

J. Denny Weaver, "Hubmaier versus Hut on the Work of Christ. The Fifth Nicolsburg Article", *Archiv für Reformationsgeschichte* 82 (1991): 171–192

Timothy J. Wengert, *Philip Melanchthon: Speaker of the Reformation* (Farnham: Ashgate, 2010)

Jakob Wipf, "Ein Schulmeisterschicksal aus der Reformationszeit (Hans Fehr, lateinischer Schulmeister in Schaffhausen 1530–1541)", *Zwingliana* 4/13 (1927): 379–400

Paul Wirth, ed., *Thomas Platter: Geißhirt, Seiler, Professor, Buchdrucker, Rektor. Ein Lebensbild aus dem Jahrhundert der Reformation* (St. Gallen: Ottmar, 1999)

Heinz Wyss, *Leo Jud: Seine Entwicklung zum Reformator, 1519–1523* (Bern: Lang, 1976)

Jason Zuidema and Theodore van Raalte, *Early French Reform: The Theology and Spirituality of Guillaume Farel* (Farnham: Ashgate, 2011)

Index of Personal Names (of Early Modern Figures)

References containing biographical or bibliographical information about the figures in question are listed in **bold**.

Agricola, Stephan   199*n*4
Alber, Matthäus   9, 18, 149*n*5
Albrecht III, Archbishop-Elector of Brandenburg   180, 180*n*2, 376*n*4
Allart, Hugo   xxv*n*24
Althamer, Andreas   **268*n*5**, 271*n*5
Ambach, Melchior   306, **306*n*16**, 325*n*6
Amerbach, Bonifatius   108, **108*n*12**, 116, 212*n*1
Amerbach, Johann   108*n*12
Ammann, Johann Jakob   392, **392*n*12**
Amsdorf, Nikolaus von   270*n*4
Arthur, Prince of Wales   419*n*6
Artolph, Hieronymus   **212*n*1**, 322*n*1
Asper, Hans   39
Atrocianus, Johannes   274, **274*n*9**

Baḥur, Eliyahu (Elia Levita)   99, 99*n*9
Baling, Nikolaus   327, **327*n*15**
Beatus Rhenanus   392*n*12
Bebel, Johannes   79*n*4
Ber, Ludwig   108, **108*n*10**, 116, 116*n*37, 169 f., 169*n*5, 262, 262*n*5, 264, 321*n*6
Bernard of Trent, Bishop   188*n*4
Bertschi, Markus   22*n*93, 90, **90*n*1**, 123, 123*n*1,4f., 211*n*5, 222, 255, 318*n*3, 348, 407, 407*n*4
Besserer von Rohr, Bernhard   413, **413*n*2**
Beyel, Kaspar   365*n*3
Beyel, Werner   24*n*99, 318, **318*n*1**, 322 f., 327, 327*n*19, 328, 356*n*6, 392, 399*n*7, 400, 402*n*12,14, 405*n*2
Bibliander, Theodor   **226*n*4**
Billican, Theobald   **105*n*5 f.**, 141, 141*n*7, 145, 149, 149*n*6, 199, 224, 224*n*5, 239*n*10,18
Billing, Heinrich   145*n*4
Bischof, Andres   307*n*1
Blarer, Ambrosius   **x**, 38f., 199, 199*n*8, 345, 345*n*3, 411*n*5, 415, 417
Blaurock, Georg   8, 215*n*10
Boleyn, Anne, Queen of England   420*n*9
Boleyn, Thomas, Earl of Wiltshire   420*n*9
Bothan, Hieronymus   26, **136*n*4**, 255, 386*n*4

Botzheim, Johann von   79*n*2
Brennwald, Felix   **202*n*2**, 205*n*15 f.
Brennwald, Hans Jakob   408*n*8, 409, 409*n*13
Brennwald, Heinrich   **202*n*1**, 408*n*8, 409*n*9
Brennwald, Jodocus   202, **202*n*1**, 205
Brenz, Johannes   **x**, 8, 18, 32, 103*n*3f., 125*n*2, 126*n*1, 127–129, 127*n*3, 128*n*1, 130, 130*n*4, 141*n*12, 142*n*17, 147, 149, 155*n*4, 220*n*1, 265, 305, 305*n*9, 333*n*1, 419
Briefer, Nikolaus   262*n*6, 264*n*4
Brunn, Urban von   164*n*2
Brunner, Leonhard   243*n*8
Bucer, Martin   **x**, xi, xvi, xix, xxiv, 9, 14, 22*n*93, 23, 28 f., 31–36, 32*n*134,137 f., 33*n*140 f., 38, 43*n*181, 44, 76, 76*n*8, 85*n*1, 94*n*13, 127*n*3, 130, 130*n*4, 149, 149*n*3, 155, 155*n*3, 175 f., 175*n*14 f., 176*n*20, 180, 185, 185*n*5, 188*n*2, 197, 199, 199*n*7, 207, 212, 230, 230*n*1, 232, 243, 244*n*1, 252, 257, 257*n*2, 260, 268, 281 f., 292 f., 292*n*2, 293*n*2,5, 298, 300, 304*n*4, 312, 312*n*9, 327, 333*n*1, 334*n*1, 338*n*8, 341, 350, 352*n*1, 353, 359*n*3, 364, 364*n*12, 366, 366*n*5, 369*n*5, 371, 374, 376, 383*n*1, 384, 386, 386*n*2, 390 f., 391*n*1 f., 394, 394*n*8, 395, 398, 398*n*2,6, 400–403, 400*n*3,15, 401*n*7, 405 f., 406*n*1, 410, 410*n*2, 411*n*5, 413–415, 417*n*8, 423, 423*n*2, 426, 426*n*2 f.
Budoti, Heinrich   378*n*1
Bugenhagen, Johannes   **x–xi**, 5, 8, 101*n*4, 103, 105, 109, 132, 132*n*2, 208*n*9, 303–305, 304*n*5
Bullinger, Heinrich   x, xiii, xvi, 12, 37
Burgauer, Benedikt   **312*n*11 f.**, 405*n*3, 416*n*5
Burnet, George   421*n*13
Butz, Peter   408*n*8

Calvin, Jean   x, xxi, xxiii, xxvi, 37 f., 40, 416*n*7
Cantiuncula, Claudius   101, **101*n*6**, 108, 116
Capito, Wolfgang Fabritius   **xi**, xvi, xix, xxiv, 4, 13, 15, 22*n*93, 23, 26, 31–36, 32*n*138, 33*n*140, 35*n*145, 43 f., 43*n*181, 49, 68*n*1, 85*n*1, 94*n*13, 96*n*6, 127, 127*n*3, 130,

Capito, Wolfgang Fabritius (*cont.*)   132*n*2–4, 133, 133*n*8, 140*n*1, 145*n*6, 149, 153*n*14, 175*n*14, 176, 176*n*21, 178, 178*n*3, 180 f., 180*n*2, 188*n*2, 196, 196*n*2, 202*n*1, 205*n*17, 206 f., 212, 212*n*1,4, 224*n*4, 236 f., 236*n*3, 237*n*9, 242*n*1, 243, 244*n*1, 249, 252–254, 256, 256*n*9, 260, 268, 271, 271*n*4, 277, 277*n*1, 281 f., 286, 286*n*2, 293, 293*n*3,5, 297, 300, 300*n*7 f., 308, 311 f., 311*n*1, 326, 334*n*1, 342, 356*n*5, 362*n*4, 369*n*5, 376, 383*n*1, 398*n*3, 401, 401*n*6, 408, 408*n*8, 423, 423*n*2, 426*n*3
Catherine of Aragon, Queen of England   29, 419*n*3, 426*n*1
Cellarius, Martin   25*n*105, 32*n*138, 244–247, **244*n*1**,3f., 247*n*1 f., 249, 249*n*2, 293, 300
Ceporinus, Jacobus   xv, 77, **77*n*11**, 79, 79*n*4, 124, 124*n*12, 136*n*2, 140, 151*n*1,3
Charles V, Holy Roman Emperor   xii, 10, 207*n*4, 234*n*5, 281*n*16, 329*n*5, 337*n*2, 357*n*3, 364*n*9, 367*n*3, 378, 378*n*2, 383*n*4
Christine of Saxony   426*n*5
Christoph of Baden-Sponheim, Margrave   296*n*8
Clement VII, Pope   168*n*8, 326*n*9
Clichtoveus, Jodocus   18, 225, **225*n*8**, 229, 229*n*2, 234
Coct, Anémond de   37, 84, **84*n*7**
Collin, Rudolf   296, **296*n*9**, 392
Comander, Johannes   263, **263*n*10**, 327
Cornarius, Janus   24*n*99, 308, **308*n*3**
Coverdale, Miles   37
Cranmer, Thomas   39 f.
Cratander, Andreas   xi, 15, 41 f., 59, 59*n*9, 71, 71*n*8, 74, 77*n*11, 79*n*4, 143, 145, 147, 152*n*8, 175, 175*n*14, 206, 206*n*21, 208, 236*n*5, 238, 238*n*1 f., 245*n*6, 256, 256*n*8, 288
Cyro, Peter   263*n*9, 277*n*2

Dangerant, Louis   411*n*2
David, Heinrich   276, **276*n*16**
Denck, Hans   xiii, 212, 218*n*6
Dürer, Albrecht   xv

Eck, Johannes   xi, xii, 10, 17, 61*n*4, 83*n*5, 134–136, 134*n*3,6, 136*n*6, 138, 140, 140*n*3,5, 143*n*1, 159, 159*n*2–4, 162, 162*n*4, 166, 169*n*4, 171*n*4, 181 f., 181*n*8, 182*n*9, 191, 199, 199*n*8, 236, 238, 252, 252*n*12–14,16, 260*n*3, 273*n*1, 274, 274*n*4, 280, 315, 315*n*4, 325
Elia Levita—*see* Baḥur, Eliyahu
Engelhard, Heinrich   400, **400*n*1**
Erasmus of Rotterdam   x, **xi–xii**, xviii*n*4, xxiii, 2 f., 3*n*12 f., 7*n*29, 13 f., 14*n*55, 19, 23*n*97, 32, 35, 35*n*148, 44 f., 54, 62*n*4, 65*n*14, 71*n*8, 79, 79*n*2 f., 81*n*2 f., 87*n*3, 98 f., 98*n*3, 99*n*6–8, 101, 101*n*6, 103, 103*n*3, 105, 107–110, 107*n*1 f., 108*n*9,12, 110*n*2, 112, 112*n*15, 115–119, 115*n*31, 116*n*35,38, 117*n*40, 140*n*4, 151*n*2, 176*n*19, 185, 214*n*7, 238, 244, 244*n*5, 270*n*4, 308, 326*n*10, 335*n*3, 342, 342*n*15 f., 347, 350*n*10, 359*n*2, 364
Erlach, Diebolt von   316*n*5
Ernst of Lüneburg, Duke   28, 401, **401*n*7**
Escher, Konrad   136, **136*n*1**

Faber, Johann   xii, 6, 6*n*25, 27*n*113, 43, 43*n*179, 53, 61*n*8, 65*n*12, 70, 71*n*1,6 f., 73, 73*n*12, 75, 75*n*2, 131*n*10, 140*n*5, 161, 161*n*3, 174, 174*n*8, 178, 178*n*1–3, 180 f., 185 f., 185*n*2 f., 188, 190 f., 192*n*17, 196 f., 208, 208*n*13, 226, 234*n*5, 238, 241, 252, 263*n*11, 266, 266*n*6, 281, 325, 362*n*4
Faber Emmeus, Johann   **274*n*5**, 276, 276*n*6, 321*n*9
Farel, Guillaume   xiii, 16, 37, 81*n*2 f., 82, 84*n*7 f., 86, 86*n*7 f., 121
Fattlin, Melchior   190–192, **190*n*3**,5, 191*n*14,16, 193*n*21, 195*n*3
Feige, Johannes   353*n*5
Ferdinand I, Archduke of Austria and Holy Roman Emperor   **xii**, 10 f., 44, 175*n*10, 185*n*2, 188*n*4, 200*n*13 f., 207, 207*n*4, 226*n*3,5 f., 234*n*5 f., 266, 268, 279*n*8, 281*n*14, 305*n*13, 325*n*2, 326 f., 326*n*9, 329, 329*n*5, 334, 337*n*2. 384*n*1
Fischer, Johannes   **166*n*5**
Fisher, (St) John   18, 39, **229*n*2**, 234
François I, King of France   356, 363 f., 363*n*7, 364*n*9
François, Dauphin and Duke of Brittany   364*n*9
Frauenberger, Peter   90, **90*n*2**, 95*n*15, 123*n*1,4, 181*n*7, 182*n*9, 211*n*5, 227–229, 291, 291*n*6 f.

Frecht, Martin   414 f., **414n8**
Friedrich II, Duke of Legnica   226, 226n1
Frey, Rudolf   346, **346n5**, 384, 384n5, 394, 394n12
Fries, Anna   184n8
Frith, John   39
Froben, Hieronymus   105n3
Froben, Johann   71n8, 99, **99n8**, 105n3, 342
Frosch, Johann   199n4
Froschauer, Christoph (*often called 'Christoph' in the letters*)   **xii–xiii**, 5, 83, 83n6, 100, 109, 126, 127n5, 128, 138, 138n2, 143, 143n2, 147 f., 147n4 f., 148n9, 152, 152n10, 162n4, 173, 173n2, 178n6, 190, 195 f., 220n7, 227, 254, 254n4, 258, 258n3, 271, 300, 304, 311, 321, 361, 361n8
Funk, Ulrich   351, **351n12**, 392, 392n13, 418, 418n2

Gemmingen, Dietrich von   130n5
Georg of Brandenburg-Ansbach, Margrave   x
Geppart, Fabian   226–228, **226n1**
Germann, Kilian   **364n10**
Germanus, Martin   **333n1**
Geyling, Johann   86n8
Glarean (Heinrich Loriti)   23, **23n97**, 61, 61n5, 108, 153n15, 392n12
Grebel, Jakob   204 f., **204n12**, 205n17
Grebel, Konrad   120n10, 157n3, 204 f., **204n13**
Grob, Hans   338n8
Grotz, Philipp   381n9
Grynaeus, Simon   xviii, **xviiin4**, 49, 130n6, 142n16, 336 f., 336n4, 419, 419n3, 421n13, 426, 426n1 f.
Guldi, Nikolaus   43n179, 352n1
Gundelsheim, Philipp von   225, **225n10**, 253n1, 321, 321n5
Gyrfalk, Thomas   16, 16n62, 24n99, **90n5**, 155n9, 211n5, 238n7, 254 f., 254n8, 303–305, 303n2, 335, 335n1

Hätzer, Ludwig (*often called 'Ludwig' in the letters*)   **xiii**, 106, 1–6n11, 109, 119–121, 119n8 f., 120n10 f., 121n10, 124–127, 129, 137 f., 142, 148, 148n9, 152 f., 152n10, 168n5, 249, 249n5

Hales, Sir Christopher   39
Haller, Berchthold   **xiii**, 163, 163n3, 166, 172, 172n6, 178, 178n2, 251, 260, 262, 262n1,3, 263n10, 265n8, 353n7, 393, 395
Haner, Johann   214, **214n7**
Hawkins, Nicholas   39
Hedio, Kaspar   68, **68n1**, 94n13, 341n7, 383, 383n1,6
Hegenwald, Erhard   68n4, 157, **157n2 f.**
Henri, Duke of Orléans   364n9
Henry VII, King of England   419n6
Henry VIII, King of England   29, 342n12, 419–421, 419n3–6, 423 f., 423n2, 426 f., 426n1,3
Hertig, Georg   263n9
Herwagen, Johann   5, 181n4, 207, **207n8**
Hess, Johannes   163, **163n4**
Hiltprant, Balthasar   374, **374n6**, 389, 389n13
Hirt, Balthasar   338n8
Hoen, Cornelis   199n7
Hofmeister, Sebastian   86n10, **97n7 f.**, 120n13, 267, 312n12
Hohenems, Wolf Dietrich von   327n13
Huber, Johannes   168n4, 174, 174n6, 234n3, 263, 263n9
Hubert, Konrad   293n3, 295, 295n1,5, 301, 301n1, 331 f., 334
Hubmaier, Balthasar (*usually called 'Balthasar' in the letters*)   83, 83n5, 87, 87n1,4, 101, 101n1, 209, 209n19 f., 238–242, 241n6, 242n4, 245, 245n6
Hübschi, Lienhart   316n5
Husschin, Eusebius   26, 26n110
Husschin, Johannes (senior)   13, 26, 403, 403n5
Hut, Hans   **241n1**
Hutten, Hans von   83n1
Hutten, Ulrich von   76, **76n7**, 78, 80, 80n7, 83n1

Immeli, Jakob   90, **90n3**, 97, 97n9, 154n4, 211n5, 238n7, 258

Jenner, Thomas   xxvi
Joham, Konrad   367, **367n1**, 398n1
Johann of Saxony, Elector   253n2, 286n3, 288n5, 290n3
Jonas, Justus   176, **176n18**, 20, 237, 237n10

Jud, Leo (*usually called 'Leo' in the letters*) xiii–xiv, 2, 77, 86, 120, 124, 177, 187, 196, 209, 213 f., 214*n*4 f., 228, 249, 256, 295 f., 345, 355, 357, 390, 392, 394, 400, 400*n*1, 402, 406*n*3, 407, 409, 409*n*10, 418
Julius II, Pope   410*n*4

Kaiser, Jakob   11
Karlstadt, Andreas Bodenstein von   xiii, 85, 85*n*2,4, 119, 119*n*6, 121, 186, 186*n*10, 282*n*23, 286*n*3, 349, 349*n*5–7, 356, 356*n*5, 362, 362*n*1, 367, 367*n*4, 369, 369*n*2, 371, 373 f., 377 f., 377*n*7, 383 f., 416, 416*n*3,5
Kautz, Jakob   293, **293*n*7**
Keller, Ludwig   xvi, xix
Kettenacker, Ambrosius   24*n*99, 78, **78*n*1**, 382
Kirser, Jakob   296, **296*n*8**
Kirser, Joachim   24*n*99, 296, 305, 305*n*11
Kniebis, Niklaus   398*n*1
Köllin, Leonhard   413, **413*n*3**
Kolb, Franz   240, **240*n*15**, 262, 262*n*1,8, 263*n*10
Kornmesser, Johannes   277, **277*n*7**, 351*n*13
Krämer, Andreas   256*n*8
Krautwald, Valentin   226, **226*n*6**, 291*n*5

Lambert, François   353, **353*n*4**
Laski, Hieronymus   257*n*2
Latomus, Jacobus   100, **100*n*10**
Lefèvre d'Etaples, Jacques   38, 363 f., **363*n*7**
Liechtenstein, Leonhart von   209*n*19
Limperger, Matthias   300, 300*n*3
Limperger, Tillmann   79*n*5, 131*n*9, 164*n*7, 300*n*3
Lincki, Heinrich   165*n*5
Lopinen, Margarethe   403*n*6
Loriti, Heinrich—*see* Glarean
Louis II, King of Hungary   186*n*6
Ludwig II von Pfalz-Zweibrücken, Count Palatine   340, 340*n*1
Ludwig V, Count Palatine of the Rhine   121, 121*n*8
Lüdin, Hans   350*n*9
Lüthard, Johannes   15, 15*n*59, 22*n*93, **90*n*6**, 155*n*9, 164*n*4, 211*n*5, 238*n*3, 255
Luther, Martin (*often called 'Martin' in the letters*)   x–xi, xiii, **xiv**, xv, xxi, xxvi, 4–6, 8 f., 13–16, 14*n*55, 18, 23*n*97, 27, 28*n*122, 29, 32–34, 40, 50 f., 64*n*6, 70*n*4, 84*n*7, 90*n*4, 94*n*12, 99 f., 99*n*4 f., 105*n*5, 107, 110, 119*n*6, 121, 132*n*3 f.,7, 149, 149*n*5,8, 155*n*4 f., 157–159, 157*n*2–5, 158*n*6, 166*n*1, 169, 169*n*3, 173, 173*n*1, 174*n*8, 175 f., 176*n*18, 178 181, 181*n*4, 184, 188, 188*n*1, 190, 190*n*6, 193, 193*n*20,22, 196 f., 196*n*1, 205, 205*n*19, 207, 207*n*5,7, 211, 214, 214*n*7, 220, 220*n*5,7, 222–224, 222*n*3, 224*n*6, 226 f., 229 f., 230*n*1,3, 232, 232*n*6, 234, 237, 244, 244*n*5, 246, 246*n*10, 253, 253*n*2 f., 256, 266*n*3, 270*n*4, 281 f., 281*n*18, 282*n*20,23, 284, 284*n*5, 286, 286*n*2, 288, 288*n*4, 290, 290*n*3, 292, 292*n*3, 293*n*2, 295, 295*n*3 f., 298, 298*n*1,3, 302*n*3, 304, 304*n*2 f., 315, 315*n*7, 337, 337*n*4, 339, 347*n*2,4, 349, 349*n*2, 353, 353*n*3 f., 362*n*2, 369, 369*n*3 f., 371, 376, 376*n*4, 391, 391*n*4, 394*n*8, 398–401, 398*n*2, 401*n*7, 403, 405, 419, 419*n*5, 426*n*2

Maer, Laurentius   4*n*15
Maigret, Lambert   411*n*2
Mangolt, Wolfgang   318*n*2
Mantel, Johann   306, **306*n*15**
Manuel, Nikolaus   316*n*5
Manz, Felix   8, 120*n*10, 215*n*10, 239*n*9
Margarethe von der Saale   426*n*5
Marguerite de Navarre, Duchess   362*n*6,8
Marius, Augustinus   **xiv**, 131*n*10 f., 195*n*3, 197*n*8, 210*n*4, 211*n*5, 213, 213*n*2 f., 264*n*5, 273*n*1, 274*n*5 f., 285*n*6
Mary I, Queen of England   419*n*7
Maximilian I, Holy Roman Emperor   xvi, 141, 141*n*9
Medici, Clara de'   327*n*13
Medici, Gian Giacomo de', Marquess of Musso and Lecco   323*n*5, 326*n*12, 327*n*13, 411, 411*n*4
Medici, Giovanni Angelo de', Bishop   326*n*12
Megander, Kaspar   249, **249*n*6**, 257, 393
Meier von Knonau, Hans   xvi
Melanchthon, Philipp (*often called 'Philipp' in the letters*)   x, xiii, **xiv–xv**, 13, 142, 142*n*18, 176, 253*n*3, 286, 286*n*1,4, 288, 288*n*4, 337, 339, 341, 341*n*2,4, 345*n*1, 362,

INDEX OF PERSONAL NAMES (OF EARLY MODERN FIGURES) 455

Melanchthon, Philipp (*often called 'Philipp' in the letters*) (*cont.*)   362*n*1f., 364, 364*n*11, 369, 383, 391, 391*n*4, 394, 394*n*8, 426, 426*n*2,5
Meltinger, Heinrich   **123*n*2**
Merklin, Balthasar   305*n*13
Meyer, Adelberg, zum Pfeil   123*n*2, 134*n*3,6, 164*n*2, 408*n*2, 410*n*3 f., 418*n*1
Meyer, Bernhard, zum Pfeil   410, 410*n*3
Meyer, Jakob, zum Hirzen   xviii, **xviii*n*3**, 123*n*3, 145*n*5, 295, 295*n*7, 343*n*3, 346*n*2 f., 360*n*6, 374, 389*n*13, 394*n*9, 406*n*1
Meyer, Johann Rudolf   394*n*9, 396*n*8
Meyer, Sebastian   86, **86*n*10**, 120 f., 120*n*13
Mülinen, Kaspar von   202*n*5
Müller, Jacob   301*n*9
Münster, Sebastian   35, 337, **337*n*7**
Murner, Thomas   191 f., **191*n*10**, 192*n*17, 210, 210*n*2, 219, 219*n*1, 260, 260*n*3
Myconius, Oswald   **xv**, 49, 76, 90*n*5, 124, 171, 177, 187, 209

Näf (Nepos), Jakob   71, **71*n*8**, 74
Nägeli, Hans Franz   **393*n*6**
Nesen, Wilhelm   **14*n*55**
Neudorffer, Georg   199*n*8
Nießlin, Agathe   382, 382*n*2

Oechsli, Ludwig   165, **166*n*4**, 208, 208*n*14
Öttli, Veit   20*n*9
Osiander, Andreas   242, **242*n*7**, 250, 250*n*3,5, 254, 254*n*4, 257, 257*n*1, 347, 347*n*2, 408
Osswald, Georg   413*n*2

Pagnini, Sante   361, **361*n*8**
Pelargus, Ambrosius   **267*n*9** f., 273*n*1, 274 f., 274*n*5, 275*n*12 f., 315, 315*n*5
Pellikan, Konrad   xi, **xv**, 15, 27 f., 35, 72*n*5, 90*n*6, 107*n*1 f., 110, 110*n*2, 111*n*5, 116 f., 116*n*35, 136, 136*n*2 f., 138, 138*n*3 f., 140, 145, 145*n*4, 149, 153, 153*n*13 f., 156, 156*n*11, 158, 160, 160*n*8, 162, 162*n*4, 171 f., 177, 184, 184*n*8, 187, 196, 209, 216 f., 221, 223, 225, 237, 249, 256, 267 f., 277, 295, 298, 302, 303*n*2, 309, 333, 333*n*2, 337*n*7, 342, 350, 390, 392, 394, 414*n*10, 418
Pellikan, Samuel   237, 237*n*12

Perkins, William   xxvi
Petri, Adam   15, 64*n*6, 160*n*8
Pfarrer, Mathis   356*n*6
Pfister, Anna   13
Philipp "the Handsome", Duke of Burgundy and King of Castile   141, 141*n*9
Philipp "the Upright", Elector Palatine   13
Philipp I, Landgrave of Hesse   xv, xvii, 12, 12*n*51, 29, 44, 121, 121*n*6, 199, 199*n*5, 214*n*7, 220, 220*n*9 f., 242*n*1, 262*n*7, 288, 290*n*3 f., 334*n*1,4, 339, 342*n*9 f., 346*n*1, 347*n*2, 353, 353*n*4 f., 359*n*2, 362*n*2, 378*n*4, 380, 380*n*3, 383*n*5
Philipp I, Margrave of Baden-Sponheim   121, 121*n*7, 183, 183*n*1,5, 196, 196*n*3, 199, 199*n*2, 292*n*4, 296*n*8, 305, 305*n*12 f., 365 f., 365*n*4
Phrygio, Paul   329, **329*n*2**, 418, 418*n*6
Pimpinella, Vincenzo   384, **384*n*1,3**
Pirckheimer, Willibald   **xv–xvi**, 18, 159, 159*n*5, 171, 176, 178, 219, 219*n*2 f., 221*n*11, 226, 242, 242*n*5 f., 250
Platter, Thomas   391, **391*n*5**, 395, 395*n*1
Prugner, Nikolaus   80*n*6

Rasdorfer, Paul   301 f., **301*n*10**
Reinhart, Anna   **xvi**, 21, 21*n*21, 86, 124, 139, 160, 209, 221, 292, 296, 301 f., 309, 331, 390, 394, 409
Reublin, Wilhelm   15, 15*n*59
Reuchlin, Johannes   xiv
Rhegius, Urbanus   **119*n*9**, 124, 124*n*9, 141, 141*n*7, 143, 147, 168, 168*n*5, 188, 188*n*3, 199, 239, 239*n*10, 252*n*16
Richter, Martin   410*n*1 f.
Ritter, Erasmus   312, **312*n*1** f., 416, 416*n*4 f.
Rivulo, Adrianus a   270*n*4
Rode, Johannes   199*n*7
Röist, Diethelm   399 f., **399*n*7**, 400*n*1, 402, 402*n*14, 405*n*2
Rollenbutz, Lukas   259*n*2, 350*n*11
Rosenblatt, Adalberg   337*n*8
Rosenblatt, Wibrandis   **xvi**, xix, 25 f., 270, 270*n*2,4, 292*n*6, 301*n*11, 331*n*3
Roussel, Gérard   38, 363, **363*n*6**
Rümling, Eberhard   263*n*9
Ruff, Simprecht   141*n*12
Ruß, Wolfgang   357, **357*n*2**, 373, 373*n*2,4, 365, 365*n*1,4, 371, 371*n*1 f.

Ryhiner, Heinrich   25, **25*n*102**, 42*n*175, 216, 216*n*1, 234*n*1, 237, 237*n*11, 407, 407*n*3
Rysysen, Egmunt   **174*n*7**, 199, 199*n*1

Saganus, Georg   199*n*7
Salamanca-Ortenburg, Gabriel von   234, **234*n*5**, 266, 266*n*4, 281*n*16 f.
Sam, Konrad   345*n*1, 411, **411*n*1**, 414*n*8,10, 415
Sattler, Michael   218*n*6, 227*n*11
Schaller, Kaspar   323*n*4
Schenk, Simprecht   **416*n*6**
Schilling. Konrad   262*n*6
Schlegel, Theodul   11 f., 263, **263*n*11**, 323*n*5, 326, 326*n*7
Schmid, Konrad   66, **66*n*15**, 262*n*6
Schmidt, Nysius   301*n*9
Schöni, Georg   263*n*9
Schuler, Gervasius   24*n*99, **332*n*1**
Schwenckfeld, Caspar   157*n*4, 226*n*6, 291*n*5, 298*n*2
Schwitzer, Claus   301*n*8
Schwyzer, Hans   **394*n*11**
Setzer, Johann   207, 207*n*7, 341, 341*n*3
Sforza, Duke Francesco Maria   411 f., 411*n*4, 412*n*6
Sichard, Johannes   188, **188*n*4**, 342, 342*n*3
Sickingen, Franz von   14
Sittich, Markus, von Ems   326 f., **327*n*13**, 383, 383*n*2
Staupitz, Johann von   306*n*15
Stör, Stephan   16, **81*n*5**
Stoll, Rudolf   316*n*4
Strauß, Jakob (*often called 'The Ostrich' in the letters*)   **xvi–xvii**, 8, 18, 43*n*179, 105, 105*n*8, 183 f., 183*n*1–3, 184*n*9, 186, 186*n*9, 193, 196 f., 196*n*2, 197*n*6, 205, 205*n*18, 208, 208*n*11
Stumpf, Simon   139, **139*n*7**
Sturm, Jakob   185, **185*n*5**, 337, 337*n*3, 341, 343, 356*n*6, 378, 378*n*5, 380*n*6, 395, 398*n*1
Sturm, Peter   367, **367*n*2**
Suleiman the Magnificent, Ottoman Emperor   186*n*6, 200*n*9
Sutor, Petrus   99, 99*n*6

Thymysen, Rudolf   329*n*1
Tillmann, Bernhard   399*n*7
Treger, Konrad   131, **131*n*12**, 396, 396*n*9

Ulrich VI, Duke of Württemberg   x, **xvii**, 83, 83*n*1–4, 86, 86*n*7 f., 130*n*3, 188*n*4, 199*n*5, 220, 220*n*9, 237, 267, 267*n*7, 351, 403*n*1
Utenheim, Christoph von   13
Utinger, Heinrich   3, 153, **153*n*15**

Vadian (Joachim von Watt)   xvii, 2, 23, 204*n*13, 210*n*3, 262, 262*n*6, 263*n*10, 312*n*11, 352*n*1, 387*n*1
Varnower, Johann   90*n*2
Vögelin, Balthasar   255, 255*n*5

Walch, Hans   301*n*9
Wehrli, Konrad   165*n*5
Wellenberg, Thomas   43*n*179, 205*n*17
Werdmüller, Jakob   316*n*4, 329*n*1
Westerburg, Gerhard   85*n*2,4
Wickler, Matthias   157*n*4, 226
Wieland, Ulrich   24*n*99, **345*n*1**
Willading, Lienhart   316*n*5
Wimpfeling, Jakob   xiv, 13, 13*n*52, 367*n*2
Winkler, Konrad   301*n*9
Wissenburg, Wolfgang   15, **90*n*4**, 94*n*12, 99*n*3, 211*n*5, 238*n*7, 255, 275, 275*n*13
Wolfhart, Bonifatius   81 f., **81*n*1**, 84
Wonnecker, Johannes Romanus   43*n*179, 6*n*4, 64, 64*n*1, 72*n*5
Wyssgerber, Christof   **174*n*7**
Wyttenbach, Thomas   2, **2*n*5**

Xylotectus, Johannes   181, **181*n*6**

Zanchi, Girolamo   xxvi
Zanger, Hans   301*n*9
Zápolya, John, Count and King   200, 200*n*9–11,14, 257*n*2
Zasius, Ulrich   70, **70*n*4**, 73*n*13
Zell, Wilhelm von   97, **97*n*8**, 100, 126, 139, 142, 175, 175*n*9
Ziegler, Barbara   205, 205*n*14
Ziegler, Jakob   410, **410*n*1**
Ziegler, Paul   326*n*12
Zwick, Johannes   x, 345, 345*n*3
Zwingli, Bartholomäus   1
Zwingli, Ulrich (senior)   1

Index of Place Names (Contemporary Swiss and Others)

Aarau 21, 388*n*8, 389*n*11, 390*n*16, 393–395, 393*n*1 f., 395*n*3, 399, 399*n*8
Aargau 332*n*1, 373*n*1, 382*n*2
Adige (river) 200
Alsace 31, 281*n*17, 325*n*2
Altomünster 14
Altstätten 416*n*2
Anwil 354*n*8
Appenzell 10, 156, 156*n*10, 163, 163*n*4, 172, 225*n*9, 279, 307*n*1
Augsburg xiii, 12 f., 29, 37, 39, 81*n*1, 90*n*2, 119–121, 119*n*9, 120*n*11, 141, 141*n*12, 181*n*7, 182*n*9, 185*n*5, 188, 199, 199*n*4, 239*n*10, 252, 252*n*15, 311*n*4, 357*n*3, 362, 362*n*3, 363*n*1, 367, 367*n*3, 371, 371*n*3, 374, 374*n*4, 376, 376*n*1, 378*n*3,5, 380, 380*n*1, 383*n*1,6, 384, 384*n*1,3, 386*n*3, 391, 391*n*1, 394, 394*n*8, 401, 401*n*8
Avignon 108*n*12

Baden (im Aargau) xii, 10 f., 10*n*43 f., 17, 28, 33, 43, 128*n*9, 134*n*6, 136*n*6, 143*n*1, 146, 146*n*8, 150*n*10, 158*n*7, 159*n*1, 162–172, 162*n*4 f., 164*n*1, 166*n*1,5 f., 168*n*1–4, 169*n*4 f., 171*n*4, 172*n*6 f., 174*n*5–8, 176*n*21, 185, 190–193, 190*n*3, 196, 197*n*2, 199, 202, 202*n*4, 208, 210*n*1, 212, 214*n*6, 218, 218*n*8, 234, 234*n*3, 236, 238, 250, 250*n*6, 251*n*7, 258, 262*n*5, 263*n*9, 307*n*1, 312*n*11, 327*n*17, 339*n*3, 346*n*3, 351*n*12, 373*n*1, 391*n*9
Baden-Baden 183*n*2, 199, 199*n*2, 305*n*12, 410*n*1
Bern xiii, 1, 11 f., 14, 20, 22, 43*n*181, 86*n*10, 90*n*3, 128, 128*n*7 f., 162, 163*n*3, 166, 166*n*1, 168*n*4, 172, 172*n*6, 178*n*2, 188*n*5, 202, 202*n*5 f., 225, 225*n*9, 240, 240*n*15, 249*n*6, 258–260, 258*n*1, 259*n*4, 260*n*1,3, 262–268, 262*n*1–3,5 f., 263*n*9–11, 264*n*1,3 f., 265*n*8 f., 266*n*1 f., 268*n*4 f., 271, 271*n*6, 275, 277, 277*n*2, 279 f., 279*n*7, 288, 288*n*6, 290, 311, 311*n*11 f., 316, 316*n*5, 322, 322*n*3, 325, 325*n*5, 327, 327*n*15, 334*n*3, 348, 348*n*6, 351*n*12, 359*n*3, 367 f., 380 f., 381*n*9, 383, 388*n*8, 390*n*15, 393, 393*n*6, 399, 399*n*7, 409, 409*n*14, 416*n*6, 422*n*2
Bernese Oberland 288*n*6, 311*n*6
Besançon 86*n*8
Betschwanden 301*n*10
Biberach 38, 416*n*1
Biel 11, 334*n*3, 388*n*8
Bingen 306*n*16
Bohemia xii
Bologna 420*n*8
Bremgarten 332, 332*n*1, 422*n*2, 423*n*4
Brugg 327*n*15
Buda 200*n*9, 266*n*3

Cambridge xvi, 420*n*8
Chartres 114*n*22, 225*n*8
Chur 12, 142, 165, 263, 263*n*10 f., 322*n*1, 323, 323*n*5, 326 f., 326*n*8, 327*n*13,15, 411*n*4, 412
Colmar xiii, 274*n*9, 377*n*8
Cologne xiii, 333*n*1
Croatia xii

Dauphiné 84*n*7

East Frisia 349, 349*n*7
Ebernburg x, 14, 76*n*8
Eguisheim 281*n*17
Egypt 200, 200*n*12
Eichstätt 329*n*2
Einsiedeln xiii, 2–4
Elgg 306*n*15
Embrach 202*n*1, 408, 408*n*8
England x, xxiv, 37, 39 f., 234*n*5, 419–421, 423, 426
Ensheim 281
Ensisheim 325*n*2
Erfurt 126*n*18, 357*n*2
Esslingen 39

Ferrara 410*n*1
Florence 363, 363*n*3

France   4, 186, 186n7, 356, 356n6, 363 f.,
    363n4–8
Frankfurt (am Main)   xii, 14n55, 98, 142n19,
    147n2, 199n6, 205 f., 206n21, 219n3,
    220n6, 223n3, 226, 306n16, 308n3, 415,
    415n14
Freiburg (im Breisgau)   xi, 108n12, 163n4,
    188n4, 255n4, 267n9, 274n5
Freising   xiv, 131, 195, 210
Fribourg (im Üchtland)   90n5, 131n12, 263
Friesland   199n7
Fürfeld   333n1

Geislingen   413, 413n2
Geneva   xiii, xxiv, 16, 38, 40, 81n2, 416n7
Gifhorn   373n1
Glarus   2, 172, 188, 188n5, 301n10
Gnadental   382n1
Gottstatt   262n6
Graubünden   204n13, 263n10, 323, 323n5,
    326n8
Guttenberg   130n5, 142n15,17, 222n4

Hagenau   xi, 207
Halle an der Saale   176n18
Heidelberg   x, xviiin4, 13, 306n16, 333n1,
    337n7, 414
Heilbronn   13
Hesse   300, 378n4
Höngg   139n7
Hohenems   327n13
Hohentwiel   83, 83n4, 86
Holland   199, 199n7
Hungary   xii, 14, 186, 186n8, 200, 200n9–11

Iffenzheim   306n15
Ilanz   142n14, 263n10
Ill (river)   30
Ingolstadt   xi, 244n1. 252n15, 274, 274n4
Interlaken   288n6
Isny   39, 312n11
Issenheim   378n1

Jura   321n5

Kamienna Góra (Landeshut)   47, 156
Kappel   xxiv, 10–12, 22, 66n15, 332n1, 335n1 f.,
    337n3, 359n1, 364n10, 374n6, 381n8 f.,
    394n11, 422n1
Kempten im Allgäu   39, 301n10, 416n6

Klybeck   15
Konstanz   x, xiii, 38 f., 61, 70, 79n2, 83n4, 134,
    134n7, 190, 190n3, 195, 199, 232n8, 279,
    279n8, 311, 311n3, 329n2, 345n1,3, 351n14,
    383, 383n6, 388n8, 408n3, 416n1, 417,
    417n10
Küsnacht   66n15

Lahr   305n12
Landeshut—see Kamienna Góra
Lecco   323n5
Legnica (Liegnitz)   157n4, 226, 226n1,4,
    291n5
Lengnau   357, 357n2, 365n2, 373n4
Lenzburg   332n1
Lichtenau   353n5
Lichtensteig   338n8
Liestal   16, 81n5
Limmat (river)   xviii, 8
Lindau   39, 408n3
Louvain   7n29, 100n10
Lucca   361n8
Luzern   10, 86, 86n8, 131n13, 140, 140n5,
    166n1, 168n4, 174, 174n6, 181n6, 191n10,
    210n1, 212, 212n2, 252n8, 263, 263n9,11,
    307 f., 383, 383n6, 390n5

Madrid   207n4, 364n9
Mahlberg   305n12
Maienfeld   204n13
Mainz   xi, 13, 68n1, 306, 306n16, 340n4, 341
Mammern   166n5
Marburg   x, xiv–xv, 8, 28, 33, 50, 185n5,
    267n7, 308n3, 337n3, 339 f., 344n1,
    345n2,4, 347–349, 347n2,4, 351n12,
    353, 353n2,4, 359n5, 362, 362n2, 384n5,
    392n13, 402n9–12
Marignano   2
Memmingen   38 f., 332n1, 408n3, 415 f.,
    415n13, 416n1,6
Metz   101n6, 311
Mikulov (Nikolsburg)   209n19, 241n1
Milan   2, 323n5, 411 f., 411n4,6
Mindelheim   97n8
Mohács   186n6, 200n9
Montbéliard   83, 83n3, 86n7
Mulhouse   11, 37, 76n7, 80n6 f., 172, 172n7,
    329n2, 334n3 388n8,11
Musso   323n5

INDEX OF PLACE NAMES (CONTEMPORARY SWISS AND OTHERS) 459

Neckarsteinach 306n16
Neuchâtel 81n2
Nördlingen 105, 105n5, 149n6, 199, 224n5
Nürnberg xv, 105n8, 159, 171, 206, 214, 214n7, 223, 223n1, 240n15, 242n6 f., 250, 268n5, 271, 271n5, 311n4, 347n2

Oloron 363n6
Orléans 420n8
Ortenbourg 234n1, 266n4
Outer Austria (*Vorderösterreich*) xii, xvi
Oxford 420n8

Padua 420n8
Paris 99n6, 108n10, 225, 225n8, 420n8
Passau 410n1
Pavia 186n7, 207n4
Pfäfers 76n7, 157n3
Pforzheim xi, 296n8, 338n8
Porrentruy 321n5

Rapperswil 418, 418n3
Ravensburg 39
Regensburg 268, 268n3
Reutlingen 39, 149, 149n5,9, 176
Rhein (river) 30
Riehen 78n1
Rome 61, 413n4
Rossano 384n1
Rothenburg ob der Tauber 186
Rothenfluh 354n8
Rottweil xv, 199, 199n8, 408

Säckingen xvi
St. Gallen xvii, 10 f., 162, 172, 172n7, 210, 210n3, 214, 225n9, 255n9, 307n1, 312n1, 352n1, 364n10, 388n8, 405n3, 418n3
St. Goar 339 f.
Saverne 96n6
Saxony 6, 300, 329, 356n5
Schaffhausen 11, 86, 86n10, 97, 97n7, 120n13, 156, 156n10, 163, 163n2, 165, 165n5, 166n4, 172, 188, 188n5, 208, 225n9, 279, 307n1, 312, 312n11 f., 334n3, 388n8, 405, 405n3
Scherweiler 96n6
Schleitheim 227n11
Schwabach 371n4
Schwäbisch Gmünd 268n5

Schwäbisch Hall x, 103n5, 128n10, 130n3
Schwyz 10 f., 307, 307n1, 390n15
Sélestat x, 266n4, 329n2
Silesia 47, 156 f., 157n4, 226, 226n6, 228 f., 291, 291n5, 298, 298n3
Singen 83n4
Solothurn 170, 170n8, 225, 225n10, 263, 263n9, 279, 353, 353n7, 381, 381n8 f., 395 f., 407, 407n4, 416, 416n2, 418n2
South Tyrol 200
Speyer 44, 50, 175, 175n10, 178n3, 180n2, 323, 323n6, 329, 329n4–6, 334, 340n4, 341, 425n1
Strasbourg x–xi, xiii, xxiv, 11 f., 15, 23 f., 30–38, 41–43, 47, 68n1, 70, 70n3, 76n8, 81n1, 85, 85n1, 92, 94, 94n13, 96, 96n6, 98, 126, 127n3, 130, 130n5, 131n12, 132n1,3 f., 133, 133n8, 140n1, 142 f., 145, 147, 149, 153, 153n14, 155, 169, 169n4, 175n14, 176, 185, 188, 196 f., 199, 202n1, 206 f., 207n8, 210–212, 214, 217 f., 217n6, 220, 222, 224, 227, 229, 232, 237, 243 f., 243n8, 244n1,4, 245n9, 247, 247n2, 253, 253n3, 257, 259 f., 259n4, 260n1, 263 f., 266, 277, 281, 281n16, 286, 286n2, 292, 293n37, 297, 301n10, 305 f., 311n1,4, 325 f., 328, 329n2, 332n1, 333 f., 334n1–3, 337, 337n3, 339, 341, 342n9 f., 343–346, 343n1,3, 344n1, 345n5, 348, 348n5, 351n12, 353n4, 356, 356n5 f., 359n3, 366 f., 367n1 f., 369, 374, 374n7, 380n6, 381, 381n7, 383n9, 388, 388n8, 389n6, 390, 390n15, 393, 395, 398 f., 398n1, 402n2, 402 f., 402n2, 408–410, 408n3 f.,8, 410n1, 414n8, 415, 415n14, 417, 417n8, 423n2 f., 425n1
Stuttgart 237n7, 306, 306n15
Sundgau 325, 325n2
Swabia 4, 105, 271, 391n3, 415, 419, 419n1
Syria 200, 200n13
Székesfelérvár 200n11

Thun 263n9, 327n15
Thurgau 166n5, 232n8, 338
Toggenburg 307, 307n1, 338n1,8
Tokaj 200n14
Toulouse 420n8
Transylvania 200n9
Trier 267n9

INDEX OF PLACE NAMES (CONTEMPORARY SWISS AND OTHERS)

Tübingen   188n4, 208, 208n13, 244n1, 268n5, 329n2,13

Ufenau   76n7
Uhingen   237n7
Ulm   xiv, 21, 29, 37 f., 166n5, 243, 243n9, 252, 252n12–14, 311n4, 345, 345n1, 357n2, 411, 411n1, 413–415, 413n2, 414n7–9,11 f., 415n13, 416n1, 417, 425, 425n1
Unterwalden   10, 288n6, 327, 327n17, 390n15
Uri   10, 390n15

Valtelline   411n4
Vic-sur-Seille   101n6
Vienna   xii, xvii, 1, 101n6, 242n4, 333n1, 410n1

Waldshut   87, 209
Waldkirch   305n13
Walenstadt   255n5
Weesen   1
Weinsberg   13

Wertheim   240n15
Weser (river)   378n4
Wettingen   373n1
Wildhaus   1
Winterthur   205n17
Wittenberg   x, xiv, 15, 84n7, 119n6, 136, 157, 157n2 f.,5, 176n18,20, 196, 207, 244n1, 253, 268n5, 288, 308, 345n1, 353n4, 401n7, 426, 426n1,3
Wittingen   373n1
Wolin   x
Worms   134, 134n7, 175n10, 199n6, 243, 243n8, 293n7, 323n6, 340n4
Württemberg   x, xiii, 13, 130n3
Würzburg   xiv, 214n7

Zofingen   47, 47n191, 80, 129
Zollikon   204n13
Zug   10, 307, 310, 381n9, 383, 383n6, 390n15
Zurzach   234, 234n3
Zwickau   308n3

Index of Personal and Place Names (Antiquity and Middle Ages)

Aeacus   251, 251*n*7
Aesop   92*n*8
Ajax   113*n*16
Alcaeus of Mytilene   151*n*5
Alexander the Great   7, 27*n*113, 70, 70*n*5
Ambrose of Milan, St,   105, 105*n*2
Apollo   114*n*21
Aristotle   337
Artemis   70*n*7
Augustine of Hippo, St   18, 85, 85*n*5, 115, 115*n*34

Basil the Great, St   51*n*201
Berengar of Tours   114, 114*n*22, 117

Caesar, Caius Julius   80, 80*n*6
Catilina, Lucius Sergius   44, 202 f., 202*n*2, 203*n*9
Catti (tribe)   378, 378*n*4, 383
Caugnista, King of Numidia   92, 92*n*8
Cherusci (tribe)   391, 391*n*3
Chrysostom, St John   4, 13*n*54, 15, 40, 51*n*201, 80*n*8
Cicero, Marcus Tullius   54, 116*n*38, 203, 203*n*9, 335*n*3
Cycnus, King of Kolonai   335*n*3
Cyril of Alexandria, St   51*n*201, 254, 254*n*7, 290, 292*n*4

Darius III, King of Persia   27*n*113, 70, 70*n*5
Delphi, Oracle of   113, 114*n*21
Duns Scotus, John   3

Edessa   420
Ephesus   70*n*7
Eusebius of Caesarea   312, 312*n*8

Gaugamela   70*n*5
Gennadius of Constantinople, Patriarch   51*n*201
Gregory VII, Pope   114*n*22
Gregory of Nazianzus   13*n*54, 51*n*201, 103, 103*n*6
Gregory Thaumaturgus, Bishop   51*n*201

Hector   113*n*16
Hercules   151*n*5
Herostratus   27*n*113, 70, 70*n*7
Hesiod   151*n*5
Hestia   44, 202, 203*n*3
Hesychius of Jerusalem   208, 208*n*16
Homer   113*n*16
Horace (Quintus Horatius Flaccus)   94
Hus, Jan   134, 134*n*7, 166*n*1

Irenaeus of Lyon   xxii, 18, 171, 171*n*4
Issus   70*n*5

Jerome, St   51 f., 155*n*6
Jerome of Prague   xxvi
John of Damascus, St   13*n*54, 51*n*201
John II of Jerusalem, Bishop   51*n*201
Julian ('the Apostate'), Roman Emperor   254
Justinian I, Byzantine Emperor   413*n*4

Lupus (Bishop)   58*n*7

Mercury   269
Mesopotamia   420
Minos   251*n*7

Nicephorus Chartophylax   51*n*201

Osroene   420
Ovid (Publius Ovidius Naso)   180

Pallas Athene   193, 193*n*24
Parnassus, Mount   114*n*21
Persia   27*n*113, 70*n*5, 202*n*4, 420
Peter of Alexandria, Bishop   51*n*201
Philip of Macedon, King   326
Physiologus   57*n*1
Pictor, Quintus Fabius   116, 116*n*39
Pindar   151, 151*n*1,3
Pliny the Elder   57*n*1, 101*n*4
Plutarch   205 f., 206*n*21
Ps. Clement, *Recognitiones*   188, 188*n*4

Rhadamanthus   251*n*7
Rufinus of Aquileia   188*n*4

Sallust (Gaius Sallustius Crispus)   203, 203*n*9
Seneca, Lucius Annaeus   153*n*11
Sidonius Apollinaris   54, 58*n*7
Solinus, Caius Julius   27*n*113, 70*n*7
Strabo   27*n*113, 70*n*7

Tenes, King of Tenedos   335*n*3
Terence   81*n*3, 108*n*9, 238, 264*n*4
Tertullian   18, 18*n*73, 39, 105, 105*n*7, 141
Thalassius, St   51*n*201
Theodectes   337, 337*n*6
Theophylactus of Ohrid, Bishop   51*n*201, 53, 209, 209*n*18
Thermopylae   44, 202*n*4
Thraso   81, 81*n*3, 103

Index of Bible References

Genesis
12:2	77n10
19:4 f.	121n3
24:60	89n12
29:15–30	420n11
41:26	240n14

Exodus
3:20	103n2
4:26	239n13
12:21	114n29, 141n11
13:7	391n8
13:21	282n21
14:21–28	418n4
20:15	111n9
32:4	141, 141n10 f.
32:32	250n5

Leviticus
18:16	420, 420n10
20:9	88, 88n11

Numbers
25:4–8	181n3

Deuteronomy
17:17	426n3
18:9–14	426n3

Judges
2:11	152n6
3:7	152n6

I Samuel
4:4	114n21
25:16	58n6

II Samuel
18:6–15	130n2
22:35	72n4

II Kings
18:17	75n4
18:19–35	75n4
19:1–7	75n4
22:2	320n3

Nehemiah
2, 4 and 6	64n8

Psalms (Masoretic/Protestant numbering)
1:1	64n4
2:2	96n4
29:5	208n10
33:10	196n6
37:28	155n8
71:4	100n12
72:6	65n10
118:22	114n24
124:3	210n2, 217n2
127:1	325n3
137:9	72n3
145:18	67n1
147:12 f.	72n2

Isaiah
1:4	72n7
37:1–7	75n4
42:2	65n10
54:1	153n17

Jeremiah
6:10	268n7
17:5	121n9

Ezekiel
1	242n1 f.

Zechariah
2:5	58n6

Matthew
3:10	215n11
3:16	282n22
5:11	73n8
5:13	391n6
5:18	62, 111n10
5:25	174n1
7:3	136n5
7:6	193n24
7:15	64n5, 157n1
7:9 f.	349n4
8:30–32	109n16

Matthew (cont.)

9:36	155n7
9:37	73n9
9:37 f.	271n7, 306n14
9:38	414n9
10:2	103n7
10:16	57n5, 135n8
10:30	108n15
10:37	181n2
11:21	273n2
12:25	274n7, 284n3
13:9	247n8
15:14	273n3
16:18	67n3
16:19	387n4
18:17	387n3
21:19	115n32
26:26	111n7, 224n7
26:26–29	188n3
28:19	87n2

Mark

1:7	134n5
9:50	64n2
11:21–23	115n33
14:22	111n7, 224n7

Luke

2:35	128n13
9:62	119n3, 156n10, 217n4
10:3	57n5
10:4	174n2
10:5	181n1
13:4	184n7
13:27	73n10
16:8	360n6
16:29	87n5
17:21	421n12
21:15	135n9
22:19	111n7, 224n7, 349n6
22:26	111n8

John

1:29	114n26
2:1–11	94n11
3:6	230n4
6:45	286n2
6:63	9, 93n9, 111n6, 129n16, 157n2, 230n5
6:69	112n14
8:12	113n17
10:12	131
14:6	78n3
15:5	114n25
17:21	91n7
19:23 f.	384n2
19:26 f.	114n27
20:22	134n1
21:16 f.	57n4

Acts

1:17	73n11
2:38	88n7
2:40	223n5
4:32	245n7
7:8	114n28
8:1–3	83n2
9:1–31	83n2
10:48	88n7
26:14	215n8

Romans

1:20	144n5
2:16	219n4
7:7 f.	239n11
8:31	131n7, 374n3
14:8	109n17
16:20	168n3

1 Corinthians

1:19	65n14
2:15	192n18
3:6	81n4, 175n13
4:20	254n5
5:5	387n2
5:7 f.	391n7
8:1–13	355n3
10:13	145, 145n5
10:16	295n4
10:17	356n4
10:24	58n8, 228n14
11:24	111n7
11:28	251n10
11:29	255n1
16:9	72n6

INDEX OF BIBLE REFERENCES

II Corinthians
1:21 f.   113*n*20
2:15 f.   57*n*2
5:17   88*n*9

Galatians
2:11   135*n*11
3:3   62*n*2
6:9   128*n*12

Philippians
1:6   284*n*4
1:21   174*n*3
3:13 f.   105*n*4
4:13   60*n*1, 129*n*15

I Thessalonians
4:9   76*n*5

II Timothy
1:12   142*n*20

Hebrews
5:7   355*n*2
12:23   129*n*4

I Peter
3:15   62*n*1
5:7   228*n*13

I John
2:18   61*n*7

Revelation
22:11   62*n*3

If you have any questions regarding this title, please contact:

Koninklijke Brill BV
Plantijnstraat 2
2321 JC Leiden
Email: info@brill.com

Batch number: 08267852